PERSONNEL MANAGEMENT
A Human Resource Systems Approach

✳

PERSONNEL MANAGEMENT
A Human Resource Systems Approach

ELMER H. BURACK
Illinois Institute of Technology

ROBERT D. SMITH
Kent State University

WEST PUBLISHING CO.

St. Paul • New York • Boston • Los Angeles • San Francisco

The West Series in Management

Consulting Editors:

Don Hellriegel
and
John W. Slocum, Jr.

Burack-Smith	Personnel Management: A Human Resource Systems Approach
Downey-Hellriegel-Slocum	Organizational Behavior: A Reader
Hellriegel-Slocum	Organizational Behavior: Contingency Views
Huse	Organization Development and Change
Mathis-Jackson	Personnel: Contemporary Perspectives and Applications
Morris-Sashkin	Organization Behavior in Action: Skill Building Experiences
Newport	Supervisory Management: Tools and Techniques
Ritchie-Thompson	Organization and People: Readings, Cases and Exercises in Organizational Behavior
Whatley-Kelley	Personnel Management in Action: Skill Building Experiences

Acknowledgments

In the preparation of this book we were fortunate to have the advice of many academicians and practitioners from the fields of Personnel, Organization Behavior, Systems Analysis, and Organization Development. We are especially grateful to Professor Don Hellriegel (Texas A & M) for his assistance. Additionally, we wish to extend our appreciation to Professors John Slocum (Penn State) and James Bowditch (Boston College) for their advice and encouragement.

Library of Congress Cataloging in Publication Data

Burack, Elmer H.
    Personnel management.

    Bibliography: p.
    Includes index.
    1. Personnel management. I. Smith, Robert D., joint author. II. Title.
HF5549.B8752   658.3   76-30886
ISBN 0-8299-0130-2

"With Ruth, Chuck, Bob and Alan very much in my thoughts"
"To Vilma, Roger, Victor and Elena: my truly remarkable family"

*

PREFACE

This book builds on basic organizational concepts of the personnel. It includes several new approaches to dealing with people in organizations. These approaches have become vital because they help fulfill the needs of organizations and the people who work for them. The concepts of (1) personnel (human resource) management, (2) career planning, (3) change management, (4) information systems, and (5) labor markets are interwoven with the more traditional interests and concerns of personnel management. Applications and examples are used to clarify important issues. The terms *personnel* and *human resources* have already found their way into a variety of business and government settings. We use them to signal modern approaches to personnel-related issues.

This book also presents and applies several models that have been found highly useful in designing personnel systems. The approaches help to crystallize problems of securing human resources, dealing with the career interests of employees and the managing personnel within organizations. These models are frameworks that provide an informed way of looking at particular problems or organizations. This approach identifies those characteristics that aid in problem solving, design or personnel systems, and understanding the connections between people, work and organization.

A realistic view of modern personnel practices goes far beyond the traditional idea (held by some) that the "company is all powerful"—that the company impersonally secures and manipulates people. New laws, social norms, and societal trends have clearly signaled an era of new concerns and approaches to human resources. This book seeks to convey this to academic and institutional audiences.

In our discussions of the personnel function we explore the individual's need for personal growth and realization and the organization's need for productivity. *Both* are important. Thus, for example, job-hunting and the hiring process are discussed from both viewpoints. Similarly, both job training and performance are interpreted in terms of the functioning of the personnel system *and* in terms of the individual's perception and response. Motivation and communication are not treated as isolated topics or general discussions. They are summarized and woven into the fabric of personnel activities. Additionally, timely materials pertaining to areas such as testing, assessment, and management by objectives are introduced and related to the particulars of human resource management. These topics, however, are not treated in depth; rather, a working knowledge is sought. A specialized literature already exists for these topics, and a bibliography provides adequate references, this lessens the need for extensive footnoting.

Material and concepts, both timely and practical, are introduced. PMIS (personnel management information systems), assessment-opportunity centers, change management, human resource planning and career designs are discussed. Also practical approaches for applications of mathematical and statistical models, new approaches to job evaluation, affirmative action in dealing with minorities, occupational safety and health, and dealing with quality-of-work-life problems are included.

Finally, the material recognizes that the world of work has changed—and continues to change. For example, lifestyles, age distribution, and the proportion of the population in various work roles in manufacturing, hospitals, and education have changed dramatically in recent years. And the changes are likely to continue. The book provides numerous applications and examples for a broad variety of careers, including industry, government, and education.

Because modern personnel (human resource) management requires a unified outlook and approach, personnel topics are treated in the context of broader organizational matters. Thus a personnel problem may involve reconciling organizational policy or dealing with changes affecting performance, or even the community.

Chapter development presents a logical basis for the reader to identify the key issues and processes related to an expanded concept of the personnel function. Some key issues and processes are systems concepts, approaches to employee problems, and the development of organizations for higher productivity and better work relationships. Developments in the environment, such as newer employment legislation, are described from the viewpoint of both organizations and individuals. Key ideas are summarized, abstracted, and employed to demonstrate their use within personnel situations. Thus the emphasis is not so much on basic theory but on why, how, and where it is to be applied.

Continuity, Demonstration, and Application

A carefully developed set of personnel models and actual applications of concepts bring theory and practice together in a realistic setting. Models are indispensable in developing a broad, flexible base of personnel concepts that can be shaped to fit the thousands of situations that define personnel. But these models are not especially interesting as such and may leave the reader in the dark. Descriptions of personnel applications and methodology can be quite interesting and informative, but they are endless. Consequently, we have used a combination of modeling and illustrative applications to capitalize on the advantages and avoid the pitfalls of both techniques.

The repeated use and application of the personnel models help to establish continuity for the reader. The models are used in the subject matter and discussed in detail. There is heavy emphasis on concept and perspective. Skills in basic personnel approaches are developed.

Finally, the examples and application problems, interspersed throughout the book, are drawn from a wide variety of research, consulting, and training/development situations. The examples are cast in a great variety of institutional settings to display the richness of personnel problems and the possibilities for improvement. Students often find these applications the high point of class sessions or the "real meat" of the course.

Chapter Development

The ordering of material parallels the logic of personnel management that emerges from environmental change and the major missions of personnel. Social, legislative, economic, and technological change, along with the workings of the "external labor market." They establish the important features of the personnel system. The personnel system varies from "gatekeeping" at the port of entry (recruiting), through wage practices and conformity to OSHA (Occupational Safety and Health Act) and EEO (Equal Employment Opportunity) regulations, to training/development practices.

Implicit within the ordering of chapter material is the patterning of human resource career development. Personnel officials, specialists, and general managers must understand how career interest, educational preparation, job alternatives, and individual mobility can motivate a person to join an organization and to produce well. These factors, vital indicators of an organization's health, are reflected in performance, absenteeism, and turnover. Thus they further mold the many characteristics of the personnel-manpower system.

The following exhibit indicates major concepts, tools, and perspectives that we consider essential to understanding modern personnel management. These important areas are translated into learning objectives that begin each chapter. They are more than simple descriptions of content; they convey the insight of working knowledge we seek to impart in chapter discussions. For the reader, they represent another form of self-testing for determining the level of learning required by enlightened personnel practitioners and general managers.

The seventeen chapters of the book place varying degrees of emphasis on various topics of importance to personnel. For example, "work" is of major interest because it is the basis for economic activity and one of the central activities in life. "Change" is a dynamic force that introduces the need for modification of work activities, organization functions, human activities, and personnel functions. The markings on the exhibit indicate the relative emphasis in various chapters. This initial view of themes that recur throughout the book suggests the need for unified approaches that move broadly across chapters' subject matter and topics.

The book is divided into six major sections. These sections present the organization, activities, and problems of personnel so that their relationship to the or-

EXHIBIT 1 Relation of Chapter Content to Important Book Concepts and Perspectives

Book Concepts and Perspectives		Chapters																
		1	2	3	4	5	6	7	8	9	10	11	12	13	14	15	16
Work	ethics, quality change, structure	†			*		*	*	*	*							
Planning	business-human resource, reserve/replacement	*		*		†				*					†	†	†
Change	environmental, social, technical, individual-group change	†		*	*	*				*				*	†	†	†
Quantitative analyses	math-statistical approaches			*			†		*								
People	behavior, communications, incentives, needs, education, experience, decision to join, participate, leave				*	*	*	*		*	*	*	*	*	*	*	*
Organization	influence of size, mission				†						*					*	
Skills	modeling, evaluation, delphi techniques	*							*		*				*		

Key: * discussion
     † heavy emphasis

ganizational whole is logical and consistent. Also, order of presentation conveys a key viewpoint on the functioning of personnel. The order of chapter development follows the sequence of establishing personnel needs, to locating and training/developing people, to the many problems of maintaining people in organizations.

*

CONTENTS

PERSONNEL MANAGEMENT
A Human Resource Systems Approach

†

Section
One

INTRODUCTION

Chapter 1

THE PERSONNEL FUNCTION IN TRANSITION: STABILITY VERSUS CHANGE

LEARNING OBJECTIVES

This chapter focuses on enlarging the reader's perspective of the trends and forces influencing the organization and activities of personnel management. In particular, the objectives of this chapter are to:

Develop a working definition and concept of the personnel-manpower function

Recognize some of the major historical developments in the emergence of personnel activities

Describe the nature of environmental forces, trends, and changes and indicate their impact upon organizations

Promote the understanding and implications of the systems-related character of modern personnel (human resource) management

Outline the legislation that has affected the specifics of personnel activities

Provide insight to the connection of changes in the work ethic, worker expectancy, and newer personnel activities

Set out clearly the impact of technological change on work, workers, and personnel–human resource management.

KEY TERMS AND CONCEPTS

bureaucratic	uncertainty, complexity
work ethic	accretion-type change
Hawthorne Study	assessment centers
change; and innovation,	welfare capitalism
acceleration of	alpha, beta, AGCT exams
systems view	position analysis
providers	questionnaire (PAQ)
labor	maintenance outlook

human relations approaches
morale
personnel–human resource
    management
system: open, input, output,
    primary, support
gatekeeping function

stable environment
validity, reliability, bias
industrial relations
social secretary
3-R skills
*Dictionary of Occupational
    Titles* (DOT)

PREVIEW

Chapters 1 and 2 set the stage for exploring contemporary personnel concepts. Chapter 1 describes some of the forces that in the last century have helped shape existing personnel systems and concepts and how these forces have created the need for new approaches. In particular this chapter will discuss:

1. The traditional bureaucratic model that evolved from the work of Weber and Taylor.

2. The expanded maintenance approach and the human relations model.

3. The role that the "outside" world (technology, legislation, and behavioral scientists, and social movements) has played in influencing business practices in general and personnel attitudes and policies in particular.

4. The human-resource model as a new approach to personnel needs.

What does a personnel manager do? At one time this was a fairly simple question. Personnel managers recruited, hired, trained, and maintained people in organizations. Such a simple, straightforward answer is no longer possible.

During this century personnel has emerged from near-total obscurity to a central position in contemporary institutional operations. The first stage (1900–30) witnessed the establishment of basic personnel philosophies. During the 1930s, the second stage, businesses established the basic personnel machinery in response to dramatic changes brought about by social, economic, legislative, and political developments. The third stage (1960–75) was marked by a new wave of social and economic changes and legislative developments that increased the power and prestige of personnel departments in organizations.

Since 1900 five forces have had a rather immediate and significant effect on personnel, management, and administrative practices:

1. union formation, development, and related legislation
2. "world of work" professionals including industrial psychologists and engineers and behavioral scientists
3. government welfare legislation
4. war and government organization and activities
5. societal changes: social and paternal programs.

BUREAUCRACY—THE TRADITIONAL MODEL

The traditional model of business organization was formulated in the early years of this century. It is associated in particular with the works of Max Weber and Frederick W. Taylor. As a response to growing unionization and the ongoing search for means of improving productivity, it flavored the character of personnel and the approaches taken to people through the first half of the twentieth century.

The *Commonwealth* v. *Hunt* case in 1842 established the legal status of trade unions. Before this case, union efforts had been modest and fragmented. This newly won legitimacy and growing industrialization encouraged the emergence of the union movement—the Knights of Labor in 1869 and the 700,000-member American Federation of Labor (AF of L) in 1886. The Knights of Labor was an industrial union, and even well into the twentieth century its growth was sporadic, dependent as it was on the ebb and flow of the industrial economy. The AF of L, on the other hand, was a craft union, and while it faced many problems, it grew slowly but steadily. Its membership was approximately three million by the eve of United States participation in World War I (1917). By 1920, unions accounted for 12 percent of the work force (Rieder, 1957).

Taylor's scientific management was the outgrowth of these changing relationships between companies and workers. The use of his approach improved management methods, procedures, and standards and strengthened production management and supervision.

Companies created organizational units to deal with union relationships and representatives. In some cases, companies sponsored (and controlled) unions as a further means of controlling their activities. Where unions brought about wage increases, organizations gave growing attention to the study of jobs, methods improvements, connecting wages to performance (monetary incentives), and the more careful selection of personnel. In turn, this "staff" work required the creation of a body of information and records and then keeping them up-to-date.

Although companies usually adopted Taylor's methods as a defensive measure, those methods led to improved wages for workers by enabling them to work more efficiently and, thus, more productively. The potential benefits of careful recruiting and selection depended on how well the new workers were trained. The joint dependency of labor and management on performance, wages, and job costs led to systematic job analysis and engineering efforts. These efforts involved time and motion studies, job classification and methods improvement, and development of information/records bases. The need to deal with unions led to functional arrangements in "personnel" units and also influenced some of the types of welfare programs that emerged.

Taylor's approach was accepted by labor and management because it placed a strong emphasis on the mutual benefits of productivity: the organization produced more and thus increased its profits, while workers made more money and thus lived better lives. One name given to this outlook is *welfare capitalism*.

Weber's approach emphasized the need for a new structuring of the functions and activities of organizations. This new structure involved extensive controls, such as clearly defined procedures and rules to handle various categories of situations and to maintain continuity in employment and levels of wages. Weber's model was based on two assumptions. First, organizations are closed "societies" that are relatively insulated from the outside world. Second, the internal functions of an organization are stable, and change that does occur is fairly predictable.

Weber's premises encouraged what has now become known as the bureaucratic form of organization. Business structure was an authority-oriented hierarchy that provided careful delegation of responsibility and subdivision of effort to assure efficient performance. This organizational structure defined the limits of the personnel function. Personnel departments were designed to meet the legal demands of employment, which were few, and to recruit and maintain employees. The purpose of personnel departments was clear and simple: ride herd over employees' activities; that is, keep them in the organization at the lowest possible cost and closely track whatever advancement they make.

This approach to personnel was reinforced in three ways. First, the internal workings of organizations were virtually a world unto themselves. Since outside interests made few demands on organizations and since management's function was efficient operation, personnel only had to be concerned with feeding employees into the production process and then keeping them there at the highest possible efficiency with the least cost and effort.

Second, the internal structures of organizations were relatively stable. Markets for goods were, by and large, well defined, though they varied considerably. The fluctuating needs of production processes were met through continuing adjustments to the work force.

Third, the prevailing work ethic of employees and the needs of people made it relatively easy to direct a bureaucratic hierarchy. Mass immigration created a seemingly endless supply of labor. Workers in the sweat shops and factories were concerned with survival and thus welcomed a steady job. They were prepared to accept strict, even arbitrary, work conditions. Craft people were conditioned by a tradition of hard work, loyalty, and dedication to work. In most cases work was the central activity of an employee's life, and many workers made lifelong commitments to a single employer. The economic crises of the 1930s served to emphasize the dependence of the worker on work for subsistence and even survival.

In this atmosphere the bureaucratic approach to personnel seemed logical, rational, and even necessary. By using this model, companies established the basic machinery of the maintenance outlook: personnel departments "maintained" workers in the production process.

Winds of Change: The Maintenance Machinery Expanded

The 1930s was a period of dramatic change. The necessity—even the logic—of the bureaucratic method of management and personnel organization had many critics. Studies conducted by the business community itself questioned the assumptions of the traditional bureaucratic model. A new social conscience both in the business community and in society in general surfaced. Business practices were criticized for their inefficiency and lack of concern for the welfare of the individual.

The various issues that had produced this criticism of the traditional model led to action from two directions. Businesses took a closer look at their employees' work conditions, and some instituted reforms that improved conditions in the workplace. However, these reforms were piecemeal, and it was the intervention of the outside world, especially through government action, that changed business organizations in general and the personnel function in particular. This legislation was primarily responsible for expanding the maintenance functions of personnel departments and for formally establishing them in the business/institutional world.

THE HUMAN RELATIONS MODEL

The traditional approach to personnel management predominated well into the 1940s. But social scientists conducting studies at the Western Electric Company's Hawthorne Works questioned the accuracy of the assumptions of the traditional model. Directed by Elton Mayo and Fritz Roethlisberger of Harvard, this group of studies, called the Hawthorne Study, eventually encouraged the development of a new personnel approach, the human relations model.

What motivates workers to produce? The Hawthorne Study showed that the traditional answer, that workers' only motivation was to produce more and thus make more money, was inadequate. First, the study noted, "rate busters"—piece-rate workers who produced more than the required number of units to be made in a day—sometimes would produce less when faced with the disapproval of their fellow workers. In other words, the employees' world of work was based on social units that could have a stronger influence than money.

Traditionalists were even more startled by another conclusion of the study. Recognition, not efficiency, seemed to improve worker productivity. When the amount of lighting was increased, productivity increased; it was increased again, and productivity increased again. Did workers simply need more light? No. Light was decreased, and productivity *still* increased! Workers' productivity increased, it seemed, because management recognized its own employees' existence and showed some interest in their work. Rather than wanting to be part of a well-honed, efficient, predictable process, workers were happier, and thus more productive, when supervisors recognized them and their work conditions, even if only slightly.

The conclusions of this study produced the human relations model, which emphasized good human relations and good employee morale. Good morale depends on communications, worker satisfaction, and the quality of management-subordinate relations: "establish good communications"; "treat them right and they'll be loyal and dependable"; "work hard and you'll be rewarded and thus be satisfied"; "strengthen your relationships with your workers."

One example will illustrate the nature of the actual change that human relations brought about. Production offices of the Taylor-Weber mode of organization usually were located physically above the assembly-line workers, possibly at the second-story level of the plant. Companies that adopted the human relations approach to personnel brought these offices out of the clouds and put them on the ground floor. This seemingly trivial move made workers feel closer to their managers.

The human relations model was a significant advance in personnel techniques. It represented business' reaction to changing social attitudes and its attempt to develop new, more efficient, procedures. Also, for the first time some important recognition was made of the psychological and social dimensions of work.

Enter: The Outside World

The changes brought about by the human relations model were only the tip of the iceberg. The most radical changes in personnel functions were caused by a frenzy of legislation that was passed and enacted between 1932 and 1938. This legislation, the expression of new social, economic, and political forces that had been developing since the turn of the century, established the personnel machinery of worker *maintenance*. Before this time personnel functions were limited mostly to the basic needs of production, such as hiring, firing, training, and wages. Even the innovations of more progressive companies were production oriented: management wanted workers to be happy because they would produce more, and while some enlightened managers enacted changes in their production operations for the well-being of their employees, many had less idealistic motives. Equally important was the fact that these new procedures existed at the whim of the company: they could be taken away at any time for any, or no, reason.

The legislation of the thirties changed much of this. Companies were forced to enlarge the scope of their personnel departments to include a wide variety of concerns of the individual worker. Some of these new duties were the result of the human relations approach, but the majority of them were the outgrowth of legislation that covered workers' wages, conditions, and general well-being. Personnel departments were forced to rationalize the growing body of knowledge into comprehensive structures that could meet the new requirements.

Legislation.   The 1930s was a period of dramatic social and economic unrest. The legislation of this period reflected and responded to this turmoil to meet the changing needs of the time. Legislation influenced organizations' structures in two ways. First, legislation pertaining only to government employees or dealing only with rather specific situations (for example, interstate commerce) set precedents for private-sector activities.

Union-related legislation played an enormously important role in institutional changes. Legislation outlined negotiating methods, such as collective bargaining and grievance procedures and the concept of prevailing-area wage rates. This early legislation restricted management's use of injunctions against unions, and the National Labor Relations Act (Wagner Act, 1935) encouraged trade union growth.

Armed with this new legal status, unions could force companies to formally recognize workers and to devise solutions related to workers' well-being as a group and as individuals. Management suddenly found itself with a new "partner"—labor—and an overseer in the form of the federal government, which also became a major participant in the establishment of wages, hours, working conditions, productivity, automation, and the disposition of displaced workers. Government agencies required business to make a strict accounting of many functions that had previously been considered its private domain. Faced with these new ground rules, company directors turned to their personnel managers for new methods and procedures.

Union-related legislation had an even greater impact in the precedents it set. Labor-management agreements established precedents in relationships, wages, and work conditions for literally thousands of workers in nonunion businesses. These changes were an important factor in the growth of personnel departments' "industrial relations" activities. Salaries, benefits, selection procedures, working hours, minimum wages, and work environments underwent significant changes.

Social welfare legislation.   Much of the legislation of the 1930s was work oriented, but the economic crisis of those years gave birth to a body of legislation that went beyond the immediate concerns of the workplace. What happened to workers and their families when they couldn't find a job? What happened to a family when the main breadwinner was injured or killed on the job? What happened to people when their working years were over? The Social Security Act of 1935 responded to these questions. It provided unemployment benefits for the unemployed and retirement benefits for those who reached retirement age.

THE EMERGENCE OF PERSONNEL

The conditions of the 1930s created a need for new organizational systems and structures. The result was the maintenance function of personnel. Business, in an attempt to put its own house in order, responded to this new climate, but other forces, especially government action, made this new approach a necessity.

Personnel as a formal, mandatory part of organizational structure really started to come into its own during this period. Many new work-related functions had to be created. Data and information analysis and reporting became regular parts of business activity that was personnel departments' responsibility. These functions were important parts of the maintenance system: personnel was still responsible for various aspects of hiring, training, and wages, but these functions were broadened to include concern for the worker as an individual. And, of course, business through its personnel officers now had to account to the government for more of its activities.

These functions, the basic mechanisms of personnel maintenance, were the central features of personnel through the 1950s. Changes during the following twenty years represented refinements of the maintenance outlook. For instance, the Taft-Hartley Act gave employees the right to accept or reject union membership and evened the power balance between labor and management. World War II accelerated the need for training programs. Personnel departments directed these programs and were responsible for reporting information about them to the government. Also, legislation mandating institutional reporting of pension and welfare activities was passed in the 1950s. The responsibility of personnel departments expanded greatly during this period. Personnel was established as a permanent and prominent part of business.

Personnel: Strictly Overhead

In spite of these changes, many organization managers still viewed personnel as overhead, a costly but necessary evil that was to be tolerated but not encouraged. "Sure," they might say, "personnel is more important than it was forty years ago. Hiring, training, and reporting are necessary, but not as important as sales or production." For managers the maintenance function was more like a holding action than a rational structure designed to promote company efficiency and employee welfare.

This view of personnel should not be seen as a long-dead dragon. Any well-traveled job-hunter has at least once experienced the confusion that can result from asking a plant security officer for the personnel director. "Who?" the security guard asks. "Oh, you want to see the *employment supervisor*, the person in charge of hiring." Unfortunately, hiring is the only word that rings a bell.

Kirby Stanat, director of the placement center at a major university, was personnel director for several large corporations. He recounts one experience that shows how strongly this attitude still exists in some companies:

> When I was a personnel manager, there were times when I started to make suggestions in executive meetings only to have the company president cut me off with, "Aw, shut up, Overhead." (Reardon and Stanat)

This outlook was anachronistic in the 1950s. Today it represents prehistory.

NEW PERSONNEL NEEDS IN AN ENVIRONMENT OF CHANGE

Through the 1950s the maintenance function of personnel management met the needs of organizations. But events of the 1960s and 1970s ushered in a whole new era of personnel developments. Changing economic conditions, radically new technology, and different outlooks and expectations of workers made the traditional view of organizational structure—and the personnel function—woefully inadequate.

Under the maintenance approach, the responsibility but not the power and prestige of personnel departments increased. But this has started to change. A new approach, the human resource model, has emerged. Using this approach, managers view organizations as complex organisms made up of parts that cut across traditional internal lines and react closely with the outside world. The traditional pyramid—even with the business' new partners, labor and government—is outmoded. The cubbyholes are gone. Personnel has played a central role in this new configuration, and the power and prestige of personnel officers have increased proportionately.

Labor

Early union-related legislation established the legal right of workers to organize and the right of unions to negotiate in their behalf. In spite of legislation in the forties that limited its power (Taft-Hartley), the labor movement grew in power and membership. As unions consolidated their early gains, they turned to health, fringe benefits (e.g., insurance), and retirement issues. These concerns became major bargaining matters in the fifties and sixties. Their prominence in institutional compensation arrangements added a whole new set of personnel activities and functionaries.

With about one-fifth of America's industrial workers organized, unions began making important inroads into traditionally nonunion groups, such as white-collar workers, engineers, teachers, public service workers, and service industry workers (e.g., hospitals). In the mid-1960s, unionism was an important force management was confronted with.

One instance of union activity has been in the extension and increase of the minimum wage. The minimum wage was intended to cover only companies engaged in interstate commerce. Through union efforts (as well as government action) the definition of interstate commerce has been broadened to include workers in most industries. In 1974 legislation extended legal coverage to service industries, such as hospitals, that had been excluded in the past. Over the years the labor movement has worked for increases in the minimum wage to facilitate an ever-increased standard of living. A detailed discussion of unions is provided in Chapter 13.

"World of Work" Professionals

The social sciences have grown and matured considerably since the turn of the century, contributing greatly to personnel by providing new concepts, methods, and analyses of personnel activities (Eilber, 1959). Stimulated by World War I and II, government and industry applied the methods of industrial psychologists and engineers on a broad scale. This activity led to the widespread growth of personnel throughout U.S. organizations. This early stage was followed by the thinking through of newer behavioral concepts as the social sciences grew in sophistication The net result has been a vast improvement in the sophistication and variety of personnel tools.

The Psychologists

James M. Cattell (Columbia University) and Hugo Muensterberg (Harvard University) were turn-of-the-century psychologists who contributed heavily to a scientifically based methodology that was important in developing testing and selection methods (Miner and Miner, 1973; Chapter 2). Cattell's work stimulated research concerning the development of intelligence testing. Muensterberg's efforts provided empirical analyses and the use of statistics, which greatly strengthened the field of testing. These test advances facilitated individual assessment and selection for a variety of situations, but the climax of their efforts was the development of the Alpha and Beta tests. With the contribution of an intelligence test developed by Arthur Otis, Alpha and Beta were a major part of the massive U.S. Army testing programs of World War I and basic to selection, training, and placement in the army.

Alpha and Beta.   The large-scale application of psychological tests, first in Alpha and then in Beta, was a tangible demonstration of behavioral scientific development and application. The war provided a laboratory for the refinement of the methodology of test construction. Millions were group tested in conjunction with military induction and the draft. In the World War I Alpha applications, the comparatively large number of low scores emphasized an implicit assumption of literacy that didn't stand up. A newer test form, Beta, was designed to place the less well educated (with poor reading or writing skills). In World War II, use of the Army General Classification Test (AGCT), a successor to Alpha, greatly facilitated selection and placement efforts to meet vast wartime needs for technical specialists.

Literacy assumptions.   The adjustments for the literacy assumption in Alpha had important ramifications for several contemporary issues and events. First, it led to an alternative test approach (Beta), which provided the important *pre*training data needed as a basis to improve the basic 3-R skills (reading, writing, and arithmetic). This 3-R training was preliminary to any specialty training and occupational placement. Thus a two-step testing model was formalized: basic skill training was followed by job skill training. This model saw widespread use in the 1960s under the manpower training legislation involving economically disadvantaged people.

The second point regarding the literacy assumption relates to the very purpose of this test and similar tests as measures of "intelligence." Where cutoff scores and/or high scores were used as a basis for placement, the number of people completing the program successfully usually was acceptable. But significant numbers of test takers who might also have been successful in training as officer candidates were overlooked by virtue of low scores on the *job* skills test.

Interpreting test scores.   Considering the literacy assumptions and 3-R preparation, cultural bias, especially for many economically/socially disadvantaged, became a serious issue. The inherent biases of these types of intelligence tests as indirect (inferential) predictors of job success came under considerable attack in the 1960s, and major reexamination of procedures was indicated under equal-opportunity legislation (1964).

Social Welfare Legislation

Unions have played an important part in changing business practices, but without minimizing the importance of the labor movement in the 1960s, the most radical changes took place in the area of social welfare legislation.

New legislation in the mid-1970s dealt with abuses that had developed in the funding and operation of pension plans. Expansion of the Social Security Act and enactment of pension welfare acts increased the diffusion of government programs and presence through U.S. industry. The government has assumed a growing role in monitoring industrial performance, not only to keep the game honest but also to legislate changes thought to be in the best interest of workers. For example, one pension reform act of the 1970s shortened the period of "vesting" for many pension plans to ten years. An employee now is entitled to a full share of the fund at the end of the vestment period.

Discrimination and employment opportunity were in the headlines and behind the legislation of the 1960s. The targets of this legislation were hiring procedures and the processing of manpower (the unemployed and under-employed) for work. The Civil Rights Act (1964, 1972), Executive Order 11245, and related acts focused on race, sex, and age discrimination and led to "affirmative action" programs by firms to correct discriminatory practices in employment.

Manpower legislation was enacted to meet the labor shortages of the 1960s, the threat of people being displaced by technology, and the challenge of accelerating change and growing business complexity. Even though the full force of technological change wasn't felt in the sixties and the employment picture changed drastically in the early seventies, a critical threshold had been crossed. The personnel function in many organizations took on vast new responsibilities. And worker participation had an impact on the destiny of organizations. However, the record of firms relative to the new manpower look was highly uneven—as we shall see in Chapter 2.

Advancing Personnel Concepts and Techniques

The behavioral scientists.   The Hawthorne Study was an important advance in the methodologies of behavioral scientists. Behavioral scientists started to use all kinds of institutions and institutional life as living laboratories for inquiry and application. Findings from freshmen college classes, penal institutions, correctional schools, Air Force squadrons, ships, planes, airport control towers, insurance offices, railroad gangs, scientific researchers, and shoe factories were derived, intermingled, and reapplied. Islands of seemingly similar results led to partial theories and new speculations regarding motivation, leadership, group influences, and the effects of organization communications on productivity and change.

Abraham Maslow (1954) proposed a theory regarding an individual's "hierarchy of needs." Frederic Herzberg advanced a "two factor theory" of motivation: some organizations used "hygiene" considerations, money, supervision, job frills, and the physical aspects of work to motivate people, but these factors served only human "maintenance needs" rather than the "job itself." Another consideration, "motivators," provided opportunities for personal realization (achievement, responsibility, advancement, interesting work, recognition, and a sense of controlling one's destiny).

Douglas Bray (1956) at the New York laboratories of American Telephone and Telegraph (ATT) pioneered some of the basic techniques of "assessment centers." These centers provided for systematic personnel evaluation. Bray organized a panel of experts to be evaluators and used multiple testing techniques to predict the future promotion and success of ATT managers and professionals, but he did not disclose the evaluations to the participants. Several years later, the prediction was examined against actual results. The outcome of the study showed that new predictive power was now realizable.

Another example of systematic study and application of personnel-related concepts concerned the job study center at Purdue University, directed by Ernest McCormick. Under governmental sponsorship, the center coordinated a ten-year study that developed new tools for systematic job analysis (the Position Analysis Questionnaire, or PAQ) and evaluations. The product of this effort was likely to influence the direction of institutional practices for many years to come.

War, the Role of Government

The two world wars stimulated much new social science research, but war also encouraged the development of other personnel tools. During World War I a

Committee on Classification assisted greatly in advancing occupational and classification methodology, and the federal government required that personnel departments be established in war plants (Ling, 1956) helping to diffuse the personnel function throughout U.S. industry. Additionally, The Secretary of Labor was elevated to a cabinet-level position during this period.

The Civil Service became a major arm of personnel work in government organization and served as an example for industry. Job classification and analysis on behalf of government employment was placed under Civil Service. This action extended personnel procedures to various types of offices and greatly increased the exposure of these methods to all types of professionals. The *Dictionary of Occupational Titles* (DOT) and the DOT job analysis schemes, found today in government as well as in industry, are traceable directly to these developments.

In the armed forces, continuing advancements in personnel technology were made. For example, research undertaken by the U.S. Air Force in Texas in the late 1950s formulated mathematical models for estimating organizational manpower needs resulting from promotions, transfers, "quits," and even deaths. These models, related to the branch of mathematics termed "Markov Processes," have proved to be of growing value in personnel studies.

The work ethic. Early in 1973 a report sponsored by the Department of Health, Education, and Welfare was prepared by the Upjohn Institute for Employment Research. It created widespread discussion in Congress, the press, television, radio, and academic circles. The report dealt with job satisfaction, work attitudes, and motivation to work among blue- and white-collar workers, professionals, and managers. The "findings" of the report should be more properly viewed as "possibilities." Since the results were derived from a modest number of studies, criticism is certainly justified. Yet the report contains so many elements of concern to personnel officials and organization policy makers that it deserves the serious attention of all organization officials (see Chapter 3):

1. For most adults, work is a central activity in life.

2. Large numbers of workers at all organization levels are dissatisfied with their jobs. (However, some research has shown that there has been no real *increase* in dissatisfaction over the last twenty years.)

3. Job dissatisfaction affects, for example, productivity, absenteeism, and even off-the-job problems (such as mental health).

4. Job dissatisfaction may emerge from a variety of causes, including over-specialization of work, lack of opportunity for personal growth, dead-end jobs, lack of job opportunities, and autocratic management.

Are we overeducating our population relative to job opportunity? Is job dissatisfaction really widespread? Do people really want a great deal of intrinsic satisfaction? Substantial research findings are lacking to either confirm or deny these questions. Yet we can rest assured that these problems exist and are likely to grow among union members and people in all walks of life—they will approach center stage in congressional deliberations and proposed legislation. The growing

TABLE 1-1 Legislation Influencing Personnel Activities

Date	Name	Salary benefits	Selection	Min. wage	Work environment	Labor Unions	Comments
1926	National Railway Labor Act					X	Procedures for collective bargaining and settling disputes
1931	Davis-Bacon Act			X			Requires federal construction contractors to pay prevailing wage rates in an area—as determined by the secretary of labor.
1932	Norris-LaGuardia Act					X	Restricts mgts. in dealing with unions, especially use of injunction—government should not interfere in union-management relations.
1935	National Labor Relations Act (Wagner Act) (NLRA)					X	Govt. intervention in labor-mgt. disputes; restrains mgts.; encourages trade union growth.
1935	Social Security Act (SS)	X					Federal tax on payrolls, unemployment benefits, retirement benefits.
1936	Walsh-Healey Act			X			Establishments with govt. contracts over $10,000 minimum hourly rate, time and one-half over 8 hours per day, and 40 hours per week.
1938	Fair Labor Standards Act (amended 1949, 55, 61, 66, 74)			X			Minimum hourly rate, time and one-half over 40 hours, and child labor.
1946	Employment Act				X		Employment is a national goal and "right."
1947	Taft-Hartley Act					X	Government supports right of free choice in seeking or rejecting union representation, rather than active union support as in Wagner Act. Administered by National Labor Relations Board.
1958	Welfare and Pension Plans Disclosure Act	X					Report of plan operation to U.S. Dept. of Labor.

Year	Legislation			Description
1959	Landrum-Griffin Act	X		Regulates internal affairs of unions and relations between union leaders and members. Eliminates "sweetheart" contracts.
1962	Manpower Development and Training Act (MDTA)		X	Retraining for those displaced by technology. Focus shifts to hardcore unemployment and economically disadvantaged.
1964 (amended 1972)	Civil Rights Act (especially Title VI)		X	Applies to employers of 15 or more people and interstate commerce. Prohibition of discrimination based on race, color, religion, sex or national origin. Implications for psychological testing. Employment records, applications, and forms. Enforced by Equal Employment Opportunity Commission.
	State Fair Employment Practices Legislation		X	Covers race, color, religion, age and sex factors, and supports earlier federal legislation.
1967	Age Discrimination Act		X	Employers of 25 or more engaged in interstate commerce. No job discrimination, ages 40–65. Includes payroll and personnel records and ok to hire.
1970	Economic Stabilization Act		X	Presidential authority to stabilize wages and salaries (among other factors). Government Pay Board Administration
1970	Executive Order 11246		X	Federal govt. contractors, subcontractors. Reporting form similar to that required under Civil Rights Act (Title VII). Requires affirmative action. Enforced by Office of Federal Contract Compliances
1970	Occupational Safety and Health Act (OSHA)		X	Compliance with safety and health standards of Labor Dept. for hazards that threaten serious injury or death.
1974	Various regulations on pension plans		X	Limits on vesting period; strengthens finances

attention of popular magazines, newspapers, and tv programs amply attests to the importance and growing interest in these questions.

Automation and computerization. Automation, and technological change have accelerated personnel-related developments. Although first used in commercial applications in the 1950s, business and government acquired thousands upon thousands of computers by 1976! Additionally, the mushrooming use of "mini" computers in the seventies promises an era of growth equal to that of the commercial units (Gross and Smith, 1976). In manufacturing, the automation of industrial processes through the use of all kinds of equipment improvements, numeric control (machine-tool) technology, and process-control computers has vastly changed the structure of jobs and use of people in most manufacturing units. These technological improvements have contributed importantly to increased output, but have caused in some cases decreases in employment (Burack and McNichols, 1973).

Some examples of technologically related change and its impact on how work is accomplished illustrate the magnitude of change employers and employees must accept.

1. *Computer automation of production control* in an automotive manufacturing plant permitted the quick determination of order-status information. However, the new information capability also has been used to predict near-term human resource requirements (three months to one year), highlight daily problems for action by department heads, and free up and reallocate time for planning and trouble spots. Department heads have become more knowledgeable of their operations and emerging manpower needs, and thus overtime scheduling has become more "plannable" and hiring practices have been improved. On the other hand, some workers who relate computer automation to their jobs have begun to fear these new procedures.

2. *Technical service people and salesmen* who sell to some of the automotive plants have found that the scope of knowledge needed in communicating with plant supervisors, managers, officials, and technical people has increased. New technologies in manufacturing and information processing are more complex because of their technical nature and relation to other procedures. Various salesmen have needed new training or retraining.

3. *Law enforcement officers* have been confronted with criminals who use advanced technical equipment for monitoring police radio bands, conversations, and phone calls. Traditional programs have had to be revised or expanded to outfit officers and investigation teams with this new knowledge. Also, the mode of police organization and work procedures have changed with the installation of computer technology for analysis and identification, and new teams of specialists have been trained for investigation.

4. *Store and plant security capabilities* in a food chain have been advanced considerably through closed-circuit tv, low-light-level cameras, two-way radios, and remote controls. Job activities have shifted considerably, from patrol to monitoring, and it has been found feasible to use women in jobs previously

occupied by males. In this situation physical exertion has decreased, the importance of mental alertness and quick response has increased, work environment and conditions are much more controllable, time scheduling has become more flexible, and the type and relevance of education and experience have changed. In this instance, previous law experience has become less important, and an added premium has been placed on education and knowledgeable action.

5. *In a hospital* new technologies have affected a wide span of activities from maintaining premises and housekeeping to patient monitoring, diagnosis, and operating procedures. Special motorized carts and cleanup equipment have decreased the number of unskilled people. But those who remain must have somewhat higher skill levels. Intensive care units, virtually built around patient-monitoring technology, have improved postoperative recovery, yet they require careful selection and specialized training of personnel. New food preparation and preservation technologies have greatly improved dietary and feeding procedures and thus changed the attendant jobs.

For these reasons—the dramatic social, economic, legislative, and technological changes, and because of a marked change in the work ethic—the world that organizations must function in is considerably more complex than it was thirty or even fifteen years ago. And when that complicated world is considered along with the complexity of present-day business operations, the conclusion is inescapable; a new approach to personnel management is badly needed.

PERSONNEL AS A SYSTEM: THE HUMAN RESOURCE MODEL

The human resource model of personnel is based on a radical assumption that sets it apart from models of the past. All organizations are systems—in other words, integrated units. The parts of any system, or unit, must be coordinated in a logical, efficient manner so that it can function in a way that benefits both the organization itself and its individual members.

The primary functions of an organization, including its work activity, are tied closely to personnel. While personnel is still a support system in the traditional sense, it is more clearly integrated into its organization's overall functions. Production planners, for instance, must rely more heavily on the judgments of personnel directors. In addition to asking a personnel director, "Will we have enough people to do such and such?" an organization planner will ask, "If we automate Division B, we will only need unskilled labor. What union will we have to negotiate with? How will other unions react?" Or, "If we computerize Section B, will we be able to hire enough programmers and system people? What will we do with the people who are displaced? How much will the new people cost us? What type of reorganization will be required?"

The human resource model represents an important advance in personnel administration in another important respect. Organizations of the present are more intimately tied to the external world than they were thirty years ago. The human resource model is an *open* system. It represents a conscious effort (and need) to relate the operations of the organization to the world outside, where the only certainty is uncertainty. A personnel director with this perspective designs plans to cope with the unexpected and to accept good rather than ideal designs—and, at times, grubby success rather than dramatic improvement.

Stages of the Human Resource System

The most distinctive aspects of the human resource model of personnel management are how it provides a way of looking at organizations as integrated systems and how it meets the increasing demands of the world they must function in. This system has four stages:

1. the acquisition of experience and structured knowledge by current and potential employees
2. the machinery (input system) to integrate people coming from schools or other employers
3. the administration-management-maintenance functions that guide and support personnel activities within the work system
4. planning and preparing individuals for career growth and development.

Stage 1. This stage (1, 6, and 7 in the diagram) includes the external forces found in society and the sources of employees for the organization. To an important extent, the internal characteristics of a specific personnel system are affected by the external environmental forces of change and features of the labor force. Legislation may mandate institutional changes; broad economic trends or technological changes may further influence the policies and purposes of personnel officials. Also, potential employees possess various social and cultural values (reflecting their educational, life, and work experiences) that may be very different from those of employees already in the organization.

There may be many reasons for personnel to accommodate and deal thoughtfully with potential organizational members. People, in their vast complexity of skills, education, professional achievements, and personal needs, comprise the central core of the *external labor market* (7). They are job seekers. According to the labor-market idea, there are both suppliers and demanders of human resources. Employers and employees come together for both economic and behavioral reasons—a mutually beneficial arrangement is sought.

Stage 2. Employees enter an organization through the recruiting, or input system (2). At this stage personnel performs a gatekeeping function by recruiting, assessing, and selecting people to meet both current and future needs and priorities.

Stage 3. Employees often receive skill training or "development" to broaden their knowledge or concepts. Planning is an ongoing organizational activity; personnel directors play an important part in this process. New production systems, for

EXHIBIT 1-1 Systems Perspective on Personnel-Human Resource Management

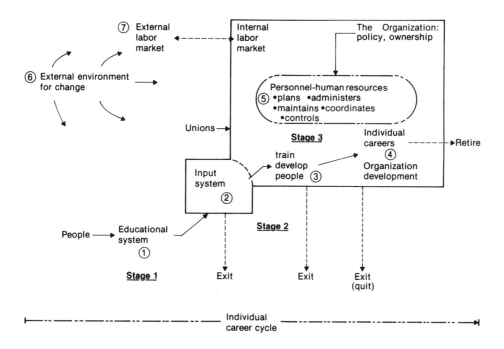

instance, can affect the internal organization and its manpower problems. As an administrator (5), the personnel director advises planners and top management about the outcome of plans and potential trouble spots. The personnel director also keeps apprised of important external trends (6) for their impact on the institution. The director's assessment of external trends may cause modifications of institutional policies.

Stage 4.   Once employees have been absorbed into an organization, both the individual and the organization must be prepared for growth and change (4). The greater the ability of the organization to tap its employees' abilities with appropriate recognition, treatment, and reward, the greater the returns to both the individual and the organization. Increasingly, however, individual accomplishments become dependent on group accomplishments (Burack, 1975, Chapters 11–14). Personnel's task is to help develop and strengthen these work teams as well.

We now add the following scenario to illustrate the impact of social and technical change upon the personnel and management functions.

SCENARIO: SANTO'S FOODS

The Santo's Food Division was one of the member families of National Enterprises, Inc., a large conglomerate with holdings in various industries. The mass
marketing retail food area, automotive production, commercial education, and
the health field were key areas of National's activity.

Santo's Foods was a seventy-store regional (Ohio-Pennsylvania) chain
founded in 1952 with an initial group of eight stores acquired from a small
chain that had gone into bankruptcy. Through superior merchandising and riding
the crest of the great surge to mass food distribution, Santo's Foods expanded
very rapidly. Most of the company's growth took place in the 1950s and 1970s.
Events in this period vastly changed the character of its operations.

Environmental and Company Change

Santo's organization and operations changed greatly in response to new conditions. Rapidly changing features of the competitive environment, newer marketing
techniques, population shifts, new legal requirements, and modifications in
distribution technology were among the key factors that accounted for the shift.

Competition and marketing. Santo's quickly moved to large-volume merchandising and the marketing of many nonfood lines. Store development followed
urban and suburban development, and stores were closed out in areas where
adequate property could not be economically obtained for expansion or where
demand would no longer support mass-distribution approaches. Price competition,
loss leaders, special promotion items, and heavy advertising were some of the
many factors causing high attrition among competitors. Stores became ever
larger as profit margins declined and units applied the economies of large-scale
operation; for example, one senior person could manage a store of forty thousand
square feet as well as he could one of ten thousand square feet. Store managers,
middle managers, and outside advertising agencies were constantly shuffled
around in the search for talent or special know-how. In the period from 1956–1976,
average store size increased threefold, and almost one-third of sales were in
nonfood items. New types of store and headquarters personnel had to be sought
out and training needs were much more evident.

New legal requirements. The era of consumerism had clearly arrived by the late
1960s. Developments such as content coding, "truth in advertising" requirements,
and pricing and content information modified general advertising and in-store
procedures. Tougher quality specifications, testing programs enforced by the
Pure Food and Drug Administration, and new legislation led to additional
warehousing and in-store procedures related to dating and coding. At times
severe disruptions took place as various kinds of suspect merchandise had to
be removed from sales. Attempts to train personnel to make these procedures
foolproof were not readily achieved.

The passage of equal employment and manpower legislation resulted in a considerable change in work force composition throughout the Santo's chain. The increasing prominence of blacks and Latins in store operations and racial minorities and women in warehousing and headquarters operations were among the shifts that took place. Also, jobs that had been traditionally reserved for women or men were being reexamined—women toted boxes and men rang out customers. A number of supervisors were never quite the same as these changes started to occur.

Technological changes.   Cash register (data) terminals (with computer capability) modified the bases for managing inventory, controlling merchandise, and monitoring the performance of store operations, managers, and employees. Further advances in freezer technology and the demand for convenience foods turned stores into "seas of refrigeration equipment." Content and carton coding permitted the use of computers to support warehousing operations. New occupational groups (for example, refrigeration maintenance) had to be hired and trained to service these systems.

Social changes and educational developments.   Various employment changes took place. Store employees went from mostly full time to mostly part time as the company expanded. Economic considerations, longer store hours, and greater need for managerial flexibility led to the greater use of part timers. The availability of part timers in the 1955–76 period was supported by the growing number of students going into higher education who needed supplementary income (yet who weren't available for full-time work) and wives or second-wage earners who made themselves available in increasing numbers. However, the full-time/part-time mix was not without its problems; company loyalty, motivation, and the search for meaningful work at times led to extraordinary absenteeism and turnover.

Redefinition of the Santo's Personnel Function

When the original group of stores was acquired and for several years thereafter, it was hoped that each store would take care of its own needs. Consequently, store managers and warehouse managers hired and trained their own employees to suit their need—and within the restrictions of their personnel budget—for floor people and supervisors. Managers, in turn were hired by the president through "walk-ins" or leads from other managers.

By 1960 Santo's had over twenty-five stores and more than one thousand employees. At this point, two marketing regions were formed, and hiring responsibilities plus wage controls were seated with the newly created jobs of regional managers.

Unionization.   Unionization of several employee groups (e.g., butchers, retail clerks) along with passage of manpower and equal opportunity legislation were all factors in the formation of a personnel department at the company's main offices in 1965. Although Santo's was acquired in the same year by the conglomerate National Enterprises, Inc., the company continued to operate for some while in largely autonomous fashion.

Personnel's role started to change as various incidents took place and needs emerged. The threatened extension of store and warehouse unionization and the whip sawing of wages (playing union off against nonunion) forced headquarters personnel to get more actively involved in wage policies.

A buying boycott by blacks for lack of black store management pushed personnel still further into the affairs of stores. One day Santo's president asked the personnel managers how many people were ready to move up to store management, as they were considering the acquisition of a small ten-store chain. Of course, the figures weren't available and couldn't even be adequately approximated—the president was very unhappy. "What have you been doing around here—is that all you are worried about—those union negotiations?" From that day on, the personnel manager took on a new set of activities, which resulted in keeping close track of people who might be eligible to be promoted. The same year, 1972, the president told the personnel manager to "go out and hire a couple of college kids—we need some new blood around here." (See discussion question number 1 at end of chapter.)

THE JANUS PERSPECTIVE: WHERE WE'VE BEEN AND WHERE WE'RE GOING

Janus was the god of hospitality in Roman mythology. He had one head with two faces looking in opposite directions. In Roman houses he occupied a prominent place over the doorway. This is an appropriate symbol to show personnel at its present stage of development.

The human resources model of personnel management did not simply appear from nowhere. It is the outgrowth of many years of response to the changing needs of organizations. These changes have produced many responses and revisions of those responses, until today personnel, once considered a frivolous addition to organizational hierarchies, has become an integral part of organizational structures. The power and prestige of personnel is likely to increase in the coming years.

But what more specifically can we say about the future? The great many disagreements among the experts, even when forecasting rather simple matters (Cetron and Overly, 1974), indicate the problem. But with a combination of brashness and humility we will describe some of the emerging events and organizational arrangements that are likely to influence personnel departments of the future.

Legislation.   The government will show continued interest and will continue to intervene in health protection and maintenance, occupational safety, transferability of benefits, benefit coverage (especially pension and disability). Also, legislation establishing a model or standard of comprehensive fringe-benefit coverage probably will be enacted in the coming years. Whatever that established standard is, it probably will influence private plans.

As more and more white-collar and professional people become unionized and as labor organizations continue to grow in maturity and sophistication, new mechanisms will be needed to solve new problems. Periodic increases of the minimum wage, welfare coverage, and forced improvement of environmental work conditions probably will continue.

Innovation and technological change.   The catch-up type of technological change that characterized U.S. industry through the mid-1960s probably will fall into a slower pattern of continuing improvement. The continuing pressure for quality-of-life improvements will sustain pressure on industry for real productivity gains. Job evaluation procedures, use of monetary incentives, retraining, and (at times) rearranging managerial structures will receive continued attention. Major one-step changes in organizational modes of production will mean that many different departments and officials will have to cooperate to assure smooth transitions in operations. For personnel, this will mean dealing with employee displacement, retraining, and reorganization (Burack and McNichols, 1973). Personnel departments will have to make periodic adjustments to deal with these situations.

Age mix and educational trends.   Pronounced shifts in the proportion of various age groups will continue. The traditional middle-management age category (early thirties to the mid-forties) will be inadequate for supplying senior managerial and top-management positions. Greater emphasis will be placed on career ladders and fast-track developmental assignments for younger people.

Growing numbers of older people will impose new demands on programs for dealing with obsolescence, phasing people out of the world of work gradually, and providing adequate benefit coverage.

The pressure for more education seems likely to decrease as new directions are assumed (U.S. Office of Education, 1974). The proportion of high school graduates who go on to college probably will stabilize, though organizational recruiting will reflect the momentum of the educational surge from 1950 to 1975 for many years to come. A major and needed adjustment appears in the offing between the number of available jobs that require higher education and specialized skills and the larger number who are trying to fill them (see Chapter 3).

Internal organization of personnel.   Formal project teams (groups organized and assigned to a specific task often taking months or even years to complete) and informal groups have been increasingly relied on in many areas of organizational analysis, planning, and decision making. The groups are a response to problems or projects that are especially complex or uncertain. Project teams have broadened the participation of institutional members by bringing people with diverse talents together. The dynamics of these teams place great importance on group processes—leadership, communications, and effective interaction. Personnel specialists will need new training approaches as these groups increase in importance.

The geographic dispersion, diversification, and conglomeration of companies have created complex organizations that were almost undreamed of only thirty years ago. Major companies have diversified drastically. For instance, Gillette, formerly in razor blades and women's hair products, has gone into games and calculators (*Wall Street Journal*, 8 Nov. 1974). This manner of organizational growth poses new demands in the training, development, and integration of large numbers of new organizational members. Communications are under considerable stress, and new media and channels must be sought.

National and international economic climate.   The longstanding economic dominance of the "advanced industrial nations" seems likely to change greatly. The growing affluence of the oil-rich "emerging nations" and continuing pressure on domestic unemployment and economic vitality indicate new areas of personnel undertakings or readjustments. If the U.S. standard of living continues to erode, new demands will be made to regularize layoff procedures (managerial and white and blue collar) and unemployment benefits. Interest in overtime work as a source of extra income may increase. If economic erosion in the United States cuts deeply, unemployment may stay at a high level, and the "no-skill" or low skilled are likely to be affected adversely.

However, economic recovery may lead to quite different bases for the seniority concept of unions and of women and racial minorities in organizations. The definition of acceptable levels of unemployment and a new international flavor in employment and organization would be likely results.

On balance, the environmental fabric surrounding all manner of organizational life seems destined to become more complex, and with it, the challenges confronting personnel management. Few organizations will be able to rest on their laurels as needed adjustments are signaled for many personnel activities. Further, demands for improving the quality of work life (discussed in the next chapter) seem destined to greatly reinforce improvements in the work climate and provision for the improvement and personal realization of work-force members.

SUMMARY

Widespread changes in the environment of organizational activities, along with the modification of employees' outlooks and work-life expectancies, have shifted the mission of the personnel function. Social, economic, and technological change, plus numerous new legislative measures, have expanded maintenance responsibilities. Organizations have become open systems that are influenced considerably by external events, which in turn may have a bearing on their internal structures. These changes and the changing character of people-related needs and growing business complexity have placed a larger premium on personnel activities.

The personnel emphasis is moving beyond "maintaining" people and requires thoughtful planning and programming for the use of human resources. For emphasis, we have termed the emerging personnel function *personnel-human resources*.

DISCUSSION QUESTIONS

1. a. What was the nature of environmental events changing the character of Santo's Foods in the 1955–75 period?
    b. What was the impact of these events on units, operations, and personnel?
    c. Describe the emergence of personnel activities, and provide key reasons for these occurrences.
    d. What new changes were likely in the offing for personnel after 1972? Be sure to state your assumptions.

2. Early in 1973 a report sponsored by the Department of Health, Education, and Welfare was made available in book form (Cambridge, Mass.: M.I.T. Press). Edited by Harold L. Shepard of the Upjohn Institute for Employment Research, the book, *Work in America*, brought together the research of a number of behavioral scientists who had probed the American work scene. The results dealt largely with matters related to job satisfaction, attitudes toward work, motivation of workers regarding their jobs, and indicators suggesting the attractiveness of work situations. Data were provided on both blue- and white-collar jobs as well as managerial and professional activities. Somewhat to the amazement of HEW and the report team, the report became a most controversial basis for discussion among congressmen, company and public officials, and union heads. Reports of widespread job dissatisfaction were both confirmed and denied.
    a. Set down some major social, cultural, and ideological developments that might account for shifts in worker outlook and attitude toward work.
    b. What is (was) *the* work ethic? Today? Yesterday?
    c. Has there been a change in the work ethic?
    d. What are *your* five-, ten-, and twenty-year projections regarding alienation, job satisfaction, and changes in the work environment? What do these developments mean for
        i. company officials
        ii. various work-force members (blue collar, white collar, managerial/professional)
        iii. government officials in the executive and legislative branches (e.g., U.S. Department of Labor; U.S. Employment Training Service; Health, Education, and Welfare; National Science Foundation)?

3. The automation of manufacturing processes and information processing has vastly changed the characteristics of work and jobs. Make and state the necessary assumptions and comment on the following:
    a. Name some jobs you are familiar with which have been affected by educational level required. Why has this requirement changed?
    b. How have technical changes affected work climate and characteristics of work?
    c. In light of the changes you have described, what would they imply for

    i. governmental officials with city and regional jurisdictions

    ii. company policymakers

    iii. personnel, industrial relations, and manpower officials of various institutions, including the manufacturing and service sectors?

BIBLIOGRAPHY

Bennis, Warren. *Beyond Bureacracy.* New York: McGraw-Hill, 1966.

Bloomfield, M. "The Aim and Work of the Employment Manager's Associations." *Annals of the American Academy of Political and Social Science* 65 (1910).

Burack, Elmer H. *Organizational Analysis, Theory and Application.* Hinsdale, Ill.: Dryden Press, 1975.

_____. *Strategies for Manpower Planning and Programming.* Morristown, N.J.: General Learning Press, 1971.

Burack, Elmer H., and James Walker. *Manpower Planning and Programming.* Boston, Mass.: Allyn & Bacon, 1972.

Burack, Elmer H., and Edwin Miller. "A New Role for Personnel in Organizations." *California Management Review* (Spring 1976).

Burack, Elmer H., James F. Staszak, and Gopal Pati, "An Organizational Analysis of Manpower Issues in Employing the Disadvantaged." *Academy of Management Journal* 15 (September 1972).

Burack, Elmer H., and Thomas J. McNichols. *Human Resource Management: Technology, Policy, Change.* Kent, Ohio: Kent State University, Division of Research, 1973.

Cetron, Marvin J., and Don H. Overly. "Disagreeing with the Future." *Technology Assessment* 1 (1974):245–53.

Cooper, Arnold, *et al.* "Strategic Responses to Technological Threats." *Proceedings of the 33rd Annual Meeting of The Academy of Management.* Boston, 1973.

DeGreene, Kenyon B. *Sociotechnical Systems.* Englewood, N.J.: Prentice-Hall, 1973.

Doctors, Samuel I. *Whatever Happened to Minority Economic Development?* Hinsdale, Ill.: Dryden Press, 1974.

Eilbert, H. "The Development of Personnel Management in the United States." *Business History Review* 33 (1959):345–64.

Gross, Paul F. and Smith, Robert D. *Systems Analysis and Design for Management.* New York: Dun-Donnelley Publishing Company, 1976.

Hubbard, Elbert. *Little Journey to the Homes of the Great.* New York: William H. Wise & Co., 1916.

Jenkins, David. *Job Power: Blue and White Collar Democracy.* New York: Doubleday, 1973.

Levitan, Sal A., and William B. Johnston. *Work Is Here to Stay, Alas.* Salt Lake City: Olympus Publishing Company, 1973.

Ling, Cyril C. *The Management of Personnel Relations: History and Origins.* Homewood, Ill.: Richard D. Irwin, 1965.

Luft, Joseph. *Of Human Interaction.* Palo Alto, Calif.: National Press Books, 1969.

McCormick, Ernest J., R. C. Mechem, and P. J. Jeanneret. *User's Manual for the Position Analysis Questionnaire.* West Lafayette, Ind.: PAQ Services, 1973.

Miner, John B., and Mary Green Miner. *Personnel and Industrial Relations,* 2d ed. New York: Macmillan, 1973.

Muensterberg, Hugo. *Psychology and Industrial Efficiency.* Boston: Houghton Mifflin, 1973.

Purcell, Theodore V., and Gerald F. Cavanah. *Blacks in the Industrial World*. New York: The Free Press, 1972.

Reardon, Patrick, and Kirby Stanat. *Job Hunting: Secrets and Tactics*. Milwaukee, Wisc.: Westward Press, A division of Raintree Publishers, Ltd. (1977): p. 90.

Rieder, George A. "Performance Review: A Mixed Bag." *Harvard Business Review*, 51, 4 (July/August 1973).

Roethlisberger, F. J., and W. J. Dickson. *Management and the Worker*. Cambridge, Mass.: Harvard University Press, 1939.

Sayles, Leonard R. "Job Enrichment—Little That's New—and Right for the Wrong Reasons." *Proceedings of the 26th Annual Meeting of the Industrial Relations Research Association*. New York, 1973.

Sheppard, Harold L. "Task Enrichment and Wage Levels as Elements in Worker Attitudes." *Proceedings of the 26th Annual Meeting of the Industrial Relations Research Association*. New York, 1973.

Taylor, Frederick W. *Principles and Methods of Scientific Management*. New York: Harper & Row, 1911.

Terkel, Studs. *Working*. New York: Pantheon, 1974.

Toffler, Alvin. *Future Shock*. New York: Bantam Books, 1971.

W. E. Upjohn Institute for Employment Research. *Work in America: Report of a Special Task Force to the Security of Health Educational Welfare*. Cambridge, Mass.: M.I.T. Press, 1973.

U.S. Office of Education. "Projection of Educational Statistics to 1978" (Washington, D.C.: U.S. Government Printing Office, 1970).

Utterback, James M., and Elmer H. Burack. "Identification of Technological Threats and Opportunities by Firms." *Technological Forecasting and Social Change* (Fall 1975).

Wortman, Max S., Jr., and Kathryn M. Bartol. "Forecast for the Future: Mobility, Promotion and Tenure." *Proceedings of the 33rd Annual Meeting of the Aacademy of Management*. Boston, 1973.

Chapter 2

ORGANIZATIONALLY SPEAKING, WHAT'S PERSONNEL?

LEARNING OBJECTIVES

Chapter 1 outlined some of the major historical forces that have shaped existing personnel functions. Yet the question remains, what specifically is the nature of personnel in the present? This chapter addresses itself to specific elements of this question. In particular, the objectives of this chapter are to:

Identify organizational factors and developments influencing the form and position of the personnel function

Describe the contingency approach to the organization of the personnel function

Describe the basis on which to formulate strategies for launching personnel and human-resource programs in organizations

Describe the basis for instituting change programs to undertake and implement personnel and human-resource activities

Apply the contingency model to a contemporary personnel problem.

KEY TERMS AND CONCEPTS

contingency plan
career management
manpower forecasting
job enrichment
critical mass
pressure points
OSHA

change strategy
authority, centralization, decentralization
contingency approach to personnel
DOT job analysis

PREVIEW

Chapter 1 painted the picture of the emergent personnel function in rather broad strokes. Chapter 2, on the other hand, uses a micro approach. In citing some of the specific needs of contemporary organizations, this chapter will:

1. Define the terminology and bases of personnel organization.
2. Discuss the contingency approach to personnel organization.
3. Explore some of personnel's new roles.
4. Identify some future trends in personnel programs.

In the opening chapter, we reviewed some of the major shifts in personnel methods and philosophies. Personnel has evolved mainly as business has responded to changing conditions. In this chapter we will analyze the more prominent organizational structures in greater detail. We also will describe the newer roles personnel managers have grown into as agents of change.

TERMINOLOGY: THE NAME OF THE GAME

Personnel; personnel management and administration; personnel-industrial relations; department of human resources; manpower management; manpower planning; industrial relations; all these and more have been used to describe personnel-related functions. Are these simply *names?* No! For some organizations these titles reflect important distinctions. They are legitimate attempts to distinguish organizational activities that can vary greatly. The following table lists only a few.

TABLE 2-1   Personnel-Related Functions

Designation	Typical activities or focus
Personnel	Recruit, select, train/develop, compensate
Industrial relations	Union negotiations, contract management
Human resource planning (narrow)	Forecasting future human needs
Human resource planning (broad)	Assuring that the right number of people with the appropriate skills are at the right place at the right time

Not surprisingly, many organizations move beyond this basic list to such things as safety responsibilities and even social welfare responsibilities (e.g., counsel on housing, personal problems, and health). *Industrial relations,* once primarily associated with industrial processes, may involve only union negotiations and contract management or some combination of traditional maintenance and industrial relations activities. Unfortunately, companies and governmental units have also used terms such as *department of human resources* to indicate the human resource types of responsibilities or, in some cases, to reflect the addition of newer employee-related activities. And the names continue. Some are accurate descriptions of responsibility; some are due to historical happenings; others are due to what's in vogue; and some simply are the whim of a key official.

In their attempts to call attention to the newer directions in personnel activities, academics and researchers have only made the problem worse. Thus *manpower planning and programming, career management,* and *human-resource management* have been added to the list to describe the newer thrust of personnel-related activities. However, these new terms have one redeeming virtue: they emphasize the need to connect planning with the implementation of plans and emphasize enlarged concern for the individual.

Usage in This Book

For subsequent discussions we will refer to the people-related function in the organization by using the terms *personnel* or *human resources* or *personnel-human resources* interchangeably. Where narrower or more specialized discussions are undertaken, these will be appropriately noted. In light of this problem it is impossible to identify precise responsibilities (e.g., to hire, train, forecast, or counsel) from these general titles. Each situation requires a functional title *and* a detailed recital of responsibilities.

BASES FOR PERSONNEL ORGANIZATION

The differing structural forms of organizations have added to the confusion with terminology. Some years ago, in a study sponsored by the American Management Association, Dalton McFarland identified four basic structural forms of personnel-related activity (McFarland, 1967). A summary of these basic models follows:

1. *Centralized organization.* The main functions are carried out at a particular location. Personnel responsibilities are separate from industrial relations duties.
2. *Centralized organization.* Personnel and industrial relations are combined at a particular location.
3. *Divisionalized organization.* A small personnel or industrial relations unit at headquarters concerns itself with personnel policy development, research, or the launching of broad institutional development programs.
4. *Decentralized organization.* Major personnel responsibilities are handled by local units.

These models may account for more than half of the personnel-type organizations of the past, but they are inadequate to describe the organizational configurations of the present. The growing complexity of business operations makes it very difficult to generalize. The rise of conglomerates and multinational operations and the wide diffusion of the personnel activity throughout governmental units and organizations (such as insurance, health, and banking) have created organizational structures that would have given executives of ten years ago nightmares. When someone mentions the words *conglomerate* or *multinational corporation,* people usually think of ITT or General Motors. But the following scenarios will show the kinds of changes many less glamorous organizations and their personnel departments have gone through in recent years.

EMERGENCE OF THE PERSONNEL FUNCTION OF NORWOOD PHARMACEUTICAL

Norwood Pharmaceutical and Chemical (NPC) is among the more volatile members of the Interstate Industries family. During nearly twenty years of operation Norwood has easily attained the conglomerate's record for highest yearly profit, return on sales, and other conventional measures of financial performance. At times profits dipped very low as a result of fierce competition, drug-test disclosures by federal agencies, and the weathervane responses of medical people and consumers. These business dips notwithstanding, the company's various divisions (chemicals, drugs, consumer) steadily increased domestic sales and successfully penetrated overseas markets. For the first time, a ten-year sales projection was prepared in contrast to the usual one- and three-year forecasts. This analysis suggested a doubling of total sales to $2 billion, including a fourfold gain in foreign sales (to $50 million). Employment was expected to grow from twenty thousand to approximately thirty-six thousand.

Many executives, including the vice president of personnel and the manager of manpower planning and development (see Exhibit 2–1), contributed to the gathering sales momentum of the company's operations. The personnel function at Norwood performed actively throughout this growth period.

Company Founding

Initially, the company was located in a small midwestern town. A multistory building served as both office and manufacturing space for the preparation of high-quality drugs for hospital and clinical use. At this early point, the personnel function consisted of a two-person department responsible for hiring, personnel record keeping, and blue-collar wages. As sales grew and the company's markets expanded, personnel took on additional responsibilities, including the office force, safety, and the outside building-maintenance group. The latter was important because the president was a maverick on "physical appearance befitting a superior company making fine quality, ethical drugs."

Growth

When sales reached $100 million per year, the company's existing facilities proved inadequate for production. Management decided to acquire a smaller drug manufacturer in another city. When this unit was established, an employee of the unit was made personnel supervisor for the new facility. The former head of personnel, Peter Ketrick, was given the new title of personnel manager, but operating department heads exercised considerable latitude in their personnel activities.

Personnel expands.   The rapid expansion of health care in the 1950s and 1960s provided a tremendous opportunity for sales development at NPC. In one five-year period, its sales doubled from some $15 million to $30 million. The corporate president and other members of top management soon realized that the pace of sales growth was outrunning the organization's ability to generate managerial talent.

To meet this rapidly emerging need for executive skills, Ketrick proposed and received approval to establish two new offices, one for management development and one for employee compensation and benefits. Also in this period, the company acquired several small companies to aid its manufacturing operations. Each plant site was provided with its own personnel supervisor to administer local plant matters. These supervisors reported to their regional or divisional managers, and only general ties connected them to "corporate personnel." The initial period of personnel's growth is traced in Exhibit 2-1.

Consolidation and Merger

Continuing growth in the 1960s and NPC's desire to continue its expansion pattern posed a major policy issue. Quality, the essence of the firm's image, was becoming a problem in the late sixties because manufacturing operations were physically dispersed. In addition, tougher and more complex governmental regulations posed new demands on quality control. Consequently, it was decided that all manufacturing operations would be located under one roof. However, the company did not have the money necessary to finance this consolidation and the construction of a chemical complex. So NPC merged with the Interstate Industries conglomerate. This merger permitted a high level of autonomy for NPC and access to new financial resources.

Reorganization

The completion of the NPC's "worldwide headquarters complex" provided the opportunity to reexplore organizational arrangements and functions. Continued growth of the managerial and professional categories led to the additional specialization of the management-development function. Also, manpower and equal-opportunity legislation of the 1960s was seen as a contributing factor in the creation of an "employee (opportunity) development function." Finally, the continuing need for new, highly educated and trained people in manufacturing, research, and marketing led to an administrative function for monitoring "new personnel development."

By the early 1970s NPC's growing international operations and product specialization led to the creation of three major domestic divisions and a foreign sales group. Each group or division had its own regional and/or foreign sales offices and warehouses. By the early 1970s, about four sales-warehousing complexes had been created. Each headquarters unit contained a division personnel group that in turn supported the various field personnel and office operations.

Emergence of the Manpower-Planning Function

The need to acquire and develop professional personnel for key managerial positions grew in importance. As a result, NPC management created the position

EXHIBIT 2-1 Evolution of the NPC Personnel Function

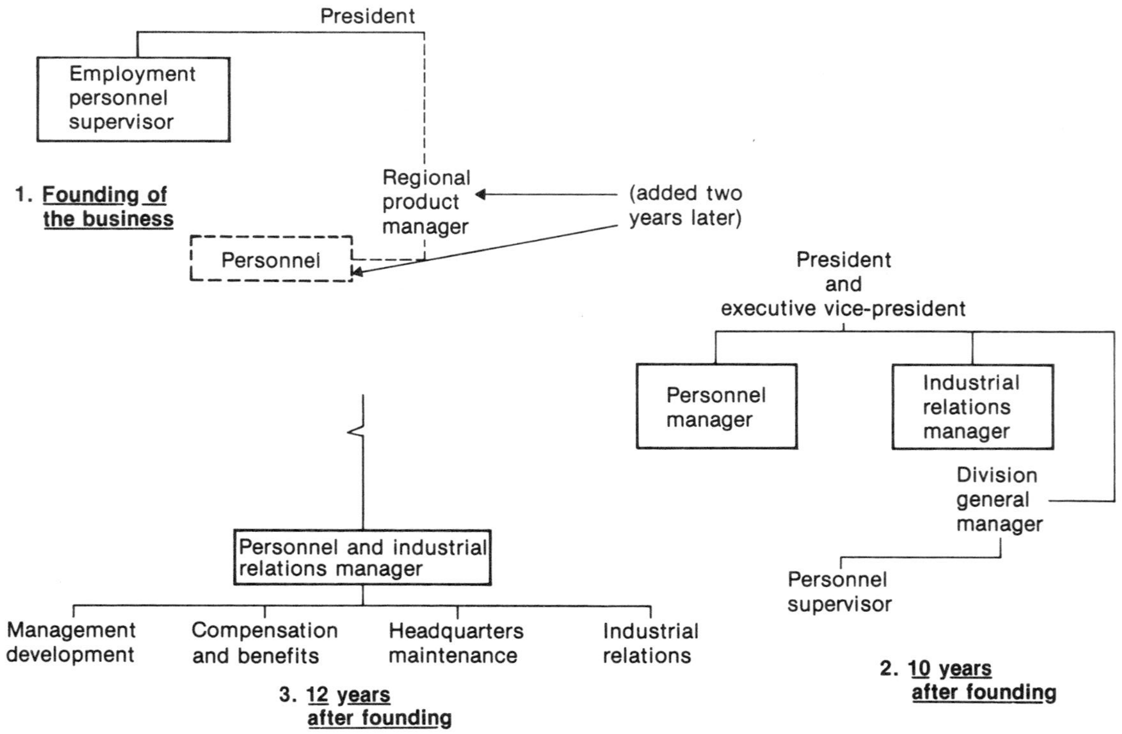

President

Employment
personnel
supervisor

**1. Founding of
the business**

(added two
years later)

Regional
product
manager

Personnel

President
and
executive vice-president

Personnel
manager

Industrial
relations
manager

Division
general
manager

Personnel
supervisor

**2. 10 years
after founding**

Personnel and industrial
relations manager

Management
development

Compensation
and benefits

Headquarters
maintenance

Industrial
relations

**3. 12 years
after founding**

of corporate manager of manpower planning and development and gave personnel "officer" status. The new manpower manager assumed responsibility for various development functions. He also directed manpower planning, which was added in 1974 to provide forecasting and modeling capabilities (see Exhibit 2–2).

What's Next?

The vice-president of personnel and the manager of manpower were justifiably elated over the results of a recent (the first) long-term manpower forecast. After an executive meeting, the vice-president of personnel asked the manpower manager to drop by.

"Bill, you really got the ball rolling with your manpower forecast. It's all they talked about at today's meeting. I think that we ought to follow up now, while everybody's interested, and do the following:

1. Develop an index (relation of number of people to sales, etc.) and model that will forecast our managerial and professional needs.

2. Prepare an approach to internal control for the short-run regulation of the hiring of professionals, one of the major personnel items in our budget. Although we have tight budgeting, cost centers, and salary controls, the president feels we should more closely monitor the hiring of division heads and various professionals.

3. Develop a solid formula that will demonstrably measure the returns of our managerial and professional training and development programs, just as is done in financial investment analysis. In other words, what are the dollar returns from training, career planning, etc.?

If we can get this material prepared over the next six months, we'll really establish personnel-manpower around here."

Analysis of the NPC Scenario

The emerging personnel function at NPC went through various changes. First, NPC used several of the basic organizational forms described in the McFarland study to meet particular organizational needs at different stages of growth. These events included the unionization of plants, the growing priority assigned to management development, the need to hire people to operate plants, and the anticipation of future manpower needs.

Second, environmental changes, including tougher food and drug legislation, led to the need for new organizational groups as well as expanded responsibility for existing groups. NPC expanded its new product testing and research facilities. When the federal government imposed higher drug-quality standards, NPC hired more highly trained specialists and assigned personnel training specialists to develop in-plant training programs to meet the growing demands of legislation.

Third, as NPC underwent changes in organizational structure, the personnel

EXHIBIT 2-2 Norwood Pharmaceutical and Chemical Division Organization Chart

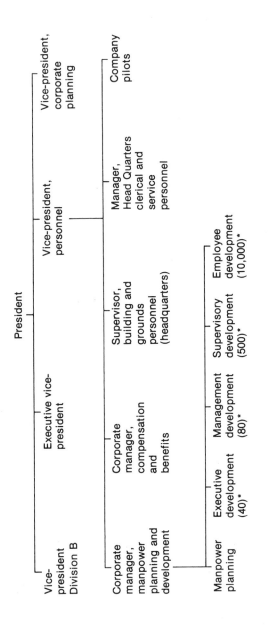

President

Vice-president Division B

Executive vice-president

Vice-president, personnel

Vice-president, corporate planning

Corporate manager, manpower planning and development

Corporate manager, compensation and benefits

Supervisor, building and grounds personnel (headquarters)

Manager, Head Quarters clerical and service personnel

Company pilots

Manpower planning

Executive development (40)*

Management development (80)*

Supervisory development (500)*

Employee development (10,000)*

* Scope of personnel responsibility in numbers of people.

department grew in importance as more and more functions became new areas of personnel responsibility. The director was elevated from "employment supervisor" to "personnel and industrial relations manager" and then to "vice-president, personnel." Thus the expansion of the personnel function and its growth in power and importance paralleled the growth and changing needs of the company.

Fourth, as personnel responsibilities increased, they were defined more sharply and then assigned to plant, division, or headquarters. Plant personnel directly serviced field operations and directed the personnel maintenance functions needed for production continuity. The headquarters personnel group became increasingly involved in counseling top management about human affairs. It recommended policy, evolved the broad designs of future development programs, and provided technical support to field operations.

Many people in the organization would admit to the necessity of personnel, regardless of how "unpleasant" or "unproductive" it might be. However, the King Brothers' General Hospital scenario which follows outlines an unusual example of how personnel has become increasingly important in all kinds of organizational structures.

EMERGENCE OF THE PERSONNEL FUNCTION AT KING BROTHERS' GENERAL HOSPITAL

King Brothers' General Hospital was a high-quality metropolitan health-care unit with a good reputation for health-care performance. It was founded in the early 1900s. Until the late 1940s, the hospital grew slowly to a 250-bed capacity.

The internal organizational structure of the hospital was traditional. There was a clear separation between medically related and general administrative functions. Thus the medical director supervised medical operating departments (e.g., obstetrics, surgical, and gynecology) and directly related medical support departments (laboratory, X-ray). A director of nursing services assumed responsibility for nursing activity, and the third area, administrative services, included physical therapy, social service, dieting, housekeeping, and laundry.

Personnel Function Emerges: "A Happy Worker . . ."

In 1920 the first personnel-related activity emerged with the hiring of an employment supervisor. He was primarily responsible for the hiring (and firing) of unskilled and low-skilled personnel. During the 1920s the hospital's directors became concerned about employee service activities. In response to these concerns the personnel department emphasized good employee relations. Personnel instituted counseling programs for employees' domestic and personal health problems, insurance, savings, and other financial needs. However, as was the case with most institutions, the hospital was caught up in the Great Depression, and these employee-relations functions and most other personnel activities were eliminated.

By the late 1930s most of the personnel functions had been restored, but they underwent a rather subtle change. The vague sense of the need for social welfare and employee relations that had been felt in the 1920s was replaced by the philosophy that "a happy worker is a productive worker." The employment supervisor attempted to create a cheerful, congenial work climate. He encouraged department heads to project this attitude and tried to make new employees feel like new "family members."

Problems of Size

In the 1940s the hospital had grown to about 800 employees. With over 200 job titles the hospital needed a more formal program of job analysis and evaluation. A new offshoot of personnel—a conscious attempt to study the job structure in a systematic way and to combine or eliminate titles wherever possible—was instituted. This personnel work required a small group of efficiency experts. These "practical people" had a primary responsibility to increase the productivity of lower-level employees.

The entire health-care industry grew dramatically during the 1950s and 1960s, and King Brothers' kept pace. It now had over 400 beds—one of the largest organizations in the community.

Growth in size transformed internal operations considerably. First, personnel had to launch a major recruiting effort to build up the employee group and to maintain it, since there was high turnover in lower-paying jobs. Second, new concepts in the nursing role and introduction of new medical technologies modified job qualifications and duties. Many employees had to be retrained to meet higher standards. Third, relationships among employees and employee groups changed. In the nursing organization, for example, a new layer of supervisors was added. Since candidates for promotion were drawn almost entirely from existing nursing ranks, all of the first-level supervisors were inexperienced—a whole new cadre of talent had to be developed. Additionally, experienced supervisors needed to be retrained to meet the demands of changing supervisor-subordinate relationships. Although the personnel department had expanded, its role still was secondary to the dominant medical orientation of the hospital. Newer human-resource developments, such as manpower planning, were largely ignored.

Analysis of the King Brothers' Scenario

Personnel initially was concerned with conventional maintenance-type activities and was confined to nontechnical personnel. When the role of personnel expanded, it reflected a new era of concern for employees—employee relations. Yet the programs that grew out of this period proved to be quite fragile and were scuttled during a period of economic crisis.

The gradual growth in size of the hospital resulted in a more complex job structure and an organization that required further changes in the personnel department. The apparatus of job analyses, employee procurement, and training had to be built. Yet, even in terms of its most recent developments, personnel displayed few human resource features.

Although the Norwood Pharmaceutical Company and King Brothers' Hospital's personnel departments developed in different ways, they are similar in several respects. They both faced the historic forces described in Chapter 1: economic fluctuation, unionization, changing societal values, radical developments in technology, and government intervention. They also are similar in another important respect: they grew in reaction, or in response, to changing conditions. This method of operation meant that they continually had to play catch up with events in the business world resulting in sporadic and sometimes haphazard program development.

THE CONTINGENCY APPROACH TO PERSONNEL ORGANIZATION

This chapter (as well as Chapter 1) has pointed to a problem that business in general and personnel directors in particular have wrestled with for many years: how to anticipate change. One result has been the contingency approach. When using the contingency approach, the personnel manager approaches a problem by asking, "*If* certain environmental, organizational, and work features exist (for example), *then* the personnel department probably will take on the following features. . . ." The contingency approach gives personnel managers more flexibility in anticipating and dealing with a variety of organizational matters.

This approach can be used for problem solving in the organization as a whole or for problems of personnel organization, systems, or methods. A manager attempts to *identify key factors* in the environment, organization, work, or individual that are causing trouble instead of working with a preconceived solution. (Frequently, the *systems viewpoint* is helpful because it alerts managers to important relationships among variables. But the systems view complements rather than duplicates the contingency approach.)

Initiating the Contingency Approach

Forward-looking personnel managers recognize the importance of the systems view (see Chapter 1)—the key variables and relationships affecting the personnel organization, such as the influence of environment, organization, and primary work systems. These variables are the contingencies. They make up the "if" parts of a personnel manager's analysis. The manager then attempts to forecast future trends in these variables to determine how they will influence the characteristics of the existing personnel system—personnel's power, its functions and maintenance responsibilities, its organization (centralized or decentralized), its special functions, and other relationships between primary and support systems.

Contingencies and Personnel Organization

The NPC company and King Brothers' Hospital scenarios provide specific examples of the contingencies that connect the environment of the overall organization with a personnel organization. These contingencies serve as a model for analyses of future occurrences or changes in organization. These organizations might take several different forms in the future. In light of Exhibit 2–3, some possible changes are:

1. A *centralized, one-location office* that has limited responsibilities (e.g., hiring). Other duties may be assigned to department heads or line managers (e.g., wage practices, training).

2. A *physical decentralization* of personnel. A headquarters with branch offices can be established. Personnel responsibilities may be separated, some handled by the branches and others handled by headquarters.

3. The *organizational growth and expansion* of responsibilities assigned to personnel. Growth sometimes results from expanding field operations or acquiring new businesses which encourages the separation of responsibilities between headquarters and field units. This kind of development may lead to greater emphasis on policy making at headquarters and more pragmatic, day-to-day activities for field units. Where higher levels of autonomy (e.g., profit responsibility) are assigned to divisions or field units, their personnel-related activities may assume a policy direction.

EXHIBIT 2–3 Emergence of Personnel Organization as Influenced by Various Internal and Environmental Features

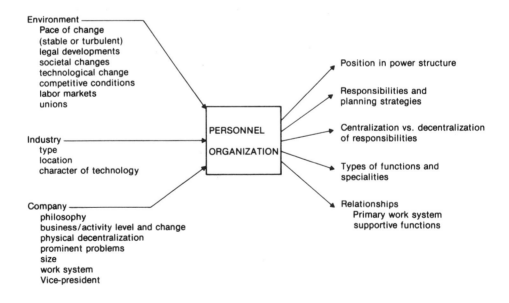

4. *Intervention of a union,* which results in the establishment of industrial-relations/collective-bargaining activity. Industrial relations sometimes is organizationally apart from the personnel function. However, personnel and industrial relations activities frequently touch on the same kinds of internal functions (pay, benefits, working conditions, etc.), so joint departments with titles such as "personnel" or "personnel and industrial relations" or simply "industrial relations" emerge. The presence of a union can lead to extremely complex, even turbulent, conditions for company officials. The size, power, or militancy of the union can exert a strong influence on the organizational strategy used.

5. *Changes in competitive conditions,* legal restrictions, or work technology can modify work requirements. When this happens, a company needs more sophisticated personnel managers (management development, training, or manpower forecasting/planning) to meet these new demands.

6. *Societal change.* Personnel directors must keep in touch with changes in society that can influence employee needs and thus require a new personnel orientation. When dramatic change occurs, it sometimes is necessary to elevate personnel in the authority structure, perhaps to the executive level.

7. *Legislative enactment.* Laws mandating fair employment practices, equal employment, and occupational safety may directly affect internal personnel organizations and activities. This kind of legislation has forced personnel departments to adopt new reporting procedures and training approaches. At times it has been necessary to install a "compliance" person who is given the responsibility of making sure legal requirements are met.

8. *Type of industry or organization.* Personnel organization is further molded by the particulars of the industry, the philosophy of ownership, the type of industry, and the location. Although it seems straightforward and painfully obvious, perhaps it is worth stating, for example, that hospital and manufacturing personnel organizations differ greatly. They may have functional similarities, but they differ in specific areas such as training, compensation, and development.

9. *Change in organization size.* Through business expansion, activities of personnel expand and become more important. Growth in size may require organizational adjustments to decentralize personnel activities to various operating units.

Emerging Trends at King Brothers' Hospital: A Contingency View Illustrated

There is one special problem with the contingency approach. A contingency is exactly what the word means: it is contingent; it depends on the specifics of a situation. The contingency approach does provide a better basis for anticipating the general structure and direction of programming personnel should take. But this strength—that it is customized to the specifics of a particular organization—makes it appear rather vague. Thus a specific illustration is in order. With one warning—this is a highly simplified example—we demonstrate how the personnel director of the King Brothers' Hospital might use the contingency approach in the future. The scenario ended with a description of the hospital's existing maintenance machinery: job analysis, training, securing people (recruiting), and employment.

The hospital's personnel director faces a problem involving two contingency factors: philosophy (organization-company category) and union (environment category). The hospital recently hired a new associate administrator for administration, John Bochner, M.H.A. (master of hospital administration). John is a graduate of a large, prestigious program in health administration. In addition to his educational development, he has had six years of general experience in hospitals so that he comes to King Brothers with an excellent background of experience and education. At an early point John discusses his philosophy of management with the head of personnel and makes it quite clear that more stress will be placed on internal management and planning for, rather than reacting to, situations.

The personnel manager, who has become more actively involved with the local chapter of Health Personnel Managers, becomes aware of a situation that may affect King Brothers. Several attempts to unionize local hospitals have been successful. The common thread in most all of the situations seemed to be poor supervision. Other problems were also present to varying degrees, but the persistent one seemed to be quality of supervision. The personnel manager follows through on his initial assessment of the situation: he talks to other hospital personnel managers and reviews training and development efforts at King Brothers, and concludes that over the next year or two they will be highly vulnerable to union organization. Supervision is very weak, and most current training is haphazard.

The personnel manager talks to John, describes the situation, and makes a proposal for a major supervisory development program. The program eventually will cover all supervision and will take almost a year to carry out. Supervisors will receive training in motivation of employees, leadership, and efficient handling of employee problems. Part of the program will also deal with developing better relationships among various supervisors and with department heads.

The scope of the proposed program is large and it is likely to be a permanent part of the organizational structure, or some type of permanent staffing seems indicated. Union organization of the hospital may be an immediate issue, but the need for bettering cost performance and productivity are likely to be important long-term interests and goals. Consequently, the personnel manager recommends 1) a change in personnel structure (addition of a personnel development coordinator); and 2) a supervisory educational program in response to anticipated organization needs.

PERSONNEL'S NEW ROLES

Formulating and Implementing New Personnel Structure

In recent years personnel has become an agent of change in organizations. Personnel directors have taken the lead in introducing and gaining acceptance of new organizational programs. As researchers and consultants in the personnel and human-resource field, we frequently have had the opportunity to move our discussions with officials and specialists beyond the official position. More and more frequently, the hidden agenda of many personnel directors appears to be how to get things going with their top managements: "How do you get senior managers to support a new personnel undertaking?" This is the first basic issue that personnel managers must grapple with. In this section some specific approaches that have proved successful in influencing change in personnel policies are proposed.

The specifics of the newer manpower technologies dealing with such matters as personnel information systems and forecasting models can be learned in a comparatively short time. Even the ideas of the human resource viewpoint are not difficult to learn. But the doing—the putting into practice—can easily take years in many organizations. Traditional individual attitudes and value systems die hard. For example, working as consultants for a large company, we discussed human-resource planning perspectives and concepts with fifty bright middle managers and other company officials over a three-month period. These discussions included ten three-hour workshops that gave various managers and officials numerous opportunities to talk about ("ventilate") many deeply rooted ideas. The workshops seemed to be a smashing success: everyone was involved in lengthy, animated discussions. Through continuing contacts with this organization, it was possible to monitor and judge the responses of senior managers over an extended period. Although more than a year passed, the organization was still heavily engaged in "management development" changes.

Unfortunately, most organizations demonstrate at least one law of physics: bodies at rest tend to stay at rest. A personnel manager must find the *pressure points*—problem areas that obviously need some kind of change—and work on them. This need for change can come from many quarters: the retirement of key people and/or a lack of qualified successors; planned expansion in the face of a shortage of key skills; threats of unionization; retrenchment; or the undertaking of multinational operations.

A case in point is the change of hospital personnel structures. For many years hospital personnel directors were unable to get the money necessary to develop training programs. The advent of equal employment opportunity changed this. Hospitals were forced to hire employees who sometimes lacked skills and often needed to be oriented to the world of health care. Thus, personnel directors finally were able to get the budgets necessary to create the rationalized training and orientation programs that hospitals had in fact needed for a long time. The result of this crisis was improved training and orientation for all facets of hospital operations, even those that were not directly touched by equal employment opportunity directives.

New Personnel Programs

The post–World War II era has been the crucible for dramatic changes in the shape and direction of personnel activities. A new, more sophisticated system has been taking shape for the past thirty years. A critical mass of legislation, social change, and growing business complexity has introduced the need for human-resource management.

For virtually all organizations, personnel maintenance activities are a must, but they are inadequate to meet contemporary needs. Whether they recognize it or not, many organizations have developed features of human resource management. Government legislation has mandated new reporting requirements, necessitated by equal employment and affirmative action practices, occupational safety and health standards, improved hospitalization coverage, and secured retirement benefits. Also, many large firms already have important elements of manpower planning and programming systems. These may involve forecasting, replacement planning (back-up people) for critical positions, a career management orientation, and human resource development and assignment.

In any event, all companies soon will need either to develop a more comprehensive human resource system (where the groundwork has already been established) or to launch human resource systems and activities (where the maintenance system is performing adequately).

What does all of this change mean for personnel departments and their directors? How will programs change? The following areas seem likely to receive more attention:

1. Continuing education, with increased emphasis on in-house programs. Also, short update courses on various modes of information delivery, including picture phone and t.v., will appear. Systems of this type have been proved technologically and will gain broader use.

2. Orientation centers and "debriefing" programs for later-life activities after completing one's work career. Such centers could be used to help retirees expand their horizons once they have left the "grind."

3. Self-assessment techniques, including computer use, for judging one's potential obsolescence.

4. Computer-based programs for preemployment analyses, career opportunity counseling information, and more powerful models and techniques.

5. Computer-based information systems for better management of the internal labor force.

SUMMARY

Personnel organization and functions are not capricious; they are not simply frills or public relations gimmicks; they serve needed roles in organizations. They are responsive to different environmental, economic, demographic, social, and institutional forces. Since the turn of the century, broad sweeping changes —wars, depression, prosperity, the social milieu and the expectations of people— have altered the forces shaping business organizations. Chapter 1 described these broad changes, and Chapter 2 gave specific examples.

The responsiveness of organizations to change has been one of its ongoing problems. Businesses, and their personnel departments, have reacted to, rather than anticipated, change. The result is that personnel managers constantly have to make seat-of-the-pants decisions to meet new circumstances.

But these days are gone or are quickly fading. As the world of business —and the world in general—has changed, executives have come to realize that they must expect and be able to predict change. Even the maintenance outlook, once considered a dramatic change, is inadequate to meet today's personnel needs.

Personnel has evolved in response to the changes of the past, and the system that has emerged, human resource management, is no exception.

But human resource management is different in one important respect: it is an attempt to anticipate change rather than simply respond to it. The foundation has been laid. *Human resource* has become part of everyday business vocabulary. Human resource approaches will become fact as decision makers realize their value and as the tools and models already developed increase in use.

DISCUSSION QUESTIONS

1. *Organizational planning.* Franklin Motors is a medium-size manufacturing firm, specializing in the production of outboard motors and small powered vehicles and employing six thousand people at three locations. A five-year corporate planning program has just been completed which, among other things, projects a 50 percent growth in sales and construction of two more plants, including one in Canada. Two company plants have employee unions, and the clerical group and engineering draftsmen at company headquarters have also joined unions. The head of the company's personnel and industrial relations department is viewed as a powerful individual who has the ear of the president.
   a. Make and state necessary assumptions and describe what you feel to be the current personnel structure. Be sure to justify your position.
   b. Using the contingency approach what new directions do you anticipate in organizational needs (considering expansion and environmental change) and how are these likely to affect the personnel structure (a)?

2. The following organization chart for personnel is derived from a relatively large insurance company located in the business district of a west coast city. What deductions would you make regarding the parent organization, its needs, and the relation and influence of personnel based on chapter concepts?

3. Provide examples for each of the following and explain how they might influence organizational practices and personnel:
   a. growing organizational complexity
   b. growing organizational uncertainty

4. Early personnel programs involving social secretaries, human relations, paternalistic attitudes, and the more recent career management thrust might well be viewed as manipulative on the part of companies. What are your opinions and comments?

5. The Industrial Relations Association of Chicago (IRAC) was founded in 1914 and is one of the oldest groups of its type in the nation. In 1934, in conjunction with a

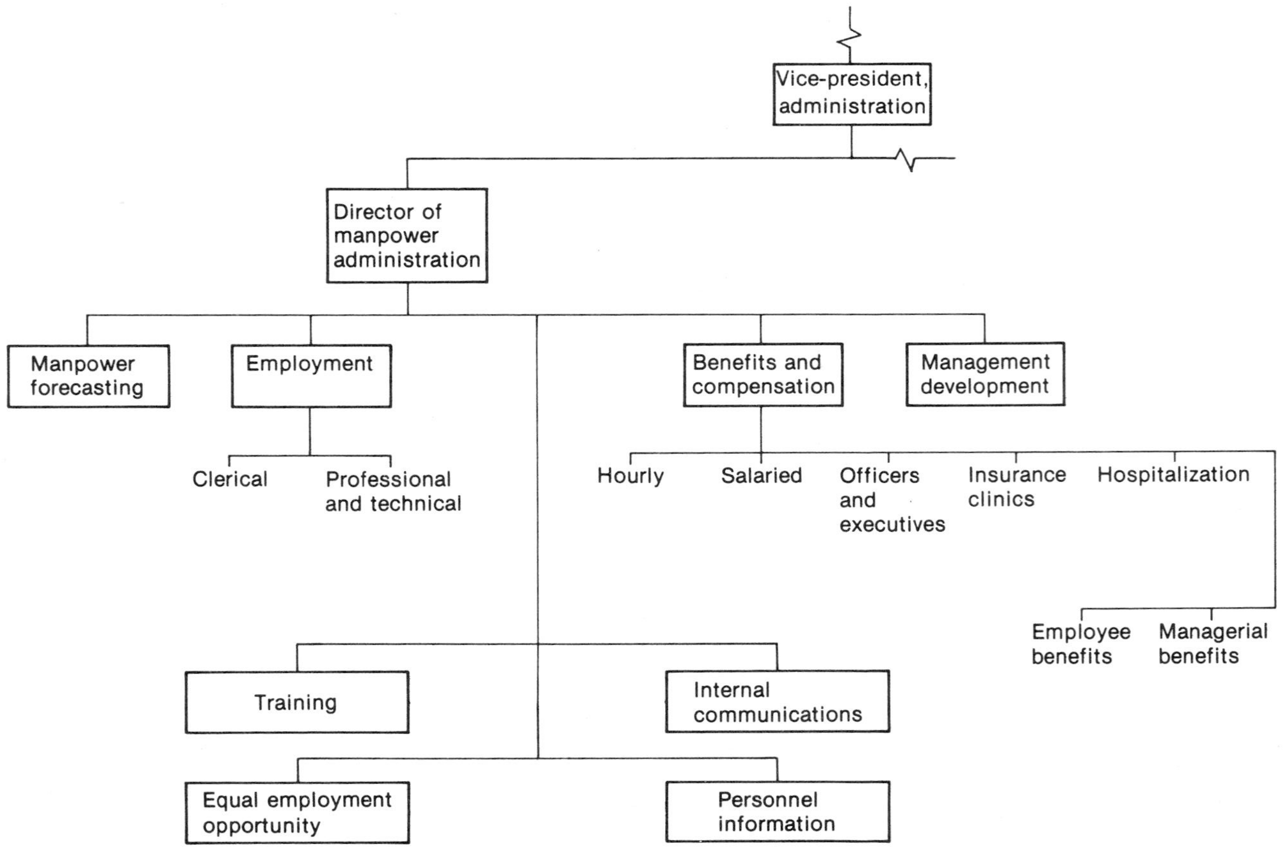

EXHIBIT 2-4 Personnel Organization of a Large Insurance Company

major university, IRAC started a series of annual fall conferences which have treated various contemporary issues (these annual meetings still take place). The 1934 program described presentations by both academics and practitioners concerning wages, hours, and working conditions; retirement benefits, needs of people, company funding, and government support; hospitalization benefits and coverage, new trends, and the likely role of government; wage determination—ability to pay, competitive wages, cost of living, and individual need; and changes in the thrust of union activity and organization efforts. To an extent, the similarities of many of the program items to those of contemporary programs of various personnel groups is striking. Have things really changed or are we still dealing with the same old problems under a new name?

6. *Blue-collar blues and the personnel function.* The majority of articles in a 1971 book entitled *Blue-Collar Workers: A Symposium on Middle America*, edited by Sar A. Levitan, suggest that there is really nothing unusual about the supposedly troubled feelings of blue-collar workers—they are the "blues" of most Americans in the 1970s. The articles center on economic matters or concern such widely different issues as to lose meaning. Some authors see the "blue-collar problem" as an old one with new terminology or dismiss it with the assertion that people today are better off than their forefathers.

a. What are your views on these issues, based on developments described in Chapters 1 and 2?

b. Based on the viewpoints presented in Chapter 2, what changes in organizational arrangement of personnel (position, responsibility, and thrust) can be linked to these changes?

c. What additional shifts, according to the chapter, seem in the offing?

d. Under what circumstances of a particular company or organization would these shifts be viewed as fully relevant? As of remote interest or little concern?

7. What new organizational stresses are likely to emerge as personnel officials seek to weld human resource functions onto an existing maintenance-type structure?

8. Central Manufacturing Company, which makes wood and plastic picture frames, is a family-owned business with more than two thousand employees. Its president and several officers and managers are members of the family and hold key positions. Younger family members have come into the business in recent years and one has become a senior manager, the other a junior officer. As personnel manager (young and with some experience), you are going to attempt to interest management in a career program for women in management. Currently, all supervisory and managerial positions are held by males, although the work force is better than 50 percent female. Outline a change strategy and identify features of the change program described in the chapter. Make and state all necessary assumptions.

9. *The Norwood case.* What type of environmental changes affected NPC activities over its merger history?

10. Did these activities affect the formation and development of the personnel function?

11. What relationships appeared to exist between corporate headquarters and personnel units?

12. Describe what you think were the major responsibilities of
a. the corporate headquarters unit
b. the regional and divisional units.

13. What opportunities and problems were inherent in the specialization of the management development function?

14. Comment on the vice-president of personnel's suggested agenda of future activities for the corporate manpower planning and development area.

15. Speculate on the future direction for the organization of the personnel function in NPC. What are your assumptions?

REFERENCES

Bray, Douglas. *Formative Years in Business: A Long-Term AT&T Study of Managerial Lives.* (New York: John Wiley & Sons, 1974).

Brayfield, A., and W. H. Crockett. "Employee Attitudes and Performance." *Psychological Bulletin* 52 (1955):396–424.

Campbell, R. J. "Selection of Salesmen by Means of an Assessment Center." *Journal of Applied Psychology* 52 (1968):36–41.

Herzberg, Frederick. *Work and the Nature of Man.* Cleveland: World Publishing Co., 1966.

Maslow, Abraham. *Motivation and Personality,* 2d ed. New York: Harper & Row, 1970.

McCormick, Ernest J., R. C. Mechem, and P. J. Jeanneret. *User's Manual for the Position Analysis Questionnaire.* West Lafayette, Ind.: PAQ Services, 1973.

McFarland, Dalton. "Company Offices Assess the Personnel Function." *AMA Research Study* 79. New York: American Management Association, 1967.

Reder, Melvin W. *Labor in a Growing Economy.* New York: Wiley, 1957.

Sheppard, Harold. *The Quality of Work Life.* Research study conducted by the W. E. Upjohn Institute on behalf of the U.S. Department of Health, Education, and Welfare. Cambridge, Mass.: MIT Press, 1973.

Section
Two

ENVIRONMENT
AND
THE
INDIVIDUAL

---

*

Chapter 3

EXTERNAL LABOR MARKETS

LEARNING OBJECTIVES

This chapter will describe many of the key features of human resources as a supply of labor for the organization. In particular, at the conclusion of this chapter the reader should be able to:

Develop the use of the labor market concept for planning and problem analyses affecting human resources

Identify important social, economic, and technical trends as they affect the features and workings of the external labor market

Clarify the role of public agencies as they affect labor markets and their connection to the personnel activity in all types of organizations

Indicate the role of educational systems in relation to labor market activity and employment

Employ labor market concepts as an approach in carrying out the functional activities of personnel.

KEY CONCEPTS AND TERMS

labor—supply and demand
wage
mobility
labor markets—internal and
   external
rate of participation

employment, unemployment
labor apparatus of
   government
discrimination in hiring
CETA
occupational distribution

PREVIEW

This chapter spans the range of material from labor market analysis to the role played by government in seeking to better organize the mechanisms and operations of those markets.

The initial discussions of the chapter provide a summary view of the various factors, trends, and groups complicating analyses in this area. Important terms and concepts are explained. The balance of the chapter is then divided into four main bodies of discussion:

1. Labor market concepts, terminology, and applications. The movement of people toward job opportunities and the relation of environmental (external) developments to organizational (internal) developments illustrate a variety of employment issues.

2. Major trends that are changing the makeup of labor markets. Women, minority, youth, and various social trends are the subject of these discussions.

3. The role of the educational system in the labor market. The education explosion, education versus employment, and career switching are key topics.

4. The complex role played by government. Government activity is described in terms of legislation, information, mechanisms of providing services, and recent trends in these operations.

PEOPLE, LABOR MARKETS, AND ECONOMIC CONDITIONS: A COMPLEX PICTURE

The subject matter of this chapter surrounds us daily. In newspaper headlines, on "Channel 20 News," in discussions at home, in school, at work, in the manager's office and in Congress, *employment, education, jobs,* or *wages* capture the attention of most people.

"What's the outlook for jobs?"

"Should I continue with my education or go out and look for a job?"

"As a black, will things be any better for me when I look for a job?"

"How come the wages across town are so much better than here?"

"When are things going to improve so I can find a job?"

These questions touch on a wide range of issues, but they involve a modest group of concepts:

1. supply of labor (people)

2. demand for labor (people)

3. forces or circumstances affecting supply and demand

4. interaction of labor supply and demand—the working out or resolution of supply and demand.

The economic crisis of the mid-1970s emphasized traditional labor supply and demand issues. Costs of energy moved "out of sight," general unemployment increased to over 8 percent (from under 5 percent), and "real" economic growth, which had increased steadily for over twenty years, came to an abrupt halt. The question of the day was, why? Various government agencies held hearings throughout the country to better understand the impact of these developments. These discussions revealed many aspects of employment and jobs that were causing much confusion among public officials, job holders and seekers, and all types of organizational officials. The following abstract suggests the type of testimony given by expert witnesses during these times.

SCENARIO: PUBLIC HEARING ON REGIONAL UNEMPLOYMENT PROBLEMS

Regional Director (U.S. Department of Labor):

Ladies and gentlemen: Normally I might start off with some lighter comments regarding the government or the economic scene; however, matters are far too serious.

We have been invited to today's session as experts or highly knowledgeable people in some of the many areas affected by the current difficulties—even near-crises for some—regarding employment and income. As indicated in correspondence to you, we would like to have each of you start off with a brief comment to stake out in better fashion the complex issues we are all facing.

I'd like to emphasize, ladies and gentlemen, a short statement so that we can devote most of our time to sifting through all the issues—and not simply those related to one area.

The first statement will be made by Mr. Calvin West, one of the department's labor economists, to establish an overview for the national, regional, and local situations. Succeeding statements will be as we have already outlined in the agenda.

Calvin West, labor economist for the government:

Nationally, overall unemployment reached 8.4 percent as compared with approximately 4.7 percent two years ago—almost an 80 percent increase. However, the situation in this region is somewhat different. Over the same two-year period, unemployment increased from 4.3 percent to 7.6 percent—about the same increase. But employment levels in the region are better than the picture nationally. However, to provide two added reference points, it may be of interest to know that in this major metropolitan area where we are meeting today, general unemployment is 7.3 percent, but there are two towns downstate with unemployment over 15 percent!

Franklin Brown, director of SHOVE (a minority-rights organization):

The real problem we're facing is jobs! You economists and managers are the "haves" in a white society that is giving us this "statistical #!@#" about 4 percent this and 8 percent that. I'll take you down to one of my areas where 25 or 30 percent of our teenagers and young people can't get jobs and the police are constantly hassling them. Never mind all the discussion—we'd do a lot more good today if you could tell me that you had ten thousand jobs for my people—*now!*

Regional Director:

Thanks, Mr. Brown. We want to assure you that we do appreciate the gravity of the situation.

Could we now have the next speaker?

Spencer Woods, director of Metro City Hospital and president of Council of Public Hospitals:

As many know, the employment situation in our hospitals stands in rather sharp contrast to the generally poor employment picture. For many years, long before the current economic crisis, we were suffering from recurring shortages of nurses, doctors, and various medical specialists. In addition, because of the generally unattractive nature of general labor jobs—orderlies, housekeeping, and cleanup people, mostly—we had high turnover. In some cases, turnover exceeded 100 percent, and we were forced to constantly rehire in these areas.

The expansion in medical education and nursing programs has helped to improve the situation somewhat, but we still have hiring problems! Nursing seems to be a chronic problem. Also, we still can't fill all the medical specialities for which budgetary authorization and real community needs exist. Still, the lower rated jobs continue to turn over, and we continue to try to hire replacements.

However, it is true that some regional unemployment patterns have started to develop in hospital-health care delivery. The delivery of health care has changed, with the central hospitals playing lesser roles and neighborhood and newer suburban units playing a greater role.

Consequently, some hospitals have actually reduced requirements for professional people. Of course, many of the doctors are quite mobile, especially the young ones, and relocate rapidly. Some of the nurses will move too, but many just seem to drop out of the work force—and may show up years later!

JoAnn McCarthy, vice-president of Women's Equality Now (WEN):

Frankly, I was rather surprised to be invited here today. It looks like most of the pressing concerns and programs have been over male jobs in organizations ruled over by male managers and male owners. Yet more women are leaving those sacred halls called the kitchen. By what rights do men get the long end of the stick and the women the short end?

Despite the recent equal opportunity laws, you know as well as I do that the first people to go when the going gets tough are the women and minorities. Employers always find some way of dumping us. If they keep us, we're tossed into dead-end or Mickey Mouse jobs that any "cluck" could hold down. Regardless of the national employment picture, we demand: 1) equal opportunity and a fair crack at the available jobs; 2) equal treatment in promotion and promotion opportunities; 3) no lesser consideration than males in lay off.

Regional Director:

Thanks, Ms. McCarthy, for your frank expression of views on a very complex question.

Ms. McCarthy:

Don't patronize us, Mr. Regional Director—we've had enough of that already. Let's have more action and less rhetoric!

William M. Lewis, Ph.D., director of State Board of Higher Education:

Ladies and gentlemen: New and far-reaching developments are taking place in education today. The 1970s will be the first time that the percent of young people going into the college system from high school will decline. If enrollment continues to go up at some of our schools, it's only due to the fact that the numbers of young people involved is sizable and that some stay on in school because they can't find jobs. Yes, there's a little statistical confusion possible here, but the facts remain the same: the percent is starting to go down, but for awhile the actual number will continue to rise.

Young people are seeking alternative education routes. A degree no longer guarantees monetary success and the good life. Vocational and trade schools have been receiving a great deal of attention. There are continuing job opportunities in this area for crafts, trades, paraprofessionals, and technologists of various kinds. It appears that a major reorienting of social and business priorities is needed if we are to match better jobs, people, and education.

Frank Wood, vice-president of International Motors (major car and truck producer):

The motor car industry receives a great deal of exposure in the media, so developments in the industry are widely known. Unfortunately, the facts are not as widely understood. We are often blamed for the unemployment in the Detroit, Cleveland, Los Angeles, Chicago, and St. Louis areas, for example, where we have large plant installations. International Motors doesn't create demand—it's people with money to spend. The buyer generates the demand for International Motors' products, and we simply produce to meet the demand—and employ or hire people relative to the demand for our product. Solve the general economic problems, and you'll solve the automotive employment problems. We have an obligation to our stockholders, who also are "the people." We need to make a legitimate profit and to acquire plant and equipment in the future. The automotive industry has always moved through cyclical employment patterns that have resulted from the shifting demands for our products—we are especially vulnerable to general economic conditions.

Harry Worth, president of Food Workers International Union:

The ranks of union labor have decreased after having reached new highs in membership in the 1960s. Yet the overall figures really hide the shameful situation that exists. Unemployment in the U.S. is at an all-time high, yet we are probably the wealthiest nation in the world. Sales of luxury cars go up, and our union members are thrown out of jobs. Imported car sales go up, and more Japanese electronics are imported—and displace our American workers. Japanese, German, and Scandinavian steel is imported; imported food or canned products of all description are brought in—and more American workers are "out of business." Many union and company supplementary unemployment funds are exhausted. Answers and action are needed. It is the responsibility of government and employers to do something now!

GATHERING THE ISSUES TOGETHER—COMMENT ON SCENARIO

The testimony at such meetings, though a bit emotional at times, reveals a number of different human-resource matters of concern to virtually anyone preparing for work or already part of the work force. The commentary of the experts suggests several issues:

1. *Demand for labor* emerges from the sale of products and services. In turn, desire of individuals, families, or businesses for the services or products of various institutions are the factors that fuel demand. A highly mixed picture is presented in which some industries (medical) or occupations (doctor, nurse) may be in relatively high demand despite general economic conditions or opposite developments in other industries. Also, certain occupations involving low skills or poor working conditions (e.g., general labor in hospitals) may provide employment opportunities but are not in demand. These jobs may

require restructuring because of high turnover. Finally, the performance of certain industries seems to closely parallel general economic conditions. Consequently, their requirements for employment are tied to economic fluctuations and become more predictable.

2. *Supply of labor* is an idea that reflects workers' race, sex, union affiliation, level of education, and skill. At one time, a particular worker represents a composite of all of these—and perhaps more.

3. *Economic conditions, imports, labor demand* are general economic conditions related to the demand for labor. Also, demand for an organization's products is vulnerable to the inroads of imported products and thereby demand for U.S. labor. Yet widely differing state, regional, and national conditions are noted in regard to unemployment levels.

4. *Unemployment* can vary greatly for women and minorities. In the past these groups have been especially vulnerable to fluctuating economic circumstances. Attempts to bring balance to the work force through elimination of past discriminatory practices have resulted in further distortion in employment patterns. Some even claim these attempts have caused "reverse discrimination" whereby the best qualified is not always hired.

5. *The educational system* is composed of programs serving widely different educational purposes. Trade schools, vocational schools, schools of technology, colleges, and universities are among the many institutions making up this system. The system provides assorted bridges connecting one type of school with another, school with work, and even school with unemployment. The bridges represent choices and realities that affect careers and the ability of people to participate in the work force.

LABOR MARKETS: CONCEPTS, TERMINOLOGY, APPLICATION

Where, when and how do people work? How do the problems of race or sex relate to labor markets and hiring practices? There are just a few very basic questions involving labor market theory and practice. Problems of the labor market are central to personnel functions, and solving them can be challenging because they involve people and organizations in all of their complexity. In approaching this subject we will clarify some basic concepts and terms and show their application in the everyday world.

Labor Market: Concept and Application

The people, processes, and places where job seekers and available jobs are joined is the *labor market*. People, the so-called labor supply, moving toward or between jobs are the core of the labor market. Labor markets serve to connect people and institutions in both the public and private sectors. For example, educational institutions (hopefully) prepare their students for employment of some sort, whether it is for a manufacturing company, a government agency, or another educational institution.

Up to this point the labor market must seem to be like a cafeteria, a small, easily defined place. In practice, labor analysts concern themselves with geographical areas, such as cities, counties, states, or statistical population areas. This idea may be considerably more complex than it at first appears. In most cases the labor market for a large city, such as New York, Chicago, or San Francisco, doesn't stop at the city limits. Why is the labor market concept important? Economists needed new concepts and tools for exploring employment relationships, predicting wage rates and wage levels, and analyzing labor supply and demand. Some of these matters go beyond the concerns of this book, but we will discuss the pertinent issues. We have made a conscious attempt to avoid taking overly generous liberties with concepts of the labor economists, but we will err on the side of simplicity and utility, emphasizing personnel-related issues.

The labor market concept provides the personnel manager and public administrator with a valuable perspective on human resources and employment processes. This concept (or collection of concepts) helps answer questions affecting day-to-day personnel activities and longer range planning:

"Where do I look for talent"?

"What's likely to be the effect of a competitive firm raising its wages"?

"What's likely to be the impact on the availability of various skills if a particular union restricts its apprenticeship program"?

"How will our employment policies be affected if the mobility of managers and technical personnel continues to increase"?

"In what ways do our internal organizational procedures involve labor market concepts and how can we use these in personnel approaches"?

Derived Demand

Although it is perhaps a bit shocking, most people are not hired for their good looks or pleasing personalities. And people usually aren't laid off because of so-so dispositions or ordinary looks. Unless you fit the model of the "old man's pride and joy" for whom room is made in the organization, it's much more likely that you were hired or laid off because of a shift in the demand for your organization's products or services. Thus if the number of school-age children declines, it's likely that teachers will be laid off or go on reduced work weeks (and reduced pay) unless the teachers' union can block it. If a major oil company is planning to expand its domestic oil exploration program, it may start hiring geophysicists or petroleum engineers in anticipation of a major program. If the U.S. government commits itself to a new ally and standby military support, recruiting quotas go up. And if we as a society decide to endorse a national health program that may assure the availability of health care for all, health personnel are vitally affected. In short, demands for human resources emerge from the current or anticipated actions affecting supply and demand for an organization's products and services.

Boundaries and mobility. What is the principal area from which a company draws its human resources? Geography—travel time or commuting distance—plays an important part in defining a company's labor supply and demand. So a labor market usually covers a definable geographic area. But it also includes the paths and processes by which people move through and between major institutions. Every June thousands of graduating high school seniors face decisions related to this aspect of the labor market. A young person must decide between attending a two- or four-year college, attending a vocational/trade school, or entering the world of work. After working for a year, the young person may face another decision—whether to leave his or her employer and seek employment elsewhere or temporarily leave employment and go back to school.

At one time boundaries were fairly clear, but the mobility of a growing number of workers has blurred traditional roles. Workers are increasingly prepared to move between employers, geographic regions, or even occupations. Thus, the notion of a local labor market is overly restrictive: a company can lose sight of good alternative sources of labor if it defines local too strictly. Consequently the notion of labor market boundaries has come to mean the geographic area that is a primary source of human resources for an organization and the bounded area within which the supply and demand forces for labor are played out.

Boundaries and organizations. Other meanings are attached to the boundary concept. For instance, the labor market boundary can refer to the area that includes those institutions competing for a common supply of labor. For example, in downtown Chicago many business offices employ thousands of secretaries, clerks, and typists. Job seekers are drawn from both nearby residential areas and distant suburbs. Traditionally, these jobs have paid quite well. Demand for people persists, and public transportation is excellent, which helps to support labor market activity.

The situation in the suburban areas is often quite different. Suburban offices have experienced chronic shortages of labor because public transportation is poor and only a modest number of people can be drawn from neighboring areas. In some cases, employers have helped to develop car pools or even provided bus transportation.

For some occupational classes the appropriate boundaries may be the entire United States, or even greater. College graduates, young people, higher-level managers, and professional personnel increasingly have displayed an inclination to "go where the action is" or to work where social or living opportunities are more attractive. Thus General Electric in New York may recruit successfully at Stanford University in California, and a vice-president of manufacturing in a northern company may display little reluctance to relocate in the Southwest.

Unions. Unions sometimes play an important role in defining a company's labor market. For example, many craft unions have long-established apprenticeship programs. In areas where unions are able to use economic sanctions, especially major metropolitan centers and areas of heavy industrial concentration, a union card is a job card: "No card, no work." Control of apprenticeship programs gives economic power to the union within a geographic area, since it determines the labor supply. For firms that must employ particular craft categories (e.g., electricians, welders, brick layers, machinists), the labor supply is often provided by union hiring halls. As one moves from centers of heavy industrial or business concentration, union influence often diminishes considerably. Consequently the lines designating control of the labor market become blurred.

LABOR MARKETS AND MANPOWER POLICIES

How does an organization determine its employment criteria? The policies a firm endorses may lead to widely different actions in regard to labor markets. Some enterprises view labor markets essentially as supermarkets, where the buyer (the organization) looks over the available merchandise (employees) and bases its selections on purely economic considerations. Planning here is for the efficient use of labor resources. On the other hand, some organizations are charged with multiple responsibilities, such as the efficient use of human resources and the provision of career opportunities that will prove economically and psychologically satisfying to the individual. In the former, the name of the game may be to hire at the lowest wage possible and get the person producing as soon as possible: "Never mind all that stuff about orientation, careers, and the like." However, some would argue that, in the long run, this economical approach may actually prove more costly.

Internal versus External Labor Markets

Many personnel managers and officials must be aware of internal and external labor markets for their basic planning and programming activities. Some organizations only fill higher-level job openings internally; that is, with people already in the organization. New employees are hired at the bottom of the promotion ladder and are expected to work their way up. Few firms today practice a pure policy of promotion from within utilizing the internal labor market. Yet for many years some extremely large firms have leaned heavily in this direction. Internal labor markets give organizations a high degree of control. Managers are in a position to guide the movement of people, and planners can predict the possible outcome of training or development programs with greater assurance. Wage relationships are established within the internal labor market, but these relationships also reflect wage conditions outside the organization. On the other hand, in the external labor market, wage levels are influenced by the actions of many firms, all of which are bidding for labor or seeking particular professional specialties on the open market.

The structuring of the internal labor market should be a conscious design and operation to meet both organizational and individual need. And the tools exist that make this kind of planning possible—mathematical procedures are available for tracing the movements of people inside organizations. Knowledge of traditional movement patterns and the potential of people provides a basis for improving future planning, for better meeting economic and individual needs, and for revising personnel policies.

Implications for Personnel

The way an organization structures its internal labor market has considerable consequences for personnel human-resources policies and programs. First, the structure of the internal labor market can influence the potential upward movement of organizational members and the attractiveness of various jobs. Second, the sensitivity with which a firm operates its internal labor market affects employees' motivation to perform, which in turn affects their sense of identification with institutional efforts and their willingness to stay on the job. Much of what the organization stands for (honesty, integrity, knowledge) can be embodied in these designs.

OTHER TERMINOLOGY, CONCEPTS, AND PROBLEMS IN LABOR-MARKET ANALYSIS

Up to this point we have discussed only very basic concepts of labor economics. The following definitions and working concepts also are important to human-resource management:

1. *Employment.* Those who are members of the labor force and gainfully at work (for wages). More precisely, employment involves those who are sixteen and over and working even part time. Those who work restricted work weeks due to cutbacks will be picked up in the employment count. But it is clear that income may vary considerably (due to variable work weeks) quite aside from the type of occupation involved.

2. *Unemployment.* Those without work who are actively seeking it. When monthly federal census takers approach people, the questions they ask include:
"How many people who are sixteen years of age or older live in this household?"
"Of those sixteen years of age or older, how many were employed last week?"
"Of those sixteen years of age or older and not employed, how many sought employment last week?"
The number of unemployed may fluctuate a good deal, and estimates of the situation are subject to a good deal of distortion. In some cases, people decide to stop looking for employment when they are unsuccessful. For instance, the chronically unemployed or economically disadvantaged (often because of poor work preparation) have dropped completely out of (un)employment statistics. Similarly, individuals who are working and become unemployed are counted in unemployment figures, but if they then decide to go back to school, they

are dropped from unemployment figures. Where should they be counted? This has become an issue governed by philosophy and method.

3. *Labor force* (total labor supply). This term involves a little population arithmetic: the sum of employment + unemployment. By itself this total figure for labor supply has limited utility for personnel and human-resource planning analyses. It must be coupled with information concerning the number of hours people are willing to work and the various skills, qualities, and abilities they represent.

The concept of the total work force on labor supply also suffers from another deficiency. This has to do with the ability and desire of job seekers (unemployed) to "hang in." When people lose their jobs and simply stop looking, they still are unemployed, but they do not show up in official statistics.

4. *Marginal workers.* These are the workers who do not always show up in unemployment figures. Some workers drop out of the labor force as demand drops and come back in a rush when jobs become available. The groups most directly affected have been members of minority groups, teenagers, economically disadvantaged, and women. These in and out tendencies have been reinforced by the great liberalization of public assistance and the spread of various supplementary income and income-maintenance arrangements.

Thus it becomes easier to understand why local or regional unemployment statistics may change very slowly in a business upturn since local conditions often vary greatly fom the national situation. The number of unemployed does not change greatly in spite of an increase in jobs because the original figures did not include these marginal workers. Newly available jobs are sought by the officially unemployed plus the unofficially unemployed, who may have completely dropped out of the work force. These developments have important implications for personnel matters, completely aside from one's understanding of how these things operate. Area unemployment goals must deal with increasingly complex combinations of general economic-business conditions and conditions affecting particular industries in regional areas. National unemployment goals must deal with social welfare trends in support of the unemployed, and various institutional arrangements that help maintain income while one is unemployed.

5. *Demand for labor.* There is a vital connection between the demand for labor and the labor supply (total labor force). The demand for labor (in other words, employment) emerges from the requirements for a firm's products or services. It is especially sensitive to economic conditions. In past years, general economic conditions appeared to establish overall needs for various occupational specialties, but highly mixed situations have emerged in more recent years. Some industries or companies produced at high levels (and sought labor) while others were affected by lack of product/service demand and might even have laid people off. These situations led to wildly different employment situations from one sector of the economy to the next.

In the classical view, the tension between the demand for labor and the supply of labor is caused by money: the wage paid. As more people are demanded, wages increase; if the supply of labor increases, but demand remains the same, wage levels "soften" and then go down. However, classical market conditions no longer exist, and the forces of labor demand work against labor supply in complex fashion.

The complexity of the labor demand/supply interplay has been brought about by many changes in society, the role of government, unions, and the like. The establishment of legal minimum wages, the decreasing likelihood of wages going down, and social welfare support have led to the need for various personnel specialists to trace the effects of all kinds of labor-market changes. Personnel specialists have dealt with problems such as the impact on institutional employment policies of changes in area wages and wage determination in union negotiations.

6. The *work day* (hours of work) reflects employer choices. In some industries such as retailing (e.g., department stores and food chains), part-time employees may account for better than 50 percent of the work force. People going to school or maintaining households, teenagers, and women have made up the great bulk of part timers in the past. In the future, however, changes in social welfare coverage and greater female participation in the work force will likely alter these figures. Minority personnel and males may comprise an increasing number of part timers.

7. *Educational credentials.* Without doubt, one of the central changes in the U.S. work force has been the elevation of its educational credentials. From a labor force that in 1950 averaged "some" high school education, twenty-five years of unparalleled growth in higher education have raised the overall average educational level by several years. To an important extent, the large number of new graduates and new specialists has been a direct response to the growing complexity, diversity, and technical nature of all business operations. At the same time, many jobs have been upgraded, though not always with proportionate increases in compensation. For some institutions this has meant "acquiring steak at hamburger prices." (The underlying question is "How many people with higher educational credentials are really needed by an organization?" This and related questions are taken up in Chapter 4.)

Underlying these discussions have been remarkable changes in the U.S. labor force. Although some have been described, even broader developments are emerging.

MAJOR LABOR MARKET TRENDS

The statistics of labor-market developments reveal important changes in composition of the labor force. The labor force is composed of the following elements:

1. type of occupation
2. relative numbers of various occupations
3. racial and sex makeup of the work force.

The composition of the labor force has changed drastically during this century (see Exhibit 3–1). Some of the major changes are described in this section.

Occupational Distribution

What kind of demand is there for an iceman's skills—or a farmer's? Distribution of occupations has shifted greatly in this century from production to service-

EXHIBIT 3–1 Occupational Distribution of U.S. Labor Force: 1900–1970

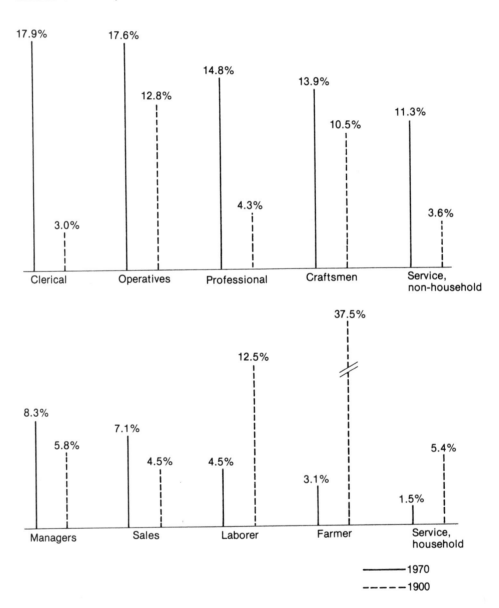

Source: U.S. Bureau of the Census.

oriented functions (sales, clerical, and professional). Also the dramatic rise of automated technologies has generated a great demand for operators and technicians, while all kinds of business and service specialists have increased steadily. The mechanization of agriculture and industry was followed by spectacular decreases in farmers and laborers (see Exhibit 3–2).

EXHIBIT 3–2 Occupational Distribution of U.S. Labor Force: 1900, 1950, 1970

	1900	1950	1970
White collar occupations	17.6%	36.6%	48.1%
Professional & technical personnel	4.3	8.6	14.8
Managerial (incl. officials)	5.8	8.7	8.3
Clerical	3.0	7.0	7.1
Sales	4.5	7.0	7.1
Blue collar occupations	35.8%	41.1%	36.0%
Operatives	12.8	20.4	17.6
Craftsmen	10.5	14.1	13.9
Laborers	12.5	6.6	4.5
Services	9.0%	10.5%	12.8%
Households	5.4	2.6	1.5
Farm workers	37.5%	11.8%	3.1%
	100%	100%	100%

Source: U.S. Bureau of the Census. *U.S. Census of Population, 1970. Occupational Characteristics* (Washington, D.C.: U.S. Government Printing Office, 1973).

Several general occupational trends are clear. First, the tendency toward white-collar jobs is revealed immediately. They accounted for almost one-half of total occupations by 1970. At the same time, the remarkable growth of these types of jobs for the 1900–50 era (17.6 percent to 36.6 percent) was not greatly diminished in the 1950–70 period (36.6 percent to 48 percent). The professional/technical and clerical occupations were leaders in these developments. The increases in professional and technical classifications reflect the growing demand for various services and the vast expansion of the U.S. educational system.

The trend in blue-collar occupations is an interesting one. The number of blue-collar workers rose during the first half of this century. It peaked in 1950, at 41.4 percent, and subsequently declined to 36.0 percent in 1970, almost matching the figure in 1900!

Major Occupational Differences

Over the years different occupations have suffered different fates. Some areas of the economy were crucial to economic growth and national defense (e.g., engineers and scientists). The trends reflect the importance of these and other high-growth areas, such as space and service trades such as banking, merchandising, and insurance. Additionally, service professions such as medical specialties (nurses, physicians, dentists), teachers and lawyers, social welfare programs, and family services have grown spectacularly (see Exhibit 3–3).

The twists and turns of the economy and particular industries are especially apparent in the 1950–70 period (see Exhibit 3–3). For example, overall growth of operatives (delivery people, welders) is reflected despite the large drop in mining (and miners) from 1950 to 1970. In this period, energy based on oil became more important than coal (e.g., due to pollution). Additionally, labor-displacing technology made great inroads in the coal mining industry, and many workers were instead employed in the oil industry. Similarly, the rapid growth of health care (1950–70) is reflected in the growth of medical practitioners, the vast expansion in nurses, and the even greater expansion of health service workers. (However, the shortages of doctors and nurses in the 1950–70 period are not indicated by the growth figures. This suggests that additional information is needed to achieve understanding of these diverse trends.)

Important Changes in the Offing: Labor-Force Participation

The gradual lowering of racial barriers to employment and new social trends have combined to effect dramatic changes in labor-force composition. These changes have been especially dramatic since 1940. Radical changes have occurred in the rate of participation of several groups of workers. ("Rate of participation" refers to the numbers of particular categories by skill, sex, or race as the employable total.)

Participation rate of women. The participation rate for women has increased greatly since 1940. The shift in women's work-force role resulted from changes in life-style, society's expectancies regarding the role of women, the pill, and federal legislation. In 1940 participation was about 27 percent; in 1947 it was about 32 percent, and by the early 1970s it had reached 44 percent. Work as a career, marriage, and family life have become elements in the complex matrix affecting women's participation in the labor force. Prior to 1970 it appeared that the traditional breadwinner role of the male had endured, and it seemed that women occupied many more part-time jobs than men. Specifically, participation of women in the work force in the early 1970s was characterized by the following:

1. One-third of clerical jobs were held by women.
2. Modest gains were achieved in professional and technical occupations (many reflecting work in health care).
3. Inroads into managerial and more senior organizational positions had begun.

This topic is discussed in greater detail in subsequent chapters.

Male participation. Since 1940 the overall participation rate for males rose and then declined. The figures were about 83 percent (1940), 87 percent (1947), and 80 percent (early 1970s). The decline in male participation rates partially resulted from the greater time spent in schooling young people and from the growing acceptance in society of early retirement.

EXHIBIT 3–3   Selected Occupational Highlights: 1900, 1950, 1970*

	1900		1950		1970	
*Professional and technical***		1,200		5,100		11,400
Teachers	450		1,400		3,200	
college	7		130		500	
Medical: nurses	12		500		800	
physicians	130		200		280	
dentists	30		75		90	
Engineers	38		540		1,200	
Accountants	23		390		700	
Drafting people	16		130		290	
Lawyers (& judges)	110		180		270	
Scientists	14		170		240	
Social workers	6		70		220	
Computer specialists, systems	—		—		330	
Managers, Administrators		1,700		5,200		6,400
Retail trade	900		2,000		1,800	
Purchasing agents	7		65		160	
Bank offices	75		140		310	
Clerical		900		7,200		13,700
Secretaries, steno, typists	130		1,700		3,800	
Bookkeeper, cashiers	230		990		2,360	
Office machine specialists	—		150		550	
Telephone operators	19		380		410	
Craftspeople and Related Workers		3,060		8,350		10,610
Mechanics, repair people	320		2,060		2,840	
Motor vehicle	—		690		800	
Linepeople (utility)	18		220		390	
Airplane	—		75		390	
Construction	1,180		2,790		2,730	
Carpenters	600		1,020		840	
Electricians	50		330		470	
Foremen	160		870		1,590	
Operatives		3,720		12,030		13,450
Manufacturing	1,820		6,610		7,390	
Delivery, route people	170		250		620	
Welders	—		280		540	
Laundry	90		460		350	
Mines	660		620		160	
Non-farm Labor		3,620		3,850		3,430
Service Workers		2,630		6,180		9,780
Food (waiters, cooks, etc.)	310		1,530		2,510	
Health service (hospital attendants, etc.)	110		370		1,180	
Protective service	135		590		950	
Farm Workers		10,890		6,950		2,370

* Figures given represent thousands and are rounded as follows: 50,000–100,000, "nearest 500"; over 100,000, "nearest 10,000."

** Major categories are followed by key subcategories; subcategory figures will not total out to category figures because of rounding.

Sources: David L. Kaplan and M. Claire Casey, *Occupational Trends in the United States, 1900–1950*, 1958. U.S. Bureau of the Census, *1970 Census of the Population, Occupation by Industry*, 1972. Garth Mangum and David Snedeker, *Manpower Planning for Local Labor Markets*, 1974, pp. 86–87.

Nonwhite participation. Participation rates for nonwhite personnel, especially males, have displayed dramatic changes. Minority employment, with governmental pressures and societal changes, finally started to take hold. Although the unemployment rates for various male categories are still low in terms of general social acceptability, improvements are evident. The following occupational shifts for blacks took place in a fifteen-year period ending in the early 1970s (Bureau of the Census, 1972):

1. The proportion of blacks as blue-collar workers decreased slightly (41.8–39.9 percent), but there have been major reductions in the laborer's jobs (14.9– 9.9 percent), while there have been similar increases in craftspeople and foremen (5.7–8.7 percent).
2. Blacks penetrated white-collar jobs in increasing numbers, registering gains in all occupational categories, to account for almost one-third of all of these job holders (from approximately 13–30 percent).

Age and participation. Age is and has been a definite factor in the participation rate. For example, although overall male rates declined, the 25 to 44 category has been essentially constant. Participation rates for categories under 24 years have been highly responsive to economic fluctuations and imposition of federal minimum wage laws. For example, poor job conditions have encouraged continuation of schooling or have led to extended periods of unemployment. Underlying some of these participation rates are many economic, social, and political considerations such as increasing personal income, federal and state legislation, societal and community values, geography (urban vs. rural area of the country), sex, race, level of education, and type of commerce or industry in a locality or region.

EDUCATION AND THE LABOR MARKET

Higher Education—The Education Explosion

The vast explosion in the U.S. system of higher education in the post–World War II era established priorities for particular types of learning. Colleges and universities were in the forefront of the expansion of post-secondary education. These were followed later by the community and junior colleges. Yet a new need exists for tradespeople, technologists, and paraprofessionals to meet the occupational requirements of vastly expanded health and service industries. College-bound students from high school increased from one in three graduates to two out of three. Additionally, the need was evident for updating and creating new industries and occupations. This need for industrial updating had further implications for the educational system. Exhibit 3–4 illustrates features of a vastly expanded educational system and an even more complex combination of jobs and educational paths.

EXHIBIT 3–4   External Labor Market and Related Systems

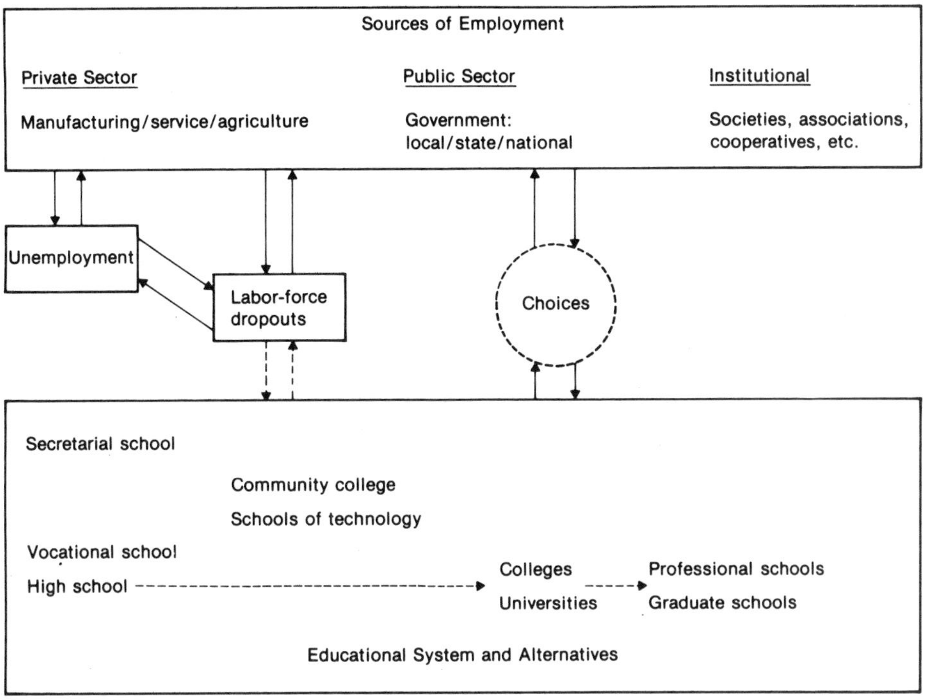

Factors Supporting Community College Growth

Community colleges have been a major factor in the advancement of educational credentials in the labor market. The growth in community colleges has been greatest in heavily populated areas because they filled a void created by a lack of educational opportunities for racial minorities and the economically disadvantaged. Other developments encouraging community college growth include equal opportunity legislation, societal emphasis on going to college, and an awakened social conscience. It was in this spirit that many community colleges adopted "open enrollment," which vastly encouraged and supported college attendance, especially among racial minorities.

Expansion of the community college system has been an attempt to teach directly a wide range of new or updated job skills. This type of educational expansion has helped to reduce the pressures on organizational training and skill-building activities. For example, a large steel facility at one time had to provide a major program of internal training in maintenance, technology (mechanical and electronics), computer systems, and various areas of production and quality control. Along with other organizations in its area, it eventually convinced legislators and state university officials of the need for technology (two-year college) programs. These were eventually established as "extension" programs of two major state universities in nearby cities and were quite successful. Another educational upgrading of the labor force took place in a southern state during the 1970s. Literally thousands of jobs in the state could not be filled for lack of appropriate trade skills. In a four-year period the state's community college system (mostly technology programs) was able to update or provide better than twenty-five thousand trained employees for employers located in the state.

Labor-Market Signals: Job Opportunity

College is also an important alternative to work when economic conditions are poor and jobs are difficult to find. For example, during the economic slump in the 1973–75 period, many colleges, especially those in the public sector (city and state), sustained enrollment increases. Additionally, to the amazement of admissions offices, many graduate programs were oversubscribed for the 1975–76 period, as graduates from earlier periods came back to the campuses because of the lack of jobs. These students were substituting educational time for work time.

Labor-market conditions send job signals to work-force members and students in the educational system. Multiple layers of Labor Department statisticians, government bureaucrats, career counselors, feature writers, and academics attempt to interpret these signals and direct educational traffic. Unfortunately, several different systems of traffic lights are in operation at the same time. What makes it unfortunate is that these different functionaries have widely different objectives. Some units are concerned only with near-term, short-run developments, while others concentrate on long-term trends. Still others are concerned with specific occupations, such as engineering, while others may concentrate on national, regional, or local developments.

Further, the information available to these systems varies widely in quality, completeness, and relevance. In some cases the information suffers for lack of basic data, which just aren't gathered. Some difficulties arise out of sheer incompetence on the part of analysts or counselors who are not trained for this type of work. Of course, additional complexities arise because all of these analyses deal with the future—a major uncertainty in its own right. No wonder students and labor-force participants have been confused: they must deal with information that is speculative, incomplete, or inaccurate. Further, they may not know how to interpret the labor-market cues in terms of their choices among job and educational alternatives.

The Student Dilemma: Narrowing Choices

Confusion regarding labor-market signals has led to switches in career preparation or job-educational choices that may have intensified unemployment problems. A student's "choice" among careers may have started with his or her parents: the occupation or biases of parents is an especially important factor in professional fields such as law, medicine, and engineering. High school "career days," student-counseling efforts, part-time work experience, and the experiences of older brothers and sisters start to focus one's notions of education-career options. The senior year in high school often forces some type of choice between a job and college, and if the latter is chosen, a general program or field of concentration must be selected.

The problem with this process involves a dimension of future shock. A student must declare a major in some field, such as accounting or engineering, almost at the point of college entry. Consequently, preparation for certain fields has required a choice of fields *years* prior to the individual's entry into the labor market. Business cycles operating during a student's college years often give strong signals to students on overall employment possibilities. The "here and now" has a powerful influence on individual choice: "Social science is poor preparation for getting a job at this time, but business management is strong; why not switch to a business program"?

Labor Demand, Career Switching, and Labor Markets: Some Cases

The continued expansion of the educational system in the sixties, new educational modes, open enrollment, "street schools," and other alternative systems of education strained teacher resources. In some cases, employment credentials for teachers were lowered simply to fill out rosters. Thousands of young people opted for teaching careers or switched out of other programs. Switching and occupational choices for teaching continued until the 1970s, when overall student enrollment peaked and then declined in a number of elementary and high school systems. The numbers of surplus teachers by 1973 and 1974 started to approximate the size of the teacher shortage in the late 1960s.

Engineering is another labor-market field that has suffered from confusion of career signals, career switching, and problems of surplus and shortage. Because of Sputnik, the vast expansion of the technology base in the United States during the 1950s and 1960s was fed by all kinds of technically trained personnel. Government agencies and major employers recruited heavily in colleges. They sponsored programs in high school, supported research, and were regularly in the news regarding the nation's manpower needs. No wonder that many students chose engineering and science as those fields rose sharply in the sixties and into the seventies, even after the peak demand for these occupations had passed and had started to decline. For instance, in the aerospace industry, opportunities dried up, and thousands of professionals on the West Coast and in other regional centers supplying this industry were unemployed. Yet, even into the seventies certain governmental departments were still forecasting aerospace job opportunities. At the same time the Engineer's Joint Council, an authoritative group, was forecasting surplus. The final result was that enrollment continued to go up for a while and finally started to decline.

Employment signals also cause movement in both directions—witness what happened in conjunction with labor demand and the energy crisis, which started in 1973. The sudden need to innovate, design, and produce new technologies in energy fields aroused all kinds of employers, contractors, and government units. By 1975 labor shortages cropped up in most basic engineering fields, starting wages went up sharply, and the switch was back to engineering fields.

Matching Educational and Occupational Needs: Future Job Opportunities

With so many people having gone or returned to college, at this point it appears desirable to look at the big picture. How well does the supply of jobs requiring college preparation match the demand for current and potential employees with college degrees and certificates? Labor supply may outrun demand for professionally oriented legal, medical, or management skills. The outlook through the early 1980s indicates that available jobs will not match the number of people coming through the educational system who have these abilities. Consequently organizations will become more selective in hiring, and some jobs may be upgraded (made more demanding) to take advantage of better-prepared people. Another development may be that some jobs will be "stuffed" with overqualified people, and wage levels, as a result, may soften. In turn, college-going is likely to undergo reexamination relative to the benefits to be derived from it (more on this in Chapter 4).

Community college programs through the early 1980s may receive increased attention as a more realistic approximation of organizational skill and ability needs. As already indicated, technology, craft, and trade needs are being satisfied by these programs. Also, the two-year educational period in business, the social sciences, and the physical sciences may become a realistic compromise. This type of two-year program may work well if it helps to meet organizational needs in updated skills and more comfortably matches real occupational need and employee abilities.

Reading Labor-Market Signals More Accurately

How can our institutions deal more precisely with labor-market behavior? How can it be understood and improved? Some major ingredients of this complex picture are:

1. organizations as sources of analyses, information, and influence
2. the need for accurate occupational information
3. the differences between the overall features of a labor market and its regional and local labor-market characteristics or employment features
4. overall labor supply and demand and their relation to the demand for various goods and services
5. distinguishing employment signals of short- from long-term business cycles or trends
6. overall population and labor-force trends, which may be counterbalanced (to a degree) by various educational and social trends
7. social trends which legitimize or encourage college-going

8. time lags in information transfer between information analyzers and information consumers (students).

GOVERNMENT, LEGISLATION, LABOR MARKETS

The Public Sector—The Role of Government

The subject matter of this chapter would be incomplete if we did not acknowledge the government's central role. We have intentionally delayed this discussion, as it has been necessary to set out basic concepts while avoiding the complications of legislation and the functions of federal agencies. Consequently, with this discussion of the role of government, a very large piece of the labor-market puzzle will be fitted in place.

The twists and turns of governmental manpower planning efforts and their effects on labor markets are of significance to organizational officials and individuals alike. For organizational officials, manpower legislation and planning have affected the number, skills, quality, and availability of work-force members. They have also affected the availability of funds that supplement internal company training efforts, at times amounting to very substantial sums of money. For individuals, governmental programs have affected the offering of marketable skills and job availability.

Human Resources and Government

Government legislation and the functions of various federal agencies underlie the entire discussion of this chapter. As a matter of fact, many discussions of labor markets center around the legislation and activities of government. In this type of approach, the impact on the general economy, employment, and job development are primary considerations. The perspective developed in this chapter has attempted to develop the human resource side of the labor market and the impact of these considerations for the personnel functions in organizations. Discussions in Mangum and Snedeker (1974) were especially useful in writing this section.

The labor-market concepts described earlier in this chapter involved both the supply of and demand for labor. In the main, manpower legislation (Chapter 2), plus the whole governmental apparatus of manpower/human-resource concerns at the federal, state, and local levels, have focused on the supply of labor or the conditions under which it is used. The complexity of the governmental apparatus that is concerned with labor matters can be appreciated from the selected listing of departments and divisions in Exhibit 3–5. It should be emphasized that this is only a selected list and that it merely suggests the many features of these operations.

Departmental Functions

Exhibit 3–5 illustrates the highly interrelated nature of the apparatus of governmental operations and legislation. Labor-market processes receive attention from

---

EXHIBIT 3–5   Labor-Related Mechanisms of Federal, State, and Local Governments (selected)

	Focus
U.S. Department of Labor (USDL)	
Manpower Administration	Planning, research, liaison with regional and state manpower programs.
Bureau of Labor Statistics	Statistical analysis in support of all USDL operations.
Fair Labor Standards Division	Enforcement of Fair Labor Standards Act and its provisions.
Wage and Hours Division	Enforcement of legislation affecting wages, hours, and working conditions.
Employment Security	Employment problems.
U.S. Training and Employment Service	Federally supported training program, employment service support, and facilities for serving local labor markets.
Federal Mediation and Conciliation	Mediation and conciliation in organization or disputes involving business and management.
State labor departments (frequently counterparts of the federal departments and divisions)	Similar concerns, but apply to various labor markets within the state and various county/city jurisdictions; major concerns in the disposition of training funds under newer, federally decentralized programs.
County and city labor departments (single or small groups of departments charged with manpower/human-resource responsibility)	Liaison with state and federal (labor) departments; at times, play a major role in the disposition of federal funds under the newer, federally decentralized programs.

---

many different types and levels (federal and local) of departments. Some agencies relate to each other procedurally, others informationally. For example, the U.S. Department of Labor's Bureau of Employment Security processes employment information based on reports from state agencies of "employment security." All of the indicated agencies deal with some aspect of preparing people for employment. Some have been formed specifically to administer or work within the framework of particular legislation. On the other hand the Federal Mediation and Conciliation Service is a direct consequence of the need for an intermediary to help work out union-management problems. The "Service" grew out of the need created by the National Labor Relations Act and the Taft-Hartley Act.

For our purposes we are especially interested in those aspects of legislation that have improved labor market mechanisms and have bettered the personal and economic welfare of labor. These areas of legislation, in conjunction with the related apparatus of government operations, are briefly discussed next.

Governmental mechanism, legislation, and the labor market. In essence, the labor-market apparatus of government has prepared many people for job roles and has facilitated the matching of job seekers with seekers of labor. Local and regional labor markets have been served by the facilities and job-finding capabilities of the U.S. Training and Employment Service and similar state and regional agencies charged with similar responsibilities. Governmental units provide a logical clearinghouse for employers seeking labor. These units maintain files on employers with jobs and workers' skills. Another key responsibility of the governmental offices is forecasting shifts in the characteristics of the labor force as they affect employment opportunity.

Training labor for improved jobs. The training of people who lack basic job skills or who are able to fill only low-skilled jobs has received growing attention in federal legislation, budgets, and agency activities. Government interest has centered on improving the human-resource planning procedures of public agencies. This planning is of growing importance in local labor markets for improving the delivery of services to and through these markets. In truth, it has been said that planning was initiated as a political stratagem to deal with the mounting criticism of federally administered programs. Many critics have charged that programs directed from Washington and other points are too removed from local problems. Consequently, much recent manpower planning has been an attempt to strengthen the organization and administration of manpower programs in various labor markets.

Improved coordination. Improved manpower planning has meant improved coordination, decentralization of responsibilities to regional and local agencies, and decategorizing many specialized agencies and activities. The activities of many agencies were felt to be overly narrow and restrictive. For example, the Concentrated Employment Program (CEP) sought to unite all manpower programs in poverty areas. CAMPS (Cooperative Area Manpower Planning Systems) sought parallel planning efforts for a variety of related programs. In one of the more recent efforts, CETA (formed by the Comprehensive Employment and Training Act of 1973), a major attempt was made to decentralize responsibilities to local officials. Of particular interest were local efforts to offer programs reflecting individual needs and community realities regarding types of jobs and skills needed.

These acts were meant to strengthen planning. They affected legislation and were further affected by manpower legislation that provided budgets for undertaking massive programs of people preparation.

As most managers and businessmen know, planning comes about only when the wherewithall is provided, namely, money or budgets. State and city planning activities to support staff and services were initiated by 1970 and were extended to counties under CETA by 1973. However, the provision of funds wasn't enough, and legislation was passed to facilitate planning and coordination.

The core of training programs aimed at assisting the poor and disadvantaged in society emerged in the 1960s. The Civil Rights Act of 1969, the Equal Opportunity Act, and the Manpower Development and Training Act (1964) established national concerns for the economically disadvantaged and minorities in work and equal-employment opportunity, with priority assigned to these groups for receiving manpower services; "on-the-job" skill training; work-experience programs for students, out-of-school youth, and economically disadvantaged adults.

Massive doses of federal training funds to help racial minorities and the economically disadvantaged mushroomed rapidly. Although the term *disadvantaged* lacked full definition, the Manpower Development and Training Act (MDTA) was assigning about two-thirds of its funds to this group by the late 1960s (Mangum and Snedeker, 1974, p. 39).

Information base for planning in labor markets.   Timely, comprehensive information is the basis for planning. In this context, the information requirements to support planning in local labor markets involves the joint efforts of public offices and private organizations.

A striking similarity exists between these information needs and those of computerized information systems for personnel (see Chapter 15). Information requirements for labor-market planning indicate the following needs (Mangum and Snedeker, 1974, p. 27):

1. Timely and accurate data from employers regarding job openings and realistic assessment of needed skills. At times there aren't enough cooperating employers, so that job seekers greatly exceed the listed jobs.

2. Detailed statistics of job seekers and those entering labor markets. Commonly, data requirements include age, location of people, numbers, skills, education, and job preferences.

3. Type and availability of educational systems for acquiring needed knowledge and skills and the role played by various institutions, such as universities, community colleges, and trade/vocational schools.

4. Administrative and management capabilities of public planning systems, availability of resources at the federal, state, and local levels, and bases for relating public to private organizations.

Comprehensive Employment and Training Act (CETA, 1973).   It is worthwhile to dwell on the CETA legislation for a few moments, for it solidified the decentralization of public manpower planning and met labor-market needs not previously covered. Most early manpower planning—even legislation—was addressed to meet urban unemployment problems, the "war on poverty," and the "needs of the day." The economic and manpower research required to document requirements was frequently incomplete. (Even this description will likely be viewed by many labor people as overly generous regarding the adequacy of background work.)

These observations notwithstanding, the 1970 census indicated that some major labor-market areas were not adequately covered in an organizational, administrative, or planning sense. The census suggested that poverty and unemployment were much more serious in non-major city areas than was previously considered. It was indicated that better than one-half, maybe two-thirds, of unemployment and poverty existed in suburban and rural areas! CETA legislation strengthened the role of "prime sponsors," public agencies, and others who were to assume planning and programming responsibilities within specified geographic jurisdictions. Generally, the areas were based on population (over 100,000), but seriousness of unemployment sometimes received special attention. For state governments and local prime sponsors, CETA provided budgets (80 percent of total funds needed) for comprehensive manpower programs and public employment programs. Other provisions of CETA served to phase out MDTA and the Economic Opportunity Act but continued the Job Corps and established a National Commission on Manpower Policy.

In summary, CETA served to decentralize responsibility and helped to organize manpower planning and programming at the state, county, and local levels. The key assumption underlying CETA legislation was that labor problems resided at regional and local levels. Consequently, funds needed to carry out these programs were placed at local levels. The centralized model of planning and control that had reigned for almost thirty years was set aside. However, the full impact of this policy shift on local labor-market activity and the management of institutions is yet to be felt.

Have We Learned?

This is a final note on manpower planning and labor-market performance related to the supply and demand for labor. The experience of the past doesn't speak too well for our efforts. This is especially true in light of our assumed capability to plan as a nation. The chaos of manpower programming in the 1960s and the overloading of educational facilities reflected a very hectic period. Additionally, the need forecasted by national planners was signaled by the great surge in births soon after World War II. A vast expansion of manpower programming and educational activity was indicated but the response was not good. Government and state planners and employers were poorly prepared for what followed. Cycles of substantial surpluses and major shortages of engineers and scientists, the glut of college-educated people on an already overburdened labor market—these and other peaks and valleys in labor supply and demand are normal in our society. Often they represent practical ways of redistributing planning efforts, jobs, and human resources, but in the future public-sector and private organizations need planning efforts that reduce the shock waves of reaction without planning. We must keep asking, Have we learned? How can we apply these experiences to the problems of today and tomorrow?

SUMMARY AND IMPLICATIONS

The management of human resources within individual organizations is tied firmly to personnel considerations both inside and outside the organization. This chapter, along with Chapters 1 and 2, has been concerned largely with external environmental developments. Labor markets are the sources of human creativity, effort, and individual capability that are central to any organization's purposes. People are one of the basic resources that permit organizational function and operation. Thus this chapter's central purpose was to describe major characteristics and changes in the composition of the labor force. These factors affect overall organizational functioning in general and personnel activities in particular. At the same time, recognizing the firm connection of an individual organization to the environment, and thus labor markets, has required developing a whole new set of tools for analysis. Labor-market concepts have played a key part in these newer tools and methods. Consequently, a second purpose of this chapter was to develop various concepts of labor-market analysis which have proven useful in planning for and utilizing human resources within organizations.

It should be clear that the personnel function within the individual organization is faced with a much more complex people picture than in previous years. Seemingly internal matters, such as training, compensation, human-resource planning, and promotion, are linked to the realities of labor markets and the restraints of government legislation. In addition, important organizational functions, such as recruiting and training, can be supported by the resources of various public agencies. But this ability to work with these public units and to administer internal personnel matters in effective fashion is linked to one's understanding of labor-market concepts and functions.

DISCUSSION QUESTIONS

1. What distinctions are made in the chapter between apparatus of government operation in the labor market and legislation related to the labor market?

2. What new labor market needs were met by CETA?

3. What has been the major shift in the role of government regarding labor-market operation? What factors account for this shift?

4. How is the new role of various governmental agencies and administrative groups likely to affect labor-related activities of the firm?

5. What recent developments have taken place regarding women's participation in the work force?

6. How are the statistics of the size of the labor force affected by inflationary and recessionary periods? Describe the actions of selected groups like teenagers and women.

7. State your assumptions and name some of the key considerations defining a labor-market.

8. Why is labor considered a derived demand?

9. What considerations work against the free flow of supply and demand for labor? How are wages involved?

10. As a member of the board of higher education for a particular state, how might you interpret current educational trends?

11. As a member of a company's personnel department, what use might you make of the government's labor-market apparatus? What considerations encourage usage? What considerations might discourage usage?

12. According to the testimony in the scenario, what were the effects of unemployment on various labor-market matters during a period of high unemployment? What seemingly contradictory trends took place? What determinations are indicated for the public?

13. How do industry considerations relate to high unemployment or employment situations?

14. As a manpower forecaster for a large material firm, what aspects of labor market trends would you be concerned with for each of the following:
   a. a department-store chain using large numbers of sales, clerical, and part-time people?
   b. a large insurance company with only a single national headquarters unit?
   c. professional and managerial personnel?

BIBLIOGRAPHY

Bakke, E. Wight. *The Mission of Manpower Policy*. Washington, D.C.: W. E. Upjohn Institute for Employment Research, 1969.

Blair, Peter M., and Otis D. Duncan. *The American Occupational Structure*. New York: Wiley, 1964.

Burack, Elmer H. *Strategies for Manpower Planning and Programming*. Morristown, N.J.: General Learning Press, 1972.

Bureau of National Affairs. "Turnover in Job Satisfaction." Survey No. 91, Personnel Policies Forum. Washington, D.C.: Bureau of National Affairs, 1970.

Doeringer, Peter B., and M. J. Pioie. *Internal Labor Markets & Manpower Analysis*. Lexington, Mass.: Heath, 1971.

Folk, Hugh. *The Shortage of Scientists and Engineers*. Lexington, Mass.: Heath, 1970.

Freeman, Richard, and S. Herbert Hollomon. "The Declining Value of College Going." *Change* 24 (1975).

Hansen, Niles M. *Location, Preferences, Migration, and Regional Growth*. New York: Praeger, 1973.

Harbison, Frederic. *Human Resources or the Wealth of Nations*. New York: Oxford University Press, 1971.

Henle, Peter. "Recent Growth of Paid Leisure for U.S. Workers." *Monthly Labor Review* (March 1962):249–57.

Hoyt, Kenneth B., *et al. Career Education: What It Is and How to Do It*, 2d ed. Salt Lake City: Olympus, 1969.

Kaplan, David L., and M. Claire Casey. *Occupational Trends in the United States, 1900–1950*. U.S. Bureau of Census Paper No. 5. Washington, D.C.: U.S. Government Printing Office, 1958.

Kerr, Clark. "The Balkanization of Labor Markets." In E. Bakke (ed.), *Labor Mobility and Economic Opportunity*. New York: Wiley, 1954.

Levitan, Sal, and Robert Taggert. "Employment and Earnings Inadequacy: A Measure of Worker Welfare." *Monthly Labor Review* (October 1973).

Mabry, Bevars D. *Economics of Manpower and the Labor Market*. New York: Intext Educational Publishers, 1973.

Mangum, Garth, and David Snedeker. *Manpower Planning for Local Labor Markets.* Salt Lake City, Utah: Olympus Publishing Co., 1974.

Moore, Geoffrey H., and Janice N. Hedges. "Trends in Labor and Leisure." *Monthly Labor Review* (February, 1971):3–11.

Oppenheimer, Valerie K. *The Female Labor Force in the United States: Demographic and Economic Factors Governing Its Growth and Changing Composition.* Berkeley: University of California Institute of International Studies, 1969.

Patten, Thomas H. *Manpower Planning and the Development of Human Resources.* New York: Wiley Interscience Publishers, 1971.

Schiller, Bradley R. *The Economics of Poverty and Discrimination.* Englewood Cliffs, N.J.: Prentice-Hall, 1973.

The Conference Board. *The Road Maps of Industry Nu's 1739, 1740.* New York: The Conference Board, 1974/75.

The Conference Board. *Job Design for Motivation.* New York: Conference Board, 1971.

U.S. Bureau of Labor Statistics. "Selected Earnings and Demographic Characteristics of Union Members, 1970." Report No. 417. Washington, D.C.: U.S. Government Printing Office, October 1972.

U.S. Bureau of the Census. *Historical Statistics of the United States, Colonial Times to 1957.* Washington, D.C.: U.S. Government Printing Office, 1960.

U.S. Bureau of the Census. *1970 Census of the Population, Occupation by Industry.* Washington, D.C.: U.S. Government Printing Office, 1972.

U.S. Bureau of the Census. *United States Census of the Population, 1970: Occupational Characteristics.* Washington, D.C.: U.S. Government Printing Office, 1973.

U.S. Bureau of the Census. *Statistical Abstract of the United States, 1972.* Washington, D.C.: U.S. Government Printing Office, 1972, Table 367.

U.S. Department of Commerce. *Occupational Trends in the United States, 1900–1950.* Washington, D.C.: U.S. Government Printing Office, 1958.

U.S. Department of Labor. *Employment and Earnings* 20.2. Washington, D.C.: U.S. Government Printing Office, January 1973.

U.S. Department of Labor. *Manpower Report to the President, March 1972, 1973, 1974.* Washington, D.C.: U.S. Government Printing Office, 1972, 1973, 1974.

Zeller, Frederick A., *et al. Career Thresholds.* U.S. Department of Labor, Manpower Administration. Washington, D.C.: U.S. Government Printing Office, 1971.

Chapter 4

WHY
PEOPLE
WORK

LEARNING OBJECTIVES

Chapter 3 analyzed external labor markets in a somewhat abstract statistical way. This chapter will explore the idea of labor as people. At the conclusion of this chapter, the reader should be able to:

Identify issues related to the work ethic and their connection to decisions affecting organization members

Describe matters related to the value of college training and alternative career paths

Describe newer needs being expressed by youth

Develop approaches to minority employment and career development

Formulate personnel strategies that respond to new occupational and human resource development.

KEY TERMS AND CONCEPTS

value of college going

work ethic

alienation

social welfare legislation

careers versus jobs

enriched jobs

alternative career paths

decisions to join, produce, maintain affiliation

new life-style

rewards: extrinsic, intrinsic

National Alliance of Businessmen (NAB)

work design

PREVIEW

Six general areas are explored in this chapter on why people work. The meaning of work is first considered in terms of the work ethic tradition and revisions in the outlook of new employees. This is followed by a discussion of related topics:

1. Why people affiliate with organizations, and what organizations seek from potential employees. This section also describes briefly some of the realities job seekers face.

2. Several major work-force components, including women, youth, and racial minorities.

3. The importance of education in job choices and employability. In particular, alternative education paths and careers are emphasized.

4. How new meanings for work and personal needs are likely to impact personnel.

THE MEANING OF WORK: THE WORK ETHIC

Curse or blessing? Although most of us spend an enormous part of our lives working, we know remarkably little about it. Many people take the idea of working for granted—an inevitability much like death, taxes, and broken political promises. Yet historically, the meaning and importance attached to work have changed greatly. The early Greeks (perhaps ancestors of some of our friends) viewed work as a curse: work was boring and meaningless activity that could enslave people, subject them to the will of others, and thereby rob them of independence. The early Hebrews similarly maintained that physical toil did not satisfy the soul because it left little time for labors of the mind.

Other views, religious and otherwise, gained importance in Western societies. Later cultures gave quite a different meaning to work and its importance in life: "Work maintains bodily health and peace of mind. It helps to keep evil thoughts at bay and helps to maintain hope and avoid despair." Clearly, this kind of attitude was a far cry from the dismal view of the Ancients.

Colonial America was founded—and the early United States grew—when the sanctification of work, in both the religious and secular sense occurred. The worth of work was all-powerful. The accumulation of wealth through work and the positive meaning of work became accepted without question. Americans of the recent past defined success—"making it"—in terms of physical possessions (which money can buy). Money, job status, and the achievements and mobility of their children became important goals. The key to this kind of success increasingly meant success in the business world, high-status professions or in white-collar jobs and skilled occupations. Work became a code word or symbol for one's position in society's pecking order.

Work and the Worker: A Dissenting View

This country was born during the Industrial Revolution. New inventions were introduced by the score. Machinery to produce more efficiently, new ways of working, and new kinds of workers were needed. *And* a new work ethic was needed. Since that time Western society has undergone a series of industrial and technological revolutions that ever so slowly, but with little deviation, have brought our industrial society to the development and form we know today. The potential risks of high levels of technical achievement and productivity are that individuals will sense a growing gulf between work and its benefits.

Early Rumblings

As early as 1844 Karl Marx predicted some key work-related issues of the modern day in his *Economic and Philosophical Manuscripts of 1844.* Although Marx admittedly was engaged in polemics, this doesn't alter the substance of his ideas. His central theme was that of the *worker's alienation from his (or her) work.* While many of Marx's ideas have been diluted or discounted, four aspects of his concept of alienation in the workplace have stood the test of time.

1. *Powerlessness.* A sense of powerlessness in the face of an overwhelming technology or massive organization. Historically, this was probably the first challenge to individual worth and dignity.

2. *Meaninglessness.* The separation of responsibility, decision making, and meaningful tasks from the worker has led to a feeling of meaninglessness and loss of a sense of purpose. The continuing division of labor and the specialization of work tasks have fragmented individual activity. In this process individuals are less able to relate their tasks to total organizational purposes.

3. *Isolation.* Isolation from the central purposes and outputs of one's organization. The inability, legally or socially, to claim the "product of one's efforts" makes workers feel apart from their organizations, and when one realizes that he has only time or labor to sell, this sense of detachment grows.

4. *Estrangement.* Finally, alienation has become estrangement for many individuals. Work, when viewed as simply a way to make a living that lacks purpose, diminishes identification, and obliterates personal control, quite naturally leads to self-estrangement. This sense of estrangement can produce anger or inner conflict because a worker must choose between his "essence" and the reality of needing food and shelter.

A Contemporary View—Work and the Work Ethic

Work has enormous economic, social, and personal consequences. It is central to our culture and society. It occupies a key place in an individual's life activity and outlook. A person's mental health, which is related to one's felt hostility, anxiety, self-esteem, and sociability, has been linked to one's work and level of job (Kornhauser, 1965). Yet many organizations stress performance and efficiency, which do little to build the factors contributing to mental health (e.g., self-esteem).

What are the consequences of alienation? An individual who loses the means of realizing the benefits of the work is beset by frustration. If a person feels he has failed in his struggle for the "good life," he feels ineffective. This is bad enough, but what is worse is that society loses a creative, productive member and instead gains discontent. This is the core of the problem.

The Behavioral Side

In recent years growing attention has been paid to the important social and psychological dimensions of work. It involves individual effort and organizational objectives. A tradeoff is worked out between individual and organization: personal effort is exchanged for a valued return. For instance, a worker receives money for working within an organization's requirements. These restraints limit a person's autonomy and independence. For example, procedures must be followed, and people are held accountable for their work effort or "contributions."

Since work meets both individual and organizational needs, it has purpose. However, work may have long-term goals as well as immediate objectives. Both parties, the individual and the organization, can be important in securing broader objectives or goals.

Many people have begun to realize that all is not well in the workplace. "If your job puts you to sleep try one of ours." This implied improvement in the world of work was not promised by one of America's supercompanies; it appeared on a Navy recruiting poster. Be that as it may, the horror stories of problems in the workplace have found their way into newspapers and feature articles. The rising tide of denials by many organizational officials suggests that some bona fide problems exist.

Changing Times and Changing Outlooks

A popular notion suggests that society in general and government in particular will reduce adversity and protect everyone from economic or personal disaster. This attitude means that people are less inclined to accept work as a destiny or fate. Rather, any change for the better *should* be made if it *can* be made.

The "right to job satisfaction" has come to dominate the thinking of many young people. Major changes in the legal and social fabric of our society have reduced the fear of economic insecurity. More and more, individual concerns have gone beyond mere survival. Social welfare legislation, including social security, wage and hour regulation, occupational safety, and unemployment benefits, has greatly reduced personal worry regarding food, clothing, and shelter for better or worse depending on one's value system.

Felt needs or wants, however vague in the past, are increasingly surfacing as individual rights. Potential employees are prepared to go to greater lengths than workers of past generations to gain their legacy from society. There is less and less feeling that individual differences, openness, expression of opinion, and personal growth need to be shelved in order to gain acceptance or survival. This new development means that people are more prepared to speak up or to challenge authority. It means that people are more frequently questioning the value of Western society's idea of efficiency, which may strip life of opportunity for real pleasure, excitement, and personal growth. It also means that people prefer to do work that promotes their idea of living, rather than simply provides money and a basis to survive.

These new values have led to a personal idealization of work: people want a "career," not simply a "job." Increasingly, young people have come to equate survival with "job" and "career" with a broader concept of work that encompasses personal growth and permits achievement of status, recognition, and work-related satisfaction. This career psychology leads the worker to consider a job as something that meets particular needs (for example, providing money for a car or as a stepping stone toward one's "career"), while a career is a source of personal and professional satisfaction as well as material gain.

What do people think about work? This question has many dimensions and evokes many different responses. Work may be considered neutral, positive, or negative for a particular individual. Virtually all aspects of the organizational environment can evoke some type of individual response. An example from a company study in England indicates the differing reactions of people to their organizations and work situations.

A Satisfaction Study: Blue Collar Blues

Summary results of an English study (Benyon and Blackburn, 1972) revealed that men on the night shift who were married, had family responsibility, and earned good salaries were "satisfied" with their jobs. Also, part-time workers, mostly women and all married, were quite satisfied with their jobs, which were seen as a means of supplementing family income. As mothers and wives, work involvement was a matter of small importance; the chance to gain social satisfaction was primary.

Women who worked full time gave their work priority, but those women without family roles to play felt they had fewer "rewards" than did the part timers.

Young people, mostly male, on the day shift had the least commitment to the organization and the least job-related satisfaction. They disliked supervision and lacked the economic incentive that family responsibility usually brings.

What is astonishing—perhaps appalling—is that this study is almost a voice in the wilderness. Statistics of worker satisfaction or dissatisfaction are of little help because comparatively small numbers of people have been studied. Also, there is a lack of comparison between time periods, studies, and countries.

Herbert Parns of Ohio State University has headed a project sponsored jointly by the U.S. Labor and Census departments that should provide some badly needed data. He initiated a study of different groups (women, young people, middle-aged workers, etc.) in 1965 and collected labor-market, behavioral, and personal data in each subsequent year. Thus data for a ten to fifteen year period (1965 to 1975 or 1980) should be available for analysis in the near future.

SCENARIO: FRAN RICHARDS

Fran Richards graduated with a specialization in computer technology from Metropolitan Community College. Metro Community is one of many schools that sprung up in the early 1970s in response to the needs for specific, job-oriented skills.

Fran's friends were surprised when they learned of her decision to go into the two-year Metro Community program, especially since she was qualified to enroll in a state university. The surprise of Fran's friends, however, in no way matched the shock of her parents. "You're a lovely, talented girl; you can go downstate to the university—maybe even meet 'somebody.' Why Metro?" For Fran the answers were simple; for her folks, they were complex and even irrational. But then Fran had always been different from her brothers and sisters.

High School Days

When Fran was in high school she had pursued her studies and personal interests very aggressively. She helped to organize the kids' march to city hall to expose the local political machine. In her senior year Fran and some friends contacted the Environmental Protection Agency concerning a local company's polluting of a small creek. When that didn't get action, the young people made placards and marched in front of the plant. When a local paper picked up the story, the company agreed to study the matter and alter its process.

Although most of Fran's friends went on to college after high school graduation, and though she placed in the upper quarter of her class, she wasn't ready for more education. She got a job with a supermarket in the area and worked at the checkout counter. One day Fran made an announcement to her parents: "First, I'm moving out—I've already rented an apartment—and second, I'm buying a used car for transportation."

Job Possibilities

Fran worked for about two years at the supermarket—she probably would have left sooner but for the rather poor job conditions. She had been carefully studying job possibilities for the future: "I'm not going to be 'ringing out' on cash registers all of my life." The computer field seemed to hold good possibilities for future employment, and Metro Community was offering a two-year certificate program; so she decided to enroll.

Job Seeking

Fran completed her computer technology program and started job hunting. At age twenty-two years she felt very confident about her ability to find a job, though the job market had improved only slightly. She developed a vita, complete with picture and descriptions, and started to interview and send material to potential employers. One company, National Scientific, a maker of test instruments, seemed very interested in her technical qualifications and the businesslike, systematic way in which she handled herself.

Scenario Commentary

Fran Richards represents the new breed of young person coming into the world of work. She had rejected the tradition (at least temporarily) of the protective shelter of the home and society's recipe of do's and don'ts.

At the same time, Fran did not ignore the realities of the job market and business needs. Her training in computer technology and a position with National Scientific may well be the vehicles she needs to build a life of her own.

AFFILIATING WITH AN ORGANIZATION: THEORY AND REALITY

People Decisions: To Join, to Switch Jobs

Attracting people *to* a job and keeping them *on* the job are two very different things. The issues related to employment have become far more than a matter of money. At one time, an individual's decision to join or leave an organization was closely related to economic conditions. And if times were poor, one took virtually any job or stuck it out with an undesirable job. Today, growing numbers of people appear inclined to look for "the job"—the job that suits them, even if it means being unemployed for a while. Job switching has tended to increase, despite recessionary conditions. For example, labor statistics indicate that during months of low economic activity in 1974, job switching was perhaps 25 percent higher than during the 1970–71 recession. Michael Brenner, head of a recruiting firm, estimates that perhaps five out of six M.B.A.s who job-switch do so because of personal and not company reasons (MBA, Oct. 1974, p. 27).

Clearly, there is no single reason for taking or leaving a job. For some, the promise of a new career, the opportunity to move up a fast track, or the chance to gain more responsibility provide more than enough reason. For others, less tension or less responsibility may be key considerations. Still others may seek a more friendly environment, a more convenient location, or better work conditions.

In any event, personnel officers who use bland, generalized approaches that ignore these aspects of employee potential and needs will fail to deal with employee problems and, consequently, fail to support the organization's goals.

One example of the complex forces that motivate workers is the case of professionals who were left jobless by cutbacks in government-related industries (such as aircraft) and research projects in the early 1970s. Some of these professionals were willing to change occupations and even accept a pay cut if necessary (Gutteridge and Ullman, 1974). However, the question of mobility (willingness to relocate) was quite a different matter, especially for those in attractive climates such as on the West Coast or in the South. In one case only about one-fourth of the displaced engineers on a large research project accepted positions and moved to another state. Generally, younger people and those with higher levels of education were the most adaptable. Previous labor market experience was also a major factor in decisions to change. Unemployed engineers were most likely to change occupations or relocate if they had *made* these changes previously.

These tendencies were reinforced as the period of unemployment increased. Ex-professionals were increasingly willing to accept salary reductions and to change occupations, but they still were reluctant to explore other geographic areas extensively. All of these factors—and many more—concern *exchange*.

Exchange: The Organization and the Individual

The notion of exchange is central to employment attitudes. It involves, simply, a *quid pro quo*—this for that, give and take. An individual brings certain skills, knowledge, and attitudes to an organization. The organization offers compensation, gratification, and a social structure. Each has what the other wants. And when each agrees on how much it will give for what it gets, they have struck a deal. They have decided on the exchange.

When the individual reports to the organization to begin working, the exchange has begun and continues for as long as the individual is employed by

EXHIBIT 4-1 The Individual-Organization Exchange

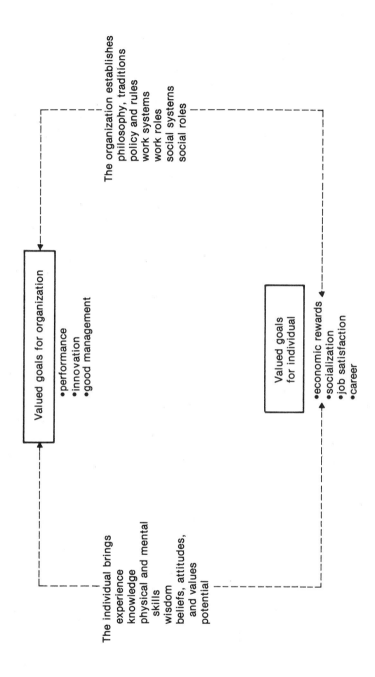

the organization. The continuity of this psychological contract is important. The process that both parties use to evaluate the advantages and disadvantages of the agreement is not mechanical: it is an ongoing process that depends on both sides' judgment of the decision.

An organization confronts many issues when it employs an individual. Human resources comprise an important part of an organization's work processes—its ability to produce. Managers or personnel officers must be able to assess the kinds of inducements a particular person brings to a job. An individual's education and skills are often a matter of record, but an organization's officials must evaluate many less tangible qualities: the individual's wisdom, behavioral traits, and potential. If a personnel manager can choose among potential employees without violating equal opportunity laws, he or she will choose an individual who *appears* to offer the most and demand the least.

We have given a rather pure definition of exchange. Realistically this pure form is complicated by several factors. For example, both sides must make decisions about future events that are yet to be played out and are, realistically, unpredictable. The information that both parties have about the other usually is incomplete and at times distorted by biases or misconceptions. Second, both parties may have little latitude because federal laws or a union may greatly reduce their choices. Third, general economic conditions and available employment may further affect the number and type of choices available to either party (see also Chapters 7 and 11).

Individual Behavior

How do people function in organizations? Again, what once was a relatively simple question has become a complex one. Individual behavior emerges from the complex interplay of two sets of variables—the individual's disposition and the work environment created by the organization. A person brings both work-related skills and various emotional characteristics to the organization. The technical side of performance involves physical and mental skills, knowledge, experience, aptitudes, and wisdom. Physical skills may include finger dexterity, motor coordination, response, and stamina. Mental skills relate to a person's ability to solve problems, coordinate, and make decisions. Several of these terms require more concrete definition. *Knowledge* concerns information and data that most frequently are secured through formal education. *Wisdom* relates to thoughtful analysis, good use of judgment, and integration of knowledge, experience, and personal skills.

The emotional makeup of the individual is as important to the organization as technical skills. Emotional features of the workplace involve attitudes, beliefs, or values that guide a person's response to people, problems, and situations. A sense of fairness, likes or dislikes, or attractiveness and unattractiveness flow from a person's deep-seated values.

Virtually every organization of any size has at least one employee with one of these emotional characteristics:

1. An excellent technician who can't work under pressure.

2. A worker who works well (or works especially well) only when staring a deadline in the face (the pressure-cooker syndrome).

3. An employee who has a personal problem (alcoholism, divorce).

4. An employee who has a family problem (a spouse or child who has a serious illness or a child in trouble with the authorities).

5. An employee who has financial problems.

In some organizations all of these kinds of employees are housed under one roof. They can have an enormous impact on organizational operations, and they can affect an individual's response to a whole range of organizational matters.

The Work Environment and Individual Behavior

The organization represents the other half of the factors affecting individual behavior. Organizations represent the product of ownership and managerial philosophies of governance and the customs and traditions that established them. But beyond this structure of philosophy and guidelines is the realization that people play various work and social roles in the organization. People respond to various organizational cues; if they misread those cues or if the cues are not given clearly they can act in unexpected ways.

Roles. Work roles are prescribed by work procedures, rules, and job descriptions. Social roles emerge from an individual's interaction with colleagues, supervisors, and subordinates. Individuals often must function in group settings, and their social roles can reflect their attractiveness to the group and the group's acceptance of the individual. Training that helps an individual blend with the personalities and the internal society of the organization may be as important as any technical or skill development. Efficient work performance and job-related satisfaction are closely related—failure to blend into an organization's social system often adversely affects work.

Needs and values. Individual performance, expectations, and the achievement of valued goals relate to work and organization life. The conduct of work and the organization's general atmosphere affect an employee's sense of purpose and identification with the objectives of the organization. These factors also affect the degree to which a person is fulfilled or frustrated in achieving valued goals. In other words, the individual, facing organization life and work, has needs and values that materialize in expectations, objectives, and desires.

Need for the Personnel Function

The personal aspirations and potential of new employees place major responsibilities on personnel-related activities. Personnel's role can be interpreted as one of communicating organizational needs to the individual. However, there is a more simple description: the personnel officer fits the organization's needs to individual expectations and desires. The organization, for its part, seeks to achieve valued results (good performance), but central to this goal will be an individual's sense of personal accomplishment while achieving the organization's purposes.

EXCHANGE: AN ILLUSTRATION

Let's consider the Fran Richards scenario. Fran had interviewed at National Scientific for employment. National was interested in hiring her for several reasons. On the factual level, her background and potential were positive (sex: female; age: 22; education: certificate from Metropolitan Community College in computer technology; experience: two years of full-time work). During subsequent interviews National's personnel director concluded that Fran seemed to know what she wanted, was well organized, and was prepared to work hard to advance. National offered several things, including salaries, benefits, training, and potentially the framework to direct the energy of aggressive young people. The organization balanced the inducements and contributions it felt existed for potential employees.

Fran's Viewpoint

For Fran, National Scientific was one of several employment alternatives she was considering. From her viewpoint, she would contribute her energies, abilities, knowledge, integrity, and belief in hard work to the organization. And she assumed several risks. She may have passed up other opportunities by working for National. If the organization failed to fully tap the talents she possessed, she would have sustained a personal and professional loss. And if the organization failed to provide sufficient opportunities for her to gain a sense of personal realization, she would lose again. Fran valued various benefits that National offered, but she also had to assess the opportunity National would give her to learn or work with other young people and to gain assignments that would help her achieve her personal and professional goals.

PROBLEMS AND CHALLENGES: YOUNG PEOPLE AND WOMEN

The considerable changes taking place in society have greatly affected the needs, expectancies, and abilities that employees bring to the exchange process. This section deals with several prominent groups of workers and their shifting needs and expectations.

Young People

The new breed of worker (whether or not young workers are a new breed or embody a new life-style is almost a moot point) has taken the lead in pressing for better work conditions and a chance for something more than a ho-hum job. The increase in education level has had some influence on young people's expectations, but a good deal more is involved—even the young who do not go to college are thinking beyond pay and/or job security to psychic rewards and personal fulfillment (Yankelovich, 1972, 1974).

There is little doubt that many young people place greater emphasis on the psychic value of work. When they consider a job, they pay more attention than do their elders to the meaningfulness of the work, the sense of accomplishment, the visible results of their actions, a sense of personal involvement, recognition, and responsibility that the job offers. Of course, all young people don't want all of these things—some don't want any—but an increasing number want some; and their goals are likely to represent the wellspring of desires for the future.

Desire for independence.   The new generation of workers increasingly desires independence and freedom and is willing to accept risk. These traits hardly distinguish young workers from earlier generations, but they are different from their parents, who bear the imprint of needs born in hard times (the 1920s and 1930s)—the need for order and security. This new breed has not known these hard times. Even the depressed economic conditions of 1970–71 or 1974–75 are a far cry from the depths of the Great Depression. And it is unlikely that they ever will face such times because of the country's social welfare umbrella.

If young people's attitudes toward work are not rooted in economic privation, what, then, is their basis? New workers are turning away from *meaningless work* in a bureaucratic or authoritarian setting that emphasizes *extrinsic rewards* (pay, work conditions, and other factors outside of work itself). In a three-year study of college students conducted by Daniel Yankelovich (1972), almost 80 percent felt that personal commitment to a meaningful career was important in a person's life, and less than one-third were hoping to "have it soft" (*Work in America,* 1973, p. 43).

The crux of the matter is the "authority tradition." For many years organizations have been based on formal position—the pecking order and age. An increasing number of students and recent graduates question the basis for and legitimacy of authority (Lawler, 1973). They value openness, confronting issues, and knowing where they stand. Thus organizational officials can expect growing mistrust of policies and actions that emerge from behind closed doors or will not bear public scrutiny. By the same token, the "way we have always done things" will convey far less legitimacy (and confidence) than in past years.

These trends emphasize the importance of good human-resource management. People's motivation to perform well starts when they are motivated to join an organization. If this motivation is to continue, it must be encouraged by work. If work is to be motivating, it must be meaningful. Personnel managers can play an important role in forming reasonable opportunities for careers that enhance individual fulfillment.

Preparing the young for work: the transition.   The "golden age of irresponsibility" for young people occurs in the "transition to adulthood," or so says James Coleman.

Coleman, who is one of the coauthors of a recent national report (Coleman *et al.*, 1974), claims that some of the most valuable years of an individual's life have been "straitjacketed in school." As young people move through the educational system, they are "kept in a state of economic and social dependency," despite the fact that many are often bright enough and resourceful enough to assume a great deal of responsibility. Instead, parents "pick up the tab," and adolescents are not held accountable for much of anything. According to the national report, high school does little to prepare adolescents to handle everyday life and also gives them poor preparation for important decisions to be made later in life. Consequently, when the time comes to leave the shelter of house and family, the golden age comes to an abrupt—and anxiety-ridden—end.

This description may be a bit overdrawn, but it helps set in place some of the matters to be discussed in this section. Preparation for the world of work, alternative educational and career paths, and some characteristics of our youth culture are discussed in the following material.

Careers, career paths, and alternatives. The preceding section makes it clear that the world of work is changing and that careers have gained added prominence. But what hasn't been clarified is the fact that many *new* career options are emerging and that a college education will not meet the needs of these fields. Further, education in a four-year college or university is not the only path to a satisfying career; it isn't clear that this path guarantees anything.

Participation of Women in the Labor Force

Not too many years ago, social clubs, the kitchen, and babies were viewed as the accepted provinces of women. However, by the 1970s these ways brought scorn from increasing numbers of women who penetrated organization life.

In the thirties, a woman who entered the work force, say as a teenager, might remain there until she was "discovered" by a husband; then she might commit herself to homemaking for most of her life. In the 1950s a vastly different pattern of female employment started to emerge. Those who chose to enter the work force might stay until their first pregnancy, drop out of the labor force until their children were in school, and return to work. The decreasing birth rate of the late fifties and sixties shortened the period of time that women dropped out of the work force.

The pill. It is difficult to grasp fully the social impact of the contraceptive pill and its enormous impact on recasting women's roles in society. The impact of equal employment legislation on female employment is not to be denied, but it hardly provides the full story behind the changes that took place. For the first time, growing numbers of women were in a position to compete directly with males for jobs.

As the number of working wives—women who had families and careers, not just jobs—increased, women became more inclined to take a leave of absence instead of quitting during pregnancy. Improvements in day care reinforced this tendency. Not surprisingly, the labor force participation rate for married women grew rapidly and essentially doubled over that of 1940.

Working women: some of the whys. The ingrained social condition of women being supportive of and dependent on men has been seriously weakened under the banner of "women's lib" and the fact of more women in the work world. Important changes affecting promotion paths, career planning, and work assignments, not to mention hiring approaches, are under way in most organizations.

Studies (e.g., Harris, 1975) make it clear that economic considerations are often neither the sole nor even major reason for the choice of women to work or not to work. Some women work in order to support themselves. They value financial independence, as opposed to simply adding to family income. The statistics from the Harris survey seem to bear out this point. From 1970 to 1975 the number of women "working to support themselves" increased from 23 to 37 percent, but the survey indicates that affluent women (and those from a family with a professional) are more likely to work than are wives and daughters of business executives (presumably with good incomes). Further, young women from affluent families are more likely to work than are those from less affluent families. Finally, women from white-collar families are more likely to work than women from blue-collar families.

Women in new roles. If the findings of the Harris study are interpreted along the lines of values held by families and the working-age populations, it appears that sharp divisions are appearing in society regarding woman's role. In some families the traditional values prevail and home and family continue as central life objectives. But it's clear that this view is giving ground to newer ones that admit an independent life-style: family *and* work; marriage *and* work but no family, etc. Furthermore, the reality of change is already with us, though not without its problems:

1. In the Women's Army Corps (WAC) the changes have been significant. Marilynn Preston (1975) claims that the "new WAC" is totally different from anything that existed before. Free high school and college education, recession-proof jobs, finding a husband are all a part of the reason for joining. Better jobs, opportunities, and training have removed the stigma of being second class citizens in the army. Changes in the law and new regulations have paved the way for the changes. Women can now be promoted to high military rank, and the dependents of military women are entitled to the same benefits as are those of servicemen. In 1975 thousands of female cadets were in training in the Reserve Officer Training Corps as compared to about two hundred in 1972. Unfortunately, many males in the army still do not fully understand what the women can do.

2. Women are entering a business world that is largely of male origin. They are starting to learn how to ask for promotions and to sell their skills rather than wait passively to be rewarded for hard work. However, for many women, work may simply represent one major responsibility among several,

while for men, work may be their primary responsibility. The work world builds on ambitious and aggressive people, but the connotations of these terms (and acceptability) for men are still quite different than for women.

3. In some business functions, such as data processing, the progress of women is far different than in the general business field. In a study carried out by *Datamation* magazine in fall 1975, many of the women employed in the computer field indicated equal status with male computer personnel in both pay and promotional opportunities. However, a lesser number felt confident about their opportunity to occupy senior positions. "They don't take us seriously" and "they treat us like *their* girls" are comments that suggest some of the problems encountered by females in business.

Impact on personnel. The new roles of women in the work force have forced major changes in personnel practices and policies. The pressure of equal opportunity legislation has forced an extensive reexamination by organizational officials of long-held ideas about "male" or "female" jobs. Female clerks, male factory help, male architects, female nurses, and "men do heavy work and females do light work" are part of the crazy-quilt pattern of beliefs that many hold to steadfastly. New organizational policies regarding pregnancy leaves, career paths for women, management training, and male and female wage differences have come to the fore in recent years.

Personnel officials need considerable understanding and sensitivity to the issues involving women. Organizational self-interest alone would dictate that key managers fully develop this area of the work force: legions of women have been underemployed, given limited opportunities, if any, to use their skills simply because they are female. In economics this is called "opportunity cost"—something an organization can't afford to waste.

Increasing numbers of women in the work force are underwritten by federal legislation and legal instruments for compliance. But even with legislative support, long-standing job practices or outright sexism won't die quickly. The situation is further complicated by the realization that the roots of women-in-work problems go back to the roles defined for females during early childhood within the family.

The issues here are not simply a matter of job skills or imparting information. Thoughtful approaches are needed to provide the skills needed for work *and* psychological support. For example, assistance is needed to help women deal with crises and beliefs regarding the ways of organization life.

MINORITIES IN THE BUSINESS WORLD

Support of Employment Efforts: The NAB

A short time ago a busload of business executives was taken to the city jail of a major metropolitan center. They were transported in large prison vans to spend a day in jail and see at firsthand the hopelessness felt by many who never had a chance to make it on their own. The executives were volunteers from the National Alliance of Businessmen (NAB) who had been loaned by their companies for one month to help find jobs for the economically disadvantaged, veterans, ex-offenders, and underemployed. The visit to the jail was part of their program of orientation to the plight of the many "job disadvantaged" in our society.

The NAB experiment has been quite successful. The federal government supplies on-the-job training funds to cover "extraordinary costs" beyond the normal cost of training job candidates. Reasonably good success in initial placement and retention has resulted from the involvement of major business firms, the enrichment of the abilities of job seekers through supplementary training, and, perhaps most importantly for the disadvantaged, a sense that someone cares. Despite "marginal qualifications," the disadvantaged who have been placed through the NAB have had a retention rate of 60 percent —three out of five were still employed after six months. This level of job stability is considered very reasonable in light of general hiring experiences.

The scope of the NAB programs is substantial; they have made a significant imprint on joblessness in labor markets. For example, the Chicago NAB placed more than thirty thousand people in 1974 despite comparatively poor job conditions. The placement of people and the funding of supplementary training (reading, shop, math, basic office skills, etc.) have been improved through the Comprehensive Employment and Training Act (CETA) of 1974. This act designates local "prime sponsors" who assume funding responsibility for an entire major city.

Organizations have reacted much more favorably to the new arrangements because bureaucratic red tape has been reduced greatly. Yet if long-term problems of unemployment of the disadvantaged are to be reduced, employment efforts must go beyond low-skilled jobs. Indications of the NAB's past success have encouraged attempts to place minorities in important managerial and professional occupations, which will further alter the composition of organizational work forces.

Minority Engineers and Managers

Several major foundations, including the Ford, Kellogg, and Sloan organizations, the American Banking Association, and dozens of corporations and other foundations, have taken important steps to get minorities into key organizational positions. The creation of business education programs for minorities at universities and large grants for engineering education have at least started to reach the level of effort and dollars that really make a difference. To be sure, the programs are self-improvement, for they help these businesses meet affirmative action/equal employment requirements for minority hiring. Yet the fact remains that the number of qualified minority engineers, managers, and specialists will increase, and organizations will be challenged to make full use of their abilities.

Screening in versus screening out. The central change in organizational hiring practices affecting the disadvantaged has involved screening procedures. Personnel managers have begun to screen in rather than screen out. The emphasis of personnel has become directed much more to developing recruiting procedures to secure desired skills. If an organization cannot find enough skilled employees, it can get financial help from the government to provide on-the-job training programs for new employees who lack necessary skills. Potential employees who were screened-out by organizational assessment procedures in the past are now given a more even break for job success. Yet the indoctrination of the new employee and the creation of stable conditions for individual growth are not without problems.

Sources of frustration in indoctrination. Many social and personal matters have been encountered in attempting to make the newly hired "stick" in the organization. For example, lack of job experiences and skills often contribute to tardiness, absenteeism, and extended training periods. At this stage, relationships are extremely fragile and frustrations can grow quickly (Burack, Staszak, Pati, 1972).

Both the individual and the organization can suffer from "culture shock." Minorities sometimes have norms, social values, language, behavior, or dress that the majority of organization members will consider different. Sometimes a failure syndrome produces discouragement and a "don't care" attitude. For other minorities, new-found racial pride may lead to aloofness that strains internal relationships. These relationships are strained further by widespread racism and lack of internal organizational policies for dealing with these issues.

Managerial philosophy and attitudes can directly affect the success of organizational programs for minorities and disadvantaged. Racism, indifference, or job competition can threaten the success of these programs. If top management refuses to make a commitment to a meaningful program or "goes through the motions" with a token minority/disadvantaged program, the program is on its way to failure.

This section on important occupational groups cannot be concluded until an important matter is addressed: college education. Various aspects of the situation are discussed throughout the chapter but need bringing together so that the full range of issues can be seen.

HIGHER EDUCATION AND CAREERS

The College Degree: Money? Status?

The twenty-five year period from 1950 to 1975 witnessed one of the most dramatic changes in higher education in America. For many, dreams turned into nightmares as the "passport" to better pay, a better job, and a better life—the degree—seemed to lose its power to work its magic. By the end of this period the day of the graduate had seemed to pass; and this was not a temporary change, it was long term

(Freeman and Hallomon). The implications of this development are likely to have far-reaching effects on the individual facing the world of work and on all kinds of personnel maintenance and planning activities.

The differences in starting salaries for college graduates and nongraduates were almost nonexistent by 1975! Even the large differences in starting salaries between college and high school graduates dwindled. In the short period from 1969 to 1973, the 53 percent difference in starting salary for college graduate and nongraduate male workers decreased to 40 percent (Freeman and Hallomon). Although a substantial difference in starting salary still existed for this category of worker, young people obviously could see what was happening and it obviously influenced their career choices.

If the status and good life promised by the college degree become somewhat uncertain, society's valuation of this path is likely to be reduced. By the late 1970s or early 1980s some young people will have less education than their parents, thus reversing a century-old trend. Additionally, they will be more likely to move into the mainstream of work earlier than in previous years.

A Dilemma: Relating Jobs to Education

If you're male, white, and a student of the social sciences—or many other liberal arts fields—chances are that for years to come you will be committed to extensive job seeking. Conversely, if you are black, female, and a college graduate in one of the professional fields in the late 1970s, a job will probably be waiting for you. These two descriptions straddle the range of situations facing graduates and potential employees.

In this game the seat one occupies is all important: employers will have a selection of job applicants that they have not had for many years. Job seekers who lack the flexibility of alternative career preparation or employment mobility will be forced to make some hard choices.

The impact of the job availability-employment situation has a direct bearing on the economics of the job market. 1975 graduates of mining engineer programs received a starting salary of $6,000 more than the average wage for many liberal arts graduates. A special instance, yes, but it illustrates the wide economic disparity in the job market.

The disparity in the job-education match is also illustrated by the overall figures, as well as by the experiences of particular vocations. The College Placement Council estimated in 1975 that college graduates will number about one million by 1980, compared to less than 400,000 in 1960. The U.S. Department of Labor estimates that the number of college graduates will exceed the number of college-level jobs into the late 1970s. According to Freeman and Halloman (1975), almost one-third of male college graduates and two-thirds of female graduates in the early 1970s had to accept positions outside their college majors. In the early 1960s these figures were far lower. In a field such as journalism, some 6,000 graduates were turned out for less than 3,000 available jobs. Yet in engineering the needs of the energy field may exceed 300,000 by 1990 while only 250,000 graduates will be available.

The situation is confused by the rapidly changing national scene, as illustrated by the energy situation, but also by change in job areas and professional fields. For example, a person *graduating* in communications in 1972 had excellent job prospects; a person *starting* a communications major in 1972 would have spent months looking for a job in 1976.

Another Side of Schooling: Career Education

Personnel recruiters and officials will surely note an important change in forthcoming years in the preparation and outlook of job seekers—at least if the nation's career programs have anything to do with it. In addition to the career programs of expanding community colleges, city, regional, and state educational systems have begun to develop comprehensive career education programs. Actually, then, far more than skill preparation may be afoot with the growth in career awareness. This emphasis is beginning in the elementary grades and extending in continuing education for advanced or new-career preparation during adult life.

According to U.S. Commissioner of Education Kenneth B. Hoyt in a September 1974 speech, the objectives of career education are to acquaint people with career options, to assist individuals in making choices, to develop skills and abilities, and to develop a realistic concept of oneself. Thus these approaches seek to prepare people for the working world who have readily usable skills and a realistic view of themselves. All of these contribute to a more satisfied worker.

What has happened to the work ethic? This question is exceedingly important because many organizations are facing problems of anger and alienation regarding work and work conditions. The problems of the work ethic and worker estrangement are not just matters of unenriched job designs. Other difficulties flow from employees' and potential employees' expectancies and attitudes, which may be very unrealistic. The career education referred to here seeks to provide individual understanding of how others see oneself, what represents an ideal state to the individual, and how one views oneself today.

Student-Employer Outlooks

Various surveys suggest that students or those coming into the work world may have motivations and attitudes toward organizational life that are very different from those of present employees. For example, a survey taken by the Bemis Company of Minneapolis (reported in NAM Reports, National Association of Manufacturers) indicated the following assignments of importance of motivation factors:

Students	*Employees*
1. Liking the job	1. Money
2. Money	2. Liking the job
3. Chance for growth, advancement	3. Recognition for good job performance

4. Responsibility
5. Friendly co-workers
6. Recognition for good performance
7. Good work conditions
8. Chance for achievement
9. Good supervision
10. Company policies

4. Chance for growth, advancement
5. Chance for achievement
6. Good supervision
7. Responsibility
8. Friendly co-workers
9. Good work conditions
10. Company policies

Some of the discrepancies could represent decidedly different outlooks by students and employees, yet factors such as friendly co-workers and quality of supervision, rated more highly by employees, could also represent a lack of student sensitivity and appreciation of important aspects of organizational life. Career education, as previously described, deals with some of these issues.

Work and life goals are closely related. This relationship is a strong argument for career education. It can help people realize their potential in meaningful and satisfying work without scuttling liberal education programs. The traditional contribution of a liberal education to a relevant life can also largely be met through a properly organized career program (Wenrich, 1974).

Consequently, organizations may increasingly encounter new employees who adjust more readily than job entrants of the fifties and sixties to business needs and the social milieu of the organization. However, nothing said here dismisses the need for organizational adjustments to people needs and an easier process of mutual accommodation.

APPROACHES FOR PERSONNEL MANAGEMENT USING HUMAN RESOURCE IDEAS

Agenda for Personnel: Human Resource Outlook

The functions of personnel relate directly to developing human resource approaches that meet organizational objectives for performance and service. Organizational needs are closely linked to individual performance, and personnel must develop approaches that meet these challenges by enlisting people on behalf of organizational objectives. This need goes far beyond recruiting warm bodies. Various motivational studies and research reports have pointed the way. In light of the changes in the climate of work and the characteristics of the work force these human resource approaches are all the more urgent.

Targets of the Human Resource Approach

In the main, research has established that human performance is linked to a sense of control over one's work space or environment. This "sense of influence" relates to one's ability to regulate personal effort (and variations in it) and make his or her work felt in the organization. Thus if this link between individual and organizational objectives is to be forged, employees must be able to identify with the organization's product or results. Exhibit 4–2 provides an expanded list of items that have a positive influence on individual job satisfaction and performance. Both groups of items relate to job satisfaction, but one emphasizes the broader context of work and work activities (Smith *et al.*, 1960) while the other (Lawler and Hackman, 1973) concentrates on work features. Not surprisingly, positive changes in one group of factors are generally associated with position changes in the other.

EXHIBIT 4–2 Job Satisfaction Characteristics

Dimensions of Job Satisfaction
    Work itself
    Influence/control over work
    Supervision received
    Compensation

Job Satisfaction and Work Features
    Skill variety needed
    Task identification
    Task significance
    Feedback from task
    Autonomy

Source: Top, Smith *et al.*, 1960; bottom, Lawler and Hackman, 1973.

Job Satisfaction

An individual's sense of satisfaction with work and organization derives from at least four different considerations. *Work itself* is one of the basic elements in building an individual's sense of satisfaction. People must feel that they are using valuable skills and that their work requires them to apply them to different situations. Thus they are challenged. At the same time, *supervision received* is important. People need to feel comfortable with the guidance, recognition, and equity in the evaluations they receive. *Compensation,* of course, is important. But it is important not only in terms of pay but also in terms of what it signals in status or promotion. Finally, people must feel a *sense of influence or control* regarding work or the results of one's efforts.

The second group of factors in Exhibit 4–2 emphasizes features of the work task. One's *variety of skills* relates directly to the span of abilities one can draw on in performing a task. Serious underutilization of abilities can cause boredom or frustration. An individual's sense of task importance—*significance*—is one of the considerations affecting *task identification* and connecting effort to organizational outcomes (product, service, or results). At the same time, *feedback* from the task should provide the information needed to judge performance, share in accomplishments, and take corrective actions where needed.

The fifth factor tied to job satisfaction and task features deals with *autonomy*—a feeling of independence and ability to exert influence, individual opportunity and ability to make decisions build a sense of autonomy.

WORK MEANING AND ORGANIZATIONAL REALITIES

There seems to be little question that participation styles of management can improve work quality for employees, but this begs an essential management question: What impact does employee participation have on productivity, performance, and labor costs? The important place of work in people's lives makes meaningless work simply a matter of putting in time and inevitably makes it intolerable. The human costs of meaningless work are all around us: worker alienation, alcoholism, drug addiction, absenteeism, and various symptoms of poor mental health (McLean, 1974).

Yet has too much blame been laid at the door of work? Some say yes. Opponents of the quality-of-work theme say that too much of the decline in productivity has been attributed to the quality issue. Research into the relationship between absenteeism and the quality of work are very inconsistent; also, employee satisfaction with a company and absenteeism do not seem to have a direct relationship—or at least it is unclear. However, evidence seems to support the idea that high absenteeism can be linked to negative attitudes regarding one's immediate supervisor. The question is, how much impact does the quality of work have on organizational operations? And, in what sense?

What Do You Mean? How Do You Measure It?

Not far removed from the controversy swirling about the quality-of-work issue is a serious semantic and measurement problem. Specifically, how do you define and measure *productivity* and *job satisfaction?* Job satisfaction has been measured through attitude surveys, interviews, and observations of various behaviors, but all have their limitations and lead to inconsistent or even contrary conclusions. The measurement-of-productivity problems didn't start with the controversial *Work in America* report. Even in the 1920s economists were battling over this one.

Another complication has been the organizational objectives against which productivity is to be measured. Short-run objectives, long-run objectives, sales volume, units, and dollars represent a wide range of performance considerations. Some of these may be especially meaningful for some industries but mean little in other industries.

Though the measurement problems are noteworthy, personnel management doesn't have the luxury of taking a pass until things are resolved. The thoughtful management of human resources requires the continuing evolution of pragmatic approaches to measuring people-work variables. A blend of experience, formal education, and understanding of people is the best combination personnel managers can use until more precise techniques become available.

The Individual and Success in the Organization

The port of entry of individuals to the organization is typically the personnel office, and in the past the passport was often issued on experience, education, age, race, and sex. The last three items have been removed: equal opportunity legislation has formed the criteria an organization can use in screening applicants for potential job success. Moreover, more and more research has knocked down old prejudices about individual differences thought to have existed because of race, age, or sex. Women prove to be as reliable as men and equal in most areas; blacks in business have demonstrated their management abilities, and older people display qualities of personal responsibility and an ability to delegate that are superior to young people's (Greenberg and Greenberg, 1974).

Additionally, education and experience have become suspect as predictors of success where matters of specific skills, techniques, or information are not involved. Even where specific skills are needed to meet the functional requirements of a job, once these have been met, the total return to the organization depends on the qualities of the individual. The challenge to the organization is to awaken competencies and motivate employees to use them in behalf of both the organization and themselves.

Individual attributes such as empathy, the desire to move ahead, the capacity to adapt to new circumstances, diligence, and ability to delegate and make decisions are among the most critical and sought-for talents in an organization. In the main, they are independent of or only loosely connected to sex, race, experience, education, and age. In summary, personnel directors, responsible for acquiring human resources and developing individual potential, are being forced to reassess measures of individual potential and the role they can play in drawing it out.

A New Role for Personnel?

The potential reduction in economic value of a college education may encourage searching for alternative routes in society, a search in which firms may play an important role. Symbols of status or achievement provided by organizations, including job titles and assignment of work responsibilities, may take on new motivational and social significance. Similarly, institutional training programs, promotion policies, and career planning within the organization can take on new significance for both the individual and the firm.

For the firm, making useful employee programs available and providing realistic job objectives can prove to be powerful attractions in individual decisions to join a firm or retain affiliation. If personnel is to play a key role in designing and launching these programs, it must have the technical competence to develop enlightened policies, an awareness of environmental trends, and the organizational power to legitimize these undertakings.

SUMMARY

The joining of an individual and work within the framework of organizational life has been described in terms of key occupational groups and issues. The wide-ranging economic, social, and psychological needs of individual work-force members rule against any type of bland, general discussion.

For people coming to the work force, many of the issues reside within the alternative paths provided by formal education. The question is, What can these alternative paths promise for future career pursuits, economic gain, and achievement of a satisfying life? Yet, to an important extent the answers must be interpreted in specific ways related to race, sex, and age, let alone the specifics of individual needs. The Fran Richards scenario provided a glimpse of the numerous interrelated issues of people in the work world. The issues for personnel involve such diverse matters as working couples and the potential complications of multiple careers, relevance of education to work pursuits, and women entering what has heretofore been largely a man's world of work. What the parties offer and bargain for, and what in fact is realized, set the tone for the whole span of personnel-related functions.

The second major discussion centered on three important occupational groups: youth, women, and minorities, groups which represent the leading edge of change in employment in the United States. The focus on youth emphasized a reassertion of the value of work and the need to review the limitations of organizational structures in light of new activities and technology. What is at stake for women is a vast redefinition of female roles within society, the family, and organizations. Personnel is challenged to equalize employment and career opportunities, not only for legal compliance, but also to gain the full benefit of women's contributions to total organizational effort.

Results of the first stage of cracking minority employment barriers are starting to be seen, but substantial personnel issues are still growing. The story of minority employment is no longer to be found in unskilled jobs. Minority managers and professionals, with significant support for their educational development, have started to move into organizations, and considerable additional changes are in the offing.

The final discussion of the chapter dealt directly with the new mission for personnel activities in light of the vast changes affecting the corporation and the outlook of people who are either preparing for or are already in the work world. Basic to personnel's program is understanding the main factors comprising an individual's sense of job satisfaction and how these factors fit into a broad career framework. Achieving motivated behavior to meet organizational and personnel needs starts with an individual's "decision to join." The considerations then move to the job itself if individual decisions to produce and maintain affiliation are to be positive. The considerations identified with valued human needs and desired accomplishments within the framework of work and careers establish basic personnel policies and programs. The perspective also provides a framework for most of the materials in subsequent chapters.

DISCUSSION QUESTIONS

1. What factors in society might account for the educational pattern and life-style of Fran Richards?

2. Suggest some ways in which her educational pattern, expectancies, and life-style differed from those of her parents, especially her mother.

3. How might an organization (potential employer) interpret Fran's active role in community affairs during her high school days? What are your assumptions?

4. What job or career experiences (short term, long term) are likely to be seen as highly valued if she secures employment at National Scientific? What are your assumptions?

5. What changes in the characteristics of work and in our society (work ethic) have affected the issues related to work and job satisfaction?

6. What distinctions were made in the chapter between jobs and careers?

7. Jack Turner, an unemployed engineer, was driving a taxi cab in San Francisco. He had been out of regular engineering work for almost two years after his West Coast electronics firm closed down. Explore this situation in terms of chapter concepts.

8. Bill Brown, sanitary engineer, age twenty-eight, has been out of regular work for almost a year. As a teenager he served a six-month jail sentence for stealing money from a paper stand. He has applied for a sanitary engineer's job at Colton Hospital, which turned out to be work with the sanitation and clean-up crew. Colton is located in the residential area of a large city and has mostly white workers. What problems are likely to arise for Bill if he is hired? What are your assumptions?

9. Lordstown is the location of a major final-assembly automotive plant. Several years ago, industrial sabotage and, finally, a strike closed the operation down. Prior to this, the new plant had rarely met production standards and its youthful work force was said to be highly dissatisfied with work conditions. Discuss the situation, but be sure to state your assumptions.

BIBLIOGRAPHY

Allen, Robert E., and Thomas G. Gutteridge. "The Career Profits of Business Majors from Ten Year Public and Proprietary Colleges." *Proceedings of the Annual Meeting of the Academy of Management.* Seattle, August 1974.

Aspey, W., and A. W. Laffman. "Women Speak out on D.P. Careers." *Datamation* (August 1975).

Benyon, H., and R. M. Blackburn. *Perceptions of Work: Variations within a Factory.* New York: Cambridge University Press, 1972.

Blumner, Robert. *Alienation and Freedom.* Chicago: University of Chicago Press, 1964.

Brayfield, A. H. "Human Effectiveness." *American Psychologist* 20 (1965):645–57.

Brenner, Michael. "The Anxiety Factor: What Happens Psychologically When You Change Jobs?" *MBA* (October 1974):25.

Burack, Elmer H., F. James Staszak, and Gopal C. Pati. "An Organizational Analysis of Manpower Issues in Employing the Disadvantaged." *Academy of Management Journal* 15.3 (September 1972).

Carnegie Commission on Higher Education. *College Graduates and Jobs.* New York: McGraw-Hill, 1973.

Coleman, James, *et al. Youth: Transition to Adulthood.* A report of the President's Science Advisory Committee. Chicago: University of Chicago Press, 1974.

Davis, Louis E. "Quality of Working Life: National and International Developments." *Proceedings of the 25th Annual Meeting of the Industrial Relations Research Association.* 1972:121–28.

_____. "The Design of Jobs." *Industrial Relations* 6 (1966):21–45.

Edgerton, Michael. "Schools Build a Shaky Bridge Over a Gap of Life." *Chicago Tribune,* 20 March 1974.

Freeman, Richard B. "Overinvestment in College Training?" *Journal of Human Resources* 10,3 (Summer 1975):287–311.

Gooding, Justine. *The Job Revolution.* New York: Walker, 1972.

Goodwin, L. "Occupational Goals and Satisfaction of the American Work Force." *Personnel Psychology* 22 (1969):313–25.

Greenberg, Herbert, and Jeanne Greenberg. *A Study Regarding Factors in Job Success.* Princeton, N.J.: Marketing Survey and Research Corporation, 1974.

Gutteridge, Thomas G., and Joseph C. Ullman. "An Analysis of the Reemployment Aspirations of Displaced Engineers." *Proceedings of the Annual Meeting of the Academy of Management.* Seattle, August 1974.

Harris, Louis. Quoted from "Harris Survey." *Chicago Tribune,* 8 December 1975.

Herzberg, Frederick, *et al. The Motivation to Work.* New York: Wiley, 1959.

Hoyt, Kenneth. *Career Education: What It Is and How to Do It.* Salt Lake City, Utah: Olympus Press, 1974.

Jenkins, David. *Job Power.* Garden City, N.Y.: Doubleday, 1973.

Johnson, Michael L. "Plan Your Career or Wing It?" *Industry Week* (September 30, 1974):32–37.

Kornhauser, A. H. *Mental Health of the Industrial Worker: A Detroit Study.* New York: Wiley, 1965.

Kotter, John Paul. "The Psychological Contract: Managing the Joining-Up Process." *California Management Review* 15.3 (Spring 1975):91–99.

Lawler, E., J. Hackman, and S. Kaufman. "Effects of Job Redesign: A Field Experiment." *Journal of Experimental Social Psychology* 3 (1973):49–62.

Lippitt, Gordon L. "Training for a Changing World." *Training* (May 1975):46–49.

Marcus, Robert J. "The Changing Work Force: Implications for Companies and Unions." *Personnel* (Jan./Feb. 1971).

Maslow, Abraham. *Motivation and Personality.* New York: Harper & Row, 1970.

McLean, Alan, ed. Special issue of the *Journal of Occupational Medicine* concerning quality of work life (December 1974).

Morse, Nancy, and R. Weiss. "The Function and Meaning of Work and the Job." *American Sociological Review* 202 (April 1953):91–98.

Neff, Walter S. *Work and Human Behavior.* New York: Atherton Press, 1968.

"The New Breed Worker: A Year Later." *Iron Age* (February 18, 1974):37–39.

Preston, Marilynn. "The WACs Move in on the Action." *Chicago Tribune,* 7 September 1975.

Prien, E. P., and W. W. Ronan. "Job Analysis: A Review of Research Findings." *Personnel Psychology* 24.4 (1971).

Ritti, R. Richard. *The Engineer in the Industrial Organization.* New York: Columbia University Press, 1971.

Ritzer, George. *Man and His Work: Conflict and Change.* New York: Appleton Century Crofts, 1973.

Ronan, W. W. "Relative Importance of Job Characteristics." *Journal of Applied Psychology* 54 (1970):192–200.

Schneier, Craig E. "Training the Hard Core Unemployed through Positive Reinforcement." *Human Resource Management* 11.4 (Winter 1972).

Shepard, Harold L., and Neal Q. Herrick, *Where Have All the Robots Gone?* New York: The Free Press, 1972.

Sigband, Norman B. *Communication for Management.* Glenview, Ill.: Scott, Foresman, 1969.

Slevin, Dennis. "Full Utilization of Women in Employment: The Problem and an Action Program." *Human Resource Management* 12.1 (Spring 1973).

Smith, Patricia. *The Measurement of Satisfaction in Work and Retirement.* Chicago: Rand-McNally, 1969.

Social Research, Inc., *Working Class Women in a Changing World.* New York: Macfadden-Bartell Corp., 1973.

Walton, Richard. "How to Counter Alienation in the Plant." *Harvard Business Review,* 50,6 (November/December, 1972):71–72.

Wenrich, Ralph C. "Is Work Still a Dirty Word?" describing work and career experiences in *Michigan Business Review* (March 1974).

Wernemont, P. F., P. Toren, and H. Kapell. "Comparison of Personnel Satisfaction and of Work Motivation." *Journal of Applied Psychology* 54 (1970):95–102.

Work in America. Special report prepared by W. E. Upjohn Institute for the Department of Health, Education and Welfare. Cambridge, Mass.: M.I.T. Press, 1973.

Yankelovich, Daniel. "Turbulence in the Working World: Angry Workers, Happy Grads." *Psychology Today* (December 1974).

Section
Three

THE
INPUT
SYSTEM

---

*

Chapter 5

MANPOWER FORECASTING IN HUMAN RESOURCE PLANNING

LEARNING OBJECTIVES

After studying the material in this chapter the reader should be able to:
Forecast within the human resource planning (HRP) perspective
Identify the rationale for organizations' undertaking and/or strengthening HRP approaches
Describe the connection between HRP and conventional personnel practices
Describe the relationships between HRP and institutional or organizational planning
Identify the considerations that influence HRP approaches for given organizations
Describe the influence of uncertainty on HRP
Identify the similarities and differences in some important forecasting-planning models
Develop and apply two important models.

KEY TERMS AND CONCEPTS

human resource planning	short-range forecasting
organizational planning	long-range forecasting
pressure points	aggregate models
uncertainty	reserve and replacement
planning horizon	policy
reaction management	budgetary models
confidence in forecast	math/statistical models
likelihood of occurrence	Markov models

PREVIEW

The need for planning and forecasting have become increasingly apparent. This chapter begins with a brief clarification of forecasting from a human resource perspective. The following topics are also discussed:

1. The relationship between human resource planning (HRP) and forecasting and general institutional planning.
2. The main reasons and concerns for the initiation and improvement of HRP procedures.
3. Specific applications that distinguish the needs and approaches of different organizations.
4. The limitations of various models.

It used to be said, with some justification, that everybody is an expert when it comes to forecasting: "After all, we're talking about the future—so my *guess* is as good as yours!" Although many planners, managers, and officials still think this is true, this chapter will provide them little comfort. Important changes have been taking place in personnel planning. In a word, everybody's guess is *not* equally good anymore—if it ever was. Forward-looking managers have begun to realize that there is a serious need for human resource planning and the quality of forecasts which support it.

Just a brief point concerning the terms *human resource planning* and *forecasting:* When we use these terms, we will use the broader human resource view. In other words, our discussion will include questions not only like How many? but also How soon?, What type(s)?, etc.

CONCEPTS AND APPROACHES IN HUMAN RESOURCE PLANNING

Forecasting What?: Institutional U.S. Resource Planning

There are two main aspects of human resource planning (HRP): forecasting and programming.

It took perhaps fifty years to bring U.S. businesses and governmental agencies to a point where general planning was considered essential to successful operation —whether in terms of profits, services rendered, or efficiency. It has taken even longer to gain acceptance for human resource planning, especially forecasting. And there still is considerable resistance to it.

It may seem to be contradictory, but our concerns with forecasting, at least at first, don't strictly concern people. Forecasting usually starts with questions about things and events: What's likely to happen? What new technologies or social concerns are emerging? How are they likely to affect our work system or the outlooks of our future work force, and when. And of course there are the more familiar questions, like What's the volume and character of our business likely to be in 19XX? What does this signal by way of human resource needs? Other forecasting approaches deal with cost problems and other specific issues. Thus a significant part of a personnel manager's manpower forecasting may start with general or imprecise questions. But then down to specifics: the numbers and qualities of people and occupations involved. In other words, the right people, at the right place, at the right time. The personnel director doesn't do this in a vacuum. In fact, a significant amount of forecasting may be done completely outside the personnel department—in the comptroller's department, the planning department, or by the market research and forecasting group. The specialized abilities, access to computers, and connection to the general institutional planning of these departments often justify locating planning activities in these areas. On the other hand, the impersonal outlook often taken by these functional groups poses a significant challenge to personnel officers who may have had little or no part in the initial planning.

A Difference in Perspective

The idea of forecasting had a difficult time winning acceptance in what—at least from hindsight—would seem to be its most logical areas of support: marketing, production, and finance, the traditional centers of corporate power. The fact that these corporate heavyweights were so skeptical might help explain why supporters of human resource forecasting have had such a tough fight.

The concerns of human resource forecasters differ from customary business planning approaches. For example, the general institutional planner might ask, How much (in sales dollars) are we likely to sell of product X over the next three years? In a similar vein a human resource planner might ask,

1. Given so many dollars of sales over the next three years, how many marketing supervisors, analysts, and field personnel are we likely to need?

But this is just the beginning. The human resource planner will ask other questions that are at least as important as the original numbers question. For example:

2. If turnover and deaths among our senior managers continue at the present pace, what will be our replacement and reserve needs in the future?

3. Given the need for new managers, how many of these can we furnish from our current work force?

4. To what extent can our requirement for new managers serve as a basis for creating promising new careers for minorities in our work force?

5. Given the current number of women and minorities in our work force and given normal turnover, how many more women and minorities must be recruited in order to *maintain* current (percentage) participation in the labor force? How can we *increase* their (percentage) participation, based on federal requirements for equal employment opportunity and affirmative action?

SCENARIO—INTRODUCING A HUMAN RESOURCE PLANNING PROBLEM

There is considerable unevenness among firms that are developing human resource planning/forecasting programs. A recent experience of one of the authors illustrates some of the many issues and practical problems encountered in this area.

Central Business Machines was one of the major operating divisions of a large corporation specializing in the manufacture and distribution of business equipment, supplies, forms, and computer readout materials. After almost forty years, the company had acquired and developed a group of knowledgeable people in sales and manufacturing. At the same time, the group that founded the company continued to play an active role in management and the maintenance of a paternal climate. Key managers in sales and manufacturing were allowed to operate in rather independent fashion so long as operations were profitable.

Institutional planning for the introduction of new products and services (forms, machine service contracts, new equipment) had been in effect for years. In the early 1960s, when the firm experienced a severe shortage of cash, financial planning was made mandatory for any type of general business planning. The comptroller, who headed the financial planning effort, worked closely with sales and manufacturing officers; he reviewed their planned programs and and determined their possible impact on profits, cash needs, and performance. All key managers quickly recognized the dependence of business planning on financial planning: "If the money isn't there, there's no use in talking about opening new sales offices, remodeling or adding new facilities, or even trying to add new benefit programs for employees."

About four years ago the manager of industrial relations, Tom Reilly, attempted to introduce a human resource planning program. His attendance at a two-day university conference convinced him of the soundness and need for such planning. Tom felt that the logical starting point was some longer-range personnel forecasts that covered a five-year period. The move seemed especially timely since the company was considering the addition of a new production plant and sales district. "Obviously, there is going to be some shuffling of people, plus the need for more warm bodies, so why not move in with a human resource plan?" Tom contacted his good friend Ed Gurstim, assistant comptroller, also seeking change. Ed thought it was a great idea; so a personnel plan was included with the financial plan. This initial effort was to include a forecast of total personnel needs over the next five years, plus a breakdown of needs according to various managerial, supervisory, sales, and worker categories—about thirty categories in all.

Implementation

The personnel forecasting approach was reviewed with the comptroller and then recommended for approval to the division general manager, who accepted the recommendation. When the line managers had to sit down with the financial planners and carry out the added work of personnel forecasting, many of them complained about the paper work; some even threatened to go to the corporate president. The comptroller, assistant comptroller, and industrial relations manager were able to calm things down when they convinced the managers of the importance of this information for staffing the new offices and facilities.

Next Year's Problems

Tom was encouraged by the way things turned out and decided to go ahead with the forecasting approach in the following year. When the time came for the managers to develop their personnel planning program, Tom met even more resistance than during the first year's effort. "We did that last year." "I don't remember the general manager authorizing this!" "We don't need any more of this stuff. It takes too much time and besides, our programs for staffing the new facilities are already under way." "I only agreed to do it last year because I understood it to be a one-shot deal."

Comments on Scenario

The situation at Central Business Machines illustrates several different points regarding human resource planning. First, there is a hierarchy of planning in most organizations: general institutional planning; functional planning, as in finance, sales, or operations; and personnel, or human resource, planning. Second, the personnel planning/forecasting approach builds on the data and information from other planning undertakings, but it also provides its own unique contributions. Managers tend to accept planning when it meets a specific need. At times, planning most readily gains legitimacy in a crisis: managers realize that they *need* it—or need something. In other words, the planner must find the pressure point(s). Finally, a personnel officer who is going to introduce approaches that run counter to past practices ("we never needed this before") must realize that he will have to demonstrate its effectiveness repeatedly.

THE CASE FOR HUMAN RESOURCE PLANNING

In Chapters 1 and 2 we described the sweeping environmental changes (social, technical, legislative, etc.) that transformed personnel's activities from mere maintenance functions to a whole new series of activities. Human resource planning is central to modern personnel management. What follows is a more precise definition of what it is.

Definition of HR Planning and Forecasting

There are two components of human resource planning: forecasting and programming. As we have stated, *forecasting* involves generating the numbers, types, and quality of personnel who will be available to or are needed by a particular organization in the future. *Programming* involves the development of activities to put the forecast into operation; these activities may involve new arrangements, relationships, training, managerial development, and the like. For many years managers equated planning and forecasting, and while they are intimately related, they are distinct. Numbers are important, but they must be related to the programs they are designed for. Otherwise they are almost meaningless.

Influence on the Specifics of HR Forecasting

Different organizations have different needs. So in a sense, forecasts must be tailor-made. The amount of detail needed can vary with the size of the organization, the accuracy of available information, and the particular plans being considered. These considerations can influence forecasting in the following ways:

1. *Type of organization.* Some organizations, such as manufacturing, tend to be more complex than service organizations, since the former contain more departments, more different types of departments, and a variety of occupations.

2. *Size of organization.* Size has an obvious and direct impact on forecasting, since greater size usually is accompanied by a larger number of employees, more staff specialties, and a greater number of occupations. Also, larger organizations tend to operate on a broader geographic basis—regionally, nationally, or internationally.

3. *Dispersion of organization.* The more an organization is spread out geographically, the more vulnerable are the numbers and features of the labor force to differing competitive labor market forces.

4. *Accuracy of information.* The preciseness of available information imposes a practical limit on the level of detail one attempts to develop. For example, the growth of electric power went along (at least for many years) in a rather orderly, predictable way. Power companies were able to make detailed plans for their personnel and organizational needs—at least before the era of concern for pollution and difficulties with fossil and atomic fuels. Accuracy may also be affected by the cost of acquiring information and an organization's ability to pay. Smaller companies may be able to afford only general information or highly judgmental approaches. Information accuracy may also be affected by the imagination and training of the planners.

5. *Specific institutional plans.* The plans or strategies of particular organizations shape their forecasting approaches and consequently each one will be different. The following are examples of specialized forecasting approaches. State departments of labor are often concerned with the level of employment or unemployment and the means of improving the job-finding process. A hospital may plan a new intensive care facility and be concerned with future patient loads and the numbers and type of medical staff to meet this development. An automobile manufacturer may plan to add a new subcompact model to its line and wish to determine the impact on plant employment. Technological improvements are introduced to a manufacturing firm, and management wants to know what the impact of this installation will be on productivity and on the level of employment.

Dealing with Uncertainty

Forecasts are approximations, not absolutes. They focus on the future—the could be, should be, or likely to be—but never the will be. Forecasts do not state ultimate facts, truths, or states of being in the future. This does not mean that one guy's guess is as good as another's: that's nonplanning or reaction management. But there is an element of uncertainty in all forecasts which personnel managers must learn to live with and, of course, attempt to minimize. This uncertainty in forecasting can be dealt with and is no justification for nonplanning.

Factors in uncertainty. Simply stated, a high degree of uncertainty wastes time (and money), causes false starts, missed opportunities, and the like. In general, the ability to influence the course of events and get good information on a timely basis reduces uncertainty. Poor information and unforeseen events increase uncertainty. These two elements—the accuracy of information and predictability of events—influence the quality of a forecast. A good rule of thumb is: the longer the planning horizon, the more tentative the forecast.

If we can find economical ways to extend our influence over future events, we can improve the accuracy or quality of our forecasts. Thus it is not surprising that short-range planning, say over a one- or two-year period, is often more precise and accurate than longer-range planning. Developing shorter-range manpower forecasts may take little more than an arithmetical conversion of past sales or service figures. In other words, the overall activity of the organization can be measured in terms of estimated sales dollars, number of patients to be serviced, estimated volume of bank deposits, and then translated into labor hours, the number of people needed, or some other convenient unit to find the number of employees needed to produce the organization's output. Examples will be provided below. To the extent that business conditions and the labor pool are stable, the likelihood that the organization's past level of production (sales, service, etc.) will continue is high and uncertainty is low. The following factors help keep the uncertainty of human resource forecasts low:

1. Stable environmental conditions
   a. business
   b. competition
   c. economics
   d. neighborhood

2. Excess of supply of labor, professionals, or specialties relative to demand

3. Good information systems design
   a. ability to capture relevant information
   b. quality of information
   c. value of information
   d. timing of information
   e. ability in processing information (e.g., computer models, programs)

4. Understanding the factors contributing to the demands for institutional services (e.g., through market research) and ability to influence them (e.g., advertising, sales personnel, highly valued product/service)

5. Ability to deal with or influence the factors affecting the supply of human resources (e.g., recruiting, training)

6. Predictability of the work system
   a. proven work system (not experimental; bugs worked out)
   b. low technical innovation (not too many improvements and no major technical improvements in sight)
   c. well-trained personnel who work with or operate the work system
   d. complete and proven procedures

7. Analysis and problem-solving abilities of key organizational personnel

Obviously, many considerations can influence confidence in a manpower forecast. An organization can't deal with all of these factors to the same degree, but it can do quite a bit to influence some of them. For example, if an organization trains its people well and has good work procedures, it will be better able to judge productivity and time of completion. Whether an organization is concerned with the average length of stay in a hospital or the time needed to process an order for a machine, clear-cut and proven procedures carried out by well-trained people will greatly improve confidence in a forecast.

Getting the right kind of information is usually the key to the performance of a system. This is a matter of system design. Often an institution can exert a great deal of control over the design of its information system. Good system design depends on an understanding of the institution's needs. For instance, neighborhood population patterns, patient load of doctors servicing a hospital, and the incidence of certain diseases may be the key areas of information for a general hospital's information system.

Many different system designs have been used to reduce the degree of uncertainty in forecasts. We will mention two of them here. One very common approach used to lessen uncertainty has been the use of a "likely range of occurrences." For example, a personnel officer might say, "It's likely that the labor force in our downtown store three years from now will be 600 to 750 people." The officer may have arrived at this figure by averaging estimates provided by various experts or by analyzing common patterns of employment growth in comparable stores. Generally, the more tentative the estimate (higher uncertainty), the wider the spread or range of the estimate.

Probability statements. Philosophers, mathematicians, and business statisticians, among others, have attempted to develop ways to predict the likelihood of events occurring in the future. These are probability statements, which have been used in human resource forecasts. Estimates may be made on the basis of, for example, a 9 out of 10 or a 7 out of 10 chance of occurrence. It is assumed that the more precise the statement (e.g., 9 out of 10), the wider the range of the estimate. In other words a relatively wide forecast range makes it likely that events will be within these boundaries. As the likelihood of occurrence decreases (e.g., 7 out of 10), the range may be narrower, or the statement may be used simply to tell the planner that a high degree of uncertainty exists.

Some probability statements and corresponding ranges are illustrated in the following:

Size of department store labor force three years from now
(Current size = 500)

Labor force size

Range	Certainty of expert opinion
675–725	7/10 (0.70 probability)
625–725	8/10 (0.80 probability)
600–725	9/10 (0.90 probability)

The experts anticipate a labor-force expansion. They seem to be relatively confident about maximum growth (725) but tentative regarding the lower end of their range. They may be more confident in the upper end of the range because of the store's size and the merchandising techniques used. The uncertainties in the lower end may reflect a wide range of business developments, including competition.

In concluding this discussion we return to the central theme underlying the confrontation of uncertainty. The type and reliability of the forecasting approach used depends on *information* (in its many dimensions) and the ability to *influence* the factors affecting the demand for an organization's institutional services or products or its supply of resources. In some situations a high level of uncertainty may be an inherent part of an institution's activities, where flexible approaches, approximation, and shorter planning periods may comprise the only feasible strategies.

FORECAST PERIODS

Different kinds of organizations have different forecasting needs. Even organizations within the same area or specialty have different needs, so they forecast for different lengths of time. They may employ short, intermediate, and long-range planning periods, which can differ greatly. For some, the long range may be ten, fifteen, or twenty years. For others, long range may be two, three, or five years. In some cases plans are fairly specific, in others the long-range plans may be drawn in much more general terms. For example, a company in a basic agricultural or food business has many competitors, faces uncertain crop yields, and is vulnerable to the state of the worldwide food demand. Its longer-range plans tend to be rather general, while its short-range plans tend to be flexible and to reflect near-term conditions (for example, the size of work forces in canning or packaging plants varies substantially, and like the farmer, these industries are affected at least indirectly by day-to-day changes in the weather). Human resource planning may concentrate on key or critical manpower, including managers and executives, and on establishing its reserve or replacement needs.

Stages of Forecasting

Short range, intermediate, and long range reflect simple differences in planning periods (horizons). Of course the purpose of the plan influences the particular planning horizon. Exhibit 5–1 summarizes factors related to two major forms of human resource forecasts: demand and supply. Short-range forecasts typically grow from budgetary processes. Variables (which can be manipulated), regular events (e.g., turnover), or imminent events (e.g., new legislation) are factored directly into these calculations. Demand for human resources can be met only by analyzing the supply of resources. A significant part of the supply emerges from within an organization by means of promotion or training. Department rosters, schedules, and anticipated transfers all influence the internal aspects of supply. If the organization must go into the external labor market for additional employees, the personnel officer can look to employment/unemployment figures for particular job categories within relevant geographic areas. This information will help him identify potential problem areas. Equal employment opportunity

EXHIBIT 5–1   Stages of Organizational Human Resource Forecasting

Length of Planning Horizon

Type of Forecast	Short range (under 2 yrs.)	Intermediate (2–5 years)	*and*	Long range (over 5 years)
Demand for labor	Budgetary authorization expansion technological change new legislation	expansion or contraction		geographic, capacity, size of system, product lines, patients served, services offered, load anticipated
	employee turnover layoffs contractual restrictions (budgets)	adjustments		labor saving equipment, efficiency, productivity, union agreements
Supply of labor— internal	departmental, division rosters promotion, transfers, expected losses union agreements (rosters, organization charts, schedule)	merger or acquisition plans managerial and supervisory development programs purchased services/contracted services shared services		
Supply of labor— external	Area employment levels	labor market projections business development plans general institutional plans to hire area trends		

(EEO) and an affirmative action policy require that both supply and demand analyses indicate the degree of geographic concentration/dispersion (average number) of females and minorities when determining the makeup of the labor force. The personnel officer must also consider another question: How can the need for minorities best be forecast and how should these individuals best be moved into the mainstream of organizational activity?

Longer-range forecasting emerges from events that shape the character of the institution many years into the future. Expansion or contraction, for example, affects the number and location of facilities and the number of employees and services and/or products to be offered. Calculations become more complex because planners must make adjustments for productivity improvement and restrictive union work rules.

FORECASTING TECHNIQUES: GENERAL GUIDELINES

As we have already mentioned, there are no hard-and-fast rules for forecasting. You can't "follow the book." The factors complicating a given organization's activities may far outweigh whatever precision is implied by a specific method or technique. However, there are some helpful general rules that can be used, and several forecasting approaches have achieved importance because they have often been used successfully. In this section some forecasting rules-of-thumb will be discussed. This will be followed by a review of important planning models and applications.

Short-Range Analyses

Short-range forecasts usually grow out of normal budgetary processes. A personnel officer develops a manpower budget by estimating work load, which reflects the character of operations (expansive or contractive) indicated by overall planning budgets. In other words, if the organization plans to increase its output, its overall budgets will be larger, and personnel budgets will be proportionately larger to reflect this increase. Work load may involve, for example, number of cars to be produced, or students enrolled, anticipated bed occupancy in a hospital, or expected volume of retail sales. The personnel planner translates work load into human resource needs by using ratios, such as nurses per room and labor hours per item produced. Of course, if overall budgets are smaller, the personnel budget also will be smaller.

Shorter-range forecasting/planning approaches relate to recent activity and relationships. Thus, unless unusual occurrences or changes are anticipated—for example, a new law or a new plant—short-range planning tends to be systematic—built around the focus of "systematic management," i.e., the budget.

Steps in short-range planning.   Exhibit 5–2 illustrates some of the key steps in the short-term forecasting/planning process.

1. Analysts in financial, marketing or administrative units anticipate both the demand for institutional services (patients, number of units to be sold, etc.) and any major external changes likely to emerge (laws, competition, fuel curtailment, etc.).

2. An overall forecast is developed for the next planning period (six months, one year, or two years) and is modified by planned-for or anticipated *internal* changes. These are the more controllable kinds of changes.

3. Working budgets are developed to reflect the work loads of individual departments or functions. These budgets and potential human resource needs are modified by possible changes in productivity, provisions of newly negotiated contracts, technical improvements, and the like.

4. Preliminary personnel requirements are determined by using conversion ratios that reflect the organization's current activity. They are suitably modified where changes are expected.

5. Labor-market forecasting analyses deal with the labor supply as it will be affected by factors both within and without the organization: *internally* by quits, deaths, promotions, and transfers and *externally* by economic or social conditions. The dashed arrows suggest that, for example, poor economic conditions may force

EXHIBIT 5-2 Short-Range Human Resource Forecasting: Organizational Perspective

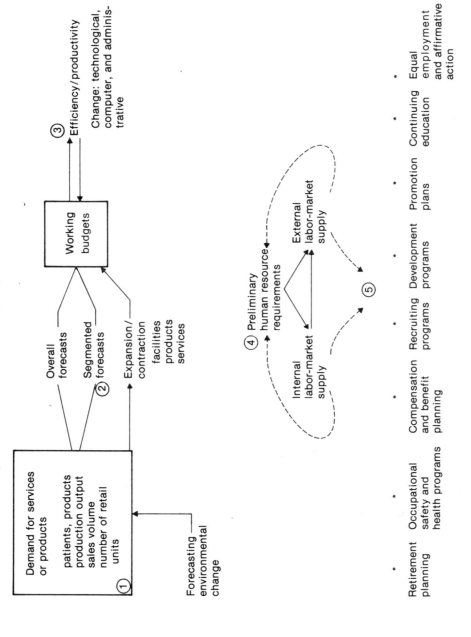

a modification of external approaches, and the reverse is also true. Also, organizational short-range planning may deal, for example, with recruiting or "affirmative action" in hiring racial minorities, the handicapped, or females.

Long-Range Analyses

The parameters of short-range forecasting usually are fairly well defined. They are handled in the normal course of budget preparation and require simple arithmetic calculating. Long-range planning is more complex. Planners are relying more heavily on mathematical and statistical models as knowledge of demand variables and appropriate measurement techniques have been developed. Although elementary statistical techniques, such as extrapolation, where past trends are extended into the future, are used by many organizations, more powerful techniques are at hand and are slowly gaining acceptance. These new techniques are helpful, yet some long-range situations are so complex that they may require approaches that are a mixture of mathematical techniques, wisdom, and just a little guessing. (As much, or perhaps more, may be learned in studying the factors affecting human resource supply or demand as in the actual application of formulas.)

An important point concerns the time-cost tradeoffs in securing more or better information. If an organization is considering major expenditures, it may be more productive to spend money for information rather than develop it over time from trial-and-error experiences. In any event, forecasted answers are only as good as the information provided and an organization's ability and willingness to deal with anticipated situations. Where long-range forecasting has become an annual "exercise" it is very costly and should be reexamined for its usefulness. Because different types of long-range planning situations arise, the human resource planning techniques that are used in these situations also vary.

Various long-range approaches. Two general kinds of forecasting techniques are used in long-range planning: indirect and direct methods. Indirect methods involve the forecasting of general rules—production figures, for example—that must be translated into specific requirements or measures. Direct techniques involve the use of models to estimate (directly) labor hours, number of supervisors, or particular occupational needs. Brief descriptions of a few common techniques follow.

Aggregate models are based on several key variables that are known to directly affect the organization's overall human resource needs. Every organization has special characteristics and problems, and a planner can use an aggregate model to get the big picture. These models may apply to a geographic region or to the overall system.

Estimation techniques and models are used for situations where circumstances make it difficult to use mathematical or statistical approaches. Here, expert opinion and experience are used. The volume of future activity or business conditions, including legislation, change, innovation, or competition—situations that are almost impossible to quantify—can provide workable answers to problems.

The Delphi technique, one of the newest of these approaches, is described later in the chapter.

Forecasting environmental change.   Increasingly, high-technology firms and all kinds of service institutions have to deal with innovations, social change, and new legislation. This has really become the age of discontinuity, where everything that "was" is not everything that is "likely to be." Recession, inflation, and reversal of roles between friend and foe are but a few examples of changes that cause great concern about an organization's environment.

Recap on Forecasting Needs and Approaches

Because both short-range and long-range forecasts deal with labor *demand*, it seems prudent to bring together some of the major portions of this discussion before we proceed further.

Supply-of-labor considerations include both the internal and external availability of human resources. Internal considerations involve budgets, promotion plans, reserve policy of qualified individuals, training programs, and recruitment plans. External analyses deal with governmental projections; listings or rosters of local, state, and national labor agencies; projections of regional or national planning groups; business/economic development in an area; union activity and training; trade/profession restraints; and professional regulatory bodies.

The demand for labor also involves internal and external approaches. Internal analyses deal with expansion, contraction, or retrenchment—reserve and replacement programs are concerned with critical or key personnel categories. Institutions compete with each other for labor regionally, nationally, or internationally. This is the subject of external analyses. In general, the greater the professionalism of an occupational group, the broader the labor market. Demand is affected by interchangeability of skills among organizations and the mobility of the work force.

Planning horizon.   Organizations can plan either on a short- or long-range basis. In short-range approaches, budgets and, occasionally, mathematical and statistical forecasting models may be employed. Conversion ratios relating need or service level to human resource requirements, estimation and judgments, or managerial consensus are used.

Long-range undertakings may employ statistical and mathematical models that incorporate external demand variables, such as the number of customers, clients, or patients. Internal variables involving people, equipment, or an organizational unit are also dealt with.

MATHEMATICAL MODELS AND BUDGETARY PROCEDURES

Some mathematical models permit the planner to make direct estimates of labor hours and even numbers of people. These models incorporate major internal and external variables that managers feel directly affect human resources. For some purposes, as in determining overall employment for planning employee benefits, a general forecast of labor hours can prove useful because they are readily converted to numbers of people. In other instances, planners may need more precise information, especially if special facilities or activities must be provided. Different models can be used for different purposes.

Aggregate Planning Models

Some models incorporate a mixture of both internal and external variables and information. Examples of various types of models follow.

A model for *forecasting overall company employment* could assume the following form:

$$E_n = \frac{[L_{Agg} + G] \dfrac{1}{X}}{y}$$

Where:

E_n is the estimated level of employment in some future period two to five years from now.

L_{Agg} is the overall or aggregate level of current business activity in dollars.

G is the total growth anticipated through year n in today's dollars.

X is the average productivity improvement anticipated over the period today to n. It is represented, for example, by 1.05, meaning an average annual productivity improvement of 5 percent.

y is the overall conversion figure relating today's overall activity dollars to personnel required.

Although this model may look complex to those who have little experience, its application is quite straightforward.

The purpose of this aggregate planning model is to forecast the overall level of employment (E_n) for an organization at some point in the future. For an organization using this particular model, it is assumed that its future employment level in the main is related to its overall (aggregate) level of business or service activity (L_{Agg}) and growth (G). Historically, perhaps, it has been found that overall activity and employment move rather closely together. If the organization is to handle a larger volume, it will need employees to meet its current needs (L) and anticipated changes—hopefully growth (G), though this factor could be negative—a reduction—for a different company in different circumstances.

This particular model has an additional feature. A company can draw on its past experience. For instance, it has been found that "so much" activity is related to "so much" employment. A million dollars of sales may call for a total employment of 100. The model provides a direct estimate of employment through the conversion factor, y.

This model has another feature worth noting. It seeks to take account of productivity, or how efficiently human and technical resources can be combined and used. Sad to say, productivity doesn't always improve; for example, machines wear out or union demands cause inefficient practices. More detailed comments on the specifics of this aggregate model and an application example follow.

Specifics of the model. First, the productivity improvement factor, X, has the effect of reducing E_n (employment) if it is possitive. If no improvements are expected, the ratio $\dfrac{1}{X}$ becomes $\dfrac{1}{1}$; if lower productivity is anticipated (for whatever reason), employment needs increase.

Second, the conversion factor, y, reflects institutional policies regarding the use of people or inventiveness in work design. For example, the decision of a large department store to go from counter assignments of people to checkout islands decreased the number of sales people required. (Unfortunately, quality of service and pilferage went in the opposite direction, so that all of the consequences of planning actions are not necessarily positive or anticipated.)

Determining the value of a factor such as G (anticipated growth) is no easy matter and may involve its own mathematics or statistical techniques, or use of expert opinion. A simple application follows.

Example: Employee benefit needs. The personnel director wants to determine employee benefit needs for an estimated level of employment (E) five years from now ($n = 5$). She used the aggregate model.

L_{Agg} (current) $= \$50,000,000$ of activity

G (total growth anticipated in millions of dollars)

n	G
1	$ 2
2	1
3	4
4	4
5	5
	$16 million

$X =$ it has been estimated by both personnel and engineering that productivity improvement should average about 3 percent.

$y =$ past analyses for some ten years of sales have indicated a rather predictable ratio of people to sales. Current analysis suggests one person per $25,000 sales, which incorporates expected improvements in work assignments, trade union impact, and top-management policy.

$$E \text{ (current)} = 2,000 \text{ employees}$$

$$E_{(n=5)} = \frac{[50\text{MM}^{**} + 16\text{MM}] \, \dfrac{1}{1.03}}{25\text{M}}$$

$$= \frac{66\text{MM}}{25\text{M}^{*}} \times \frac{1}{1.03}$$

= approximately 2,500 people five years from now.

*   M = 1,000
** MM = 1,000,000

What would the employment be without any productivity improvement? Here $X = 1$ and $E_n = 5 = 2,600$, or approximately 100 more people. Note, in either case, the substantial change in anticipated employment and the potential impact on benefits planning. Added funds must be made available from future income or profits.

A second example of this common forecasting approach follows.

Example: College staffing requirements.   Columbia Commercial College has found over a period of years that the best indicators of next year's enrollment are (1) current enrollment; (2) intentions of current students regarding further education; (3) average influx of new students based on the past five years; and (4) general adjustment (+10% of current enrollment for "strong" to − 10% for "poor") based on the state of expected business.

Current enrollment	= 3,000 students
plans for	
continued education	= 2,500
average influx	
of new students	
(last five years)	= 600/year
business outlook	
(U.S. Dept. of Commerce)	= strong.

Total forecasted enrollment E_{est} (next year):

$$E_{\text{est}} = 2,500 + 600 + 10\% \text{ (of current enrollment)}$$
$$= 2,500 + 600 + 300$$
$$= +3,400 \text{ students.}$$

Staffing and enrollment figures from past years indicate that class size has averaged 25 students. Furthermore, a full-time teaching load consists of four classes. Thus, on the average, one teacher handles 100 students.

Estimated enrollment *increase* = 3,400 − 3,000 = 400 students

$$\text{Estimated additional staff} = \frac{400 \text{ students}}{100 \text{ students/teacher}} = 4 \text{ additional teachers.}$$

However, classes are not always staffed with the same type of teachers; Columbia employs both junior and senior staff members. In the past the school has employed one senior person for each two junior people. Since no neat division is possible here, it is likely that next year Columbia will try to hire

Senior people $= 1$
Junior people $= 3$
total $= \overline{4.}$

Notice how the arithmetic for this short-range forecast draws on historical relationships and understanding of the factors influencing Columbia's enrollment figures. The largest part of next year's enrollment is likely to be students who are already enrolled in its classes (2,500). As a school, Columbia influences the certainty of this outcome simply by not goofing up—that is, by maintaining the quality of teaching and support of a good marketing program for developing new students—as it has done in the past. Columbia's accountants and analysts tell us that the school has maintained steady growth over the past five years. If it maintains community image and reputation and if business people and young people maintain a positive view of continuing business education, the expected influx of new students should continue.

Finally, the adjustment for enrollment due to a general assessment of future business conditions has proved quite reliable, although some judgment is exercised in the actual percent employed. For those interested in a more concise statement of Columbia's forecasting model:

$$E_{est} \text{ (next year)} = E \text{ (intended)} +$$
$$E \text{ (avg. new students)} +$$
$$E \text{ (business adjustment)}$$

$$\text{New staff needs} = \frac{E \text{ (estimate)} - E \text{ (current)}}{100.}$$

STATISTICAL FORECASTING APPROACHES

Aside from budgetary procedures, statistical approaches are among the oldest and most widely used means of forecasting procedures. These procedures are similar to statistical models used in personnel research studies, behavioral research, economic forecasting, quality control, and production control. Since statistical techniques have been in common use for better than fifty years, it's little wonder that a large, complex family of statistical approaches has emerged. These approaches include *linear* and *curvilinear* models; *two-variable, multivariable* approaches; and techniques suitable under some conditions of risk or chance (*probabilistic*). For the purpose of our discussion, simple linear models will be considered. (All involve the same basic assumptions, but some possess greater power for applications involving more than two variables or nonlinear relationships.) The linear model assumes that the relationship between the variables is fixed and unchanging.

The Simple Statistical Model

The principles underlying this approach have to do with *association*. The central question is, does some type of association or relationship exist between two variables such that they behave in systematic or predictable fashion? For example, can we predict (better than by chance or coin flipping) how much absenteeism or turnover there will be based on the way people are handled? That is, does it follow that the better we supervise or deal with people, the less the absenteeism?

If annual sales over the past five years have increased each year by $1 million, does it follow that next year's sales will also increase? If our needs for managers and supervisors have grown each year on the average of ten people, can we also expect this growth next year?

All of these questions can be considered statistical matters because they potentially involve relationships between supervision and absenteeism, sales growth and the passage of time, and needs for managerial resources with the passage of time. The more remote the involvement or relationship between the variables, the more uncertain the relationship or predictability. For example, supervisory action can be tied closely to problems of absenteeism, but, it is much less clear why sales or the need for managers may be going up each year. Yet even in the case of rising sales or the need for additional managers, if the manager decides that these are due to specific (controllable) actions (advertising, providing new products or services, hiring of specialists, or a growing reputation for quality), the growth or change of these variables overtime will make more sense.

Thus if the organization continues its level of advertising, meeting competition, and introducing new services (products) and if outside conditions don't change very much, a manager will have a basis for anticipating the level of future sales, future hiring, or whatever. A manager forecasting human resources pays special attention to manpower-related variables that change regularly over time. By the same token, if a manager forecasts major business variables (level of sales, production, service) over time, he will make the human resource forecast by converting these variables to various manpower or labor measures.

For the purposes of this section, two types of associations will be discussed: those where human resource variables can be related to business variables and those where a human resource measure is projected into the future based on past relationships.

Does a Relationship Exist?

The answer to this question is at times difficult to establish. One way to start to get at the answer is to develop a "scatter" diagram and visually judge whether some relation appears to exist (see Exhibit 5–3). For example, in Company A a distinct relationship appears to exist between its use of sales representatives and level of sales dollars: the higher the sales volume, the larger the number of "reps." Not so for Company B, where it appears that the number of reps bears little relation to sales. How come?

The explanation might be quite simple. Company A sells strictly with sales reps and must develop more reps to get more sales. Company B may sell through several channels, only one of which is reps. In the past, significant levels of sales may have been secured from these other sources, and B's reps have trouble developing new business.

A second and rather obvious point, yet one which is often neglected, is the logic of the relationship. Is there a good reason why one factor *should* be related to another? Ridiculous answers (the statisticians call them "spurious relationships") will often be avoided if just a bit of thought is directed at the logic of the association.

EXHIBIT 5–3   Scatter Diagram

 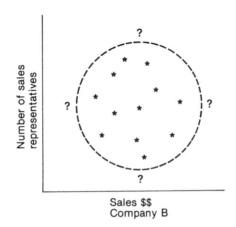

Formulas for Calculations

The simple, two-variable statistical model basically is directed toward determining a *line of best fit*. This line best represents the data in the sense that the distance from all the data points to the line is the minimum distance. The regression line in the scatter diagram is the best balance, fit, or compromise for the ten data points shown on the diagram (see Exhibit 5–3). The sum of the distances under the regression line matches the sum above the line.

The intent, then, is to determine the equation of the line of best fit. In a linear regression model, the two central features of the line of best fit are the y intercept (a) and the slope of the line (b), which equals P/t. Because computations involve numerous arithmetic calculations and mathematical operations, statisticians use a standard format to avoid mistakes and to lessen computation time.

Application Example of Linear Regression Model

For the purposes of these illustrations, simplified data are used so that we can emphasize the procedure. Typically, much more comprehensive and complex sets of data are involved.

EXHIBIT 5–4 Linear Regression Model

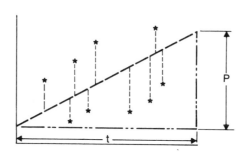

1. *Relation of number of registered nurses to size of hospital.* A 300-bed hospital in a large metropolitan area expects to expand substantially—to 450 beds—over the next four years. The director of nursing and the personnel director are attempting to plan future requirements for registered nurses. To get figures for planning purposes, the personnel director calls five similar hospitals in the area (smaller, similar size, and larger size) and gets the following figures.

Size of hospital (no. of beds)	Number of registered nurses
200	250
300	270
400	450
500	490
600	640

If these area figures were to be used for planning purposes, how many nurses would be indicated for the future 450-bed hospital?

EXHIBIT 5–5 Format for Carrying Out Calculations to Determine Linear Regression Line

---

	(1) List of x values	List corresponding y values	$(x) \cdot (y)$	(x^2)
(2) Determine sum of each column	$\overline{\Sigma x}$	$\overline{\Sigma y}$	$\overline{\Sigma(x) \cdot (y)}$	$\overline{\Sigma(x^2)}$

(3) x (average of x's) $= \dfrac{\Sigma x}{n}$ (n number of sets of x/y values)

(4) y (average of y's) $= \dfrac{\Sigma y}{n}$

(5) b (slope of regression line) $= \dfrac{\Sigma(x) \cdot (y) - n(x) \cdot (y)}{\Sigma(x^2) - n(x)^2}$

(6) a (intercept) $= y - bx$

(7) Equation of regression line: $y = a + bx$

EXHIBIT 5-6 Application Example of Linear Regression

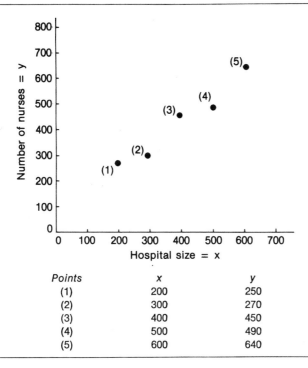

Points	x	y
(1)	200	250
(2)	300	270
(3)	400	450
(4)	500	490
(5)	600	640

Solution a) scatter plot. Hospital size is taken as the independent variable and is plotted on the *x* axis. (see Exhibit 5–6). The scatter data suggests that hospital size and number of nurses reflect a good relationship.

Solution b) calculation of regression line (using format).

x Hospital size	y No. of nurses	$(x) \cdot (y)$	(x^2)
200	250	50,000	40,000
300	270	81,000	90,000
400	450	180,000	160,000
500	490	245,000	250,000
600	640	384,000	360,000
2,000	2,100	940,000	900,000
$\Sigma(x)$	$\Sigma(y)$	$\Sigma(x) \cdot (y)$	$\Sigma(x^2)$

$$x = \frac{\Sigma x}{n} = \frac{2,000}{5} = 400$$

$$y = \frac{\Sigma y}{n} = \frac{2,100}{5} = 420$$

$$b = \frac{\Sigma(x) \cdot (y) - n(x) \cdot (y)}{\Sigma(x^2) - n(x)^2}$$

$$= \frac{940,000 - 5\,(400)\,(420)}{900,000 - 5\,(400)^2}$$

$$= \frac{940,000 - 840,000}{900,000 - 800,000} = \frac{100,000}{100,000}$$

$b = 1.0$ (slope)

$a = y - bx = 420 - (1)\,(400) = 20$ nurses (intercept)

$y = 20 + (1)\,(450)$

$y = 470$ nurses

2. *Extrapolation of linear regression over time.* Alpha-Omega, a leading research and development organization, uses large numbers of scientists and engineers. If the company continues to develop government and private contracts as it has in the past, it expects to maintain its growth pattern. What is its forecast of needs for scientists for 1980 based on its five-year growth pattern from 1970 to 1975?

Year	Average number of scientists used
1970	20
1971	35
1972	55
1973	85
1974	110
1975	140
.	
.	
.	
.	
1980	?

Solution a) scatter plot (*values from past*) (see Exhibit 5–7).

Solution b) calculation of regression line.

x Year*	y No. of scientists	$(x) \cdot (y)$	(x^2)
1970	20	1,400	4,900
1971	35	2,485	5,041
1972	55	3,960	5,184
1973	85	6,205	5,329
1974	110	8,140	5,476
1975	140	10,500	5,625
435 $\Sigma(x)$	445 $\Sigma(y)$	32,690 $\Sigma(x) \cdot (y)$	31,555 $\Sigma(x^2)$

$$x = \frac{\Sigma x}{n} = \frac{435}{6} = 72.5$$

$$y = \frac{\Sigma y}{n} = \frac{445}{6} = 74.17$$

$$b = \frac{\Sigma(x) \cdot (y) - n(x) \cdot (y)}{\Sigma(x^2) - n(x)^2}$$

$$= \frac{32,690 - 6\ (72.5)\ (74.17)}{31,555 - 6\ (72.5)^2}$$

$$b = \frac{32,690 - 32,264}{31,555 - 31,537} = \frac{426}{18} = 23.67$$

$$a = y - bx = 74.17 - 23.67\ (72.5) = 74.17 - 1716.23$$

$$a = -1,642$$

$$y = -1,642 + 23.67x \text{ (the prediction model)}$$

Calculation of estimated needs for scientists in 1980:

$$y = -1,642 + 23.67x$$

$$x = \text{"80" (1980)}$$

$$y = -1,642 + 23.67\ (80)$$

$$y = -1,642 + 1894^{**}$$

y (in 1980) = 252 scientists (estimated need) compared to the 140 employed in 1975.

* Only last two digits of the year are used since all are in the 1900s.
** Number is rounded.

Final Note on Statistical Forecasting

We have given simple examples of statistical applications using very modest amounts of data to focus on technique. Ordinarily, much more comprehensive sets of data would be required if the data were to be employed confidently. The confidence with which data are employed is affected by:

1. size of the body of data
2. data characteristics, including dispersion and accuracy
3. conformity in future of the assumptions related to past data.

There are additional statistical measures from which the human-resource planner or forecaster can judge the relevance or usefulness of past data. These measures relate to both the size of the body of data and its dispersion or scatter. One of these measures is called the "standard error of the estimate." Calculation of this measure goes beyond the current discussion, but a commonsense, working understanding of this concept is easy to grasp. Scatter diagrams are a good vehicle for indicating the nature of the data. Loosely speaking, the more the data "hugs" or "packs around" the regression line, the greater the accuracy of the predicting equation (see Exhibit 5–8).

The three diagrams in Exhibit 5–8 each contain eight observations (x) and the same regression equation: each illustration reflects a closer and closer conformity of the data to the predicting equation or regression line (marked with the dashed line). Thus, other things being equal, the more closely the data approach the regression line, the greater our confidence in their ability to represent past *relationships*. Then, the more closely future conditions approximate past conditions, the more confidence we have in the usefulness of the forecasting model.

EXHIBIT 5–7 Application Example—Alpha-Omega

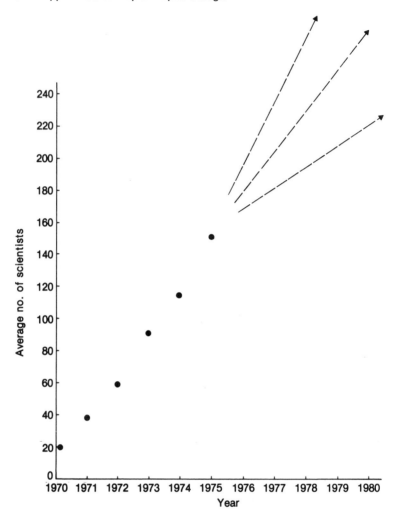

NEW FORECASTING MODELS

The *budget* model and the *statistical forecasting* approaches have been presented as vehicles in contemporary forecasting practices. Two newer approaches, which have been gaining attention because of their usefulness are, *group estimation* techniques, including *Delphi* approaches, and the *Markov model*. These approaches will be described briefly in the following section.

Group Estimation Approaches including Delphi

An old adage says that "two heads are better than one," but to this day many managers refuse to believe it. This brief section concerns matters where two

EXHIBIT 5-8   Scatter Diagram

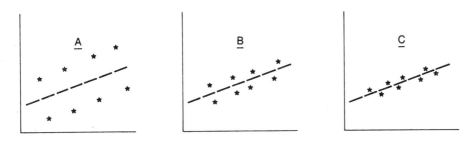

heads, three heads, or even more are much better than one head (but it doesn't exclude the possibility that in some cases one head may be better for forecasting purposes).

Owners, senior managers, officials, and bureaucrats have regularly employed personal guesses about the course of future events. And in simpler times, or where one person was the acknowledged expert, one informed guess may have been better than five, ten, or twenty uninformed guesses, even if they were averaged. Times, however, have become more complex because environmental events and institutional circumstances contain many more elements that interact in ways that outrun individual comprehension. Increasing complexity has made it more and more likely that existing events may occur or elements that affect developments remain unidentified because they are outside an individual's realm of experience or knowledge.

Application.   A large, integrated steel firm, considering its future level of demand and related human resource needs faces a very difficult situation. If it furnishes steel sheet to the auto industry, estimating the number and size of domestic cars poses considerable problems. Second, the use of steel products in construction is influenced by the level of economic activity, housing starts, design innovations, and fluctuations in industrial construction activity. These same types of issues have to be faced in all of the other product lines of the company, which also have to reckon with the introduction of new products to these markets. The company also must examine its present facility and its technology plans for the future in response to its estimates of product and market developments, as well as the possible developments of new machines and processes that affect productivity and human resources.

All of this can be boiled down to a simple notion: More and more forecasting situations are emerging that require the insights, knowledge, and judgment of several experts or knowledgeable people.

Bases for group approaches.   The contribution of management and behavioral research to human resource forecasting efforts has been to 1) Recognize where group (as opposed to individual) efforts are appropriate, and 2) Structure groups and guides for interaction so that the groups will work efficiently and be able to take advantage of the information members of the group have.

For the purposes of the discussion in this section, the main sources of information for group structuring are the work at the Rand Corporation concerning the "Delphi technique" and "nominal group techniques," developed by Andre Delbecq and Andrew Van de Ven.

A note on the concepts. We should make a brief comment about the concepts of Delphi and nominal group interactions before we proceed. Both assume that the group possesses the necessary knowledge or expertise and that the product of the whole is often much greater than the parts (individual members). In Delphi approaches, face-to-face individual interaction is avoided to eliminate the force of individual personalities dominating the activity. Instead, individuals interact through an intermediary, who summarizes information and coordinates group activity. This intermediary clearly plays a key and central role. Information is developed in successive rounds, and each new round of information development capitalizes on the previous rounds. Between each round, the intermediary summarizes and advances the information toward an area of common agreement. For example, typical problems might be the types of new medical technologies most likely to be in common usage ten years from now, the degree of penetration of foreign auto manufacturers in domestic markets, or the likelihood and type of new labor or safety legislation.

It's not an accident that these examples lie beyond a particular institution and in the external environment. The environments that are external to an organization's activity are those that at the outset establish a base plan for internal operations. There's little point in making internal plans if they are not fully compatible with external developments.

In nominal group techniques the experts may be physically present, but the procedures are structured so that initial information gathering permits all participants to contribute before group processes take over. For example, there may be an initial statement of the problem or issue and all members of the group write down their initial ideas, which are then listed on flip charts for all to see and discuss. Group interaction serves to narrow possibilities and occasionally combine some of the best features of individual contribution and group processes.

General guide for group estimation. Several general points can be made regarding group processes for forecasting which may prove helpful in using this approach.

1. This type of forecasting problem goes beyond the power of statistical or other systematic approaches (social, legislative, economic, or technological developments sufficiently far in the future require more than a simple extension of current deliberations or trends).

2. The problem/issue is often found in the external environment and is of such complexity as to involve multiple, often interacting, forces.

3. Understanding or judging the nature of the developments is beyond the knowledge or information possessed by a single individual.

4. Convergence on a feasible set of possibilities or general agreement will require successive rounds of information giving, feedback, and discussion before the narrowing of possibilities can be accomplished.

5. Information gathering among participants is such that all group members can contribute their knowledge or expertise to the development so that the influence of dominant personalities is minimized.

6. Information gathering, processing, and dispensing techniques will affect the efficiency of these procedures and the quality of the subsequent answers. A brief example of group estimation is provided below.

Application example of group estimation. The director of nursing for a large metropolitan hospital was concerned with various future economic, social, legislative, technical, and medical events. He was especially concerned about events that would affect the number and type of nurses needed in the future and, consequently, lead to potential problems in recruitment and training.

It seemed clear that the problem contained a number of different facets; therefore the overall forecasting problem was broken down into parts. One of these was to determine *population shifts* in the service area and, consequently, possible changes in patient load and new or potential problems in attracting nurses to their particular physical location. The director of nursing and the personnel director were able to get the following people to serve as members of a forecasting panel: the city public health director, the assistant director of a regional health planning agency, a specialist from the city' chamber of commerce (specializing in business and population movements), the vice-president for planning of the hospital, and an economist from a local university (specializing in regional economics).

The methodology for determining population shifts was based on a questionnaire designed to bring out key features of the changes (Delphi-type approach). Construction of the questionnaire was based on preliminary discussions with members of the panel, on readings, and on various contacts maintained by the personnel director and the vice-president for planning. Examples of the types of questions follow:

1. The current composition of the hospital's service area is 20 percent minority and is experiencing rapid changes. The area can be expected to achieve 30 percent minority composition in (a) two years, (b) four years, (c) six years, (d) ten years, (e) never.

2. Moderate-rent apartments, which are well lighted and secure, have been very important for housing our nurses. A need for more of this type of rental housing can be expected in (a) two years, (b) three years, (c) five years, (d) ten years, (e) never.

Questionnaires were submitted to individual panel members. On questions where large disagreements existed, the coordinator (personnel director) went back to the experts to get the thinking underlying the responses. For the second round, controversial questions were resubmitted to the panel wih comprehensive explanations.

Rather than additional rounds, final areas of differences were resolved by a meeting of those available. Prior to this meeting they were asked to submit brief written statements of their positions, and the remaining issues were resolved in open discussion (nominal group technique).

Recap of steps in group estimation. The steps described in the preceding example of the group estimation method reflect the following key steps:

1. breaking the overall forecasting problem down into key segments that re-reflect different forecasting concerns

2. preliminary research on each segment to identify main variables, problems, or developments that are to become the subject of group estimation

3. identifying specialists or experts who are to comprise the group representing various areas of knowledge or expertise relevant to the forecasting problems

4. developing questions with appropriate response scales reflecting the planning horizon and concerns of human resource planning

5. designing the structure for group interaction—assuring the solicitation of information under efficient conditions that maximize the quality and quantity of feedback—and providing for coordination of group efforts and assuring that the coordinator is aware of behavioral issues in this technique

6. attempting to gain general agreement on the problem.

The final technique to be described in this chapter is also rather new in forecasting efforts, yet it has received considerable attention.

Systems Approach to Human Resource Planning

People probably are the most dynamic aspect of organizations, whether the business or activity is growing, declining, or static, simply because they are so varied and unpredictable. People are recruited, enter, and quit, or are promoted. Positions are created temporarily or permanently or are eliminated, thereby imparting further motion to people-related affairs. Unfortunately, people movements don't always take place in the best fashion. Inefficiency or poor strategies regarding people frequently result from poor information or no information. For example, how long does it take, on the average, for a competent person to reach a middle level in the organization? Could this rate of progress be improved? To what extent are we forced to rely on recruiting as opposed to internal training or development of people? If a key manager should quit or die, will a replacement be available? When? Answers to these types of questions require a great deal of information and serve quite different needs of the organization. Some of this information pertains to career planning, some to recruitment or to institutional policy. The answers to some questions may be satisfied by relatively specific types of information while others may require a comprehensive set of data.

For the purposes of this section, however, a modest but important type of analysis will be described. It pertains to the movements or transitions of personnel to jobs, between jobs, and from jobs. This approach is often termed "Markov-type" analysis.

The Markov model. The Markov model is a mathematical technique that analyzes personnel movements to show recruitment and development needs and provide a more objective basis for career planning. *If* the pattern of personnel movements to/between/from jobs is relatively stable, the procedure is carried out in straightforward fashion.

1. Historical records provide information for a five-to-ten-year period. These records include personnel information on hirings, date of job entry, promotion, new jobs, and time of departure from jobs (quit, leave of absence, retire, etc.).

2. Historical data are examined to determine how *stable* the job transitions have been (i.e., patterns of movement in the past that can be expected to predict patterns of distribution of existing personnel among jobs in the future).

3. If movements appear stable, figures are averaged so that the probabilities of one's position, transfer, or promotion "next year" can be determined. For example, what are the chances of a salesperson being a sales supervisor next year? of remaining a salesperson? of being transferred to production or merchandising?

4. The probabilities determined in number (3) can be used to determine or predict the distribution of personnel in subsequent years by using matrix algebra concepts.

Example. Consider the divisions (see Exhibit 5–9) of a sales and engineering organization containing two types of functions (sales and engineering), regular employees and supervisors, and general management people.

Exhibit 5–10 is exactly the same as the previous one, except that:

1. Arrows have been added to show movements between positions plus movements into and out of these divisions.

2. Probabilities have been added for the indicated movements, based on analyses of payroll and personnel records.

What at first seems quite a muddle becomes clearer after brief examination. Let's trace one position through and see what the human resource forecast is for the following year. This chart tells us that sales people have a 78 percent chance of remaining in their present positions the following year. However, some people from sales transfer to engineering (on average, there's a 2 percent chance);

EXHIBIT 5–9 General Organization Structure

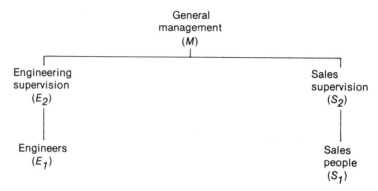

a rather large number leave (around 12 percent); and our experience has been that none are promoted to engineering supervision.

So much for the mechanics of this initial chart. But several other observations can be made:

1. Exits from supervising positions are less than those from worker positions (10 percent vs. 4 percent in engineering; 12 percent vs. 8 percent in sales).

2. Sales people are never promoted to engineering supervision, but a few engineers may be transferred to sales supervision (2 percent).

3. Some people from general management are shifted to supervisory positions in engineering (4 percent) or sales (2 percent).

4. Shifts to general management are twice as great from engineering (6 percent) as from sales (3 percent).

EXHIBIT 5–10 Managerial Movement between Positions

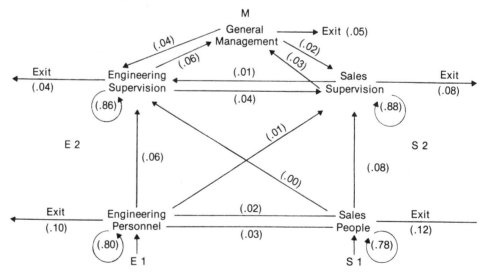

The pattern of movements shown in the previous chart can also be represented in tabular form, which is more compact and lends itself to mathematic operations. In Table 5–1 two areas of information have been added: the distribution of personnel in 1976 and distribution of this same group the following year.

TABLE 5–1   The Distribution of Personnel in 1976–1977

1976 distribution of personnel	E_1	E_2	S_1	S_2	M	Exit
300 E_1	.80	.06	.03	.01	0	.10
40 E_2	0	.86	0	.04	.06	.04
500 S_1	.02	0	.78	.08	0	.12
50 S_2	0	.01	0	.88	.03	.08
20 M	0	.04	0	.02	.89	.05
Total 910	250	53	399	88	22	97

Distribution of 1976 personnel in 1977.

Note: Numbers don't quite "add" because of rounding.

The shift in personnel assignments from year 1976 to 1977 is dramatic; for example, the number of engineers remaining in engineering (E_1) decreased from 300 to 250; engineering supervision (E_2) has grown substantially, from 40 to 53 people, while sales supervision (S_2) increased to 88 from 50. Also, the number of exits is substantial—some 97 employees from the previous year's total of 910 are expected to leave (recruiting will face a substantial challenge). If this division was being used as a training division to prepare personnel for supervising tasks, the relatively large number of people being moved to supervising or general management positions, (E_2), (S_2), (M), calls for a carefully coordinated and well-organized training and development effort.

The mathematical principles underlying the calculation of the 1977 figures can be used to determine the number of the original 1976 group remaining in subsequent years—so long as the stability of the probabilities of people movements remain valid. This same technique can be employed for a number of other human resource planning purposes. It can be used to trace the career path of a specific employee, predicting where this person is likely to be two, three, or four years from now. Another important area is calculating total recruiting and/or training-development needs on a year-to-year basis, or determining an inventory or expected supply of people from the internal labor market. Markov analyses may also be useful for probing turnover, detecting changes in promotion or transfer policy, or assessing the most popular paths upward.

Further applications of the Markov-type analysis are beyond the scope of our discussion, but it should be evident that this approach provides a basis for exceedingly rich analysis. This approach will probably be used more extensively in the future.

Computers, Analytic Methods, and Forecasting for the Future

Before closing this chapter it seems appropriate to call attention to several important trends that are changing the usefulness of planning/forecasting designs. The widespread use of computers in the 1970s has given power to forecasting approaches that was largely absent in the past. Computers have facilitated simulation forecasting estimates under sets of widely different assumptions, and the use of more powerful mathematics and statistical techniques. The technology of computation has been further bolstered by a new generation of specialists who have been trained to take greater advantage of the computer and analytical approaches. As a result, people working in these areas will be increasingly forced to rely on those with formal training and education in these approaches. However, there is also a trend in the offing which can widen the base of personnel who employ these approaches.

Various forecasting models can be incorporated into the computer so that all kinds of department heads, managers, or planners can recall needed information. The ability to ask "what if" questions or derive estimates under various input assumptions or changes can bring the power of these planning approaches to all manner of functional officials. Extensive discussions of computer applications in personnel management are found in Chapter 15.

SUMMARY

The forecasting of human resource needs must be viewed in the broader context of human resource and institutional planning. Forecasting is much more than a numbers game; it is part of enlarged analyses that must also deal with issues in career planning, recruiting, training and development, and reserve and replacement analyses for key positions. And it must relate to overall institutional planning, prove responsive to overall needs, and signal caution when it appears that organizational plans will be limited by human resource considerations.

Human resource planning/forecasting must deal with varying degrees of uncertainty. Ability to influence key forces in an organizational environment, accessibility to information (quantity and quality), and information-processing ability affect the breadth of an organization's planning horizon. Consequently, terms such as *short range, intermediate,* and *long range* are only relative; they will vary greatly from organization to organization.

Human resource forecasting approaches deal with several different classes of problems, and the perspectives and methods used differ accordingly. Some approaches are directed toward internal labor markets while others deal with external labor markets. In one area of approaches, institutional concerns are directed toward forces or variables that will affect the number, type, timing, and use of labor categories by an institution. Here, forecasts of technological change, new (labor-related) legislation, and changes in labor supply serve as examples of these approaches. A second area of human resource planning/forecasting approaches deals specifically with various occupational and specialty categories, assessments of reserve and replacement needs for officials, and movements of people through the organization.

In this chapter, four types of planning models (two methods that are used extensively and two new ones) were described. Budgeting models were described as essentially short-range planning approaches. The basic two-variable linear statistical model can be used for a variety of situations involving relationships between human resource and institutional variables and changes in human resource variables over time.

The two newer models described were group estimation techniques (Delphi and nominal) plus Markov-type math procedures. The continuing diffusion of these methods and other new capabilities brought about by computers will help managers meet the forecasting needs of the future.

DISCUSSION QUESTIONS

1. The comptroller for a commercial college uses forecasts of student registration hours to determine the number of teachers who will be authorized for various academic departments. Based on past experience, it is assumed that one teacher will be required for each 300 semester hours of student registration. What assumptions underlie the determination of authorized teacher staffing, using future enrollment, future hiring, and so on?

2. The president of Fairfield Manufacturing Company has asked the personnel director for a report on the company's progress in minority employment and possible long-range planning goals for three and five years from now. "Also, when can we expect to reach a level of at least 20 percent minority employment if we continue our current program?" The company's program has now been in effect for five years and indicates the following:

Year of minority program	Percentage minority
1	2
2	5
3	6
4	7
5	9

a. Develop a regression model that describes past accomplishments to project future planning objectives in years 8 and 10.

b. When will Fairfield Manufacturing reach 20 percent minority employment if the current recruitment and training program is continued?

3. In the Columbia School example, how do teaching techniques and technology affect the use of conversion factors?

4. The chapter frequently refers to the concept of uncertainty. How would the following considerations be expected to affect the uncertainty confronting human resource planners? Why?

a. A firm produces many different products selling in diverse markets.

b. Construction of facilities takes a considerable length of time.

c. A company prides itself on highly flexible operations.

d. A firm is unwilling to spend much time training its people.

e. A labor surplus is expected.

f. A labor shortage is expected.

g. An organization has undertaken an extensive study to develop a "skill bank."

5. What distinctions between a pure forecasting approach and the human resource planning/forecasting concept are made in the chapter?

6. What two characteristics are considered crucial in determining a firm's ability to deal with uncertainty?

7. In developing human resource planning/forecasting approaches for a large regional department-store chain, what types of information would probably be of environmental interest to planners for incorporation into their forecasting effort? Why?

8. Compare and contrast the four forecasting approaches described in this chapter.

BIBLIOGRAPHY

Berg, Sanford V. "Determination of Technological Change in the Service Industries." *Technological Forecasting and Social Change* 5 (1973):407–26.

Bezdek, Roger H. *Long-Range Forecasting of Manpower Requirements.* New York: EEE Monograph, 1974.

Bezdek, Roger H., and Barry Getzel. "Alternate Forecasts of the Job Content and Skill Requirements of the American Economy in 1980." *Technological Forecasting and Social Change* 5 (1973):205–14.

Bryant, Don R., Michael J. Maggaid, and Robert P. Taylor. "Manpower Planning Models and Techniques." *Business Horizons* (April 1973):69–77.

Burack, Elmer H., and James W. Walker. *Manpower Planning and Programming.* Boston: Allyn & Bacon, 1972.

————. *Strategies for Manpower Planning and Programming.* Morristown, N.J.: General Learning, 1972.

Cressy, J. E. William, Robert M. Kaplan, and Louis H. Grossman. "Matrix Models for Planning Executive Development." *MSU Business Topics* (Summer 1969).

Dalkey, N. *The Delphi Method: An Experimental Study of Group Opinion.* RAND R,–5888–PR, 1969.

Dalkey, N., and O. Helmer. "An Experimental Application of the Delphi Method to the Use of Experts." *Management Science* (1963).

Delbecq, Andre, and Andrew Van de Ven. "Group Process Model for Problem Indentification and Program Planning." *Journal of Applied Behavioral Science* (1971).

Folger, John K., Helen S. Austin, and Alan E. Bayer. *Human Resources and Higher Education.* New York: Russell Sage Foundation, 1970:76–84.

Foltman, Felecian F. *Manpower Information for Effective Management: Part 2: Skills Inventories and Manpower Planning.* Ithaca, N.Y.: N.Y. SSIL.R, Cornell Univ., 1973.

Gray, Duncan S. "Corporate Manpower Planning and Forecasting: Canadian Experience." *The Business Quarterly* (Summer 1971):60–65.

Haire, Mason. "Managing Management Manpower." *Business Horizons* (Winter 1967): 23–28.

MacCrimmon, Kenneth R. "Improving Decision Making with Manpower Management Systems." *The Business Quarterly* 36.3 (Autumn 1971):29–41.

Morton, J. E. *On Manpower Forecasting*. Kalamazoo, Mich.: W. E. Upjohn Institute, 1968.

National Science Foundation, Office of National R & D Assessment. *First Annual Report —Fiscal Year 1973*. Washington, D.C.: Office of National R & D Assessment, 1973.

O'Neal, Charles R., Hans B. Thorelli, and James M. Utterbach. "Adoption of Innovation by Industrial Organization." *Industrial Marketing Management* 2 (1973): 235–50.

U.S. Department of Labor, Bureau of Labor Statistics. *The U.S. Economy in 1980*. Washington, D.C.: BLS Bulletin 1606, 1970.

Utterback, James M., and Elmer H. Burack. "Identification of Technological Threats and Opportunities of Firms." *Technological Forecasting and Human Performance* (Spring 1974).

Van de Ven, Andrew, and Andre Delbecq. "Nominal Versus Interacting Group Processes for Committee Decision-Making Effectiveness." *Academy of Management Journal* (1971).

Vroom, Victor H., and Kenneth R. MacCrimmon. "Towards a Stochastic Model of Managerial Careers." *Administrative Science Quarterly* 1.11 (June 1968):26–46.

Chapter 6

JOB ANALYSIS: A SYSTEMS VIEW

LEARNING OBJECTIVES

This chapter presents descriptions and examples of basic concepts and approaches used in job analysis and design. This chapter should provide the reader with the information to:

Relate job analysis approaches to other central personnel functions such as job evaluation and compensation

Develop job descriptions for a wide variety of basic jobs

Identify sociotechnical systems concepts

Apply the concepts of job analysis to various work situations

KEY TERMS AND CONCEPTS

average time	job structure
critical incidents	learning function
extrinsic work features	man-machine model
intrinsic work features	motion and time study
job design	normal (work) pace
job enlargement	primary work system
job enrichment	representative work conditions
job evaluation	secondary support system
job specification	sociotechnical systems

PREVIEW

This chapter provides the basic concepts of job analysis. These concepts provide a logical link to techniques and functions, such as recruiting and evaluation, taken up in following chapters.

Entire books have been devoted to job analysis, so we have been highly selective in sorting out topics. Our experience in the field (and biases) has led us to emphasize:

1. Job analysis and its fit in newer personnel-human resource programs and undertakings.

2. Descriptions of important procedures and content of job analysis that are crucial to understanding both maintenance and planning processes of personnel.

3. Newer techniques and concepts in job analysis, such as the DOT job analysis (based on *Dictionary of Occupational Titles*).

OVERVIEW AND NEW DIRECTIONS IN JOB ANALYSIS

What is work? How can a "job" be defined? These questions provide the framework of job analysis (JA). Analysis of jobs and job structures can be an important source of understanding many human resource activities. In light of the growing national concern for improving productivity, spiraling costs (as in health care), and sustaining economic growth, this area deserves attention. Finally, a basic understanding of those aspects of jobs or job structures that can be varied to improve work and work conditions is an integral part of the "quality of work life" issue.

Approaches, Results

Job analysis combines long-standing observational techniques used in industrial engineering (e.g., motion and time study) and newer behavioral approaches. Standard JA techniques include interviewing job holders, observing work, and studying personnel relationships in conduct of work. "Work" is an organization's *primary* function. Ideally, JA enables managers to understand jobs and job structures to improve work flow or develop techniques to improve productivity. It also involves job design or redesign, coordinating demands on available time, individual psychological needs, technical procedures, and desired performances.

More frequently, JA is concerned with "job enriching" activities that expand the worker's sense of personal accomplishment and challenge or satisfaction. Finally, job analysis may assist the creation of personnel documents and procedures, such as *job descriptions*, which highlight responsibilities and job relationships; *job specifications*, which define skills and education experience; and *job evaluation*, which establishes the relative value of jobs for wages and salaries. JA is necessary to assess performance and training needs and provides basic information for recruiting.

Job Analysis versus Job Evaluation

Job analysis is concerned with the study of jobs or work routines from a systems perspective. It is a way to look at both people and process. Human and machine are viewed as a unit; the analyst attempts to understand their relationship (a sociotechnical view). Job evaluation—the worth of work performed—starts when job analysis—*how* work is performed—has been completed. Job evaluation is used to establish the relative value of particular jobs to provide a basis for compensation. Various approaches to job evaluation will be discussed in Chapter 11.

Informal versus Formal Approaches in Job Analysis

Job analysts use a variety of approaches, not all of them formal. Many workers know their jobs from tradition, a great deal of experience, or "gut feel." Some managers have good memories or display an uncanny ability to describe work activities in their areas, but the growing complexity of work has made it increasingly risky to rely too heavily on this approach. The degree of formalization of JA procedures depends on the size of the organization, so that the larger the organization (1,600 to 2,000 employees), the more formal the analysis.

But the *type* of the organization also makes a difference. Organizations numbering only a few hundred employees may take advantage of JA if many different jobs exist or large numbers of professionals are involved, as in research groups or architectural firms.

Areas of Application

While JA is concerned with the *primary work function* (e.g., flying, retail sale of food), it also is concerned with *secondary* activities supporting the main work system (e.g., flight mechanic, purchasing, warehousing) (see Exhibit 6–1, item 1). Primary and secondary work systems relate jobs to job structures (2). The immediate product of JA procedures is description of work methods, techniques, responsibilities, and relationships that can be analyzed and studied further (3). For example, the relationships among jobs can touch on questions of technology, human understanding, and communications.

JA also can concern job redesign to improve operational performance or to enrich job content and employee involvement (5). Managers may develop ways of giving their employees an increased sense of personal accomplishment and control over themselves and their work. Closure is the employee's ability to sense how his activity fits into the total activity; closure reinforces a feeling of personal accomplishment and job satisfaction.

Results

Job analysis (3) produces four kinds of documentation and procedures that are crucial to personnel activities: job descriptions, job specifications, job evaluation, and personnel assessment. In turn, the procedures and documentation are basic inputs for diverse personnel functions (4).

New Perspectives for Job Analysis and Design

At long last, organization theorists and behaviorists, job analysts, and engineers can meet in a joint effort to redesign the basic units and systems of work activity in organizations. The "man-machine model," introduced more than seventy years ago and frequently attributed to Frederick W. Taylor, has dominated the thinking of management, personnel, and workers for virtually this entire period. Findings in the behavioral sciences are now advanced enough so that at least the broad outlines of alternative job-design approaches can be drawn.

The new behavioral approaches can frequently meet output or performance

EXHIBIT 6-1 Job Analysis and Allied Studies

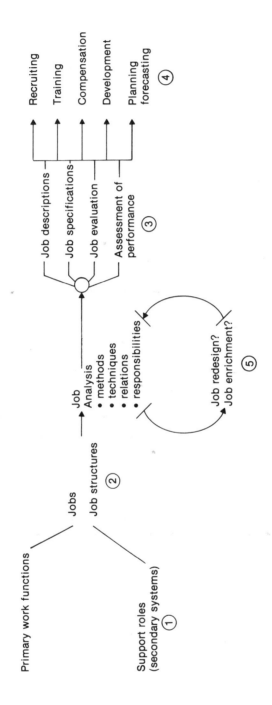

154

requirements and at the same time permit higher levels of personal achievement, and they can be a message to the employee that his supervisors care about his individual worth, dignity, and ambition. The growing number of experiments with systems design—both the successes and failures—indicate that the time is at hand for more general incorporation of these methods (Davis, 1971). These newer approaches are described in Chapter 10. However, because of the prominence of the man-machine model and widespread use of various traditional job-study practices, these too will be described, along with their key assumptions and limitations.

A final point concerns a long-standing debate regarding the designing of jobs for people or fitting people to jobs. The viewpoint expressed in these discussions is that both approaches are useful. Jobs and work systems can be extensively modified, even beyond previous expectations of "experts," while still meeting performance requirements. At the same time, there are major limitations to design modifications of some systems. For example, companies that have committed themselves to expensive, large-scale technologies will resist significant modifications. Also, where a job title represents a large number of jobs, any attempt to modify an individual activity must deal with the results of this action on other jobs, wages, etc. Nevertheless, more care in personnel assignments and the construction of jobs and job structures can result in better matching of job and individual requirements.

BASIC CONCEPTS AND TOOLS OF ANALYSIS

Motion and Time Study (M&TS)

Industrial engineering approaches emerged from the work of F. W. Taylor and his associates in the early years of this century (roughly 1900–20). Their work provided the first major, systematic, and enduring attempts to analyze jobs. These are often identified as "motion and time study" (stop-watch oriented) and "work analysis." These studies (mostly in manufacturing facilities) identified the key elements of a job function and arranged them so that workers could use work implements at "optimal" levels. But even in these early years, optimal performance was seen as bringing about a highly desired *joint product.* High productivity was—and still is—a highly valued goal because it was thought that productivity increased the worker's earning potential. In a sense, Taylor's approach attempted to get the best of both worlds: higher profits for an organization and higher earnings for employees. Much literature exists in this area describing work study and the interested reader is referred to the bibliography.

An example and some definitions. Early work-study procedures sought to describe the key elements needed to complete a job task. This technique led to breaking down a whole task into its key elements for study and improvement. An example of a simplified list of job elements for drilling holes in an aluminum casting is shown below:

	Standard time allowed (minutes)
1. Remove previously drilled casting from holder (to keep it secure during drilling).	.30
2. Clean holder and table.	.45
3. Remove casting from bin, place in holder, and clamp.	.15
4. Activate drill by pushing button.	.05
5. Check holes with gauge while piece is still in holder.	.55
Total standard time	1.5 minutes

Challenges to the analyst. The isolation of the five elements of drilling enables the analyst to find a standard number (average) of times needed to complete the task after he has developed a one best way of performing the operation. Also, it is probably clear that viewing a total work task (drilling holes in an aluminum casting) in this form (namely, as job elements) permits analysis and possible improvement. On the other hand, if the analyst's task is to identify good performance as well as a job-enriching task, he may consider incorporating more related or similar operations (job enlargement) to increase the scope of activities. He may attempt to tie the worker's task to a related department to improve a larger group or set of operations (broader perspective and sense of closure) or possibly to include nonroutine responsibilities (e.g., a quality check).

Standard time. This concept is commonly employed in work analysis, and it should be understood by both the worker and the analyst. The study of a job and, more particularly, job elements in the motion and time study approach leads to an estimate of the time needed by an "average" person. It is assumed that figures are gathered under representative work conditions (temperature, light, work pressures, delays, etc.) and at a "normal" work pace. Thus the analyst relies on his judgment or on time-value tables in at least three areas:

1. *Average person.* This seeks to take into account a fair sample of physical characteristics, intelligence, and motor abilities. In the past, little thought was given to the interests, attention span, susceptibility to boredom, or other worker behavioral characteristics. Job analysts, especially those oriented to socio-technical concepts, attempt to factor in these aspects of job performance.

2. *Representative work conditions.* It's commonly known that work conditions can vary greatly. Such things as periodic delays involving breakdowns, lighting, temperature, shortages, absenteeism, breaks, washroom time and meals can affect performance and must be analyzed. Adjustments for these conditions are made by averaging events that are likely to arise over the period of job performance.

3. *Normal work pace.* Work analysts or tables of standard time values give the amount of time needed to perform an operation. These figures are based on

the assumption that the pace they set represents a level of energy that can be maintained over extended periods of time without undue fatigue. It's further assumed that the employee has been adequately trained for the work task and that he displays only those time variations in the work cycle that typically accompany work startup, fatigue, and energetic feelings.

Learning time versus time to perform.   Considerable differences exist between the time it takes an employee to learn the basics of a job as opposed to standard, or job, times. The standard times for hole drilling referred to previously, *assume* the worker's job familiarity. Job familiarity of course varies with the task. It may be a matter of hours, days, months or even years before a person really learns a job. (Exhibit 6–2 suggests some of these periods.)

Exhibit 6–2 contains two representations of time. In 6–2A, a learning function is depicted: the sketch indicates that the full benefits of training may not be realized for a substantial period of time—and that learning is not uniform over

EXHIBIT 6–2   Learning Time and Worker-Cycle Variations

A. Learning function (curve) for various types of jobs

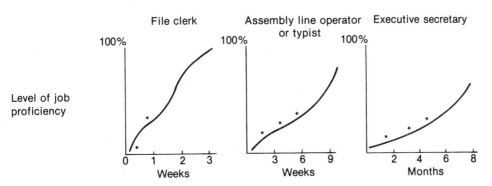

*Area of high individual tension and learning difficulty

B. Variations in worker energy expenditures over a single work day

the period. Technical and behavioral improvements in training procedures (e.g., sense of help or support) seek to reduce the time needed for the worker to gain proficiency (see Chapter 8, Learning and Training). Also, the learning time varies greatly with the type of job to be performed.

Exhibit 6–2B depicts energy–time relationships in the course of a typical day of a worker who already is familiar with a job. For example, when Mary says, "I don't really wake up until 10 A.M.," the chart suggests that this is a typical situation and that many workers do reach a type of "high" at this time of the day.

Complications: Monetary Incentives and Time Standards

The standard times for task completion become the basic building blocks in establishing the expected level of work performance. In turn, the standard times and expected performance form the basis for monetary incentives and serve as a managerial control. This is a major source of friction, even conflict, between management and workers, especially those in unions. The standard time value is derived from a series of assumptions regarding work conditions, technology, and the amount of energy needed by the worker. Management and unions often disagree greatly as to what constitutes an accurate or fair time standard.

The notion of standard time is a complex subject and the reader needs at least a nodding acquaintance with its assumptions and terminology because of the close relationship with personnel practices and problems. The next section describes a historically important and central vehicle for job analysis which has of late assumed a number of new features—the job description.

Job Descriptions

One of the earliest tools of personnel management, the job description, continues to play an important, basic role in a wide variety of maintenance activities. In this section the purposes, form, and techniques of job description development will be presented. New concepts in job descriptions that incorporate behavioral, communications, and leadership concepts will be presented in Chapter 9. Practical problems in the use of job descriptions are considered in this section. One problem is how to capitalize on job-description usage in personnel procedures. Another deals with the implications of job-holder characteristics that do not precisely match those of the job description.

Purpose. The purpose of a job description is to provide both organizational information (location in structure, authority, etc.) and functional information (what the work is). It defines the scope of job activities, major responsibilities, and positioning of the job in the organization. Precision and detail, the two most important aspects of job descriptions, can vary greatly. The specifics are tailored to the needs of a particular organization, but in any case, if done carefully, the description should provide the worker, analyst, and supervisor with a clear idea of what the worker must do to meet the demands of the job. A manager must be able to use it for recruiting, as a realistic assessment of the worker's performance, as a guide for training programs and planning. In this sense the outline of the position description is no different for the president than for the department supervisor or clerk. Admittedly, detail and preciseness will vary but a common structure must be present.

Jobs, not people. Job (or position) descriptions describe jobs, not job holders. The movement of employees due to promotion, quits, and the like would lend much instability to job descriptions if people rather than jobs were described. However, there are exceptions. For unique positions—for example, the head of an organization or a new specialty—the description may reflect the philosophy of management or skills of the soon-to-be job holder. Thus, who may be available may be one of the practical considerations in job-description development which must be confronted.

Economic conditions that affect labor markets. If the job description is developed realistically and external labor market conditions are good, filling jobs with qualified people should be routine. If an occupation is in short supply (e.g., engineers, managers, and skilled craftsmen), an organization may be forced to make realistic adjustments in its hiring practices. Although the job description may call for certain skills, managers may have to settle for someone with significantly different abilities. If erratic labor-market conditions come to be the rule, the job description may have to be reevaluated and modified. Under extreme conditions, the job may be fragmented and its parts assigned to other positions.

Description and performance assessment (evaluation). Obviously there can be an enormous difference between what a job is supposed to do and what it actually does. This is the basic difference between job descriptions and job assessments. Job description concerns such functions as planning, coordinating, and assigning responsibility, while assessment concerns the quality of the performance itself. It is easy to see how the two are related. While job description is not assessment, it provides an important basis for establishing assessment standards and objectives.

There usually are four main components of job descriptions:

1. *Organizational (structural) position and descriptors.* Title and reporting relationships ("reports to" and "supervises"). This portion of the description is a direct translation of the location of the job in the organization structure—title assignment: To what higher level job is this job accountable? and Who is supervised directly?

2. *Summary highlights of job.* Briefly, what are the critical accomplishments needed for success in this job? These highlights often take the form of a summary statement describing the day or the week in review.

3. *Major responsibilities in detail.* This description contains a brief profile of the requirements critical to job success. Often these requirements are organized in descending order of importance. They may be organized in a composite list or within functional categories such as planning, controlling, directing, co-

ordinating, and administering. Action language such as plans, monitors, and directs, is used. The detailing of major responsibilities is often drafted as variations of basic organizational functions, but in action form: plans, directs, coordinates, controls, administers, and innovates.

4. *Principal working relationships.* Communications and interpersonal (i.e., position-to-position) relationships are the key considerations. Special emphasis is placed on those relationships involving work or positions in other departments—that is, beyond the worker's authority or jurisdiction.

Relation of the job description to work and organization. The main elements of the job description can be related more specifically to the work activities and organizational functions they represent. See Exhibit 6–3.

EXHIBIT 6–3   The Job Description—Its Relation to Work and Organization Structure

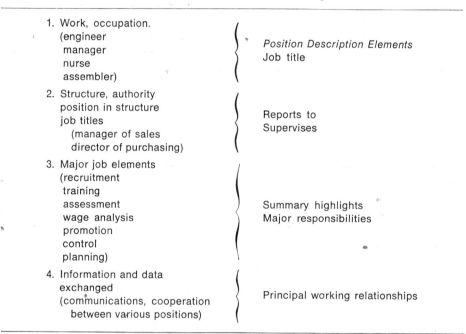

1. Work, occupation.
   (engineer
   manager
   nurse
   assembler)

   Position Description Elements
   Job title

2. Structure, authority
   position in structure
   job titles
     (manager of sales
     director of purchasing)

   Reports to
   Supervises

3. Major job elements
   (recruitment
   training
   assessment
   wage analysis
   promotion
   control
   planning)

   Summary highlights
   Major responsibilities

4. Information and data
   exchanged
   (communications, cooperation
   between various positions)

   Principal working relationships

Job description versus job specification. Confusion continues regarding the purposes of *descriptions* versus *specifications.* This confusion is natural because in some quarters these terms have been used interchangeably. For purposes of our discussions, the distinction between these two documents will be based on:

1. *Job description.* Deals primarily with organization, structure, responsibility, and relationships. It is an organizational "map" that tells us job objectives and what is to be done.

2. *Job specification.* The emphasis here is on the physical tools, knowledge, educational experiences, physiological and motor abilities, and intellect needed

to carry out the responsibilities assigned to the job. For example, responsibility for sales planning (position description) may require a number of years experience in field selling, knowledge of advanced statistical concepts, and perhaps even understanding of an organization's computer system and capabilities.

Why job descriptions? Organizations use job analysis procedures to varying degrees and for many different reasons. Some use them often while others have never used them. Unfortunately, in both instances, managers often don't really know what functions job descriptions serve. Many nonusers argue, "We don't want to be tied down by descriptions; if we document every job, we lose flexibility and creativity." If flexibility and creativity are needed on the job, a description can be designed to meet these needs. But in too many cases, a manager attempts to incorporate an unrealistic amount of detail. In other words, descriptions are sometimes used incorrectly. And, of course, like any tool, a job description won't work properly if it isn't used properly.

There are, in fact, compelling reasons for using job descriptions. The following three items provide a self-check of potential shortcomings of existing approaches and suggest the importance of job descriptions to organizations.

1. Avoid confusion and provide understanding or clarification. Research suggests that clearly describing what the individual will be held accountable for (House, Filley, and Kerr, 1971) can reduce misunderstanding and ambiguity. A clear description of responsibilities supports performance and job satisfaction. Failure to clarify the organization's or supervisor's expectations regarding job performances (of a subordinate) will almost certainly lead to confusion and people working at cross-purposes.

2. Clarify job relationships. The nature of work in organizations, whether dealing with information, things, or people, requires the division of the activity and interdependence among jobs and workers. A credit department's activity may involve salespeople, order-entry, and accounting people. Producing a television set may involve fifteen or twenty production and staff departments. Developing a roster of patients on a hospital floor may involve admitting, surgery, medical departments, and an accounting office. Good job descriptions will assist in bringing these diverse functions together to meet system objectives. Exhibit 6–4 illustrates how the system can be improved with job descriptions.

Gaps or overlaps in responsibility should become apparent immediately. If the work has been done well, the logic of information/work flow will be reflected in position descriptions. A worker won't feel that his activity has been covered or perhaps substantially overlapped by another. As illustrated in Exhibit 6–4, the comparatively straightforward work procedure of credit check can easily cut across four or five different departments and involve rather complex information. The processing of sales orders, for example, requires a check of credit, past billings, unpaid items, and current orders. A side-by-side comparison of responsibilities of these different job descriptions will identify the thoroughness of these procedures, or time delays, or omission of needed information.

Of course there's nothing magic about a description; it doesn't get the work

---

EXHIBIT 6–4 Involvement of Related Jobs in a Credit Check

Work activity: Credit Check	Impact on related job descriptions: Title	Item statement or description
1. Sales order, receipt	Sales order clerk	Receives and processes sales orders. Determines orders requiring a credit check.
2. Credit department	Credit assistant	Routinely processes orders from sales order department to determine credit status.
3. Check accounting for status of past billings	Accounts receivable clerk	Checks customer accounts to determine credit status based on past payment schedule, outstanding payables, and/or current status information from outside sources.
4. Check order department for current orders	Order clerk	Provides order status information to credit department as requested.
5. Sales department	Sales supervisor	Contacts existing or new customers regarding credit matters, terms of delivery, etc.

---

done. People, not paper, get jobs done. The road map is provided by the job description, but the success of the system ultimately depends on people.

3. Facilitate recruiting, training, and various personnel-human resource procedures. One of the first questions asked by a firm's recruiters is, "What kinds of people are we looking for?" The latter is answered by a job description. The focus of training or development must ultimately be the job for which the person is being trained or developed. This point seems so obvious that it shouldn't have to be stated, yet the aimlessness of some programs is truly amazing. But aside from defining objectives, the job description helps the manager determine more precisely the types (qualities, abilities, knowledge, knowhow, experience) of personnel who will be needed in the future—a matter substantially beyond the numbers issue.

SOCIOTECHNICAL SYSTEM CONCEPTS IN JOB ANALYSIS

Background

Two important developments that took place in the period from roughly 1950 to 1975 permitted a decidedly different approach to work design and analysis. First, research in England led to development of a concept of *sociotechnical* systems. This viewpoint approaches work activity as a combination of both technical (impersonal) and human elements. The combination of the two—and the dependency of one upon the other—accounts for work, performance, and output. This idea was subsequently advanced and applied in various countries and organizational environments (Davis and Taylor, 1972, and Robert Dubin, 1973). This systems concept is discussed in the next section.

Second, behavioral scientists developed a new motivational concept: *path-goal* expectancy theory. It presents a powerful new way to view motivation-performance which also can incorporate various other motivational theories. In the past the approach has often been overlooked but in recent years some managers have begun to see how useful it can be in job design.

EXHIBIT 6-5 The Sociotechnical Approach

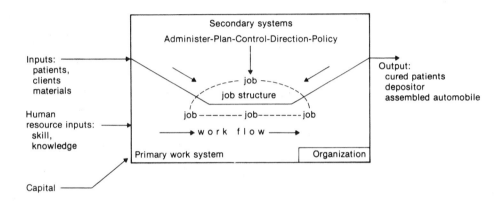

Secondary System

Primary systems are the essence of the central work function of an organization. But they don't function in a vacuum. They depend on various support systems. These secondary work systems (subsystems) support the primary system by providing supervision and technical knowhow. Secondary systems also assure that the other activities—for instance, maintenance functions such as accounting as opposed to production operations—are carried out. The functioning of the primary work system is critically dependent on working out the interactions and relationships within the primary system and between the primary and secondary subsystems.

General Perspective

In an increasingly complex world, the survival, growth and performance of organizations depend on the effective coordination of the technical and human components of work. Developing procedures that are technically efficient and also socially satisfying is the problem that the sociotechnical approach addresses.

Personnel is part of an organization's secondary system. Yet it provides an important link to the primary system. In addition to overseeing traditional maintenance functions, personnel directors are in a position to solve people-related problems, which can exert an enormous influence on the primary efforts of an organization. The personnel director might use the following sociotechnical guidelines for job analysis and design:

General guidelines

1. Design of an individual job requires specific recognition of its functional relation to other work activities.

2. Activities or functions that are part of the primary work system directly affect overall performance.

3. Members of support systems bolster the activities of the primary work system. They tend to emphasize nondirective administrative and coordinative efforts that reinforce and guide the main work function.

4. Interdependence, control, and coordination among system components stress communication processes and the role of information (amount, frequency, and quality).

Human considerations

5. Personal fulfillment of workers (for example, job satisfaction, valued goals) depends on intrinsic characteristics of jobs. Intrinsic refers to aspects of the job that give the opportunity to use one's abilities and skills.

6. Operational performance (e.g., items produced, number of people served), whether in qualitative or quantitative terms, is affected by social performance (people and the quality of their relations). The greater the number of human linkages (as in service organizations like hospitals, schools, banks, etc.), the greater the dependence of organizational performance on that of the human system.

Up to this point our discussion has been somewhat abstract. The remainder of this chapter will explore application of these new systems notions.

APPLICATIONS AND GUIDELINES

Developing Job Descriptions

Any discussion of job descriptions must be related to the job context. We will describe the "how to" with a real-life example of description development.

Jack Barnes, Manager at Acme Motors

One of our organization studies was concerned with the "development division" of a large automotive company. The group of particular interest within development was an engineering group charged with the design of new products. Jack Barnes, who managed the group (New Products Development), reported to the director of development and supervised some fifteen engineers and specialists. A manager can learn much by observing the procedures related to a particular job, department, or activity before interviewing organization members. Consequently, when we met Jack we already knew quite a bit about his department. His group was charged with designing new mechanical and electronic products that might eventually become part of Acme's vehicle or appliance lines. This was one of several similar groups, each specializing in some type of applied engineering science or supportive service.

Outside contacts.   In chatting with Jack it became apparent that he and various group members frequently had to contact other groups in the development department and occasionally consult outside suppliers and specialists. Jack had a Master's Degree in Mechanical Engineering from a leading school of technology, which, in conjunction with a Bachelor of Science in Electrical Engineering, equipped him quite well for the planning of design projects assigned to his group. The group head was also expected to provide technical assistance to group members and carry out liaison with various technical specialists.

Available knowledge.   One of the underlying reasons for initiation of the study was that department managers had almost no idea of the scope of services available from staff and other development managers. Even more to the point, the relationships (responsibilities and obligations) of one development group to another were poorly defined. The result was that, in some cases, extensive duplication and confusion, even bitterness, had led to conflicts that undercut the purposes of the department.

Preliminary description.   At the completion of our interviews with development personnel, including the director and individual engineers, as well as our review of minutes of meetings and records, we developed preliminary job descriptions and reviewed them with the job holders. Exhibit 6–6 is a version of the description for New Products (electro-mechanical) Development manager.

The job description in Exhibit 6–6 reflects several concepts described in this section:

1. *Identification of the job* and its positioning in the organization structure through the insertion of title, reports to, and supervises information.

2. *Overview of the job,* which highlights its key responsibilities, relationships, and the desired results.

3. *Major job responsibilities* in detail (and descending order of importance), drafted in action form and incorporating extensions of functional activity (plan, direct, coordinate, control, administer).

4. *Important working relationships* needed for job success, which fall outside the formal jurisdiction of the position.

EXHIBIT 6–6   Job Description, Acme Motors Corporation, Fairbanks Division

---

Title: New Products Development Manager, Electro-Mechanical
Reports to: Director of Development

1. Supervises
    Development engineers (10)
    Project engineer
    Cost engineer
    Junior engineer
    Analyst
    Secretary
    Clerk

2. Overview of job
    Plans and supervises the development and assessment of newer electro-mechanical products destined for automotive and appliance applications under the general direction of the director of development.

3. Major responsibilities
    a. Plans the overall development approach and assessment of new products applications assigned to the group by the director of development.
    b. Assigns group members to project teams based on availability of personnel and needed technical requirements.
    c. Provides technical assistance to team leaders in resolving technical problems or the use of newer development and analysis techniques.
    d. Reviews test results and cost analyses with the team head and cost engineer.

4. Major work relationships
    a. Works closely with the heads of the metallurgical group in resolving problems pertaining to such things as fatigue, wear, electrical properties, and thermal features.
    b. Works closely with the purchasing department in arranging for the acquisition of special test and development equipment budgeted for new products projects.

Preliminary Draft	March 14, 1976
Prepared by	F. Bishinski
Final Draft	
Prepared by	
Reviewed	
	dept. head
Reviewed	
	personnel
Issue date	

The job description in this exhibit is only a portion of the preliminary draft prepared for this position. As indicated earlier, this initial form is reviewed with the worker and various differences or inaccuracies reconciled. Notice that at the bottom of the form, preparation and date information is provided. Also, there is information indicating review by the job-holder's supervisor (director of development) and of personnel.

Control of Job Descriptions—And Some Important Benefits

A manager preparing a job description must act cautiously. A job description can influence a wide range of human resource activities, salary determination being only one of the more obvious ones. At the same time, procedural controls that result from job descriptions can produce substantial benefits. Two control procedures are commonly employed: review by the job-holder's supervisor and review by a personnel wage specialist or supervisor.

Supervisory review. A job description should be reviewed by the relevant supervisor before it is issued. This control assures that description of the job, its responsibilities, and scope of activities reflects the supervisor's idea of what the job involves. Importantly, preparation of the job description often provides a forum where supervisor and job holder work out philosophies or differences and secure common purposes. It has been our experience that this process of review including supervisor and job holder interaction is often a revelation to both.

Example—a "revelation." One of our work-analysis projects involved a manufacturing planning department. The manager of planning had always shown little interest in the "grubby" details of the work activity of the planning staff. One of the planning positions analyzed was production scheduler. When the manager was asked to review and comment on the first-draft job description, he wanted to beg off: "Why don't you initial it for me. I don't have time to shuffle through this paper work." But we persisted and he agreed to take it with him and look it over. In the evening the job analyst received a phone call from the manager (he couldn't wait until morning): "Where did you ever get such crazy ideas about that job? It's incredible!" With considerable reserve the analyst explained that the content to a large extent reflected activities performed for a long period of time. In fact, it was only the ingenuity in scheduling displayed by "manufacturing planning" that had kept the schedulers out of trouble.

At last the manager began to grasp the significance of the situation faced by the scheduler and was able to add constructively to the scheduler's understanding, responsibility and activity. But more important than the needed strengthening of the job was the understanding achieved by the planning manager. Additionally, the working relationships within the department improved enormously through the improved communication offered by the job description exercise.

Personnel review. A second element in control procedures is judging the potential impact of job modifications on salary/wage structure, (new) training, recruiting, and related matters. If a job description is modified and consequently upgraded, a higher salary will often be justified. At times, upgrading a position may cause distortions in job relationships or a "domino" effect involving a large number of jobs. Some supervisors use this strategy to force change: they request reevaluation of a position because of "significant new responsibilities"—as part of gamesmanship to justify a wage increase. Where descriptions involve union jobs, the final adjustments of job descriptions may well become a negotiated matter. Review by the personnel department can help to prevent or soften some of these possible negative impacts of new job descriptions.

Behavioral Considerations in Job Analysis

When job tasks are fairly clear, design is simpler. In a sense it consists of writing down what everyone already knows—and making certain that everyone knows the same things. But in many cases a true dilemma exists between the desire for specificity and the desire for flexibility. In the past, job designs were often created with the express purpose of creating predictability, a certainty of performance, and complete accountability of the worker. This approach, in the best tradition of the bureaucratic model, has serious behavioral consequences. Yet going to the other extreme of simply listing general job objectives can be highly ambiguous—and useless. What guidelines, then, should be established to resolve the degree of detail or prescription? Exhibit 6–7 suggests some of the major criteria to be considered under the behavioral and work accomplishment categories.

EXHIBIT 6–7 Behavioral and Work Accomplishment Criteria

Behavioral:
Clarify objectives of activities
Avoid ambiguity
Permit sense of involvement
Provide "sense of job" as a means to other accomplishments
Clarify what job holder will be held accountable for
Gain personal commitment
Show task as feasible, capable of accomplishment
Clarify job relationships, dependencies, sources of assistance
Enrich job to extent feasible, within economic and technological restraint
Convey sense of personal achievement
Afford degree of independence
Provide opportunity to exercise alternatives and degree of personal judgment

Work Accomplishment:
Secure performance, work objectives (quality, quantity)
Permit internal control of job activity
Minimize lost time in training at inception of new job
Provide sufficient detail to permit job evaluation, performance assessment
Assure wage/salary structure comparability

Jointly resolving behavioral and work needs. Clearly, many behavioral aspects of a job should be met at all times and don't involve any tradeoffs with productivity. On the other hand, accurately predicting performance may deny the worker any options or degree of freedom. In this regard the overused example of the auto assembly line applies. When jobs reach this point (little variety, paced by line), some say automate and get rid of the human operator.

It is difficult to give hard-and-fast rules regarding the degree of job specification because many organizational and personal variables are involved. Our orientation is toward a contingency approach that can meet the needs of a specific situation. Specification of individual, job, and environmental variables—including, for example, the philosophy of organization, traditions, and leadership—are helpful in deciding how much detail is necessary. Generalizations concerning behavioral considerations are:

1. Extend job options and exercise of choice where jobs involve higher levels of education or exercise of creativity. Provide more options for people with high achievement orientation (as often found among senior managers, designers, architects, and sales personnel). Recognize, however, that even professionals such as engineers require job structuring to minimize conflict or ambiguous instructions or objectives.

2. Provide detail and considerable specification where these are indispensable to job performance. Pursue personnel assignment policies that appropriately match job and job holder.

SUMMARY: JOB DESCRIPTIONS, JOB ANALYSIS

The job description is an important vehicle for carrying out a wide range of personnel–human resource functions. The success of these efforts is critically dependent on the quality of job analysis and job description efforts.

Job descriptions that emerge from job analysis and design have important behavioral implications for workers. A job description can encourage potential frustration or lively interest. It contains notions of formal authority which raise questions about the leadership effectiveness of managers, work groups, or others and about supervision in general. It also describes what the organization can expect. But what, in fact, does the organization get? When expectation and reality are reasonably alike, little more can be done through these descriptions or procedures.

EQUAL EMPLOYMENT AND NEWER ANALYSIS APPROACHES

Job Analysis and Equal Employment Opportunity (EEO)

An organization's problems with hiring procedures or meeting a federal complaint of discriminatory practices can be firmly linked to job analysis practices. Recruiting, hiring, promotion, job evaluation, or salary activities can only be as accurate as the job analysis. As the computer people say, "garbage in, garbage out." Job analysis must provide an accurate and realistic picture of job content, and it requires good judgment in filling jobs and in training and assessing the performance of job holders. Often times, JA requires the conversion of what a person does to more general descriptions involving education or various skills. For example, if a job questionnaire indicates that a receptionist spends a good part of the day at a front-office desk, a general description might be "sedentary" or "low level of physical effort required." If a planner has to deal regularly with scientists and engineers in order to prepare forecasts of technical products, the planner's analysis might emphasize the importance of education. A typical educational specification might be "a B.S. degree in science or engineering" or, perhaps, "knowledge of statistics and modern mathematics." It is in this translation from what a person *does* to what a person *needs* in order to be qualified that considerable problems arise related to EEO (see also Chapter 7).

Past Practice

In the past, job analysts, personnel officials, and managers frequently made generous translations of work requirements. They were often unconcerned about the precision of these translations, their potential racial bias, or (occasionally) even their accuracy.

For example, the job description for a receptionist might have called for "receives visitors" or "answers phones and talks with a wide range of people, including managers, professionals, and executives of other firms." The job specification for this item in the past (and until quite recently) indicated "a college degree" or "dresses well" or "has a good appearance." For a white society, color of skin, whether black or brown or yellow, has not always met the good appearance criterion. Also, are the only people who can meet these needs for talking to or receiving various people college trained?

Clearly, the long-standing assumptions of job analysis have not been questioned often enough. Racism and sexual bias have often been part of these job activities. However, increasing societal pressure has necessitated reexamination of existing practices. We've come a long way, but we still have a way to go.

Shift in Job Analysis Focus: Critical Incidents Approach

A direct outcome of equal employment considerations has been a shift in job analysis toward direct descriptors of job requirements. More emphasis is being placed on objective indicators of what people have to do to meet job and broader organizational requirements and less emphasis on indirect measures. This use of direct job descriptors is at the very heart of the *critical incidents approach*. A job is literally described in terms of the key elements of what people do—each hour, each day, each month. Obviously, similar and related items are combined into clusters of job functions. For example, a supermarket (canned goods) department head might perform recurring activities that include "preparing next month's warehouse order," "checking with the district sales manager on new canned goods promotions," and "planning the next quarter's manpower budget." These three items might be seen as related to the broader managerial functions of the department head's job, especially planning. Thus a critical-incidents approach in job analysis might list all of the activities under planning and then enumerate specific duties.

Critical-incidents procedures are a process of identification, comparison, classification, and simplification (where possible) of important job activities. A typical list of critical incidents may initially contain more than one hundred items and be ungraded and unclassified. Sentences are translated into tight statements or phrases of the type illustrated previously in this chapter. The final product of this effort reflects both grading for importance and classification into related groups. Perhaps six to eight groups or clusters will emerge and maybe a total of twenty-five to thirty incidents.

Example

An earlier example in the position description section concerned the job of manager in the New Products Development Department at Acme Motors.

Developing critical incidents. Discussions with the manager, review of his appointment book, and observation produced the following types of critical incidents:

1. "Talked to department members regarding their availability to work on a given project."
2. "Checked with department members on a new assignment to see if they had needed technical background."

These and related incidents led to the job responsibility:

3. "Assigns group members to project teams based on availability of personnel and needed technical requirements."

Equal employment considerations. Another job specification in the product development group (at one time) called for *male* engineers to work with customers under *field* conditions. These field conditions were especially difficult (weather, remote locations, poor roads). However, recently hired female engineers proved they could do quite well under the same conditions.

SUMMARY

Clearly, major changes have taken place in job analysis techniques. The tradition of the motion and time study (M&TS), initiated at the turn of the century, has been vastly altered, or even replaced, by behavioral research and applications. M&TS sought to identify the individual work elements in jobs, identifying steps that were critical to output or performance potential, and then reassemble them into a more efficient structure. This approach, the man-machine model, made the worker a junior partner in the work process. Taylor and others created the most efficient work pattern, with the worker as an adjunct to the machine and the work procedure, because they viewed the worker as the weak link in the production chain.

More contemporary job-analysis approaches have introduced various behavioral concepts into the workplace. Concepts related to motivation and leadership approaches (Chapter 9) and the growing emphasis on what people *do* (direct measures) versus emphasis on indirect measures of job function have become especially important.

The use of M&TS in conjunction with the systematic study of work for control or compensation led to the use of various descriptors for characterizing work accomplishment and energy expenditure. *Normal, standard,* and *average* were some of the terms employed in this regard.

Job descriptions are being applied to a wide range of organizational activities. Side-by-side inspections of job descriptions have assumed increasing importance in documenting both authority and work flow (system) relationships by emphasizing inconsistencies, gaps, or overlaps.

The final discussion covered an important contemporary issue in job analysis pertaining to discriminatory practices. The critical incidents approach is a job analysis technique that seeks to meet the deficiencies of indirect job specification factors through direct enumeration of requirements, thus reducing the chances that discriminatory and subjective biases can enter the specification.

REVIEW AND DISCUSSION QUESTIONS

1. Define *job analysis.*

2. Distinguish between *job analysis* and *job evaluation.*

3. Name some important personnel activities that are built on job-analysis studies.

4. What part does the sociotechnical perspective play in job analysis?

5. Distinguish between the following concepts employed in a time study of jobs: *standard time, average person, normal work pace.*

6. Why do learning functions (curves) seemingly vary between occupations and people?

7. What are the principal areas of job description information?

8. What is meant by the *interrelated character* of job descriptions?

9. What behavioral needs and work accomplishments, on balance, are to be satisfied by the job description?

10. What is the *critical incidents* approach? How does it relate to EEO practices?

11. The manager of a movie theater has many different tasks. At times he may have to deal with dissatisfied patrons, city inspectors, absent employees, unions (camera operator), popcorn suppliers, etc. For a movie theater you are familiar with,*
    a. Develop 15 to 20 *critical* (important) *incidents* in carrying out the manager's job.

    * To help you get started, one incident might be: orders supplies for ticket sales, candy counters, washrooms and maintenance.

b. Organize the incidents into similar groups (i.e., items that appear to be related).

c. Indicate the responsibilities suggested by your groups of incidents.

d. Explain how your incidents and groupings would help in meeting the needs of various personnel functions.

e. Indicate if any of your incidents involve particular people regarding sex, race, or type of education.

f. Develop a job description and job specification.

12. A job analyst in an insurance company developed a job description for a new position in the marketing department: "market analyst." Because of the press of time, the job analyst didn't have a chance to thoroughly check out his information with the employee or other department members. How should a manager view the information provided in this job description document? What are your assumptions?

13. For a number of years many companies have installed a wide variety of automated equipment. In the steel industry, many new processes were introduced. In the insurance industry many computers were installed. Speculate on the types of changes to be made in job descriptions and your assumptions for the following:

a. supervisors

b. workers (plant-steel; office-insurance).

14. Comment: The job specification for a "clerk-typist" position in an office calls for (among other things):

a. High school graduate plus at least one year of college

b. Neat appearance

c. Pleasant personality.

What assumptions were probably made by the person writing the specification?

15. A job analyst in a manufacturing plant carried out a motion and time study on an assembler's job and later set a rate on the job of 100 pieces per hour. This rate was to represent the normal, or standard, time—"good workers should make 125." Operators assigned to the job claimed that the rate was too tight and that they couldn't make out. Since this was a monetary incentive system, the worker's income was being penalized and they protested to the union. A union time study engineer then studied the job and reported that the rate was set incorrectly and really should have been 90 pieces per hour. If the rate was set incorrectly, what factors could have accounted for the situation? What difficulties exist in attempting to establish the right or wrong rate for this type of situation?

16. Select a job you are familiar with and develop a job description. Be sure to clarify your assumptions. Indicate how aspects of the description might change in other organizations.

BIBLIOGRAPHY

Baehr, Melany E. *A Factorial Framework for Job Description*. Chicago: University of Chicago Industrial Relations Center, 1967.

Davis, Louis. "The Coming Crisis for Productive Management: Technological Organization." *International Journal of Production Research* 1 (1971).

Davis, Louis, and James C. Taylor, eds. *Design of Jobs.* Middlesex, England: Penguin, 1972.

Dickman, R. A. *Handbook for Supporting Staff, Job Analysis and Job Evaluation.* Baltimore: Johns Hopkins Press, 1971.

Dubin, Robert, ed. *Handbook of Work, Organization and Society,* Chicago: Rand-McNally, 1973.

Fine, Sidney, and Wretha W. Wiley. *An Introduction to Functional Job Analysis.* Kalamazoo, Mich.: W. E. Upjohn Institute for Employment Research, 1971.

_____. "Functional Job Analysis Scales." Kalamazoo, Mich.: W. E. Upjohn Foundation for Employment Research, 1973.

Hemphill, J. K. *Dimensions of Executive Positions.* Columbus: Ohio State University, 1960.

Holley, William H. "Effect of Modifying Job Design to Employ the Hard Core Jobless." *Personnel Journal* 50 (April 1971):288–92.

House, Robert, Allen Filley, and Steven Kerr. "Relation of Leader Consideration and Initiating Structure to Raid D Subordinate Satisfaction." *Administrative Science Quarterly* 16, 1 (March 1971):19–30.

McCormick, Ernest J., P. R. Jeanneret, and R. C. Meecham. *"The Development and Background of the Position Analysis Questionnaire PAQ."* West Lafayette, Ind.: Purdue University, Occupational Center, 1969.

_____. "The PAQ." *Journal of Applied Psychology* (August 1972).

Price, Charlton R. "New Directions in the World of Work." Kalamazoo, Mich.: W. E. Upjohn Institute for Employment Research, 1971.

United States Department of Labor. *Handbook for Analyzing Jobs.* Washington, D.C.: U.S. Government Printing Office, 1972.

Chapter 7

RECRUITING
AND SELECTION

LEARNING OBJECTIVES

After studying this chapter and exercises, the reader should be able to:
Define the elements of an effective recruiting and selection system
Discuss the problems and benefits of government regulations in the areas
of affirmative action and equal employment opportunity
Conduct an effective employment interview
Point out the key advantages and disadvantages of important selection tools
Explain the relationships among recruiting, evaluation, and compensation
as components of a total personnel system.

KEY TERMS AND CONCEPTS

weighted application blank
structured interview
affirmative action
Equal Employment Opportunity
    Act of 1972
Civil Rights Act of 1964
Griggs v. *Duke Power* case
Age Discrimination in Employ-
    ment Act of 1967
cooperative education program
internship

computerized selection models
labor inventory communication
    system
fair employment practice
psychological testing
test validation
personality test
interest tests
achievement test
job interview
reference letter

PREVIEW

A productive work force and good employee relations are based to a large extent on recruiting and selection procedures. The effects of a good hiring decision—and a bad one—can often be felt years later. This chapter will discuss the following topics, which can establish sound recruiting and selection practices:

1. The importance of accurate and realistic job descriptions.
2. The legal aspects of recruiting.
3. New employee selection methods and techniques.
4. Effective use of applications and testing methods.
5. Effective interviewing techniques.

EXHIBIT 7-1   Recruiting and Selection as Part of the Total Human Resource System

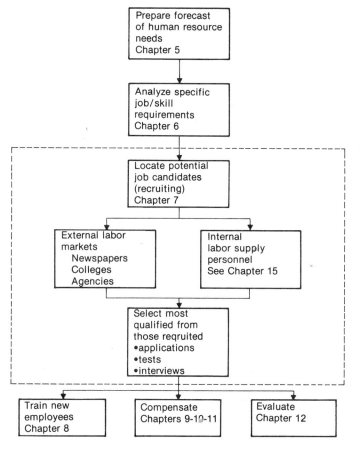

RECRUITING

Every organization faces the problem of recruiting applicants and then selecting actual employees from among those applicants. But in the seventies, personnel managers and recruiters are finding that they face new problems as well. Many recruiters are not presenting a realistic picture of their company to job seekers. Consequently, those finally selected to fill a position are often surprised and unhappy when they find themselves with more—or less—than they bargained for. Turnover percentages are high at a time when training costs have been pushed to new levels by the demands of specialization and complexity. Recruiters and personnel officers must wrestle with legal and ethical problems caused by new legislation mandating equal employment for minority group members and for both sexes. The burden of proof rests more and more on the organization: it must prove that it has complied with new laws; lawmakers don't have to prove the organization delinquent.

Managers have reacted to this new climate in many different ways. For example, they have compiled overviews of jobs to give job seekers a better idea of what will be expected of them. They have used studies of compensation in order to apply variable methods of payment, including fringe and benefit packages and, in some cases, combinations of salary and benefits suited to the potential employee's desires.

Attracting Good Candidates

Who are good candidates and how does an organization attract them? Recruiters have been the personnel departments' first-line troops, talking to potential employees for the first time and presenting their companies to mostly uninformed prospects. But with high turnover rates—a high percentage of new employees leave their jobs within six months to a year—organizations have begun to question long-standing assumptions about recruiting, training, and subsequent personnel procedures.

Many organizations have placed too much emphasis on training potential of employees. This philosophy has tended (consciously or unconsciously) to produce a "cannon fodder" approach—"give me a body with a few brains and I'll fit it into the program." Because managers have tended to view technology as the "productive" element—and employees as mere extensions of that technology—they have tended to train "anyone" to do the job and not put enough emphasis on the worker's interests and potential contributions. The product of this attitude has sometimes approached trying to fit a size twelve foot into a size nine shoe. And, in more and more instances, when the manager puts down his shoehorn for a moment, the foot takes a walk.

On the other hand, organizations spend precious little time training their own recruiters. In a study of recruiting practices (Drake *et al.*, 1973), 195 responding firms indicated that only 41 percent evaluated their recruiters and that only 51 percent had training programs for campus interviewers, even though the interview was used primarily to screen college graduates for the second interview. Three out of four companies responding felt that the interview carries more weight than the applicant's grades or resume. Campus interviewers rely on their own judgment to identify candidates for second interviews and their opinions have a great deal of influence on the final decision to hire or reject. Campus interviewers attempt to evaluate such hard-to-measure areas as ambition, interpersonal skills, communication ability, creativity, and fit with the organization. A great deal of emphasis is placed upon having a "congenial personality."

Realism in Recruiting

As organizations face the problems of employee disenchantment leading to poor work and a high turnover among recently trained and highly skilled personnel, the difficulty caused by the potential employee's picture of what his or her job will be like becomes increasingly clear. Numerous studies have shown that the organization and the job seeker must leave their first meeting with a realistic picture of the other.

One technique, "realistic job previews," has begun to appear as a significant part of the initial meeting (Wanous, 1975). These job previews have been designed to give the applicant a more realistic picture of what he or she would face on the job. They may include candid, unrehearsed films of an actual department in operation or interviews with current employees. The key approach to these films is they must not be structured *only* to make the company look good. Before the use of realistic job previews, the philosophy seemed to be to present the company as "one happy family," a place where the employee would find peace and happiness while seeking greater rewards. But recruiters are now aware that the best possible new employee is not only one who has the capability to perform as needed but also one who will stay with the company long enough to return a fair value for training. Effective recruiters now consider it an absolute necessity that the new employee have a realistic picture of his or her new position. Of course, a firm may lose some applicants who are "turned off" by what they suddenly discover to be the reality of the situation, but they have only lost someone they would likely lose later, after they had invested a sizable amount of money and effort in training.

In addition to realistic job previews, the employee should have a precise description of the job itself. When a phrase such as "a sharp individual" is replaced with a description of the potential employee as "one who must be able to work quickly and accurately with large amounts of figures and calculations in the following fields . . . ," the recruiter has a more precise knowledge of the task—and so will the applicant.

In the early 1970s, U.S. Army Intelligence refined its job-needs description from "an individual of high character and good intelligence with better than average ability to communicate" to "a college graduate in liberal arts who has previously demonstrated the ability to learn a new language, has previously demonstrated outstanding fluency and command of both written and spoken English, and can type at least forty words per minute." Field work had proven precisely what the real job required. The new job description provided recruiters a better chance of filling the job with potentially effective agents.

Many recruiting professionals have also suggested a better and tighter use of such old standbys as the application blank, structured interviews, and personal data forms. Interviewers themselves must be taught to record their exact impressions of an individual both from the application form and from what has verbally crossed the table between them (Kessler, 1975). However, some of these procedures are subject to biases of the evaluator and the use of application forms has brought out new, potentially dangerous problems. Many application forms ask questions that are patently illegal under new legislation or are so demanding that they serve to keep worthy applicants away rather than help usher them in (Fox, 1975).

Legal Aspects of Recruiting

Some of the legal problems now confronting recruiters and personnel officers seem staggering. The requirements of recruiting a percentage of minority group members and women for positions that have seldom been filled by these people in the past have brought forth the following suggestions: 1) a company truly interested in fulfilling the new law must not attempt to restructure a job so that it is more suited to a male employee; 2) the firm must have some proof that theirs is an organization where the employee really will have a fair chance to succeed (specifically, the use of success stories should be considered); 3) the organization must make every attempt to advertise in minority magazines or in special group literature (Straka, 1975; Sharf, 1975; Gery, 1974).

The key is that the firm must assume that it has the responsibility to seek out the potential applicants who would fill its needs. Companies cannot simply wait for the special applicants to come to them. In many fields, the latter option would be downright impossible, as the supply of female, black engineers, for instance, is very limited.

Affirmative Action and Equal Employment Opportunity

One of the first equal opportunity bills proposed in Congress was introduced in February 1943, but two decades passed before decisive action was taken by the federal government to guarantee employment opportunity without regard to race, color, religion, age, creed, sex, or national origin. Title VII of the Civil Rights Act of 1964 and the Equal Employment Opportunity Act of 1972 are important events in the history of fair employment practices. The purpose of this section is to briefly outline the contents and implications of these events for the field of personnel management.

On June 11, 1963, President Kennedy announced in a televised conference that he would seek Civil Rights legislation from the Eighty-Eighth Congress. On July 2, 1964, after bitter battles in both houses of Congress, President Johnson signed the bill into law. This original law was modified by the Equal Employment Opportunity Act of 1972.

These acts have broad coverage and apply to any activity, business, or industry in which a labor dispute would hinder or obstruct commerce or the free flow of commerce and include any activity or industry affecting commerce. The acts originally applied to organizations employing at least fifteen persons on each working day in each of twenty or more calendar weeks in the current or preceding calendar year. Title VII was amended in 1972. It now covers state and local governments, governmental agencies, political subdivisions and departments, and agencies of the District of Columbia. Senators Ervin and Allen introduced an amendment that provided an exemption for elected officials, their personal assistants, and their immediate advisers. An excellent guidebook for personnel administrators concerned about these important pieces of legislation is the *Equal Employment Opportunity Act of 1972* (Bureau of National Affairs, Inc., 1973).

Guidelines for Equal Employment Opportunity Implementation

1. It is unlawful for an employer to fail or refuse to hire, or discharge, any individual or otherwise discriminate against any individual with respect to compensation, conditions, or privileges of employment because of race, color, religion, sex, age, or national origin. This applies to applicants for employment as well as current employees.

2. Employers may not limit, segregate, or classify employees in such a way

that would deprive them of employment opportunities because of race, color, age, religion, sex, or national origin.

3. Discrimination is permitted when those being discriminated against are members of the Communist Party or a Communist-front organization.

4. Discrimination is permitted when religion, sex, or national origin is a bona fide occupational qualification reasonably necessary to the normal operation of the organization, such as with teaching faculty in a Catholic seminary for training priests.

5. Discrimination is permitted when the employer is subject to a government security program and the persons involved do not have security clearance.

6. A business operating on or near an Indian reservation may accord preferential treatment to Indians.

7. Differentiations in pay based on sex are authorized under the provisions of the Equal Pay Act of 1963 where the jobs performed are not equal.

8. Nothing in the law shall be interpreted to require an employer or training program to grant preferential treatment to any individual or group because of an imbalance that may exist with respect to the total number or percentage of persons of any race, color, religion, sex, or national origin already implied. Affirmative action plans for government construction and manufacturing contractors, however, often require the establishment of goals for employment quotas.

9. All regulations apply to labor unions and employment agencies.

10. The EEOC now has the power to file action in a federal district court if it is unable to eliminate alleged unlawful employment practices by the informal methods of conference, conciliation, and persuasion.

11. Employment tests may be used if it can be proven that they are related to the job or promotion sought by the individual. Tests should be validated for each company but need be validated at only one location of a multioperation firm where no significant differences exist between units, jobs, and applicant populations at the various locations. In cases where validation is "technically impossible," such as in those instances where the size of the test group is inadequate, the employer may rely on validity studies conducted by other organizations. Professional supervision of testing activities will not substitute for evidence of validation.

12. The Age Discrimination in Employment Act of 1967 precludes discrimination against persons between ages of 40 and 65, with enforcement of the act assigned to the Deparment of Labor.

13. No discriminatory statements may be included in any advertisements for job opportunities.

Equal Employment Opportunity: Practical Examples

The following examples give an idea of the complexity of the Civil Rights Act and the nature of recent court decisions. It should be noted that judges interpret the law differently, and decisions are often reversed in higher courts.

A U.S. Court of Appeals held that an employer violated Title VII by refusing to hire a black job applicant because of his arrest record. The court's position was that blacks are arrested substantially more frequently than whites; thus a hiring policy that takes arrests into account is discriminatory against blacks. The same rule would not apply to convictions. Additionally, a federal district court ruled that an employer may violate Title VII by discharging a minority-group employee for incurring a number of wage garnishments, stating that such employees are more subject to garnishments than nonminorities.

In most cases employers may have no obligation to accommodate the work schedule to employees' religious beliefs. A district court upheld the decision supporting Reynolds Metals discharge of an employee who refused to work on Sunday because of religious beliefs. In a case involving the New York act, a court affirmed the discharge of an employee who refused to get rid of his beard because of religious belief.

Hiring policies followed by airlines were the subject of two important decisions. One held that female sex is not a bona fide occupational qualification for the job of flight cabin attendant. Another held that an airline's policy that stewardesses must be single is unlawful where no other female employees were subject to the policy and there was no policy restricting employment to single male stewards. Another court ruled it illegal to fire a female employee because she is pregnant and unmarried.

In general, a court has ruled it illegal to reject women on the basis of general assumptions regarding physical capabilities. Women must be judged as individuals and may be excluded from a job only after showing individual incapacity. In the state of Ohio, however, statutes excluding women from working more than forty-eight hours a week, lifting more than twenty-five pounds, and not being furnished seats when not engaged in active work were held contrary to Title VII and therefore invalid.

In this section we have provided an overview of the effect of government legislation on recruiting and selection processes. Table 7–1 summarizes lawful and unlawful inquiries that may be made of job applicants prior to hiring. Subsequent sections will deal with tools to be applied to the selection of likely candidates with emphasis on application blanks, testing, and interviews. A tool of many purposes, the assessment center, is also used for selection but is discussed in the chapter on performance appraisal.

RECRUITING ADVICE FOR JOB APPLICANTS

Recruiting with Flexible Benefits

Recruiting and compensation are closely related—a prospective employee seeks a job in return for compensation *of some sort*. Some organizations have now begun to use a flexible combination of benefits that allows the potential employee to structure his or her own type of compensation plan. For instance, an employee might have the option of taking a larger salary with few benefits, a small salary with many benefits, or some combination of the two. Harris (1975) has shown that fringe benefits, if used in a flexible program, can be a deciding factor in the job applicant's decision to join the firm.

What the Job Applicant Should Know about a Prospective Employer

Many college graduates begin their careers on the wrong foot, making a serious mistake: they fail to get sufficient information about their first employer. People who take a position with an organization that doesn't fit their personality and background risk their future. Table 7–2 contains a listing of questions that should be answered before accepting a position, and it is important to do one's homework before the actual job interview. Answers to questions are not difficult to obtain. A number of sources—acquaintances or school alumni who work with the organization, company brochures and annual reports, discussions with others who may have interviewed with the same company—will provide information a candidate needs to make an informed decision.

EMPLOYEE SELECTION

Traditionally, personnel selection processes consist of a series of obstacles: initial application blank screening, personal interviews, reference checks, physical examination, and perhaps some form of psychological testing. An applicant must hurdle each of these in order to qualify for a particular position. While methods vary, the objective of the selection process is fairly consistent: to determine whether an applicant meets the qualifications for a specific job and to choose the applicant who is most likely to perform well in that job.

The development, refinement, and updating of decision rules to use during the selection process is a continuing problem for personnel management, a problem not immune to halo, bias, inconsistency, and other errors of commission and omission. The more scientific of the traditional selection procedures begin with the identification of statistical relationships between predictor and criterion measures for a sample of employees. The manager forms a decision rule based on the relationship of predictor and criterion and then cross-validates the rule for a second sample of workers. The *predictor* may be a single score or a combination of scores on a battery of psychological tests, while the *criterion* usually is some measure of job performance. These terms are more fully defined in the following section.

According to Mahoney (1965), this approach has several shortcomings. First, it fails to consider the actual probability of success or failure because it assumes that both probabilities are equal (one-half). It also does not show the cost consequences of selection decisions. For example, under tight labor market conditions, a personnel director may be willing to select an applicant whose probability of succeeding in a position is only 70 percent if the costs of recruiting a second candidate are high, say $2,000 or more.

184

TABLE 7-1 Questioning Applicants for Employment: a Guide for Application Forms and Selection Interviews*

Inquires before hiring	Lawful	Unlawful
1. Name	Name.	Inquiry into any title which indicates race, color, religion, sex, national origin or ancestry.
2. Address	Inquiry into place and length of current and previous addresses.	Specific inquiry into foreign addresses which would indicate national origin.
3. Age	A. Request proof of age in form of work permit issued by school authorities. B. Require proof of age by birth certificate after hiring.	Require birth certificate or baptismal record before hiring.
4. Birthplace or national origin		A. Any inquiry into place of birth. B. Any inquiry into place of birth of parents, grandparents, or spouse. C. Any other inquiry into national origin.
5. Race or color		Any inquiry which would indicate race or color.
6. Sex		Any inquiry which would indicate sex.
7. Religion/creed		A. Any inquiry to indicate or identify denomination or customs. B. May not be told this is a Protestant (Catholic or Jewish) organization. C. Request pastor's recommendation or reference.
8. Citizenship	A. Whether a U.S. citizen. B. If not, whether intends to become one. C. If U.S. residence is legal. D. If spouse is citizen. E. Require proof of citizenship after being hired.	A. If native born or naturalized. B. Proof of citizenship before hiring. C. Whether parents or spouse are native-born, or naturalized.
9. Photographs	May be required after hiring for identification purposes.	Request photograph before hiring.
10. Education	A. Inquiry into what academic, professional or vocational schools attended.	A. Any inquiry asking specifically the nationality, racial or religious affiliation of a school.

	Acceptable	Unacceptable
	B. Inquiry into language skills, such as reading and writing of foreign languages.	B. Inquiry as to what is mother tongue or how foreign language ability was acquired, unless necessary for job.
11. Relatives	Inquiry into name, relationship and address of person to be notified in case of emergency.	Any inquiry about a relative which is unlawful.
12. Organization	A. Inquiry into organization memberships, excluding any organization, the name or character of which indicates the race, color, religion, sex, national origin or ancestry of its members. B. What offices are held, if any.	Inquiry into all clubs and organizations where membership is held.
13. Military service	A. Inquiry into service in U.S. Armed Forces. B. Rank attained. C. Which branch of service. D. Require military discharge certificate after being hired.	A. Inquiry into military service in armed service of any country but U.S. B. Request military service records.
14. Work schedule	Inquiry into willingness to work required work schedule.	Any inquiry into willingness to work any particular religious holiday.
15. Other qualifications	Any question that has direct reflection on the job applied for.	Any non-job related inquiry that may present information permitting unlawful discrimination.
16. References	General personal and work references not relating to race, color, religion, sex, national origin or ancestry.	Request references specifically from clergy or any other persons who might reflect race, color, religion, sex, national origin or ancestry of applicant.

1. Employers acting under approved Affirmative Action Programs or acting under orders of Equal Employment law enforcement agencies of federal, state, or local governments may be exempt from some of the prohibited inquiries listed above only to the extent that these inquiries are required by such programs, agreements or orders.

2. Federal Defense Contracts: Employers having Federal defense contracts are exempt to the extent that otherwise prohibited inquiries are required by Federal Law for security purposes.

3. Any inquiry is forbidden which, although not specifically listed among the above, is designed to elicit information as to race, color, religion, sex, national origin or ancestry in violation of the law.

* These guidelines were prepared and distributed in 1974 by the Ohio Civil Rights Commission.

Improving the Accuracy of the Selection Process

Psychology has provided methods for increasing the rate of success in selecting job applicants by developing standard observation techniques. These standardized observations enable managers to make systematic comparisons and evaluations and guard against poor memories. Schein, an organizational psychologist, provides an excellent summary of the steps required to improve the accuracy of selection (1970).

TABLE 7–2   Questions to Answer Before Accepting a Position

Promotion criteria
    Does the organization use a formal evaluation system?
    How often is a person evaluated?
    What are the major criteria upon which a person is evaluated?
    Are evaluations discussed with persons being evaluated?
    Is career counseling available?
    Does the organization encourage publication in professional journals?

Professional development
    Does the organization offer a formal training program?
    If so, what is the nature and duration of the program?
    Is there any formal training in computers and information systems?
    Does the organization support travel to professional meetings?
    Is there any form of tuition refund program for college degree programs? for continuing
        education nondegree programs?
    What type of responsibility is offered during the first year on the job?

Organizational background
    What are the objectives of the organization?
    What has been the general trend in sales, growth, employment, earnings, research expenditures, and leverage (i.e., debt/equity)?
    What universities have senior officers attended?
    What is the nature of the organization's affirmative action program?
    What is the opportunity for women in management?
    How many persons left the staff during the past year? (compute turnover)
    What is the absentee rate for hourly personnel? Is it above the average for the industry?

Financial considerations (to be discussed and considered last)
    What are normal working hours? Is overtime pay granted for staff?
    Is overnight travel required? What is reimbursement policy?
    Is there a profit sharing plan?
    Is retirement plan vested?
    Vacation policy? Hospitalization? Life insurance?
    What would starting salary be?

---

1. *Develop criteria.* Jobs to be filled must be accurately described to the person responsible for selection. Written job descriptions (Chapter 6) are very useful in this regard. It is important that actual performance on the jobs be measurable in some way. This measure of job performance is known as the *criterion variable.*

2. *Identify predictor variables.* The job applicants must then be observed on variables that are considered (hypothesized) good predictors of job performance.

3. *Obtain sufficient candidates to ensure adequate variation on predictors.* An organization usually wants to get the best person for the job. However, test scores at best are relative measures. They are abstractions that must be related to the needs of the moment—what is available—to provide some kind of comparability, so that a manager can decide just how good a prospect is and separate the "ideal" from the "real" needs of the job.

An example will illustrate two aspects of this issue. A test on *basic* engineering or mathematical concepts for nuclear engineering candidates probably would not be very useful. Any candidate who is remotely qualified for a position in nuclear engineering undoubtedly would score well. Anyone who scored poorly probably would have been screened out at an earlier stage. Tests to determine spatial aptitude, design ability, and creativity probably would give a manager a better basis for comparing candidates.

A good variation of predictors also helps deal with a practical problem. Department heads understandably want the best candidate they can get—that one candidate in a million who scores 100 percent. In most cases, 85 or 90 percent is perfectably acceptable if other indications are good. If the personnel director has data that show that a particular candidate is the best among available talent and is an attractive employee in other ways, the department head can make an intelligent and realistic decision.

4. *Hire a group of applicants who have not been "selected."* Even though the applicants have been subjected to various predictors such as tests, assessment center, interviews, reference check, or others, some applicants should be hired without consideration of their scores on any predictor variable. This "random" procedure serves as a check on selection decisions based on formal procedures.

5. *Evaluate the applicants' job performance.* Accurate measures of job performance are needed in order to correlate these criteria with predictor scores obtained prior to the hiring of the applicants.

6. *Correlate scores on predictor variables with job performance.* Predictors can be wrong and the only way of knowing which ones are right and which ones aren't is by checking them. The manager can check the accuracy of a predictor by correlating it with performance. If the correlation is not significant, other predictors must be tried. If a meaningful correlation between predictor and criterion is established, it is possible to improve the accuracy of the selection process by hiring future applicants who score similarly to those of the unselected group who actually did well on the job.

As scientific as it might seem, there are several problems with this approach. For many types of jobs it is difficult to obtain accurate measures of performance. This is especially true at managerial and professional levels. For other jobs it is quite difficult to locate predictors. Also, if the number of applicants is less than or nearly equal to the number of open positions (i.e., the selection ratio is low), it does not pay to invest in the development of expensive selection procedures.

The selection procedure outlined in this section depends on good predictors. Regardless of the logic (i.e., face validity) of the predictor or the "feeling" of confidence the selectors have, if the predictor does not correlate with the job performance criterion, it will not improve the existing selection method. The correlation obtained between predictor and criterion is called the *validity of the predictor,* its capacity to predict what it is supposed to predict: successful job performance. Guion (1965) has developed tables of validity and selection ratios that help a manager predict how much improvement can be expected from use of selection tools (predictors).

General Weakness of Selection Methods

The development of useful selection procedures is difficult at best. Besides difficulty involved in designing valid predictors, there are several other roadblocks to success. Jobs are becoming more complex and interdependent, making it difficult to write good job descriptions and accurately measure performance. The use of computer technology and information-processing systems for all kinds of work, both "physical" and "mental" has increased enormously in the last thirty years. It has led to a great deal of complexity, especially at managerial levels. These changes have made correlation difficult. Correlations between short-run and long-run performance by individuals in a particular position are generally low even though criteria applied to job performance tend to be short run. Thus, what may predict successful job performance in the short run may not predict success in the long run.

Computer Models for Improving the Selection Process

The development of analytical models and more comprehensive techniques for personnel decision making have emphasized the importance of personnel records and other data as inputs to selection decisions. This is especially true in large organizations where the mass of data makes computer storage an attractive alternative to drawer upon drawer of manila file folders.

Personnel information systems become a real possibility as management creates new applications for its human resource data. For instance, a system can improve planning by providing an immediate picture of the corporation's manpower resources; in selection, the computer information system permits managers to consider all logical candidates within the corporation as the first step in filling a position. The same code numbers are used in accounting and personnel, so these departments can perform integrated analyses. The data base can be used to work out consistent procedures by storing corporate policy documents on tape for retrieval by a key-word index. A five-year projection of corporate needs for personnel in such areas as engineering, mathematics, and physical sciences is possible for various corporate growth rates. A thorough discussion and examples of personnel management information systems are provided in Chapter 15.

Information systems have been used in many other ways. Personal history data have been found to be very valuable in predicting certain criteria of job success for clerical and sales positions. Studies have shown that such data can be weighted (given a relative value) successfully for predictive use for one or a variety of jobs (Kirchner, 1957). Once a personnel data base is computerized, application blank weights can be updated continuously to reflect changes in organizational goals, labor supply, supervision, product, and so forth. Such updating can be achieved with reasonable cost since data are available in the computer memory and the same program can be applied each time an update is made.

Managers can use a computer-assisted selection procedure to balance recruiting costs against misclassification costs. (Misclassification costs are those opportunity costs associated with the selection of a candidate who subsequently fails to perform on the job and rejecting a candidate who would, in fact, have succeeded in a particular position.) The relative costs of the two types of selection errors can be allowed to vary with the situation. For example, if training costs are much higher than recruiting costs, a recruiter will want to use a selection decision rule that places more weight on the probability of rejecting a potentially successful candidate than on the probability of accepting an unsuccessful one. Prior to the availability of the computerized personnel data base, these types of calculations were too costly and tedious to make.

Large-Scale Automation of Selection Decisions

A number of independent agencies have been established to aid employers in their recruiting and selection processes (Huber, 1969). The primary function of such agencies (e.g., Career-Ways System, Comp-U-Job, Graduate Resume Accumulation and Distribution) is to identify potentially compatible applicant-employer pairs (i.e., there is a good chance that the recruit accepts a job offer).

Data on the qualifications of each candidate who volunteers to join the system are stored in the computer. The data base also lists employers' requirements, job characteristics, and candidates' job preferences. Upon request from either the candidate or employer, a computer search is made for all combinations that satisfy the minimum requirements of both parties. Those that match are printed and the employer and candidate are encouraged to establish a time for an interview. Some systems provide additional information via television screen, on-line video terminals, in computer jargon.

Sophistication has been added to this matching process in some systems, through computation of a relative ranking of potential candidate-employer pairs. The Labor Inventory Communication System (LINCS) of the California Department of Employment uses a "key word" approach that compares job requirements with candidate qualifications. A count is made of the number of key words that appear in both requirements and qualifications (hits), and pairings are printed in rank order from highest to lowest number of hits.

The computer does not make the actual selection decisions; it only presents selected information and recommendations for the candidate and the employer to consider. Holt (1969) proposes a computer-aided model that identifies those interview situations that will tend to maximize expected gains in labor productivity and job satisfaction for all employers and job candidates participating in the labor market. The primary objective of including the computer in this particular selection model is to provide a better distribution of effort between person and machine, so that both the employer and the job candidate can concentrate time-consuming interviews on a relatively small number of promising applicants and vacancies. Holt suggests that a good computer-generated list would result in better selections measured by increased productivity, job satisfaction, and job tenure. Needless to say, measures of productivity and satisfaction present a complex, subjective problem, which goes beyond the scope of this book. For our purpose it is sufficient to understand that large-scale selection problems are being studied by researchers in various disciplines. But without the aid of the computer, little progress can be made in improving traditional selection methods.

The reader may question the reliability and validity of computerized approaches to employee selection. It is true that personal contact between potential employer and applicant yields valuable information not contained in mechanized storage. Such factors as facial expressions, photographs, voice intonations, firmness of handshake, and width of tie tell something about an applicant. However, these factors also tend to bias some interviewers and often override the job applicant's other qualifications.

The authors are not suggesting that machines totally replace human contact in personnel selection. But at least during the initial screening phases, the computer can be much less biased toward subjective characteristics and more likely to select on the basis of qualifications (objective criteria). Given consistent inputs, the machine will be reliable; that is, the outputs will be consistent, which generally is not true for human decision processes. For example, research evidence (Mayfield, 1964) points to the lack of both reliability and validity in the personal interview process. And Meehl (1954), found that in nineteen of twenty studies, predictions based on statistical approaches were more effective than those based upon the personal judgment of selection interviewers.

APPLICATION BLANKS

Contents

The most widely used written selection tool is the application blank. Items included on the blank vary from organization to organization, but generally include routine biographical data, formal education, criminal offenses resulting in convictions, and work experience, including job title and major duties. The blanks should contain requests for pertinent information only since applicants may be discouraged by the length of time required to provide much of the same information already contained in the resume. Exhibit 7–2 provides a typical example of application blank design.

When seeking background information, care should be taken not to request data in violation of federal or state equal employment practices legislation.

It may seem incredible, but in 1976 a national firm still had a place on its application for "wife's name." Since there was no corresponding request for "husband's name," it could only be assumed that the intent to discriminate existed. The company has since changed the blank to read "spouse's name."

Weighting

Some firms weight the items on application blanks and score job applicants based on their responses. The manager relates specific items on the blank to some criterion of job success (e.g., job tenure, performance index, salary increments). The basis for weighting application blanks is research evidence that indicates past behavior. Experience, acquired habits, and achievements predict future behavior. For example, Buel (1972) concludes that "there is great utility and validity to biographical information when tailored to fit organization and job."

In order to establish the validity of a weighted application blank, two samples should be taken. The first sample involves many different items on a lengthy questionnaire. This information is then correlated to some measure of job performance, such as sales ability, productivity, tenure, or promotability. Since all of the items on the long questionnaire generally do not correlate, a shortened version is constructed using only the valid items. The second sample, different from the first, uses the shortened version and establishes total score validity for the job.

Three studies (Buel, 1972) relate biographical scores and performance ratings for 122 engineering salesmen, 100 production supervisors, and 175 field representatives. In all cases, biographical scores were related to job performance, both with respect to score magnitude and the number of individuals falling into particular score ranges.

A variety of techniques exists for weighting application blanks (Guion, 1965). One method uses a sample of present employees that is divided into high and low groups based on a criterion such as job performance. Previously completed application blanks are then examined to determine how many in the low and high groups selected each alternative on a given item. For example, if 70 percent of married salespersons were in the high group, while 20 percent of divorced salespersons were in the high group and 30 percent of single salespersons were in the high group, then the response married might receive a weight of 7, divorced a weight of 2, and single a weight of 3.

In a similar manner, all categories can be weighted with an overall score attached to a particular application blank. After weights are developed for a sample, they should be cross-validated with another sample taken from the same category of employee (e.g., sales personnel).

PSYCHOLOGICAL TESTING

Effective participation in modern work and society requires intellectual skills learned during the formal education process. Important among these skills are verbal fluency, reading comprehension, and mathematical comprehension that

EXHIBIT 7-2

APPLICATION FOR SALARIED EMPLOYMENT

COLONIAL HOSPITAL IS AN EQUAL OPPORTUNITY EMPLOYER

NAME IN FULL _____

(LAST)   (FIRST)   (MIDDLE)   (MAIDEN NAME)

POSITION DESIRED: FIRST CHOICE _____

SECOND CHOICE _____   YEARS EXPERIENCE _____

EMPLOYMENT: PERMANENT ____ TEMPORARY ____ SUMMER ____ DATE AVAILABLE TO START WORK _____   YEARS EXPERIENCE _____

WILLING TO WORK ANY hours? YES ____ NO ____

PERSONAL DATA

PRESENT
ADDRESS _____

(STREET ADDRESS)   (CITY)   (STATE)   (ZIP CODE)   TELEPHONE NO. _____

PERMANENT
ADDRESS _____

(STREET ADDRESS)   (CITY)   (STATE)   (ZIP CODE)   TELEPHONE NO. _____

SOCIAL
SECURITY NO. _____

ARE YOU A CITIZEN OF
THE UNITED STATES? _____ IF YOU ARE NOT A U.S. CITIZEN, DO YOU HAVE THE LEGAL RIGHT TO REMAIN PERMANENTLY IN THE U.S.? _____

DO YOU HAVE ANY PHYSICAL ____ DEFECTS? ____ EXPLAIN _____

HAVE YOU EVER RECEIVED WORKMEN'S COMPENSATION? ____ WHEN? _____

HAVE YOU EVER BEEN CONVICTED OF A MISDEMEANOR OR FELONY? ____ YES ____ NO ____ IF SO, COMPLETE THE FOLLOWING: (Do Not Include Minor Traffic Violations)

DATE	OFFENSE	PLACE	RESULT

U.S. MILITARY SERVICE

BRANCH OF SERVICE	FROM	TO	RANK OR RATING	TYPE OF DISCHARGE

EDUCATION

INSTITUTION	NAME AND LOCATION OF SCHOOL	NO. OF YEARS ATTENDED	COURSE TAKEN	YEAR GRADUATED	DEGREES ACQUIRED
HIGH SCHOOL					
COLLEGE					
OTHER TRAINING					

EXPERIENCE

HAVE YOU EVER WORKED FOR COLONIAL HOSPITAL   YES   NO

(PLEASE LIST ALL PREVIOUS EMPLOYMENT AND BEGIN BY LISTING YOUR LAST OR PRESENT EMPLOYMENT FIRST)

EMPL'T DATES		COMPANY NAME AND LOCATION	POSITION	SALARY	STATE DUTIES CLEARLY AND BRIEFLY	REASON FOR LEAVING
FROM	TO					

IN APPLYING HERE FOR EMPLOYMENT IT IS UNDERSTOOD Colonial Hospital reserves the privilege of contacting PAST EMPLOYERS REGARDING REFERENCES. MAY WE ALSO CONTACT YOUR PRESENT EMPLOYER AT THIS TIME?   YES ☐   NO ☐

ARE THERE ANY ADDITIONAL COMMENTS YOU WOULD CARE TO MAKE REGARDING YOUR EXPERIENCE OR SPECIAL SKILLS?

WHY ARE YOU INTERESTED IN EMPLOYMENT WITH Colonial Hospital?

WHAT DO YOU CONSIDER YOUR GREATEST QUALIFICATIONS?

I HEREBY REPRESENT THAT EACH ANSWER TO A QUESTION HEREIN AND ALL OTHER INFORMATION OTHERWISE FURNISHED IS TRUE AND CORRECT

I UNDERSTAND THAT ANY INCORRECT, INCOMPLETE, OR FALSE STATEMENT OR INFORMATION FURNISHED BY ME WILL SUBJECT ME TO DISCHARGE AT ANY TIME. IN THE EVENT THAT I AM EMPLOYED,   I AGREE TO COMPLY WITH ALL OF ITS ORDERS, RULES AND REGULATIONS. I HEREBY AUTHORIZE MY FORMER EMPLOYERS TO G VE ANY INFORMATION REGARDING MY EMPLOYMENT WITH THEM, AND IN ADDITION, TO FURNISH ANY OTHER INFORMATION THEY MAY HAVE

APPLICANT'S SIGNATURE _____   DATE _____

INTERVIEWER'S COMMENTS _____

DATE INTERVIEWED _____   INTERVIEWER _____

can be measured and evaluated in order to predict the type of work a person can learn.

Individuals vary enormously in verbal competence, mathematical comprehension, and reasoning ability. Accurate and prompt information about competence levels of prospective employees is essential if they are to be selected, placed, and motivated according to their abilities.

During both world wars, the U.S. government quickly mobilized millions of persons to participate in the nation's defense. Persons were not always given tasks that matched their abilities (and certainly not with their wishes), but the fact that so many were selected and placed so quickly to accomplish the end results is largely attributed to use of the Otis Mental Ability Test. Some of those tested for reading and numerical competence were found to be illiterate and could not be used at all; others were competent enough for simple tasks performed under close supervision. A third group could learn technical and command tasks. A few could learn more complicated tasks such as theoretical physics, foreign languages, and weapon systems design.

Most modern work tasks require at least a minimum level of reading and numeric comprehension. Many require verbal and mathematical reasoning for more difficult and rewarding assignments. Since there is inflation in the evaluation (grading) systems used by both secondary and higher educational systems, it is important that organizations develop valid selection tools for independent assessment of prospective employees.

Definition of a Psychological Test

Psychological tests are commonly thought of as a measure of intelligence or emotional stability. Actually, any objective and standardized measure of a sample of behavior can be considered a psychological test. However, only those tests that are valid predictors of job performance can legally be used for personnel selection purposes.

Types of Psychological Tests

Four basic areas are considered reasonable to measure through the use of psychological tests: intelligence and aptitude, interests, specific abilities and skills, and temperament or personality.

Intelligence tests. These tests indicate general intellectual capacity and may result in an intelligence quotient (IQ), which represents an individual's mental age compared to chronological age. It is generally believed that the ability measured by intelligence tests loses some importance after adolescence, making the IQ score less meaningful. In personnel selection, tests of mental ability often use the raw score (number of correct answers) rather than an IQ. The raw scores are converted to percentages and applicants are ranked. Government Civil Service Tests are scored in this manner, with applicants ranked according to the percentage score received. Examples of tests used to measure intelligence are the Wonderlic Personnel Test, Wesman Personnel Classification Test, and the Adaptability Test.[1]

Since there is little agreement among psychologists as to what "intelligence" really is, there is no unanimous support for use of intelligence tests in personnel selection. Many argue that intelligence is a broad combination of factors such as numerical reasoning, verbal fluency, inductive and deductive reasoning, and memory skills. Since these skills vary in importance from job to job, it may be difficult to validate general intelligence tests for use in personnel selection. In fact, the correlation between job demands and intelligence may be inverse (negative). That is, the more intelligent a person is, the less likely he or she may be able to cope with the routine demands of some jobs, such as assembly line activity. Further, there is some reason to believe that intelligence tests may be culturally or environmentally biased in favor of certain educational and linguistic backgrounds. In view of these limitations, personnel officers must be extremely cautious in applying intelligence tests to selection of new employees.

Aptitude tests. Aptitude tests supposedly measure a person's overall ability to learn. Specialized aptitude tests have been designed to predict the chances that an applicant can learn a particular job, such as computer programming. Since people possess significant differences in logical, mathematical, and verbal abilities, it is very reasonable to use valid aptitude tests to select candidates for special tasks such as doctor of medicine, aircraft pilot, lawyer, repair person, and so forth. Intelligence and special aptitude tests cannot measure motivation, however, so once again the predictability of such tests for job performance must be carefully determined.

Interest tests. Interest tests, although easily faked, are useful for selection, placement, and some training decisions. Such tests (inventories) are also quite useful for counseling purposes where the motivation to fake may not be as high as when seeking employment. Popular interest inventories include the Strong Vocational Interest Blank, Minnesota Vocational Interest Inventory, Kuder Preference Record, and the Michigan Vocabulary Profile Test.

Specific abilities tests. A third area often measured by tests is job ability, knowledge, or achievement. These tests are used to measure learned skill or knowledge about a specific occupation in which an applicant claims to have experience. Examples include the SRA Typing Test, Purdue Blueprint Reading Test, and the DAT Language Usage Test. Of course none of these tests should be used to hire personnel who would be expected to learn their skills on the job.

Personality tests. A fourth measurement area is that of temperament, more commonly referred to as personality. In reality, personality inventories measure some aspect or set of aspects of one's total personality, and consequently the

---

[1] For a complete listing of tests and uses, the reader may wish to refer to O. K. Buros, ed., *The Mental Measurements Yearbook.*

term *temperament* is probably more appropriate. Temperament tests are much like interest inventories in that neither has right nor wrong answers. Interest tests are designed to predict whether someone will like to perform a particular task, while the temperament test assists in predicting such areas as whether people will be able to accept high-tension situations as well as relate well to other employees. Since managerial positions require effective interpersonal relations, accurate assessment of an applicant's "personal traits" (e.g., dominance, flexibility, sociability, achievement orientation) is of great importance in management selection.

Temperament tests are also subject to faking, although attempts have been made to build "lie" factors into many of them. Also, personality profiles may not be stable over time. However, since motivation and temperament are often more important to job success than intelligence or technical skill, efforts should be made to integrate valid personality assessments into the selection process, especially for leadership positions. Widely accepted instruments for this purpose are the Minnesota Multiphasic Personality Inventory (MMPI), Gordon Personal Profile, and California Psychological Inventory (CPI). Patterns of behavior measured by personality tests are chosen by comparing the responses of people with psychiatric disturbances (e.g., severe depression, paranoia) with those given by emotionally stable people. The MMPI was developed in this manner. The CPI, on the other hand, measures different patterns of behavior. It focuses on such items as responsibility, dominance, sociability, and achievement orientation. Thus the CPI scales are probably more useful for personnel selection than are the psychiatric behaviors measured by the MMPI.

A recent approach to personality testing is the group oral performance test. This type of test is particularly useful in the selection of management personnel and is often a part of the assessment center battery discussed in Chapter 12. In the group test, interviewers determine the most significant traits desired of the employee, and questions and problems are formulated to bring out these traits. Applicants are seated around a table with a moderator and observer(s) during the group oral performance test.

The Predictive Value of Tests

The predictive value of a test depends on the degree to which it indicates a significant area of behavior (Anastasi, 1968). Test items need not closely resemble the behavior the test is to predict, since it is only necessary that a statistical relationship between test items and the predicted behaviors exists. To the test taker, however, tests are generally more acceptable if there is a resemblance between the test items and the particular job. A test is said to have face validity if such a resemblance exists. For example, an actual road test taken as part of a driver's examination has high face validity, whereas questions such as "Are you afraid of snakes?" found on some personality tests bear little relation to the job and consequently have little face validity, even though answers may have a strong empirical (statistical) relationship to job performance.

Methods Used in Test Development

A test designer may simply sit back in a large chair and dream up a set of stimulus materials (e.g., verbal statements, pictures, inkblots, etc.) to be used in generating responses from future test takers. The designer may employ a favorite theory in both the development and evaluation of the test. According to Dunnette (1966), "This armchair approach is often employed in personnel selection with poor results and little relationship to later behavior on the job." Tests developed in this fashion include handwriting analysis tests, inkblot tests, thematic apperception or picture interpretation tests, and others. The U.S. Supreme Court has made the use of arbitrary tests illegal since they have not been shown (in most instances) to be valid predictors of job behavior for given organizations and therefore might be used to discriminate unfairly among job applicants.

Statistical techniques such as factor analysis provide a scientific approach to test design. Factor analysis typically begins with a long list of common behavior-related terms or statements that observers use to rate actual behavior shown by persons well known to them. For example, a psychiatrist might use a lengthy list of terms to describe her patients. She then uses factor analysis to reduce the long listing to a set of basic dimensions (taxonomy) of human behavior. It is noted that the factor analytic approach attempts to reduce observable behavioral tendencies to a minimum number necessary for describing the behavior demonstrated by people in "normal" day-to-day living situations.

A third approach to test design bases the selection of a test item upon a relationship between success on the item and some observation of nontest behavior, such as a supervisor's rating of job proficiency. This method was used by Binet in developing his early intelligence tests. It has also been used with some noteworthy success to identify the patterns of likes and dislikes of persons who enter and remain in various professions and skilled trades. The behaviors chosen for analysis are occupational choice and occupational persistence with statements of likes and dislikes associated with people belonging to each skilled trade or profession. On this basis, people considering a career may determine whether their own likes and dislikes are comparable to those who have chosen and stayed with the same career such as lawyer, electrician, computer programmer, or nurse.

Limitations of Testing

There are many criticisms leveled at psychological testing. Aside from the possible cultural bias attributed to intelligence tests, criticism, some of which has been unfair, has been leveled at their validity, reliability, invasion of privacy, fakeability, cost, age, incompleteness, irrelevance, and excessive emphasis on results.

Validity of tests. It is true that some tests show little correlation to job success since a test may well predict ability without predicting job performance, which also requires motivation. Thus, managers must keep a close watch on tests involving predictive validity, that is, the correlation between test measures and criterion measures. The factors contributing to validity may change over time as a result of increased competition for particular jobs, changes in the nature of the job itself, new evaluation procedures measuring job performance, or revised job incentive plans. Thus even though a test may have been valid at one point, changing conditions require ongoing efforts to reassess validity.

Reliability of tests. Many tests are not reliable (consistent). When the same person is retested with the same test, different scores are obtained. Reliability of tests should be checked with reference to time fluctuations, the role played by different examiners or examining procedures, and the selection of items in the test. Some people have a difficult time taking tests but perform well on the job. Some may have a bad day when the test is first administered. Persons seeking entrance to an accredited graduate school of business generally are required to take the admissions test for business schools. It has been demonstrated that, on occasion, a person scoring 390 on a scale of 800 can retake the examination and score as high as 500 on the same scale. Does this mean the test should be eliminated? Probably not, since the objective of testing is not 100 percent predictability but merely increasing the odds of selecting those who are likely to succeed and those who are likely not to succeed. However, any test that has not been proven reliable over time and under various testing situations should not be used for personnel selection.

Discrimination by tests. In current times, a major area of criticism of tests is that they discriminate against minorities. In fact, since the Civil Rights Act was passed in 1964, the use of tests for employment selection has become a fairly controversial issue. The Civil Rights Act recognizes the employer's right "to give and to act upon the results of any professionally developed ability test provided that such test, its administration or action upon the results is not designed, intended, or used to discriminate because of race, color, religion, sex, or national origin." The law states that any test used for selection of personnel must be related to the job and validated for the organization intending to use it.

Anxiety and test performance. The test taker's level of anxiety can have a dramatic influence on the validity and reliability of test results. In 1970 the Division of Research and Special Projects of the Pennsylvania State Civil Service Commission studied the question of test anxiety in order to determine the effect anxiety has on psychological tests (Berkley, 1973). College students were used as research subjects and were divided into five levels of scholastic ability. Each student's state of anxiety was measured through the use of a structured test-anxiety scale. Then a comparison was made between degree of anxiety and test performance.

Results indicated several interesting items. Anxious students in the middle level of ability obtained lower grades than nonanxious students of the same ability level. Students with low ability earned low grades regardless of their level of anxiety. It was also concluded that anxiety may have enhanced the academic performance of high-ability students. In general, the author concluded that except for extremes, test anxiety is inversely correlated with test performance.

The Impact of the Duke Power Decision on Personnel Testing

Petersen (1974) evaluates the effects of the Supreme Court ruling in the *Griggs* v. *Duke Power* case. Basically, the Court ruled that tests can be used for employment decisions only if they are proven to predict job performance and are related to the job itself. A survey was made of industrial organizations to determine: 1) whether or not the firms would discontinue tests rather than validate them; 2) the degree of effort firms would use to validate their tests, who would do the validation, and techniques to be employed for validation; and 3) the future impact of the decision on employee selection procedures.

Sixty usable responses were received to a mail questionnaire sent to 185 organizations varying in size from 780 to 500,000 employees. Governmental agencies were not included in the sample, since the researcher felt they were probably not able to answer the questionnaire for various reasons. Results indicated that, prior to the *Duke Power* case, 53 of the 60 companies were using testing programs. After the decision, 8 companies dropped them completely. Prior to the court decision, 14 of the 53 did not validate factory-level tests, 15 did not validate clerical tests, and 10 did not validate managerial tests. After the case, among the 45 still testing, the numbers not validating dropped to 2, 4, and 3 respectively. Most of the firms responding to the survey were using in-company statisticians to perform the validation of tests. Many of the executives responding to the survey felt that the future impact of the *Duke Power* case would be to cause more emphasis to be placed on "good" interviewing techniques, with tests of skills being used much more than aptitude and personality tests, which are more difficult to validate.

Psychological Testing: A Summary

Tests can be used to predict job proficiency if criteria can be found that indicate job success. By eliminating applicants who do not meet a certain standard, the proficiency of an organization should be higher and indeed will be higher than with no testing if proper leadership and planning are evident.

Tests can also be used to select trainees who are likely to succeed in specialized training efforts. Turnover rates may be reduced by eliminating applicants who apparently have no interest in the type of work for which they are applying or have far greater intelligence than that demanded by the job. Differential aptitude tests can indicate various areas in which a new employee is likely to excel, thus aiding in the placement of recent trainees in jobs that may be better suited to their skills and interests.

Psychological tests, then, are a valuable tool for the hiring and promotion processes, but in many instances they are poorly used. Tests cannot make up for unrealistic job descriptions. They must be carefully validated before they can predict job success. The person tested should be told of the results if such results are to do the applicant and the organization any good. Tests may also be followed with specific, workable training programs to get the full benefits —the time, energy, and expense—of testing programs. Tests will never be infallible, but they can effectively serve to maximize the selection of probable job successes and minimize selection of probable failures.

INTERVIEWING

Every professional person should develop skill at interviewing since it is one of the most common methods known for generating information from and about people and problems. In organizations interviewing is used for a variety of purposes, including selection, appraisal, disciplinary action, promotion, counseling, and general problem solving. Even when an employee leaves the company an exit interview is often given in an attempt to learn the reasons behind the departure.

Employment Interviews: Problem Areas

In the personnel field, interviewing is almost always treated as the final hurdle in the selection process despite the fact that it is often a costly, inefficient, and nonvalid procedure (Mayfield, 1964). After the *Duke Power* decision, interviewing became even more widespread as a major selection practice (Ruch, 1971) due to pressures to validate all psychological tests which, in turn, made these tests less attractive to management. Unfortunately, the interview is generally less valid and reliable than many tests because many interviewers are not trained or evaluated on their effectiveness.

Wiener (1974) demonstrated that interviewers give more weight to irrelevant information when unfavorable relevant information is present than when favorable relevant information exists about an applicant. Additionally, he suggests that an interviewer's confidence in a selection decision increases as the amount of unfavorable information (either relevant or irrelevant to the position in question) increases. The next highest level of confidence in decisions exists when information is positive and consistent. As one would expect, confidence in selection decisions is lowest when information is inconsistent.

An interesting aspect of this and other research dealing with the interview process is the apparent tendency on the part of interviewers to seek out negative data, relevant or not, on which to base a selection decision. For example, Hollman (1972) used 39 experienced employment interviewers to show that decisions about job applicants with a good possibility of being hired were affected more by negative information than by favorable information. Each unit of negative information about an applicant had a much greater impact upon a rejection decision than a positive unit of information had upon a decision to hire. Additionally, the order in which positive and negative information is introduced seems to have no effect on the final decision.

Single interviewers are generally consistent in successive evaluations of a particular individual, but different interviewers will probably arrive at significantly different conclusions about a single candidate. The use of "leading questions" (e.g., Don't you feel good grades are easier to obtain these days than they were a few years ago?) is generally discouraged and probably says more about the training of the interview*er* than the qualifications of the interview*ee*. It has also been shown that the interviewer's personal biases can influence both the responses as well as the final selection decision. Another negative finding is that untrained interviewers, during open-ended (unstructured) interviews, are likely to make a final decision very early in the discussion, most generally before the interview is half finished.

Improving Employment Interviews

With these weaknesses in mind, is it any wonder that the interviewing process is beginning to receive the same type of criticism that psychological tests received a decade ago? In reality, most interviews are less valid than the tests ruled illegal by the Supreme Court decision. To improve the validity of interviews, a structured format should be employed. That is, each question on the interview form should be asked in the same way of all applicants, and the responses should be compared with successful and unsuccessful employee responses over an extended time period. In other words, validation should be undertaken with interview questions just as with the questions used in psychological tests.

Standardized evaluation and prediction forms will help the interviewer summarize information gained during the interview. Additionally, systematic feedback should be provided to the interviewer regarding the job performance of candidates interviewed. Finally, intensive training for interviewers is necessary if they are to increase the probability of obtaining valid selection interviews.

Table 7–1, used in our discussion of recruiting (pp. 182–183), provides a summary of lawful and unlawful inquiries that may be made during a preemployment interview. (Notice that much of the information that is unlawful for businesses to gather may be collected by government agencies or contractors working on government contracts.) Table 7–3 is a summary of items that are appropriate for structured interview forms and, in fact, have been used by various organizations during the mid-seventies. The reader probably has encountered many of these items during previous interviews and will undoubtedly encounter them again in the future since they represent common questions used in employment interviews.

Exhibits 7–3 and 7–4 are provided to assist the reader in understanding how two major organizations evaluate job applicants. These forms guide the interviewer in evaluating candidates, but the reader should note that there is ample opportunity for personal bias and subjectivity to interfere in the interpretation or completion of both forms. For readers who are interested in performing well during the interview process, the following paragraphs should be helpful.

TABLE 7–3 Suggested Items for a Structured Interview: Supervisory Position

---

Tell me about your most recent job. Why did you decide to change?

As you look back on your recent job, what did you like most about it? What did you like least about the job?

What do you feel were your three most significant achievements in your past position?

You have probably developed some idea of what you think an effective manager should do. Could you tell me about your image of the effective manager?

How do you feel your subordinates would describe you as a supervisor?

Were you satisfied with the progress you made on your previous job? Why? Why not?

What plans do you have for self-improvement during the next twelve months?

What does success mean to you?

What do people criticize about you the most?

Many of us improve our ability to relate to people as we develop more maturity. In what way would you say you have improved over the past two years?

What or whom has contributed most to your self-development?

Think about a difficult decision you have had to make recently regarding your work. Tell me how you went about making this decision.

How do you plan your work?

What has been the heaviest pressure situation you have had to face in the past year? Describe the circumstances.

Give me examples of the types of problems that create the greatest stress or strain for you.

What goals have you set for the next year? For the next three years?

How Job Applicants Should Approach the Interview Process

We have heard countless personnel administrators bemoan the fact that so few college graduates are well prepared to participate in a job interview. Consequently, the following paragraphs are included to assist the interviewee in establishing immediate and positive rapport with the interviewer and, hopefully, perform well in future interviews.

Preparation of a resume. An effective, typed biographical summary—a resume or vita—is of primary importance. This summary must be a concise reflection of demographic data, career objectives, education, work, and military experience. Demographic data should be limited to name, permanent and local address, local telephone, marital status and dependents, and birthdate. Career goals should be stated for the short range (e.g., staff assistant, labor relations) and, where possible, for the longer range (e.g., contract negotiator). Educational background should include high school, college, and postgraduate studies. Scholastic achievements and *leadership* positions in clubs, athletic teams, student government, and social organizations should be emphasized. Previous work experience is a key factor in most selection decisions even if it is limited to part-time or summer employment. Prospective employers are also interested in knowing the amount of educational expense covered by personal work efforts as opposed to parental, governmental, or scholastic awards.

Since past achievements have been found to be good predictors of future achievements, it is important that short statements reflecting past accomplishments appear on the resume. Some examples are provided below:

1. June 1974–May 1975; part-time assembler, Mason Tool and Die Works, Ravenna, Ohio; promoted to assistant foreman in charge of all night shift assembly work, January 1975.

2. May 1975–June 1976; systems analyst, Mason Tool and Die; designed and programmed order entry, accounts receivable, and payroll subsystems for computerized information system.

3. Coeditor high school yearbook; responsible for coordinating photography, advertising, and copyediting functions.

4. June 1972–September 1972; assistant manager, Arby's International Fast Food Unit, Sharon, Pennsylvania; responsible for employee scheduling, equipment maintenance, customer relations, and all night shift supervision.

The length and form of a resume will depend on an individual's age and quality of experience. As a general rule, recent college graduates attempt to stay within a one- to two-page, single-spaced, typed format. Correct grammar and spelling are vital. Salary requirements probably should not be stated although geographical preference should. References are generally not specifically named but "are supplied upon request."

Preparing for the interview itself. In preparing for the interview, the applicant should study some literature about the company, such as a recent annual report, in order to ask specific questions about product, process, goals, or competition. These questions are important because they demonstrate interest in the organization.

It is also advisable to prepare a list of questions and practice them before the interview. Questions about job duties are expected; those regarding salary, fringe benefits, vacations, and so forth should be avoided during early discussions.

During the interview. Interviewers frequently form their final judgments within the first few minutes of an interview, and most judgments are made before half the interview is completed. Thus the old maxim about first impressions being important is apparently sound for the interview process. Dress and bearing are significant. A cordial, relaxed (but not lackadaisical), interested attitude is helpful. The interviewee should *not* initiate opening small talk. Responses should be weighed, precise, and relevant, emphasizing the interviewee's strong points without appearing pompous or egotistical. Eye contact is important. A clear statement of the next action should be obtained before concluding the interview and a followup letter from the interviewee acknowledging the interview should be sent within a few days.

ment maintenance, customer relations, and all night-shift supervision.

EXHIBIT 7-3 Sample Interview Evaluation Form

Candidate evaluation guide	Top 10% of class (outstanding)	Top 25% of class (very good)	Top 50% of class (good or average)	Bottom 50% of class (Marginal or below average)
1. Personal characteristics Poise, manners, friendliness, bearing, appearance	Usually outgoing but not overbearing, confident without being abrasive. Has natural enthusiasm and friendliness. Unusually mature for age. Very impressive in stature, dress and grooming. Has demonstrated leadership ability.	In spite of any apparent nervousness, comes across as friendly and reasonably confident. Record shows some degree of social success and a sense of responsibility. Neat, well-dressed and groomed in spite of any long hair or moustache.	Generally bland personality, may have some minor quirks or mannerisms. Nervousness may cause some fuzzy thinking. Lacks enthusiasm. Seems unconcerned about appearance which is generally unimpressive.	Has some definitely unpleasant traits, may be too reserved or too overbearing. Lacks maturity or has a negative attitude. Appearance poor in one or more respects.
2. Communication Command of language, voice tone, sincerity	Unusually well-spoken without any distracting speech habits. Has consistently well-organized presentation. Answers questions in depth without hesitation. Has strong, pleasant voice and unusual sincerity.	Speaks easily and clearly. Generally presents ideas in a logical and concise manner. Has pleasant, if undistinguished voice and apparent sincerity.	May have some hesitation due to nervousness but gets most ideas across fairly well. May tend to ramble or may not go into depth on any subject.	Has difficulty with self-expression due to mental blocks, limited knowledge of English or simply a low level of intelligence.

204

3. Academic achievement Grades, standing in class, honors	Has outstanding GPA* (normally 3.5 or better depending on the school) or may have made a strong showing in spite of major obstacles such as a heavy outside work schedule or extra-curricular involvement.	Has above average GPA* (3.0 or better, depending on school). Appears to be a reasonably hard worker who takes things seriously. Or may have high-level of intelligence but be coasting academically while involved in other pursuits.	Has average GPA* (around 2.5) and no reasonable explanation for not doing better.	GPA* (below 2.5) and no extenuating circumstances.
4. Other accomplishments Organizations, offices held, intercollegiate competition, work experience	Has, through personal efforts and by choice obtained some relevant work experience. Hard worker in any situation. Has held a major office in a campus or community organization. Has unusual drive.	Has shown above average sense of responsibility in obtaining summer or part-time jobs. Has had some in-depth involvement with a campus or other organization.	Has had some paid employment experience but has shown no great initiative. Has been only a passive member of extra-curricular groups.	Has had little or no work exposure and no significant accomplishments in any field.
5. Overall appraisal	A near perfect candidate with maximum long-term potential.	In spite of minor faults, could command respect in our profession. Has no obvious limit on potential.	Average all-around, limited potential. Employable only under special circumstances.	Unacceptable.

* GPA—4.0 system assumed.

EXHIBIT 7–4   Sample Interview Evaluation Form

REPORT OF INTERVIEW

Interviewer _____

Department _____

Location _____

Please complete and return this Immediately after interview.

Name of Candidate Jane Doe   Degree MSME   Interview Date 6-20-76

Weights		0 Not Acceptable	1 Below Average	2 Average	3 Good	4 Outstanding
1	Appearance & attitude (grooming, courtesy, appropriate attire)	0	1	2	3	4
1	Personality (poise, bearing, rapport, total impact, business manner)	0	1	2	3	4
1	Communication (ability to adequately express himself/herself)	0	1	2	3	4
3	Education (appropriateness of degree and course work for job)	0	3	6	9	12
3	Work experience (appropriate to field of benefit to ABC Manufacturing.)	0	3	6	9	12
3	Technical competence	0	3	6	9	12
2	Ambition (in line with anticipated job progression)	0	2	4	6	8
2	Potential (ability and motivation to grow or advance, capable of developing, scientific curiosity)	0	2	4	6	8
16	Total points					

Score _____ (Interviewer need not tabulate)

Overall Evaluation Scale

├┼┼┼┼┼┼┼┼┼┼┼┼┼┼┼┼┼┤

0 4 8 12 16 20 24 28 32 36 40 44 48 52 56 60 64

Other comments: _____

_____

_____

_____

Number of years applicable experience
   (to be completed by section chief): _____

Specify requisition number
   (to be completed by section chief): _____

Recommendation: Offer _____ Reject _____

For what area(s) is applicant best suited? _____

There is very little that can be said about how a person is evaluated during an interview. Much of the evaluation is based upon the whims, biases, emotions, experience, intuition, and other subjective criteria used by the interviewer. Even structured situations are easily biased, as indicated in Exhibits 7–3 and 7–4.

The reader has probably concluded that the state of the art with regard to job interviews is far from scientific. If so, this section has achieved its major objective.

REFERENCE LETTERS

Another method used quite frequently to obtain information about prospective employees is the reference letter. Unfortunately, the use of such information has not proven to be of much value in improving the selection decision. Information gathered through reference letters has been correlated with subsequent ratings obtained of on-the-job performance with very little significance between the two. Since it is fairly easy for almost any person to find several friends who will write something positive, the use of personal references is not highly recommended for the selection process. Previous employers and supervisors tend to be the most critical, and if references are to be used perhaps it should be the previous employers who supply the data. Since reference letters are now open for review by the person about whom they are written, they may have become even less valuable as a selection instrument. Now that the letter writer knows that his or her words are no longer confidential, there will be even less of a tendency to state anything of a negative nature. Moreover, organizations are increasingly following the policy of not providing letters of reference regarding prior employees other than to indicate their period and status of employment. A possible substitute for the reference letter is a personal telephone call to the former employer.

SELECTION THROUGH COOPERATIVE
EDUCATION (INTERNSHIP) PROGRAMS

A growing number of organizations are using the cooperative education, or internship, approach to evaluating potential employees. The student intern works for a semester or two for the company before graduation. This process benefits both parties. The company gains an insight into the student's qualifications and potential, and the student can determine whether or not he would be interested in full-time employment after graduation.

Jarrell (1974) compared the effectiveness of NASA research employees hired through the following methods: participants in the cooperative education program, bachelor's degree holders with no experience, those hired immediately after receiving a graduate degree, and those hired after some postcollege work experience. Effectiveness was based on four criteria: awards for exceptional performance, turnover rate, continuing education, and number of research papers authored. Former cooperative students received a greater number of performance awards than all others combined. Their turnover rate was 9.5 percent as compared with 26.4 percent for the other groups combined. The conclusion drawn from this particular study, which has its limitations, is that student internships represent a very good investment both in cost and performance for the organization that provides *meaningful* work experiences for part-time student employees as well as for the employees themselves.

SUMMARY AND CONCLUSION

As new problems confront personnel officers, they have opted for new solutions. They offer more realistic appraisals of what they have to offer in a job and what they need from the job applicant. They use interviewing techniques based on the idea that the interviewer is the company's first link and adopt new methods of minority-group recruitment borne of the realization that the company must actively search out opportunities to comply with existing legislation. In addition, flexibility as to what the company actually has to offer an applicant is becoming a key consideration in recruiting. Overall trends lead away from the idea of finding the best applicant from the *company's* point of view and towards finding an applicant who will be compatible with the company and who will perform as desired. This reduces the risk of training a person in a specialized skill only to immediately lose that person and the investment in him or her.

Research indicates that there is no single, predominant method used in recruiting (Ericson, 1974) and that the method employed is heavily influenced by the condition of the labor market. Any large, economically dominant organization in an area has a significant influence over all personnel functions of other organizations in that area. But in any case the trend is definitely toward more scientific approaches to finding the best possible match between applicant and organization. Selection must be the end result of a well-defined notion of what the job involves, the type of skills necessary to perform the job well, a valid set of instruments used to measure the skills, and a definite commitment to the welfare of the employee as well as that of the organization.

DISCUSSION QUESTIONS

1. Identify the major problems personnel officers are facing with regard to recruiting and selection.

2. "Many companies' advertising gives a picture not only of their product but also of the company itself." Do you think this statement is true? Do you think a company should take this into account when it considers its recruiting effort? Explain.

3. Do you think a campus recruiter should be prepared to defend a company product? Would he be better off to change the subject? Discuss.

4. Some people feel that realistic job previews have a fatal flaw: they make the organization appear less attractive and therefore the best recruits go to other organizations. Do you agree? Why or why not?

5. Discuss the high points of realistic job previews. How do they help the recruit? the company?

6. What functions do precise job descriptions perform for the company? for the applicant?

7. Everyone knows that students, given the chance, would hire ideal professors to teach their classes. Write a brief job description for the "ideal" professor.

8. Look up Title VII of the federal equal opportunity legislation. What does it really say? What are its potential dangers for business?

9. Do you agree that compensation is among the most important of recruiting factors? Why? Why not?

10. Can you work out for yourself some possible combinations of compensation? Include salary, discounts, vacations, bonuses, sick leave, and insurance as possible types of compensation.

11. What do you see as the differences between recruiting and selection?

12. If a company has a high turnover rate within the first year of employment, what are some of the things that could be done to improve the situation?

13. Do you think letters of reference are worthwhile? Do they help an employer select an employee? Explain.

14. What do you think has been the effect of new laws allowing employees to examine their own personnel file, including letters of reference written on their behalf?

15. Do you feel more scientific evaluation of prospective employees is a good idea? What are its strengths and weaknesses?

16. Discuss briefly some of the problems in minority testing.

17. Recalling the job description you wrote for a professor, what now are the selection criteria you would use to decide on hiring an applicant for a position in your school?

18. If you were assigned the task of validating your company's selection interview, what variables would you begin to use for analysis? (Hint: think in terms of a success criterion, interview length, type of position being applied for, information provided in advance to the interviewer, etc.)

19. What do you see as the major advantages and disadvantages of using interviews for personnel selection?

20. Why might the structured or patterned interview be superior to other types of interviews such as group interviews or open-ended discussions?

APPENDIX A
MEETING AFFIRMATIVE ACTION GOALS: A CASE STUDY

Darlene Blakely has worked as an assembly line operator for the past three years and is now being considered for promotion to supervisor of the line. The assembly team consists of thirteen males and three females, and there has never been a female supervisor in the department. Darlene has three small children at home being cared for by their grandmother. Darlene's work record is good, although she has missed the allotted number of sick and personal days primarily because she wanted to be with her children when they were ill. A male in the department is also being considered for the same position.

The personnel manager, attempting to meet affirmative action goals, is anxious to have Darlene promoted and interviews her on several occasions about the position. She claims to like the idea of trying her hand at management but admits she is somewhat worried that the men on the assembly line will not accept her as a supervisor. She also freely admits that she is concerned about her responsibility to her family.

The personnel manager now becomes very aggressive in getting her to accept the position, pointing out a survey recently conducted in the plant. The survey indicates that 80 percent of the males working in the organization would accept a woman supervisor if she is the best qualified, while only 15 percent responded that they would resent a woman supervisor. Some of the reasons stated for the resentment were: many women become quite emotional when there is serious human conflict in the shop, many women work primarily for extra money to supplement family income and may not have the desire or dedication necessary to put in the extra hours required of all managers, some women place first priority on their family and may not be able to place their job ahead of personal concerns for their children.

The plant manager feels Darlene is very capable, but he too worries about her responsibilities to her family and he also feels her husband, a sales manager for a local computer manufacturer, will soon be transferred to another state. The plant manager hears from several of the hourly people, who claim that Darlene is a very good worker but really not "tough" enough to put up with the pressures of day-to-day production and union demands.

Frank, the plant manager, comments to the personnel manager, "We realize your commitment to meet government-imposed hiring quotas but I am judged on the basis of how well my departments perform, not on how well you meet your affirmative action goals. I really can't afford to gamble this year since we have a very important contract which could make or break the company." The personnel manager exclaims, "We just have to get more women into management. I'll do everything in my power to help you over the rough spots if you take this woman on as a supervisor." Frank replies that he cannot go along with the hiring of Darlene and that the case will have to be taken up with the vice-president for manufacturing as soon as possible.

Assume you are the vice-president. What would you recommend? How do you feel the organization will function if Darlene is promoted? What steps should the personnel manager take next?

APPENDIX B
SELECTION TRAINING AND PLACEMENT FOR COMPUTER PROGRAMMERS:
A CASE STUDY

(The following case is taken from real life. The reader is asked to evaluate the personnel procedures used by the company pointing out major strengths and limitations of these procedures.)

A multiline insurance company headquartered in Maryland had 3 billion dollars in policies in force in 1975. The firm has 61 branch offices with centralized data processing in the home office in Baltimore. Branches communicate with the home office via intelligent computer terminals.

The data processing staff was increased from 32 persons to 109 over a period of four years through the careful selection, training, and placement of *inexperienced* personnel (Siegel, 1975).

Prior to 1971, the company used the Programmer Aptitude Test (PAT) as a screening device, considering for employment any candidate who passed. Subsequent analysis of the performance of these people showed that those who did well on the test might or might not do well as programmers. (People doing poorly on the test generally did poorly as programmers.) The company still uses the test as an initial screening device and requires candidates to score an A. Employees of the company are given the same opportunities as nonemployees. No other testing is used.

All candidates who score an A are scheduled for an interview which is considered by the company to be the most important part of the selection process. At least four people are present with the applicant during the interview: two managers of divisions who use data processing (DP) services, the DP education coordinator, and the training-class coordinator.

The interview is scheduled for an hour, during which the interviewers try to determine the candidate's potential job longevity, verbal facility, personality, curiosity, maturity, judgment, drive, motivation, and growth potential, with greatest importance given to longevity, motivation, drive, and growth potential. Course content and grades dating back to high school play an important part in evaluating these traits. As an example, doing well in one major course of study but poorly in another may indicate lack of drive. Summer employment during college is considered a plus. Nonsocial and nonathletic extracurricular activities are also considered traits of a good employee.

The tone of the interview changes from one of stress at the beginning to friendliness at the conclusion. After the interview, the team discusses the candidate and each member writes an individual critique. All decisions on whether to make an offer must be unanimous. A goal is to hire the brightest people possible since the company has found that the best qualified people write better programs quicker, and even if they quit, lasting work remains. Prior work experience, although part time and not in the computer area, is considered a definite plus.

Successful candidates are all hired at the same salary regardless of educational degrees, but experience shows that those with advanced degrees progress much faster. Applicants are then assigned immediately to a training program under the direction of a class coordinator, usually a middle-level staff programmer who assigns laboratory problems, keeps records, and administers tests. Each class has about fifteen students and four faculty members in addition to the class coordinator. Each faculty member must attend a corporate teachers' training seminar, which involves being videotaped while teaching.

The training class begins to write computer programs on the first day. The course extends nine weeks, with nine periods each day. All periods are prestructured so that the students move through the course together. In addition to computer subjects, the students are taught business subjects and must pass a basic insurance exam to graduate from the program. Heavy emphasis is placed on how the programmers are to serve the users.

At the beginning of the final week of class, the division managers meet to place their requests for trainees. These requests are not for a particular individual but for a type of person they need. Before the class graduates, the systems and programming manager meets with the class coordinator and faculty to assign the trainees. An attempt is made to match trainees' strengths and weaknesses with the future supervisors' strengths and weaknesses. Care is also taken to break up cliques that may have been formed during the training class.

The following day students are told of their assignments. They spend the rest of the morning with their new supervisors.

Approximately one thousand hours are spent on interviewing for each class. Another one thousand hours are spent in instruction. The total investment per trainee is about $3,400 (1975), although the company has found the expense to be less than if "headhunters" (agencies) were used. Turnover has been low among the employees thus far selected under this approach.

Comment on the strengths and limitations of this approach. What potential problem areas do you foresee? Can you identify side benefits that may result from the approach?

APPENDIX C
POLICY ON PERSONNEL TESTING

The following five paragraphs represent the policy on personnel testing for a major corporation. Point out the strengths and any possible weaknesses you may observe in this formal statement of testing policy.

1. The Personnel Testing Section will communicate to management that tests do not provide, by themselves, an adequate basis for hiring. The function of testing is to furnish additional information. Tests indicate what an applicant is potentially *able to do*, not what he *will do*.

2. Personnel tests are used to aid in the hiring, placement and upgrading of personnel in order to select employees who have the ability and knowledge to meet immediate and future job needs. Tests and procedures will be fair to all regardless of race, nationality, sex, color, or creed.

3. No test results will be provided to the employee without their meaning and

significance being adequately discussed according to accepted counseling procedures. No test results will be available to any outside agency without the written consent of the applicant or employee concerned. No test materials may leave the Personnel Testing Section without the consent of the supervisor of testing. Only those individuals trained in the administration of tests shall be permitted to give such tests.

4. Personnel Testing's tests and procedures shall comply with the *Guidelines for Employment Testing* issued by the Equal Employment Opportunity Commission and with *Executive Order 11246*, "Validation of Employment Tests for Contractors and Subcontractors," issued by the Office of Federal Contract Compliance.

5. It is the intent of Personnel Testing that its efforts will be conducted in accordance with American Psychological Association's *Ethical Standards and Psychological Testing* and *Standards for Educational and Psychological Tests and Manuals*.

BIBLIOGRAPHY

Anastasi, Anne. "Nature and Use of Psychological Tests." In *Contemporary Problems in Personnel*, W. C. Hamner, and F. L. Schmidt, eds. Chicago: St. Clair Press, 1974:102–9.

Berkley, C. S., and C. F. Sproule. "Test Anxiety and Test Unsophistication: The Effects and Cures." *Public Personnel Management* 2 (January 1973):55–59.

Britton, D. B. "Are Job Descriptions Really Necessary?" *The Personnel Administrator* 20.1 (January 1975):47–49.

Buel, W. D. "An Alternative to Testing." *Personnel Journal* (May 1972).

Buros, O. K., ed. *The Mental Measurements Yearbook*. Highland Park, N.J.: Gryphon Press.

Burton, G. E. "How to Prevent Dry Rot in College Recruiting." *The Personnel Administrator* 20.5 (September 1975):56–58.

Drake, L. R., H. R. Kaplan, and R. A. Stone. "Organizational Performance as a Function of Recruitment Criteria and Effectiveness." *Personnel Journal* (October 1973): 885–91.

Dunnette, M. D. *Personnel Selection and Placement*. Belmont, California: Wadsworth Publishing Company, 1966.

Equal Employment Opportunity Act of 1972 (Bureau of National Affairs, Inc. 1973).

Ericson, R. W. "Recruitment: Some Unanswered Questions." *Personnel Journal* (February 1974):136.

Fox, W. F. "A Job Seeker's View." *The Personnel Administrator* 20.5 (September 1975): 51–55.

Gael, S., D. L. Grant, and R. J. Ritchie. "Employment Test Validation for Minority and Nonminority Telephone Operators." *Journal of Applied Psychology* 60.4 (August 1975):411–19.

Gery, Gloria J. "Hiring Minorities and Women: The Selection Process." *Personnel Journal* 53.12 (December 1974):906–9.

Greenlaw, P. S., and R. D. Smith. *Personnel Management: A Management Science Approach*. Scranton: International Textbook Company, 1970.

Gross, A. L., and W. Su. "Defining a Fair or Unbiased Selection Model: A Question of Utilities." *Journal of Applied Psychology* 60.3 (June 1975).

Guion, R. M. *Personnel Testing*. New York: McGraw-Hill Book Co., 1965.

Hackman, J. R., and G. R. Oldham. "Development of the Job Diagnostic Survey." *Journal of Applied Psychology* 60.2 (April 1975):159–70.

Harrell, T. W. "High Earning MBA's" *Personnel Psychology* 25 (1972):523–30.

Harris, R. L. "Let's Take the Fringe out of Fringe Benefits." *Personnel Journal* 54.2 (February 1975):86–89.

Hollman, T. D. "Employment Interviewers' Errors in Processing Positive and Negative Information." *Journal of Applied Psychology* 56 (1972).

Holt, C. C., and G. P. Huber. "A Computer Aided Approach to Employment Service Placement and Counseling." *Management Science* 15.11 (July 1969):573–94.

Huber, G. P., and C. H. Falkner. "Computer-based Man-Job Matching: Summary of Current Practice." *Proceedings of the Twelfth Annual Midwest Management Conference*. Des Moines, Iowa: Drake University, 1969.

Jarrell, D. W. "An Evaluation of Recruitment Sources for R&D." *Research Management* (March 1974):33.

Jenkins, G. D., D. A. Nadler, E. E. Lawler, and C. Cortlandt. "Standardized Observations: An Approach to Measuring the Nature of Jobs." *Journal of Applied Psychology* 60.2 (May 1975):171–81.

Kessler, C. C., and G. J. Gibbs. "Getting the Most from Application Blanks." *Personnel* (Jan–Feb 1975):53–61.

Kirchner, W. K., and M. D. Dunnette. "Applying the Weighted Application Blank Technique to a Variety of Office Jobs." *Journal of Applied Psychology* 41.4 (1957): 206–8.

Leiman, J. M. "Man-Job Matching and Personnel Information Management." Paper presented at the NATO Conference on Operational and Personnel Research in the Management Manpower Systems, Brussels, Belgium, August 1965.

Luke, R. A. "Matching the Individual and the Organization." *Harvard Business Review* 53.3 (May–June 1975):17–34.

Mahoney, T. A., and G. W. England. "Efficiency and Accuracy of Employee Selection Decision Rules." *Personnel Psychology* 27 (1965):361–77.

Matteson, M. T. "Employment Testing: Where Do We Stand?" *The Personnel Administrator* 20.3 (January 1975):17–34.

Mayfield, E. C. "The Selection Interview: A Review of Research." *Personnel Psychology* 27 (1964):239–60.

Meehl, P. E. *Clinical Versus Statistical Prediction*. Minneapolis: University of Minnesota Press, 1954.

Petersen, D. J. "The Impact of Duke Power on Testing." *Personnel* (March–April 1974).

Ruch, F. L. "The Impact on Employment Procedures of the Supreme Court Decision in the Duke Power Case." *Personnel Journal* 50 (October 1971):777–83.

Schein, E. H. *Organizational Psychology*. Englewood Cliffs: Prentice-Hall, 1970.

Sharf, J. C. "How Validated Testing Eases the Pressure of Minority Recruitment." *Personnel* (May–June 1975):53–59.

Sharma, J. M., and H. Vardan. "Graphology: What Handwriting Can Tell You About an Applicant." *Personnel* (March–April 1975):57–63.

Siegel, C. "Investing in New Employees." *Datamation* (1975):65–67.

Smith, R. D. "Models for Personnel Selection Decisions." *Personnel Journal* 52.8 (August 1973):688–96.

Smith, R. D., and P. S. Greenlaw. "Simulation of a Psychological Decision Process in Personnel Selection." *Management Science* 13.8 (April 1967):B–409.

Straka, J. "Guidelines on Affirmative Action Recruiting." *The Personnel Administrator* 20.2 (April 1975):36–39.

Wanous, J. P. "Tell It Like It Is at Realistic Job Previews." *Personnel* (July–August 1975):50–60.

Wiener, Y., and M. Schneiderman. "Use of Job Information as a Criterion in Employment Decisions of Interviewers." *Journal of Applied Psychology* 59 (1974).

Zeira, M. "Overlooked Personnel Problems of Multinational Corporations." *Columbia Journal of World Business* (Summer 1975):96–103.

*

Section
Four

MANAGING AND MAINTAINING PEOPLE IN THE ORGANIZATION

*

Chapter 8

TRAINING

LEARNING OBJECTIVES

As a result of studying and understanding this chapter, the reader should be able to:

Give a clear definition of learning, training, and development

Explain the importance of training to individuals and organizations

Discuss underlying theories of learning as they apply to training

Design an employee orientation program

Provide a general design for effective training programs

Evaluate the various methods of training as to their effectiveness in reaching training objectives.

KEY TERMS AND CONCEPTS

affective learning

cognitist

cognitive learning

connectionist

criterion referenced measurement

employee orientation

feedback

Gestalt

law of diminishing returns

learning curve

learning theory

norm of referenced measurement

operant conditioning

positive reinforcement

probation period

psychomotor learning

skill oriented

the discovery method

training assessment

training methods

vestibule training

PREVIEW

In many cases a company is ahead of the game if it can promote from within. This kind of policy can be less expensive, more efficient, and a morale builder. Training is a key to this kind of policy. In this chapter we will discuss:

1. Major learning theories and principles.
2. A variety of employee orientation programs.
3. Design of effective training programs.
4. Effective training methods.
5. The importance of training evaluation.

Training represents an important opportunity for an organization to deal formally with a new employee. As an initial stage in personnel maintenance, training can have an enormous effect on an employee's behavior on the job. It can create—or kill—individual motivation and give an employee an impression of the organization's communications and reward structure. In this chapter we will discuss the training of lower-level, nonmanagement employees. In light of increasing worker alienation, especially at lower levels, training can be an important first step in the right direction by encouraging a positive attitude as well as improvement of skills.

THE NATURE OF TRAINING

Training is a planned, organized, and controlled activity designed to improve some aspect of present job performance. Training is skill oriented and it usually is intended for the short-run welfare of the company, the employee not withstanding. Development, on the other hand, is generally aimed at the long-run growth potential of the employee, expanding present skills and possibly opening new opportunities for advancement to high-level positions.

Training is a key ingredient in the motivation of individuals. An untrained, unskilled employee feels very insecure, lacking the self-confidence necessary for comfortable group relationships. If the employee is not trained, higher management will have little opportunity to motivate workers with various kinds of positive reinforcement and other forms of recognition. Almost every human need is somehow threatened by a lack of effective training. It is quite understandable why turnover is very high in the first few months (at times *days*). If new employees do not know their job, they will be unable to develop good relationships with fellow employees by demonstrating a sound knowledge of the job. Also, the untrained or poorly trained individual undoubtedly sees little opportunity for self-fulfillment, achievement, and growth within the organization.

Well-trained workers take more pride in their work, provide fewer supervision problems, are more productive (given the presence of other motivational ingredients), produce less waste, and generally show a higher degree of concern for the company, its policies, and its leadership.

Technology has had an enormous effect on how work is done. Yet training is becoming more important with every increase in the *rate of change in technology*. Bookkeepers, machine operators, key punch operators, and many others are being replaced by systems analysts, numeric controlled machine tools, and optical scanning instruments. New technologies require new skills and patterns of work activity. Resistance to changing technology is quite explainable. But it is very expensive. People in fear of losing their jobs will not accept new methods or equipment.

Changing technology and expanding foreign competition force organizations to establish training programs to meet the needs of more complicated and specialized jobs requiring cross-disciplinary skills. Affirmative action requirements (equal employment opportunity for minorities) and social responsibility also demand effective training efforts. However, if managers maintain a socially and technically progressive climate and select and train individuals carefully, then change will occur in an orderly and rapid fashion.

The first problem with training is the illusion that it has taken place. Training managers and line managers alike feel that explanation and demonstration are all that is necessary to learn "simple" tasks. What must always be kept in mind, however, is that a simple task for the manager/trainer can be quite complex for the insecure, unaffiliated, and/or unrecognized newcomer. Consider the following situation which occurred in a major automobile plant.

THE LORD MOTOR TRAINING CASE

Computer controlled machine tools were installed at the Kenton Plant of the Lord Motor Company. These tools reduced the number of machinists required at the plant from twelve to five. Each of the displaced machinists was sent to another job within the plant. One of these machinists, Bill Quinton, was placed in the floor panel area to learn the job of spot welding.

When Bill arrived at the Floor Panel Department, John Schwitter, his new supervisor, commented, "We aren't sure whether you'll be around this department very long. Things are slow and there is no real need for an extra welder. But just to make you feel at home, let me show you where the coffee machine is, get you a bench to sit on, and a place to hang your hat." For the next several days Bill stood around and watched the other welders. Toward the end of the first week John came over to Bill and exclaimed, "Hey fellow, work is coming in now. Maybe we can put you to some useful purpose on Monday. Have a good weekend."

Early Monday morning, Bill was placed at a vacant welding machine. The task was not complex. The welding was done automatically at the touch of a button. The operator merely positioned a panel against a fixture as it passed the welding machine, held it in place for a few seconds, then helped lift it onto a conveyor hook.

The supervisor told Bill to watch him do the weld operation saying, "It's so simple anyone can do it." John demonstrated the task slowly and explained each step as he was performing it. He repeated the task a few times and then told Bill to try it. Bill did it correctly the first time and several times thereafter as John stood by and watched. Finally, John said, "See, I told you it was so simple a moron could do it. I bet you could do it with your eyes shut. See you later."

The supervisor did not come back until the next week, after some news had reached him about Bill's work performance and attitude. It seemed that Bill had been welding panels even though they had readily visible defects and had to be scrapped. On several occasions the welding machine jammed and while Bill waited for a repairman, the entire line was stopped. Bill's safety glasses constantly steamed in the high humidity, and he had taken them off for several hours each day. Bill did not communicate with his fellow workers except when he had to ask a question about his job. On Tuesday of the second week of welding, Bill arrived an hour late for work and complained of severe headaches after reporting to the dispensary. After hearing these facts the supervisor approached the personnel manager and asked to have Bill transferred since he did not seem to fit into his operation.

Analysis of the above situation will demonstrate a common set of errors made in organizations throughout the country. Can you define the major problems and symptoms before reading further?

LEARNING THEORIES

Behavioral change is called learning. Training is what is done *to* the trainee. It should cause learning, a process that takes place *within* the trainee. Effective training must be closely tied to job responsibilities and should include the skillful analysis of human resource needs and proper methods for bringing about controlled behavioral change. To provide a solid base for training design, we now discuss important aspects of learning theory.

The Connectionist School of Learning

Learning theorists may be divided into two major schools: the connectionist and the cognitist. The connectionists are represented by Thorndike, Guthrie, and Skinner, who believe primarily in the stimulus-response approach. For the connectionist, learning involves the operation of laws of association, such as assimilation, frequency, contiguity, intensity, duration, context, acquaintance, composition, individual differences, and cause-effect (Seagoe, 1961).

Thorndike, for example, places major emphasis on the law of effect. He suggests that when an act produces satisfaction, it will be associated with a particular situation and probably will be repeated when the situation arises again. On the other hand, if an act produces psychological or physical discomfort, a person will tend to avoid that behavior in a similar situation. Thorndike later modified his approach to suggest that reward strengthens an act but punishment does not necessarily diminish an act in the same proportion. In other words a teacher can increase the amount of learning in a training situation significantly by reinforcing correct responses rather than by giving some form of sarcastic (punishing) feedback when the task is performed incorrectly.

Positive reinforcement.   Skinner attempts to control behavior through the positive reinforcement approach. He suggests that through a process of operant conditioning, organisms will make a predetermined response to an external stimuli. If the stimuli are controlled, the desired type of learning can occur. Programmed learning and computer-based instruction (described later in this chapter) are methods being employed to bring about such conditioning since they can be used for any kind or rate of reinforcements.

Operant conditioning: fad or reality? Conditioned responses are divided into two classes, which are acquired in different ways. The first class, commonly referred to as classically conditioned responses, describes responses that are controlled by prior stimulation. Examples are salivation and emotional responses, which are reflexive, or involuntary.

At first, an unconditioned stimulus will draw a specific response from a person. For instance, if food is put on a person's tongue, he will begin to salivate. If food is put on a person's tongue every time a bell rings, after a while that person's mouth will salivate every time a bell rings, even without food. Through this process a stimulus that previously had no effect on behavior (bell) now can be used as a source of behavior control. Political indoctrination is often based on such unquestioning, unknowing, and reflexive responses to preconditioning used during childhood in tightly controlled countries.

The second class of responses is called operant responses. They are usually considered voluntary. To develop an operant response, a person should reinforce or follow the desired behavior immediately with a pleasing consequence. If the outcome or reinforcement is pleasing, according to Skinner, the probability of repeating the response is increased. If the consequence is displeasing, the probability of repeating is decreased. The process of changing behavior by such reinforcing techniques is called operant conditioning.

An important factor in operant conditioning is the frequency with which a given consequence follows a response. A consequence can be continuous, following the response every time the response is made. This pattern of reinforcement is used at marine shows. The dolphin is rewarded with a small fish each time it performs a desired task. Consequences can also be intermittent, where reinforcement is given only after a certain number of responses rather than after every one. One variation of intermittent reinforcement is the random reward; the number of responses the subject must make to gain the reward is obtained in a random manner. Intermittent reward patterns tend to generate a high rate of response. The highly variable, random pattern produces longer lasting responses than either the continuous pattern or the more predictable intermittent pattern.

Punishment is widely used in most societies to control behavior. This strategy for behavior control may be inefficient for several reasons. First, the probability of undesired response may be reduced only when the threat of punishment is seen to exist. Thus, when the punisher is not present or visible, the undesired behavior may occur at its initial pace (when the cat's away, the mice will play). Second, punishment only reduces the probability of undesired responses rather than necessarily increasing the probability of desired responses. Third, punishment may interfere with positive responses. For example, if a subordinate uses initiative in solving a crisis situation and management reacts by criticizing the employee for overstepping her authority, creative problem solving may be suppressed for all future conditions. Punishment can also lead to avoidance and disdain for the punisher. If this happens it can break down communications and raise hostility and conflict levels in training situations and in work groups.

No one likes everything about his work. It is inconceivable that the day will come when everyone will be able to do only work that is personally pleasing.

Positive reinforcement is helpful, but it is not a panacea for management's problems. But if organizational behavior is at least partially a function of the consequences of positive reinforcement, then human relations training programs will produce at least some important on-the-job changes. The organization is the determining factor. If the organizational climate supports (reinforces) the content of the training programs, the programs will produce positive results. Empirical research has demonstrated this point (see Fleishman, 1967).

Bread and butter. Traditional annual merit reviews and yearly salary increments are probably very inefficient in promoting higher performance. Rewards are too widely dispersed, and workers do not always relate them to their personal level of performance.

Responsibility. Job assignments are similarly inefficient. Generally speaking, when given the choice, most individuals will select routine over problem-solving or planning activities. The reason for this behavior is that routine activities provide a constant reminder that the individual is contributing to the organization. Problem-solving and planning activities, on the other hand, do not produce the same type of feedback reward since they are not as easily measurable and because the reward givers do not encourage and recognize such activity. Another factor involved is that problem solving implies a much higher degree of risk (and consequent threat to security need) than routine, programmed, predictable activities.

Social approval. Social forces in organizations often restrict learning and output by rewarding conformity rather than achievement. The need for belonging to one's peer group often overshadows the motivating influence of individual monetary rewards. The transformer experiment at the Hawthorne Works gave one of the first publicized clues to this important social phenomenon. Individuals in this study who performed beyond what the group considered standard were given a "friendly" slap on the wrist to remind them to cooperate.

After a certain level of skill and monetary income is achieved, the need for social approval often outweighs the motivational impact of such management strategies as piece-rate incentives. Thus, reinforcement based on group incentives may become more effective than individual piece-rate methods in increasing learning and productivity, especially where strong peer and union influences exist. The Scanlon plan at Lincoln Electric demonstrates the powerful motivating impact of group incentives. In fact, the group incentive has been so successful at Lincoln Electric that repeated attempts at unionization have failed.

Positive approach to absenteeism. Some organizations now follow a policy of rewarding attendance rather than merely punishing absenteeism. For example, for a month of perfect attendance coupled with no tardiness, an employee may be given 1,500 trading stamps, something of importance to many families. If a worker's spouse sees the possibility of getting stamps, the spouse may join with the management in encouraging good attendance.

The Cognitist School of Learning

The other major school of learning theory is represented by the cognitists, or "gestaltists," who define the learner as one striving to reduce tension caused by a problem. They see all learning as leading toward a goal—that in fact, all human behavior has a purpose. Unlike the connectionists, cognitists believe in latent, or collateral, learning (i.e., the formation of enduring attitudes, likes, and dislikes) in addition to learning in order to acquire a particular skill. Additionally, the cognitists suggest that if training is goal oriented, training must take into consideration the goals of the trainee. A corollary to this conclusion is that trainers should structure learning situations so that relationships among stimuli, responses, and individual goals are emphasized. The cognitists also claim that the trainee should be able to develop a pattern of the total learning situation and be able to view the task as a complete structure.

A good example of the application of cognitive theory to training practice is found in a U.S. Army training approach which includes five major components:

1. performance orientation (a clear statement of expected achievements)
2. self-paced learning
3. insistence on mastery
4. rapid and detailed feedback to trainees
5. rapid and detailed feedback to trainers on the adequacy of their efforts.

PRINCIPLES OF LEARNING

Following is a summary of widely (if not totally) accepted principles of learning that can be adopted as pragmatic guidelines for prospective and practicing trainers. We have attempted to summarize widely accepted tenets of both the connectionist and cognitist schools, since the future will likely see a merger of these two approaches to learning.

Motivating the Learner

The learner must be able to see that learning will satisfy some active personal need. For example, the learner might see that training is somehow related to job security, better relationships with peers, advancement, or rewards from the organization.

Task Analysis

Any human task may be divided into a set of component tasks that are distinct from each other and affect the final task performance (Gagne, 1962). Gagne concludes that the basic principles of training design consist of 1) identifying the component tasks of final desired performance, 2) assuring that each component is fully achieved, and 3) arranging the total learning situation in a sequence that will bring about optimal interconnecting effects from one component to the next. Thus task analysis, intratask transfer of activity or information, level of achievement in component tasks, and sequencing are viewed as important variables in learning and training design.

Specification of Objectives

Learning objectives should be established for every training program. These objectives guide the instructor in planning the training, guide the trainee, and provide criteria for evaluating how much learning has been achieved. A complete statement of learning objectives clearly specifies the behavior expected of the trainee after the instruction has taken place, the conditions under which the trainee will be required to demonstrate the prescribed behavior, and the standards of acceptable performance.

Learning objectives can be classified into these major categories: cognitive, motor skills, and affective. Cognitive, or intellectual, abilities deal with the acquisition of knowledge; objectives can be specified in terms of thinking, knowing, and problem solving. Motor-skills objectives include such activities as building, performing, manipulating, and designing. Affective learning relates to feelings, with objectives expressed as values, interests, attitudes, or appreciations. Affective learning forms a continuum of attitudinal behavior beginning with a mere awareness, then acceptance, and finally internalization leading to a preconceived willingness to behave consistently with the learned value system. The degree of a worker's affective learning will be reflected in a willingness to pay attention to an event, respond with a positive attitude toward the event, give priorities to events according to some learned values, or act in accordance with the values.

Each learning objective should be stated as clearly as possible so that trainers and participants have equal understanding of what is expected. Stating objectives is a demanding task and requires a good deal of planning activity that many instructors dislike. However, such difficulties will become less frustrating as the value of learning objectives is recognized.

Effective learning objectives should begin with an action verb followed by specifications of learning content. For example, in the area of cognitive learning, action verbs can be sequenced into five categories (not listed in any given order):

1. comprehend (compare, recall, state, explain, summarize, give examples)
2. apply (use, solve, predict, arrange, demonstrate, interpret, distinguish)
3. analyze (select, relate, infer, contrast)
4. synthesize (plan, organize, justify, generalize)
5. evaluate (judge, discuss, justify, interpret).

Verbs such as list, define, and recall represent the lowest level of cognitive learning. A higher level of learning is suggested by the verbs identify, recognize, and compute. The next level involves more complex mental operations and includes the action verbs prove, analyze, relate, justify, and interpret. The highest level of cognitive learning, that of original thought, includes the verbs infer, reorganize, generalize, discuss, predict, synthesize and evaluate. When participants are able to perform at this level, they demonstrate a solid grasp of the subject material.

An example of a set of learning (performance) objectives for a skilled filter press operator might be as follows:

1. *set up* and *operate* a filter press
2. *obtain* a representative *sample* from a centrifuge; and
3. *operate* a batch distillation unit.

Words and phrases such as appreciate the value of, grasp the significance of, become familiar with, and understand the meaning of are vague and almost meaningless when associated with learning a task. The objective for skill development programs should be explicit: list, identify, solve, choose. They will help the trainee identify what he or she will be *doing* as a result of the learning exercise.

The Trainer as a Catalyst for Learning

Trainers are an important ingredient in the learning environment. They should know the material, be able to communicate, and be aware of the learner's needs. The old military expression that says "if the student failed to learn, the teacher failed to teach" may not be totally accurate, but it contains a great deal of truth.

The role of first-line supervisors in training is critical. They must be involved in establishing the learning objectives because they are the people who best know what training is required. The first-level supervisors should do as much of the training as possible since it helps them establish an effective working relationship with their subordinates. The use of supervisors in training reinforces them as leaders, and the supervisors themselves are likely to be motivated to train effectively since it is they who will have to supervise the workers they train. Realistically, however, some first-line supervisors will never be effective trainers.

Action-Oriented Learning

One of the direct effects of learning is that people tend to act almost exactly as they did during the learning process when they translate newly acquired skills to the work environment. Because of individual differences, it is probably best if learners can proceed at their own pace, from relatively easy steps leading to more difficult or unknown steps. Learners should be asked to express the answer themselves and be given immediate positive reinforcement when a correct response is achieved.

Research supports the principle that persons learn best when they are actively involved in the learning process. Some researchers have argued that people remember 10 percent of what they read, 20 percent of what they hear, 30 percent of what they see, 50 percent of what they see and hear, 70 percent of what they say, and 90 percent of what they say as they perform a task. While a great deal of faith should not be placed in these percentages, it is worthwhile to consider the value of multisensory learning exercises.

Different training methods are required for different types of learning. *Cognitive learning* stresses visual and audio experience to gain understanding. It may involve reading, lectures, audio-visual presentations, case problems, examinations, and computer-based instruction. *Affective learning* (i.e., attitude, value, and interest acquisition) may best be achieved through field trips, role-playing, open-ended discussion, counseling, or reflection. *Psychomotor learning* (doing skills) can be acquired best through practice, drill, behavior modification, simulation games, demonstration, or internships (e.g., assembly line, military drill, computer operations, drafting, and machine-type tasks).

Feedback

Feedback is a vital principle of learning. Feedback should be specific rather than general. It is better to say that "you aren't drilling according to the specifications" than "you are not operating the machine like I taught you." Feedback should be precise and diagnostic rather than evaluative. Saying something like "you have missed three defects in the last five minutes of inspection" is not something a person likes to hear but is probably more effective than suggesting that "you certainly are slow at learning how to recognize defective material." Feedback should be directed at behavior, not at values or individual personality traits. It should, in addition, be directed toward behavior that the learner can do something about. Frustration will only be heightened if a person is reminded about a fault over which he or she has no control.

Learning and the Aging Process

The *rate of learning*, not the *capacity to learn*, decreases slightly with age, usually beginning to deteriorate at about one-half of one percent a year until it reaches a level approximating what it was at the age of sixteen. It is thought by many that the capacity to learn continues to expand well past middle age since the older individual has greater experience, tenacity, directiveness, and is more fad resistant. Of course, as values and attitudes become more deeply ingrained, it can be more difficult to bring about change in these attributes.

Learning Curve Analysis

Improvements in employee performance usually occur as additional units of a product are manufactured. Such increased efficiency is often attributed to the process of learning and researchers have designed quantitative models to aid in the prediction of changes in output that are likely to occur as a result of learning. These models have been given various names—progress curves, improvement curves, experience curves—but they are most commonly referred to as learning curves.

   The concept of the learning curve was introduced within the aircraft industry during the 1930s. T. P. Wright (1936), one of the first to publish on the subject, showed that the cost of producing private aircraft could be reduced as the amount of production increased. World War II saw extensive use of learning curve analysis applied by the federal government in the procurement of land and water vehicles and aircraft.

Early research in the area of learning as applied to industrial production indicated that as workers repeatedly performed a task, the amount of direct labor required per unit of output decreased according to a regular and, consequently, predictable pattern. The fact that the pattern is fairly constant for different companies within an industry led to the formulation of the theory of learning curves, which states that as the quantity of output is doubled, the number of direct man-hours required to produce the output decreases according to a constant ratio. A commonly used ratio is 4/5, often referred to as the 80 percent learning curve. This implies that only 80 percent as much direct labor is required to produce the second unit as is required to produce the first unit. Another way to express this point is to say that for airplane production, the fourth plane produced will require 20 percent less direct labor than the second plane produced. This relationship is represented symbolically by the following mathematical equation:

$$y = ax^b.\text{*}$$

* The definition of terms for the learning curve equation is as follows:
y = the amount of direct labor required to produce the xth unit,
a = the amount of direct labor required to produce the first unit,
x = the unit number,
b = a constant factor representing the rate of learning such that $-1 < b < 0$.

If the values for y, a, and x are known, b may be found by taking the logarithms of both sides of the equation and solving for b:

$$y = ax^b$$
$$\log y = \log a + b \log x$$
$$b = \frac{\log y - \log a}{\log x}.$$

For example, if $a = 100$ hours, $y = 80$ hours, and $x = 2$, b would be calculated as follows:

$$b = \frac{1.903 - 2}{0.301}$$
$$= -0.3219.$$

If one wishes to approximate the number of direct labor hours that are required for the third unit, the following formula can then be used:

$$y = 100(3)^{-0.3219}$$
$$\log y = \log 100 - 0.3219 \log 3$$
$$= 2 - (0.3219)(0.477)$$
$$= 2 - 0.154$$
$$\log y = 1.846$$
$$y = 70.2 \text{ hours.}$$

The reader will note that the equation
$$\log y = \log a + b \log x$$
is a linear equation of the general form
$$y = a + bx.$$

Consequently, if the values for a and b are not known, they may be computed through the use of correlation (regression) analysis as discussed in Chapter 6.

Learning curves have a number of practical applications, some of which include:

1. They provide a method for establishing production goals and evaluating performance toward these goals.

2. More efficient production scheduling is possible when approximate improvement in worker performance is predictable.

3. Hiring and termination of employees over the life of a contract can be controlled more efficiently.

4. An alternative to hiring and firing would be production leveling through increasing lot sizes as the direct labor per unit decreases.

5. Government procurement officers apply the learning curve in contract negotiations for repeat business. By extending the curve developed during a first contract to the total cumulative units called for in a second contract, the direct labor hours for the second contract can be more accurately established. In fact, government regulations often specify that learning curve data be collected during the entire period of a contract.

When considering the application of learning curve theory to industrial situations, one must remember that factors other than learning are likely to affect changes in output over time. Other variables that may influence the shape of the curve include changes in 1) the motivational aspects of the job, 2) product design, 3) supervision, and 4) work methods.

In the following sections we will explain the important ingredients of an effective training program for hourly employees. The program we discuss includes orientation, training design, selection of a trainer, training methods, and finally, evaluation of training efforts. In a subsequent chapter we will focus on management development.

EMPLOYEE ORIENTATION PROGRAMS

The Importance of Effective Orientation

The first—and critical—phase of an employee's training occurs during the initial day and week on the job. This introductory phase of the training cycle is referred to by various names: orientation, induction, indoctrination. There is no choice as to whether or not orientation will be needed: new employees are taken on and other employees are transferred in every organization. The only option is whether or not this process of orientation is going to be controlled.

In far too many organizations the new employee is told, "Go down to line two and ask for Sam. He'll be your boss." This is the extent of "orientation." The employee has many questions during the seemingly endless walk to meet Sam. He is insecure in his new surroundings; he is worried about the job and what it involves; he wonders about his new work team. What will he tell Sam? What will Sam be like? What are all these parts doing lying around on the floor? What is that machine? By the time he reaches Sam, he might wish he had never joined the unit.

The new employee finds Sam who starts him on the job. This is where the indoctrination begins. Sam tells him what to do and what not to do. His co-workers tell him what he can get away with and how the management is "ripping them off." He learns about the company through the opinions of his new boss and his new co-workers.

Psychologists suggest that the more conscientious and eager to please a person is, the more he or she will be upset and frustrated by ignorance of the job, dependence, and mistakes. Indifferent or irresponsible newcomers are better able to weather early confusion, so they stay on. Sensitive, eager-to-contribute employees are much more likely to quit, convinced that they are unable or unwilling to master the new task (Famularo, 1972). It is quite possible that the best employees will be "short-timers" and the worst will be "lifers." Even the ones that stay will probably be frustrated and discontented.

A well-designed employee orientation program will help to alleviate these feelings of insecurity in a new environment and assist the new employee in getting started in the right direction. The orientation process actually starts with the employment interview. Too often however, considerable information is being received from the prospective employee (i.e., application blank, psychological tests, interviews, references, etc.), but little job-related information is being given in return (Scott, 1972). Thus the new employee doesn't really know, in many cases, what to expect on the job. Scott also points out that in the life insurance business it was found that those agents who said the manager misrepresented the job or job possibilities during the hiring interview were more likely to terminate than those who did not agree with this statement. It was also found that there was a significantly larger number of terminations among those new life insurance agents who did not receive a booklet describing required job duties than from another group that did receive this booklet.

Thus to avoid "organizational shock" and disillusionment, the job should be explained with detail and honesty. If the new recruit doesn't like what he sees and hears, it is better to find out before he starts than to have him leave after the expenditure of training time and money. The new employee needs assurance, confidence, and a nudge in the right direction. He needs confidence and pride in himself and the company. He needs to feel a part of the team. He also has an interest in benefits, salary, promotions, opportunities, and job knowledge. It is at this point where a supervisor can make or break the new person.

Orientation Procedures

The orientation procedures for a new employee should basically follow these steps. First, the new person needs a time and a place to report to work. Surprisingly, many managers forget to tell the new employee exactly where and when to report. Second, it is very important that the new supervisor meet and welcome the new employee to the organization. The supervisor shouldn't let newcomers start on their own or with a group of strangers. Next, administrative work should be completed. Here such items as vacations, probationary period, medical absences, tuition refund plans, credit union, suggestion system, etc. should be covered. Then the departmental orientation can be conducted. This should include a get-acquainted talk, introduction to the department, explanation of the functions of the department, and job instruction.

Table 8–1 illustrates a new employee orientation checklist. It is important

---

TABLE 8–1 Guidelines for Helping the New Employee Get Started

---

1. When new employee first reports to job:
   Welcome to company, job, and people
   Show coat rack, locker, and washroom
   Show cafeteria, vending machines, lunch hours
   Review security regulations, badge system
   Cover safety rules
   Introduce worker to his or her work place and to co-workers
   Explain how worker's job fits into the total job
   Review working hours and use of time card
   Start new employee on task:
       Determine training needs
       Define purpose of training to new employee
       Give detailed explanation of task
       Demonstrate the task
       Discuss the task and ask for questions and feedback
       Drill the worker and follow-up on performance
   Remind employee to come to you for information and assistance

2. In the afternoon of the first day:
   Review pay procedures
   Discuss parking and car pools
   Explain available medical facilities
   Review safety rules discussed during the morning
   Talk about work of department and how it fits in total company
   Shortly before quitting time check back with new employee for questions and comments

3. Sometime during the first two weeks:
   Review benefit plans
   Discuss company suggestion system
   Check on safety habits
   Follow-up on task performance and progress

---

to have such a checklist to help all concerned and to assure that everything has been covered. The attention and retention ability of people is limited; the law of diminishing returns applies. It also is advantageous to utilize supplementary material such as flyers, handbooks, or employee manuals so they can be referred to at a later date. A personnel manual (employee handbook) may include:

1. an introduction—brief history of the company and a statement of its purpose
2. a general statement about cooperation and teamwork
3. personnel policies and procedures (discrimination)
4. terms and conditions of employment (pay, hours, transfers)
5. benefits (vacation, insurance)

6. grievance procedures

7. rules and regulations with appropriate disciplinary actions which may be taken for breaking the rules.

Managing the Orientation Process

The personnel manager is responsible for coordinating the formal employee orientation program. He should select experts from different departments to conduct the different parts of the program (e.g., finance, security, safety, quality control). However, the supervisor has the most important role. The supervisor is *expected* to have a complete understanding of the company's policies and procedures. Many times supervisors say they just don't have the time. A supervisor who takes a more active role in the orientation program will spend less time on subsequent problems like disciplining subordinates for unacceptable behavior and filling out reports on absenteeism, tardiness, and low productivity. Because he or she can provide some of the most useful follow-up and feedback, the supervisor must make the time available to help new employees to adjust.

The initial introduction to the department setup and work atmosphere will probably have the most impact on the attitude of the new employee. If the orientation program is handled shabbily, a credibility gap will be created. The supervisor must destroy the idea that management and employees don't converse with each other by getting out and talking with new employees. This is the time to develop an effective communications relationship.

Unions play an important role in the workplace. This subject is, in many cases, avoided. Managers often reflect an attitude of competition for loyalty (it's me or the union); others just ignore the union's existence. Others believe that the new employee should learn about unions and collective bargaining procedures through the initiative of union representatives or the grapevine. The union could participate in the formal orientation program by having a representative brief the new employee.

We can now see the importance of a quality orientation program to the employee. It builds the employee's sense of identification with the organization and stresses the importance of the job to be accomplished. It helps to gain acceptance from other employees and facilitates movement into a smoothly functioning team operation. It also provides a clear, understandable picture of the many things the new person wants and needs to know.

In conclusion, orientation refers to the process in which new employees develop an understanding of their relationship to other workers and to the mission of the agency or firm. We have also developed an understanding of the importance of new employee orientation. We see the value of effective orientation in the results of recent research. For example, a study made in England explains that of 140 women operators interviewed in a survey in seven electrical engineering factories, only 4 had forgotten their first impressions. Of the 136 that remembered, 54 said they would never go through their first day again, 48 said the job appeared to be too difficult, and 8 said they were extremely nervous about making mistakes. Initial reaction to the work tended to be dislike and dismay, and the operators became chiefly concerned with the problem of survival in their environment.

Probation period. Many organizations have a probation period during which workers prove their competence and fitness. The probation period is mainly used for the protection of management, and managers should see that they get proper feedback during this period so the employee can be properly evaluated. Feedback may be accomplished through testing, questionnaires, checklists, evaluation forms, discussion with the immediate supervisor, interviews, and/or terminal interviews.

TRAINING DESIGN

In early 1974, the manufacturing manager of a motor assembly plant approached the personnel director and suggested that a training program might be needed since the number of product rejects during final assembly had increased 100 percent over the previous month. The personnel director, realizing that he had a well-funded training budget and had not offered any skill training for the past few years, jumped on this opportunity. He immediately started rummaging through his files looking for the outline of a programmed learning course he had written in 1968 to train new operators in motor assembly skills. When he located the package, he called the plant manager and said he was ready to begin the course on the following week and asked the manager to select a convenient day and time to begin the instruction program.

There are, of course, a number of errors in this approach to training. Somebody thinks there is a problem that can be solved by training. Somebody else finds some money to carry out the training, and perhaps a third party is called in to conduct the training session. Much good money can be wasted in this approach and, even worse, the performance after training could be worse than if no training had been conducted at all.

An effective training program design consists of six major steps:

1. Assess training needs.
2. Define behavioral objectives (what the learner should be able to do as a result of the training, as discussed in the earlier section on learning theory).
3. Define the abilities, interests, and attitudes of the prospective learners.
4. Select the appropriate personnel and methods for presenting the training.
5. Make the presentation.
6. Evaluate the effectiveness of the training effort.

Assessment of Training Needs

There are three types of analyses that should be performed in order to accurately assess training needs: organizational analysis, job analysis, and manpower analysis (McGehee and Thayer, 1961). The first step in an organizational analysis for training purposes is to determine the short- and long-range goals of the organization as well as the strategies being established or used to achieve these goals (Bass, 1969). Next it is necessary to determine which performance standards are being used to measure the degree of goal attainment. For example, employee turnover and absenteeism are measures of supervisory effectiveness; product quality, direct labor and material cost ratios, the number of late deliveries, and so forth are all possible standards of performance. Failure to meet these standards may be traceable to a lack of proper training, but of course, other factors such as poor communication, incorrect accounting procedures, obsolete equipment, defective raw materials or subassemblies, lack of inventory control, poor job design, and so forth can cause difficulty. Thus, the organizational analysis will point out whether problems are attributed to training or other systems and human causes.

Assessment of organizational attitude is also important. What is the attitude of top management toward training in general? Without adequate support from upper levels, most training will not be effective. What is the attitude of the first-level supervisor toward training? Since this individual is the primary responsible manager for training all hourly personnel under his jurisdiction, it is vital that he be motivated and capable to carry out long-range training efforts.

Analysis of specific jobs is a necessary ingredient in assessing training needs. Systematic collection of data should lead to a clear definition of what tasks are to be performed, how they are to be performed, who is to perform them, and where they should be performed. Data can be collected through questionnaires, direct observation, group meetings, discussion with supervisors, formal job descriptions, motion pictures or video tapes of the job as it is performed by a skilled worker.

Human resource analysis concentrates on the individual in the job. The analysis should be conducted to determine whether current employees are performing at a reasonably high level. Next it must be ascertained whether or not current employees who are performing below standard are capable of being trained in their present positions or should be transferred or released.

Selection of a Trainer

Selecting a trainer is one of the most important steps in the training process. The following represents an adequate definition of what one would look for in an effective trainer: The trainer should have skills in analyzing training needs, scheduling, content analysis, curriculum design, analysis of methods and materials, and training evaluation. A trainer should be aware of self and others, understand group dynamics, possess a thorough knowledge of learning theory and communications, and have a keen understanding of the subject matter being presented.

TRAINING METHODS

A wide variety of approaches exists for transferring knowledge. The purpose of this section will be to briefly define and point out the advantages and shortcomings of the mostly widely used training techniques and methods. We have also added a relatively new technique to the list, the discovery method of training.

Unfortunately, many training programs have been designed with an emphasis on technique rather than needs. The best technique for one situation may not be best for different groups or tasks. Care must be used in adapting the technique to the learner and the job. An effective training technique will generally fulfill the following objectives: provide motivation to the trainee to improve job performance, develop a willingness to change, provide for the trainee's active participation in the learning process, provide a knowledge of results about attempts to improve (i.e., feedback), and permit practice where appropriate.

On-the-Job Training

A practical, although not necessarily effective, approach to training is referred to as on-the-job training (OJT). Trainees earn as they learn under the watchful eye of a master mechanic or craftsman, receive immediate feedback, practice in the actual work environment, and associate with the same people they will work with after training. If the teacher-coach has a supportive personality, provides adequate reinforcements, and has sufficient time to work closely with a new worker, this method can be most effective. On the other hand, expensive machinery and work space may be unnecessarily taken out of the production process. Waste can be high. New workers may not be able to find out the reasons for their mistakes if they are appraised along with experienced workers. This approach, since it generally interferes with optimal production output, and since the purpose of business is to produce, has serious drawbacks. Training can become quite haphazard when the production function faces interference from the training function.

Internships, apprenticeships, and coaching are other methods of on-the-job training. Apprenticeships are generally used to impart skills requiring long periods of practice such as found in trades, crafts, and other technical fields. Internships are usually applied to managerial personnel and provide for a wide variety of job experience, often involving job rotation or an "assistant to" type of position. This approach is also widely used for the highly specialized fields of medicine and law.

Job-Instruction Training

Job instruction training (JIT) was developed by the U.S. government during World War II as a way of mobilizing large numbers of new workers during emergencies. The JIT method requires skilled trainers, extensive job analysis, training schedules, and prior assessment of the trainee's job knowledge. The actual training follows a four-step process, beginning with the preparation of the trainee for instruction. This includes putting him or her at ease, emphasizing the importance of the task, and giving a general description of job duties and responsibilities.

The next phase requires the trainer to demonstrate the job to the learner. The trainee is properly positioned at the work site, and the trainer tells and shows each step of the job at least twice, stressing how and why each step is carried out as it is shown. Third, the learner is required to perform the job at least twice, with errors being corrected. During the second performance, the trainee is expected to tell how and why each step is being performed. Finally, questions are encouraged, the employee is permitted to work alone, and the trainer follows up regularly.

JIT has several attractive features. It provides immediate feedback on results, quick correction of errors, and provision for extra practice when required. However, it demands a skilled trainer and, like OJT, can interfere with production and quality.

Vestibule Training

Some of the drawbacks associated with JIT and OJT training methods can be avoided through use of the vestibule approach. This is a laboratory-type training method designed to give new employees some preliminary learning experience before they are actually placed into the real production environment. A special area or room is set aside from the main production area and equipped with furnishings similar to those found in the actual production area. The new employee is then permitted to learn under simulated conditions without disrupting ongoing operations.

Vestibule training minimizes the problem of transferring learning to actual work situations. It permits the trainee to practice without the fear of peer observation and possible ridicule. Active participation helps to assure effective training. Of course, the cost of duplicate facilities and a special trainer are obvious disadvantages.

Programmed Instruction

Many workers find the entire task too big a bite to swallow. Programmed instructional materials have been devised on the assumption that workers can learn tasks better in smaller parts. The material or task to be learned is broken into small bits or frames that learners must respond to individually. The response reveals whether or not the learner has learned the necessary material. Programmed instruction recognizes individual differences, provides immediate feedback, involves the learner in the process of learning, and permits the individual to proceed at his or her own pace.

The learning materials are expensive and time-consuming to develop and are relatively inflexible. For programmed instruction to be effective and efficient, it should be based on material that will remain static and can be taught to large numbers over a lengthy period of time. With these limitations in mind, however, programmed instruction can be an effective management tool. It ranks high in learning effectiveness, long-range cost economies, learner reaction, and broader employee coverage. Buckley (1967) reports that experiments in over 1,500 companies showed improved learning at lower cost when the programmed instruction approach was used.

Programmed learning can be achieved through the so-called teaching machine, which in turn can be a textbook, combination text and audio-visual presentation, or a computer. This latter method is gaining in popularity and consequently is more carefully explained in the next section.

Computer-Based Instruction

Computer-based instruction refers to all uses of computer technology to support or facilitate learning. It includes computer-assisted instruction (CAI), which adapts computer terminals to the function of tutoring, and the application of computer terminals to problem-solving and simulation techniques, which permits the learner to interact with models representing real-world situations. It also includes the concept of computer-managed instruction, which applies technology to the diagnosis of learning deficiencies, and record keeping related to progress in learning.

Various computer-related techniques are better suited to different populations of learners. For example, the student who has a minimum level of understanding of a well-structured subject can be aided by drill and tutorial assistance using computer presentation of material. Such material includes grammar, vocabulary, mathematics, and basic reading skills. "Underachievers" or slow learners benefit most from the drill and practice of computer-assisted instruction.

"High achievers" and those who already have good skills tend to become easily bored with drill and practice. For these learners, higher success has been found using problem-solving approaches that employ the computer as a complement to existing educational methods. In these situations, the computer presents problems to be solved and helps the trainee develop a solution by providing additional information, performing calculations very rapidly, and representing practical applications of theory.

Early hope for tutorial application of the computer grew out of work in programmed instruction, which grew from the work of Skinner and his positive reinforcement approach to learning. Programmed instruction does not allow sufficient flexibility to be called a completely individualized approach, and computers, which are more flexible than programmed textbooks in terms of their ability to make decisions about branching (developing alternative learning paths), were looked upon as a better source of individualized instruction. However, at this point they have not lived up to their potential.

One of the primary reasons for the lack of widespread acceptance and use of CAI is that the preparation of materials depends on the artistry of the program writer rather than on theoretical or scientific approaches to learning. Intuitive feelings for learning problems are about all that the program writer has to go on. Decisions as when to branch, anticipation of alternative answers to questions, and the type and frequency of feedback are up to the discretion of the programmer or course author.

When CAI programs are able to treat learning and memory, which are actually processes of association, in a more scientific manner, the application of computers to human development will be much more fully realized.

The Discovery Method

Making an appearance in the literature and in practice in recent years is a training technique known as the discovery method. Research on the discovery method indicates that it may be superior for certain learning situations, especially with older workers (Belbin, 1973).

The discovery method involves a style of teaching that permits the learner to find out principles and relationships for himself. Unlike programmed instruction, it does not present information in a bit-by-bit fashion with immediate and frequent feedback. Rather, the discovery method avoids expository instruction and presents tasks that engage the learner in the search for and selection of clues on how to proceed. The design of learning tasks seeks to achieve two goals: to provide an intrinsic means for unassisted learning and to provide the experience upon which insight into key relationships can be developed by the learner without the *direct* intervention of a teacher.

The initial stage in implementing the discovery method is to identify the critical concepts involved in the learning task while simultaneously removing all nonessentials. Next, the training designer must somehow get inside the learning situation and decide major obstacles to learning. Experts have great difficulty in accomplishing this feat and probably best succeed if they observe those trying to learn the task. The third phase is to select a training design followed by a pilot training program that can be modified as experience is gathered.

A concrete example will illustrate this approach to training. A demonstration project in the United Kingdom involved the training of eighty-three steam locomotive drivers in electrical theory in preparation for their transfer to diesel-electric trains. Trainees, working in pairs, were given controlled experiences to permit them to discover principles of electricity. Forty-seven trainees were taught by the discovery method, thirty-six by traditional methods. In one experiment, the teams were provided a test board with a battery, ammeter, switch, three pairs of motors connected in parallel, and circuitry simulating the power circuit of a diesel locomotive. Trainees were directed by the instructor to change the apparatus and make observations on meter readings and periodically draw conclusions. The instructor was available to help out in difficulties but gave no formal lectures. His response to a question was a further question.

The teams engaged in excited discussion, confirmed each other's readings, rechecked the behavior of the equipment, pointed out discoveries (such as closing the circuit caused all motors to rotate, isolating two pairs of motors caused a current fall of two-thirds, etc.), and argued points extensively. Learning was judged by posttesting. Performance on the tests showed the discovery method to be significantly better than the traditional methods, although the traditional methods were not specifically defined nor were the possible differences in instructors mentioned.

In an industrial experiment in the United States, 242 trainees divided into 20 groups participated in three different learning activities: machine shop, data processing, and electrical work. The discovery method improved performance scores in machine shop and data processing by a factor of one-third to one-half. The electrical area trainees did not reach the same measure of performance, although the electricity instructor approached the subject matter differently.

The discovery method gives immediate feedback as to whether the trainee is learning. It seems to work especially well with older workers who are required to develop new concepts and understanding, since adults do not learn well by passive listening and are often handicapped by past learning experiences, habits, and misconceptions.

Video Training

This training technique has had wide publicity and application in both educational and industrial organizations. Participant acceptance has been relatively low, especially when used to teach basic materials such as accounting and statistics to large numbers of undergraduate students. The effectiveness of films and TV can be increased if discussions regarding the contents are conducted either before or after the film is shown and if the films do not cover too much material. A summary of the findings of 114 studies indicates that whether a lecture or demonstration is presented in person or by television does not seem to affect learning or retention one way or the other (Schramm, 1962).

Lectures

Lectures, as generally employed, do not contribute much to the effectiveness of training. Little opportunity exists for learner involvement, no consideration is given to individual differences, and it is difficult to obtain feedback. Its major advantage is that large amounts of material can be presented in a short time period.

Case Studies

In this method, certain aspects of real world situations are written for analysis by the learner, who is usually asked to define problems, evaluate alternatives, and make recommendations on the basis of information provided. Team discussions on cases are very effective in producing solutions to organizational problems. The cases do not teach general principles and lack guided instruction, but they can be used to reinforce theories provided under a different training technique. The adequacy of the case method, which is well accepted by participants, depends almost entirely upon followup discussion and reinforcement of the individual or team approach to problem definition and solution.

Other training techniques such as role playing, sensitivity training, gaming, laboratory exercises, in-baskets, and conference-discussion are used primarily for management development purposes. Management development is treated as a separate topic and is discussed in Chapter 16.

TRAINING EVALUATION

Effective performance on the job is the ultimate criterion of training quality. But how can a program's ability to provide effective performance be measured? Participants in training programs, if asked to rate the program during one of its final sessions, will generally give very positive feedback. To get a valid measure of training effectiveness, the personnel manager should accurately assess trainees' job performance two to four months after completion of the training.

Questionnaires or structured interviews with the immediate supervisor of the trainees are acceptable methods for obtaining feedback on training. The supervisor is asked to rate the former trainee on job proficiency directly related to the training objectives. It should be made clear to the supervisor exactly what is to be expected of a recent training program graduate. For example, most training program graduates are not at 100 percent proficiency upon completion of the program. Perhaps it is sufficient if the graduate can do all of the tasks without assistance except in the most difficult situations. The graduate is considered proficient if he or she can name the steps in the task and tell how each is done.

Objectives of training evaluation should be to determine the ability of recent participants to perform jobs for which they were trained, the specific nature of training deficiencies, whether graduates required any additional on-the-job training, and the extent of training not needed for participants to meet job requirements.

There are several traditional approaches to training evaluation. An experimental design may involve the use of experimental and control groups (no change). Each group is randomly selected, one to receive training (experimental) and the other not to receive the training (control). The random selection helps to assure the formation of groups quite similar to each other. Measures are taken of the relevant indicators of success (e.g., words typed per minute, quality pieces produced per hour, wires attached per minute, etc.) before and after training for both groups. If the gains demonstrated by the experimental group are significantly greater than those of the control group, the training program is labeled successful.

Another method of training evaluation involves longitudinal, or time series analysis. A series of measurements is taken before the program begins and continues during and after the program is completed. These results are plotted on a graph to determine whether changes have occurred and remain as a result of the training effort. A control group may also be added to the time series approach to further validate that change has occurred as a result of training and not some other variable.

The simplest of all evaluation designs requires that pre- and posttests be applied to the training group. Prior to the training, a test related to the training material is applied, and the results of this pretest are compared with results on the same or similar test administered after the program has been completed.

Why Training Fails

In 1973 the Bureau of Training of the U.S. Civil Service Commission studied the factors preventing the implementation of effective employee training (Salinger, 1975). Those factors inhibiting successful training in government organizations (and undoubtedly related to training effectiveness in private industry) were identified as follows:

1. The benefits of training are not clear to top management.
2. Upper management rarely rewards supervisors for carrying out effective training.
3. Upper management rarely plans and budgets systematically for training.
4. Middle management, without proper incentives from top management, does not account for training in production scheduling.
5. Without proper scheduling from above, first-level supervisors have difficulty meeting production norms if employees are attending training programs.
6. Behavioral objectives of training are often imprecise.
7. Training external to the employing unit sometimes teaches techniques or methods contrary to practices of the participant's organization.
8. Timely information about external programs may be difficult to obtain.
9. Trainers provide limited counseling and consulting services to the rest of the organization.

SUMMARY AND CONCLUSION

This chapter has been designed to provide insight into the psychology (why) and techniques (how) of employee orientation and training. Every indication is that the field of training is growing in importance and professionalism as workers insist on the opportunity to become meaningful contributors to the organization, at the same time that their skills are becoming obsolete at increasing rates.

Present emphasis in the training field is on improving performance rather than merely increasing knowledge or making people feel better. Techniques focus on individual and group problem solving as related to real work situations. This focus signals increased use of simulated, computer-based, and individualized training techniques such as gaming, vestibule training, case analysis, programmed instruction, and computer-aided instruction. Continuing emphasis will be placed on action-oriented training sessions, reinforcement and followup on the job, teaching people how to learn, self-motivated learning, and goal-oriented learning. Finally, constant pressure will exist to evaluate the results of all training efforts.

Effective learning and training depend a great deal on the type of job to be performed. A thorough job analysis is required prior to training-program design in order to assure that proper training objectives are established, a rational sequence of activities is presented to the trainee, and ultimately a means of evaluation of training effectiveness is defined. The following chapter provides a thorough coverage of the work design function as it relates to training compensation, and job enrichment.

DISCUSSION QUESTIONS

1. Distinguish between the terms "training" and "development."

2. Discuss the relationship between training and employee motivation.

3. How might a well planned training program reduce the "resistance to change" tendency that exists in the minds of many workers?

4. Explain what is meant by "operant conditioning."

5. Why may the majority of employees favor routine to problem solving work activities? (Use the concept of "positive reinforcement" in responding to this question.)

6. Distinguish between the Connectionist and Cognitist Schools of learning.

7. What are the advantages of establishing learning objectives for a training program?

8. Explain why employee orientation, especially that which occurs during the first day on the job, is so vital to building a psychological linkage between manager and subordinate.

9. Think about your first day on your present job or the first day you spent on a summer or part-time job which you just completed. Can you identify anything that happened on that day? Be prepared to provide the class with your reaction to the treatment you received during your first day.

10. Identify the steps in training program design.

11. Why should training programs be evaluated?

12. The following is a communication from the production manager of a major automotive parts manufacturing corporation. Discuss the probable impact upon the employees receiving this written memorandum.

> CONGRATULATIONS! We did it again! For the second time in the history of our division, the manufacturing section has successfully met the monthly shipment schedule. This represents outstanding efforts on the part of each employee in meeting our goal of shipping 15 OCTA assemblies in the month of November; and one which we must recognize as being essential to our continuing as an automotive parts manufacturer.
>
> To celebrate your accomplishment, arrangements have been made with Servomatics to dispense free coffee and soft drinks on Monday, December 5.

13. Northeastern Company, which was in need of eight to ten operators of a highly complicated machine in its processing department, decided to initiate an off-the-job classroom training program with some on-the-job exercises during the course of the training. John Waters, a man who had worked with the machine, was chosen to instruct the course. Waters often bragged to his fellow employees how difficult it was to learn to run the machine.

Once ten semiskilled machine operators were hired, the classroom training began. All ten of the new hirees were operating it excellently, especially Terry Jones, a bright ambitious worker. Terry's progress was coming along well until it seemed that John Waters started to ignore all of Terry's questions and refused to explain certain aspects of operating the machine.

When on-the-job training began, it seemed that Terry always received the hardest parts to machine, and even though he was the best trainee, he had to scrap much of his work. Finally, Terry got so discouraged that he quit. What are the obvious problems in this case? What may be some of the not-so-obvious problems?

14. Marie Goodman was a sewing machine operator at one of New York's large clothing manufacturers. Recently, the company had a decline in sales and was forced to lay off some of the operators. One of these was Mrs. Goodman.

During the time that Marie was off, the company purchased all new sewing machines to help streamline its operations. After six months Marie received notice to report for work the next morning. When Marie arrived at work, she was given a brief description of how the machines worked. The company felt that anyone with as much experience as Marie could easily master the new machine in a day or two.

Having heard how quickly the company expected an operator to master the new machine, Marie was embarrassed to ask for any assistance when she had problems with the machine. She was content to stumble along producing below her capacity.

Do you feel this is an uncommon occurrence in industry? What problems can result when experienced people are expected to adapt quickly to changing conditions?

15. Smith and Mason, a local CPA firm, has increased its business nearly three times during the last five years. During this time of growth, most new hirees were assigned to the staff and received on-the-job training from the seniors on the job.

This year the firm is faced with a problem of how to train new staff members. Because of continued growth and the loss of some experienced personnel, Smith and Mason has only five senior staff members to train the ten college graduates who will be joining the firm in the next two months.

Without hiring additional senior accountants, how would you propose to solve the training problem?

16. Tom Boggs, a recent college graduate, obtained a position with the personnel department of a medium-sized wholesaler. The company has a history of promoting capable people who have worked in the plant for at least two years to the position of order-taker because plant workers know the stock. Often personnel are later promoted to sales positions.

One day, Tom's supervisor called him into the office to explain that he wanted Tom to study the educational requirements a person needs to make the transition from laborer to order-taker and to make recommendations for training these people.

How should Tom go about obtaining information necessary to develop an adequate program of training for these people?

17. During the summer months, Marine World hires many students to help run its

park. In previous years these employees were assigned a job and reported to that job without any introduction to company policies or procedures. They were trained on the job by their supervisors.

This year, a member of the personnel department recommended that these employees be given an indoctrination to the company by spending the first day in classes learning to fill out time cards, how to handle emergencies, and to promote customer goodwill.

If you were head of the personnel department, how would you justify the expenses of such an indoctrination?

BIBLIOGRAPHY

Argyris, C. *Interpersonal Competence and Organizational Effectiveness.* Homewood, Ill.: R. D. Irwin, 1962.

Bass, B. M., and James A. Vaughan. *Training in Industry: The Management of Learning.* Belmont, Calif.: Wadsworth Publishing Co., 1969.

Belbin, R. M. "The Discovery Method." *Training in Business and Industry* (November 1973):38–44.

Buckley, J. W. "Programmed Instruction in Industrial Training." *California Management Review* 10.2 (Winter 1967).

Duet, Claude P., and John W. Newfield. "Sources of Information for the Development of Training Programs." *Personnel Journal* 54.3 (March 1975):162–64.

Famularo, J. J. *Handbook of Modern Personnel Administration.* New York: McGraw-Hill, 1972.

Fleishman, E. A. "Leadership Climate, Human Relations Training and Supervisory Behavior." In Fleishman, ed., *Studies in Personnel and Industrial Psychology.* Homewood, Ill.: Dorsey Press, 1967, pp. 350–63.

Franklin, William S. "A Comparison of Formally and Informally Trained Journeymen in Construction." *Industrial and Labor Review* (July 1973):1086–94.

Gagne, R. M. "Military Training and Principles of Learning." *American Psychologist* 17 (1962):83–91.

_____. *The Conditions of Learning,* 2d ed. New York: Holt, Rinehart and Winston, 1970.

Gibson, Richard F. "Apprentice Training Gets Back on the Road." *Industry Week* 179.10 (December 3, 1973):41–45.

Hess, L., and L. Sperry. "Psychology of the Trainee as Learner." *Personnel Journal* 52 (September 1973):781–85.

Hill, Winfred F. *Learning: A Survey of Psychological Interpretations,* rev. ed. Scranton, Pa.: Chandler Publishing Co., 1971.

McGehee, W., and P. Thayer. *Training in Business and Industry.* New York: McGraw-Hill, 1961.

Morano, Richard. "Determining Organizational Training Needs." *Personnel Psychology* 26.4 (Winter 1973):479–87.

_____. "Continuing Education in Industry." *Personnel Journal* 52.3 (February 1973):106–12.

Pfeiffer, J. William, and John E. Jones. *The Annual Handbook for Group Facilitators* and *A Handbook of Structured Experiences for Human Relations Training,* Vols. I–V. San Diego, Calif.: University Associates, 1975.

Quick, Thomas L. "Putting Responsibility for Training Where It Belongs." *Personnel* 52.2 (March–April 1975):45–51.

Saint, Avice. *Learning at Work: Human Resources and Organizational Development.* Chicago: Nelson-Hall, 1974.

Salinger, R. D. "Why Training Fails." *Training* (February 1975):28–33.

Schramm, W. "Mass Communication." *Annual Review of Psychology* 13 (1962): 251–84.

Scott, R. D. "Job Expectancy: An Important Factor in Labor Turnover." *Personnel Journal* 51 (May 1972):360–63.

Seagoe, M. *A Teacher's Guide to the Learning Process.* Dubuque, Iowa: W. C. Brown, 1961.

Stumm, D. A. "On-the-Job Training: Make Learning Theory Work for You." *Supervisory Management* 18 (January 12, 1973):7.

Thorndike, R. L., ed. *Educational Measurement,* 2d ed. Washington, D.C.: American Council on Education, 1971.

Wenig, Robert E., and William D. Wolansky. *Review and Synthesis of Literature on Job Training in Industry.* Columbus, Ohio: The Ohio State University, ERIC Clearinghouse on Vocational and Technical Education, The Center for Vocational and Technical Education, June 1972.

Wright, T. P. "Factors Affecting the Cost of Airplanes." *Journal of Aeronautical Sciences* 3 (February 1936):34–40.

Chapter 9

WORK
DESIGN AND
ENRICHMENT

LEARNING OBJECTIVES

This chapter provides descriptions and methods of using newer work design approaches that incorporate behavioral and system concepts. After reading this chapter the reader should be able to:

Describe and employ a limited but important group of newer work system and job concepts and techniques

Link system and job concepts to job redesigns for enriching work

Gain familiarity with techniques of growing utility in work environments characterized by human in addition to technical processes

Incorporate behavioral, communications, and leadership concepts in work design and enrichment efforts.

KEY TERMS AND CONCEPTS

work design

path-goal model

job enrichment

communications analysis

leadership contingencies

organization design

PREVIEW

The newer approaches to work design described in this chapter deal with three main areas of concern:

1. Analyses in service-type industries. These people-oriented environments have grown in importance in recent years. One new technique, functional job analysis, is described.
2. Enriching work through job or work redesign.
3. Use of leadership and communications concepts in carrying out job analyses and work design studies.

SCENARIO—"THE JOB ITSELF" IS WHAT COUNTS

Frank Kay was personnel manager for Mid-States Telephone Co., a small telephone utility serving a number of commercial and residential areas outside of several large cities. Frank was considered an "active personnel guy" who made it his business to know what was new in training, development and other personnel areas. Over the last year or so, Frank noticed that meeting announcements he had received from various personnel groups referred to "job enrichment," "job redesign," and similar subjects. Although Frank was interested in new materials and ideas, he had figured that most of this stuff was a gimmick. Yet, he kept thinking, "Who knows, maybe there's something to it."

The Work Shop

Frank decided to attend a half-day work shop on "Enriching Workers and Work Performance," which was to be conducted by a professor from a nearby university. According to the announcement, the professor was a former student who had studied under the direction of Dr. Frederick Herzberg, a noted authority on "job enrichment."

The work shop consisted of a lecture, a movie, and exercises related to motivating people through the redesign of jobs. Considerable attention was given to Herzberg's theory of "hygiene" factors and "motivators"—a classification of factors 1) said to be needed by people and external to the job but not likely to affect performance ("hygiene") and 2) likely to bring about good performance through design of the job itself. However, the professor did describe some other motivational theories, including one called "expectancy theory," which also helped explain the possibilities of job redesign.

As part of the presentation on job enrichment (JE), reprints of an article that had appeared in a popular business publication were distributed. The article presented a case study of a JE installation, including several sketches of office layouts. Frank was very interested in the case because of the relatively large part of Mid-States Telephone Co. given over to various office and administrative activities.

According to the professor, job enrichment was not without its problems. Work systems required careful job analyses to get a complete picture of job activities. This meant understanding work methods, as well as such things as the role of supervision, means of communicating information, and the workers' desires and needs.

When Frank got back to Mid-States the following day he called a meeting of his staff. After everybody had arrived, Frank started things off by announcing, "We've got our homework cut out for us—Personnel may be able to make a real contribution to performance at Mid-States if we can do something about enriching jobs around here."

Comments on the Scenario

This scenario describes a concept of enriching jobs that has captured the interest of managers and academics alike. Job design (or redesign) has important potential. It can improve an organization's performance *and* workers' interest. The growth in importance of administrative functions has made organizations increasingly dependent on people performance.

Studies directed toward job enrichment draw on a wide range of techniques, including industrial engineering and newer behavioral concepts. Understanding the work system as a sociotechnical system (Chapter 6) is an important basis for carrying out organization analysis. Communications, leadership, and motivational concepts are some of the contributions of the behavioral sciences to dealing with this complex but promising area.

ENRICHING WORK, JOB (RE)DESIGN

Motivational Perspective

Recently developed job design procedures are directed at motivating good levels of employee performance. This is not always the case. Forty years ago—and in some organizations today—job design (which is based on job analysis) dealt mainly with work equipment, procedures, and physical aspects (e.g., lighting) of work. But this approach is no longer enough. The changes we have described in previous chapters have required job analysis approaches that explicitly *include* the job holder as a *person*—someone with needs, ambitions, and desire for a reasonable life today and realistic hope for tomorrow. The motivation perspective in job-analysis approaches is both proper and necessary if a job design is to meet the needs of both the individual and the organization.

Much can be said for developing an ability to see various personnel situations from several different viewpoints. Although one model can be broadly applied, managers need even more flexibility. Some models or approaches are especially helpful for specific situations. In Chapter 4, which dealt with the individual and work, some basic motivational tools were presented. In this section we present two additional models and then focus on job analysis/design tasks.

Path-Goal and Expectancy Theory in Design

Until recent years little research was conducted to discover what workers' outlooks were, why they held them, and why they acted as they did. The purpose of work design is to determine if a particular new design will better meet personal needs than the existing one. Understanding the outlook of job holders and the factors motivating their actions (and performance) is an important and necessary first step.

Conscious choice. All of us face a range of choices in our daily lives. Level of job performance, absenteeism, job selection, and our concern for the organization as a whole reflect the choices we make. We may accept a situation passively or express wholehearted support. We may choose one employer over another, stay in a particular position, or leave. New design approaches inevitably raise such questions as will an employee feel that a new design will help him reach valued personal goals? The path-goal approach (a part of expectancy theory) helps answer this kind of question.

People may not be conscious of why they act as they do in a particular situation, why they feel the way they do about their jobs or employers, or even why they feel the way they do about themselves. Their immediate actions are connected to longer-term personal objectives. Being well known in business; securing the "good life"; getting along better with others; achieving financial independence; having a happy family life; securing power; or gaining a sense of personal fulfillment and accomplishment are examples of long-run personal objectives. The path-goal model connects short-term actions (daily, weekly, monthly) and long-run goals. But individuals act in more complex ways than this implies. One action may not be as efficient as another in attaining a particular short-term "pay-off," let alone a long-run target.

An example or two will give a general sense of the path-goal approach.

Decision to join. Jim is trying to decide whether to join Franklin Insurance Company or United National Insurance Company. Franklin offers a relatively high starting salary and good job opportunities, but many of the managerial positions Jim is interested in are filled by young people. At United, the starting pay is substantially lower, but several key managers are nearing mandatory retirement. With the importance Jim places on achieving a top managerial position, he chooses to go with United and is willing to pass up the short-term salary gain. This type of analysis led to a new understanding of trainee positions. When it became apparent to Franklin's personnel department why the company was not attracting young, talented people, they revised their recruiting and promotion policies.

Job design and work space. A second example illustrates a specific aspect of job analysis/design. In an architectural firm, personal interviews and surveys indicated high job dissatisfaction among senior architects. These architects had expected that their long years of work would bring increased independence and the ability to contribute creatively to projects undertaken by the firm. But these aspirations were largely unrealized. On the other hand, maintenance features, or short-run returns, for senior architects were very attractive. The firm had outstanding benefits, attractive pay, private offices, and contracts with many noted people. Yet the interviews and study of the work system indicated that internal work patterns and the location of various staff groups made it difficult for people to get together and discuss ideas or progress on projects. Additionally, the partners frequently interfered in important projects and overrode the senior architects' design decisions—the very essence of their creative effort.

Viewing the results of the interviews and work study in the path-goal framework made it clear that the organization's emphasis on salary and other job factors (e.g., office assignments, benefits), compounded by the frustrations of daily work arrangements, made it difficult for the architects to realize longer-run objectives. Job redesign led to the creation of small, self-contained studios, possessing a full complement of support personnel. Second, an agreement on a new way of working out final design decisions between partner and senior architect gave the latter greater prominence in design decisions once ground rules were agreed upon by the two parties.

Sense of Achievement, Valued Goals

These examples provide the general framework of the path-goal model. However, two other points should be clarified further to show the power of this approach. First, alternative actions vary in the payoffs, or sense of achievement, they may provide the individual. Put simply, an employee may feel one alternative is more beneficial than another. However, individuals may not see all of the alternatives available to them. Second, the likelihood that a particular action or short-term result will meet a longer-run goal is increased. In other words, an individual should have access to information or feedback on progress. What is most important is how the employee views his or her *own situation* and possibilities, not the boss/analyst's detached viewpoint.

In the architectural example, rearranging work groups and access to staff groups improved daily work. The new groups fulfilled the architects' desires to increase their creative time and reduced frustrating administrative detail. But what was most important to the architects was that revamping the partner-architect relationships in design decisions increased their chances for achieving an increased sense of personal contribution.

Essential Aspects of the Path-Goal Model

The path-goal model in Exhibit 9–1 shows how two steps relate individual shorter-term outcomes to longer-run objectives. The immediate results of individual choices or performance are a means to an end, not the end itself. Short-term payoffs from a job design may be thought of as affecting the job holder's sense of an enriching work experience. The job designer's challenge is to understand individuals and help them reach personal objectives and simultaneously to further institutional objectives.

Job-Enrichment

We briefly discussed the idea of enrichment earlier in this chapter and in Chapter 4. Having described and defined path-goal motivation, we will discuss enrichment—a key basis for motivation—more fully.

The seminal work leading to job-enrichment concepts is usually ascribed to the research of Frederick Herzberg (1959). Though his work has been subjected to considerable criticism, several useful concepts have endured. Herzberg's formulation suggests that two sets of essentially different factors affect worker performance in quite different ways. One set of factors—motivators—is related directly to job content. These are the primary source of job satisfaction. These factors include sense of independence, responsibility, accomplishment, recognition, advancement potential, and "closure" (understanding the whole task and how one fits in the total scheme of things).

EXHIBIT 9–1 The Path-Goal Motivation Model

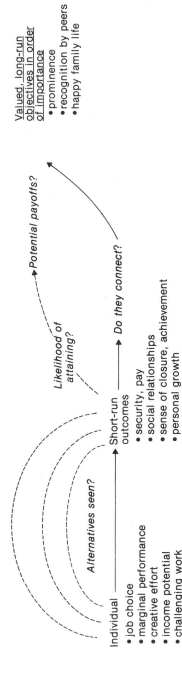

254

The second set of factors comes from the environment of work and is termed "hygiene," or maintenance, factors. These include pay, the quality of supervision, social amenities, and physical work conditions. Herzberg's theory suggests that people need and expect both kinds of satisfaction; if they're not there, they will be dissatisfied. If hygiene factors are present (the traditional amenities), dissatisfaction potential is likely to be lessened, but people won't be satisfied.

Degree of Job Enrichment—An Alternative Approach

Herzberg's concept has great historical significance, and it is highly referenced. Difficulties in using the Herzberg framework for assessing the level of job enrichment have led to alternative proposals. One is described in the following.

The degree of enrichment found on a job may be said to depend on five factors:

1. *autonomy*—the sense of self-containment, or independence. What choices exist? Can self-control be exercised?

2. *task identification*—the extent to which an individual can relate to the work being performed and its relationship to the general work system. Does the task have visible, recognizable features?

3. *task significance*—the contribution of one's job to total work performance. How critical or essential is the performance of one's job in servicing customers, developing profits, etc.?

4. *task variety*—the number of different job elements that indicate different skills, or routines, on the part of the worker.

5. *feedback*—information communicated to the job holder regarding acceptability of work performance, quality, bases for self-improvement.

These five factors have several distinct advantages over the Herzberg model. They provide a specific agenda of criteria for judging the degree of job enrichment content. They are divorced from the technical detail or specifics of a task and can be dealt with specifically in a wide variety of job situations.

The central concern of the enrichment approach to job analysis and redesign is to improve individual performance and personal realization through the job itself. Much greater latitude exists for modifying jobs than was thought possible in the past, so that performance is improved or not greatly blemished. This supersedes the old approach, "If jobs can't be improved to benefit the job holder, automate them out of existence." If changes are made, however, they should do more than simply enlarge the job with more activities of the same kind. Content must be enriched.

Job-Enrichment Procedures

Although some companies, such as American Telephone and Telegraph, have had many years of experience with JE approaches, results have not been uniform (Ford, 1974). Much information still must be developed from installations. Un-

---

EXHIBIT 9–2 Highlights of Job-Enrichment Procedures

---

1. *Criteria.* Criteria must be selected which will signal success or failure of job changes. Absenteeism, turnover, productivity, job attitudes, and sense of cooperation are among the many factors commonly considered.

2. *Controls.* Experimental and control groups should be available (if possible) to more accurately assess the changes in performance and behavioral indicators.

3. *Commitment.* The key people essential to success are job holders and supervisors. They must actively endorse the JE approach and typically request or volunteer participation.

4. *Design latitude.* Jobs and tasks must be capable of modification and upper management must be in agreement with these approaches.

5. *Joint benefits.* Job analysts and others must be understanding of both organizational and individual needs.

---

fortunately, the results from installations in the past often have not been examined rigorously. Consequently, a cautious approach is urged in considering work study approaches based on enrichment designs.

Exhibit 9–2 presents important steps and conditions required in JE approaches. They are noteworthy because of the growing importance of these investigations in the design or redevelopment of jobs. Often they take the form of an industrial experiment. First, the success of JE and design efforts must be measurable and acceptable to managers and officials. Second, since changes may take place regardless of how well an employee works, a control group is needed. This control, unaffected by the modification of job conditions, is helpful for making comparisons. This exhibit also points out the importance of management support for job-enrichment. Thus critical conditions for the success of job-enrichment rest on important organizational considerations aside from those in the job itself.

Traditional Work Tasks Under Job Enrichment

A production example in Chapter 6 described a job carried out in a traditional way—a job with five steps requiring a total of 1.5 minutes. The viewpoint and thrust of job-enrichment approaches have been to expand job content and achieve a more behaviorally satisfying experience. This production task (after enrichment) might appear as follows:

1. Inspect aluminum castings; although done once per batch, this might require, on the average   0.50 min.
2. Drilling operations   1.50
3. Replace drill bits and check out production setup periodically   .25
4. Assemble impeller into casting   1.50
5. Test (worker affixes name and "inspected" stamp)   .25
    Total standard time (under enriched conditions)   4.00 min.

Note the changes that have taken place in this job under enriched (and enlightened) job analysis. First, the time cycle of 1.50 minutes has been extended to 4.0 minutes, with 15 cycles per hour rather than the 40 cycles using the other procedures. Second, work content has changed dramatically as the simple operation of hole drilling has been expanded to include inspection and assembly operations. Third, the character of the job has changed. Not only have other tasks been added, but they require the worker to judge acceptability and permit a more complete functional grasp of the tasks. The new procedure also requires personal certification and identification of acceptability and performance.

Commentary and Critique: The Herzberg Approach

Few people would argue with the inherently attractive notion of enriching jobs. Disagreements begin on the practical level—where the theory is applied. The nagging question—What specific factors are likely to be enriching for a particular professional, manager, or work?—won't go away (Hackman and Lawler, 1971). The distinction between motivators and hygiene is much easier to draw on the level of theory than in practice.

However, the Herzberg motivational formulation is widely used. Many consultants and behavioral scientists feel that the Herzberg formulation contains observations and prescriptions that square with the facts. Many of Herzberg's contentions seem to reflect situations and behavior observed in widely different circumstances. Researchers have begun to identify which of Herzberg's concepts are really relevant and which ones must be modified (Cummings, 1974).

For example, work values may differ at various organizational levels. Top-level managers and professional personnel may tend to place most emphasis on job content and opportunities for personal realization (motivators), while white-collar and blue-collar groups may place equal stress on both hygiene and content factors.

Another set of developments is operating in favor of a behavioral approach to job design or some variation of it. The continuing uses of the man-machine model are becoming more and more inappropriate as societal needs continue to shift. Organizations are providing entry-level jobs with increasing opportunities for achieving a sense of closure, achievement, and self-direction. This increasing emphasis on motivators is the result of long, and sometimes painfully expensive, years of experience in those areas where job holders with advanced educational credentials are employed. But increasing numbers of blue-collar workers are rapidly catching up with their white-collar and professional counterparts. They are seeking similar kinds of gratification. This new attitude is also felt by experienced workers—especially professionals—who have become increasingly aggressive in seeking tasks and opportunities that permit greater personal realization.

Tactics for Increasing Employee Involvement in the Job

Motivators, as they relate to personal accomplishment, are not stable. Considerable variations appear to exist between and within occupational groups, levels of management, and levels of educational attainment. Money, for example, may be an important motivator for some people because it represents accomplishment, power, or the means to important, valued ends. For others, money may indeed be less important. Still, many workers at all job levels may adhere rather closely to traditional job values and stress the job satisfaction derived from hard work, loyalty, and dependability (for example), irrespective of specific job features.

In general, an analyst begins to determine important job features by identifying the particulars of the job holders, climate of the organization (e.g., cordiality, support, rewards available), and the economic features and flexibility of the work system. Tactics for increasing employee involvement include:

1. employee evaluation of supervisor
2. employee participation in problem solving and work improvements
3. job rotation to increase individual understanding of job roles
4. group counsel in hiring decisions involving formal group membership.

These tactics can lead to the development of longer-run strategies that will meet the different enrichment needs of employees.

JOB ANALYSIS IN SERVICE ORGANIZATIONS

Functional Job Study Approach

The growth of the service industry (e.g., insurance, banks, and government) has opened a new area of interest for job designers and analysts. Service organizations traditionally have been dependent on people and information for carrying out work. The need for better information systems for these occupations has become apparent as the number of people in them has increased. Government programs have sponsored basic research to establish the groundwork for job studies. A major document is the DOT, the *Dictionary of Occupational Titles,* which provides information and classifications of jobs (over 22,000 in 1974) for statistical and employment purposes. The DOT provides a ready base for systematic job studies.

DOT/JA approaches classify job features into "data," "things," and "people." Each of these classes is studied and the level of ability, complexity, or judgment is identified. Highly rated, or more difficult, jobs are characterized by unstructured situations, poor information, and the need for exercising judgment. These tasks require extensive education and/or experience. Coversely, jobs requiring little judgment, experience, or formal education get lower ratings. This is the essence of rating scales. A typical set of data-people-things scales is reproduced in Table 9–1.

A rating such as a 6 or 8 indicates low ability requirements in the data-people-things (DPT) categories. A number of different sets of work field categories has been established so that DPT descriptions are more easily applied to particular

TABLE 9-1 Data-People-Things (D-P-T) Analysis

Data	People	Things
0—synthesize	0—mentor	0—setup
1—coordinate	1—negotiate	1—precision work
2—analyze	2—instruct	2—operate, control
3—compile	3—supervise	3—drive, operate
4—compute	4—divert	4—manipulate
5—copy	5—persuade	5—tend
6—compare	6—speak-signal	6—feed
	7—serve	7—handle
	8—tube instruction	

fields. At this date about one hundred fields (sets) have been established. Each field is thought to reflect typical machines, tools, or equipment (technologies) or standard techniques to meet particular purposes (e.g., baking/drying, healing/caring, saving, and writing).

Categories of jobs and industries.   Another aspect of work performed is a classification of MPSMS—the materials, products, subject matter, or services connected with a particular job. About six hundred categories are organized into fifty-five groups (e.g., bacteriology, banking, business services). The rating of the appropriate DPT set plus specification of the MPSMS category identifies 1) level of skills required (DPT) and 2) services, or activity associated with the particular job. These functional job studies provide fifteen different categories of data (details of these are provided in the appendix to this chapter) beyond that already described. Information is made available for such areas as educational preparation, aptitudes (mental and physical) commonly associated with the job, special requirements in temperament, experience, and equipment commonly employed at work.

Complications.   The earlier discussions in this chapter pointed out the growing trend in job analysis to employ direct measures of job requirements (what people do) as opposed to indirect measures, which traditionally included educational level or broad descriptors such as skill or aptitude. Enactment of equal employment opportunity legislation supports the shift to direct measures and places indirect measures in the suspect category (requiring close study and validation). Various indirect categories have appeared in some of the functional job analysis approaches employed. Thus this method can be useful but it should be used carefully.

Work Design Applications: What Can Be Done?

Precisely because functional job study separates data, people, and things, it provides considerable potential for redesigning work and improving job assignments. For example, a clerk's job may be at the lowest category of data—namely, a number 6, which indicates "compare." Additionally it may only require to "serve" people (7). These two categories would place the clerk at a very low point in degree of job enrichment.

The clerk's job probably would be low on at least four factors: autonomy, task identification, task variety, and task significance. For the clerk's job there would be a need to redevelop the data and people categories in order to meet the job enrichment criteria we have discussed. This would be the basis of the job redesign.

Data. The clerk might be made responsible for "copying" or even "computing." For example, additional tasks that are now a part of another job could be incorporated into the clerk's job, or several different jobs might be recombined in a different way. The clerk might also be given tasks that would lead to more active involvement in the work activity. The clerk might check information with others (number 6—"speak") or secure needed information. Increasing responsibilities in both categories—data and people—would increase task variety and task significance.

Training needs. In the process of creating an enriched job, new work demands are made on the job holder, and new skills must be developed. The job analyses that provide the basis for enrichment take into account the new skill demands along with the aptitudes, abilities, and interests of the job holder. A delicate balance is implied—weighing enriched work content against the interests and potential limitations (physical and mental abilities) of the workers. At times a series of adjustments might have to be made in the redesigned job before the worker and the work can be well matched.

APPLYING LEADERSHIP AND COMMUNICATION CONCEPTS TO DESIGN PROBLEMS

Organization Design, Work Systems, and Job Analysis

The design of jobs and work systems is an important part of job analysis (Chapter 6) and organization design. How does a manager design jobs and work systems? He must have a working knowledge of the elements of the job, job analysis techniques, and the impact of work on individual performance. In other words he must have a picture of the overall organization.

Organization design deals with the broader aspects of authority structure and the allocation of responsibilities to subdivisions (department, section, etc.). Logically one would expect the grand design of the organization to precede job design. This is the theory and its logic is probably solid. But in practice the opportunity to work with total organization design is rare. Organization problems are approached on an individual basis. More often, a particular organization design problem will arise from the creation (or elimination) of a department and the need to reorganize a portion of the total organization. Even a simple problem such as the number of workers which should report to one supervisor will raise many questions and, probably, not be readily resolved. Consequently we have not devoted extensive material to organization design matters because of the wide range and depth of subject matter involved. This subject matter goes beyond the scope of this book and the interested reader is directed to the references at the end of the chapter.

Leadership, Communications, and Work Design

Two interests that are closely related to organization design, leadership and communications, are treated in this section. Both topics are deeply intertwined with modern approaches to designing jobs.

Leadership style and approaches of supervisors vary according to the situation or particulars of a job. Thus, in designing a job we cannot take supervision as a constant.

Communication channels for information transmission, control, and coordination are the basic media for exchange among workers or between worker and supervisor. Communications are also the vehicle through which motivated performance—or confusion and alienation—can and do emerge.

Leadership: formal responsibility and behavioral issues. Wide differences frequently exist between the formal authority of a position and the kind of leadership the day-to-day situation requires. Much recent work has been done in this area, with important implications for job design practice. (Fiedler, 1971; House, 1971; Hunt and Hill, 1971) Explicit recognition of formal authority is evident in the job title "supervisor," but simply delegating formal authority to a position does not guarantee leadership. Subordinates must eventually accept their supervisor's authority if work potential is to be realized. The specific needs of a situation may involve matters that go beyond a simple recounting of authority or responsibility. Sometimes the real leader doesn't have that title.

A contingency approach to design. Managers have recognized the need for more realistic approaches to defining leadership responsibilities. Increasing need for flexibility points up the potential value of the contingency approach. When using this approach, a supervisor assumes that the job holder will be able to exercise a variety of leadership roles: 1) consideration—fostering a supportive, cordial relationship; or 2) structuring—defining job objectives, procedures, and at times recognizing the need for close supervision to insure control. Central contingencies are shown in Exhibit 9–3.

Design studies. The categories of situations influencing job analysis reflect the organization's main productive functions. These features apply to all cases, regardless of work system, job holder's preparation, the relationship of the supervisor to higher authority (the "boss"), and the formally designated leader of the group. The latter point requires amplification: What the boss expects *does* make a difference. Frequently, top management may expect the supervisor to get tough, but this approach may be far from what the situation requires or the

EXHIBIT 9–3   Leadership Contingencies in Work Design Studies

Typical situations and job description approach for supervision

1. *Work Situation* *
   (technology, physical)
   Degree of work standardization
   - high — Low need for direction; "structuring" up
   - low — Tough direct supervision; "structuring" minimized

   Workers' creativity need
   - high — Supervision less
   - low — Supervision depends on other situational or personal factors

   Physical dispersion
   - high — Supervisory time available lessened
   - low — Depends on other situational or personal factors

   Adversity of conditions
   (depending on leader: threat, death, severe penalty)
   - high — Increased dependence on leader
   - low — Little or no influence

2. *Typical group member preparation regarding work task* †
   - good
   - marginal — The poorer the preparation, the greater the supervision required; good preparation diminishes required supervision
   - poor

3. *Breadth of supervisory activity* ††
   - wide — The greater the span of responsibilities, the less supervisory time available
   - narrow

4. *Type of group supervised* *
   - blue collar
   - white collar — The greater the professionalization of the group, the greater the existence and exertion of colleague norms of behavior and performance quality and the less the supervision
   - professional

5. *Power of supervisor in organization* (able to secure services/arrangements) ††
   - high — Diminishes supervisory need
   - low

6. *Boss's expectations for supervisor* †
   - "Consideration"
   - "Structuring of work task, objectives, procedures — Where these coincide, tension and conflict lessened

Key: * Explicit in job analysis approach.
     † Explicit if a regular and recurring condition.
     †† Practical factors posing supervisory and organizational problems.

supervisor wants. Thus, beyond the immediate job design requirements there are a variety of behavioral issues including conflict. Although the job analyst or work designer may not be concerned directly with these matters, top management and the personnel manager certainly are.

Points not considered. For this discussion of leadership considerations in job design, the points concerning the quality of relations (supervisor and worker) and preparation (experience and education) are disregarded. However, they would form a practical part of any personnel assignment involving problem solving in a leadership situation.

The remainder of this chapter is devoted to communications. While our discussion will focus on the internal communications system of organizations, it will also have some bearing on the contingency model of leadership.

Communications Analysis

The importance of communications gets a lot of "lip service," but unfortunately many organizations think they have a communications program if they have a bulletin-board campaign. Many also see communications as safety promotion or "getting our message to the stockholders." These are aspects of communications, but they do not in themselves constitute a program. Personnel officials and line managers alike frequently mistake techniques for strategy. They fail to follow the basic guidelines needed to identify strategies and successful programming efforts. As noted in Chapter 6 (job descriptions), cooperative working relationships are critically dependent on good communications. The following discussion on communications will primarily concern organization members and will not include matters that ordinarily are grouped under advertising, though these ideas may have useful applications in this area.

Managers and personnel officers need a basis to judge how well they're doing in communications. Two perspectives (see Exhibit 9–4) of communications flow help identify the needs of the situation: 1) behavioral, which emphasizes flow between job holders, and 2) systems, which stresses relationships, information flow, media, and performance features (e.g., timing). Several criteria are good indicators of an organization's communications effectiveness.

Behavioral perspective. Communications flow two ways. The work needs and the behavioral support of group members, not supervisory whim, should determine the degree, the direction, and the content of communications. "Behavioral support" means that work situations make their own particular demands on the individual (attentiveness, isolation, pace of work, precision, etc.) and communications may be able to absorb or reduce the adverse behavioral consequences that may result.

Feedback. Feedback should be explained further. Communications flow may be two way in form, but one way in actual content. If one channel is passive (e.g., when the supervisor doesn't actively seek a response), a subordinate simply

EXHIBIT 9–4   Communications Perspectives: Behavioral and Systems

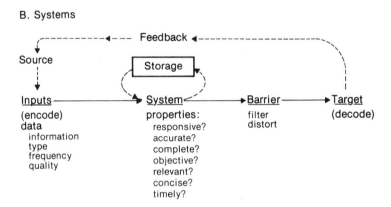

A. Behavioral, "Person to person"

"I hear you.....do you hear me?"

B. Systems

complies with requests for information which are passed down the line. Feedback stresses the interactive nature of communications flow, the give-and-take and convergence on mutual understanding. Feedback also relates to a number of other important matters involving training (How am I doing?), interaction in group settings, judging individual progress toward career and business objectives, and evaluating personal improvement.

Information content.   Information flow may involve impersonal content such as data, objectives, rules, and the like. It may also involve behavioral overtones or specific behavioral content (e.g., emotional). Impersonal content is necessary for an organization's activities (orders, economic data, performance information, policy, etc.) to function properly.

Virtually any communication contains the seeds of various behavioral issues. Communications can help give subordinates a meaningful sense of participation and contribution that support organizational goals and individual needs for security, recognition, achievement, and growth.

Many seemingly impersonal situations can have behavioral overtones. Goals, for example, may help to build individual loyalty and identification or may neutralize conscientious, individual efforts. For example, A tells B that the target for next month is 1,200 sales units. B, knowing full well that he won't have enough time to make the number of calls needed to sell 1,200 units, becomes upset and lets A know in no uncertain terms that this is completely unrealistic. How and what a supervisor communicates with subordinates may express confidence or desire for participation, contribution, and opinion feedback. Supervision may communicate in such a way as to build on acceptance (or conviction) of the formal leader's ideas or in a way that creates frustration and conflict.

Job Design—Interpersonal Communications

Hopefully we have shown that the thoughtful construction of communications relationships can bring important returns to an organization and its members. Some guidelines emerge from wide-ranging industrial experiences and research:

1. B must *think to* tell A (of his problems, concerns, or ideas for improvement). Something must initiate this flow.
2. B must *want* to tell A.
3. B must have *the opportunity to* tell A.
4. If B finds the opportunity to tell A, A must *listen* with understanding.
5. A must be *responsive* to B—reflecting understanding, approval, sympathy, or cooperation. In some instances, A becomes a channel through which meaningful actions for both parties come about. Alternatively, A and B may reach a mutual understanding, regardless of whether they agree on content or not.

Scenario—A Problem in Communications

The following scenario illustrates the five criteria that must be met if two-way interpersonal communications flow is to take place. In this scenario, A is Alice, office manager, and B is Bill, credit supervisor, who works for Alice.

Background.   For a considerable time Bill has been bothered by the phone situation in the office. He has a direct-dial phone but it is on the left side of his desk (the most convenient installation). Bill's calls are often so long that he likes to do other work while hanging onto the phone. The trouble is that he is left-handed, and the phone gets in the way. Almost every day, when Bill is on the phone, he promises himself to talk to Alice about changing the installation, but he is constantly very busy (B must have the opportunity to tell A), and Alice never seems to be in her office when Bill is looking for her. In fact, other matters have arisen in the office in recent months involving other office people which, though minor in nature, have not been resolved and have been left to corridor discussion.

Narrowing the problem.   One day Bill is talking to Catherine, who handles receivables; she also has a problem. When Bill spots Alice walking hurriedly through the office, he calls out, "Alice, can we see you for a couple of minutes? There are some things we just have to talk about." Alice agrees. Bill and Catherine go into Alice's office, and they discuss a variety of issues. While they are talking Alice receives several phone calls and engages in some short conversations. Finally Catherine says, "Why don't you have your secretary take the calls for a few minutes—how can you understand the importance to us of getting these things straightened out if you are constantly interrupted? (A must listen if B or C has found the opportunity to tell A.)

Agreement. After additional discussion, Alice is convinced of the importance or these matters to Bill and Catherine (reaching a common understanding) and agrees to correct the matters, although some exceed the current budget and will have to be delayed. (A provides the action channel.)

Communications Systems in Job Design

Exhibit 9-4 displays an additional perspective drawn along systems lines; it requires clarification. Communications is the organizational cement that joins people, units, and work activity. This perspective emphasizes the quality of information that is available (completeness, accuracy, relevance, objectivity, and timeliness). The systems perspective also deals with the following:

1. Selection of information channels and their appropriateness for particular needs.

2. Storage and information accessibility; completeness relative to work processing, planning, and decision making. There is no point in storing something that can't be delivered where and when it is needed.

3. Barrier—that is, filtering or distortion, whether intended or unintended. Filtering means the removal of relevant points in communications. Filtering can result from poor listening or it can represent a subtle form of fighting the organization or individuals within it. For example, if conflicts exist among various departmental personnel, people often hear what they want to hear, or veiled threats. Consider the difference between "hospital turnover is 8 percent" and "nursing turnover is 8 percent."

Another point about barriers is that where they are significant, rumors flourish. Failure of officials to provide enough information encourages organization members to construct their own stories.

Good communication systems design can greatly assist work flow and help create a climate of understanding and mutual purpose within an organization.

Other information considerations. Systems design for communications or exploration of problems indicate that the following types of questions should be answered.

1. What are the objectives of the information exchange? understanding? warning? cooperation? enlist support?

2. Who are the senders and receivers of information (A's and B's)?

3. What are the information requirements in terms of type, frequency, accuracy, access, privacy, security, etc.?

4. What information media (verbal, written), channels (face-to-face, written message, computer terminal, teletype, TV, phone, etc.) or forums (casual meeting, committee, project group, etc.) will provide maximum understanding and information exchange?

Cooperative working relationships involve behavioral and systems features of communications. A, for example, is production general foreman on the final assembly line of Franklin Motor's plant in Cleveland. He is responsible for door, window, and trim assembly on the auto chassis. For several months he has had problems with the poor fit of many purchased components. When a foreman has a problem, he calls A and tries to work things out. If this fails, A calls process engineering, purchasing, or quality control, but somehow the problems don't get solved permanently. The general foreman's job description indicates that three key cooperative work relationships are with purchasing, process engineering, and quality control, but it doesn't describe the mechanism for working out problems.

A specialist with experience in communications studies, called in from personnel, talks at length with the general foreman, line foreman, and the contract people in process engineering, purchasing, and quality control. The specialist also spends considerable time observing the production line and draws up a "communication interaction matrix." It shows the direction of communications flow, the content of the messages, and provides comments on the transmission media. A sample work sheet for recording frequency and direction of flow is provided in Exhibit 9–5.

EXHIBIT 9–5   Communications Analysis Work Sheet Format

Date _____
Analyst _____
Time_____

Direction of information flow

	General foreman		Foreman		Purchasing		Process engineering		Quality control	
	From	To	From	To	From	To	From	To	From	To
General foreman	—	—								
Foreman			—	—						
Purchasing					—	—				
Process engineering							—	—		
Quality control									—	—

The communications study indicated that the general foreman initiated all contacts with process engineering, purchasing, and quality control after the foreman complained of a particular difficulty. Second, the study indicated that the general foreman discussed the problems individually with the support staff so

EXHIBIT 9–6   Communication Network

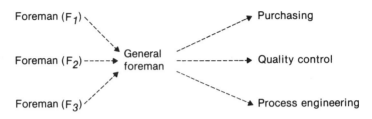

that the opportunity for everyone to get together to compare notes never occurred. This system of communication is illustrated in Exhibit 9–6. Information disclosed by this job study led to a group meeting in which both operating
and staff support personnel compared notes and problems. This meeting
clarified problems, generated possible solutions, and helped establish a climate
of understanding. As a result, subsequent feedback and communication relationships were improved greatly. The study also resulted in a better system of communications between the general foreman and support people. A committee was
established to hold short meetings to discuss progress on previously identified
problems and to identify new problems as they arose.

EXHIBIT 9–7   Revised Communication Network

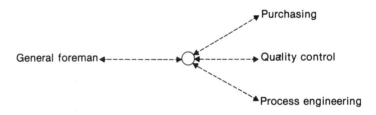

The communications system study identified existing information flows and
the needs of the system. System improvements emerged from mutual understanding of problems and the benefits of group versus individual action. A better
internal organization and a new communications format helped assure continuing
attention to chronic problems.

SUMMARY

The job enrichment approach introduced in this chapter is one way of dealing
with problems of worker performance and fulfillment. This approach consists
of two factors: extrinsic factors, which are outside of the job, and intrinsic factors,
which are part of the job itself. Expanding intrinsic factors can be used to provide
work challenge, independence, sense of closure (completeness) and personal
accomplishment. According to the path-goal view, job enrichment can prove a

motivating force to the extent that the job holder sees job outcomes as securing valued long-range goals. The perspective in this chapter has been that those work design approaches that meet the test of the path-goal model could well result in better job performance and a greater sense of personal realization through job design or redesign.

This chapter also described approaches to work design based on behavioral and systems analyses involving leadership and communications. Use of these concepts makes design a broader, more complex idea, beyond the specifics of a particular job. One job links to another job and communications provides the connections. Leadership considerations also link jobs, worker and job, and the worker to other areas of the organization. Jointly, leadership and communications form an important part of design approaches because of their impact on both performance and behavioral aspects of the worker.

DISCUSSION QUESTIONS

1. Regarding the scenario concerning Mid-States Telephone and Frank Kay:
   a. In what way were the traditional and more recent approaches of job analysis said to differ?
   b. In job (re)design, which job factors received the primary attention of the analyst?
   c. In what way do leadership considerations complicate the job analysis activity in relation to the officially designated authority person?
   d. What is the general role of motivation in job design?

2. Briefly describe the path-goal model and its use as a criterion for judging the relevance and desirability of a particular job design.

3. What are some of the central features of the job enrichment concept and what assumptions underly it?

4. What are some criticisms of the Herzberg theory as employed to job enrichment?

5. What aspects of leadership are explicit or implicit in job descriptions?

6. What differences exist in approach when distinguishing behavioral views of communication from the systems view?

7. What job prerequisites were outlined for effective communications?

8. What are some of the highlights of the DOT functional job analysis approach (see Appendix)?

9. Select a common job or one you are familiar with that possesses job characteristics likely to lead to unrewarding or dull work.
   a. Outline your approach to job analysis and the information you would need to undertake a job redesign.
   b. What specific proposals would you make for improving this job, considering both the operational and behavioral features.
   c. Justify your approach in terms of work considerations (sociotechnical analysis) and in terms of the path-goal model. State your assumptions.

d. What organizational support would you seek for your program?

e. How would this job enrichment undertaking be handled as a research activity yet be dealt with in a practical manner?

f. Provide a job description of the redesigned job.

10. At Central States Telephone, a small independent phone company in the Midwest, a variety of work activities are carried out to support the main activity of providing phone service for better than 200,000 subscribers. One portion of the support work deals with the maintenance and updating of the subscriber list for the directory. Additions, changes, "suppression" of numbers, and cancellation of service (temporary or permanent) are some of the many activities that concern this department. Currently the directory department is set up as follows:

Directory Department
Supervisor

Order Entry:	Directory Look-up:	Field Service	Exchange Service	Special Operator Listing:	Customer Service	Clerks
Entry	Current listing	Contact: Installation, removal, change	Contact: Adds/changes service at exchange	Apprises callers of change in listing	Contact: Customer contacts to clarify or secure information	

Employment: 15 people

The organization chart depicts the main activities of the directory department and some of the key functions of each section. Over the years, this work has become highly specialized, and each section carries out some phase of the total activity related to the modification of phone service and subsequent changes in the directory. Turnover and absenteeism in these jobs are extremely high. Exit interviews typically reflect fatigue, boredom, or unimaginative work as reasons for leaving the company. As a member of the personnel department, your assistance has been requested in recommending ways of improving this operation through job redesign. State necessary assumptions and answer the following:

a. How does the directory department's activity relate to the main work function of telephone service?

b. Write a simple job description for one of the section employees (directory look-up, etc.) as the job currently stands.

c. What are some alternatives for job redesign? (advantages and limitations?)

d. What approach would you propose? Justify your response in terms of work considerations and the path-goal model.

e. What criteria would be employed to gauge performance improvement? What research design would provide the information needed to evaluate the success or needed changes in this project?

f. What organizational strategy could be employed for undertaking this work and enlisting the support of key people?

11. Review the DOT functional job analysis form in the Appendix and suggest areas that could be questioned in light of E.E.O. legislation.

APPENDIX
FUNCTIONAL JOB STUDY: INFORMATION DEVELOPMENT

The range of information generated in job analysis studies based on the data-people-things concept is extensive and more easily understood by considering the information gathered.* The following description is reproduced from job analysis materials employed by the U.S. Department of Labor, Manpower Administration. It generally parallels the information on the form but some modifications have been made for illustrative purposes. Other modifications or complications due to equal employment opportunity legislation will be described shortly.

1. *Job title*

2. *Industry assignments*—general description of industries using indicated job

3. *SIC code(s) and title*—a number (based on DOT) indicating the type of establishment

4. *Job summary*—summary description of major job features

5. *Work performed*—rating of worker activities in terms of data-people-things. The example below is one of some 600 different sets of scales.

Data	*People*	*Things*
0. Synthesize	0. Mentor	0. Setup
1. Coordinate	1. Negotiate	1. Precision work
2. Analyze	2. Instruct	2. Operate,
3. Compile	3. Supervise	control
4. Compute	4. Direct	3. Drive, operate
5. Copy	5. Persuade	4. Manipulate
6. Compare	6. Speak-signal	5. Tend
	7. Serve	6. Feed
	8. Tube instruction	7. Handle

6. *Education, aptitude, interests, and behavioral features*

a. *GED (general educational development)*—a composite rating of reasoning, mathematical, and language development. For example, a rating of 1 might correspond to commonsense understanding and ability to follow simple instructions (reasoning), addition and subtraction (math), and speaking and writing simple sentences. A 6 might involve logical/scientific thinking (reasoning), use of calculus, modern algebra or statistics, ability to read the literature and write precisely, and to speak in a persuasive manner.

b. *SVP (specific vocational preparation)*—refers to the time required to learn techniques or acquire information.

* This approach is also tied into the *Dictionary of Occupational Titles*, which gives it great applicability in better than 20,000 jobs referenced in the material.

c. *Aptitudes*

G—intelligence

E—eye/hand/foot coordination

V—verbal

N—spatial

P—form perception

Q—clerical perception

C—color discrimination

K—motor coordination

F—finger dexterity

M—manual dexterity

Each aptitude is rated on a five-point scale.

d. *Temperament* (relevant items noted) or personal traits of workers

D—direction

F—feelings, ideas

E—influence

J—sensory, judgment

M—measurable criteria

P—dealing with people

R—repetitive work

S—perform under stress

T—set limits, tolerances

V—variety and changes

e. *Interests*—patterns of interest often held by job holders. Possibilities include:

1a. preference for activities dealing with things and objects versus

1b. preference for activities concerned with the communication of data;

2a. preference for activities involving business contacts with people versus

2b. preference for activities of a scientific and technical nature;

3a. preference for activities resulting in prestige or the esteem of other versus

3b. preference for activities resulting in tangible production

f. *Physical demands* (appropriate item checked)

strength ("sedentary" to "heavy" to "very heavy")

climbing

stooping

talking

seeing

g. *Environmental conditions*—aspects of the physical environment imposing specific demands on a worker's physical capacity

1. work location (inside, outside, or both)

2. cold extremity

3. heat extremity

4. wetness, humidity

5. noise, vibration

6. hazards

7. atmospheric conditions

7. *General education*—general assessment of overall educational requirements

8. *Vocational preparation*—includes college, trade preparation (vocational school apprenticeship), training in companies (in-plant training), on-the-job or other training

9. *Experience*

10. *Orientation*—overall elapsed time to understand job duties (while employed)

11. *Licenses*

12. *Relations to other jobs*—concerns promotion or transfer from particular job and indicates immediate supervisor and supervision requirements

13. *Machines, tools, equipment*

14. *Materials and products*

15. *Detailed description of task*

16.–17. *General information*

18. *Preparation information*

The form just described is the product of considerable job study efforts, which include observation and questionnaires filled out by the job holder and supervisor. The completed form, and discussion between supervisor and job holder, become the basis for job modifications (redesign). When the analysis is finally agreed upon, it becomes the basis for job descriptions, recruiting programs, work redesign, improved matching of individual and job, and compensation.

In attempts to more precisely define job or work-related needs, the DOT-type analysis continues to undergo modifications. Scales for "general educational development" (illustrated) and "worker instruction" (autonomy or degree of supervision required) represent some of these additions.

BIBLIOGRAPHY

Burack, Elmer H. *Organization Analysis: Concepts and Applications.* Hinsdale, Ill.: Dryden/Holt, Rinehart & Winston, 1975.

Cummings, Paul. "Does Herzberg's Theory Really Work?" *Personnel Administrator* (October 1974):19–22.

Fiedler, Fred E. "Twenty Years of Considerations and Structure." *Symposium on Contemporary Developments in the Study of Leadership.* Carbondale, Ill.: Southern Illinois University, 1971.

Ford, Robert N. "Work Itself Programs." American Telephone and Telegraph Company, 1974.

Grote, Richard C. "Implementing Job Enrichment." *California Management Review.* 15 (Fall 1972):16–21.

Hackman, J. R., and Edward Lawler. "Employee Reaction to Job Characteristics." *Journal of Applied Psychology* (June 1971):259–86.

Hellriegel, Donald, and John Slocum. *Organizational Behavior: Contingency Views.* Minneapolis, Minn.: West Publishing, 1976.

Herzberg, Frederick, B. Mausner, and B. Synderman. *The Motivation to Work,* 2d ed. New York: Wiley, 1959.

House, Robert J. "A Path Goal Theory of Leader Effectiveness." *Administrative Science Quarterly.* 16.3 (September 1971):321–33.

House, Robert J., Alan C. Filley, and Steven Kerr. "Relation of Leader Consideration and Initiating Structure to R & D Subordinate Satisfaction." *Administrative Science Quarterly.* 16.1 (March 1971):19–30.

House, Robert J., and L. A. Wigdor. "Herzberg's Dual-Factor Theory of Job Satisfaction and Motivation: A Review of the Evidence and a Criticism." *Personnel Psychology.* 20 (Winter 1967):369–89.

Hulin, Charles L., and M. R. Blood. "Job Enlargement, Included Differences and Worker Responses." *Psychological Bulletin.* 69 (1968):41–55.

Kerr, Steven, *et al.* "Toward a Contingency Theory of Leadership Based on the Consideration and Initiating Structure Literature." Working paper, Ohio State Univesity College of Administrative Science, 1973.

Lawler, Edward E. III, and J. L. Suttle. "A Causal Correlation Test of the Need Hierarchy Concept." *Organizational Behaviors and Human Performance* 7 (November 1972):265–87.

Luthins, Fred. "Contingency Theory of Management." *Business Horizons.* 16.4, 9 (June 1973):67–73.

Maslow, Abraham. *Motivation and Productivity.* New York: Harper & Row. 1956.

Miles, Raymond E. *Theories of Management.* New York: McGraw-Hill, 1975.

Rizzo, John R., Robert J. House, and Sidney E. Lertzman. "Role Conflict and Ambiguity in Complex Organizations." *Administrative Science Quarterly* 15 (1970): 150–53.

Rosow, Jerome W., ed. *The Worker and the Job.* Englewood Cliffs, N.J.: Prentice-Hall, 1974.

Schwab, Donald P., H. W. De Vitt, and Larry L. Cummings. "A Test of the Two Factor Theory as a Predictor of Self-Report Performance Effects." *Personnel Psychology.* 24 (1971):293–303.

Shepard, Jon M. "Specialization, Autonomy, and Job Satisfaction." *Industrial Relations.* 12 (October 1973):274–81.

Sheppard, Harold L., and Neal Q. Herrick. *Where Have All the Robots Gone? Worker Dissatisfaction in the 70's.* New York: Free Press, 1972.

Strauss, George. "Job Satisfaction; Motivation; and Job Design." In *Organizational Behavior: Research and Issues,* George Strauss *et al.,* eds. Madison, Wis.: Industrial Relations Research Assoc., 1974.

Vroom, Victor H. *Work and Motivation.* New York: Wiley, 1964.

Wahba, Mahmond A. "Maslow Reconsidered: Review of Empirical Evidence of the Need Hierarchy Theory." *Proceedings of the 33rd Annual Meeting of the Academy of Management.* Boston, August 1973.

Wofford, J. C. "The Motivational Bases of Job Satisfaction and Job Performance." *Personnel Psychology.* 24.3 (Autumn 1971):504–6.

Yukl, Gary. "Toward a Behavioral Theory of Leadership." *Organizational Behavior and Human Performance.* 6 (July 1971):414–40.

Chapter 10

JOB
EVALUATION

LEARNING OBJECTIVES

After reading this chapter, the student should be able to:

Define and distinguish between job analysis and job evaluation

Describe traditional approaches to job evaluation

Identify problem areas in job evaluation

Describe new approaches to job evaluation

Apply different job analysis and evaluation techniques to actual job situations.

KEY TERMS AND CONCEPTS

compensable factors

job analysis versus job
   evaluation

job structure

basic methods:
   nonquantitative schemes
   quantitative schemes

ranking method

job classification

point method

factor comparison

overlap

key/benchmark jobs

factor degrees

curve fitting: linear, curvilinear,
   constant value

DOT

PAQ

factor analytic techniques

dimensions of managerial positions

factor clusters

Hay Plan

PREVIEW

How well are employees producing? Can it be improved? These are important questions that job evaluation can help answer. This chapter discusses four topics:

1. Basic job evaluation methods and procedures. The concepts and terminology critical to a general understanding are explained.

2. Newer job evaluation techniques. We review some of the newer job evaluation approaches that are in use today in various organizations. Some of the techniques described in this section are especially applicable to managerial positions.

3. Important behavioral issues.

4. Future trends and directions in job evaluation.

Job analysis should provide considerable understanding of what a specific job involves. It also can provide a basis for relating a particular job to other jobs and broader aspects of the organization and work system.

Some job descriptions give a sense of content or relationships solely on the basis of societal norms or general experience. For example, if a job entails management responsibilities, it probably is more important (at least in terms of salary, though other points may be debated) than a blue collar job. Also, the manager probably is considered more important than the foreman, and the officer more important than both. Yet these crude assessments don't need job analysis—they can more or less be determined by looking at job titles.

However, if we move across an organization and make comparisons between titles such as production manager and marketing manager, or clerk and assembler, we need more than crude inferences or general impressions of work content to establish the relative importance of jobs. This is the task of job evaluation.

An organization bases wages on *compensable factors*. Managers frequently use job analysis content and descriptions to translate job requirements into degrees or levels of compensable factors and, subsequently, into points and dollars. Examples of compensable factors include physical work conditions, influence on sales, mental dexterity, and level of education needed. Traditional plans, such as those used by the National Metal Traders Association (NMTA) or Midwest Industrial Management Association (MIMA), employ relatively small numbers of factors, perhaps six to eight.

The traditional approach to job evaluation includes three factors: job structure, job analysis, and the evaluation itself. Job analysis is used to determine the job design, responsibilities, and specifications needed to complete a job successfully. JA takes the needs of both the work and the worker into account. Job evaluation is a process for establishing the relative importance of a job in order to assign monetary rewards. The factors used to determine the monetary importance of a job are called compensable factors. When all jobs have been evaluated so that their relationships are established, they form a job (wage) structure.

The problem of translation.   Unfortunately, job analyses most frequently *cannot* be used as measures to translate relative job importance into dollar figures. For example, JA may cite required educational or physical skills for a position. But what importance is to be assigned to them? JA may provide ratings of the ability needed to handle people or use information. But how are we to combine multiple measures of job requirements so that different jobs can be compared and given relative importance? This is the task of job evaluation specialists.

None of the job analysis techniques described in Chapter 9 can be directly translated into measures of relative job importance. All of the data and information from JA must be translated before the relative importance of a job can be determined for compensation purposes. Traditional job evaluation (JE) approaches have performed this transformation, but some relatively new approaches have shown promise for direct translation of job analysis efforts; they will be briefly described in the following section.

EXHIBIT 10–1 Relation of Job Analysis to Job Evaluation

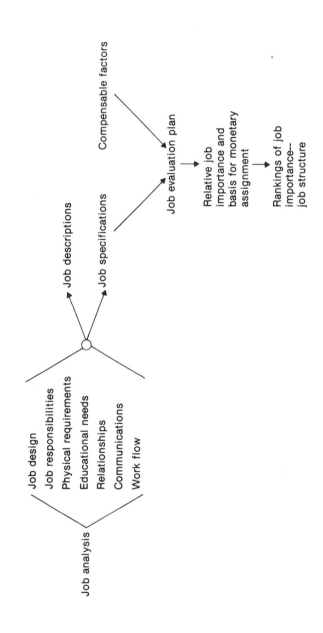

BASIC JOB EVALUATION METHODS AND PROCEDURES

Traditional Approaches to Job Evaluation

There are two broad categories of traditional methods and four basic plans:

1. Nonqualitative schemes
   a. Ranking method
   b. Job classification method
2. Quantitative schemes
   a. Point method
   b. Factor comparison method

The principal differences between these methods reflect 1) consideration of the job as a whole versus consideration of compensable factors, and 2) judging and comparing jobs with each other rather than assigning numerical scores on a rating scale. Plans commonly in use today represent variations of these basic methods.

Ranking method. This is the simplest and oldest of the four basic plans. Jobs are considered as a whole, and an attempt is made to establish a job's importance by comparing it with another one. In small organizations or where a small number of different jobs exist (say around thirty or less), the scheme is fast, quite manageable, and easy to explain to employees (or a union). Raters, who should be knowledgeable managers, and a personnel analyst establish the ratings based on job descriptions. The process is initially based on judgment and tends to be influenced by a variety of personal biases (Akalin, 1971). Perhaps the most serious shortcoming of this approach is its lack of comparison criteria.

Attempts have been made to develop more systematic ranking procedures. A "paired comparison," or "card sorting," approach forces job comparisons and lends some order to this approach. Also, job analysts have sought to define a set of *comparison criteria* for use by the ranking committee as the sole guide for establishing rankings. Ranking techniques, although they may establish an acceptable order of differences, provides no basis for establishing relative amounts of differences. It's good to know that X is more important than Y and that Y is more important than Z, but how much more important? That is, ranking techniques can establish orders of importance, such as X–Y–Z, but the relative differences remain undefined.

Classification method. When the classification method is used, overall job assessments are still made (as in ranking method), but they are related to job grades or general classes of jobs arranged in order of importance. This technique, though still judgmental (and a qualitative approach), seeks to remedy one of the serious deficiencies of the ranking method. The use of fully described job classes meets the need for employing systematic criteria in ordering jobs as to their importance. Many workers tend to think of jobs in, or related to, clusters or groups, and this approach makes it easier for workers to understand rankings. If an organization consists of five hundred people holding sixty different jobs, the jobs might be broken up into perhaps five classes, arranged in order of importance from low to high, and described class by class. The class descriptions might broadly reflect level of education, mental skill, profit impact, or some combination of these.

Perhaps the most serious problem in attempting to employ the classification method is the basic difficulty of developing descriptions for job grades. If an analyst tries to incorporate specific duties or responsibilities in the class grade description, it will be difficult to make generalizations. It is difficult to develop sufficiently broad categories that include many different jobs and are still specific enough to allow grading. Although not widely used in industry, Civil Service classifications of job classes/grades are used extensively for most federal government jobs. In the Civil Service system some eighteen job classes are employed and span a range from entry level, to grade no. 1, to skilled clerical jobs, to senior managers and officials (grade no. 18). Salary ranges correspond rather directly to the job grades, although there are overlap situations (one may earn more in the highest level of one grade than in the lowest level of the next higher grade).

Factor comparison method. This approach is one of the two basic *quantitative* schemes. Using this approach, a personnel manager compares how many compensable factors jobs possess, selects comparable factors of job A and job B, and compares them. (A compensable factor represents an essential element or skill needed to perform the job in a satisfactory manner—"it's what we pay people for." At times it may also represent adversity (e.g., heat or cold) that the job holder must live with.

The factor comparison approach is carried out as follows:

1. *Key,* or, *benchmark* jobs are identified that reflect
   a. the full range of importance and salary
   b. job titles that are commonly found in other companies or industries and thus facilitate comparisons with conditions outside of the organization. (With care in selection, a small number of benchmark jobs, perhaps a dozen or less, can meet the needs of large organizations.)

2. Compensable factors are identified and described.

3. Benchmark jobs are ranked within each of the categories of compensable factors. In other words, if five compensable factors are employed, five separate comparisons will be made. The result of this analysis is the ranked order of importance of each benchmark job relative to the extent it utilizes the factor. For example:

Compensable factors

Mental requirements	*Skill requirements*
1. Estimator	1. Tool designer
2. Draftsman	2. Draftsman
3. Tool designer	3. Estimator
4. Clerk	4. Clerk

4. These jobs are then ranked under each factor by the relative cost or amount it is thought each is worth. For example:

Value ($/hr)	Mental requirements	Skill requirements
3.00		
2.75		
2.90		
2.25		Tool designer
2.00	Estimator	
1.75		
1.50	Draftsman	
1.25	Tool designer	Draftsman
1.00		Estimator
.75		Clerk
.50	Clerk	
.25		
.00		

Thus if the estimator were paid $6 per hour, the indicated allocation for two of the job factor requirements (mental and skill) would have accounted for $2 plus $1, or $3, of the $6 per hour pay. Other requirements would account for the other $3.

5. The accuracy of this judgmental process is established by comparing the simple rank ordering from step 3 against the monetary allocation of step 4, and differences are reconciled.

The factor comparison method has some important advantages. The scale of monetary units permits direct translation into an individual's total pay by simply adding the allocations for the job factors. Second, scales must be constructed for each salary–job evaluation application, so that the applications tend to be built around the specifics of particular situations.

On the other hand, the very considerations providing advantages may lead to problems. For example, monetary scales are likely to encourage rate bias. Factor scales are difficult to construct. A matter of serious difficulty is the underlying structure of key jobs which form the basis for comparisons: jobs are no more universal than people—various real differences exist even for key jobs. Finally, the content of jobs changes over time, and this may not be accurately reflected (Akalin, 1971, p. 192).

Point method. This approach is the most widely used type of job evaluation plan. There are many variations but the concept is simple and comparatively easy to explain. As in the factor comparison technique, job factors are identified and several points that reflect their relative importance are assigned to each. If four compensable factors are selected and a maximum potential of 25 points is assigned to each, the factors are equally important. For instance, experience is as important as education or physical requirements. No person can score higher than 25 points on any of the four factors (theoretically, a "super" worker would score 100, but this is unlikely). If experience is considered more important than education and education more important than physical conditions, the following weighting (assignment of points) might be used:

Experience	35
Education	30
Physical condition	25
Speaking skill	10
Total	$\overline{100}$

In general, comparable job factors are not standardized. Many different ones are used. Traditional plans (e.g., National Electrical Manufacturers Association) typically use indirect measures for job performance (e.g., education, experience, working conditions). Contemporary approaches increasingly emphasize what people do or the scope and depth of experience and knowledge that must be brought to the job. The newer approaches are popular for a variety of reasons, not the least of which is their compatibility with Equal Employment Opportunity regulations.

The steps in the point plan procedure are as follows:

1. Compensable factors must encompass all the jobs to be considered in the plan.
2. Compensable factors are defined. To facilitate the assignment of points to specific jobs, job factors are usually broken down into points. For example, if 20 points are assigned to job skill, the total might be broken down into four degrees: A (20), B (15), C (10), and D (5). Each degree is also defined. For instance, the difference between two degrees may be the difficulty of work ordinarily assigned to the job holder.
3. The relative importance of each factor is based on the number of points assigned. The total assignable number of points (100, 500, 1000) is arbitrary and largely a matter of convenience and the number of degrees in the plan.
4. Key, or benchmark, jobs, which will then serve as a skeletal structure of point allocations by which the organization jobs are assigned, are often identified.
5. All jobs are then rated on each factor, based on the factor (or factor degree) definitions and using benchmark jobs as additional guides.

The use of points has a number of advantages, including ability to handle large numbers of jobs, ease of communication, ease of numerical analyses, divisions into classes of jobs, and reasonable stability as long as the factors remain relevant. Where major changes occur in a job structure, say as a consequence of new technology, the point plan (and others described previously) must be reexamined.

Quantitative approaches, as in the point method, unfortunately often give their users a sense of security or accuracy because of the numerical scores. In some cases, this sense of security is false. The definition of various factors and degrees (or subfactors) requires skill and extensive knowledge of the jobs involved. Because of the widespread use of point plans, two examples are provided in subsequent sections.

Application of the Traditional Point Plan

Doctors' Hospital used a traditional point evaluation plan based on five job factors for nonmedical employees:

1. skill requirements
2. mental requirements
3. physical requirements
4. responsibility
5. working conditions.

A condensation of the factors, their general definitions, point assignments, and degrees are indicated in Exhibit 10–2.

EXHIBIT 10–2   Doctors' Hospital Point Evaluation Plan: Factor Definitions and Point Assignments

---

		Points
1.	*Skill requirements*—dexterity of finger, arm, and/or eye movements and motor coordination. High skill indicates one who is able to carry out precision work with a major impact on the patient.	25

	Points
Degrees A–High	25
B–Intermediate	15
C–Low	5

		Points
2.	*Mental requirements*—knowledge and experience needed on the job. Complex problem solving, proper response under emergency conditions, and decision making under difficult conditions exemplify high mental requirements.	30

	Points
Degrees A–Very high	30
B–High	20
C–Rather low	10
D–Low	5

		Points
3.	*Physical requirements*—the level of energy that must be expended on a continuing basis in order to meet job requirements.	15

	Points
Degrees A–High	15
B–Intermediate	10
C–Low	5

		Points
4.	*Responsibility*—impact on patient care, dollar value of equipment (which one can likely affect adversely), monies handled, people supervised, health of patient.	20

	Points
Degrees A–Very high	20
B–High	15
C–Rather low	10
D–Low	5

5. *Working conditions*—conditions surrounding the conduct of work, including   10
substantial temperature variations, noise, lighting, high humidity, etc.

	Points
Degrees A–High	10
B–Intermediate	5
C–Low	–

Point assignment to two representative jobs

	Skill	Mental	Physical	Responsi-bility	Working conditions
Corridor Orderly (moves patients or things, assists nurses as requested, and may secure equipment/implements for a doctor)	5	5	15	10	5
				Total points	40
Registered Nurse (patient care: administers medications under doctor's direction, provides therapy as directed, assists doctors)	15	20	10	15	5
				Total points	65

Exhibit 10–2 illustrates several aspects of the point evaluation plan in use at Doctors' Hospital.

1. This is a 100 point plan.

2. Five compensable factors are employed, each weighted somewhat differently in relative importance (25 for skill, 30 for mental, etc.). Additionally, the total weightings (point assignments) for each factor indicate that the mental requirements factor (30 points) is three times as important as the working conditions factor (10 points), two times as important as physical requirements, etc.

3. Factor degrees are provided: the highest-ranking job achievable under this plan is 100 points, the lowest-ranking job achievable is 20 points. Consequently, all jobs score some points. None can score less than 20 or more than 100.

4. Mental requirements are considered most important for Doctors' Hospital. They emphasize problem solving, decision making, and response under difficult or emergency conditions. Working conditions is the least valued factor; and if temperature extremes are encountered, this is apparently an occasional thing with only modest value to the hospital.

5. The general observations concerning the relative importance of factors are borne out by the two jobs depicted in the exhibit. The orderly job involves manual chores, surveillance, and low-level skills, while nurse requires a high order of mental skills and educational preparation.

In a manner similar to that described for the jobs of corridor orderly and registered nurse, the assignment of points for other representative benchmark jobs might be as follows:

	Points
Orderly	40
X-ray technician	50
Registered nurse	65
Accountant	65
Personnel manager	75
Assistant administrator	70
Office manager	75

Notice that at Doctors' Hospital all of these benchmark jobs cover only 35 points (40 to 75 points) of the full range. The compensable factors in the hospital's plan and the point assignments make only a portion of the 100 point range functional:

1. Everybody gets an automatic 20 points (the minimum score for four of the five factors).

2. At the upper end of the point range, it is highly unlikely that a job would entail both high mental and physical requirements.

3. A very high point assignment is given to physical features of the job, with two factors (working conditions and physical requirements) equaling 25 points.

Making Dollar Assignments

At this stage of analysis, a manager does not have enough information to determine compensation. But we will discuss the mechanics of connecting point values with dollar values. Two common schemes are illustrated in the hospital example below, and two common benchmark jobs are selected. The general procedures are identical.

1. *Points are assigned a uniform monetary value.* For the Doctors' Hospital example, wage surveys in the city might have disclosed that these two benchmark jobs at time of hiring paid, on the average, $3.00 per hr. for orderlies and $4.75 per hr. for nurses. Orderlies' jobs were valued at 40 points, or approximately 7.1¢ per point ($3 per 40 points), while nurses' jobs were valued at 65 points, or about 7.3¢ per point ($4.75 per 65 points). Checking these figures against those for other benchmark jobs, we might decide to compensate jobs at the rate of 7.2¢ per point if most of them were similar. The tentative multiplier of 7.2¢ per point would then be tried against other job/point assignments, and comparisons would be made with wage-survey figures. The greater the convergence of the average figures, the greater the likelihood of this approach. If differences start to emerge in the order of, say, 15 percent or higher, major adjustments or an alternative approach would be necessary.

2. *Curve fitting.* Typically, figures don't behave as neatly as just described, and it becomes necessary to establish statistical plots of points and compensation for benchmark jobs. Next, this structure of relationships is employed to judge the value of various jobs in the structure. A typical plot of dollars and point assignments is presented in Exhibit 10–3. These plots permit the assignment of dollar

values relative to points, virtually by inspection. This exhibit displays several common forms of job importance and wage relationships.

Linear regression line. Where the line of best fit shows a linear relationship, the task of calculating the dollar value of jobs of intermediate importance is straightforward (see Exhibit 10–3). For example, a job valued at 60 points would be valued at $5.50 per hr., a job valued at 50 points, $3.50 per hr., and one valued at 70 points, about $7.50 per hr. This linear regression line can be determined, based on the benchmark job values. When jobs are evaluated subsequently for points, their dollar values may be determined visually from the linear plot or by substitution into the regression equation. The derivation of this linear regression line is given in this chapter's appendix.

EXHIBIT 10–3   Job Structure: Doctors' Hospital Benchmark Jobs

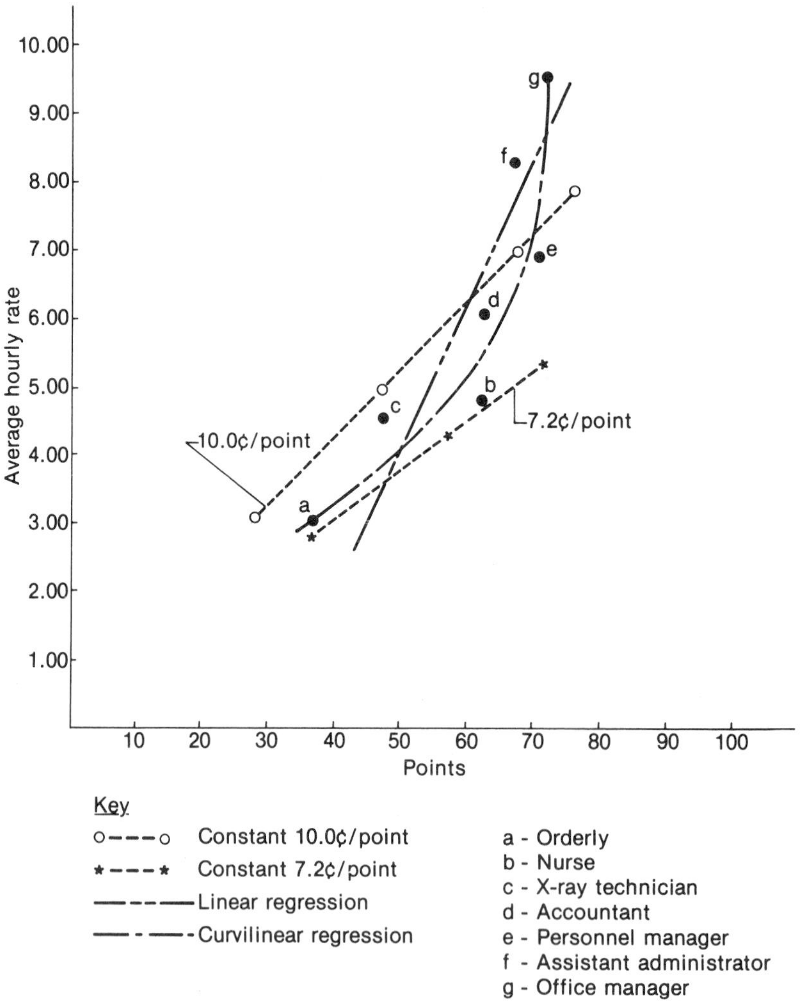

Key

o – – – o   Constant 10.0¢/point
★ – – – ★   Constant 7.2¢/point
——– –——Linear regression
—— · ——·Curvilinear regression

a - Orderly
b - Nurse
c - X-ray technician
d - Accountant
e - Personnel manager
f - Assistant administrator
g - Office manager

Curvilinear regression line. This is a situation where the line of best fit curves to accommodate the data (see Exhibit 10–3). Solely on visual grounds, the curvilinear plot is a much better approximation of the benchmark wage data. It can be seen that the linear regression, at least for these particular data, forces considerable compromises with the plotted value. Using the curvilinear regression line, it is possible to read job values directly from the plot; for example, 60 points equal about $4.80 per hr., 70 points equal $6.50 per hr., and 50 points equal about $3.70 per hr. Notice the rather wide differences in the values derived from the linear versus the curvilinear plot. If these plots are used for convenience or ease of calculation, considerable accuracy may be lost. It is clear from observation of Exhibit 10–3 that the dollar values corresponding to a given number of points (the linear versus the curvilinear plot) are quite different. If approximation is to be used—that is, a linear plot instead of a curvilinear plot—it is well to check out points and values using both techniques to see if major errors may occur.

Line of constant value. The line of best fit is based on the constant relationship of 7.2¢ per point. Although this plot provides an excellent fit for the nurse and orderly jobs, it is clearly unacceptable for all of the others. If the constant value— the multiplier—is changed, to say 10¢ per point, a somewhat better compromise is reached with the benchmark job values, but it is still unacceptable. The difficulty encountered with this constant value approach results from an initial calculation that represents a compromise between the nurse and orderly jobs—as if no other jobs existed. Wage surveys seek to embrace the full range of benchmark jobs, and it is this set with which one must contend if point-wage relationships are to be derived which reflect competitive wage conditions in the organization's labor market.

NEW TECHNIQUES: APPLICATION AND LIMITATIONS

As we have mentioned, job analysis techniques do not yield data that permit job evaluation for compensation purposes. However, these data may be useful in understanding a job. An outstanding example of this problem is functional job analysis, which is based on the *Dictionary of Occupation Titles.* DOT fits into the government's scheme of job classification and permits interindustry comparison of particular jobs and facilities training. Yet in itself it is not a job evaluation approach. DOT information cannot be translated directly into a common denominator, such as points. It is more properly described as a job analysis or job classification scheme. While research is under way to extend its use to job evaluation, its use for evaluation at this time is questionable.

The PAQ (position analysis questionnaire) developed at the Purdue University Occupational Center (Ernest McCormick *et al.*, 1949) is also a job analysis scheme, but research has also shown it to be useful in job evaluation.

Several new job evaluation approaches are quantitative schemes based on points that permit correlations with salary data (see Chapter 11). For example, the Hay Plan (Hay, 1967) has been in use for some years; it provides a complete job evaluation–salary package. Occupational research at several major universities (e.g., Ohio State, Chicago, and Purdue) has produced evaluation approaches that show promise for use in the analysis and evolution of managerial and professional positions. In contrast with the PAQ approach, which is also numerical, the Hay Plan and other similar programs focus specifically on the a) factors for which people are paid, b) amount of the (compensable) factors in a particular job, and c) correlation of the amount of the factors in the job to wage or salary.

Dimensions of Managerial Positions (DMP)

Research undertaken by Hemphill (Ohio State University, 1960), Melaney Baehr (University of Chicago, 1967), Ernest McCormick (Purdue University, 1969), and others has identified incidents that are common to many managerial and professional positions. Although they often have employed somewhat different terminology and techniques, their results show some similarity. Much of this research has dealt directly with job positions and emphasized what people do. It has shown that there are many more common factors among these positions than one might suspect. Compensable factors are job related and thus tie in with newer study techniques, such as the critical incidents approach. Also, new equal opportunity legislation is forcing a much more direct job-work approach.

This matter of direct connection to the job (see Chapter 9) is very important. Older plans contain factors such as education and experience, which provide indirect assessment of skill and knowledge. Even a factor such as physical requirements reflects only a general assessment of the conditions confronting the job holder; it emphasizes what the individual brings to the job and the conditions confronted on the job. Newer approaches have emphasized *doing*, using factors that indicate such direct conditions as "setting objectives" and "supervision applied."

The dimensions of managerial positions approach organizes twenty-six individual factors into six bundles, or clusters, of generally related factors. The titles for the clusters of factors are arbitrary, but organizing them into these groups makes it much easier for a personnel officer to analyze and evaluate jobs. The relationships among factors that comprise a cluster are often obvious—they provide a starting point. But from this point the personnel officer can apply more precise factor analytic techniques to determine less obvious correlations and relationships.

Application of dimensions of managerial positions. The dimensions of managerial positions listing can be used directly as a point evaluation scheme. An architectural-engineering firm employs almost five hundred people, including almost four hundred in various managerial-professional-technical categories. The job analyst will use the DMP scheme to determine the relative importance of various activities in both handling current business and developing new business by considering the following issues:

1. The essence of the business is the art form or design, closely supported by technical or engineering capabilities. Securing profitable new business requires a high level of creativity, wide contacts (in the community, nationally, internationally), client-handling abilities, a sound knowledge of cost estimation, and negotiation abilities.

On the other hand, execution of construction contracts requires a high level of internal organization, sound leadership, and good decision-making ability. Budgets require high reliability and reflect both the quality and quantity of work. Also, future business will depend on reliability, quality of work, and cost-budget performance.

2. Relying on preliminary data, the analyst described each cluster of factors.

EXHIBIT 10–4   Dimensions of Managerial Positions*

---

1. *Organizational*
   Setting objectives
   Establishing long-range plans
   Developing, implementing technical ideas, products, solutions
   Work practice, procedure improvement

2. *Administration and decision making*
   Supervision received—structuring of work
   Judgment use in decision making
   Data analyses, reasoning, information synthesis
   Promote safety
   Administer, direct operations

3. *Leadership*
   Promote organizational relationships, cooperative teamwork
   Supervision applied (number, type)
   Competency to exert leadership
   Delegation of responsibility
   Coping ability (emergencies)
   Communication skills (advise, negotiate)

4. *Human-resource management*
   Develop employee potential
   Supervisory practice (discipline, etc.)
   Promote union-management relations

5. *Professional, personal qualities*
   Quality of work
   Quantity of work
   Reliability, sense of timing
   Innovation
   Ability to adhere to schedules, follow directions

6. *Community, customer, external environment*
   Community-organization relationships
   Outside contacts, customer relationships
   Sales (technical service, persuasion)

---

* Source: Hemphill and Baehr, Purdue Occupational Center.

Before determining the relative importance of factors (by assigning points or weights), the analyst reexamined the DMP to make sure that all important items were included and unimportant ones omitted. Concluding that the initial listing was adequate, the analyst then visited a number of people in the firm at all levels to further understand various jobs and to make some initial determinations of the relative importance of factor clusters (based on a 1,000 point scheme). These analyses led to the following:

Factor groups	Initial point/ weight assignment
Organizational	300
Customer, community, external environment	200
Professional, personal qualities	200
Leadership	150
Administration, decision making	100
Human-resource management	50

The high point value given to the organizational set of factors reflected the primary importance of goal setting and identifying new business opportunities. The customer and professional categories indicated the dual and interdependent needs for generating business and the business' critical dependence on quality and creativity. Leadership factors were central to internal organization, as were time-cost-quality performance and administration factors. The assignment of weight to human-resource management underscored the organization's concern for developing the person.

3. Next, the individual job factors were defined more precisely. An illustration of cluster and factor definitions is given in Exhibit 10–5. Then the points assigned to the clusters of factors were broken down according to individual job elements. The product of this job evaluation appears in Exhibit 10–6.

4. Detailed point-factor assignments were then reviewed with various officials and managers. Note that in all cases the individual factor assignments add to the cluster total and that the total of all clusters is 1,000 points. These point assignments represent the maximum assignment possible, although a particular job holder may bring more to the job than required.

EXHIBIT 10–5   Example of Cluster and Factor Descriptions

Cluster description ("organizational"):
   Those job abilities related to establishing institutional goals and the formulation of plans for carrying them out, including both established and innovative concepts.

Factor description ("develop, implement, [technical] idea"):
   Ability to propose useful ideas or technical solutions to complex design problems involving individual structures and city centers.

EXHIBIT 10-6   Applying the Dimensions of Managerial Positions Approach

Description of factor set	Points	Individual job factors	Points
Organizational	300	Setting objectives	100
		Establish long-range plans	90
		Develop (technical) ideas, solutions	70
		Practice, procedure improvement	40
Customer, community, external environment	200	Sales	120
		Outside community	80
Professional, personal qualities	200	Innovation	70
		Quality of work	50
		Reliability	30
		Ability to adhere to schedules	30
		Quantity of work	20
Leadership	150	Coping ability	50
		Communication skills	40
		Promote organization relationships	30
		Supervision applied	20
		Competing to exert leadership	5
		Delegation of responsibility	5
Administration, decision making	100	Judgment in decision making	40
		Data analysis, reasoning	30
		Administer, direct operation	15
		Promote safety	10
		Supervision receiver	5
Human-resource management	50	Develop employee potential	30
		Supervisory training	10
		Promote union-management relations	10

Hay Plan

This comprehensive approach to job evaluation and compensation uses a point-oriented approach and updated salary data from participating companies. The materials are patented, and members of the plan pay an annual fee to Edward N. Hay & Associates.

Three aspects of jobs are assessed, including a) "know-how" (total possible = 1,400 points), b) problem solving, taken as a percentage of "know-how" (maximum = 1,400 points), and c) accountability (up to 920 points). The scope and depth of each of these three factors is assessed. Eight different levels of knowledge are possible, from "primary" to "advanced vocational" to "professional mastery." Scope of understanding required is broken down in a similar way so that "limited," "related," "diverse," or "comprehensive" designations might be possible.

A simple example illustrates how points are assigned to both scope and depth. Consider a factor such as know-how (maximum is 1,400 points). A clerk's job may require only a primary level of knowledge ordinarily gained from elementary school (depth) and only a limited or narrow understanding of job and job relationships to operate satisfactorily (scope). This clerk's job could be evaluated as low as 50 points. In contrast, a research director might require professional mastery of subject matter (depth) and a very broad understanding of techniques, products, work systems, and their relationships (scope). The research director's job could be evaluated for perhaps 1,000 points in the Hay approach. In other words, for a factor such as know-how, the requirements for the research director are seen as being many times that of the clerk. Total points for each factor can be translated into dollars. The sum of these three factor evaluations establishes the basis for an individual's salary or wage. The Hay procedure also uses wage surveys to keep the point-dollar relationship up to date and for many firms results in a practical, workable system of salary evaluation and administration.

The assessment of job requirements varies with assumptions. In the case of the research director, it might turn out that both the scope and the depth of know-how are rather superficial because much work is prescribed and only a narrow field of scientific knowledge is needed. In this case, the point assignment might be considerably lower—say, 200 to 400. Conversely, research directors in scientific units and high-technology industries frequently must demonstrate considerable scope and depth of know-how. In this case, the evaluation might go from 700 to 1,200 points. In short, job analysis procedures must accurately disclose the character of the job before any meaningful evaluation can be made.

Job Evaluation Example: Claremont Commercial College

National Industries, Inc., a large conglomerate with holdings in several major industries, acquired Claremont Commercial College in 1971. Located in northern Los Angeles, the school specialized primarily in the secretarial sciences, computer sciences, and management institutes for sponsoring companies as a part of continuing education. With an administrative staff of twenty and a professional staff of eighteen full-time and forty-two part-timers, the school was considered large for its type and was viewed as a fairly profitable and successful operation. An organization chart for Claremont Commercial College is presented in Exhibit 10–7.

The vice-president of administration, Martin Luther Davis, was a highly energetic, bright individual who had quickly worked his way up to an officership. Martin, just twenty-nine years of age, had graduated from Los Angeles State University with a major in business administration. He was hired initially to supervise the office and "get things running smoothly." In just a short time he substantially improved credit and collection operations and straightened out the publications department and the general flow of work. Subsequently he was made administrative manager, a position that was phased out when he became the vice-president of administration.

Martin rarely "turned the job off." One situation was "bugging" him. He wanted to develop a more systematic way of evaluating job responsibilities, the relative importance and worth of jobs, and the efforts of current employees. Also, if Claremont were to facilitate the personal and professional growth of an organization member, management would have to know far more than it currently knew

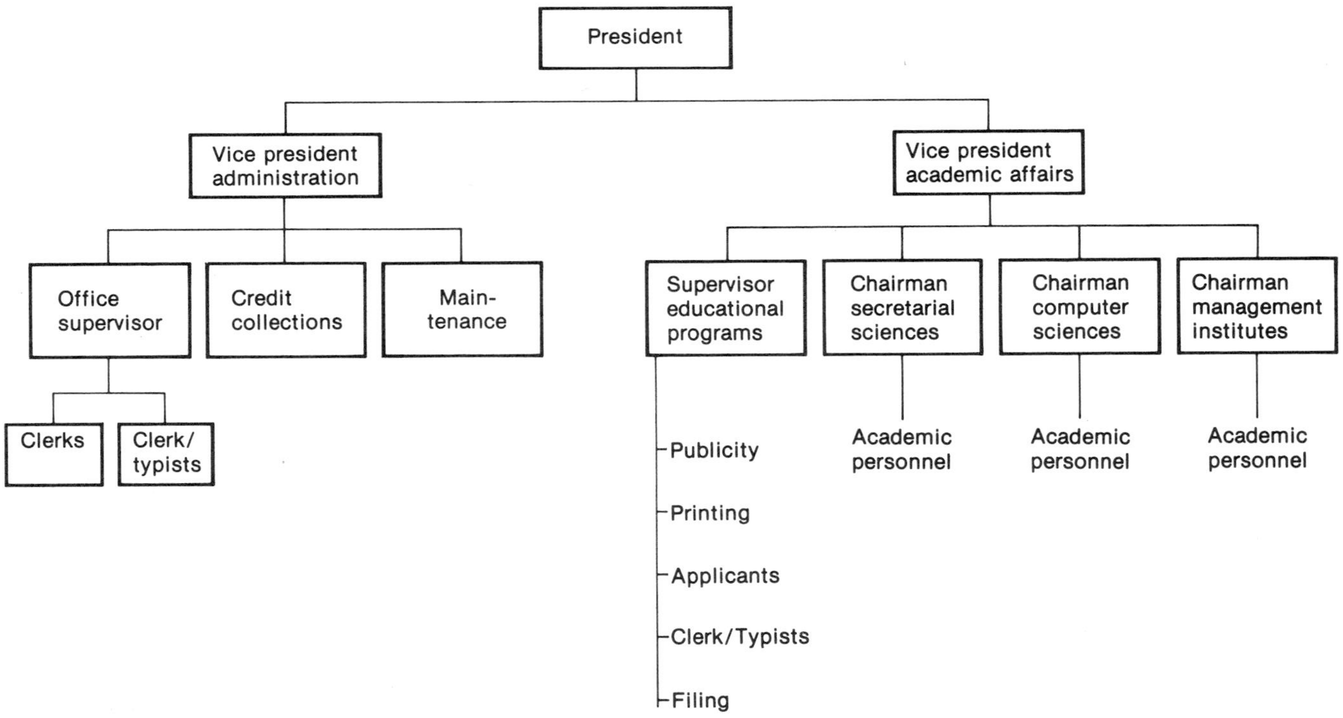

EXHIBIT 10-7 Organization Chart: Claremont Commercial College

regarding individual work activities. Martin was especially sensitive to the manner in which he had "lucked in," a situation not likely to occur for other people and thus perhaps a detriment to the organization.

Martin had recently attended a personnel management workshop where the subject was "job evaluation for performance assessment and compensation." Two different procedures were presented. Though both were point evaluation plans, one was presented as a traditional plan and the other as a newer approach. He decided to try out these two approaches informally, just to see what results might emerge.

Traditional approach: 100-point, 5-factor plan.   To cover the various officer, supervisory, specialist, and clerical jobs in the office, Martin selected five factors and assigned points as follows:

	Maximum possible points	*Basis for distributing points*
Experience needed	25	15 yrs.: 25 10 yrs.: 15 5 yrs.: 10 1 yr.: 5
Education required	30	M.S. or higher: 30 B.S.: 20 High school: 10
Planning, decisions, administration	20	Major impact on welfare: 20 points to 0
Directive responsibility	15	Direct five or more persons, 15 points to 0
Physical demands, accuracy	10	Estimate of exertion

The purely arbitrary basis for distribution was an attempt to reflect Martin's understanding of various jobs. Using this five-factor plan, he assigned points to various jobs, based on his estimate and knowledge of the jobs. The jobs for this initial analysis were chosen to represent a cross-section of demands, similarities, and differences.

Using a traditional type of five-factor plan, a preliminary assignment of points indicated that the vice-president of academic affairs received the greatest number of the jobs analyzed (Exhibit 10–8). The vice-president of administration, with 80 points, was a close second. Both of these jobs were assigned almost four times as many points as filing clerk and about twice as many as supervisor of credit and collection. Since the vice-president of academic affairs received about $25,000 per year, each of his points might be worth about $300 ($294 to be exact: $25,000 per 85 points). On the basis of about $300 per point, the filing clerk job would be valued at about $6,000 per year (20 points $\times$ $300 per point). It occurred to Martin that the order of difference

EXHBIT 10–8   Point Evaluation Approach in Analyzing Claremont Commercial College Jobs: Traditional Factors

	Factors					
Jobs	Education 30 max	Experience 25 max	Plan- ning 20 max	Direc- tion 15 max	Physical demands 10 max	Total
Vice-president academic affairs	30	20	20	15	—	85
Vice-president, administration	20	25	20	15	—	80
Chairman, secretarial sciences	20	20	15	10	—	65
Credit/collections	10	20	10	—	—	40
Clerk/typist	5	10	—	—	10	25
Filing	5	5	—	—	10	20

Job value (annual salary) based on $300 per point:

Vice-president, academic affairs	$25,500
Vice-president, administration	24,000
Chairman, secretarial science	19,500
Credit/collections	12,000
Clerk/typist	7,500
Filing	6,000

between these two jobs was about right, even for a first approximation. The valuation of each point (about $300) and the difference it made in salary calculation were striking and emphasized the need to go slow with this type of approach.

Newer approach.   The second approach Martin tried resembled the traditional approach in several ways. First, the point assignment could be identical (100 points), and it contained factors (six in this case, instead of five). However, at this point the resemblance stopped. The factors in this approach were really the titles of clusters of factor elements; there were actually six clusters comprising twenty-six different job-related elements. Because this appeared to be a much more complicated but perhaps realistic scheme, Martin decided to work initially with the clusters as a whole and make a more detailed analysis later if necessary. The assignment of 100 points to the six clusters, based on his assessment of influence on Claremont welfare and survival, was as follows:

	Maximum points
Organizational (setting objectives, planning, improvements)	20
Administration, decision making (supervision, judgment)	25
Leadership (delegation, relationships, communications)	5
Human resource management (development, personnel practices)	10
Professional, personal qualities (innovation, reliability)	20
Community, customer, external environment (external sales)	20

The point assignments to individuals are shown in Exhibit 10–9.

EXHIBIT 10–9   Point Evaluation Approaches Using Dimensions of Managerial Positions

Jobs	Orga-niza-tion 20 max	Admin. 25 max	Leader-ship 5 max	Human resource manage-ment 10 max	Pro-fessional, personal quali-ties 20 max	Com-munity 20 max	Total
						Factors	
Vice-president, academic affairs	15	25	5	5	15	15	80
Vice-president, administration	15	25	5	10	15	5	75
Chairman, secretarial science	10	15	5	10	15	10	65
Credit/collection	5	10	5	5	15	5	45
Clerk/typist	—	5	—	—	10	—	15
Filing	—	5	—	—	10	—	15

Job value (annual salary) based on $320 per point:

Vice-president, academic affairs	$25,600
Vice-president, administration	$24,000
Chairman, secretarial sciences	$20,800
Credit/collections	$14,400
Clerk-typist, Filing	$ 4,800

The completion of the preliminary study, based on dimensions of managerial positions, identified some internal relationships that were different from those identified by more traditional analysis. Although the totals for the two vice-presidential positions were not much different, clerk/typist and filing clerk were lower and credit/collection was somewhat higher using DMP. When a dollar per point figure was applied ($320 per point to approximate the $25,500 figure from the first calculation), various internal relationships seemed different and the lower-level jobs appeared to be too low. It seemed that the newer approach, though perhaps more precise, was not well suited to lower-level jobs and might have to be modified with other factors, such as physical effort.

BEHAVIORAL ISSUES AND FUTURE DIRECTIONS

Job Evaluation: Some Behavioral Implications

Establishing the relative worth of an organization's job evaluation procedures can benefit both employer and employee. Job evaluation procedures help an organization spell out its pecking order and at least indirectly establish its priorities and objectives, which are not always as obvious as they might seem at first glance. By the same token, employees get an important indication of where they fit into the organization's plans. The specific features of work that the organization values—and the degree to which it values them—are clarified. People's motivations are as different as workers themselves: everyone wants and needs a certain amount of money, but many value a sense of accomplishment or prestige or social environment more highly than a higher income. If job evaluation procedures are used wisely, they can help employees identify personal goals, compare them to the organization's goals, and help them identify the best ways to fulfill those goals. Both workers and managers can gain a sense of direction, a sense of fairness, and a sense of knowing what the issues are—where the "rub" is—if they are dissatisfied.

Two motivational theories can prove useful in identifying some of the benefits of job evaluation efforts for employees. Although little attempt has been made to validate Maslow's hierarchy of needs theory, it contains some helpful ideas for assessing job evaluation results. Some common motivational needs are the need for shelter, security, social acceptance, recognition, and self-fulfillment.

All of these needs may operate simultaneously, yet different people will value them differently. If the evaluation for a particular job emphasizes physical skills or experience, but if more and more people applying for the job have extensive academic preparation or are otherwise overqualified, conflict will grow. Put another way, where compensable factors emphasize wages in response to security and shelter needs but ignore other desires of people (e.g., the social climate or opportunity for self-fulfillment), job evaluation may be technically sound but not especially useful for those positions that require individual creativity.

Another consideration in job evaluation is equity or fairness of points assigned. An individual's sense of justice regarding the job evaluation plan is flavored by work-related and non-work-related attitudes. Job evaluation may place high value on, for example, physical abilities and dexterity in the traditional skilled trades, but technology may have eliminated the need for individual craftsmanship. Within a particular organization, other workers in traditionally unskilled or semiskilled jobs may view the higher wages received by those workers in the *formerly* skilled trades' positions.

More of these equity notions will be discussed in Chapter 11. At this point we conclude that compensable factors and the value assigned to tasks turn on far more than technical correctness. They involve a wide range of behavioral issues, both expressed and implied.

SUMMARY

Job evaluation is going through substantial changes. The traditional techniques such as nonquantitative ranking schemes and quantitative techniques, as in the point evaluation method, have given ground to several new approaches. The PAQ, dimensions of managerial positions, and the Hay Plan are gaining popularity. The Hay Plan, for instance, is some improvement over traditional schemes—in this case the point evaluation plan—because it provides a comprehensive job evaluation–salary program that permits more precise point determinations. All of these newer techniques are more job related.

Ideally, a particular job study will span the complete range from job analysis through job evaluation and permit wage/salary assignments. Unfortunately, most approaches are not this thorough. The DOT is an example of an incomplete approach. It provides considerable insight into job structure but fails to meet the need for evaluation. Developmental work with the PAQ approach provides the possibilities of some real gains in this regard. Undoubtedly it will receive close attention in the future.

All job evaluation approaches have two components: identification of compensable factors and the determination of relative importance or worth of a job. Whether compensable factors are used as a reference in qualitative ranking schemes or for point assignment in the quantitative techniques, they provide the organization's basic rationale for wage and salary payments.

Once the compensable factors have been determined, wage survey techniques become feasible and necessary. The compensable factors permit a more accurate assessment of the wage and salary data gathered in a survey. The framework of jobs employed in the survey is the *benchmark*. This benchmark provides a representative selection of organizational jobs, encompasses the full wage/salary range, and is general enough in character to permit reasoned comparisons. Benchmark jobs, compensable factors, and wage/salary surveys are central to job evaluation methodology. The organization may have to adjust its requirements if conditions in the labor market change. But at least there is a standard upon which a rational change can be based.

Job evaluation plans involve far more than simple technical considerations; they also imply a great deal concerning features that attract people to organizations and the value given by the organization to internal abilities and accomplishments. The comparison of evaluations and people's needs and expectations, both current and future, furnishes a useful check on the effectiveness of job evaluation programs.

In addition to behavioral considerations, job evaluation approaches must now contend with equal employment opportunities legislation. EEO imposes further limitations on the extent to which point assignments may involve racial or sex biases or differences that cannot be established in actual work. Reexamination of plans is necessary in any situation where possible discrimination may exist.

DISCUSSION QUESTIONS

1. Name some traditional types of compensable factors that could prove useful for:
   a. supermarkets
   b. manufacturing companies
   c. city transportation systems.

Suggest the relative importance you would assign to them in each institutional situation and the assumptions you have made.

2. Distinguish between job analysis and job evaluation.

3. For the organizations described in question 1, propose some benchmark jobs and your justification for their selection.

4. Using the Doctors' Hospital case, take two hospital jobs that have not been analyzed. Present a hypothetical point distribution and your underlying assumptions.

5. Compare DOT and PAQ.

6. Considering the dimensions of managerial positions developed for the architectural firm, how would these point assignments change for a smaller firm that places more emphasis on renovation projects than it does on new and creative designs?

7. For the Hay Plan factor "know-how," what would be your point assignment for an elementary school teacher? An elementary school principal? What are your assumptions?

8. Take a job with which you are well acquainted and apply two sections of the PAQ form (see Appendix) to this activity. Provide an interpretation of your point assignments.

9. Develop a 100-point evaluation plan for a firm with which you are familiar, based on
    a. traditional compensable factors
    b. job-related factors.
Be sure to clarify your assumptions.

10. Describe the development of a wage survey, benchmark jobs, and survey approaches for the firm described in question 9.

APPENDIX
THE POSITIONAL ANALYSIS QUESTIONNAIRE

The PAQ is a highly systematic procedure for understanding job analysis. It provides scores on numerous dimensions for all kinds of jobs. Recent research on the PAQ suggests the possible translation of job dimension scores directly into overall job comparisons for compensation purposes. This results from work undertaken at the Purdue University Occupational Research Center, directed by Ernest J. McCormick and supported by funds from the Office of Naval Research. (We discuss the PAQ in the job evaluation rather than job analysis section because of the rather unique potential it represents for connecting JA and JE.)

Structure of the PAQ

The PAQ contains 194 individual questions grouped into six main categories. Most of the questions are of the scale or rating type; that is, the job is rated in terms of degree of an attribute it possesses, how often something is performed or occurs, etc. The six main divisions of the PAQ are:

1. *Information input.* These questions deal with "where" and "how" the worker gets the information needed to perform the job. For example: Rate the importance to the job of the worker who "may use any or all of the senses, for example, sight, hearing, touch, etc." This particular section provides for the following ratings:

DNA–does not apply
1   –very minor
2   –low
3   –average
4   –high
5   –extreme.

One question asks the respondent to estimate the speed of moving parts used by the worker (the moving parts associated with stationary objects—for example, the revolutions per minute of a motor, the speed at which a lathe turns).

2. *Mental processes.* This refers to planning, decision making, and information processing activities necessary to perform the job. Question number 37, for example, deals with the level of reasoning in problem solving. The respondent is asked to judge the worker requirements in applying knowledge, experience, and judgment to problems. The possibilities range from 1 to 5:

   1–very limited (use of common sense in carrying out simple instructions, e.g., a delivery person)
   5–very substantial (use of principles of logic or scientific thinking to solve a wide range of intellectual and practical problems, e.g., a corporate president, branch manager, nuclear engineer).

3. *Work output.* This refers to work activities and tools employed. The possibilities range from DNA (does not apply) to 1 (very minor) to 5 (extreme). One question, number 50, refers to manually powered tools and the extent to which they are employed in precision work ("very accurate" or "extreme," say, for a watchmaker's tools).

4. *Relationships with other persons.* To develop information on relationships required in performing one's job, question number 101 deals with "persuading" (influencing others). The possibilities range from 1 for immediate supervision (close supervision or frequent surveillance by supervisor) to 5 for no supervision (people operate independently as owner-managers or independent consultants).

6. *Other job characteristics.* These include work schedules and job demands. The last item involves such factors as "specified work pace," "time pressure of situation," "vigilance," and "updating job knowledge" (to stay current with job demands). It is highly unlikely that all 194 questions will be relevant for any job, although it is not uncommon for perhaps 60 to 75 percent to apply to virtually any job.

PAQ and Job Evaluation Potential

McCormick and his colleagues at Purdue University have collected an extensive body of job information, derived from the PAQ as well as from salary information. The relationship between raw point total and salary, for example, has not been especially promising, for this procedure would assign the heaviest weight to "work output" (44 questions), somewhat less weight to "information output" (35 questions), "relationships with others" (35 questions), and "other job characteristics"

(40 questions), and the least weight to "mental processes" (14 questions), and "job context" (18 questions). Yet the facts of work life are that "mental processes," "information processing," and "relationships" probably are the highest rewarded of the six factors. Thus, if these categories are weighted heavier than the other categories, with "mental processes" receiving perhaps the heaviest assignment, correlations between the readjusted points and salary received are improved considerably.

Since the process here is a common one, employed in various personnel techniques, it might prove useful to summarize this discussion in the following tabulation:

Section	No. of questions	Weighting based on questionnaire	Revised weighting to illustrate market (wage) valuation of factors
Information input	35	18%	25%
Mental processes	14	7	25
Work output	49	25	15
Relationships	36	19	20
Job context	19	9	10
Other job features	41	21	5
Totals	194	99%*	100%

* Rounds to 100%

This tabulation anticipates some of our subsequent chapter discussions, but organizations erect a complex set of procedures and controls to assure work flow and high performance (i.e., related to "work output," "job context," and many of the "other job features"). Wage mechanisms in the external environment frequently place high values on jobs that are built on higher levels of education (related to "information input"), high orders of "mental processes," and people management ("relationships") abilities. It is true, however, that in the era initiated with the seventies, some major structural shifts occurred in the job market, extension of union influence (white collar and professional areas) and gains for their members, and society's valuation of various skills and abilities which will bear watching.

For example, a union settlement for garbage collectors in one large city boosted annual salaries to almost $15,000—considerably above the 1973 average for many white-collar jobs. In another large city, a new union contract for bus drivers and motormen resulted in a $20,000 annual salary in 1975. Members of an airline pilots union were moving toward annual salaries in excess of $50,000 in 1975. Yet in the mid-1970s many teachers with advanced educational credentials weren't even working as teachers but had been forced to take low-skill and low-pay jobs for lack of employment opportunities. In white-collar and professional jobs, the traditional gap between professional jobs (and salaries) and craft trades had narrowed appreciably—a "comparison" effect.

Indeed, important changes are afoot, affecting fundamental assumptions regarding the relative value of occupational skills. They will bear close scrutiny in the future.

BIBLIOGRAPHY

Akalin, M. T. *Office Job Evaluation.* Des Plaines, Ill.: Industrial Management Society, 1971.

Atchison, Thomas, and Wendell French. "Pay Systems for Scientists and Engineers." *Industrial Relations* (October 1967):44–96.

Baehr, Melaney E. "A Factorial Framework for Job Descriptions for Higher-Level Personnel." Paper prepared for Industrial Section, Illinois Psychological Association (Springfield, Ill., March 18, 1967), and Industrial Relations Center, University of Chicago.

Bakke, Robert L., *et al. Task Analysis by Selected Criteria: A Manual.* Cambridge, Mass.: Technical Education Research Centers, U.S. Office of Education, 1972.

Belcher, David W. *Compensation Administration.* Englewood Cliffs, N.J.: Prentice-Hall, Inc., 1974. See especially Chapters 6 and 7.

Boshoff, A. B. "A Comparison of Three Methods for Evaluation of Managerial Positions." *Psychologic African* 12 (1969):212–21.

Fine, Sidney A. "Functional Job Analysis: An Approach to a Technology for Manpower Planning." *Personnel Journal* 53.11 (November 1974):813–18.

Fine, S. A., and W. W. Wiley. *An Introduction to Functional Job Analysis.* Kalamazoo, Mich.: Upjohn Institute, 1971.

Goodman, Paul S. "An Empirical Examination of Elliot Jacques' Concept of Time Span." *Human Relations* (May 1967):155–70.

Guilford, J. P., and Ralph Hoepfner. *The Analysis of Intelligence.* New York: McGraw-Hill, 1971.

Hay, Edward N. and Associates. *Hay Guide Charts* (S). New York: Edward N. Hay and Associates, 1967.

Hemphill, J. K. *Dimensions of Executive Positions.* Research Monograph 89. Columbus, Ohio: Bureau of Business Research, The Ohio State University, 1960.

Jaques, Elliott. *Equitable Payment.* New York: Wiley, 1961.

McCormick, Ernest J., P. R. Jeaneret, and Robert C. Mecham. *The Development and Background of the Position Analysis Questionnaire (PAQ).* Lafayette, Ind.: Occupational Research Center, 1969.

Pasquale, A. M. *A New Dimension to Job Evaluation.* New York: American Management Association, 1969.

Prien, E. "Development of a Clerical Position Description Questionnaire." *Personnel Psychology* 18 (1963):91–98.

Primoff, Ernest S. *The Job-Element Procedure in Relation to Employment Procedures for the Disadvantaged.* Washington, D.C.: U.S. Civil Service Commission, 1972.

Shaw, Edward A. "The Maturity Factor as an Aid in Administering Personnel Salaries." *Personnel* 39.5 (September/October 1962):37–42.

U.S. Department of Labor. *Dictionary of Occupational Titles,* 4th ed. Washington, D.C.: U.S. Government Printing Office, 1975.

_____. *Handbook for Analyzing Jobs.* Washington, D.C.: U.S. Government Printing Office, 1972.

_____. *Estimates of Worker Trait Requirements for 4000 Jobs.* Washington, D.C.: U.S. Government Printing Office, 1956.

Wiley, W. W., and S. A. Fine. *A Systems Approach to New Careers: Two Papers.* Kalamazoo, Mich.: Upjohn Institute, 1969.

Wilson, Michael. *Job Analysis for Human Resource Management: A Review of Selected Research and Development.* Washington, D.C.: Manpower Management Institute, 1974.

Yaney, Joseph P. *Personnel Management.* Columbus, Ohio: Charles E. Merrill, 1975. See especially Chapter 7.

Chapter 11

COMPENSATION: A HUMAN RESOURCE PERSPECTIVE

LEARNING OBJECTIVES

This chapter has the purpose of presenting the key ideas employed in traditional compensation and benefit plans plus newer approaches based on human resource concepts. In particular, the following learning objectives should be achieved. The reader should be able to:

Distinguish between traditional and human resource approaches to compensation

Recognize the motivational aspects of wage and salary payments

Relate evironmental and organizational factors to wage/salary determination

Use supply and demand concepts in compensation analyses and wage determination

Establish a working knowledge of the application of major motivational models

Define and critically evaluate monetary incentive schemes

Structure basic compensation approaches to particular organizational situations

Identify newer trends in compensation and their contribution to human resource management.

KEY TERMS AND CONCEPTS

direct compensation

benefits, fringe benefits

wage rate determination

economics of supply and
   demand

going wage, wage leaders

wage structure

ability to pay

wage level

wage progression

wage survey

area wage differences

exchange

delphi technique

decisions to join, to stay, to
    produce
contingency approaches
hygiene factors, motivators

monetary incentive
benchmark jobs
salary-experience curves
"cafeteria compensation"

PREVIEW

Compensation—wages and benefits—has received increased attention in recent years. This chapter focuses on the following issues:

1. The terminology and concepts of compensation.

2. Compensation administration within organizations, the role of money, and some of the practical problems of developing and administering compensation programs.

3. The motivational factors related to compensation. Several important motivational models and their uses are described.

4. The importance of monetary incentives and the potential relation of salaries to career development.

5. The motivational features of benefits, the role of government and recent trends in benefit packages are discussed.

CONCEPTS AND PERSPECTIVES IN COMPENSATION

Compensation Defined

At one time, compensation was a relatively simple matter—it was pay for work. An employer hired an employee, the employee worked for a certain length of time, and the employer paid the employee. But those days are gone. The idea of compensation still involves this basic kind of relationship, but it also encompasses a good deal more. Organizations have become much more complex, the government is more actively involved in employer-employee relations than in the past, and people are compensated in many different ways.

We have already implied that compensation can be a very complex idea, so we will begin with a working definition. For our purposes, we will consider compensation as money received in the performance of work, plus the many kinds of services and benefits that organizations provide their employees. Unless we state otherwise, we will call the former *direct compensation* or *wages* (gross pay), and we will call the latter *benefits* (*fringe benefits* or *indirect compensation*), which include life, accident, and health insurance, the employer's contributions to retirement, pay for vacation or illness, and employer's required payments for employee welfare such as social security.

We will use benefits rather than *fringe* benefits to emphasize their importance. Benefits are not "fringes"—they are not "little extras." They are important and in the not too distant future may equal direct compensation. In 1940, benefits amounted to about 5 percent of direct compensation and about 20 percent in 1950, but in 1975 they were almost 35 percent of direct compensation and were continuing to move upward. According to the U.S. Department of Commerce (USDC), in the period 1965–73, average factory wages rose 72 percent, while fringe benefits increased 126 percent. The importance of benefits relative to wages is illustrated by the fact that a factory worker who earns $9,100 also gets about $3,000 in additional benefits.

Many people have questioned the whys of these increased benefits. "What's in store for the future?" And even more basic questions arise. For example, "Why does Ruth get more than Mary—is it because Ruth is well educated?" "Is the determination of wages solely an inside function or is it mandated by outsiders?" And "Why is it that Jim works one day a week, earns $20, and thinks he has a terrific deal, while Frank works five days a week, earns $200, and says his job is a drag?"

Surprisingly, all of these questions can be explored with the small group of concepts developed in this chapter.

Environmental and Institutional Factors Shaping Compensation

An employee's starting wage is a fact. How much she brings home is also a fact. Most people take these facts for granted, but there is a lot more here than meets the eye, and a job seeker should be aware of the underlying forces involved. Managers, in particular, need to understand all of the factors that affect wage/salary matters and can lead to enlightened, profitable programs (economically and behaviorally) for both the organization *and* its employees. Exhibit 11–1 brings together many of these considerations.

Wage Levels and Structure

Exhibit 11–1 identifies international, national, regional, and local forces and trends that influence an organization. Economic, social, and legislative developments and the general economic climate create the possibilities and limitations of compensation administration. Economic forces that directly affect human resource needs work through supply and demand. These forces influence the occupational or educational choices of workers' *wage levels* and *wage structures.*

Wage levels, from national to local, represent the money an average worker makes in a geographic area or in his or her organization. It is only an average; specific markets or firms and individual wages can vary widely from the average. For example, the clerical wage level in Dayton, Ohio, may be $2.95 per hour but a particular office clerk may make $3.10 per hour in Dayton.

The term *wage structure* is used to describe wage (salary) relationships within a particular grouping. The grouping can be according to occupation, political jurisdiction, or organization. So we can refer to the wage structure for craftsmen (carpenters, mechanics, bricklayers, etc.) nationally or, for example, in Milwaukee. We can also refer to the relationships among all salaries/wages in a particular organization.

Wage level and wage structure can also be used to describe wage relationships within an organization. Wage level might describe the average wage paid to a particular group of employees, such as blue collar workers. In this instance, wage structure might define wage levels for all categories of blue collar workers, such as carpenters, electricians, and janitors.

The terms we have defined point to one obvious element of compensation: the criteria used. What may not be so obvious are the many different kinds of criteria. Exhibit 11–1 describes some important ones:

1. an organization's ability to pay or concern about productivity
2. the influence of wage leaders (dominant organizations in a local labor market or in an industry sometimes dictate wages)
3. the going rate, or customary average wage for the industry
4. compensation equated to individual productivity
5. the value of the product of one's labor.

Union negotiators, individual job hunters, and managers all take a close look at these considerations. This is true of both formal union-management negotiations and individual discussions with "the boss."

External Forces and the Organization

Most banks, hospitals, city governments, and manufacturing companies have an outside constituency. It's the framework within which they operate. They have little, if any, effect on this outside world in wage matters. Yet within the organiza-

EXHIBIT 11-1 Perspective on General Environmental and Institutional Factors Shaping Compensation Plans

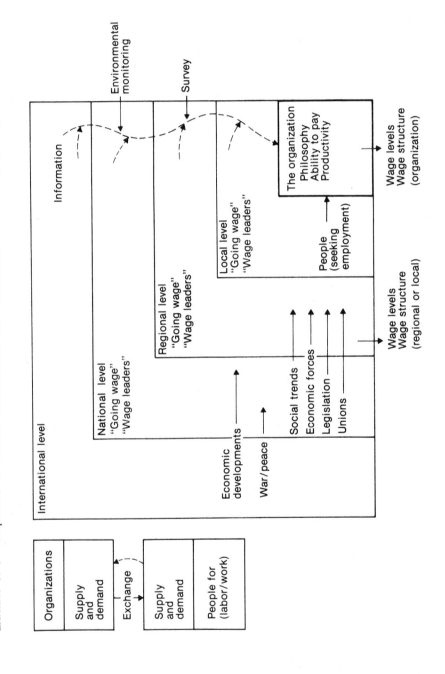

tion the situation is different. Managers often have a great deal of influence over wages within their organizations.

Examples. If the owner of a small company (say, under 250 employees) in a large city like Los Angeles or Cleveland decides to pay office help $7 per hour (when $4 is average), there may be a small article about it in a major newspaper. But that is about all the attention it will get. On the other hand, if the company is located in the rural community of Twin Hollows, Kentucky (population 1,000), which has only a general store and two or three factories that employ 50 or 75 people, an owner's wage policy would get quite a bit of attention—it might cause farmers, wives, or young people to pass up the plow for the "buck." Yet at the same time it would most likely provide continuing irritation to other owners who must compete with these wages. In these situations, the following variables are at work:

1. *Relevant external environment.* Considerable differences may exist between isolated rural areas and urban centers or, for that matter, regions and states.

2. *Size of organization* relative to others and its visibility in a particular market or geographic area. The greater the size, the greater the visibility and potential impact—at least in local areas.

3. *Wage power of a particular employer.* An offer of $7 per hour versus a general wage of $4 per hour is likely to appear attractive to job seekers.

4. *Choices.* Due to whatever circumstances (including owner philosophy), different choices are made by different individuals or organization officials.

Wage-Related Information for Analysis and Decisions

Information plays a specific—and important—role in wage matters. Awareness of a situation (or wage) is one thing; having a legitimate opportunity to do something about it is quite a different matter. Visibility of opportunity and alternatives was one of the factors related to our previous example of the owner who paid clerical help $7 an hour. And in both examples, the quantity and quality of available information was directly related to visibility. Television, newspapers, and radio are basic communications vehicles; they can build impressions, influence attitudes, or provide information on a wide range of general interest. Exhibit 11–1 shows that environmental monitoring and surveys tap these information sources.

For several years now, critics have noted that some people completely rely on the evening news for information about public events. They have no other source of information. Thus the media can be an extremely influential source of information. Reports often create a sense of opportunity (jobs available or an attractive wage), although they frequently lack specifics and, at times, accuracy. The problem of accuracy, along with great variation in viewing, reading, and listening abilities, results in highly uneven and uncertain information from these sources. So the actual amount of visibility the media provide varies greatly.

Second, there is an enormous difference between knowledge and real opportunity. Even if a person is aware that a particular organization pays $X per hour, all the jobs may be filled or there may be a long waiting list. The individual may not have the skills needed for the job, or the job site may be too far away.

Wage Surveys

Another point in Exhibit 11–1 concerns getting information about wage practices, trends, benefits and the like. "What are other firms doing by way of health insurance?" "What's the level of pay offered by other firms for similar occupations?" The *wage survey* seeks to answer these and related questions by regularly gathering information about benchmark jobs which are generally known and good indicators. If a wage survey is to be useful, it must satisfy the following points or questions:

1. Frequency—affected by the rapidity of changes, current and contemplated. Once per year is common.
2. Scope (number of firms)—influenced by the geographic area from which people are drawn, the number of units competing for this labor, accuracy requirements, and willingness of organizations to share information.
3. Accuracy—the diversity in job titles and specific job duties is staggering. The greater the detail and accuracy needed, the greater the requirement for careful description and specification and surveyor's reliance on person-to-person interviewing rather than mailed questionnaires.

Regional Wage Differences

Wage surveys provide many kinds of useful compensation information. For instance, a wage survey often shows the regional differences in wage levels for particular kinds of occupations. Surveys can be especially useful for organizations that have facilities in different parts of the country because they provide valuable information about regional labor markets. This kind of information can have a great influence on an organization's compensation policy. The following wage survey information reveals how greatly these data vary:

Occupation	Midwest	Southeast	Middle South
Secretary A (executive)	$11,000	$ 7,700	$ 8,400
Secretary B (typist)	7,000	5,520	5,200
Personnel manager	18,000	16,000	17,000

There are logical reasons for regional wage differences. But at the same time, several forces also work to level these differences:

1. *Forces that favor uniformity:* high mobility between regions and/or employees; access to timely, reliable information; widespread unionization efforts (often along industry/occupational lines).

2. *Forces that favor regional differences* (as in secretaries A & B): low mobility; lower-skill jobs; major cost-of-living differences between areas; added sources of income (e.g., farming, multijobs); area characteristics (rural versus urban or industrial); seasonal occupations as in agriculture versus stable occupations.

Supply and Demand—The Economist's Perspective

Although the wage survey we presented shows the great variability that can be found between various organizations and regions, we still need to make two more distinctions: 1) between the *individual* and the *population* and 2) between a *single establishment* and an *industry*. The outlook and tools of the economist are especially helpful for these purposes. The point is simply this: the working population in the mid-1970s consisted of better than 90 million people. Individual actions, outside of those of a few politicians or social leaders, had little effect on total population features. Similarly, there were over 2 million manufacturing and service establishments in the United States. Even the largest domestic employer, Sears, accounted for less than half of 1 percent of the working population, although admittedly its wage practices have had some impact on other retailers. The reason is that the forces of supply and demand are strong influences in the labor market and wages play an important role in resolving differences between them.

Wages, Employment, Supply and Demand

Supply and demand forces operate within various contexts. They operate at the national, regional, and local levels (see Exhibit 11–1). They comprise the playing field on which organizations and individuals interact. Some specific examples of these forces are:

1. The supply of and the demand for products and services influence product prices and the prices of services. Falling product demand discourages the entry of new firms and decreases the need for workers.

2. The supply of and the demand for people establish wages and wage levels. High wages or earning opportunities, as in some trades, in medicine, or law, have attracted far greater numbers of people than could be absorbed at the high wage rate.

3. The restrictions imposed by professional groups, trade unions, and the like have greatly reduced the number of people who enter these systems and thus have preserved high compensation levels.

Two Sides of Supply and Demand

The relationship between supply and demand for products or services and for people is complex and interdependent. People are consumers of the goods and services that organizations provide. But at the same time they are employees—and producers—of the goods they consume. There is a fundamental exchange between producing unit and consuming unit—goods and services are exchanged (sold) for money, which enables organizations to continue functioning and also to invent and provide a reservoir of funds for future needs. People, in the role of labor, also make an exchange—abilities, time, and energy for wages and benefits.

At the national or international level many forces affect supply and demand. Adverse weather affects crops, farm prices, processed foods, and the work forces of food processors. Legislation concerning equal employment opportunity and affirmative action forces equalization of wages, employment of minorities, and the use of uniform promotion criteria. Technological changes in the automotive industry, for example, reduce the average amount of labor needed to produce a car. This means there will be less need for auto workers. A union succeeds in raising average employee wages. So managers are encouraged to introduce labor-saving devices. Increased energy costs raise fuel prices and decrease the demand for certain cars and thereby certain types of labor. But at the same time this change spurs the demand for engineers and scientists (and raises their salaries) in a search for new energy sources. All of these events, of course, happen within the total economic system which provides the framework for wages.

The Exchange: Organization and Member

The notion of exchange is interwoven with the process of supply and demand because it involves individual motivation and performance. Exchange shapes wages and benefits, and it is the basis of an employee's decision to join or leave an organization. Organizations and employees exist in the world, and changes in that world (competition, social change, recession) influence how they react to wage levels and structures. But it would be naive to believe that these decisions are made purely on economic grounds. All sorts of noneconomic considerations (geographic area, organization climate, opportunity for promotion) play an ever increasing role in wage matters.

Exhibit 11–2 illustrates some of the main features of exchange as they affect decisions "to join" (affiliate), "to stay" (maintain affiliation), and "to produce" (motivation to attain high levels of performance or achievement). Exhibit 11–2 suggests that exchange involves much more than pay for ready hands. Many economic, psychological, and sociological considerations are involved. A company's personnel manager makes a salary offer based on his or her judgment (perception and translation) of a person's usefulness and potential—this is how the organization sees it. Jim thinks he got a good job offer (pay, training, etc.) from a company and intends to accept it. Yet, Sam may think the wage offer was a "ripoff" and wouldn't consider it under any circumstance.

Exchange: Variations Beyond the Basic Decision to Join

When a person joins an organization, he is influenced by even more considerations than at the time of employment. His decision to stay in the organization may be based on good treatment by supervisors, on the presence of friends at work,

EXHIBIT 11-2 Economic/Behavioral Perspectives of Exchange

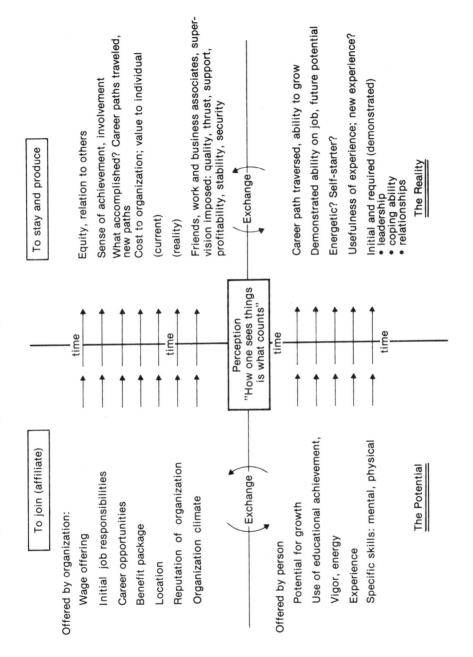

313

or on a sense of satisfaction. The person and the organization weigh their bargain against the elements of the exchange.

COMPENSATION ADMINISTRATION AND APPROACHES

Compensation Administration

For most of us, an amazing amount of money seemingly disappears for taxes, contributory benefits (the part the employee pays) for health insurance, profit sharing, and other payroll deductions. But for the company, all of this represents a cost; in fact, many officials have stated that "it's a cost no matter how you slice it up." Yet it does matter how things are allocated between wages and benefits. There can be quite a difference between compensation programs. One can be much more beneficial—for both employee and employer—than another.

Questions Regarding Money

Few areas have greater interest for an employee than compensation. "This is what it's really all about. You can talk all you want about self-fulfillment and that stuff—which may be OK—but one thing I know for sure is what I get paid." However, even if our friend knows this for sure, are there other important considerations that have not been specified? How does a person rank priorities when it comes to wage-related matters? And how about an individual confronting a potential employer as opposed to one who is already employed? Money will reenter the discussions of this chapter many times. However, before we can make even partial responses to these questions, we will discuss additional concepts related to wages and salary.

Compensation Program Objectives: The Human Resource Perspective

In too many cases managers take the compensation program for granted. They never really define the purposes the program is to serve. The attitude that "we pay people for work performed" misses the point completely. From the human resource perspective every organization needs to be able to attract potential employees, to maintain the continuity of its operations by having a stable work force, and to renew itself with new ideas generated by all employees. These objectives support profitable operation and continuity and minimize disruption. A good compensation program can do much to fulfill these objectives. The human resource perspective of compensation administration emphasizes the central role played by people in all the activities of an organization.

Essence of Compensation Approaches

The essential form of compensation programs results from basic decisions that managers make:

1. total dollars allocated to compensation

2. timing—cash flows, now or deferred; when the employee is entitled to a pension, and health/life insurance; variable coverage over an employee's career

3. direct pay versus benefits and the division among benefits (vacation, health provisions, holidays, insurance coverage, provision for retirement).

Using the human resource perspective, a compensation manager attempts to link the organization's options to individual needs so that each reinforces the other. An employee's sense of worth, desire for mobility, career development, and/or sense of equity can be linked to programs involving, for example, career paths. Thus the compensation options can be the *means* of motivating employee performance and creativity, which the organization needs in order to prosper. The use of compensation programs as part of a firm's human resource strategy concerns much of the material of this chapter.

Compensation: Its Relationship to the Organization and the Individual

Exhibit 11–3 illustrates the relationships among compensation options, organizational (personnel) programs, individual need, and organizational goals. Further discussions will expand on these relationships.

The Role of Money in Compensation Approaches

At first glance most people would think that employees value money above all else. But research findings, comments of consultants, and observations of managers and employees suggest this emphasis on money is not as strong as it appears.

How does a compensation administrator handle this situation? The most reasonable approach he can take is to be flexible—to attempt to meet individual needs. People's needs for money vary widely, and what is perhaps most relevant is determining "what's important to Joe or Dorothy" at a given point in time.

Assessing the importance of money to a current employee depends on a variety of work situations and personal factors. These factors are so intertwined that often it is unrealistic to try to separate them. With this limitation in mind, we will define these factors and present them in a realistic setting.

MOTIVATION AND COMPENSATION

Behavioral Perspective

How do employees react to compensation? How do they view it? Their motivations include the following:

1. Situational factors involving (for example) type of supervision, work group, task activity, and the reward climate of the organization.

EXHIBIT 11–3   Compensation: Where Does It Fit?

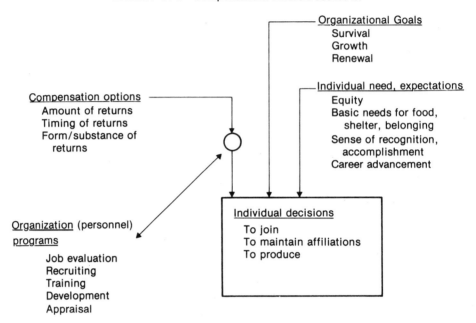

2. Organizational abilities and limitations in changing or modifying situational factors.

3. Personal satisfaction(s) and motivation to perform.

4. What one "sees," whether it is viewed as opportunity or a problem, as attractive or unattractive, affects one's sense of equity, felt needs, and the importance assigned to them. Each person sees and values things differently.

5. Individual needs change over time and the distinctions can be very unclear. They can occur in complex combinations, with several active at the same time. Additionally, certain needs appear to be endless, others may be satisfied quickly.

6. Individual performance, job satisfaction(s), and actions (e.g., decision to leave) can reflect a variety of factors coming together at the same time. These factors include elements of the work situation, felt mobility of the individual, an individual's sense of unfulfilled needs, and one's judgment of the value of personal actions.

These six points are the result of a wide variety of research and compensation investigations, yet it must be emphasized that there are ongoing disagreements among researchers and practitioners regarding these points.

Exhibit 11–4 suggests that a wage and benefit strategy is only one way an organization can improve performance and job satisfaction. No wonder that money isn't everything or that when a union secures wage increases or an enlarged benefit package, employees may still have many unfulfilled desires.

EXHIBIT 11-4 Compensation Matters: A Situational Perspective

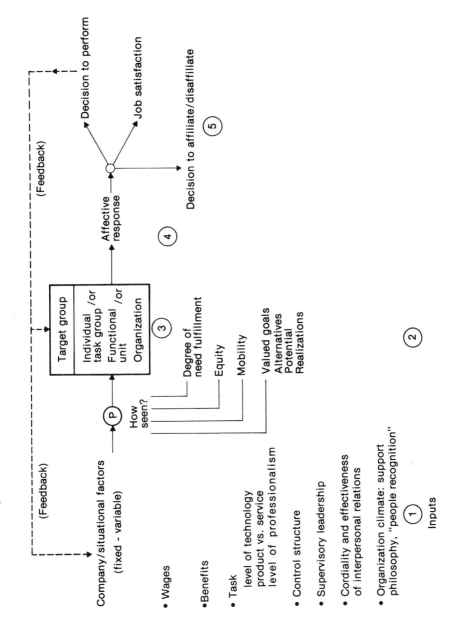

As indicated in Exhibit 11–4, wages and benefits (1) are only two factors that influence an employee's performance and job satisfaction (5). The type of work, controls, and supervision may "turn people on" or "off." Every individual (2) has a personal sense of fair treatment and a sense of mobility that may reflect age or education. These are some of the many things that color an employee's outlook. The target group (3) is what a personnel manager analyzes. Like any target, the target group can be big or small. It may be a particular person (e.g., engineer, executive), a work group, or perhaps an entire organization. How well the individual responds to the wages, job features, or other work-related concerns strongly influences an employee's performance and sense of accomplishment (4). The success or failure of past actions (feedback) sets the tone for subsequent actions. Many inputs (1) are fixed for the most part and organizations can do little to change them (some supervisors may have basic, personal limitations) or can make only minor adjustments in work systems (in the short run).

The following scenario is drawn from our research studies in organizations. It illustrates the complex interplay of situational and personal factors we have described.

HOWARD BEER, SALESPERSON

Toward the end of Howard's second year of college he became convinced that further schooling would be a waste of time. He was tired of the hassling over grades and homework. He wanted to be out in the real world, dealing with real problems.

Howard dropped out of school and for almost five years moved through a succession of jobs, trying to find one that would help him identify interests, abilities, and income possibilities. He thought that several retail fields looked promising because they required little experience and because he was interested in meeting people. These early jobs included selling sporting goods, men's articles, and floor covering. Howard's desire to meet people included Dorothy, and at age twenty-seven, Howard was married.

Most of Howard's early career jobs in the retail field paid little and had minimum benefit programs—a characteristic of the jobs and job structures in the retail field at that time. And after Howard and Dorothy were married, it became clear that two couldn't live as cheaply as one. Thus Howard looked for a job that paid more and offered better benefits. Star Clothing seemed to be the answer.

Star Clothing

This firm was located in the central business district of a large midwestern city. However, it was situated in a fringe area to take advantage of somewhat lower store rentals and shoppers seeking bargains.

Star Clothing was a multimillion-dollar, family-owned concern, consisting of four floors of men's, women's, and children's apparel. With the retirement of the founder, the sons, Al and Joe, took over the business. Al managed retail sales and Joe ran the office. When Howard applied for employment at Star he was interviewed by Al and given a deal "he couldn't refuse." Howard would be a floor salesman with a guarantee of $100 per week (gross pay). He would get a 6 percent commission on gross sales, special premiums on high-markup items, and either the $100/week guarantee *or* the commission on sales, *whichever was higher.* Howard was told that matching the guarantee was no problem and that "most salespeople consistently earn $140, $180, and not uncommonly over $200 a week." Howard was to work a six-day week. His day off would be mutually arranged, dependent on store sales. The company's vacation policy was five days off for up to five years' service and then one additional day for each year up to a maximum of ten days vacation. Fringe benefits consisted of a free health policy (spouse extra), a $5,000 life insurance policy, and four paid holidays.

The sale of clothing at Star was very competitive, and Howard learned this quickly. Salespeople drew numbers that determined their order of approaching potential customers. Customers who couldn't be sold were to be "turned over" to other salespeople.

However, work-related issues were not confined to salespeople; supervision of selling also was a problem. It was store policy that:

1. Nobody was allowed to sit down while on floor duty.

2. Customers were to be "turned over" if the sale couldn't be made quickly.

3. Salespeople were to attempt to push hard on high-markup items.

4. No time off was allowed without a formal OK from Al, and in no case was this to be compensated.

According to Al, supervising salespeople was "like trying to deal with animals in the jungle. They are always trying to put one over on you. Try to be a good guy, and they sock it to you. So you have to be tough."

Howard worked very hard at Star Clothing; he managed to consistently earn over his guarantee and averaged about $150 per week. However, many nights Howard came home and complained bitterly about Al, who was always on his back, and about some of the salespeople, who were constantly trying to beat him out of a sale.

One day, after Howard had been at Star for two years, he talked to Al at the close of the work day about getting some time off. He had an almost flawless record. Dorothy wanted to get away, and he did too. Al told Howard that his basic responsibility was his work, he was provided a vacation for time off, and that "there's no way I can keep the floor covered while you're gone." Howard started looking for a new job the following day.

The Clothing Mart (TCM)

After a while Howard found another job with a five-store chain called The Clothing Mart, Inc. Although a bit unhappy, he agreed to an initial salary of $110 per week, with the promise that he would be watched and promoted if he showed potential. Although The Clothing Mart was family owned, it used professional managers. Howard's initial assignment was a five-week rotation period among the five stores to gain familiarity with their operations. At the end of this period he was assigned to one of the stores.

Star versus The Clothing Mart

Although TCM sold the same type of merchandise as Star, Howard found most other aspects of his new work, aside from the basis of payment, quite different. TCM's vacation policy provided five days for the first year of employment, ten days for the next three years, and then one day per year of employment to a maximum of fifteen days vacation. Second, Star permitted a 10 percent discount on employee purchases, while TCM provided 15 percent—and 20 percent after five years' employment. The hospitalization, health, and life insurance package was similar to Star's. In the development of merchandising policy, each store manager was given some degree of latitude. In turn, store managers commonly met with sales personnel to discuss sales programs and get suggestions for better handling of customers or confirming sales.

Job-Related Experiences

Howard found that TCM's store supervision was quite different from Star's. At TCM the store manager periodically asked for his opinions and those of other salespeople. He didn't always go along with the ideas, but at least he seemed interested. In the matter of time off or tardiness, floor supervisors appeared to be quite different at TCM. Howard occasionally met with the salespeople from other stores and compared notes, finding that their situation was much like his. There was a willingness to discuss situations and resolve them on a one-at-a-time basis.

One incident stuck with Howard. He got started a little late one morning and arrived about a half-hour past his normal starting time. At the end of the day the store manager asked for an explanation of his tardiness. When Howard explained the circumstances, the manager indicated that he felt Howard had been a bit irresponsible in not calling; then he dropped the subject.

When Howard got home that evening he was quite upset and told Dorothy about his "lousy treatment" despite "all the hard work" he had been putting in. Dorothy listened patiently and then said that she felt the manager was right. After sulking for a while, Howard went over the events of the morning in his mind and the problem they had created in handling customers—especially with a sale in progress.

Pay Raise

At the end of the year, during the holiday season, Howard (along with other salespeople) had been putting in long hours to service the holiday trade. Just before Christmas the store manager spent some time with Howard and mentioned the store's appreciation for his good work. He was given a small bonus and a $25 per week pay raise for the new year. When he got home he told Dorothy about the pay raise and his good luck in going to work for The Clothing Mart.

Scenario Summary: Factors in Individual Response

This scenario provides the opportunity to reexamine the six points regarding an individual's response to compensation matters. First, Howard changed jobs because of his negative reaction to harsh supervision, response to other employees, and boring work. These were reasons to leave an employer despite relatively good earnings (situational factors). Howard took a job at TCM despite a low starting wage. He was able to visualize considerable *career opportunities* at TCM but only limited opportunities at Star.

Howard's *motivation to perform* and *sense of job satisfaction* were negatively affected at Star, given its technique of supervision and impersonal atmosphere. At least this was how Howard saw it. He felt unjustly treated and considered the treatment very insensitive.

When Howard was married, his *needs changed*. The responsibility for supporting another person and moving ahead became much more important. Consequently, the decision to move to TCM reflected a complex resolution by Howard of the availability of a new job that *appeared to better suit high-priority needs* and overcome the limitations of his current situation. The idea of incentive schemes discussed in the next section introduces some newer pay-job-motivation considerations as compared to those of Howard Beer.

Incentives in a Motivational Framework

An incentive scheme is a plan or program to motivate individual or group performance. An incentive program is most frequently built on monetary rewards (incentive pay or a monetary bonus), but may include a variety of nonmonetary rewards or prizes. Virtually all incentive approaches can be analyzed in path-goal motivational framework (see Chapters 4 and 8).

The use of incentives assumes that people's actions are related to their ability to achieve important longer-run goals. Unfortunately the issue isn't always this simple. Over the years the issue of incentives has become greatly confused with claims and denials by supporters and critics of monetary incentives: "Salary is necessary to reward work, but it does not motivate people to work more effectively." "There is no direct relationship between incentives and performance due to a variety of mediating circumstances." "One-third of all company bonus plans examined do no motivating and are quite expensive." And so the argument rages on.

All of this "flak" is reason for concern, but it should not be too discouraging. We will establish a more complete perspective from which to view the potential of incentives. As we have described, effective use of incentives depends on many situational and individual factors—incentive plan, work situation, and individual—and they can be used effectively and productively. Three areas of contingencies will be considered here, and they must be viewed collectively in designing or assessing incentive programs.

The individual. Different people value things differently. A manager who uses the path-goal perspective and has a dynamic view of individual needs will realize all people do not attach the same value to monetary incentives, bonuses, prizes, or trips. Employees view these things differently because of age, marital status, economic need, and future objectives. However, even though employee reaction to incentives varies greatly, incentives must have *some* redeeming merits; in some industries (see Exhibit 11–5) incentive programs are a very important part of employee benefits. And these programs attract many new employees.

Sales plans and programs provide a good example of how incentives can influence motivation. Some sales executives seem to have an unending number

EXHIBIT 11–5 Percentage of Production and Related Workers Paid on Incentive Basis in Selected Manufacturing Industries, U.S. 1963–68

Industry and payroll reference	Percentage of workers on incentive basis	Industry and payroll reference	Percentage of workers on incentive basis
Work clothing (Feb. 1968)	82	Cotton textiles (Sept. 1965)	34
Men's and boys' shirts, except work and night wear (Apr.–June 1964)	81	Farm machinery (Mid-1966)	**34**
		Malleable iron foundries (Nov. 1967)	33
Men's and boys' suits and coats (Apr. 1967)	74	Motor vehicle parts (Apr. 1963)	31
Footwear, except rubber (Mar. 1968)	70	Meatpacking (Nov. 1963)	30
Women's hosiery (Sept. 1967)	70	Structural clay products (July–Aug. 1964)	28
Children's hosiery (Sept. 1967)	70	Wool, yarn and broadwoven fabrics (Nov. 1966)	27
Basic iron and steel (Sept. 1967)	66	Synthetic textiles (Sept. 1965)	26
Men's hosiery (Sept. 1967)	65	Steel foundries (Nov. 1967)	26
Cigars (Mar. 1967)	57	Candy and other confectionery products (Sept. 1965)	25
Leather tanning and finishing (Jan. 1968)	53	Office and computing machines (Mid-1966)	24
Glass containers (May 1964)	38		
Fiber cans, tubes, drums, and similar products (Nov. 1964)	37	Gray iron pipe and fittings foundries (Nov. 1967)	23
Corrugated and solid fiber boxes (Nov. 1964)	36	Engines and turbines (Mid-1966)	22
Glassware, except glass containers, pressed or blown (May 1964)	36	Gray iron, except pipe and fittings, foundries (Nov. 1967)	21

Source: George Stelluto, "Report on Incentive Pay in Manufacturing Industries," *Monthly Labor Review* 92 (July 1969).

of monetary and nonmonetary incentive programs to stimulate sales. Money, trips, and gift certificates are part of the continuous parade of promotions. The fact that some bomb while others stimulate considerable competition, discussion, or excitement further attests to the readily observable differences in values that people assign to incentives.

However, there is such a thing as satiation (diminishing returns). Steak is great, but would you like to have it every week? How about every day—day in and day out, month to month, year to year? Even the most ardent steak lover would throw in his knife and fork at some point along the line. Thus even in production-oriented monetary incentive programs, a worker reaches a comfortable and profitable performance level and work pattern. So piecework rates should depend on personal energy, machine, or technological limitations. "Rate busting" (earning more than the "rate") should not be a superhuman feat. If it is, something is wrong with the rate. By the same token, if an employee's earnings decrease rapidly (for instance, during a job change), one reason for the variation may be that the worker is having problems learning a new skill (see Chapter 7). Or the rate may be unrealistically high. Managers should keep a close watch on piecework rates. After all, they are set by people and for people—hardly a faultless arrangement.

However, there are times when great variations can't be blamed on work matters. For instance, an employee may suddenly need a gift, a new car, or tuition payment. There is a type of spontaneity or "elation effect" (Halpern and Chapman, 1968; Goupert et al., 1969) as this worker realizes that his extra effort is tied to his goal (extra payoff). Elation effect usually is short-term because it involves an unusual level of mental or physical effort.

The work situation.   The work situation is made up of four important elements:

1. *Technology, machine, or work system.* If the speed of equipment operation can be varied, it can establish the range of the incentive. But equipment has its limits. If the speed of the equipment is fixed, the use of incentives will be highly restricted and often not feasible. Exhibit 11–5 illustrates this point: motor vehicles, yarn and textile production, and meat packing are examples of industries where many parts of the system or equipment speeds are fixed. Also, many new technological changes may make systems more inflexible. The result is that productivity is limited even more and the usefulness of incentives may be limited. This problem is one target of job enrichment (see Chapter 10). Managers have tried to make rigid production systems, including automobile assembly lines, more flexible. This experiment has been tried by the Volvo automobile company in Sweden, for example, with encouraging results. In some cases these experiments reestablished work groups and provided greater latitude for the individual worker. The outcome, as far as monetary incentives are concerned, is thus far uncertain, but it is worth watching.

2. *Satisfying job assignments.* Job analysis can tell a manager quite a bit about employee satisfaction. One question goes to the very heart of motivational matters: To what extent does a job permit a worker to achieve personal objectives that

may involve social interaction, a sense of independence, or accomplishment? Is the job narrowly focused on quantity or does it permit additional realizations?

This is not to ignore productivity, but productivity should be only one of several considerations. For example, a worker's job may incorporate a range of activities that he or she finds more satisfying than simply one element. Incentives may take the form of earned time off, greater flexibility in hours worked, extended vacation times, or other privileges that an individual values.

3. *Feedback.* Individuals need a sense of closure—that is, reliable information about performance on a timely basis. In other words, a worker needs to be able to see the connection between his work and rewards. These responses provide important reinforcement.

4. *Equity.* Workers consider fairness or reasonableness as part of the exchange for their work.

Features of an incentive plan.

1. Monetary plans. Most of the elements underlying these incentives have already been discussed. Mixed strategies can provide the diversity needed to match the needs of individual employees. The size of the incentive is clearly a matter of equity. This in turn relates to custom, general values held in society, etc.

2. Feedback. The timing, accuracy, and frequency of incentives can influence the success of a program.

3. Communications. Managers need to devote special attention to the type of communication used to encourage individual performance, provide feedback, and encourage redirection. Face-to-face exchanges and written appraisals are two of the alternatives a manager can use. Their suitability will vary according to the individual or situation.

Summing up these points on incentive systems, we note that there are three variables (individual, work situation, and incentive plan). These features are contingencies. All of them affect the suitability and design of incentives to varying degrees. Managers must consider all of these areas in any approach they use.

Managerial Bonus Plans

Bonuses are one-time payments, usually money, for a specific time period and accomplishment. Various tax reforms and fluctuations in the stock market, including some substantial periods of declining prices, have encouraged the use of bonus plans.

Early bonus plans were often used for especially valuable senior managers. Yet, understandably, the contribution of a particular manager is often difficult to establish. In addition, bonus plans proliferated as they were moved to successively lower organization levels. The addition of "turkey giveaways" and the like, which tend to separate accomplishment and effort, eventually led some organizations to look at bonus approaches more selectively.

Why managerial bonus plans? Bonus plans tie the income of key managers directly to the destiny of the business. If a company's profits increase, it is assumed that this is due to the key people—and their share in the profits increases. If profits decrease, so does their share. But what happens if all the key people are really working hard and profits go down—won't this be demoralizing? There is disagreement on this point. One side of the argument is that poor markets and severe competition are a part of business operations. These problems are why key people are "key." They are important because they can—or are supposed to be able to—deal with these problems. On the other hand, if profits go down because of inventory adjustments (an act attributable to the president or to long-term price inflation), key people may wail, "Why should we suffer?"

Thus successful operation of a managerial or executive bonus system poses a variety of problems and makes some demanding assumptions regarding people, situations, and planning. Some guideposts to successful programming have included:

1. *Selection*—only for key people whose efforts are indispensable to short- and long-term operations.
2. *Substantial return potential*—enough to really count. Some plans result in 20 to 50 percent of base salaries.
3. *Correlation to institutional destinies*—up or down.
4. *Individual achievement*—requires an institutional philosophy that encourages individual achievement, sense of participation, and willingness to have others share in its destinies.
4. *Profit stability and potential*—reasonable earnings stability or evidence of good growth potential to assist in building realistic expectations.

A final note on bonus plans concerns organizations that have revised managerial bonus schemes. Chrysler Motors Corporation has revised its managerial bonus program to increase emphasis on individual effort and reduce consideration of (not eliminate) profits. The purpose of this revision is to improve performance. The results will be of considerable interest.

CONTEMPORARY ISSUES AND NEW DIRECTIONS

Salary Level and Career Development: The Case of the Engineer

It seems entirely reasonable that as an employee gains experience beyond her college education, her total salary becomes higher because her value increases. Studies of engineers generally confirm this. A typical salary/experience (maturity) curve is depicted in panel A of Exhibit 11–6. The fact that these salary curves are rather consistent, at least for the first fifteen to twenty years of an engineer's career, suggests that a) individual career planning regarding income and b) long-term salary costs for technical personnel are predictable, at least to a limited extent.

EXHIBIT 11–6   Relation of Salary to Years of Work Experience: The Engineering Situation

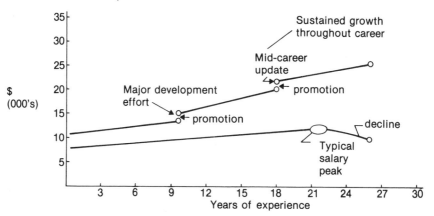

Panel A: General Experience

Panel B: Individual Experience

Of course this type of predictability may also apply to other occupational groups. However, results may simply suggest a community of interests and development patterns in certain careers. The community of interests of professional groups is less apparent among semiprofessional groups; for low-skilled groups it is virtually nonexistent.

Salary Development in the Human Resource Perspective

Of course, salary doesn't go up just because a person sits in a chair over an extended time period. Usually it is the result of experience, performance and academic preparation. This brings us to the second point concerning salary/experience curves.

The general or average path of salary growth for large numbers of people will often differ greatly from individual experience. Personal aptitude and interest, and quality of initial and ongoing organizational training and development change the salary curves. Also, a good supervisor and a work climate that encourages individual growth (Burack and Calero, 1972) are important. And the ups and downs of business contributions may greatly alter the character of the salary-experience curves.

Exhibit 11–6B traces two careers. One is a high performer. He has received good training and has been lucky to work in organizations that encourage individual growth. The second individual has not matched experience and education. Perhaps there has been a dismal trail of jobs and his salary has suffered. When salary and experience do not match, when salary does not increase with experience, the stories about "playing favorites" or "he was either lucky or knew the right guy" lose credibility. Most people have been lucky once or twice, but luck hardly represents a general or recommended strategy for moving ahead.

Other Salary-Experience Characteristics

Exhibit 11–6A also shows that a person's real income decreases with age. Various explanations have been advanced for this development. Clearly, many people do slow down in later years, and this may be why the salary curves fall off. In a few cases, senior engineers are subject to salary cuts, especially when their firms hire younger engineers who have higher levels of education. This is a compelling reason for an individual to anticipate professional obsolescence. Other reasons why the curve falls off are fewer hours of work, shifts to other jobs, curtailed work weeks, or the gradual shift of personnel to less demanding (and lower paying) jobs.

Salary–Human Resource Development Policy

People can either act or react to the development of human resource potential. There are potential rewards for both. The individual gains the monetary rewards and a sense of achievement resulting from promotion and higher levels of responsibility. The organization gains from higher levels of performance and greater employee loyalty and dedication.

The performance of "knowledge workers" (such as engineers), who do not work by the rhythm of the production line, depends on personal control, sense of duty, and pride. A thoughtfully developed compensation system connects individual gains and advancement with monetary rewards and expanded choices in benefit options, work schedules, and the like. They deemphasize "money-as-an-end." Money becomes a symbol of achievement, but it is tied to long-term goals and objectives. A practical interpretation of the path-goal model can guide the design of compensation programs.

Obsolescence

What can and should an individual do about potential obsolescence? As a person becomes older, she is drawn toward family and community activities (among others) that lead her away from work. The time devoted to an occupation or profession must compete with these other demands. Research in obsolescence and the character of salary-experience curves sound the warning that an individual's value to the organization and, potentially, to himself may decline over time. Compensation systems that support personal development and are reinforced by sensitive management and enlightened personnel policies can help to prevent this obsolescence.

"Cafeteria" Compensation

By this time it's probably clear that we favor rather flexible approaches in dealing with individual compensation matters. The idea of a single, rigid wage-benefit system moves further and further from the interests of individuals, especially those who are coming into today's organizations (Yankelovich, 1974), as well as growing numbers of incumbents. Today's workers want flexible arrangements that meet individual needs. Flexible arrangements are already being employed in the following areas:

1. "buying" time off by working extra hours
2. "banking" vacation days
3. options between direct payment and various benefits, such as deferred compensation or selection among various benefit options.

The key point with regard to flexible arrangements is that their cash value is equivalent but their value to particular individuals may vary greatly.

Benefits

Benefits are an anomaly: "You can't afford to live with them and you can't afford to be without them." Executives constantly bemoan the "money giveaway": "Every employee wage dollar is costing us more than 25 cents *additionally* in indirect costs and benefits and most of them don't even know it, or care. They expect it, and I guess that's what counts." The fact that in the 1940s most fringe benefits were almost nonexistent and today assume such a large part (see Exhibit 11–7) of organizational costs is indeed striking. But this hardly begins to reveal the sometimes confused, often agonizing thinking with which officials approach these matters.

Benefits as Incentives

The executive's quip in the previous section was cut off a bit prematurely, for he had far more to say concerning benefits. Aside from their expense, our executive wonders how beneficial benefits really are. Frederick Herzberg lumps benefits, along with other factors such as working conditions, into the "hygiene" area: they are needed, and the human appetite for them is limitless. Yet they don't motivate people to perform better. In Maslow's need structure, benefits may affect the

EXHIBIT 11-7 Wages and Benefits

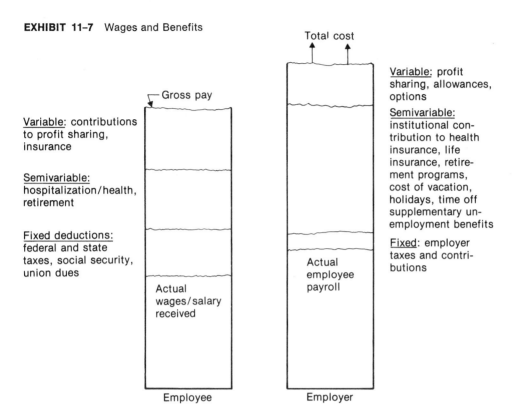

Employee   Employer

various aspects of "security" (e.g., individual felt needs to cover hospital costs, retirement, support during unemployment, or life insurance monies for the family's protection in case of death) but little else. In fact, if one views the major dimensions of job satisfaction, such as satisfaction with supervisor, co-workers, the job itself, pay, and work environment, the benefit is seen as entering into little of this and therefore may have little effect on the employee.

Then Why the Increases in Benefits?

Without much question, in recent years, unions have tried to increase benefit packages. At times, company negotiators have displayed less resistance to benefit increases than to direct wage increases because benefit increases distort salary structure relationships less and are often more easily explainable to stockholders as social responsibility or the company conscience. Also, they often involve complex financial arrangements and underwriting so that their true cost may not be discernible by employee or union.

Social Conscience and the Good Life

Since about 1950 there has been a considerable change in young people's outlook and expectations (see Chapter 3). As far as benefits are concerned, the growing demand for a good and secure life (without financial worries) has centered on the two major stages of young lives: 1) the *working period*, which once spanned perhaps forty years and is decreasing due to more education and earlier retirement, and 2) the *postwork* experience, traditionally called retirement but now apparently involving much more of the "good life."

Further, general trends suggest that financial security and the quest for a better life have become a matter of social conscience and public and private-sector responsibility. Three central ideas follow from this:

1. Impairment of individual earning capacity due to illness or lack of work should not unduly compromise the individual or family during the work years.

2. In the course of the individual's work years, he or she is entitled to enjoy some of the fruits of life—and at a point when young enough to enjoy them.

3. Financial provision for the postwork years can't be fully met by even the well-intentioned social security program of the government.

These three points help account for the growing number of benefit programs in private and public institutions and the new governmental legislation that has encouraged them. Exhibit 11–8 summarizes various benefit developments related to these three recognitions.

Benefit Trends

Exhibit 11–8 suggests just how pervasive benefits have become and why organizations have established departments and officials devoted to these matters. For the during-work experience, health insurance occupies a key role and is often the

---

EXHIBIT 11–8   Benefits: Growth and Shifting Focus

Work years
  A. Income continuity and financial solvency
      Health insurance (regular and major medical)
      Dental insurance
      Life insurance
      Accident insurance
      Job insurance
      Supplementary unemployment benefits

  B. The better life—now
      Longer vacation periods
      Vacation entitlements (sooner)
      Profit-sharing funds
      Shorter vesting periods
      Informational programs (alcoholism, addiction, etc.)

Postwork years
      Retirement / pension funds
      Employer contributions to social security

---

largest cost (outside of vacations) to the company. Health benefits include ordinary hospitalization, surgical, and major medical costs. And these provisions continue to grow. Provisions for dental insurance are relatively new but are starting to grow rapidly in importance. Various aspects of benefits related to the "good life" have changed remarkably in recent years. Two-week vacations after a year of employment have become more common, and three weeks after perhaps five years of work are increasingly seen in plans. Profit-sharing plans have also changed considerably in recent years. Plans have shorter periods of vesting—a period of time an employee must wait before getting full rights to the complete share.

Individual entitlements. An individual is always entitled to make a contribution to the profit-sharing fund. However, in the past many plans had vesting periods of up to fifteen years and were arranged so the employee gained a proportionately greater amount with length of employment. If, for example, the company contributed $100 in an employee's first year of employment, the entitlement might be $20 after five years, $50 after ten years, and $100 (the full amount) after fifteen years.

The postwork category in Exhibit 11–8 deserves a few comments, especially about pension funds. Until quite recently, pensions were mainly funded by the government, especially through Social Security. Pensions have run into several problems. Continuing inflation has eroded the real value of "later-year dollars" that people saved when they still worked. Second, life expectancy has increased throughout this century. Unfortunately this great benefit has created serious financial problems for retirement programs. Meeting just the basic needs for health, housing, and recreation has become a serious problem. This has led to a new era of private pension funds (manufacturing, service, profit and nonprofit institutions) to meet some of these financial requirements. The central assumption underlying private funds has been that a combination of Social Security, company pension funds, and personal savings should meet the needs of retirement.

Before we proceed further it would be well to clarify the role of the government in the development of benefits, aside from its rather well known role tied to Social Security.

The Role of Government in Benefit Developments

The visibility of public policies and actions has often made the government the showcase or "whip" for social actions long before they became important in the private sector. The Railway Labor Act of 1926 and equal employment opportunity legislation are just two examples. In benefit-related matters, extended vacation periods (up to four weeks) and liberal hospitalization and sick leave provisions have characterized numerous areas of federal government employment for many years.

In recent years, however, federal legislation has started to focus on such key areas as health coverage and pension funds. The potential for major changes is in the offing or already under way. In 1974, the Pension Reform Act (ERISA) established a maximum vesting period of ten years for profit-sharing funds. Also, it has provided for a stringent reporting/auditing system to deal with the many abuses in this area. Second, major health legislation seems likely to mandate health coverage for many in the work force who are not yet covered. These acts also seek to establish alternative health programs (e.g., through health maintenance organizations) to those currently offered by institutions—and employees will have to be given a choice.

POTENTIAL DIRECTION OF FUTURE BENEFITS

Benefits have come to play such an important role in compensation matters and the lives of all of us that the pattern they form over the next five to ten years is of more than passing interest. Directly related to these concerns is a study undertaken by T. J. Gordon and R. Lebleu regarding the probable thrust of future benefits and the contributing events.

First, a word about the technique and approach for developing these projections. The Delphi Technique involves a panel of experts and control of feedback among the experts to achieve thoughtful opinions and judgments to gain general agreement. The Institute for the Future utilized twenty-two experts in these analyses to establish a) key developments likely to shape future benefits and b) the relative impact on benefits. Also of interest to the current discussion are four classes of benefits covering both the work and the postwork years:

1. *legally required payments,* including unemployment compensation and health insurance
2. *hazard protection,* involving life insurance, termination payments, and pension
3. *time not worked although employed* (e.g., holidays, vacations, and sick leaves)
4. *miscellaneous programs,* including tuition, profit sharing, and employee savings plans.

Key forces shaping future benefits. The panel of experts in the Gordon and Lebleu study felt that several major environmental forces would provide the driving forces affecting benefits. First, organized labor would constitute a major force pushing continually for large extensions of benefits in institutions and through new legislation. Union pressure would affect existing programs and provide a model for people or organizations not in unions. Second, continuing advances in medicine would affect diagnostic possibilities, health care, preventive therapy, and life expectancy. Additional forces for changes in benefits included more governmental social legislation and militancy among minorities, especially blacks.

A summary view. Abstracted from the Institute for the Future's study, Exhibit 11–9 summarizes some of the key forces and their potential impact on benefits. The exhibit suggests three levels of force for change thought likely. For example,

EXHIBIT 11-9 Factors Likely to Shape Future Benefits and Their Relative Impact

Relative impact of force on benefits *

Some	*Moderate*	*Strong*
Better labor-force education	Rise in individual affluence	More leisure time, vacations, holidays
Growth in white-collar versus blue-collar occupations	Extension of unionization, new unions	Pressure from established unions
Relative growth of minorities and increased participation in work force	Medical advances (e.g., transplants, life extension)	New public welfare program
Growth in relative youthfulness of work force	Participative planning with institutional members	Minority frustrations and pressures
Growth in female component of work force		
More technological change		
More urbanization		

* A judgment that jointly takes into account a) the importance of the force in benefits and b) likelihood of occurrence.

Source: Based on a report by T. J. Gordon and R. Lebleu, "Employee Benefits, 1970–1985," Institute for the Future.

the shift from blue-collar to white-collar work is virtually certain. Yet this force may have only a modest effect on benefits, but a big impact on improving work conditions. In this exhibit, we have attempted to consider the likelihood of occurrence and importance of benefits by using the column headings "some," "moderate," and "strong."

Key forces. It appears that forces such as unions, more social legislation, and increased leisure time will lead the benefit parade for the future. These will be followed by increasing affluence, extensions of unions, medical advances, and participative planning (which will draw employee and employer closer together). In the vanguard of the parade may be found the growing youthfulness of the work force and more technological change.

Outcomes. What do all of these likely developments suggest? Simply that benefit coverage is going to be extended in the future. Also, the relative costs of providing the benefits will march in step with the new music. Perhaps we can even imagine the "chorus" from financial officers as these changes emerge.

Specific Benefits

We have not tried to exhaust the subject of benefits (or the reader) with these descriptions. But this is a complex and important subject and there are many unanswered questions: What medical benefits are likely to emerge? What new employee services are likely to be provided? The following suggests a few particulars of benefits emerging from the Gordon and Lebleu study:

1. *income security*—annual wage guarantees, job guarantees, and minimum annual income
2. *medical/health coverage*—extension of coverage (e.g., transplants), health plan coverage, and custodial coverage
3. *postwork coverage*—variety of assured services, including medical, education, and residential
4. *employee services*—flexible work hours and work days.

SUMMARY

Compensation administration has gone far beyond yesteryear's concentration on wages or salary. More and more, programs have been described as the *motivation* and *compensation* of personnel. Our approach suggests that the array of options within the compensation framework be viewed in terms of their behavioral implications for the individual and performance overtones for the organization.

But even if behavioral or human resource planning concerns were set aside, the vast growth of all manner of benefits has committed compensation officials to a new era of specialized activity. The growth of benefit schemes has in turn been exceeded by the emergence of newer compensation schemes, such as "cafeteria" compensation, by concepts such as "salary maturity curves," and by a revitalization of traditional incentive schemes. However, things have hardly stopped at this point.

The viewpoint in this chapter has been that compensation approaches are intimately tied to motivational notions. Decisions to join, stay, or produce can be usefully viewed in terms of their monetary and nonmonetary dimensions—aspects of the issue which satisfy valued needs of the individual and serve to meet organization requirements. The path-goal formulation, the motivator-hygiene scheme of Herzberg, and Adams's equity model represent useful ways of viewing the various key decisions of individuals and organization compensation officials.

Organizations and individuals exchange valued abilities, investments, monies, and benefits to establish mutually acceptable arrangements where both parties feel they have gained from the association.

Although various compensation criteria are described in the chapter, they are only a portion of the complex fabric of considerations underlying compensation. "Going wage" and "ability to pay" obviously influence institutional salary levels and structures. Yet these in turn are tempered by the behavioral considerations previously described. It is true that institutions must, as a minimum, maintain timely benefit and salary arrangements, and thus periodically use survey techniques. But the essence of compensation approaches is found in human resource concepts rather than in the mechanics of programs.

Human resource approaches to compensation argue for an artful blending of organizational and individual needs which is maintained on a timely, ongoing basis. Flexibility is central to maintaining a viable scheme, which bends with the continuing changes in organizational, individual, and environmental circumstances.

DISCUSSION QUESTIONS

1. Distinguish direct wages/salary from benefits. Give examples of each. List any qualifications that seem appropriate.

2. Distinguish environmental and institutional factors in wage rate determination. How will assumptions regarding city size, firm size, and type of occupation further affect your response?

3. Betty has a degree in electrical engineering and is applying for work with a large electronics firm near a large city. Use the concept of exchange to describe a) her considerations in joining the organization and b) the organization's view of her becoming a part of the institution.

4. Jeff Storey is personnel manager for an advertising agency with over two hundred employees, including some one hundred professionals. One department is a small, youthful market-research group, charged with assisting various account executives and clients regarding relevant information on neighborhood changes, media effectiveness, shopping center patterns, etc. At one time or another, various members of the department have complained about the "slave wages" being paid and the "poor work conditions." As a

pattern of complaints started to emerge, Jeff probed the situation—into several vague references regarding poor supervision. When he checked area wage rates for senior and junior market research staff, he learned that the rates of other companies were close to those paid by his organization. He started to wonder what the real problem was. Use the situational perspective diagram in Exhibit 11–4 to suggest problem approaches.

5. Irma Finch was an RN and practicing nurse at Garfield Hospital (three hundred beds in an urban location) before she was put in charge of the hospital personnel department. The former head had been promoted from a service group but "never seemed to get the hang of it." With Irma it was quite a different matter and she had things humming in less than a year. The mother superior and hospital administrator, encouraged by Irma's performance, asked her to take a look at the hospital's wage and benefit program and to make recommendations for possible changes over the next year or two. Because of the program's considerable cost, the administrator wanted to make sure it would be able to cover employees in the future and, further, that it was right for the present. Irma surveyed various hospitals in the area and came up with information of the type described by Gordon and Lebleu in their survey of future employee benefits. Using information on wages and benefits from the chapter, propose a preliminary wage/salary-benefits plan to the hospital administrator. Be sure to state your assumptions.

6. Tuition benefits, as in the preceding question, might occasion a lot of speculation. One way to handle this might be a Delphi design with an expert panel. Assume the conditions of question 5 and suggest a design for a Delphi, including some examples of the questions to be asked and how this type of study is to be structured.

7. The chapter references three central areas of contingencies in designing incentive programs. a) Name the general categories and some of the key subpoints; and b) Apply these concepts to an audit of the following programs: Rex Drug Company, a West Coast company, owns over 100 drug stores. Store managers are paid $250/week and a bonus. Store sales vary from a low of $140,000/year to $600,000/year in high traffic areas. The store manager bonus system operates as follows: The bonus is paid once per year, and managers receive a year-end statement. They receive 1.5 percent of annual sales for the first $25,000/year and 0.5 percent for all annual sales in excess of $25,000/year.

8. Salary maturity curves
   a. Joan Franks is a recent engineering graduate for whom aptitude tests and ratings by instructors suggest a future with great promise. Estimate her peak salary relative to starting salary both in dollars and as a percentage change in starting salary.
   b. Marty Adams is an engineering graduate, and many feel he made it only as an "accommodation." His experiences in his first two jobs seemed to bear out his ineptitude for engineering. If Marty stays in engineering, estimate his maximum salary expectation relative to starting salary in dollars and as a percentage change in starting salary.
   c. Describe the possible consequences for these young people of changes in their job structure, change of employers, shift of occupations, and continuing education. State your assumptions.

9. Apply "cafeteria" compensation concepts to the following situations. Clearly state your assumption and indicate likely approaches.
   a. Young Alfredo Sanchez, a recent graduate of a community college, is on his

first full-time job. He is unmarried and living in his own "pad"—in an apartment complex with many other single people. Although only on the job a short time, he is well liked and doing well.

b. Georgio Sanchez is Alfredo's father. He works in the same company as Alfredo and has been there some twenty years. He is married, living with the family, and has four other children.

10. Provide the indicated commentaries for the Howard Beer scenario.

11. *Case: Frank Acropolous, Management Major.*

Frank received a B.S. in management almost ten years ago and went to work for a large insurance company headquartered in New York City. Although Frank graduated from Purdue University, he had always wanted to live in New York. He wanted to visit the United Nations, see the sights, and to enjoy the shows. The insurance company's offer, although among the lowest in starting pay, provided good training and experience opportunities. Most importantly, the offer meant a key to the "empire city." Competition and high insurance losses were among the key factors severely restricting the ability of Frank's company to pay the going wage in the New York area for similar work. This situation was compounded by a steep rise in the cost of living, which eroded Frank's takehome pay.

After a few years Frank started to look for another job. An opportunity to become a management trainee with a large retail firm appeared attractive. Frank entered its employ and worked in its Dallas store as part of his training. Since Frank had long ago broken away from his family's influence, and was unmarried, his "felt" mobility was high and new opportunities were very appealing.

Frank's first managerial assignment in the department store chain was supervisor of sporting goods in one of its B-size stores on the West Coast. (In the chain, A was the largest unit and C a small, limited-line store). Among Frank's important responsibilities was that of interviewing prospective employees—a never-ending task because of relatively high turnover. The department store maintained a rigid wage structure which specified the entry level, or hiring, wages for a given job. Also, wage progression, or salary increases with time and experience were specified.

Frank was now in the position where he had to justify wages to employees and potential employees, which at times was a difficult job. For example, one sporting goods job called for an entry level wage of $2.47 per hour. A female graduate of a community college who applied for the job, when apprised of the starting wage, pointed out that Fairchild's, one of the town's leading stores, was starting people out for almost 50 cents more per hour. "How come?" she asked. She also wanted to know why Frank's store offered two weeks vacation after two years of work (one week immediately) while "*they* give two weeks after only *one* year of work."

Subsequently Frank started taking graduate courses. He felt that this would help to qualify him for higher pay and a better job. When he told his supervisor about his graduate work, Frank was shaken up to learn some new compensation facts of life. "The company uses education as one of its job evaluation factors, but you're already getting the maximum by having a college degree. It's nice that you are expanding your knowledge, but we can't pay you more for it."

a. Comment on the role of compensation in this case as opposed to nonmonetary benefits.

b. Was Frank mobile? Why?

c. What factors seem to have accounted for salary differences between firms? Be sure to state your assumptions.

BIBLIOGRAPHY

"Bonuses as Usual, But Not for All." *Business Week* (January 1, 1972):19–20.

Buchenroth, Kenneth J. "Motivation: Financial and Nonfinancial." *Management Accounting* 51 (December 1969):15–16+.

Burack, Elmer H. "Dealing With Managerial Obsolescence." *California Management Review* 15.2 (Winter 1972).

Burack, Elmer H., and Thomas M. Calero. "Managerial Manpower Development: Design or Default?" In Elmer H. Burack and James W. Walker, eds., *Manpower Planning and Programming*. Boston, Mass.: Allyn & Bacon, 1972.

Carroll, S., and H. Tosi. *Management by Objectives: Application and Research*. New York: Macmillan, 1973.

Dacher and Mobley. "Construct Validation of an Expectancy Model." *Journal of Applied Psychology* 58 (1973):379–418.

Gardner, David M., and K. M. Rowland. "A Self-Tailored Approach to Incentives." *Personnel Journal* 49 (November 1970):907–12.

Gordon, T. J., and R. Lebleu. "Employee Benefits, 1970–1985," Institute of the Future.

Goupert, Peter, Morton Deutsch, and Yako Epstein. "Effect of Incentive Magnitude on Co-operation." *Journal of Personality and Social Psychology* 11 (January 1969): 66–9.

Halpern, Joseph, and R. C. Chapman. "Positive Contrast Effects as a Function of Method of Incentive Presentation." *Journal of Experimental Psychology* 80 (March 1968):157–89.

Herzberg, Frederick W. "Does Money Really Motivate." *Purchasing* 69 (August 6, 1970):57–58+.

"Incentive Bonuses Are Great for Sales." *Advertising Age* 41 (November 16, 1970):66+.

"Incentive Pay for Purchasing Staffers." *Purchasing* 75 (July 10, 1973):33.

"Incentives Work." *Personnel Journal* 49 (November 1970):942–3.

Lawler, E. E. "Job Design and Employee Motivation." *Personnel Psychology* 22 (April 1969):426–35.

————. *Pay and Organizational Effectiveness: A Psychological View*. New York: McGraw-Hill, 1971.

Lawler, E. E., and J. R. Hackman. "Impact of Employee Participation in the Development of Pay Incentive Plans." *Journal of Applied Psychology* 53 (January 1969): 467–71.

Martin, Neal A. "What's Wrong with Bonuses." *Dunn's Review* 97 (April 1971):42–44+.

McCabe, Thomas B., Jr. "Non-Cash Incentives: The New Frontier." *Sales Management* 103 (September 10, 1969):26–27+.

McClelland, David C. "Business Drive and National Achievement." *Harvard Business Review* 40 (July 1962):99–112.

————. "Achievement and Motivation Can be Developed." *Harvard Business Review* 43 (November 1965):6–25.

McManis, Donald L., and William G. Bick. "Monetary Incentives in Today's Industrial Setting." *Personnel Journal* 52 (May 1973):387–92.

Mobley, W. H. "Link Between MBO and Merit Compensation." *Personnel Journal* 53 (June 1974):423–74.

Patton, Arch. "Why Incentive Plans Fail." *Harvard Business Review* 50 (May, 1962): 58–66.

Perham, John C. "Pay Off in Performance Bonuses." *Dunn's Review* 103 (May 1974): 51–55.

"J. C. Penney: The Deft Motivator." *Dunn's Review* 102 (December 1973):54–59.

Pitts, Robert A. "Incentive Compensation and Organizational Design." *Personnel Journal* 53 (May 1974):338–44+.

Porter, Lyman W., and Edward E. Lawler III. *Managerial Attitudes and Performance.* Homewood, Ill.: Irwin, 1968.

Roberts, Reed M., Jr. "Tie Bonuses to Corporate Profits." *Financial Executive* 41 (June 1973):12–19.

Roethe, Harold. "Output Rate Among Welders." *Journal of Applied Psychology* 54 (December 1970):549–51.

Schrieber, David E., and Stanley Sloan. "Incentives: Are They Relevant, Obsolete, or Misunderstood." *Personnel Administration* 33 (January 1970):52–57.

Stelluto, George. "Report on Incentive Pay in Manufacturing Industries." *Monthly Labor Review* 92 (July 1969).

Wilson, Stanley R. "The Incentive Approach to Executive Development." *Business Horizons* 15 (April 1972):15–24.

Winning, Ethan A. "MBO: What's In It For the Individual." *Personnel* 51 (March 1974):51–56.

Yankelovich, Daniel. *The New Morality: A Profile of American Youth in the 70s.* New York: McGraw-Hill, 1974.

Chapter 12

PERFORMANCE EVALUATION

Everyone wants to "know the score." People want to know what is expected of them in their jobs and how well they are performing. Workers' enthusiasm for the present and future is closely connected to past performance and how information about this performance is communicated. The detailed review of performance evaluation provided in this chapter will relate closely to our discussions of training, development, job analysis and compensation.

LEARNING OBJECTIVES

As a result of studying this chapter, the reader should be able to:

Understand and explain the values and limitations of performance evaluation as an aid to self development, selection for promotion, recruiting, training, and wage/salary decisions in organizations

Illustrate the important steps in designing a performance evaluation system

Discuss the interrelationships between the performance review process and the total personnel management information system

Discuss the positive contributions that an effective management by objectives program can make to the performance evaluation and development processes

Describe the assessment center approach and design an effective assessment center model for human resource selection, evaluation, and development.

KEY TERMS AND CONCEPTS

rater bias	critical incident
graphic rating scale	forced distribution
forced choice	field review

group appraisal
systems feedback
individual performance ratio
grading

halo
management objectives
peer group appraisal
assessment center

PREVIEW

Earlier we emphasized the importance of planning and forecasting. The other end of this process—evaluation—is equally important. Every organization, regardless of objectives, whether public or private, nonprofit or profit oriented, must ultimately stand or fall on the performance of its people. This chapter will explore performance evaluation, including:

1. The nature and importance of performance evaluation.

2. Traditional approaches to performance evaluation and the strengths and weaknesses of these approaches.

3. New approaches to performance evaluation.

4. The usefulness of assessment centers in performance evaluation.

THE NATURE AND IMPORTANCE OF PERFORMANCE EVALUATION

Evaluation obviously involves feedback. Personnel systems provide many kinds of feedback, but the regular and, as far as humanly possible, objective measurement of employee performance is the most important. An employee's performance in the present and progress toward higher level positions depend on many factors. But recruiting, selection, and placement and development policies are very important. The type of standard used to measure performance influences decisions on promotions and merit increases. Also, performance measures link information gathering and the decision-making processes, which provide a basis for judging the effectiveness of personnel sub-systems such as recruiting, selection, training, and compensation.

Accurate performance measures also play a key role in the organization as a whole. They help pinpoint weak areas in the primary systems (e.g., marketing, finance, and production). It is easier for managers to see which employees need training or counseling, because jobs are grouped by categories (e.g., production foreman, sales manager, financial analyst). These categories can be broken into smaller and smaller groups if necessary. If valid performance data are available, timely, accurate, objective, standardized, and relevant, management can maintain consistent promotion and compensation policies throughout the total system.

Performance evaluations have existed in a whirlwind of criticism for many years. People have both praised and criticized their accuracy, validity, and use. But the criticisms generally involve techniques, methods, and measures rather than the use of the evaluation itself. Indeed, the critics of the evaluation process offer alternatives to the existing methods; in general they accept the concept (McGregor, 1957). These critics realize that an organization must be able to measure its employees' performance in some way and that if it is going to grow, it must be able to evaluate employee potential.

The real issue about performance evaluations, then, is not Should they be done? but How should they be done? The challenge is to find a method that can succeed by learning from initial failures. It is with this approach in mind that we will examine both the conventional and some of the more recent methods of performance evaluation. We will consider their strengths, and weaknesses, and applicability to specific types of problems, the relative merits of ratings by peers, subordinates, and supervisors, and the uses of the evaluation data after initial ratings are recorded.

What Is Performance Evaluation?

All of us evaluate the people around us. They, in turn, size us up. We choose friends on the basis of an evaluation: we judge their values, education, and interests. We go to several lawyers, doctors, or dentists before we decide on one. People call the Better Business Bureau for an evaluation of a contractor before agreeing to a major remodeling job. Priests and other religious leaders are evaluated by their congregations. These evaluations are, for the most part, informal, easily biased, incomplete, and often inaccurate. Nevertheless, the process continues and will continue as long as at least two humans are alive.

Organizations, on the other hand, use evaluations for a variety of purposes. They require a higher degree of formality than we use as individuals. Organizational evaluations are systematic, periodic, and, as far as possible, objective.

Purposes of Employee Evaluation

Many types of evaluation systems are available. Before choosing one, a manager should establish objectives. In other words, he should decide the reasons for the evaluation. For instance, a manager may want to motivate and develop employees. This is a fairly common and very important use. If the system is well designed, the manager will have accurate and timely feedback on employees' present performance and potential. Depending on how the manager relays this feedback to employees, he will be able to affect all kinds of important human needs: security, affiliation, recognition, and self-fulfillment. If a good employee knows where he stands, he will feel more secure. If supervisors clearly tell employees what they want and need, the employees will have a sense of belonging and feel they really count. Performance feedback gives a manager the chance to praise a job well done and to help overcome problems. A manager will have an effective way of motivating workers and helping to reduce the frustrations that inevitably result from a lack of information.

Evaluations are made for many other reasons, such as promotions and raises. Most officials feel that evaluation sessions dealing with salary (promotion) should be kept separate from those dealing with counseling, career guidance, or personal development. For example, if an employee receives a very high rating but then receives only a token salary increase, the employee may feel that he's been "had." In fact, the company may be in poor financial condition, and the manager may have had to fight for even a small raise for a valuable employee. If the employee doesn't know the whole situation, he may think that the evaluation is worthless.

Another important purpose of performance evaluation is to provide research data for improving the overall personnel information system (Hamner, 1974). Effectiveness of recruiting, selection, and placement techniques can be evaluated by comparing the employee's performance with recommendations that were made before he was hired. For example, if employees selected through college campus interviews perform significantly better than those obtained through agency advertisements, the manager has isolated a problem. The personnel department should find out how the agencies select candidates for interviews. An investigation may reveal that these two classes of employees are motivated differently.

This kind of approach is clearly much better than a "knee jerk" or "seat of the pants" solution. Instead of blaming the agency and refusing to see its candidates, a manager can take one of two constructive kinds of actions. He can use different kinds of motivational approaches—in this way he recognizes employees as individuals who simply happen to value different things. Or he can direct the employment agency to screen employees differently.

Performance data also provide a base for planning, training, and development programs. Areas of general weakness (for example, communication skills) can be identified and studied.

Performance evaluations, when properly carried out, provide consistency in salary and promotion practices. They also identify effective lower-level managers. A manager who develops good workers through counseling and feedback is a valuable asset and is a good candidate for promotion. In all cases evaluation systems should focus attention on organizational objectives.

Stages in Developing an Effective Performance Evaluation System

The old army situation-analysis technique is a good starting point for discussing decisions that managers make when using performance systems. A personnel evaluation system should address the questions: Who, What, When, Where, How much, and How often?

As we have shown, evaluations can be made for a variety of reasons—counseling, promotion, research, salary, administration, or a combination of these. So it is necessary to begin by stating very clearly the objectives of the evaluation program.

Who should perform the rating.   Once a manager has set objectives, he must decide who will perform the evaluation. Most appraisal forms used today are designed to be completed by the immediate superior of the person being rated. Most employees appear to prefer evaluation by their immediate superior rather than by peers or subordinates (Lopez, 1968). (An important exception to this principle occurs in research teams, universities, and other professional associations, where individuals prefer to have their work evaluated by peers who have the technical competence to assess their efforts.)

Peer evaluations and self-evaluations tend to be higher than ratings given by superiors (Miner, 1968). Self-ratings emphasize human relations, while superiors focus on technical knowledge and initiative.

Lawler (1967) favors a combination of superior, peer, and self-ratings. Both self-assessment and feedback from co-workers are very useful. Perhaps future evaluation systems will incorporate a combination of feedback depending on the objectives of the appraisal and wishes of the person being rated (Kraut, 1975).

It is good to use more than a single rater because an average of ratings made by several persons helps lower the effect of a biased rating. Knowledge that a rating will be reviewed (endorsed) by the rater's immediate superior also helps to improve the quality of ratings (Barrett, 1966).

When to rate.   Informal performance counseling should occur continuously. The manager should discuss an employee's work as soon as possible after he has judged it. He should use good work as an opportunity to provide positive reinforcement and use poor work as a basis for training.

In most organizations employees are formally evaluated once a year. Forms are completed, endorsed, reviewed, filed, and sometimes returned to the evaluator for personal review. Research conducted at General Electric indicates that employees should not receive feedback about their performance at the same time they receive information about salary action (Meyer, 1965). When an employee receives negative feedback about job performance at the same time he is told about salary adjustment, he spends more time rationalizing and generally learns very little. The employee worries about defending his job and self-respect rather than developing his abilities.

The impact of direct feedback on rating validity. Employee ratings usually are much higher when the rater is required to confront the employee face to face with the results of the rating. At Lockheed Aircraft, 485 persons were rated twice. The first rating was secret, and the second one was discussed with the employees. The average of the second rating score was 40 percent higher than the first one (Stockford and Bissell, 1949). Also, derogatory information contained in an open file is easily subject to challenge through legal action. The full disclosure act of the federal government almost assures that employees will be able to read their performance reviews. Consequently such ratings will probably be inflated.

Traditional approaches to performance evaluation. There is little agreement on the best way to evaluate managerial, professional, or salaried performance. Leading industrial organizations have used many approaches. American Telephone and Telegraph has used an assessment center to observe how managers behave under standardized and simulated conditions. Union-Carbide once used peer-group appraisal; and Equitable Life has used a job discussion program that included lengthy interviews about a manager's responsibilities, accomplishments, and performance results expected and achieved.

In the late 1960s, IBM shifted from the rating scale method (described at a later point in this chapter) to an objectives-oriented appraisal for managers. The latter approach required that projects be outlined at the beginning of the year and evaluated at the end of the year. Many different rating forms were used: a performance planning and evaluation document, a promotability document, and an employee development plan. The appraisal was job oriented, with weights established for each listed job responsibility. A major automobile manufacturer uses a similar job-oriented appraisal that lists a hierarchy of objectives. A great deal of emphasis is placed on making the rater responsible for what he says. (Rater responsibility and accountability could be improved if a personnel information system as discussed in Chapter 15 were used to record and evaluate all ratings made by a series of supervisors. Significant variations would signal a change in employee attitude, a need for training, or an ineffective rating.)

Many evaluation systems focus on personal traits, such as initiative, dependability, drive, responsibility, creativity, integrity, leadership potential, intelligence, and so forth. However, many organizations are placing more emphasis on the evaluation of work results—job achievements—than on personality traits. Results-oriented appraisals tend to be more objective and worthwhile, especially for counseling and development purposes. We will discuss this approach in some depth in a later section. At this point, however, we will describe the more traditional approaches to performance evaluation.

Graphic Rating Scale

The graphic rating scale is the most common evaluation tool in use today. It lists a number of characteristics, usually quite ill defined, that rate an employee on a point scale ranging from three to five. A three-point scale may consist of the headings excellent, average, unsatisfactory. Sometimes a five-point scale is used: exceptional, very good, satisfactory, marginal, inadequate.

Rating scales usually are used to rate such characteristics as job knowledge, judgment, dependability, human relations, appearance, attitude, planning ability, and creativity. The rating scale is simple to use, and the manager can rate many people in a short time.

When these ratings are objectively given, they can provide useful feedback. But they have severe limitations. They assume that each characteristic is equally important for all jobs. Perhaps worst of all, they assume that everyone's definition of dependable is the same. An example of a conventional graphic rating scale is shown in Exhibit 12–1.

It is easy to make an improved version of this scale. If a manager prepares short definitions of each characteristic *and* each degree of performance within a given characteristic, the rating scale will be much more effective. Exhibit 12–2 illustrates an improved rating scale, while Exhibit 12–3 provides a humorous approach to the same concept.

Critical Incident Method

The critical incident approach avoids the pitfall of attempting to measure subjective personality characteristics. The manager bases his ratings on specific instances of actual job behavior. When a "critical incident," either good or bad, occurs, the manager records the incident in the employee's file. Feedback is then provided about the incidents during performance review sessions. This approach definitely reduces the "recency" effect (most recent incidents, good or bad, get too much emphasis) of most performance ratings.

However, French (1970) points out that the critical incident approach has significant limitations. These include:

1. Negative incidents are generally more noticeable than positive ones.

2. The recording of incidents is a chore to the supervisor and may be put off and easily forgotten.

3. Overly close supervision may result.

4. Managers may unload a series of complaints about incidents during an annual performance review session. The feedback may be too much at one time and thus appear as a punishment. More appropriately, management should use incidents of poor performance as opportunities for immediate training and counseling.

EXHIBIT 12–1 Employee Review Report

PROBATIONARY EMPLOYEE REVIEW REPORT

| (Probationary Employee) | (Clock No.) | (Date employed or transferred) |

| (Department) | (Classification) |

Rate the above named new/reclassified employee as accurately as possible. Your <u>OVERALL EVALUATION SHOULD BE IN CAMPARISON WITH OTHER EMPLOYEES WITH THE SAME LENGTH OF SERVICE ON THIS JOB.</u> Your analysis determines the employee's desirability and worth. Your thorough appraisal now may well prevent a critical problem later. No employee shall be retained beyond the probationary period if he/she fails to fulfill your specific requirements for the position. Termination form should accompany the review if the employee is unsatisfactory. (See instructions on reverse side of duplicate.)

RATING TABLE

	Not Applicable	Unsatisfactory	Below Average	Average	Above Average
Quality of work Accuracy, neatness	_____	0	1	2 3 4	5
Quantity of work	_____	0	1	2 3 4	5
Ability to follow directions	_____	0	1	2 3 4	5
Conscientious about work	_____	0	1	2 3 4	5
Use of judgment and imagination	_____	0	1	2 3 4	5
Initiative and responsibility	_____	0	1	2 3 4	5
Observance of departmental and safety rules	_____	0	1	2 3 4	5
Attendance	_____	0	1	2 3 4	5
Promptness	_____	0	1	2 3 4	5
Response to supervision and instruction	_____	0	1	2 3 4	5
Courtesy and cooperation	_____	0	1	2 3 4	5
Attitude toward work, public visitors, patients, co-workers, etc.	_____	0	1	2 3 4	5
Appearance	_____	0	1	2 3 4	5

COMMENTS _____

_____

_____

_____

_____

12 week's recommendation: Retain __ Dismiss __

Orig: Personnel
cc: Department Head

This will acknowledge that this review has been discussed with me.

Date Reviewed_____

| (Employee Signature) |

| (Rater Signature) |

EXHIBIT 12-2   Company Grade Officer Effectiveness Report

IDENTIFICATION DATA (Read AFM 36-10 carefully before filling out any item.)

1. LAST NAME-FIRST NAME-MIDDLE INITIAL	2.AFSN	3.ACTIVE DUTY GRADE	4 PERFORMANCE GRADE

5. ORGANIZATION, COMMAND AND LOCATION	6.AERO RATING	CODE	7. PERIOD OF REPORT
	8. PERIOD OF SUPERVISION		FROM: THRU:
			9. REASON OF REPORT

II. DUTIES-PAFSC _____ . DAFSC _____ .

III RATING FACTORS (Consider how this officer is performing on his job.)

1. KNOWLEDGE OF DUTIES

NOT OBSERVED	SERIOUS GAPS IN HIS KNOWLEDGE OF FUNDA-MENTALS OF HIS JOB.	SATISFACTORY KNOWL-EDGE OF ROUTINE PHASES OF HIS JOB.	WELL INFORMED ON MOST PHASES OF HIS JOB.	EXCELLENT KNOWLEDGE OF ALL PHASES OF HIS JOB.	EXCEPTIONAL UNDER-STANDING OF HIS JOB. EXTREMELY WELL INFORMED ON ALL PHASES.

2. PERFORMANCE OF DUTIES

NOT OBSERVED	QUALITY OR QUANTITY OF WORK OFTEN FAILS TO MEET JOB REQUIRE-MENTS.	PERFORMANCE MEETS ONLY MINIMUM JOB REQUIREMENTS.	QUANTITY AND QUALITY OF WORK ARE VERY SATISFACTORY.	PRODUCES VERY HIGH QUANTITY AND QUALITY OF WORK. MEETS ALL SUSPENSES.	QUALITY AND QUANTITY OF WORK ARE CLEARLY SUPERIOR AND TIMELY.

3. EFFECTIVENESS IN WORKING WITH OTHERS

NOT OBSERVED	INEFFECTIVE IN WORK-ING WITH OTHERS. DOES NOT COOPERATE.	SOMETIMES HAS DIFFICUL-TY IN GETTING ALONG WITH OTHERS.	GETS ALONG WELL WITH PEOPLE UNDER NORMAL CIRCUMSTANCES.	WORKS IN HARMONY WITH OTHERS. A VERY GOOD TEAM WORKER.	EXTREMELY SUCCESSFUL WORKING WITH OTHERS, ACTIVELY PROMOTES HARMONY.

4.LEADERSHIP CHARACTERISTICS

NOT OBSERVED	OFTEN WEAK, FAILS TO SHOW INITIATIVE AND ACCEPT RESPONSIBILITY.	INITIATIVE AND ACCEPT-ANCE OF RESPONSIBILITY ADEQUATE IN MOST SITUATIONS.	SATISFACTORILY DEMON STRATES INITIATIVE AND ACCEPTS RESPONSIBILITY	DEMONSTRATES A HIGH DEGREE OF INITIATIVE AND ACCEPTANCE OF RESPONSIBILITY.	ALWAYS DEMONSTRATES OUTSTANDING INITIATIVE AND ACCEPTANCE OF RESPONSIBILITY.

5. JUDGEMENT

NOT OBSERVED	DECISIONS AND RECOM-MENDATIONS OFTEN WRONG OR INEFFECTIVE	JUDGEMENT IS USUALLY SOUND BUT MAKES OCCASIONAL ERRORS.	SHOWS GOOD JUDGEMENT RESULTING FROM SOUND EVALUATION OF FACTORS.	SOUND, LOGICAL THINKER. CONSIDERS ALL FACTORS TO REACH ACCURATE DECISIONS.	CONSISTENTLY ARRIVES AT RIGHT DECISION EVEN ON HIGHLY COMPLEX MATTERS.

6. ADAPTABILITY

NOT OBSERVED	UNABLE TO PERFORM ADEQUATELY IN OTHER THAN ROUTINE SITUATIONS.	PERFORMANCE DECLINES UNDER STRESS OR IN OTHER THAN ROUTINE SITUATIONS.	PERFORMS WELL UNDER STRESS OR IN UNUSUAL SITUATIONS.	PERFORMANCE EXCELLENT EVEN UNDER PRESSURE OR IN DIFFICULT SITUATIONS.	OUTSTANDING PERFORM-ANCE UNDER EXTREME STRESS. MEETS THE CHALLENGE OF DIFFICULT SITUATIONS.

7. USE OF RESOURCES

NOT OBSERVED (M) (P)	INEFFECTIVE IN CONSER-TION OF RESOURCES.	USES RESOURCES IN A BARELY SATISFACTORY MANNER.	CONSERVES BY USING ROUTINE PROCEDURES.	EFFECTIVELY ACCOMPLISH-ES SAVINGS BY DEVELOP-ING IMPROVED PROCE-DURES.	EXCEPTIONALLY EFFECTIVE IN USING RESOURCES.

8. WRITING ABILITY AND ORAL EXPRESSION

NOT OBSERVED (W) (S)	UNABLE TO EXPRESS THOUGHT CLEARLY. LACKS ORGANIZATION.	EXPRESSES THOUGHTS SATISFACTORILY ON ROU-TINE MATTERS.	USUALLY ORGANIZES AND EXPRESSES THOUGHTS CLEARLY AND CONCISELY.	CONSISTENTLY ABLE TO EXPRESS IDEAS CLEARLY.	OUTSTANDING ABILITY TO COMMUNICATE IDEAS TO OTHERS.
	WRITE SPEAK	WRITE SPEAK	WRITE SPEAK	WRITE SPEAK	WRITE SPEAK

IV. MILITARY QUALITIES (Consider how this officer meets Air Force standards.)

NOT OBSERVED	BEARING OR BEHAVIOR INTERFERE SERIOUSLY WITH HIS EFFECTIVENESS.	CARELESS BEARING AND BEHAVIOR DETRACT FROM HIS EFFECTIVENESS.	BEARING AND BEHAVIOR CREATE A GOOD IMPRES-SION.	ESPECIALLY GOOD BEHAV-IOR AND BEARING. CREATES A VERY FAVORABLE IM-PRESSION.	BEARING AND BEHAVIOR ARE OUTSTANDING. HE EXEMPLIFIES TOP MILITARY STANDARDS.

Nov. 66

COMPANY GRADE OFFICER EFFECTIVENESS REPORT

EXHIBIT 12–3   Cold Hard Facts

COLD HARD FACTS

IDENTIFICATION DATA			
1. LAST NAME-FIRST NAME-MIDDLE INITIAL KNOWITALL, JOSHUA G.	2. NO FOD00000	3. ACTIVE DUTY GRADE MAJOR	4. PERMANENT GRADE 2/LT
5. ORGANIZATION, COMMAND AND LOCATION Commercial Airline Liaison Secret Command Hong Kong Airfield	6. AERO RATING CODE Aviator ?	7. PERIOD OF REPORT	
		FROM: July 1970	THRU: June 1972
	8. PERIOD OF SUPERVISION Undetermined	9. REASON FOR REPORT Upcoming court martial	

II DUTIES-PAFSC 0000. DAFSC 0001/2.   PRESENT DUTY:

Instruct stewardii in hand to hand combat. Acts as personal bodyguard for stewardii after duty hours in foreign ports. Reads the riot act to military passengers on R & R flights. Searches for and confiscates live contraband on return flights.

1. JOB CAPABILITY

NOT ○ OBSERVED	CANNOT RECOGNIZE BUILDINGS. [X]	CRASHES INTO BUILD-INGS TRYING TO JUMP OVER THEM [ ]	CAN ONLY LEAP OVER SHORT BUILDINGS. [ ]	NEEDS RUNNING START TO LEAP OVER TALL BUILDINGS. [ ]	LEAPS TALL BUILDINGS WITH A SINGLE BOUND. [ ]

2. PERFORMANCE OF DUTIES

NOT ○ OBSERVED	WOUNDS SELF WITH BULLETS. [X]	CAN SHOOT BULLETS. [ ]	NOT QUITE AS FAST AS A SPEEDING BULLET. [ ]	IS JUST AS FAST AS A SPEEDING BULLET. [ ]	IS FASTER THAN A SPEEDING BULLET. [ ]

3. ADAPTABILITY

NOT ○ OBSERVED	HATES PILOTS. [X]	HAS TROUBLE FLYING. [ ]	ONLY FLIES AS HIGH AS TRANSPORTS. [ ]	DOES NOT LEAVE ATMOSPHERE WHEN FLYING. [ ]	FLIES HIGHER THAN A MIGHTY ROCKET. [ ]

4. LEADERSHIP CHARACTERISTICS

NOT ○ OBSERVED	NEVER HEARD OF LOCOMOTIVE. [X]	GETS RUN OVER BY LOCOMOTIVE. [ ]	LOSES TUG OF WAR WITH A LOCOMOTIVE [ ]	AS POWERFUL AS A LOCOMOTIVE [ ]	MORE POWERFUL THAN A LOCOMOTIVE [ ]

5. HUMAN RELATIONS

NOT ○ OBSERVED	TALKS TO WALLS. [X]	TALKS WITH ANIMALS. [ ]	TALKS WITH HUMANS. [ ]	TALKS WITH ANGELS. [ ]	GIVES POLICY GUIDANCE TO THE ANGELS. [ ]

Rank Order

There are two common varieties of rank order evaluation. Using the *alternation ranking method,* the supervisor ranks the best employee first and the worst one last. Then, from the remaining unranked employees he selects the second best and second worst employees. This process continues until all are ranked. The *paired comparison method* involves a series of comparisons and a tally system to develop the relative ranks of employees.

Both methods are fairly reliable in developing rankings within a given department. However, there are several problems. Ratings cannot be compared because they do not have an objective base, and there is no safeguard against the bias of a rater. A relatively small number of people must be used; otherwise comparisons become virtually meaningless. Another disadvantage of these ranking methods is that the ranks suggest how a person stands relative to the others in the group, but they do not tell how much better or poorer one person is than another.

The same general weaknesses and strengths of the ranking methods apply to the *forced distribution method,* which is no more than an attempt to give percentage values to the rankings. Thus, a manager may be asked for a list of the top 10 percent and bottom 10 percent of his subordinates.

Checklist

The checklist method is made up of a set of questions about the employee. The supervisor makes responses that are evaluated by the personnel department. The questions may be weighted equally or certain questions may be weighted more heavily than others. But the checklist has a major disadvantage: the rater is able to bias the evaluation because he can distinguish positive and negative questions. Also, a separate checklist must often be developed for different classes of jobs. This process can be expensive and time consuming.

Essay Method

The essay evaluation has been used for many years. The supervisor makes a free-form, open-ended appraisal of an employee in his own words. There are several advantages to this method. An essay can provide a good deal of information because the supervisor is not restricted by a list of choices. Because the essay does not have a necessary form, it can provide a good deal of information, especially if the supervisor is asked, for instance, to give two or three examples of each judgment he makes. The explanations will give specific information about the employee, and can reveal even more about the supervisor. However, essays have several important drawbacks. They generally cannot be compared. Rater bias is easily introduced into essay-type ratings, since the essay is in the supervisor's own words. Finally, appraisals often depend more on the skill and effort of the writer than the real performance of the people being rated.

Forced Choice

The forced choice approach was developed by a group of U.S. Army psychologists during World War II. It was a response to widespread dissatisfaction with the results of rating scales, forced distributions, paired comparisons, and checklist techniques. The forced choice performance scale consists of a series of tetrads (sets of four phrases about job behavior or personal qualities, two of which are positive, two negative). The rater is asked to indicate which of the four phrases is most and least like the subject. If one of the positive (favorable) is checked as most characteristic, the subject receives plus credit. The subject also gets plus credit if one of the negative phrases is checked as being least characteristic. Rater halo and bias are significantly reduced by this method since only one of the favorable and one of the unfavorable phrases in each tetrad is related to success or failure on the job.

Considerable research was performed on the validity of the forced choice technique in the 1950s (Cozen, 1959). Although the method does provide greater objectivity, its validity is not clearly superior to traditional rating methods. There are several reasons why it is not more attractive than other rating methods. Trained technicians are required to prepare tetrads for each occupational group. And most managers don't like to "rate in the dark." Forced choice tests are expensive to develop, and most raters become irritated with the tests because they feel they are not being trusted. Oberg (1972) notes that comparisons of the graphic scale and the forced choice technique show that the two are fairly close in validity.

Field Review

Field reviews can take several forms. One form relieves the supervisor from the paper work necessary in the other evaluation methods. A member of the personnel department interviews the supervisor about his subordinates. This method has at least one disadvantage: it ties up two professionals at the same time.

In another form of field review, previously completed ratings are discussed by several raters and a member of the personnel department. This method involves a good deal of time, but it can be a valuable aid to identify disagreements between raters, help the group arrive at a consensus, and assure that each rater similarly understands the rating standards.

The *group appraisal* is similar to field review. A panel consisting of the employee's supervisor and other supervisors familiar with the employee's work makes the evaluation. Single-rater bias can often be reduced or eliminated, but the process is time consuming. (See Assessment Centers, pp. 354–359.)

Grading

State and federal government civil service agencies use a grading system. A supervisor defines important categories and gives them values. The persons being evaluated within a grade often are assumed to have a similar level of ability.

This approach may force the rater to assign a certain percentage of the total group to each category.

Descriptive Evaluation

Like the essay method, description evaluations use narrative discussions of employee performance. They use word pictures: the rater selects a descriptor that best describes a candidate. These ratings are difficult to compare, but they give the rater more opportunity in what can be said.

Inherent Weakness in Traditional Evaluation Programs

Many traditional performance evaluation systems have internal weakness. Managers generally are not qualified to assess personality traits, and research indicates that most managers are not properly trained to conduct evaluation and performance interviews. They have only vague notions of the purpose of the evaluations. Although they try very hard, they usually do a poor job (Conant, 1973). Some managers discourage good performance by overemphasizing shortcomings and almost neglecting good work. Others have little effect on poor workers because they tend to sugar coat their criticisms (many people do not like to criticize others, especially face to face). Consequently, the real message is lost.

The rater's personality also plays an important part in the effectiveness of evaluation programs. Some raters are, by temperament, overly harsh and give low ratings to all subordinates. Others are too lenient and give everyone a good rating. Some raters play favorites, some are victims of the "halo effect" (an employee demonstrating one or two outstanding traits is automatically rated high on all other traits).

The relative status of raters in their organization is a factor that is important to the validity of performance evaluations. Using more raters or endorsements by a superior reduces rater bias and increases the validity of appraisals. It would seem logical to assume that rater discontent might affect ratings and their validity. However, rater attitudes towards rating scales have little effect on the validity of those ratings (Brumback, 1972). The implication is reasonably clear. The personnel department can apparently choose the type of evaluation instrument best suited to provide necessary information without worrying about rater reactions.

A MODERN APPROACH TO EVALUATION AND CAREER DEVELOPMENT: RESULTS-ORIENTED MANAGEMENT

We have discussed several traditional approaches to performance evaluation. They emphasize either the task or the worker's personality. In the context of the sociotechnical systems approach to management emphasized in this book, it is only natural to seek an approach to employee evaluation that provides a balanced approach to the task and the humans involved in performing the task.

Definition and Advantages

Management by objectives (MBO), or results-oriented management, as it is often called, is an important performance evaluation tool. MBO is a management system and philosophy that stresses goals rather than methods. It provides responsibility and accountability and recognizes that employees have needs for achievement and self-fulfillment. It meets these needs by providing opportunities for participation in the goal-setting process. Subordinates become involved in planning their own careers. People generally want to do the right thing, and MBO helps them to know what they are expected to do.

Consider the manager who thinks it is important to paper the walls of his office with colorful control charts showing planned and actual daily output for *past* months. One day, the vice-president visits the office and asks about plans for the *coming* months regarding capital investment expenditures. "Well," says the subordinate, "I never realized that this was important at my level. I really thought this was all done by headquarters." Obviously, a communication void existed. MBO is effective because it improves internal communication through direct feedback.

MBO increases employee motivation because it relates overall goals to the individual's goals. It helps to increase an employee's understanding of where the organization is and where it is heading. Managers are more likely to compete with themselves than with other managers. This kind of evaluation can reduce internal conflicts that often arise when managers compete with each other to obtain scarce resources. For example, individual goal setting can help a sales manager identify different conditions in different sales territories. A fast food unit located in a retirement community should probably not be expected to compete, on the basis of sales volume, with a unit located in a large shopping center.

MBO helps the individual manager to develop personal leadership, especially the skills of listening, planning, counseling, motivating, and evaluating. This approach to managing instills a personal commitment to respond positively to the organization's major concerns as well as to the development of human assets. Such a manager has a far greater chance to move ahead within the management hierarchy than the non-MBO type.

Psychological Basis for the MBO Program

According to widely accepted psychological theory, human needs exist in a hierarchy, beginning with the lowest level physiological needs for food and drink and progressing upward through needs for security, a sense of belonging, esteem, and self-fulfillment. Higher level needs become operative before the lower level needs are *fully* satisfied. More traditional management strategy has viewed the worker as an "economic person," one who is indolent, motivated by money, and naturally lazy. This economic person therefore must be supervised closely and have all objectives set for him. Douglas McGregor and other members of the human relations school of management strongly disagree with this approach.

They suggest that people are social beings; they need recognition, responsibility, and challenge. They are motivated by more than just money. Neither attitude is true of everyone. Some individuals work better in an authoritarian environment, while others work best in a permissive environment.

If we assume that most workers are conscientious and do seek some level of responsibility in most situations, the strict authoritarian approach to leadership is unnecessary. However, this does not mean that objectives and standards are unnecessary. Standards reinforce the motivation provided by personal responsibility. If a person does not know what he is expected to achieve, he will not know if he has, in fact, achieved anything. Thus, the need for self-fulfillment, esteem, and a sense of belonging probably will not be effectively satisfied in the absence of goals.

Fusion of Individual and Organizational Goals

If the goals of individual managers can somehow be integrated with the goals of the organization, management as a whole will benefit. The organization as a whole undoubtedly will be better off if the individual worker can see how securing his personal goals contributes to company goals. Unfortunately, this is easier said than done. Take, for example, a top-flight aeronautical engineer who expresses a desire to become involved in community problems. The manager might discourage this, feeling that this kind of outside activity will only detract from time spent on the job. In situations such as this, social psychologists see a real opportunity to integrate personal and organizational goals for the benefit of both. If the manager knows what kinds of community activities the company wishes to emphasize, he can advise the engineer about which ones would be most useful—from the company's viewpoint—for him to participate in. This will do a lot more good than discouraging such participation. This applies whether the person's interests direct him toward participation in a fund drive, education for the hardcore unemployed, international trade exhibits, the chamber of commerce, or simply the design of a product that is closely tied to social progress.

Practical Research in Management by Objectives

At the Hovey and Beard Company, women were allowed to participate in deciding how fast a conveyor line should move in front of them. The company found that the women accepted a higher average speed than managers had originally planned to set as the standard. In England, the Tavistock Institute of Human Relations (Buffa, 1974) demonstrated that groups of workers can design effective procedures and methods. This was particularly true when the work required considerable flexibility.

Vroom (1959), in a study of 108 first-, second-, and third-line supervisors working in a large corporation, found that participation in the establishment of goals had positive effects on attitudes and job performance. But the most important element was certain personality characteristics of the participants. Those with "authoritarian" personalities, or those who did not need to feel independent, did not seem affected by the opportunity to participate in making decisions. In other words, a management by objectives program probably would not have an effect on such personalities. On the other hand, equalitarians and those who had strong needs for independence developed more positive attitudes toward their work and greater motivation. Vroom's study lends support to the hypothesis that management must give greater attention to participative strategies than it did even five years ago.

Vroom also concludes there is no evidence that increased participation harms the attitudes or performance of low-level supervisors. The reader is cautioned not to extend this reasoning beyond the sample or to immediately apply it to workers in general. While the MBO approach appears to bring either positive or neutral results at supervisory and professional levels, there may be cases when individual workers who have strongly authoritarian personalities or have a very high need for dependence would rebel against participation.

A manager of integrated circuit manufacturing for an electronics firm explains his company's approach. New employees are given an entire day to become acquainted with the company. Each is then given a learning curve and quality goals for his or her particular job. These employees are told that the learning curve was developed from the last 250 people on the job. This enables them to plot their own progress. This approach, claims the manager, is to get people used to goal-setting as soon as possible. Especially noteworthy are the results achieved among a group of workers who assemble radar equipment. By setting their own targets and somewhat managing the job themselves, they reduced assembly time from a money losing 138 hours per unit to 32 hours per unit.

Carroll (1969) reports a research project studying management by objectives in another firm. Out of 150 managers, 129 responded to a survey indicating that the success of an MBO program is highly related to the perceived relevance of the goals and the frequency of feedback. When workers felt that goals were realistic, MBO was successful.

Establishing Objectives

As we mentioned earlier, organizations need to establish and communicate their objectives. In businesses, market share, innovation, growth, profitability, social responsibility, management development, worker development, and product mix in particular need objectives that are expressed clearly and concisely and can be measured accurately. Most of these objectives will have to be periodically revised to avoid rigidity.

Objectives should be challenging: high enough to provide motivation but not so high that they are out of reach. Unattainable goals cause frustration, which may in turn lead to defensive behavior by workers. Consider the Olympic athlete who is driven to exert maximum effort. He has a clearly definable goal in mind—a challenging goal which, if attained, leads to personal recognition and satisfaction. The same principle applies to workers.

Goal setting requires balance. For example, if a manager is told that she is going to be evaluated on the basis of cost performance, she probably will make every effort to reduce costs. In general, people will try to act in ways that will help them attain their goals, but they must be told clearly what is expected. This approach requires a systems outlook. In other words, the final, agreed-upon goals should reflect consideration for all areas affecting the performance of the system rather than emphasizing one or two goals at the expense of all others (Werther, 1975).

Perhaps an illustration from the real world will help clarify this point. A middle manager at a large automobile firm realized that he would be evaluated on the basis of his department's profit performance. When preliminary statements indicated he was 19 percent below plan, he considered all of the following strategies: 1) eliminate his $30,000 advertising budget for the latter half of the current year, 2) postpone the addition of two engineers until the following year, and 3) further reduce purchases of raw materials to improve return on assets. Each alternative would improve profitability for the current year but would also probably hurt long-range performance. Thus, management, through participation, must establish objectives that will benefit both the short- and long-range goals. They should not conflict. This is not an easy task, but it is necessary. For instance, maximizing cash flow is not necessarily compatible with minimizing maintenance expenditures.

Implementation of a Management by Objectives Program

As we have already mentioned, the first stage of an MBO program develops and communicates the organization's long-range goals. The next phase is to get top management support for the MBO program. Once workers realize that the chief executive thinks the program is important, they will be more likely to accept it.

Individual managers then must clarify in their own minds the responsibilities of their subordinates. Organization charts and job descriptions can be helpful, but other tools can be used. The manager should ask each subordinate to write down his personal goals, while in turn the manager writes out the goals he thinks subordinates should have. The manager and subordinate can discuss them, reach an agreement about them, and put them in writing. The manager should then ask his subordinate how he personally can help achieve those goals, request suggestions, and evaluate progress at regular periods.

If both the manager and the subordinate are satisfied with past objectives and results, the past objectives can be used as a basis for selecting future objectives. These objectives should be flexible enough to accommodate new ideas, and they should stress individual responsibility. Of equal importance, good work should be quickly reinforced through feedback.

Of course, some persons will purposely attempt to set their personal goals low in order to make the target easy to reach. This quirk of human nature demands that the manager be constantly alert and exercise sound judgment. The manager cannot deny responsibility for achieving results merely because goals are set in mutual consultation with subordinates. As subordinates learn to establish objectives and direct activities toward their goals, the rate of control and amount of checking gradually can be decreased. During the initial stages of the

MBO program, monthly reviews may be used and then extended to quarterly reviews. For maximum effectiveness, reviews probably should be made more often than once each year.

Goals, of course, should be specific, and if possible they should be quantified for easier measurement. Individual goals should also have a strategy for implementation. One of the greatest benefits of managing by objectives is also one of its dangers: MBO stresses results rather than means. The danger is that managers will not place *enough* emphasis on *how* results will be achieved. Consider the production superintendent who is in the process of setting goals in the areas of inventory, quality, records, communications, training, innovation, maintenance, safety, and absenteeism. Examples of goals and substantiated strategies might appear as follows:

1. *Inventory.* Reduce out-of-stock to 1 percent of total inventory items through installation of order-cycling method by March 15.

2. *Quality.* Establish a 3 percent outgoing quality level through the installation of statistical sampling techniques; have charts posted by August 15.

3. *Records.* Have 90 percent of required reports in by due date by hiring and training an executive secretary.

4. *Communications.* Hold weekly meetings with all supervisors.

5. *Training.* Install job-training program for new machine operators by December 1.

6. *Innovation.* Use program evaluation and review technique (PERT) for all new plant layouts.

7. *Maintenance.* Reduce machine breakdowns to three per month through preventive maintenance program.

8. *Safety.* Reduce serious injuries to 15 per million hours worked through weekly plant tours, supervisory meetings, and a poster campaign.

9. *Absenteeism.* Reduce hours paid for but not worked to 4 percent through increased effort in human relations and participative management.

A Note of Caution

In spite of its theoretical soundness, MBO has had extensive failures since its official introduction in the middle 1950s. About 40 percent (200) of the *Fortune* 500 largest industrial firms had MBO-based programs in 1974 (Singular, 1975), while only 35 of these companies reported that their programs were successful.

Primary among the reasons for extensive failure in the MBO process are hasty implementation, unknowledgeable users, lack of top management follow-through, overemphasis on structure (e.g., filling out forms on time), treatment as another gimmick, and failure to carefully monitor and encourage the MBO process during the hard initial years of implementation. MBO is a long-range organizational development process requiring very effective and persevering managers (Odiorne, 1974).

It is quite possible to use MBO as a management *control* device rather than a system to achieve participation. Companies that have tied their MBO programs to salary adjustments and annual performance evaluations have had trouble increasing motivation and productivity. As with the more traditional forms of performance review, it is necessary to separate the counseling, developmental, and motivational aspects of the appraisal process from the salary and promotion aspects.

Management by objectives is far from a panacea. Those executives who have been involved very often find it difficult to apply MBO concepts to their own work habits. They find it hard to think about the results of work rather than the work itself. They tend to overemphasize goals that are easy to quantify, sometimes forgetting that workers often behave almost like children at play—when the game no longer challenges, interest soon is lost.

MBO: A Case Study of Failure

As a final note of caution, we present an example of an MBO program that has failed and give some of the reasons for its failure. The managers involved in this real-life example are all members of a state vocational rehabilitation system and are in charge of individual counselors dealing with alcoholics, parolees, and the mentally and physically disabled.

Fifteen such executives and counselors were polled for their reactions to the one-year-old MBO program that central headquarters instituted. The response was unanimous—and negative. They stated some of the reasons why the program failed: since people are not predictable, it is not possible to establish specific goals; we did not have previous experience in decision making; we cannot control our environment; our superiors were not sold on the program, and consequently we got a hazy picture of what was expected; our organizational units do not agree about what the goals of the organization actually are; and finally, we did not have sufficient information regarding budgets to be able to establish our goals for the coming year.

Each of the above statements is, in itself, sufficient reason for lack of success. In contemplating an MBO approach, management can learn much from this program that failed.

Managing Change by MBO

It is fruitless to seek an ideal philosophy of management. Frustration would undoubtedly be the primary result of such a search. Rather, management must be concerned with moving in the right direction by balancing technological advancement and human need for achievement. As the information revolution continues to provide greater challenge, we must seek to narrow the gap between technology and our capability to understand and use it to the betterment of human dignity. At this time, very few generalizations can be made about the management of human resources. Management scientists and behavioral scientists should be able to integrate their research efforts. Fortunately, we are moving in a positive direction, and future generations will undoubtedly benefit from the successes and failures of our experimentation.

It is unlikely that a management by objectives program can harm an organization. In fact, research indicates that in most cases it will do some good without costing much. As McGregor (1957) points out, "Under proper conditions, participation and consultative management provide encouragement to people to direct their creative energies toward organization objectives, give them some voice in decisions which affect them, and provide significant opportunities for satisfaction of social and egoistic needs."

Designers of computer-based management information systems, for example, should provide their systems the flexibility needed to react effectively in non-programmed or crisis situations. Tightly controlled, highly efficient and centralized computer systems do not provide such flexibility: they react with limited alternatives or even fixed responses in crisis situations. As DeCarlo (1967) points out, however, new information technology makes it possible to develop flexible goals more suited to human needs where "purpose-centered units are coordinated through a network representative of the corporate entity."

For example, the profit center concept (use of profit objectives by a department or division that has control over its activities) can be extended through the addition of other quantitative measures of effectiveness as spelled out in this section.

In this way, organizations can encourage autonomy and pluralism rather than centralization (rule by few) and rigid control. In other words, managers must design personnel systems that maximize the opportunity for individual initiative, creativity, self-determination and self-control by coordinating systems objectives.

If the MBO approach is to be truly effective, executives at all levels must be able to communicate with one another. Those at the bottom must be willing to listen to the voice of experience, and those at the top willing to accept fresh ideas from lower-echelon employees. Similarly, executives must keep abreast of new programs, especially the modern ideas that recent university graduates possess.

Management by objectives provides a useful tool for developing personnel and providing feedback for evaluating how well they are doing in terms of what the organization expects of them. MBO does not, however, provide sufficient information about an individual's promotability to a higher level. Assessment centers, a relatively new tool, look promising because they may be used to evaluate how a person will probably perform if promoted to a more advanced position.

ASSESSMENT CENTERS: A MULTIPURPOSE PERSONNEL TOOL

Performance can more easily be evaluated when it can be described in terms of objective standards, physical output, or dollar amounts. As we have noted, it is much more difficult to measure abstract performances, such as mental activities, creative contributions, interpersonal and leadership skills, or planning activities.

As a result, the activities of relatively high-priced personnel are guessed at more than assessed. Important promotions are often based on performance in the present rather than on potential. The most important feature of the assessment center is job-related simulation. These simulations involve characteristics that managers feel are important to job success. The evaluators, who are familiar with the needs of particular jobs, observe and evaluate participants as they perform activities commonly found in these higher level jobs.

How Assessment Centers Started

The assessment center concept was initially applied to military situations by Simoneit in the German Army in the 1930s and the War Office Selection Board of the British Army in the 1940s. The purpose of assessment centers, then and now, is to test candidates in a social situation, using a number of assessors and a variety of procedures. Of course, the dimensions of behavior assessed and the type of procedures employed have been changed during the transition from wartime to peacetime application.

Station S of the U.S. Office of Strategic Services used a series of simulations in which each candidate had to develop and maintain a cover story that would hide his identity. Intriguing tests were designed to trick the candidate into revealing his true identity. Leaderless group discussions, as well as group exercises with assigned leaders, were also employed. The exercises were very physical and designed to simulate conditions behind enemy lines. Tests of stress and frustration tolerance were very important in the OSS Centers. A life history interview conducted by a psychiatrist was given heavy weight in the total score. The wartime assessors made a distinction between intelligence as measured by pencil-and-paper tests and intelligence applied to practical situations, a distinction that is recognized in most modern business assessment centers. In the wartime centers any assessment effort had to test the validity of its decisions, including agreement on criteria measures, before the first group of candidates was assessed (MacKinnon, 1975).

This technique has been refined during the past two decades. Modern business, spearheaded by American Telephone and Telegraph (AT&T), has since developed the assessment center approach into a highly refined method for performance evaluation, personnel selection, and human development.

Purpose of Assessment Centers

Since participants are observed in controlled situations, managers can compare the performance of candidates more fairly using assessment centers which are found in AT&T, IBM, Sears Roebuck, General Motors, Standard Oil, General Electric, Ford Motor Company, and the Department of Agriculture. Assessment centers can be used for the following:

1. To measure potential for first-level supervision, sales, and upper management positions. Because it is difficult to evaluate supervisory skills in most nonmanage-

ment jobs, the greatest use of assessment centers is the identification of potential for first-level supervision. However, because the assessment center looks so valid and reasonable, organizations are increasingly using the technique at higher levels of management for development purposes (Byham, 1971).

2. To determine individual training and development needs of employees. Assessment and training are often combined due to the "unfreezing process" that occurs during assessment. Most participants in the assessment center become highly aware of individual weaknesses and thus are more open to training and development.

3. To select recent college graduates for entry-level positions.

4. To provide more accurate human resource planning information.

5. To make an early determination of potential.

6. To assist in implementing affirmative action goals. The 1973 EEOC/AT&T Compliance Agreement established the company's assessment centers as an unbiased means of identifying management potential among previously overlooked employees.

As a result of the *Griggs et al.* v. *Duke Power* case (1971), which upheld EEOC guidelines, organizations must be able to prove that methods used for selection and appraisal are job related. If exercises result from an accurate and complete job analysis and measure criteria related to job success, assessment centers can be shown to be job related. The job relatedness of an assessment center can be measured by statistically relating on-the-job performance ratings with previously obtained assessment center scores.

What do Assessment Centers Measure?

Dimensions often measured in assessment centers include: organizing and planning, interpersonal competence (getting along with others), quality of thinking, resistance to stress, orientation (motivation) to work, dependency on others, oral communication, and creativity. It is hard to imagine how these qualities can be accurately assessed, but several studies clearly conclude that inter-rater reliabilities in assessment evaluations are sufficiently high to justify continued use (MacKinnon, 1975).

Research (Wilson, 1973) indicates that the main factor influencing the total rating obtained in an assessment center is the candidate's ability to influence others. Two factors, the ability to apply interpersonal skills and the ability to be sensitive to the human aspects of situations, are especially important. The ability to organize, plan, and make decisions, as demonstrated by in-basket simulations and by scores obtained on paper-and-pencil psychological tests, also are important to the overall assessment score.

Chevrolet sales divisions select candidates for assessment centers by using nine dimensions for measuring management potential. These are: responsiveness to job demands, interpersonal communications, relations with supervisor, practical judgment, market strategy, work problems, use of time, job knowledge, and developing subordinates. Candidates with the highest overall ratings are then assigned to assessment centers, where their potential for higher-level positions is tested (McIntyre, 1975).

Types of Exercises Commonly Used in Assessment Centers

There is no recognized best set of exercises used in assessment centers. As a minimum, however, most programs contain the following procedures. A leaderless group is established; each member supports a predefined position, but the group must arrive at consensus. This procedure is used to measure interpersonal skills. Another common exercise uses a task force with an appointed leader. The group must decide on a course of action. Simulation games and in-basket exercises are used to test organizational and planning abilities. The in-basket exercise nearly always includes a simulation of the problems an executive faces during the course of a day or week. Often, the candidate must make an oral job report. This report tests the candidate's communication skills and insight into his present position. Personal interviews and projective tests are used to assess work motivation, career orientation, and dependency on others. Paper-and-pencil tests measure intellectual ability. Procedures which contribute most significantly to overall predictions appear to be group and in-basket exercises (Bray, 1974).

Duration of Assessment Center Programs

The number of exercises and time required for completion of the assessment vary with the purpose and level involved. Centers designed for selection of first-line supervisors, sales personnel, and management trainees generally last a day or less. Centers used for higher-level managers may run for two or three days or longer if used for developmental as opposed to selection purposes.

Moses (1973) demonstrated that a one-day center can yield reliable information for selection and placement of recent college graduates. The program consists of a group exercise and an in-basket based on a university scenario. An interview, biographical data form, and manual test complete the day's work.

Problems with Assessment Centers

Research studies suggest the need for caution in using an assessment center for performance evaluation and selection purposes. Wilson (1973) demonstrates that strong correlations exist among scores obtained on a verbal intelligence test, the California Psychological Inventory (CPI), and assessment center ratings of 297 female job candidates. Specifically, CPI scales related to interpersonal behavior (dominance, capacity for status, social presence, and self-acceptance) clearly predicted high assessment center evaluations and recommendations for management positions.

Bray (1974) concludes that assessment center staffs are strongly influenced by subjective elements, such as the personality of the candidate. Judges tended to evaluate the quality of the individual's social skills rather than the quality of the decisions themselves. Based on these and other studies, assessment center ratings seem to be strongly influenced by the participants' interpersonal skills.

A second predictor is the demonstration of organizing and decision-making ability measured by in-basket exercises. Other predictors are verbal ability and personality traits. Thus, the relatively inexpensive paper-and-pencil tests for measuring potential may be as accurate as the high cost–high stress assessment center.

Another important study conducted at IBM (Hinrichs, 1969) demonstrated that assessment centers may be quite valuable for early identification of potential for those with little or no job history. However, Hinrichs concluded that careful analysis of job history and accomplishments may be a more valid predictor of

EXHIBIT 12–4 An Assessment Center Model

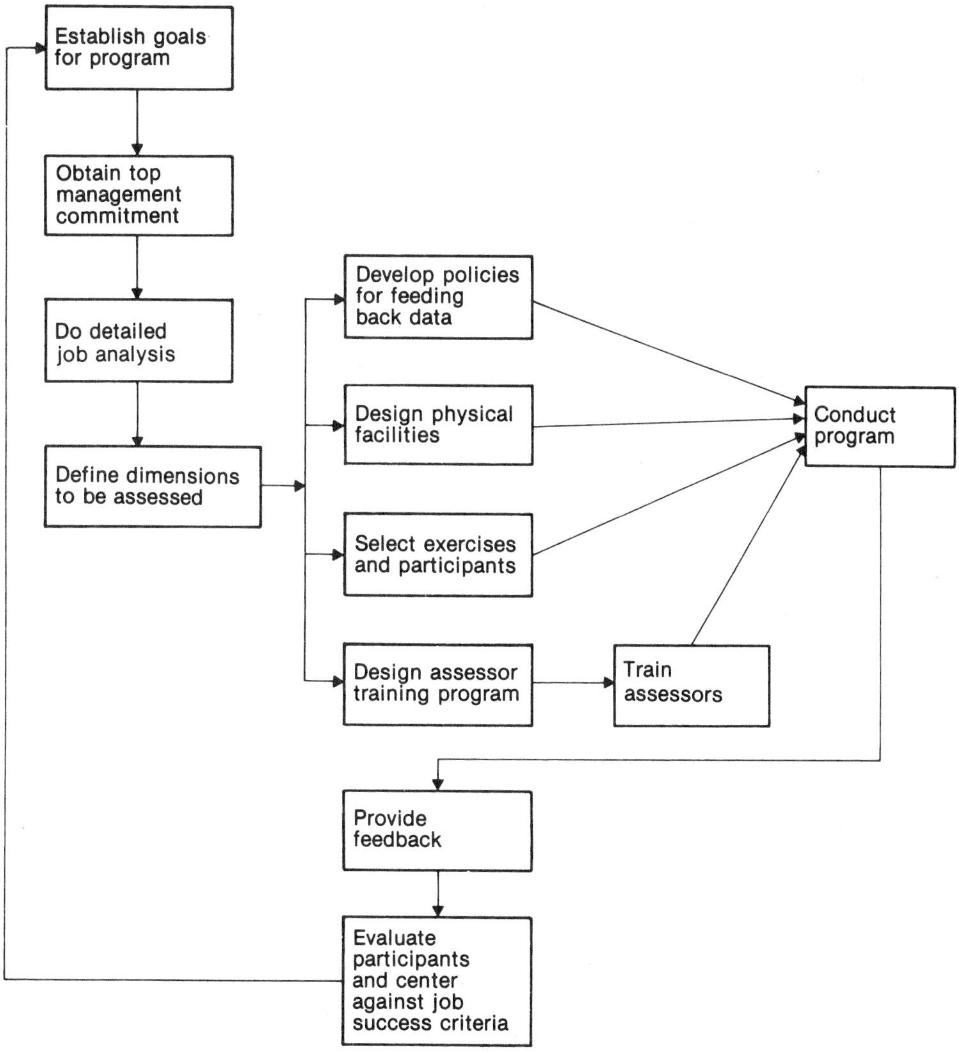

future performance at middle and upper levels than the situational tests used in assessment centers.

As with all techniques dealing in the area of human performance measurement, the assessment center approach involves real hazards. One of the most obvious is the exam-taking syndrome. Solid performers in day-to-day operations suddenly choke in the simulated environment. Another drawback is the potential bad effects on those *not* selected to participate in the exercise. The cost of assessing every person in a particular job level or category could be prohibitive. Yet, to ignore a part of the work force represents a strong silent message. Rejection could virtually destroy an employee's motivation.

Many assessment centers have one particular weakness: immediate supervisors nominate participants. Employees who are curious, independent, aggressive, and intelligent may never be selected because such traits, while important at higher levels, are not always accepted by lower-level supervisors. Some companies have attempted to avoid this problem by self-nomination or by putting everyone at a given level through the center regardless of cost.

Employees who receive a poor report from the center may react in negative ways. (This, of course, is true with all performance appraisal techniques.) Ideally, a rejected employee would return to his former job, satisfied—maybe relieved—that he would not be promoted to a job he could not handle. However, a perfectly good performer at one level may leave the organization in order to remove the bad assessment report from his work record. Thus a poor report can demoralize an employee who was once an asset.

Exhibit 12–4 illustrates the important steps in developing and using an assessment center. Heavy emphasis must be placed on a clear statement of goals, the obtaining of top management commitment, job analysis, assessor training and program audit and evaluation.

SUMMARY AND CONCLUSION

Performance appraisal and feedback are basic ingredients of the manager-subordinate relationship. Employees want to be told where they stand. But, naturally, they expect to hear all good things about themselves. Consequently, anxiety and dread unfortunately accompany the feedback process. Conscientious managers try to be straightforward about positive as well as negative aspects of an individual's performance. The manager's anxiety increases since it is well known that employees react defensively to negative feedback. The dilemma is how to communicate constructive suggestions without harming motivation.

This chapter contains the important reasons why evaluation must be conducted and the descriptions of the most common approaches to measuring performance. Few managers really document performance as it occurs, so there are significant distortions in measurement, including the recency and halo effects, unclear criteria, peak performance bias, changing job conditions, differences in values among raters, and the desire to be a nice person.

To compound the problem, employees often hear criticisms about problems they have wrestled with most of their lives. Thus, they may not appreciate being made aware of these defects again by their superiors. Conant (1973) suggests that feeding back negative data poorly or inconsistently can have serious psychological effects. Overreaction, increased anxiety, erosion of self-confidence, insecurity, regression to earlier childhood behavior, breakdown in superior/subordinate relations, and weakening of self-esteem can occur as a result of negative feedback.

Does this mean that we advocate the abandonment of performance appraisals? Not at all. What is needed, however, is a less biased and threatening approach. In this book we suggest management by objectives as a viable alternative to the more traditional graphic rating scale techniques for assessing performance. Individuals involved in setting their personal goals are aware of measurement criteria in advance rather than after the fact, when many types of biases can intervene. MBO is an instrument management can apply to provide equitable, reasonable, flexible, and concrete standards to the appraisal process. The approach can enhance the respect employees have for their managers, increase identification with the organization, and help motivate many employees.

In the final part of the chapter we evaluated assessment centers. Simulating the work environment and then testing a person's performance in the mock environment has been proven to be a realistic approach to evaluation. It has avoided some of the mistakes in promotion and increased the chances of selecting good personnel. As with the MBO technique and philosophy, it must be said that no method is any better than the people who design and implement it.

In the following section, we will discuss two important aspects of modern organizations which play a significant role in determining how effectively employees can and will perform in their jobs. The first is collective bargaining and its impact on both blue-collar and white-collar performance. The second deals with overall working conditions, with special emphasis on the health and safety of employees.

DISCUSSION QUESTIONS

1. How might managers be convinced that they are doing themselves, their subordinates, and their organization a favor by being as honest and objective as possible during performance appraisals (both written and oral)?

2. *Average* performance for a Royal Air Force officer is defined as "effective and competent in performance of assigned duties." What is the likely impact upon personal motivation when an "effective and competent" performer is rated average? What does it mean to be "average" within an elite group? Should the word "average" be used in any evaluation system?

3. What is likely to happen when a superior with a low performance rating is asked to rate subordinates with relatively high qualifications?

4. Should appraisal systems differentiate between present performance and potential? Why?

5. Should raters be held accountable for the ratings they assign? Why? Can this be achieved with a good personnel management information system? How?

6. Within the Department of the Army it was discovered that junior officers complained much more about performance appraisals than did senior officers. Why do you suppose this was the case?

7. In the early 1970s, a large computer manufacturer adopted a performance review system using several rating documents: 1) performance planning and evaluation, 2) promotability, and 3) employee development plan. The first form requires a job analysis when an employee is hired, after six months on the job, and each year thereafter. It requires justification for any salary increase. It uses an MBO approach with weights for each job responsibility, while providing for changes in these weights during the year. An overall rating is made at the end of the year. Satisfactory performance is divided into four categories: 1) far exceeds job requirements, 2) consistently exceeds job requirements, 3) exceeds job requirements, 4) meets job requirements. Unsatisfactory performance is graded as marginal or inadequate. An employee in the last category is "on notice" for termination. The form provides for a counseling summary, rater's and employee's signature, employee's comments.

The promotability form is simple in format, and it is optional. It merely states: promote now, reassign now, not ready for promotion yet. Space is provided for comments and signature. The employee development plan attempts to project two- to five-year training needs, outside assignments, and action plans.

Managers seemed relatively satisfied with the system, although only 10 percent used the optional promotability and development plans. The same forms were used at all levels, no inflation in scores was evident (although central tendency did occur), and managers had authority to increase salary between 4 and 12 percent within each level. Each rater was given a four-hour training session on the purposes of the system.

Comment on the viability of this approach based on the material covered in this chapter.

8. Pinpoint several areas in which performance evaluation data can be effectively used to improve the overall human resource system. (Hint: If engineers with computer training and business backgrounds tend to perform more effectively in managerial capacities than do those engineers without such backgrounds, what might one conclude about the selection of engineering managers and how might a computer data bank assist in this selection?)

9. Do you feel there is inherent conflict between the MBO and assessment center approaches to personnel evaluation and development? Explain.

10. Identify positive features of assessment center methods for performance evaluation. What are the major limitations of this approach?

11. York Graphic Services of York, Pennsylvania, uses managers' wives as assessors in addition to traditional methods. Discuss the implications of this strategy, which was initiated to provide "broader based evaluations."

12. Define the special skills you feel an assessor ought to possess before being permitted to evaluate a center participant (listening, observing, counseling, etc.).

13. It has been suggested that assessees be given carbon copies of all reports written by assessors before the assessors prepare a final report. The assessee would be asked

to reflect on his overall performance, explain inconsistent behaviors, add new insights, and finally write a preliminary conclusion to his own final assessment report. Discuss the potential merits and drawbacks to such a procedure.

14. Peer ratings among Army ROTC officer candidates would not be as valid as those among career officers at the captain level attending further schooling as a requirement for promotion to field grades such as major. Comment.

15. Using the critical incident technique, Wolfe (1975) collected 1,453 examples of effective and ineffective performance by 211 students playing a management simulation game. Students were organized into teams of four to five players. The most effective teams used greater foresight and adopted a stance of positive adaptation and experimentation and were offensive rather than defensive. Effective players were characterized by enthusiasm for the game, openness, and trust. Discuss the implications of these findings as they might relate to assessing human performance in real, as opposed to simulated, situations. Do the results of this study add any validity to what was claimed about the assessment center approach in this chapter? Why? Why not?

16. Top-level organizational leaders must trust subordinates to carry out objectives while they concern themselves with setting and modifying organizational goals in their competitive environments. Comment.

17. When chief executive officers of major business firms were asked about how top-management performance appraisal is conducted, they overwhelmingly stated that the performance criterion overshadowing all others is the ability to develop plans for making operations profitable and to achieve the planned profits (Reeser, 1975). Discuss this finding.

18. Which are the major methods for assessing human performance in organizations? Identify the advantages and limitations of each.

19. Develop a graphic model for the activities involved in designing and implementing a management by objectives program.

20. The City of Fort Collins, Colorado, and Colorado State University Police evaluated 108 potential patrolmen using assessment center techniques between 1971 and 1973 (Hamilton, 1974). The center was composed of seven exercises, in addition to a paper-and-pencil test, physical examination, and polygraph test. Three situational exercises evaluated applicant behaviors in simulated police situations. Applicants were given a concise set of facts, placed in a room with a confederate "citizen," observed through one-way windows, and then evaluated on the basis of interactions. In addition, an individual interview was held with a psychologist; two leaderless group discussions were held on controversial police topics (rated by three assessors); and a structured panel interview was conducted with the panel comprised of a police officer, psychologist, and community representative. Discuss the values and limitations of this approach to the assessment of future performance of law enforcement officers.

21. The production manager of a large division of a major United States corporation wrote the following memorandum to all employees. Discuss the impact such a memorandum would have on you if you were on the receiving end of the communication. How might you have gotten this message across?

When I first met with you several months ago, I promised to keep you informed on the state of our business and to discuss our problems and their effect on you and your jobs frankly. We are now faced with a problem that threatens your job security, and it's a problem that will require your help to solve.

To put it bluntly, I'm talking about the theft of tools and the willful damage to the very products on which our jobs depend. Quite honestly, this is one of the most baffling situations I've ever encountered in my twenty years in manufacturing.

Power drills, grinders, air hoses, tool boxes, and separate tools too numerous to mention are being stolen from our building in numbers that far exceed any incidence of what could be termed "occasional theft." Equally as serious is the problem of careless workmanship and malicious damage to automobiles in the process of production.

Shortages of materials and high costs are, as you know, making it extremely difficult for us to meet customer delivery demands and to quote competitive prices. In addition, stolen tools, poor quality workmanship and YES, even *sabotage* by our own people continue to plague us. In fact, one recent incident occurred where someone jumper-wired a control system which kept the product energized although the power controls were shut off. Someone could have been killed!

These are some of the problems. The question is what to do about them. There is no question we've got to put an end to the thefts, deliberate damage, and the concealing of poor workmanship. They're hitting hard at our ability to produce our product and if we can't produce, it's obvious we can build nothing in the way of job security. It's no exaggeration to say "OUR JOBS DEPEND ON IT." It's more than Management's problem; we can't do it alone. We both know that the vast majority of employees are not involved, and we need the help of this majority to end these problems once and for all.

If you are aware of any individuals who are involved in theft or the deliberate damage of tools, materials or automobiles in process, I ask you to report the incidents through a call or an unsigned note to me or to any member of Management listing all the information you can provide. We will promptly and confidentially follow-up on all information we receive and discipline as well as prosecute if appropriate.

22. Ronald Blakeman, supervisor of twelve people who perform teller functions in the branch office of a large bank, is in the process of completing rating forms on his subordinates as required by the main office. Upon completion of the forms it is his intention to interview each employee concerning his or her performance during the six-month period covered by the ratings.

One of Blakeman's subordinates, Mary Stevens, was completing a year's service with the bank. She has shown considerable interest in her job, is very proficient, and accomplishes her tasks in a very efficient manner. However, in her relations with fellow workers and with customers, she is quite lacking in tact and tends to upset others' feelings. There have been a few complaints but nothing serious enough to warrant action at the time the complaints were received. Two of the items on the rating form, "relationships with others" and "promotability," remind Blakeman of the complaints he has received about Miss Stevens.

    a. If you were Blakeman, how would you discuss the problem with Miss Stevens?
    b. Prepare to role play the performance interview between Blakeman and Stevens.

BIBLIOGRAPHY

Barrett, R. S. *Performance Rating*. Chicago: Science Research Associates, 1966.

Bray, D. W., R. J. Campbell, and D. L. Grant. *Formative Years in Business: A Long-Term AT&T Study of Managerial Lives*. New York: Wiley, 1974.

Brumback, G. B. "Acceptability of an Employee Rating Form and Its Validity." *Personnel Administration* (November–December 1972):28–30.

Buffa, E. *Modern Production Management*. New York: Wiley, 1974.

Byham, W. C. "The Assessment Center as an Aid in Management Development." *Training and Development Journal* (December 1971).

Carroll, Stephen J., and H. L. Tosi. "Superior/Subordinate Relationships and the Success of a Management by Objectives Program." Paper presented at the Midwest Meeting of the Academy of Management, April 1969.

Conant, James C. "The Performance Appraisal." *Business Horizons* (June 1973):73–78.

Cozan, L. W. "Forced Choice: Better Than Other Rating Methods?" *Personnel* (May–June 1959):80–83.

Cummings, L. L. "A Field Experimental Study of the Effects of Two Performance Appraisal Systems." *Personnel Psychology* 26 (1973):489–502.

DeCarlo, R. *The Impact of Computers on Management*. Cambridge, Mass.: MIT Press, 1967.

French, W. *The Personnel Management Process*. Boston: Houghton Mifflin, 1970.

Glasner, D. M. "Patterns of Management by Results." *Business Horizons* (February 1969):37–38.

Hamilton, J. W., and J. F. Gavin. "Small Community Police Assessment." *Assessment and Development* 2.1 (April 1974):3.

Hamner, W. C., and F. L. Schmidt, eds. *Contemporary Problems in Personnel*. Chicago: St. Clair Press, 1974.

Hinrichs, J. R. "Comparison of Real Life Assessments of Management Potential with Situational Exercises, Paper-and-Pencil Ability Tests, and Personality Inventories." *Journal of Applied Psychology* 53 (1969):425–33.

Kraut, A. I. "A Hard Look at Management Assessment Centers and Their Future." *Personnel Journal* 51.5 (May 1972):317–26.

_____. "Prediction of Managerial Success by Peer and Training Staff Ratings." *Journal of Applied Psychology* 60.1 (1975):14–19.

Lawler, E. E. "The Multi-Trait-Multirater Approach to Measuring Managerial Job Performance." *Journal of Applied Psychology* 51 (1967):369–81.

Lopez, F. J. *Evaluating Employee Performance*. Chicago: Public Personnel Association, 1968.

MacKinnon, D. W. "An Overview of Assessment Centers." *Technical Report No. 1*, Center for Creative Leadership, Greensboro, N.C. (May 1975).

McGregor, D. "The Human Side of Enterprise." *The Management Review* (November 1957):91–92.

_____. "An Uneasy Look at Performance Appraisal." *Harvard Business Review* (May–June 1975):87–94.

McIntyre, F. M. "Unique Program Developed by Chevrolet Sales." *Assessment and Development* 2.2 (January 1975).

Meyer, H., E. Kay, and J. French. "Split Roles in Performance Appraisal." *Harvard Business Review* 43 (1965):291–98.

Miner, J. B. "Management Appraisal: A Review of Procedures and Practices." *Business Horizons* (October 1968).

Moses, J. L. "Development of an Assessment Center for Early Identification of Supervisory Potential." *Personnel Psychology* 26 (1973):569–80.

Oberg, W. "Make Performance Appraisal Count." *Harvard Business Review* (January–February 1972):61–67.

Odiorne, G. A. "The Politics of Implementing MBO." *Business Horizons* (June 1974): 15–21.

Patton, A. "Does Performance Appraisal Work?" *Business Horizons* (February 1973): 83–91.

Reeser, C. "Executive Performance Appraisal: The View from the Top." *Personnel Journal* (January 1975).

Singular, J. "Has MBO Failed?" *MBA* (October 1975):47–50.

Slusher, E. A. "A Systems Look at Performance Appraisal." *Personnel Journal* (February 1975).

Stockford, L., and H. Bissell. "Factors Involved in Establishing a Merit-Rating Scale." *Personnel* 26 (1949):94–116.

Strong, E. P., and R. D. Smith. *Management Control Models.* New York: Holt, Rinehart and Winston, 1968.

Vroom, V. H. "Some Personality Determinates of the Effects of Participation." *The Journal of Abnormal and Social Psychology* 59.3 (November 1959):326–27.

Weiner, J. B. "Texas Instruments: All Systems Go." *Dun's Review* (January 1967).

Werther, W. B., and H. Weihrich. "Refining MBO Through Negotiations." *MSU Business Topics* (Summer 1975):53–59.

Wilson, J. E., and W. A. Tatge. "Assessment Centers: Further Assessment Needed." *Personnel Journal* (March 1973):172–79.

Wolfe, J. "Effective Performance Behavior in a Simulated Policy Decision Making Environment." *Management Science* 21 (April 1975):872–82.

Section
Five

COLLECTIVE BARGAINING AND EMPLOYEE WELFARE

*

Chapter 13

UNIONS AND THEIR IMPACT ON PERSONNEL MANAGEMENT

LEARNING OBJECTIVES

This chapter should enable the reader to:

Specify the positive and negative impact of unionism on American free enterprise

Explain why workers join or refrain from joining unions

Identify major legislation affecting the American union movement

Explain the steps used in the bargaining and contract negotiation processes

Discuss recent trends in unionism, especially those leading toward public sector, white collar, and international unionism

Clarify priorities being assigned by courts regarding collective bargaining and equal opportunity issues

Understand the relationships between mediation, conciliation, grievances, and arbitration

Evaluate a company's industrial relations organization.

KEY TERMS AND CONCEPTS

collective bargaining	union shop
negotiations	closed shop
arbitration	agency shop
mediation	past practice
Wagner Act	discipline
Taft-Hartley Act	due process
ILO	grievance
wildcat strike	work stoppage
slowdown	National Labor Relations Board
industrial relations policy	just cause

PREVIEW

Since the turn of the century, unions have become an increasingly powerful force in the work place. This chapter discusses:

1. The evolution of collective bargaining.
2. The pressures for changes in union procedures, organization, and tactics.
3. The legal aspects of unionism.
4. The collective bargaining process.
5. International unionism.
6. New approaches to labor relations.

Very often personnel managers become so involved with labor relations activities that they have little time left to plan, organize, and control recruiting, selection, training, evaluation, and compensation activities. Smaller organizations, which cannot afford to have separate labor relations and personnel managers, often are in this position. The major purposes of this chapter are to acquaint the reader with the pressures associated with collective bargaining, the changing nature of unionism both domestically and internationally, necessary approaches to discipline under a union contract, and how computers can be used to aid the negotiation process.

EVOLUTION OF COLLECTIVE BARGAINING

Historical Perspective

The first attempts at collective bargaining were made in the early nineteenth century. Fledgling unions attempted to organize workers into cohesive groups that could force management to improve working conditions. By the end of the century, the American Federation of Labor had become strong in several skilled trades. Total union membership reached approximately one million. Unskilled workers, however, were not organized successfully until the 1930s. The economic despair of the Great Depression increased cohesion among workers, increased public acceptance of unions, and caused a relaxation of government regulation. These factors, combined with sometimes arbitrary management practices, led to a strong, rapid, and often violent growth in unionism. As the American dream of owning one's own business or constantly moving upward to better jobs temporarily weakened, workers attempted to protect and improve their present situation. They wanted job security and guaranteed income. Unions promised to meet these basic needs and were able to attract large numbers of employees from the mass production industries.

Unions grew more slowly after World War II. Most of the easily organized workers (in such industries as mining, transportation, utilities, and manufacturing) were already in unions, and the number of low-skilled workers in these industries began to decline while the number of professional and other white-collar workers began to rise dramatically. Management also learned more about participative leadership: it discovered two-way communication, worker needs, and social responsibilities. This new strategy weakened the influence of unions.

Since the mid-1960s, union membership has begun to grow again, but the character of the membership has changed dramatically. Faced with declining membership, organizers turned to offices, mail order houses, and especially federal and state government agencies. Farm workers also began to organize. When coverage of the National Labor Relations Act was extended to hospitals in the 1970s, this also became another area of union activity.

Organized labor has won significant victories for the working class. Job security, improved work conditions, improved pensions, and insurance and health benefits are the more important victories. Formal work rules, disciplinary procedures, and grievance channels are less glamorous but equally important contributions of the labor movement. Finally, the American working class has been provided a voice in national and state governments through the work of union officials and lobbyists.

These victories do not come without bitter struggles and violence. At times management and labor are in direct conflict, which ultimately involves much of American society. Over the years, unskilled or unwary managers have often yielded major concessions to skilled union negotiators without compensating increases in productivity. Inflation and loss of competitive position can be partially attributed to these concessions.

Bases for Union Success

Successful organization of workers requires, among other things, irritating conditions leading to widespread dissatisfaction. These conditions were flagrant in the 1930s. Lack of job security, low wages, unhealthy and unsafe working conditions, mistreatment of child labor, and ineffective managers were extensive. Workers felt powerless to change these intolerable conditions. Thus they saw unions as the only way to right the wrongs—to get improved conditions and a voice in some of the affairs directly affecting their lives. Similar needs, and some new ones, may well lead many white-collar workers, engineers, and even supervisors to unionize in the 1980s, unless an enlightened management implements effective human resource systems.

The union's most important weapon is the power of the strike. It was used extensively in the early days of unionism, but in the future, strikes may become less frequent. One large and militant union even accepted a no-strike clause when its contract came up for renegotiation in the mid-seventies. Other unions are attempting to abolish strikes. Why?

In the words of George Meany, a giant among labor giants, "Labor is becoming middle class. We started out to become something other than 'lower class'; now we are paying the penalty of success. When you strike, you have a lot more to lose." Labor is now much more "middle class," at least in terms of income. Unions are full participants in many managerial processes. Thus a strike is a symbol of the failure of both union and management to fulfill workers' needs. Union members may see a call for a strike as a failure of their own leaders, especially since the average wage of union members is relatively high ($11,500 in 1975).

Pressures for Change: Changes in Internal Practices

As with almost every other institution in our society, unions have been rocked by change in recent years. They face many of the same challenges that management must contend with.

Nevertheless, unions are an important part of the system. In 1973, approximately 23 million Americans belonged to a union or similar association, such as the National Education Association. This figure represents one out of every four nonfarm workers in the United States. Managers must learn to coexist and bargain effectively with labor. Otherwise, they will have to contend with work slowdowns, stoppages, trivial grievances, strikes, and the like. They will lose an important contact—even at times an ally—with their own workers.

Unions are coming under increasing attack. They have been found guilty of practicing race and sex discrimination. Members are voting out their leaders more often. Young people are not joining as often as in the past. Union leadership is being pressured by the government to improve productivity and to curb wage/benefit demands that have hurt the economy. All in all, the American labor force is the best paid in the world, but its benefactor, the once powerful union, is struggling to increase membership.

Union leaders are treated well by their members and often will fight to stay in office. The 1974 retirement of the president of the National Maritime Union provides an example of why union leaders stay in office: when he left office he received a pension of $4,400 per month and a lump sum of $250,000 in severance pay.

Education of Union Leaders

The typical union official of today is a far cry from the prototype of the militant blue-collar agitator of the past. Union leaders often are well trained and educated, and unions help officials learn how to organize and bargain effectively. For example, the AFL-CIO opened its new Labor Studies Center in Silver Springs, Maryland, in 1974. The union negotiators are taught sophisticated negotiating principles. For instance, they are taught to avoid taking a hopeless case to the bargaining table. They are given information from current labor studies and taught related subjects, such as claims, grievances, mediation, group dynamics, economics, civil and women's rights, pensions, insurance, leadership skills, and union administration.

Subjects are taught by a variety of sophisticated methods such as simulation models of arbitration cases. Students participate in role playing on closed circuit television. Would-be negotiators get an idea of what to expect and how to handle difficult issues. The center also offers an opportunity to earn a college degree in labor studies through a mid-western college.

Unions and Productivity

One of the oldest criticisms of unions is that they decrease productivity. The matter remains controversial though some claims have been documented.

An interesting, though perhaps extreme, example is the case of the U.S. Borax Company. A thousand workers went on strike. Before the walkout the unionized employees were producing 3,100 tons of borax per day. After the strike was called, 325 untrained managers took over the operation. Much to the embarrassment of the union, the managers averaged 3,600 tons of borax per day. The productivity of the managers was two to three times greater than that of the striking workers. Needless to say, the company drove a hard bargain before settlement. When the dust cleared, 450 union members were no longer employed at Borax (Alexander, 1974).

John E. Healy, national president of the Associated General Contractors of America, an organization of owners, contends that the work ethic has been lost and must be regained if this country is to compete effectively in world markets. He claims that, in spite of forty-one years of technological advancement, three revisions of labor legislation have seriously hurt productivity. For example, Healy estimated that it would take three and a half years to reconstruct the Empire State Building if work began in 1972, although it required only fourteen months to complete it in 1930–31. The construction industry is an important case because wages in that industry have surpassed gains made in any other field (Modic, 1972). However, there have been serious declines in construction-related fields, and they are a major national problem because the construction industry is large and has an important effect on inflation.

Charles Smith, chairman of Sifco Industries of Cleveland, explained why his firm no longer makes truck axles in its Cleveland plant. When he learned that his major customer was planning to buy axles in Japan, he managed to block the move and get the business for Sifco's plant in Brazil. Sifco buys steel in Japan, ships it 12,000 miles to Brazil, hauls it 100 miles inland to the plant, packs the axles for export, ships them 6,000 miles to the United States, pays a 10 percent duty and a 10 percent surcharge on imports, pays inland freight, and delivers them to the customer cheaper than if they were made in Cleveland, only five miles from a U.S. steel producer (Campbell, 1974).

The preceding cases illustrate our concern for productivity and the United States economy. For its part, management too must be included and we feel that concern must be given to both sides. Poor engineering practices, inept planning of facilities, ineffective training programs, poor organization, clogged communications, and red tape hurt productivity as much as outrageous union demands.

Both labor and management should be warned. Reasonable demands, open communications, and trust are vital to the survival of the American industrial system. Carpenters who will not touch prehung doors, painters who will not use a brush wider than four inches, plumbers who rethread pipe already threaded at the factory, meat cutters who won't permit centralized wrapping, managers who won't manage—all must recognize that short-run wage gains that are not supported by increased productivity will only cause more serious problems in the long run.

LEGAL ASPECTS OF UNIONISM

Labor Law

U.S. labor law is based on the National Labor Relations Act (Wagner Act as amended), which was passed in 1936. This act defined the conditions under which employees may bargain collectively. For our purpose, *collective bargaining* is defined as that situation in which authorized representatives of the employees and employer bargain together to establish wages, working hours, or working conditions.

The Wagner Act covers most industries except railroads and airlines, which are subject to the Railway Labor Act. Both acts are designed to promote order in labor-management relations. They define the rights and responsibilities of employees and employers, prescribe methods of settling various types of labor disputes, and establish agencies for reaching a decision when labor and management become deadlocked. These acts devote a great deal of attention to unfair labor practices by management. Later in this chapter some of these practices are defined specifically.

Other significant labor legislation includes:

1. The Landrum-Griffin Act of 1959, which deals with reporting and disclosure of union activities.

2. The Norris-LaGuardia Act of 1932, which establishes when court injunctions may be used in labor disputes. It also makes yellow dog contracts (pledges by individual workers not to unionize or join a union) illegal.

3. The Walsh-Healey Act, which sets wage, hour, and working conditions for government contractors.

4. The Davis-Bacon Act, which regulates wages for personnel involved in the construction or repair of public buildings.

The Taft-Hartley Act (Labor Management Relations Act) of 1947 substantially amended the Wagner Act. The Taft-Hartley Act prevents unions from forcing an employer to discharge workers for not joining a union, forbids unions from forcing workers to join, outlaws secondary boycotts, subjects union officials to the same surveillance as management regarding its organization and member practices, and prevents unions from forcing management to pay for work not actually performed. While the Wagner Act defines unfair management practices, Taft-Hartley defines unfair union practices. Also, it requires a sixty-day notice of contract termination and permits employees to bargain directly with management as long as neither side violates the existing labor agreement.

The Taft-Hartley Act also established the National Labor Relations Board. The National Labor Relations Board (NLRB) is the chief agency responsible for administration of federal labor law. The purpose of the NLRB is to balance the bargaining power of labor and management. It is headed by five members appointed by the president of the United States for five-year terms. The board has several thousand employees, who handle over thirty thousand cases in each year, scattered throughout the country. The board investigates alleged violations of management or union rights. It has the right to condemn and prosecute such violations as unfair labor practices (Byrd, 1963).

At first glance, U.S. labor law may look like an uncharted wilderness. Labor law is enacted at three levels of government: the federal, state, and municipal levels. Arbitration boards interpret labor law in opinions that are equivalent to laws. These boards, in effect, function as legislatures. Volumes of arbitration opinions take the place of a uniform code.

The general framework of labor law is established at the national level. State and municipal law develops within this framework. State and local conditions that are not covered at the national level are interpreted in the light of principles set down in federal law. For instance, federal legislation covers such broad items as occupation, health and safety, child labor, pension reform, and workmen's compensation. In this section we are concerned with a brief review of those laws related to labor-management relations (see also Chapter 1).

Unfair Labor Practice

Unfair labor practice refers exclusively to actions of management regarding unions or union formation. Unfair labor practices are subject to "cease and desist orders" and occur under the following circumstances:

1. Employers attempt to dominate and control unions by such activities as financial support, provision of meeting places, circulating petitions for a company union, assisting in drafting bylaws, or extension of credit to unions.

2. Employers interfere with the rights of employees to form, join, or assist labor unions. Threats of reprisal, keeping employees from voting in union elections, or questioning employees about their union intentions can all be considered unfair labor practices. Employers, on the other hand, may remind workers of benefits they get without a union and state arguments in opposition to unionism so long as the arguments pose no threat or promise of benefit for not joining a union. It is also legal to prohibit union activity during working hours.

3. Except in cases of incompetency or violation of work rules, employers may not demote or discharge workers because of union involvement. All discrimination against union organizers or union members because of their union affiliation is considered an unfair labor practice.

4. Labor law prohibits employers from refusing to bargain with representatives of employees. Agreements need not be signed, but it must be shown that good faith discussions actually took place.

Unions also are restricted. Unions are considered to be in violation of the law (especially since Taft-Hartley) when they engage in such activities as the following:

1. Coerce or otherwise interfere with employers in their selection of bargaining or grievance-handling experts.

2. Coerce employees (or their families) regarding union membership.

3. Attempt to force employers to discriminate against employees who engage in activity supporting a rival union or no union.

4. Refuse to bargain in good faith.

5. Engage in secondary strikes and boycotts.

THE BARGAINING PROCESS

Negotiating the Labor Agreement

The purpose of an effective labor-management program is the negotiation and administration of a collective agreement or contract. The contract defines relationships between management and labor and the conditions under which employees are to work; it normally includes wage rates, due process, benefits, seniority rights, and layoff procedures.

The term *negotiation* is simple to define but difficult to apply. Whenever people exchange ideas with the intention of changing relationships, they are negotiating (Nierenberg, 1973). Labor negotiation is the discussion of any work-related issues. Because practically any issue can be brought into the negotiating process, negotiations can be extremely complicated. They require extensive communication.

Management pays its employees for their work, but each side has different ideas about the conditions of the exchange. This is the starting point for negotiation since each side has a policy about how its needs are to be met. The two sides then communicate to determine how each set of needs can be met within the limits of the other side's policy. Both parties generally enter the negotiation with a plan that includes a willingness to give. For example, labor may enter with a demand for a 15 percent increase in wages and management originally may offer 7 percent. A final agreement may call for a 6 percent increase the first year and 4 percent the second.

If negotiation is formal, it generally leads to a collective bargaining agreement. (Informal negotiation occurs when an existing contract is in effect; it is part of contract administration.) If the two sides cannot reach an agreement during a formal bargaining session, special mediating services can be called in to settle differences.

The Effect of the Negotiator

An effective negotiator needs many skills (Karrass, 1970). Research indicates the most important skills a negotiator can have are: planning, the ability to think clearly under stress, practical intelligence, verbal fluency, production and product knowledge, integrity, the ability to perceive and exploit power, tolerance for ambiguity, understanding of human behavior, and a good deal of self-confidence. Obviously a good negotiator is a special kind of person, not easily found and, once found, prized!

Labor negotiations are strategic; they require a plan of attack as well as positions to be adopted in response to the other side's counterproposals. A negotiator must be able to sense the pattern of the sessions quickly and view them within the broader context of union and management. No single move of a single participant should be viewed in isolation. Like a chess player, the effective negotiator must look at the total board at once, judging the opponent on the basis of all the pieces and in view of either the strength or weakness of the current position.

Negotiating skills can be learned. Role playing, cases, and videotapes are effective training tools. The Central Electricity Generating Board of England hires retired union officials to train its young managers in the art and science of negotiation (Pocock, 1970). When asked why they would assist in such training, the union officials replied that their organizations "prefer to deal with management teams that understand how to negotiate."

Management's first step in the negotiation process is to select a bargaining team that has status and authority to make a binding commitment. Hopefully the chief negotiator, at minimum, will have the qualities mentioned earlier. Should a lawyer be used as the negotiator? Gitlow (1971) suggests that the disadvantages of using a lawyer include 1) a lack of knowledge of the operation and the workers, 2) an inclination to give too much weight to technical matters, 3) use of obscure legal language, and 4) an approach similar to that used in court, aiming at total victory. Possible advantages include: skill in drawing contracts, skill in arguing, and knowledge of labor law.

Preparing for Negotiation

Negotiators don't begin preparing their strategy a few weeks or even months before the end of a contract. Preparing for negotiations is an ongoing process. More and more companies are using computers to store and analyze bargaining data, such as grievances and records of their resolution. Management should give its negotiators specific goals and clear directions about priorities—in other words, where to give ground and where to stand ground.

The site of negotiations also is important. A large conference room, comfortable chairs, easily accessible rest rooms, chalkboards, air-conditioning, two smaller rooms nearby, pencils, pads, drinking water, and ashtrays should be available. Soft light and a restful atmosphere are preferred by many negotiators. From management's standpoint there are advantages to meeting on company premises. Information, advice, and approval are more readily available. There also is a slight psychological advantage for the "home" team and a savings in travel time. The negotiating team usually enters the session with prearranged signals to be able to communicate with each other about when not to talk about a subject, when a team member is talking too much, when an unforeseen demand requires a caucus, and so forth.

Fact-finding sessions are often used before formal negotiations to clarify the negotiating objectives and lay the ground rules for bargaining. Once the management team knows what general areas are to be discussed, it can gather information regarding previous grievances, the expiring contract, working conditions, breakdown on the distribution of the sales dollar, regional and national productivity and wage data, fringe benefits, absenteeism, and economic indexes.

The team must be aware of all aspects of the major issues, since resolution of important questions generally resolves minor but related issues. A skilled negotiator realizes that a chain of events occurs when bargaining on any issue:

assumptions—facts—issues—position—decision—implementation. Thus, in a rational bargaining session, changing an opponent's decision means first changing his assumptions. Since new facts may alter the priority of given issues, the negotiating team must be ready to exploit such changes quickly.

The following are guidelines provided to union negotiators to assist them in preparing for and conducting collective bargaining negotiations. Union representatives attend special schools to develop a scientific approach to negotiation. The list below is adapted from the school for negotiators at the University of Missouri.

Before negotiations begin

1. Review grievance file to determine which complaints have occurred most frequently during the previous contract period.
2. Interview members about their present complaints and suggestions.
3. Make sure which issues can be negotiated and which cannot.
4. Obtain copies of agreements from other locals that negotiate with the company and from other unions in the industry.
5. Stay in contact with your international union representatives.
6. Collect all facts necessary to substantiate the union proposal.
7. Make sure to file all necessary notices of interest to reopen the contract.

Drafting the proposal

1. Consider the interests of *all* groups in the local when drafting proposals.
2. Be prepared to substantiate all proposals with facts.
3. Put the proposal in writing.
4. Present the final proposal to the membership for discussion and action.

Selecting the negotiating committee

1. Committee size will vary but should include officers of the local and a representative designated by the membership.
2. The committee should represent all major parts of the union, but have *one* spokesperson who is principal negotiator.
3. The spokesperson must be well acquainted with union policies and problems; a leader respected by members; firm, patient, a good listener, and skilled in communication.

Conducting the negotiations: the union approach

1. Union and management spokespersons act as co-chairpersons with equal rights.
2. The first session(s) is devoted to formalities: introductions, agreements on

procedures and time schedule, and exchange of written proposals if not previously submitted.

3. During first discussions of proposal, give only a general outline of issues and do not discuss points in detail. Then agree on the order in which individual issues will be discussed (take up easier issues first so as to avoid immediate impasse).

4. Make sure there is another room available for meetings of the union committee to hold caucus during recesses.

5. In case of impasse, postpone the disputed issue or ask for caucus to redefine the union's position.

6. In case of disagreement among the members of the union committee, the spokesperson should call for recess (caucus) upon request from anyone on committee. Never argue with a committee member in front of management.

7. In case of total impasse, seek assistance from the international union. If impasse still cannot be broken, consider mediation.

8. If necessary, prepare for and conduct a vote for strike authorization.

Keeping union members informed

1. Before negotiations, explain the final proposal; don't try to impose the proposal on the membership; be patient in explaining the committee's thinking, and accept any amendment that would improve the committee's proposal. To have full membership support, make sure as many as possible understand the full meaning of all items in the proposal.

2. During negotiations, keep the members informed about the general trends of the negotiations.

3. After negotiations, the negotiating committee should explain the terms of the agreement to secure its approval. Ratification of the agreement is obtained by secret ballot of the membership in accordance with the local bylaws. The negotiating committee should sign the written agreement only after approval. All employees, members and nonmembers, should receive copies of the contract.

Information to have prior to negotiations

Prior to entering a negotiation session to establish a new labor contract, it is critical that the negotiating team have certain facts and figures at their fingertips. The following is a detailed listing of the data necessary for effective bargaining, as compiled and edited by J. J. Mikrut, Labor Education Specialist, University of Missouri. It should be noted that this information is provided to union negotiators as part of their extensive training courses.

1. Wage data
    a. internal wage structure by job
    b. external wage data by occupation and by industry and geographic area

    c. description of plan for employee progression in wage
    d. description of job evaluation plan and incentive plan
    e. beginning rates for male and female employees
    f. plan for employee upgrading
    g. average hourly earnings, average weekly earnings, straight-time earnings
    h. description of recent increases such as a cost-of-living increase

2. Hours data
    a. number of hours in normal workday, workweek
    b. number of hours in average workday, workweek
    c. starting and quitting time for each shift

3. Employee data
    a. number of employees by sex and seniority for each shift
    b. age distribution of employees
    c. employee services available (medical, credit, recreational, cafeteria, etc.)

4. Productivity data
    a. production per labor-hour
    b. labor costs per unit of production
    c. equipment added during contract period
    d. percentage of labor costs to total product costs

5. Fringe data
    a. description of shift differentials
    b. description of overtime payment plan
    c. description of pension, group insurance plans
    d. description of safety program
    e. description of employee policies such as call-in, pay, sick leave, severance pay, holiday pay, rest periods, wash-up rules, etc.

6. Important documents to have on hand
    a. employee handbook
    b. copy of last contract
    c. grievance procedure
    d. pension plan
    e. wage progression plan
    f. group insurance policy
    g. incentive plan
    h. job evaluation plan
    i. memoranda circulated to employees or posted for review
    j. accident compensation policy

Union Objectives

Unions, of course, have special priorities. A training manual for union negotiators (Mikrut, 1975), spells out union objectives in collective bargaining in detail. The primary objective is to "protect the union's strength as an organization," which includes: more members; stronger treasury; increased prestige; control over jobs; increased seniority for union leaders; and limitation of employer's right to hire, fire, promote, demote, transfer, and discipline. Improved "wages, security, leisure, job control, voice in setting work standards, and elimination of discrimination due to race, creed or color" are immediate goals. The particular goals of union officers are "increased respect of workers, educational development, break in monotony of factory work, and money."

Union Security

Union security is an important contract provision. It describes an employer's obligation to the union in hiring new employees. The most important forms of union security are:

1. Union shop. An employer may hire nonunion members, but the employee must join the union within a specified period. This is the strongest form of union security permissible under U.S. federal law. However, many states have "right to work" laws that override the federal statutes by outlawing any form of union security.

2. Closed shop. A company may hire only union labor in a closed shop. This form of security is banned by federal law but allowed in several states. If a company is not involved in interstate commerce, then a state law permitting the closed shop overrides the federal law banning it.

3. Agency shop. Employees are not forced to join or remain in the union, but those who elect not to join must pay a "service charge" equal to the dues charged by the union.

Grievances

An employee who feels that management has violated the labor contract files a grievance. The employee must file the grievance according to the terms of the contract. The contract specifies filing procedures, including who can file a grievance, who should receive it, who should be notified, the time limits for each step, and how the grievance is to be settled (arbitrated).

Grievances are put in writing. Under the law, they may be brought directly to the immediate supervisor, who may handle them, and the union must be given the opportunity to be present when they are discussed. If an employee files directly with management, the union should be immediately notified of the date and time set for discussion or hearing. Good communication on these points may produce a more cooperative atmosphere between labor and management; in many cases the contract requires or encourages this communication.

The employee has a right to be present when his or her grievance is settled. The union must be given an opportunity to have a representative present at every stage in the grievance process, including the final stage, which may be conducted by a neutral arbitrator or arbitration board.

Arbitration

Arbitration is not a legal proceeding, though it is generally the final step in the grievance process. Arbitration is not collective bargaining. It is a process in which a decision is reached based on the merits of an issue by an expert (neutral) third party. The neutral third party, usually selected by the parties to a dispute, listens to both sides of the case and issues a decision that both sides must accept. An arbitrator is not a mediator. A mediator tries to find a solution satisfactory to both sides, while at least one and possibly both sides probably will not like the arbitrator's decision.

First, the arbitrator must be selected. Sometimes one is named in the existing contract. Most contracts provide that the arbitrator will be chosen from a list or panel supplied by the American Arbitration Association or a government agency. Next, the arbitrator is provided a statement outlining the issue. If the sides do not agree on the problem, each issues its own statement. Since the arbitrator's decision is final and binding, these statements are very important. Then the initial hearing is held, once the date, time, and place have been agreed to by all concerned parties. These hearings usually are informal. There are no oaths or written transcripts. Arbitrators try to maintain as much informality as possible to reduce hostility between the parties.

Since the union is usually the grieving party, it must prove that management has violated the labor agreement. Unless an employee has been fired or disciplined, the union presents its case first. But if an employee has been fired or disciplined, management presents the evidence for the action, and the union then attempts to disprove the evidence or argue about the severity of the penalty. Both sides use legal rules of evidence to establish the facts and circumstances. Both sides can call and cross-examine witnesses. After both sides have presented their evidence and final arguments, the hearing is closed. In many instances, both sides include written briefs. The arbitrator sends both parties a copy of his decision (award) and a written opinion. The decision is enforceable by court action if necessary.

Unions usually have nothing to lose in arbitration except the expense. Companies, on the other hand, have a great deal at stake. In addition to the cost of paying for arbitration and back wages, a lost decision can hurt managers' morale and motivation. So it is critical that witnesses understand how important their testimony is. The company's attorney must review witnesses' testimony before the hearing. Managers should be counseled on those matters that are likely to come up in cross-examination. Facts should never be altered, but management must present the strongest possible case.

Witnesses should always appear straightforward, concise, calm, and objective. They should be told to expect attacks as a matter of course and to remain unemotional. They must be definite and firm but not antagonistic or argumentative. A manager must be able to support his opinions about an employee's job performance with facts or critical incidents, including date and, if possible, time of occurrence. A witness should not guess; if he is not certain about the answer to a question, he should say so. Management, in summary, should be accurate in recording the details upon which the organization will act in the event of arbitration.

CASES IN LABOR LAW APPLICATION

The following cases illustrate many points we have made. Each is taken from an actual situation, and arbitrators' findings are presented at the end of the cases. Labor justice, as with the judicial system in general, is subject to the interpretation of facts based upon individual values, biases, attitudes, and other such human variables. The arbitrator's findings provide precedents for future hearings and actions.

The Dangers of Past Practice: A Case

A corporate official visited an arbitration hearing and noticed a union steward sitting in as the observer during normal working hours. The company officer asked the steward whether he was being paid to listen even if he was not a witness. The steward answered yes and added that the company had been doing this for several years.

When the company officer reviewed the labor agreement, he found absolutely nothing to support such payment, so he issued an order that union stewards would no longer be paid for attending an arbitration unless they were to testify in the case being heard. The union filed a grievance saying that management was in violation of the agreement by unilaterally doing away with an established practice. The company defense was that nothing in the contract supported payment.

The arbitrator decided in favor of the union. He stated that the company had violated the contract because meaning may be drawn from *conduct* as well as from writing. Management's behavior and action over a period of time can be made a binding part of a labor agreement even though it is not part of the agreement itself. Even a statement such as "this agreement shall become the sole agreement for the bargaining unit" will not do away with so-called past practice. There are two ways for management to avoid the abuse of labor privileges. It must not allow them in the first place or be prepared to bargain something away for their removal once they are established practice.

Work-Rule Enforcement

The enforcement of plant rules arises frequently in labor situations. The following case is a general example of work-rule enforcement.

Foreman Buddy Miner found Art Browne smoking in the company washroom in the chemical plant where they worked. Several months previously, the company had posted a written notice limiting smoking to the washroom, but after abuse of the privilege, the company posted a notice that banned all smoking on the property. Because of the dangers involved from fire, violators were suspended on the spot.

The foreman however, told Browne and the union representative that he was fired. Later that day the plant manager sent a written notice to Browne that he would be fired immediately after his suspension. (The labor contract provided that an employee could not be fired on the spot; a ten-day suspension had to be issued during which time written notification had to be sent to the employee and the union.)

Browne objected, and the case went to arbitration. The union admitted that Browne broke the posted no-smoking rule and that smoking in certain areas was extremely dangerous. But it argued that the punishment was too severe, that Browne had taken only one puff, and that the suspension rule was violated when he was fired on the spot. The company responded that the rules were necessary to prevent serious explosions, that all employees had been notified of the rule and the penalty for violation, that Browne knew the rule, and that the on-the-spot firing was a spur-of-the-moment act that did not violate contract provisions.

During the hearing it was brought out that other employees had broken the rule but that Browne was the first one to be caught. It also became evident that customers had complained to the company that smoking was endangering their orders.

The arbitrator denied the grievance and held that the company was justified in discharging Browne. He commented that the rule was related to the safe and efficient operation of the company and that, due to the hazardous nature of the business, the rule was not too harsh. He further stated that all employees were given opportunity to know the rule and penalty and that there was no evidence of discrimination in applying the penalty. The fact that the foreman issued an improper oral discharge prior to the proper, written notification did not prejudice Browne's rights under the contract and therefore was irrelevant.

It should be pointed out that one of the most common errors companies make is not providing extremely detailed instructions and training for supervisors for interpreting and implementing labor agreements. The first-level supervisor is the "responsible agent" of the company and, unfortunately, often makes expensive mistakes. In the Browne case, the company was fortunate. Many arbitrators may have ruled in favor of the union on the basis of a technicality.

This kind of situation can place a supervisor in a very awkward position. If his action is overruled, he may lose the respect of his subordinates, peers, and superiors. If a supervisor is "burned" once by being overruled by higher management or an arbitrator, he will be reluctant to take future disciplinary action. In this type of situation, past practice begins to evolve and discipline falls apart. Well-trained supervisors are therefore the key to the success of effective management involvement in labor relations.

EXPANDING UNIONISM

International Unionism

Multinational corporations reach their customers by direct production and sales in the foreign marketplace rather than through domestic production. In the early

1970s international production was increasing at a rate three times greater than the average rate of growth in the gross national domestic product (Levinson, 1972). The growth in size and number of multinational companies has caused many changes. It has led to a global economy and changed the nature of collective bargaining.

Many U.S. companies have moved their operations to foreign countries because of lower wages overseas, unreasonable wage demands in the domestic market, and favorable tax advantages offered by developing nations. Damaging slowdowns and strikes have led some firms to move their production facilities to more hospitable and productive climates.

Ironically, while production facilities are being located throughout the world, companies have centralized their industrial relations policies. Companies' international headquarters use integrated and computerized information systems to get greater control over regional labor activities. For example, the economic power of national unions is weaker in the face of a worldwide corporation because the economic importance of any one segment of the corporation is less important. A strike in one division of a multinational corporation will probably have less impact than a strike in a segment of a purely national corporation, especially if the multinational can shift its production to another country on short notice.

U.S. labor unions have not remained idle. They have attacked the multinationals through legislative processes. The AFL-CIO, for example, is attempting to limit the foreign operations of U.S. multinationals through regulatory schemes that would decrease the outflow of capital and technology, increase taxes, and establish reporting requirements about wages paid in foreign countries. The AFL has also lobbied to get mandatory labeling showing the country of origin of products and all components. The purpose of gathering such information is to assist in international collective bargaining and product boycotts (Gunther, 1972).

A concerted effort is being made to develop single master contracts to cover all aspects of a multinational industry, regardless of the countries involved. Unions are compiling files on forty of the largest multinationals, covering such items as structure, location, finances, labor agreements, employee profiles, state of union organization, and working conditions. Integrated computer data banks are being developed and will be accessible around the world. The International Metalworkers Federation, for example, has developed one computer data bank for all auto plants in Latin America and another in Europe.

Many obstacles stand in the path of international unionism. A principal stumbling block is the involvement of unions in the political structure of their respective countries. Unions, for the most part, are anti-capitalist. In most nations, the anti-capitalistic tendencies of unions are manifested in strong labor, socialist, or communist political parties whose primary goal is the nationalization of all industry. Additionally many of these same countries distrust the United States, and their unions distrust American labor organizations.

There are other obstacles to international unionism. Differences in wage levels, bargaining strategies, legal attitudes toward secondary boycotts, and sympathy strikes all present formidable barriers. Cultural differences among workers in various countries present a significant roadblock to international unionism. Japan represents a particularly relevant example of such cultural differences. The very concept of collective bargaining is quite different from the traditional attitudes, values, and customs that govern relations between Japanese workers and employers. The traditional relationship between employer and employee is one of master and servant, a relationship of control and subordination.

Grievance procedures in Japan are relatively ineffective because workers find it difficult to *demand* satisfaction of personal wants. The concept of job "rights" is psychologically foreign to most workers and managers. Provisions on job content, promotion, and transfer in labor contracts are very ambiguous (Taira, 1970). Collective bargaining is used only in times of conflict and seldom manifests itself in peaceful negotiations. In Japan, unions operate primarily through confrontation and force rather than by discussion and negotiation (Okochi, 1974). Bargaining also tends to occur within a single company, although the "spring labor offensive" focusing on industrywide coordination seems to have gained momentum in the past several years.

In spite of the problems, significant progress is being made by some international unions. In 1970, there were eighteen international trade secretariats in operation. The International Metalworkers Federation (IMF) is the largest; it represents about 11 million members in 80 unions in 49 countries. Its headquarters is in Geneva.

The IMF has established world councils for four industries: automotive, including farm implements; steel; shipbuilding; and electrical/machinists groups. The IMF has supplied skilled negotiators from the country of the parent company. These negotiators help local unions organize workers in foreign subsidiaries and provide help during strikes.

The International Federation of Chemical and General Workers Unions (ICF) has 2 million workers in 33 countries and is also headquartered in Geneva (Barovick, 1970).

An especially important breakthrough for the ICF occurred in the early 1970s, when affiliates in France, Germany, Italy, and the United States negotiated a master agreement with the French glass company, Saint-Gobain. The agreement stipulated that a contract could not be negotiated in any country without approval of a standing committee. If there is a strike in one country, all affiliates have agreed to provide financial support to the striking union; they have agreed to prevent the company from shipping among countries to break the strike and to stop overtime work in all Saint-Gobain plants in the event of a long strike. In the United States, the Glass and Ceramic Workers Union forced the Saint-Gobain Company to bargain on its very profitable world consolidated financial position rather than on its U.S. profit, which showed no earnings in the immediate preceding years. Despite the absence of local profits, the union was able to win a wage increase of 9 percent.

While the Saint-Gobain experience may appear as a victory for international unionism, it should also be viewed in terms of its long-range impact on the welfare of labor. Companies cannot stay in business without the necessary profits for reinvestment, dividends for shareholder support, and incentive for investment capital. Multinational collective bargaining imposes severe restrictions on the nature and extent of foreign investments and could probably have adverse effects on labor in the parent nation. Loss of a competitive advantage in foreign markets could prevent growth of the total system, and there would be less or no capital for investment in the parent company. The result would be a loss of jobs. On the other side, developing nations would be deprived of additional investment capital if multinational unions used collective bargaining to make these countries unattractive for investment purposes.

United Rubber Workers and the ICF

An important example of the growing power and influence of international unionism occurred in April 1976 during the strike of the United Rubber Workers (URW) against the major U.S. tire producers. In the midst of negotiations, the international president of URW left Akron, Ohio, to meet with the president of ICF (International Federation of Chemical and General Workers Unions) in Geneva, Switzerland. Discussions in the United States stopped for four days. At the Geneva meetings were Dr. Charles Levinson, secretary general of ICF; Karl Havenschild, president of the 600,000 member West German Chemical, Paper, and Ceramic Workers Union; president of the Paperworkers International; a Teamster official representing 750,000 members who pay dues to the ICF; and a member of the House of Commons from Great Britain representing Britain's 1.8 million-member Transport and General Workers' Union. Also at the meeting were union leaders from France, Italy, Japan, Spain, Norway, Denmark, and Belgium. Every speech was simultaneously translated into six languages. For the rubber workers, the ICF pledged aid in fourteen key countries. Workers at foreign Firestone and Goodyear plants would refuse overtime work, initiate consumer boycotts, and generally disrupt the foreign subsidiaries enough to help settle the U.S. strike in favor of the URW. Although it is unclear as to the impact these pledges had upon the eventual settlement, the very fact they were made is significant.

This activity represents the first time that the worldwide labor movement joined an American union in action against a multinational company. The consequences of such interlocking unionism are staggering and could easily alter the nature of global economics.

The ICF, which claimed 5.5 million members in 60 nations, has attempted to control companies like Goodyear and General Motors through worldwide strikes. To achieve this, Dr. Levinson claims he will need union contracts in many countries with the same expiration dates. The ultimate goal of such organization is the "direction of property by the workers."

In mid-1975, American labor leaders asked the U.S. government to withdraw from the International Labor Organization (ILO), claiming it had become a forum for the denunciation of free enterprise economic systems. The ILO, with 126 member nations, was established in 1919 with the assistance of Samuel Gompers, also the founding father of the American Federation of Labor. The

International Labor Organization, an arm of the United Nations, is housed in Geneva and heavily supported by the U.S. government.

White-Collar Unionism

As we have mentioned in earlier chapters, the number of white-collar workers has increased throughout this century. White-collar employment represented 28 percent of the U.S. labor force in 1900 and 47 percent in 1960, when white-collar workers began to unionize. They include clerical, professional, technical, sales, and similar occupations.

Department of Labor statistics reveal that union membership among white-collar employees rose from 2.2 to 3.4 million from 1960 to 1972. Another 1.8 million belonged to employee associations. In 1974, unions won 622 white-collar elections involving 18,864 workers; they lost 484 elections involving 25,896 workers. This represented the largest number of white-collar elections ever held (Houston, 1975).

Management has strongly resisted the tide of white-collar unionization. Companies have given tandem benefits (benefits negotiated by blue-collar unions) to their white-collar employees in an attempt to reduce the financial incentive to unionize.

Specific conditions have encouraged white-collar workers to unionize. When management has used its authority arbitrarily or created a strong sense of inequitable treatment, or as other workers have attempted to unionize (steamroller effect), conditions have been ripe for a unionizing effort. Naturally, job insecurity and frequent layoffs also encourage unionization. For example, there were virtually no secondary school teachers' unions in early 1960, but by 1970 there were over 3,500 contracts covering over 1 million teachers.

Worker Attitudes

An analysis performed by the Opinion Research Corporation reviews the attitudes of clerical and blue-collar employees toward management during the past years. This analysis reveals that clerical employees are becoming markedly more critical of their managers.

The study used the average favorable ratings of management for the 1955–65 period as the median. The researchers then computed the percentage of change in favorable ratings since 1966 for both clerical and blue-collar employees. Both groups agreed that basic employment conditions of pay, benefits, job security, and working conditions were less attractive than in the past. But clerical workers were most critical. Their favorable ratings declined by an average of 14 percent, while the ratings of blue-collar workers declined 11.5 percent.

In the area of personnel practices and communications, the change was even greater. Clerical workers showed a marked decline in attitudes, while blue-collar workers showed a slight increase. For example, for the issue "Promotes environment where management and employees can work together," favorable ratings by clerical workers declined by 14 percent, while blue-collar ratings improved by 4 percent.

Of course, these are measurements of relative declines and increases. Clerical employees still have more favorable attitudes toward management and will express less criticism than blue-collar workers do. However, the study does illustrate that the gap is closing between the needs and outlooks of both blue- and white-collar workers.

The White-Collar Mystique

There are many obstacles to white-collar unionization. The mass media has tended to emphasize union strikes and violence rather than peaceful negotiations, which are not "newsworthy." This has created a poor public image. On top of this, older union leaders often lose touch with the wants of the rank and file and lack imaginative solutions to their problems.

These impressions are not lost on white-collar workers. They have a certain self-image that is inconsistent with picketing, violence, strikes, and hard-nosed bargaining. They feel that union membership would decrease their prestige. Many look forward to moving up the management ladder and feel that unionizing would interfere with such opportunities. Most professionals with special skills feel that they can gain more through individual bargaining than through collective agreements, which bring equal benefits to all regardless of skill or productivity.

Clerical unions. Growth in technology, especially computers, in office and sales work has changed many clerical jobs. Clerical workers have resisted these changes in the same ways that blue-collar workers have opposed mechanization. Office personnel dislike monotony and fear loss of jobs just the same as the factory workers resented automation in the early part of the century and still do today. A second industrial revolution, the computer revolution, will bring increased unionism in those organizations unwilling to treat their personnel in a humane manner.

Supervisory unions. Another group of employees who are becoming increasingly dissatisfied with their role is the first-line supervisor, especially industrial foremen. These managers are badgered by the union, harassed by management, annoyed by increasingly apathetic subordinates, and ill-trained to deal with the constant flow of human problems they must face in their daily work. Many supervisors believe their working conditions are the worst in the plant, their prestige is nil, and that there is little hope of improvement in the future.

Most supervisors have no effective formal grievance procedure. The Wagner Act permits supervisors to organize, but it also allows an employer to act against supervisors who become involved in the process of organizing. Thus, one can readily understand how frustrated a group of supervisors might become.

Public sector unions. Self-employed professionals, including physicians and lawyers, have been organized for many years, although they call their organizations associations rather than unions. The associations perform many of the same functions of unions, such as limiting membership and maintaining common fee structures.

It is among public sector professionals, however, where unionization of white-collar workers has been most successful. The advocates of unionism in the public sector see a bright future. Conditions that have caused employees to organize in the private sector exist in public employment. Although pay has increased substantially in the public sector, employees must deal with a vast government bureaucracy.

The poor communication between employees and decision makers is feeding a growing militance in public sector bargaining (Bakke, 1970). Many managers in the public sector oppose collectivism and are unlikely to negotiate rationally. All of this has increased workers' reliance on direct, coercive pressure to achieve their ends.

Jurisdictional disputes between trade unions and so-called professional associations (particularly in public education) will probably add to tensions and radical activism. Unions will probably use their political power to pressure executive and legislative branches of government to overrule the decisions of public managers. True collective bargaining under these conditions will be difficult. Uniform work rules probably will be replaced by regulations for each bargaining unit. The public will pay a high price in the form of increased taxes and interruptions in public services.

In 1964, 900,000 federal and 556,000 state and local employees were members of unions. By 1974, according to U.S. Department of Labor statistics, 1.4 million federal and 1.5 million state and local workers were unionized. This means that one in five public service employees belonged to unions in 1974, compared with one in seven in 1964. Another 2.4 million government workers belong to associations that are not technically considered unions but do bargain collectively on behalf of their members. Thus, more than one-third of all civilians who work for the government were in collective bargaining units in the mid-seventies.

During the recession period beginning in 1974, strikes among public service employees began to increase, particularly at the local level. Prior to these hard times, strikes would not have occurred because governments were quite generous with newly unionized workers.

As financial conditions worsened, mayors and governors approached negotiations with grim offers of less money or fewer jobs. In August 1975, the lame duck mayor of San Francisco initially refused a union request for a 13 percent increase in the salaries of police and fire employees. After a short strike the mayor reversed his decision, in spite of the vehement opposition of the city board of supervisors and granted the union's request. The average patrolman's salary was increased to $19,500 per year plus another $10,000 in fringe benefits. Such action, in the face of devastating inflation, was condemned widely throughout the United States. San Francisco also paid its firefighters the maximum earned among other large California cities. For twenty-three years through 1974, the board of supervisors automatically had voted the maximum pay raise permitted.

Many examples of totally ineffective labor relations can be found in municipal labor negotiations. Politics plays an important role in the problem. For example, in San Francisco, the chairman of the Civil Service Commission in 1975 was an officer of the Plumbers Union Local 38. The city plumbers in San Francisco, incidentally, earned $15.39 per hour, or $24,993 per year in 1975. Not all blame can be placed on city officials for the apparent ineptness in dealing with public employee bargaining units. They often face a no-win situation: grant exorbitant demands or allow law and order to disintegrate. The taxpayer loses in either case.

Some officials find that standing up to unions is not only a matter of hard economics but also good politics. When the mayor of Seattle fired a popular fire chief, the firefighters union forced a special recall election. The mayor received two-thirds of the vote in his favor. The following day the union quietly settled a long-standing wage dispute (*U.S. News and World Report*, September 1, 1975). The near bankruptcy of New York City led to the dismissal of 13,240 city employees in 1975, which resulted in only one very brief strike. In Cleveland, city employees were offered the startling low pay increase of 10 cents per hour in 1975, and only one small union chose to strike. Effective labor negotiations and disclosure of financial conditions is necessary for the survival of the cities.

Compulsory arbitration may become the only answer for public unions and public welfare since any strike by civil servants works against the social welfare of the total community.

If management wants to stop the rising tide of white-collar unionism, the following strategies should be included:

1. Candid communication between management and employee about those issues of vital concern to the employee (organization goals, performance standards, work rules, job responsibilities, and performance feedback).

2. Two-way communications at all levels, to include periodic attitude surveys.

3. A personalized statement of benefits issued annually (or more often) to each employee.

4. Avoiding overreacting when organizing efforts are first noticed, since this will drive most middle-of-the-roaders to the union side.

5. Administering all discipline promptly, fairly, objectively, and consistently. The issue of discipline is so important to effective personnel administration that we have included the following section on the subject.

EFFECTIVE DISCIPLINE IN LABOR RELATIONS

Discipline

Discipline is attitude, not punishment. It is the attitude employees have toward regulations and supervision. Discipline is good when subordinates willingly follow the rules of the organization; it is bad when they willfully disobey regulations. Good discipline should be positively reinforced as suggested by motivation theory. Poor discipline demands feedback, counseling, and a penalty system professionally administered in accordance with contractual arrangements and standard practices.

The result of either good discipline or bad discipline should be organizational action. Poor discipline should be approached initially as an opportunity for corrective rather than punitive action. In other words, the manager should view poor discipline as an opportunity for counseling and training. The negative aspects of discipline actually can be quite challenging. A good manager needs to communicate promptly with a worker about faults, mistakes, violations, and ways to correct them. He also needs to be flexible. Different approaches work better with different people. When a manager's attempts to change negative attitudes toward rules fails, he must build a case. This means prompt action: *written* records of warnings and acquisition of evidence needed to justify a penalty.

The most effective form of discipline is based on "due process." Rules are stated in advance, and if a penalty is required, it is also stated in advance. The penalty matches the severity and frequency of the violation. Employees must know in advance what the rules are and what the penalty is for breaking them. Penalties should be heavier as rule infractions are repeated. For example, a first offense could be dealt with by verbal discussion; the second offense could merit a written warning; a third offense might require suspension without pay for a week, while the fourth offense would require dismissal.

Absenteeism is one of the most frequent and difficult to solve disciplinary problems. Absenteeism costs American business over $12 billion each year. Some of the loss is unavoidable. Employees do become ill or have personal emergencies, but as much as half of the absenteeism can be avoided. There should be a set of rules regarding absences. The manager must enforce the rules and never overlook the first absence. By talking to the employee as soon as possible to find out the reason for unexcused absence, the manager should let people know they are missed, request that it not happen again, and give written warnings to persons who are absent three or more times without excuse. If counseling doesn't help, stronger disciplinary measures will be required.

Exhibit 13–1 provides a series of questions regarding the application of discipline in a unionized organization. It also brings up many difficult questions that managers must answer carefully to be consistent with contracts. Exhibit 13–2 provides a set of guidelines that can be applied across all organizations in the area of discipline. Answers to many of the issues raised in Exhibit 13–1 can be found in this set of questions. An example of an actual disciplinary action, coupled with an arbitrator's ruling after the action was grieved, follows. (The names and dates in the case have been changed, but all events are real.)

COMPUTER SYSTEMS IN LABOR RELATIONS

The use of computer systems has resulted in the modernization of the labor relations activities in many firms. Before the computer, labor relations specialists spent a lot of time hunting records (busy work), but now they are able to deal with the human element of their jobs, such as discipline, counseling, union-

---

EXHIBIT 13–1   Tests and Problems in Determining "Just Cause" for Discipline

---

A. Did the organization give the employee forewarning of the possible disciplinary consequences of the employee's conduct?
   1. How should such forewarning be given?
   2. Is it necessary that such rules have been negotiated with the union? Is it advisable to negotiate such rules?

B. Was the organization's rule or managerial order reasonably related to a) the orderly, efficient, and safe operations of the business, and b) the performance the organization might properly expect of the employee?
   1. Obligation to obey.
   2. Exceptions to such obligation.

C. Did the organization, before administering discipline to an employee, make an effort to discover whether the employee did, in fact, violate or disobey a rule or order of management?
   1. "Day in court" principle, right to know the offense charged, right to defend behavior.
   2. Is it essential that the investigation be made before disciplinary action is determined?

D. Was the investigation conducted fairly and objectively?
   1. How to assure that judicial fairness towards the employee in management attitude and conduct?
   2. Handling the no-witness situation—i.e., supervisor versus employee; questioning the management "participant" by the management "judge."

E. Was the evidence of guilt substantial?
   1. Determining the amount of proof required?
   2. Assuring that an aggressive search (versus passive acceptance of testimony) has been made.
   3. Resolving conflict in testimony.

F. Has the rule, order, or penalty been evenly applied to all employees?
   1. What warrants a finding of discrimination?
   2. How to go from lax to tighter enforcement of a rule?

G. Was the degree of discipline administered reasonably related to the seriousness of the proven offense?
   1. Avoiding the hazard of determining guilt by the past record?
   2. What is the proper use of "past record"?
   3. Can you administer different degrees of discipline for the same offense?
   4. How can charges of discriminatory treatment be avoided?
   5. How can modification of penalty by the arbitrator be avoided?

---

management relations (contract interpretation, grievance procedure, etc.), and employee relations. As business organizations have grown more complex, so have the problems of how to deal with the employees. Fairness and communication—these are the issues that labor relations people deal with every day. And information systems are helping them.

When a labor relations specialist is trying to prevent or solve a problem, timing and accuracy are very important. A prime example of the use of computers in labor relations work is in disciplinary cases. Most personnel people agree that discipline must be administered fairly but firmly if it is to do any good at all. Fairness involves the relationship of penalty and offense, the right of the employee to know what the charge is and who brought the charge against him, and his right

EXHIBIT 13-2 Guidelines for Improving the Disciplinary Process

1. Reprimanding should be done in private whenever possible.
2. Disciplinary action should be looked upon as *corrective* in initial stages and *punitive* when training and counseling have little or no effect.
3. Good discipline is more effectively maintained if the manager has a written set of guidelines to follow.
4. Make certain you have all the facts before taking disciplinary action. Reversal of a penalty is detrimental to morale and lowers respect of employees for management.
5. Sarcasm should be avoided when dealing with employees.
6. Don't threaten, argue or show anger.
7. Suit reprimands to the individual and situation.
8. Discipline promptly.
9. Criticize the behavior, not the employee.
10. Suit the severity of the discipline to the seriousness of the offense.
11. Disciplinary action requires follow-up.
12. It is important for the manager to reestablish friendly contact with an employee soon after disciplinary action is taken.
13. An employee should be told when he is doing poorly on the job.
14. The immediate supervisor should be involved with any disciplinary action involving a subordinate.
15. An employee who is a chronic disciplinary problem is not likely to improve simply through a transfer.
16. Managers must take disciplinary action on continued infractions of rules even though the infractions are minor. Laxity breeds laxity.
17. Remember that the primary function of disciplinary action is to prevent recurrence.

TIGER MANUFACTURING COMPANY
AND
UNITED WORKERS OF AMERICA, LOCAL NO. XXX

GRIEVANCE NUMBER: 21–739
DATE OF DECISION: 1/6/75

NATURE OF CASE: PROTEST AGAINST DISCHARGE OF ELWOOD MILES

THE FACTS

Elwood Miles was hired on November 11, 1969. His disciplinary record since that time has been as follows:

Date	Nature of Discipline
4/3/70	Counseled for irregular attendance.
5/3/70	Reprimanded for irregular attendance.
10/2/71	Suspended one week for participation in illegal work stoppage.
6/3/73	Reprimanded for excessive personal time (55 minutes in lunchroom).
6/22/73	Suspended one day for insubordination (swearing at foreman).
8/5/73	Counseled for irregular attendance.
12/22/73	Suspended balance of shift plus 10 work days for possessing alcoholic beverages

in plant during regular work shift. Placed on probation and informed next incident of misconduct or infraction of established rules or practices would result in discharge.

9/6/74   Reprimanded and lost .3 of an hour's pay for taking shower sixteen minutes before end of shift.

9/6/74   Informed still on probation and that any infraction of the established rules or practices or any misconduct will result in discharge.

1/2/75   Counseled for irregular attendance.

3/18/75   Suspended three working days for leaving work area early without authorization, failing to ring out clock card. Lost .3 hour's pay and informed such violation of Company rules not to be tolerated. Above action if continued with other type of infraction listed, will result in further serious disciplinary action.

6/17/75   Reprimanded for irregular attendance.

On June 17, 1975, Miles was given a notice distributed to all employees, reiterating a series of frequently violated rules including one which stated "Employees are not permitted to take a shower until after the end of their work shift."

On June 26, 1975, grievant was found showering prior to the end of his work shift and indefinitely suspended. This suspension was changed to a dismissal on July 1, 1975, giving rise to the instant dispute.

CONTENTIONS OF THE PARTIES

The Company argues that Miles has had a long career of unsatisfactory attendance, an insubordinate attitude toward Management, and a record of various forms of improper conduct. It asserts that it has made many efforts to restore Miles' record, through corrective discipline, to a satisfactory level without success. In view of his inability, or refusal, to respond to these efforts, the Company concludes that it had no alternative course but to discharge the grievant.

The Union acknowledges the content of Miles' disciplinary record but asserts that all notations of discipline should be considered in the light of the contract which requires disregarding violations more than twelve months old, except for participation in illegal stoppage, in administering future discipline. In this regard, the Union concludes that the violations which took place within the prior twelve months were at most "second offenses" the normal penalty for which is a three-day suspension. Accordingly, and in view of Miles' record for good work performance, the Union requests the Arbitrator to direct the Company to return the grievant to his job with all rights and privileges but with a one-day penalty for offenses.

DISCUSSION BY ARBITRATOR

The facts of this case are undisputed. Miles had been reprimanded and penalized for taking a shower sixteen minutes before the end of his shift on September 6, 1975, when he was on probation for a prior offense. On June 17, 1975, he was given a copy of a general notice reminding him that this was a violation of plant rules. Nine days later he was found taking a shower before the end of his shift. There is no question that this justified the imposition of a penalty. The Company imposed the discharge penalty as being appropriate in the light of grievant's whole previous record. The Union challenged the penalty on the grounds that the contract precludes consideration of any violations not repeated within twelve months in levying discipline.

This provision is calculated to recognize improvements in an employee's behavior in response to discipline when there has been no repetition of an offense within a twelve-month period. There is nothing therein which precludes the employer from considering the employee's overall record within the recent twelve-month period to determine whether his acts and attitude justify imposition of a particular penalty—or indeed, his continuing on the job.

Thus in the case, the seventeen-month span between 8/5/73 and 1/2/75 during which grievant had no reprimands for irregular attendance eliminates consideration of his earlier transgressions in that area of discipline but does justify consideration of the latter reprimand and the succeeding one on June 12, 1975, in determining the employee's overall attitude toward his job. Likewise the 1973 insubordination suspension not having been repeated within a twelve-month period must be bypassed. However his March 18, 1975, suspension for leaving early must be considered, particularly in the light of the warning of serious disciplinary action, in future infractions. Naturally under the contract, his participation in the 1971 illegal work stoppage remains on his record.

Grievant's record during the last twelve-month period includes two violations of the shower rule, one immediately following a general notice, as well as a three-day suspension for leaving a work area early for which he was warned that future infractions would lead to further "serious disciplinary action," and two reprimands for irregular attendance. Although claimant can hardly be described as having accumulated a desirable record during the period under examination. I do not believe that he has adequately demonstrated disregard of his responsibilities to be deemed incorrigible so as to justify discharge at this time. This is particularly true in that the final infraction, early showering, appears to have been a sufficiently widespread problem with other employees as well to have justified the General Notice to all employees. Indeed there was testimony that another employee was discovered showering early, at the same time as the grievant during the second occurrence.

This is not to say that a strenuous penalty is inappropriate. Claimant must be rapidly and forcefully apprised of the urgency for response to his employment commitments and for abiding by the essential rules of conduct that are necessary if any industrial organization is to operate effectively and continue to provide its employees with jobs. It is hoped that Miles' reinstatement will provide him the opportunity to demonstrate his abilities with due regard to the rules of good conduct in the plant. In providing him with an opportunity to return to work, I am withholding any back pay—such deprivation to bring home to the employee the impropriety of his past conduct and the need for immediate improvement.

DECISION

Grievance No. AW–22–613 is sustained in part. Elwood Miles shall be reinstated but without back pay.

Discuss the implications of this decision upon company management, both at top and first level supervisory levels. How might the problem have been avoided?

---

to union representation if the situation is covered by a union contract. Firmness includes such points as the degree of supervisor's security and the ability to stand in the face of pressure. Of course, the computer cannot guarantee that a supervisor will handle a disciplinary situation correctly from a human relations viewpoint, but it can give the supervisor necessary information. In a matter of minutes, the labor relations person can have the employee's complete disciplinary record in front of him, including dates, offenses, and penalties. Figures on absenteeism, productivity, job assignment, and payroll can also be obtained. The availability of such information will help avoid mistakes that could later be overturned in a grievance procedure.

Using computer data banks for disciplinary matters is only one example of how labor relations can take advantage of computers' record-keeping abilities. These abilities can also be used for grievance investigations and job-promotional postings, where skill banks and the time and accuracy factors are important. For example, most union contracts allow employees to bid on higher paying jobs. Merit, ability, and seniority are the standard criteria used to pick the people who will fill the openings. A labor relations specialist can use printouts from skill banks which show all employees who have had the necessary experience for the job. In a matter of minutes, the bidders and qualifications for a certain job can be matched. Skill banks are also useful when replacements are needed to cover sickness, vacations, and absenteeism.

The "information-decision" system is more sophisticated, going one step beyond the pure information system. The information-decision system stores data and provides it upon request. The system includes decision rules for application within the organization. The system makes calculations (decisions) based on specific rules that are programmed into the system. The computer provides these decisions in a few minutes or seconds with near perfect accuracy if the initial data are correct. It can save an enormous amount of time and trouble. Such information-decision systems are helpful in union-management negotiations and compulsory arbitration (Greenlaw and Smith, 1970).

A number of major unions, notably the International Association of Machinists and the United Steelworkers, have developed elaborate information-decision systems for use in contract negotiations with major corporations. These systems enable the unions to compile facts and figures about all contracts covering their members, feed these figures into the computer, analyze the various contracts, and provide information to be used in bargaining demands. In order to keep up with the progress of unions in the field of information systems, labor relations departments must utilize their computer facilities in the same manner as unions do. Facts about various contracts within the industry can be stored and analyzed much the same as is done by the unions. In this way the labor relations departments can anticipate union demands and take steps to meet these demands. Advance knowledge of possible union demands is labor relations' dream, for the elements of surprise and timing are key factors in the union's battle plan in bargaining negotiations.

Some labor relations experts have suggested the possibility of using computer simulation for planning negotiation strategy. Quantifiable proposals can be coded and stored in the computer. With this set of reliable information on possible offers and alternative union demands, the company could plan its strategy. This possibility is questionable, however. Many demands, such as changes in work rules or contract clauses are not quantifiable because they involve the human element and would be difficult to predict or program.

Support of Arbitration: Computer Analyses

Arbitration is an area in which computers can save both time and money. A record of past arbitration cases can be stored in the computer's data bank, and each case coded according to a number of predetermined key factors relevant to arbitration cases. A probability rule would tell the labor relations department whether or not to proceed to arbitration with a case. The rule would be based on precedents in similar cases and coded on the key factors mentioned previously.

The information-decision system will indicate whether it is worthwhile to take a case to arbitration. This type of decision can be crucial. Losing a case in arbitration can result in disastrous precedents for disputed cases in the future. Rather than take such a risk, the grievance may be granted or some type of compromise attempted by the company.

An Application Case

In 1970, a large manufacturing company implemented a personnel data system for use by its labor relations departments in various locations. This system is an example of how computers can increase the effectiveness of staff functions and is basically concerned with the storage and retrieval of personnel data. Federal law requires employers to maintain records of current employees for promotions, demotions, transfers, layoffs, recalls, discharges, and disciplinary proceedings for a minimum of one year. Company policy requires storage of such data for seventy-five years, the most recent ten years of which must be "easily accessible." These requirements made it necessary for the Labor Relations Department to develop a system that could store accumulated data while providing for quick and accurate retrieval (Kish, 1970).

In this particular system, data are placed on cards or magnetic tape and fed into the computer. The cards are divided into various informational areas, such as the usual spaces for name, address, etc., but codes have been added for such informational areas as job classifications, disciplinary records, and medical restrictions. Codes for job classification (P18060 for Production Department, 18060 for job title), actual pay rates (4675 for $4.675), disciplinary records (D1 for interview, D4 for one week off), and medical restrictions (C1 for protective glasses, C7 for ground level work) allow vast amounts of information to be stored in the data bank for each individual. The Labor Relations Department has total responsibility for the operation of the system. Its personnel input the data and operate the computer. A daily report lists all of the day's transactions. (A real-time system was in the planning stages in 1970.)

Labor relations information is provided to all production departments as well as the Labor Relations Department. All foremen and general foremen are able to obtain information by using a security code that is changed at specified times. The foremen or labor relations people simply type the correct security code and then feed a specific employee number into the system. Information is provided in a matter of minutes. Thus the data system not only provides the department with updated files on each employee, but these files become action documents for the supervisors to use in their work.

The Labor Relations Department uses the system primarily for disciplinary actions and grievance investigation. Both of these subjects involve the foremen and labor relations people, and both involve great amounts of time that could be more effectively utilized if directed toward other things. The system, hopefully, enables members of management to reduce time spent on these matters and devote more time to preventing these problems from happening.

As was mentioned in a previous section, timeliness and accuracy are important in both disciplinary cases and grievance investigations. At many industrial locations, the main problem with disciplinary actions is failure to follow the proper sequence in assessing penalties. Incorrect information about employees' past disciplinary records often results in improper penalties being assessed. These penalties can then be reversed in the grievance procedure, and the effect of the action is lost. The supervisor loses face in front of his subordinates, and the Labor Relations Department must take the blame for not providing correct information or for failing to win the grievance. Computer systems ease many of the problems by providing the foreman with the most timely and accurate information available. Each prior disciplinary action is listed in sequence, and the supervisor then should have little trouble deciding on the proper penalty. If he is not sure of the proper penalty, the official penalty sequence can also be obtained from the computer.

The computer system also makes grievance investigation much easier for Labor Relations. A majority of grievances involve job assignment and overtime assignments. Data available in the system permit faster investigation and can even result in fewer grievances being filed. Each employee has a list in his record of classifications held, department, and date assigned. The number of grievances filed may even be reduced so that a union committeeperson may question a job classification or assignment and Labor Relations can then answer the question with information from the system. Depending on the facts provided, the committeeperson may find that no violation existed and consequently will not file a grievance.

The advantages of the computer system have been in saving time, accuracy of data obtained, and better employee relations. Employee relations can be improved as a result of use of computers because the employees begin to understand that the machine practically eliminates bias from information storage and retrieval. Employees cooperate more when information is requested of them. Employees seem to develop a greater understanding of management's position and realize that the computer is there to help them as well as the company. Local management has taken great pains to orient employees to the uses of the system, and many potential problems have been avoided.

The most notable disadvantages of this approach have been cost and the problems between computer specialists and labor relations people. Computer systems do not always bring substantial savings to the company. Machines have not replaced people in the Labor Relations office. Extra people have been hired and present personnel given special training in how to administer and operate the system. The costs of these extra people, training sessions, and machines themselves have been quite substantial. These increased costs can be justified on the basis of increased efficiency and effectiveness of the Labor Relations Department. In the long run this may produce actual cost savings.

Adoption of the system forced the company to hire more computer specialists to work with present personnel in initial development of the system. In many instances, these two types of specialists came into conflict over who had what authority and who was right or wrong in establishing priorities. Neither group seemed to want to understand the other's role. Such behavior has to be resolved in order to ensure the effective operation of similar systems.

SUMMARY

Labor unions have played a very significant role in the development of business and personnel practices. This chapter has focused on the positive and negative aspects of domestic and international unionism, with emphasis on the reasons workers join or do not join a union. The successful organization of workers requires irritating condition(s) that create widespread employee dissatisfaction. Such conditions include substandard pay, lack of job security, dirty or unsafe conditions, unreasonable management, and others. White-collar, supervisory, and public sector unions were also discussed.

Illustrations of union power were noted along with examples of how the misuse of power can actually lead to significant decreases in worker productivity. Important labor legislation was briefly described, including the Wagner, Landrum-Griffin, Norris-LaGuardia, Walsh-Healey, and Taft-Hartley Acts. Unfair labor practices by management were defined and illustrated. Examples of how unions might violate the law were also given.

Negotiating a labor agreement is the heart of the collective bargaining process. Successful negotiations require well-qualified personnel who plan, think clearly under stress, communicate effectively, and are honest, self-confident, tolerant, and exploitive. Grievance proceedings, arbitration, and mediation were also briefly covered.

The rapid growth in multinational firms has led unions to develop on a worldwide scale. Computer data banks have been used by both multinationals and international unions.

Since the discipline process is so closely related to industrial relations effectiveness, considerable attention was devoted to the analysis and design of workable disciplinary systems. It was noted that computers play an increasingly important part in labor-management relations by serving as important ways to store and retrieve information quickly.

DISCUSSION QUESTIONS

1. Using motivation theory as a base, explain why a group of bank tellers might tend to unionize if an electronic deposit system were discussed informally at an executive meeting and the news leaked out.

2. What major events in the United States prompted widespread attempts to organize labor during the first half of the twentieth century?

3. Identify the major factors contributing to successful organization of workers.

4. What major factors might have played an important role in increasing productivity at U.S. Borax when management stepped into production jobs during the 1974 strike?

5. What is collective bargaining? Do you believe it is possible to have three major parties (e.g., administration, faculty, students) involved directly in the bargaining process? Explain your reasoning.

6. Differentiate between contract administration and contract negotiation.

7. Describe the personal qualities likely to be found in an effective labor negotiator.

8. How might physical arrangements and conditions affect the negotiating process?

9. Differentiate among union shop, closed shop, and agency shop.

10. What are the major steps in an arbitration proceeding?

11. Explain some of the possible effects of international unionism upon the monetary and social systems of countries.

12. Explain the potential advantages and disadvantages of a supervisory union to a manufacturing plant.

13. What are some reasons for recent growth in white-collar unionism?

14. Do you believe that public servants such as firefighters, police officers, nurses, and doctors should have the right to strike? Why? Why not?

15. In early 1976 doctors joined to effectively halt the practice of medicine in California's private hospitals. As a result of this work stoppage, many patients who needed surgery could not get it. The reason for the work stoppage was to protest escalating costs of malpractice insurance. Do you believe the work stoppage was justified? Explain.

16. Explain how computers can improve the effectiveness of contract negotiation, grievance handling, and arbitration sessions.

17. What can be done to improve the process of collective bargaining in the United States?

18. What is the impact of current collective bargaining on managerial efficiency and effectiveness?

19. What is the relationship between collective bargaining and inflation? What might be done to reduce the inflation created by collective bargaining?

20. What are likely to be the new issues for collective bargaining in the private sector in the years ahead?

21. What does management generally seek to achieve through collective bargaining?

22. Which factors contribute most to the union's power at the negotiating table?

23. *The Longren Bearing Case.* The Longren Bearing Corporation, with headquarters in Springdale, Ohio, has subsidiaries in Roundtree, Ohio, and Louisville, Kentucky. The company was formed in 1960 and by 1975 had 267 employees in its three manufacturing plants. During the initial stages of growth, the president made a special effort to know each employee by name and even visited the hospital when someone was sick or when a new child was born to an employee's family. As the company grew, the president couldn't continue this kind of personal involvement, although the older employees never forgot the "way things used to be."

When the founding president retired in 1973, Mr. Green was brought in from the outside as the new president of Longren. He was very concerned about improving the company's national image and product design. He redesigned the organization to provide functional leaders for engineering, sales, accounting, manufacturing, and research. He also noticed that the employee bonus system was serving as a negative motivator since the amount set aside each year by the board of directors was not growing in proportion to the size of the work force. Thus, even though people were working harder, their actual bonuses received around Christmas time were decreasing. In addition, Mr. Green felt that the reward for perfect attendance (a day off or a day's pay if no absenteeism over a three-month period) should be discontinued since employees were expected to be at work.

The new president took special care to assure that wages and fringe benefits were better than the average in surrounding areas for all plants. In fact, the personnel manager, who also served as the president's executive assistant, assured us that the benefit package was better than 99 percent of all benefit packages in the country.

In 1974, a letter was circulated to all employees and supervisors announcing the end of the bonus and perfect-attendance awards. Shortly thereafter, wages and dental benefits were increased. In spring 1975, a union vote was taken in one plant. Even though the union was defeated, management was shocked that such a thing could even occur. In fall 1975, another union move was actively started in a different plant.

What do you feel are some of the reasons behind the apparent increase in interest being shown by the workers in collective bargaining? What should the president do as the second election is about to take place? What should be done after the election?

BIBLIOGRAPHY

Akron Beacon Journal, 24 November 1974:G1.

Alexander, T. "How the Tenderfeet Toughened Up U.S. Borax." *Fortune* (December 1974):159–66.

Bakke, E. W. "Reflections on the Future of Bargaining in the Public Sector." *Monthly Labor Review* (July 1970).

"Bargaining by Electronics." *Business Week* (June 5, 1971):78.

Barovick, Richard L. "Labor Reacts to Multinationalism." *Columbia Journal of World Business* (August 1970):40–46.

Byrd, S. F. *Front Line Supervisors' Labor Relations Handbook.* Waterford, Conn.: National Foremen's Institute, 1963.

Campbell, W. J. "Our Jobs are on the Line." *Industry Week* (January 3, 1972):s-1.

Denison, G., and W. Schulz. "Let's Enforce our Labor Laws Fairly." *Readers Digest* (August 1968):120.

Gitlow, Abraham L. *Labor and Manpower Economics.* Homewood, Ill.: Richard D. Irwin, 1971.

Greenlaw, P., and R. Smith. *Personnel Management: A Management Science Approach.* Scranton, Pa.: Intext Publishing Company, 1970.

Gunther, Hans. *Transnational Industrial Relations.* New York: St. Martin Press, 1972.

"Heating Up: The Battle Over Automation in Printing." *U.S. News and World Report* (May 6, 1974):87–89.

Houston, J. "More White Collar Workers Join Unions." *Chicago Tribune,* 9 February 1975.

Karrass, Chester Louis. *The Negotiating Game.* New York: World Publishing Co., 1970.

Kish, J. L. "Personnel Records Required by Law." *Office* (November 1970):160.

Levinson, Charles. *International Trade Unionism.* London: George Allen and Unwin, 1972.

Mikrut, J. J. *Labor Education Manual.* Columbia: University of Missouri, 1975.

Modic, S. J. "Odds Favor Labor." *Industry Week* (January 3, 1972):s-5.

Nierenberg, Gerard I. *Fundamentals of Negotiating.* New York: Hawthorn Books, 1973.

Okochi, Kasuo. *Workers and Employers in Japan: The Japanese Employment Relations System.* Princeton, N.J.: Princeton University Press, 1974.

Pocock, Pamela. "A Change of Roles." *Personnel Management* 2.3 (March, 1970):40–42.

"Quit the KO, AFL-CIO Asks." *U.S. News and World Report* (August 11, 1975):70.

Taira, Koji. *Economic Development and the Labor Market in Japan.* New York: Columbia University Press, 1970.

Chapter 14

CONDITIONS OF WORK: HEALTH, SAFETY, WORK DAY

LEARNING OBJECTIVES

This chapter introduces several newer developments affecting the work environment and thus all kinds of workers and managers. In particular, the objectives should permit the reader to:

Gain familiarity with the general requirements of the Occupational Safety and Health Act of 1970 (OSHA)

Describe and analyze the potential impact on organizations of newer working hour arrangements

Develop models and approaches to personnel motivation in the light of changes in organizational work conditions

Prescribe personnel planning strategies for human resources based on health, safety, and/or other work condition changes.

KEY TERMS AND CONCEPTS

Occupational Safety and Health Act (OSHA) of 1970
standards, health and safety
compliance
consensus standard
flexible working hours
flexitime
work conditions: a personnel strategy
unannounced inspection

PREVIEW

Health and safety can influence productivity and worker morale. This chapter analyzes OSHA (Occupational Safety and Health Act), one of the most controversial pieces of legislation ever enacted. In particular, we discuss:

1. The origin and coverage of OSHA.
2. The problems of developing health and safety capabilities.
3. Some problems with OSHA.
4. New arrangements in working hours.

Good is a relative term. It depends on what is acceptable. Society's definition of good health, safety, and working conditions has been undergoing continuous change since the start of the Industrial Revolution. What is good, or permissible, or desirable, or acceptable combines a whole complex of social ideals and realities. The ideas of employee and the employer, and the influence of one's family, technological considerations, economic and political considerations—in short, the intermingling of all these forces produces part of what society feels is "acceptable." It may not be everything that could be or should be; it may not be everything we want. But we have to live with it, at least for the present.

The Practicality of Good Health and Safety

According to some employees, "If we didn't gripe about hours or work conditions, we wouldn't be alive—it's just part of working for a living." However, some union leaders and employee associations are less tolerant: "The high accident rate in this industry is disgraceful in the light of proven technologies to remedy this situation, and it's time for companies to correct things—once and for all."

Everyone wants "good" health, safety, and working conditions. They are as important as apple pie, patriotism, and motherhood. Most people agree that it is important to have "good" conditions. But few agree about who should pay for safe and healthy work conditions and the part the government should play in deciding what is good. Despite the laws on the books, including the most controversial one, the Occupational Safety and Health Act of 1970 (OSHA), most people agree about *what* we should have. Few agree on how. OSHA is one of the main themes of this chapter.

Other Elements of Work Conditions

Other attempts have been made to improve working conditions. Managers have tried to make rules and regulations more flexible. The purpose of this has been to give employees some freedom in establishing their work day so that they feel that they exert greater influence over their work.

SCENARIO: AN INCIDENT IN OCCUPATIONAL SAFETY AND HEALTH

Tony Marcello worked in the soldering department of a large manufacturer of electronic equipment and components. The department had been in existence for many years, and although many older techniques had been automated out of existence, the department still had plenty of work.

One night at the dinner table, Tony was reading *The Evening Bulletin* and noticed an article on the front page about health and safety: "Major Industrial Firm Cited for OSHA Violations." After reading the headline of the article to his wife Tony said, "They probably got what they deserved—these guys never take care of that safety stuff until somebody gets hurt—or killed."

When Tony was at work the following day he took his usual coffee break at 10 A.M. with a friend and mentioned the health article. Tony asked his friend Jimmy, "What is this OSHA business?" Jimmy, who considered himself well informed, responded to Tony:

Jimmy: Wow! You're really stupid. Congress passes a law to protect us workers and you don't even know about it—all you have to do is complain and the government inspectors are out on these guys.

Tony: You mean all we have to do is call up these OSHA guys, and the managers have to correct it?

Jimmy: That's about it—of course it's got to be legitimate. But we can really make these bosses dance if we want to.

Tony: How about our soldering room?

Jimmy: What about it?

Tony: You know—for years we've complained about the fumes, and they've done nothing about it.

Jimmy: Hey Tony—you're right.

Tony: Who do I call?

An employee complaint was formally registered with OSHA offices regarding "excess and potentially dangerous fumes in the soldering department—in direct violation of OSHA standards."

An OSHA inspector made an unannounced inspection of the plant. In part, the report prepared by the OSHA inspector indicated that "the complaint concerning soldering fumes was largely unjustified—the company maintains adequate ventilation equipment. However, I found a number of electrical outlets in the plant which do not conform to our electrical outlet standards. Therefore I am recommending that a citation be issued for these electrical violations."

Comments on the Scenario

Potency of the legislation.   The reaction in the plant gives an idea of the power of the OSHA legislation. First, the awareness of the act and some of its general provisions had sifted down to the work floor and into the consciousness of some workers. Workers know when complaints can be filed by a worker. But this was no ordinary dead end, where complaints are registered and go into the wastebasket. Apparently the nature of the complaint suggested a violation of a standard described in the legislation. The fact that this was an *action system* was revealed by the appearance of the OSHA inspector for an unannounced inspection of the production facilities. Here was a government inspector who had the right to actually come into a private enterprise plant and conduct the inspection.

OSHA's power was also revealed by the nature of the complaint that was eventually issued against the company. The OSHA citation (electrical hazard) was not for the "hazardous condition" that was the basis for Tony's initial complaint (fumes in soldering department). Consequently, the ability of a worker to initiate action by a powerful agency, the apparent scope of OSHA's coverage, and the idea of an unannounced visit make for a lively new dimension in the work world. Understandably, much controversy has swirled about OSHA and its provisions.

The original complaint.   A final note concerns the original complaint about fumes in the soldering department. Tony's complaint about these dangers may have been a legitimate concern about a health hazard, but the company had provided equipment that, in the light of existing practices, was appropriate for the situation. There are lingering problems here. Some work conditions pose continuing health hazards, yet an organization may be able to do little about it because the technology needed to correct these problems isn't available or is extremely expensive. These problems pose some basic, tough philosophical (and economic) questions: How far should an organization go? These matters are certain to be subjects of growing discussion in future years.

THE OCCUPATIONAL SAFETY AND HEALTH ACT (OSHA)

OSHA legislation has had an enormous impact on commerce and industry in this country. It has affected three out of four workers in American industry and organizational practices in about 5 million firms. Because it touches on so many organizations' internal practices, it has created controversy among all sorts of employers and employees. The intensive lobbying efforts of the AFL-CIO and other major union groups were largely responsible for the legislation, which sought to reduce on-the-job illness, sickness, and death of "shocking proportions."

Scope and major issues.   The legislation has sought to make the workplace virtually free of hazards. Some people believe that the law applies primarily to manufacturing or processing firms that have large amounts of equipment. This simply isn't true. Banks, insurance firms, offices, hospitals, and professional associations are frequently as concerned as their manufacturing cousins about OSHA requirements.

OSHA requirements—housekeeping and the house.   In general, OSHA requirements are an attempt at keeping the house in order and at keeping the house itself intact. A number of housekeeping provisions outlaw specific kinds of arrangements that may present health and safety hazards: organizations must keep areas uncluttered, clean, etc. However, some of the health and safety standards also require changes in equipment, processes, and procedures. These structural changes in the house itself can be serious matters. They can require investment to modify or replace equipment, processes, and building structures. Needless to say, this can be very expensive.

Authorization.   The law established and authorized the Occupational Safety and Health Administration to set up federal regulations and standards covering health and safety for virtually all business activities in the country. In theory, compliance was to be "voluntary," with simply an occasional poke or two provided by the

OSHA system of random inspections. Occasionally OSHA might impose a penalty or fine for serious violations.

So much for theory. Right from the beginning, an adversary relationship emerged. OSHA's lawyers interpreted the law's provisions to mean that if managers asked for on-site advice, they were subject to an official examination and possible penalty. In short, it became dangerous even to ask for advice or an opinion from an OSHA official. Efforts to improve this distasteful situation were underway in the mid-1970s, and the outlook for revision to permit on-site consultative visits without penalty is promising.

The complaints. It didn't take long for the controversy and complaints to start. Much of the initial wave of complaints had to do with the highly technical language and possible interpretations of its provisions. Second, qualification for coverage—"Is my business affected by OSHA?"—was cloudy. When questions were asked, still more confusion resulted. Third, many business persons felt that the cost of compliance was ridiculously high.

Unfortunately much of the big picture of controversial legislation like OSHA can get bypassed by small picture gripes and complaints. Yet this is a reality to be faced. Congressional committees and congressmen generated all kinds of anecdotes and tales that were widely circulated in the media. These stories added to the boiling controversy. For example:

> "One OSHA requirement is for fire extinguishers to be at eye level, but at whose eye level?"

> "It is incredible. . . . that hundreds of thousands of taxpayers' dollars go to finance government emloyees. . . . who pontificate the fact that there must be coat hooks in toilet stalls" (*Akron Beacon Journal,* 25 August 1974).

The provisions in brief. The OSHA legislation and descriptive literature have grown so large that only a few highlights can be presented. Yet the legislation is so important, called by some a "safety and health bill of rights for the worker," that some attention to its specifics is warranted. OSHA regulations cover every employer "engaged in a business affecting commerce who has employees." Public employees (federal, state and local) are excluded from the general provisions, but other specific provisions cover them.

OSHA is the administrative responsibility of the Department of Labor. However, administration is the joint responsibility of the secretaries of Labor and of Health, Education, and Welfare. Cases involving alleged violations, corrective orders, and determination of penalties are heard and reviewed by the Occupational Safety and Health Review Commission.

Standards. The heart of the OSHA enforcement program is health and safety standards, which establish the basis of comparison used by investigators. Standards that apply to all industry or particular industries or types of work have been developed (Guenther, 1972). Thus in some instances 1) *all employees* may be affected, or 2) *all employees in a particular industry,* or 3) only *particular types of employees and employment.* The safety and health standards are defined as those "practices, means, methods, operations, or processes, reasonably necessary or appropriate to provide safe and healthful employment and places of employment." This general doctrine is backed up by highly specific standards such as "Aisles and passageways shall be kept clear and in good repair with no obstruction across or in aisles that could create a hazard." With such a broad view of health and safety, it is no wonder that OSHA has affected so many companies, employees, and practices.

Setting standards. Three different approaches are permitted under the legislation:

1. Initiation of standards by the secretary of labor (Department of Labor) or in response to petitions from "interested parties."
2. Interpretation of any existing federal standard or in conjunction with a national "consensus standard." Consensus standards are agreed-upon standards as issued by the National Fire Protection Association or the American National Standards Institute. They require no administrative rule-making process (Guenther, 1972).
3. Issue of temporary or emergency standards where workers may be in "grave" danger.

Enforcement and variations. Who, precisely, are the people who enforce this controversial legislation? OSHA compliance officers include engineers, industrial hygienists, and specially trained inspectors. They are the key to enforcement of standards. They make inspections of industries that (historically) have high accident rates. They choose specific companies by random selection, in response to worker complaints, and in connection with serious accidents that have taken place.

Compliance officers can't be "unduly delayed" when they are investigating an establishment or questioning its managers. Representatives of the employer *and* employees are entitled to accompany the inspector. Where violations are noted, the compliance officer makes a report and issues a citation. Citations must be posted for a prescribed length of time at or near the point of the violation. The public relations effects of these tactics are obvious and potent. Penalties may also be assessed depending on the specifics of the situation.

Variances. An employer can get a temporary variance if it can be shown that there has not been enough time to comply or that a plan is already being developed. If alternative safety measures that are not specified in the standard are employed, a *permanent variance* may be granted.

Developing a health-safety capability. Passing an act is one thing; administering it can be something quite different. One of OSHA's main administrative problems has been the inability to enforce rulings. First, health and safety statistics for the most part have been lacking. Second, there was a severe shortage of experts.

Several programs were launched to remedy these deficiencies, including the establishment of schools and regional training centers. These programs were quite effective in strengthening the enforcement of OSHA, yet much remains to be done in this area.

The five-year experience: 1970–75. OSHA's training programs for new compliance inspectors and officials have made considerable progress. A national training institute was established in Rosemont, Illinois. The institute provided training for almost 7,900 people in a three-and-one-half-year period (*Training*, July 1975). Courses and programs also were started at community colleges, university extension campuses, and with various societies.

Controversy and complaints about OSHA still abound. The cost of compliance, illogical interpretations, red tape, complexity, and the adversary position of OSHA inspectors have caused many of the complaints. Also, business people complain about OSHA being staffed with "labor-union sympathizers" (*U.S. News and World Report,* November 24, 1975).

In all fairness, OSHA has tried to clean its own house, but progress has been slow and the lobbying and political pressures from all sides have been enormous. OSHA directors are trying to reduce the adversary role of its inspectors by providing more counsel and by modifying its penalty structure by eliminating minor items, or providing exemptions for equipment that has already been installed (*U.S. News and World Report,* November 24, 1975).

NEW ARRANGEMENTS IN WORKING HOURS: FLEXITIME

Permitting employees to adjust their own work hours is a rather recent development in the United States. Although a few U.S. organizations have experimented with these programs for the past ten years, most of the experiments with variable work hours came from West Germany during the mid-1960s. These programs deserve closer attention.

What is it? The term *flexible working hours* is deceptively simple. It actually describes several different kinds of working arrangements. A "flexitime" program is an arrangement that permits the employee to decide when he works given the total hours remain constant (e.g., eight-hour day). (Programs that reduce total time worked go beyond the basic flexitime concept. We have excluded them from our discussion.)

Flexitime programs can be quite complex. The specific kind of program used depends on different ideas of 1) what time period is to constitute the work period, and 2) which hours within the work period are to be considered variable. Exhibit 14–1 gives three examples of possible flexitime programs. All of the following arrangements have actually been used in particular companies. These arrangements are based on a forty hour work week to simplify the illustration.

The major variable in these flexitime arrangements is the relevant work period—the day, week, and month. The plans have both *fixed and flexible* elements: some work hours or starting times are considered mandatory for everybody

EXHIBIT 14–1 Examples of Flexible Work Week Arrangements

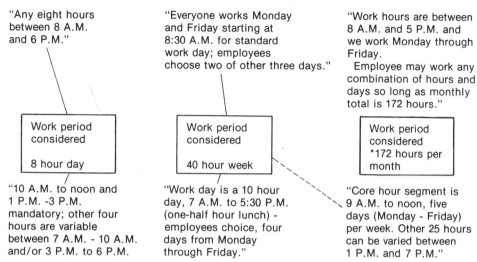

"Any eight hours between 8 A.M. and 6 P.M."

"Everyone works Monday and Friday starting at 8:30 A.M. for standard work day; employees choose two of other three days."

"Work hours are between 8 A.M. and 5 P.M. and we work Monday through Friday.
Employee may work any combination of hours and days so long as monthly total is 172 hours."

Work period considered	Work period considered	Work period considered
8 hour day	40 hour week	*172 hours per month

"10 A.M. to noon and 1 P.M. -3 P.M. mandatory; other four hours are variable between 7 A.M. - 10 A.M. and/or 3 P.M. to 6 P.M.

"Work day is a 10 hour day, 7 A.M. to 5:30 P.M. (one-half hour lunch) - employees choice, four days from Monday through Friday."

"Core hour segment is 9 A.M. to noon, five days (Monday - Friday) per week. Other 25 hours can be varied between 1 P.M. and 7 P.M."

*Note: 4.3 weeks/month 40 hours/week = 172 hours.

because of customer hours, customary business hours, or work load. Within these limitations, an employee can choose starting time, hours of the day, days of the week, etc. Also, some plans use the *work month* as the basic work period. Within this framework employees can carry hours over from week to week as long as they work 172 hours during the month.

Why the variations?   Some of the reasons for variation in working hours should already be clear. Customer habits or general business needs make this kind of flexibility attractive. Regional or local business patterns sometimes encourage the approach. In some organizations, especially manufacturing or process plants with major capital investments in equipment or processes that can't be shut down, flexitime is greatly restricted.

Why consider flexible work periods?   Obviously, companies haven't adopted flexible work schedules purely to benefit employees. One of the first companies in West Germany to initiate a flexitime arrangement was an aerospace company (around 1967). It did so for purely pragmatic reasons. Traffic congestion around the plant caused many employees to arrive late for work. There was considerable loss of production time. The tight labor market in West Germany ruled out the possibility of severe discipline (layoffs or firing). The possible introduction of a flexible work hour arrangement was viewed with great skepticism, but few of the dire predictions materialized (Elbing, 1974). The amount of employee sick days and tardiness decreased.

In general the experience has been quite good. According to a 1973 company survey by the German Personnel Management Association, companies indicated that the work environment, the situation with paid absences, and individual self-adjustment have improved. Other important benefits may be reduced overtime, increased productivity, and better results in recruiting. Experts have estimated that 15 to 20 percent of all workers in Switzerland were on a flexitime arrangement (*Business Week,* October 7, 1972) in the early 1970s.

In the United States, the popular press has accorded considerable space to several well-known companies, such as Scott Paper, Sun Oil, Hewlett-Packard (Elbing, 1974) and Control Data (*Nation's Business,* September 1973), that have adopted these plans.

The motivational value of flexitime.   In many instances management has introduced flexible work plans at the suggestion of its employees. Thus right from the start, management was able to get employees to identify with the program. Under these circumstances, employees were committed to giving the program a fair test. This wasn't something management had dreamed up that employees would look at suspiciously. Management and labor were on the same side.

A flexible work period program can give employees a sense of control over their work. The opportunity to exercise some range of personal choice is real, and the feeling of self-control can realistically help an employee identify with his work. Here is a specific means to join important individual and organization objectives. In these programs, employees are given the degrees of freedom and range of choices necessary to demonstrate responsible action. If employees do not act responsibly, the program fails, so employees can best reach their goals by helping the organization reach its goals (see Exhibit 13–2, p. 392). Responsible action on the part of the employee boosts the interests of the organization and at the same time advances those of the individual.

PERSONNEL STRATEGIES: WORK CONDITIONS

Newer Approaches

Human resource management has encouraged personnel managers to approach legislation such as OSHA in imaginative ways. The key questions to be asked are:

1. Should an organization assume a passive role in simply seeking to comply with the letter of the law?
2. Can conformity to legal requirements affecting health, safety, and work conditions be viewed as potential benefits rather than costs in seeking to achieve the purposes of the organization and individual?

The issue involves alternative strategies for personnel management where managers can identify the real costs and benefits attached to different courses of action.

Historically, many organizations have complied with legislation and regulations only when they had to do so. The experiences of the past forty years with wages, hours, work conditions, equal employment, and collective bargaining make this virtually undeniable. And there is nothing necessarily wrong with this position. After all, why should an organization spend the money when it doesn't have to or install a procedure simply because it might be desired? However, years of behavioral research suggest some new answers. Perhaps there are *good, sound economic as well as human reasons for an organization to take aggressive leadership in improving work conditions prior to any legalistic requirements.*

The purpose of a human resource model is to plan approaches like those found for many years in finance, production, and marketing. Competent personnel planning and programming of activities can take place only when they can be justified to officials and policymakers. Admittedly the evidence may not be as tight or as numbers oriented as it is for other areas, yet personnel activities can be every bit as productive. Behavioral research already discussed in previous chapters has indicated that organizations can better achieve their performance objectives when employees are actively involved.

Flexible Work Period—A Management Strategy

Not all organizations can use the same kind of program, but the one we present here will show what the possible uses and benefits of flexitime are. In some cases, flexitime is not feasible, simply because some managers cannot philosophically accept their role in this kind of arrangement. Evidence of good faith and developing a good working relationship with employees are necessary before flexitime can be successfully introduced.

Flexitime can be viewed as a deliberate management strategy to gain employee involvement and more closely align individual and organization goals. It is just one of a wide range of options organizations may use. Other options may involve vacation schedules, cars, contests, insurance options, etc. Exhibit 14–2 serves a dual purpose: it illustrates the possible application of a specific personnel strategy (flexitime) and presents a format for exploring other personnel strategies and how they influence employees. More importantly, the exhibit shows how organizations can make constructive changes in work conditions instead of following the path of least resistance.

Motivational Opportunities

A manager can use health and safety to motivate workers in many ways. Some are fairly obvious; others are quite subtle. Let's briefly recount the necessary conditions for dealing with or increasing employee motivation:

1. Decrease the sense of alienation; that is, increase identification with the organization's purposes.
2. Enlarge a worker's sense of control over his work and/or work space.
3. Make work itself more meaningful.
4. Provide opportunities for developing satisfying social relationships.
5. Help build a sense of self-worth.
6. Support approaches leading to individual recognition and achievement.
7. Provide feedback so that a person can judge progress and need.

EXHIBIT 14–2   Adjustment of Work Conditions as an Organization-Personnel Strategy

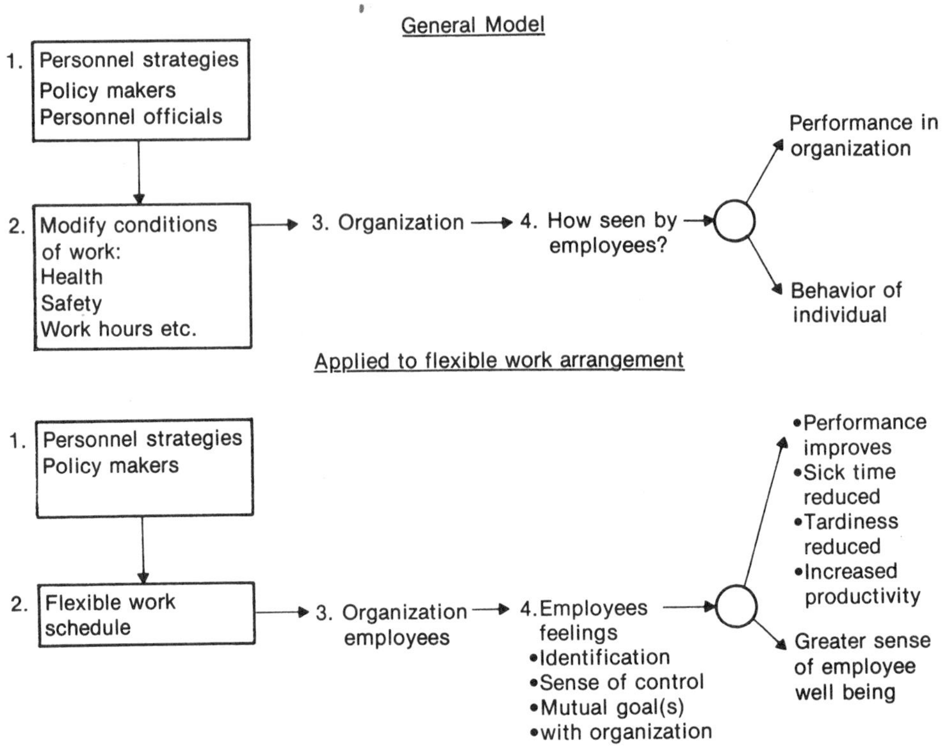

General Model

Applied to flexible work arrangement

Organization leadership.   Organizations can tap important employee motivation by taking the lead in occupational health and safety matters. First of all, managers should view this type of legislation as inevitable and, second, they should realize that it will become even more comprehensive in the future. But in addition to resigning oneself to fate, a manager can take several positive steps.

The general model depicted in Exhibit 14–2 indicates that various changes in work conditions (2) can be introduced as conscious designs (1). Legislative regulations such as OSHA need not be seen as a curse. Management can make the first move to let employees know that it cares about employee welfare and well-being. If an organization makes and communicates honest efforts to its employees, it can start to establish a high degree of employee loyalty (3).

Employee commitment.   The key to long-term success usually involves employee commitment. An organization can get this kind of commitment if employees feel they have some control over their work—that they have a say. If an organization plans well, it will be able to see positive results (5).

Adversary and cooperative relationships.   If an organization grudgingly complies with the minimal requirements of laws, it will simply emphasize the adversary relationship of management versus employee. If an organization acts on its own, without pressure from the government or outside groups (e.g., in minority employment), it will have taken the first step in a positive program. Second, an organization must thoughtfully communicate its intentions and concerns. This will alert employees to changes and the reasons for them. Third, the results of these programs (feedback) should provide clear evidence of accomplishment.

More than security. At first glance health and safety programming appears to be a response only to Maslow's theory of individual safety or security needs. Even if this were the only motivation, it is important—in many cases individuals place high priority on security. But management's message can cut a lot deeper than this. Employees will interpret an honest attempt to improve health and safety as a sign that management is really concerned. In an era of rising expectations, a well planned health-safety program can bring quite positive results.

SUMMARY

This chapter has dealt with the improvement of the work environment, especially the health-safety aspects of work conditions. Government legislation in this area is not new. It goes back over thirty years. What is new is the fact that legislation like OSHA and arrangements like flexitime are modern developments that can be traced to a whole new social ethic of bettering the world of work. Regulatory legislation concerning hours, work conditions, and the like which have been in force for many years in industry were not discussed in this chapter. These developments have assumed the maintenance type of personnel activities.

OSHA was described as very comprehensive. Its provisions touch the housekeeping ways of organizations as well as needed changes in all kinds of equipment, process, and techniques to establish "safe and healthful conditions." The core of enforcement are the standards, unannounced inspections, opportunity for employee-initiated complaints, and enforcement machinery, including the assignment of penalties. Both the provisions and techniques of OSHA enforcement have resulted in great controversy. It appears likely that some important changes will be made in both areas.

Flexitime was described as a new type of management action designed to improve employee relations, work performance, and individual satisfaction. Modifications in work hour scheduling can provide potent motivational benefits for organization and individual.

Finally, this chapter has sought to establish a human resource viewpoint and interpretation for health, safety, and work condition programs. At issue here is that of personnel approaching these application areas as part of a strategic plan for bettering organizational performance and the lot of its members. Human resource planning and programming notions, laced with motivational concepts, were set out as growing in importance as overall organizational strategies for survival, renewal, and growth.

This chapter concludes the descriptions in this and previous sections of personnel organization and concepts, and techniques for dealing with human resources. Section 6 will introduce and develop some of the dynamic qualities of personnel management in establishing the bases for growth of individuals and organizations.

DISCUSSION QUESTIONS

1. What distinguishes the housekeeping provisions of OSHA from more basic provisions regarding equipment, processes, and procedures? Provide some simple examples of each.

2. How broad is OSHA coverage regarding organizations and employees?

3. What are the key enforcement provisions of OSHA?

4. What are your views on unannounced inspections? Defend your views.

5. Do you feel that changes are needed in OSHA strategies? Why?

6. Suggest some examples of situations or organizations where flexitime would be
   a) feasible
   b) difficult to install.

7. Defend or attack the proposition: Flexitime arrangements represent a powerful new tool for employee motivation.

8. A large company recently announced that it was going to take the next step in its flexitime program for its administrative offices. This large manufacturer of business equipment removed all time clocks and indicated that in the future all office personnel would fill out their own time cards. What are your views on this approach? Be sure to clarify any assumptions you have made.

9. The company described in question 8 was visited by a small team of management professors from a local university. These professors were especially interested in the motivational aspects of the flexitime program and the elimination of time clocks. Propose a model and define the assumptions under which the company program could be considered
   a. successful
   b. unsuccessful.
Diagram each situation.

10. In January 1976, a legislative subcommittee was debating the merits of the OSHA's enforcement program and the adversary relationship that had grown between OSHA inspectors and organizations.
   The legislative committee was going to take testimony on a proposal to modify one of the key interpretations of the legislation. A proposal was made to permit inspectors to visit with organizations on an unofficial basis and to provide advice regarding practices or situations that might be in violation of OSHA standards. Take the role of the following parties, clarify your assumptions, and debate or write an argument for:
   a. union officials
   b. National Association of Manufacturers (owners or officials)
   c. representatives of the American Medical Association.

BIBLIOGRAPHY

"Business May Win Easing of U.S. Job Safety Law." *Akron Beacon Journal* (25 August 1974):F13.

Elbing, A. O. et al. "Flexible Working Time: It's About Time." *Harvard Business Review* 1 (January, February 1974):19.

"Europle Likes Flexitime Work." *Business Week* (October 7, 1972):80.

Guenther, George C. "The Significance of the Occupational Safety and Health Act to the Workers in the United States." *International Labor Review* 1.09 (January 1972):59–67.

Hedges, J. N. "New Patterns for Working Time." *Monthly Labor Review* 96 (February 1973):3–8.

Hellriegel, Donald. "The Four Day Workweek: A Review and Assessment." *MSU Business Topics* 20.2 (Spring 1972):39–48.

Jenkins, David. *Job Power*. New York: Doubleday, 1973.

McGregor, Douglas. *The Human Side of Enterprise*. New York: McGraw-Hill, 1960: especially 33–67.

"Pick Your Hours, Experiment in Germany." *Time* (July 19, 1971).

"Picking Your Own Working Time." *Nation's Business* (September 1973):71–73.

"Protecting People on the Job: ABC's of a Controversial Law." *U.S. News and World Report* (November 24, 1975):61–71.

"OSHA: Five Years Later." *Training* (July 1975):21–25.

*

Section
Six

PREPARING THE INDIVIDUAL AND ORGANIZATION FOR GROWTH AND/OR CHANGE

*

Chapter 15

PERSONNEL MANAGEMENT INFORMATION SYSTEMS

LEARNING OBJECTIVES

After studying this chapter, the reader should be able to:

Develop an appreciation for the wide gaps that exist among existing personnel methods, human needs in organizations, and available computer technology

Understand that computer technology can be an important tool for humanizing and enriching jobs rather than an encroachment on individual privacy

Gain insight into the analysis, design, and evaluation methods for personnel information systems as they apply to decision making and reporting

Develop the ability to apply design and evaluative principles to on-going personnel systems.

KEY TERMS AND CONCEPTS

information system
time-sharing
data base
system design
measures of systems effectiveness
integrated system
feedback

skills inventory
decision outputs
data/information
information files
remote access
random access update and inquiry

PREVIEW

Twentieth-century technology has revolutionized the business world. The need for information is greater than ever. In this chapter we will describe some of the new developments in information systems, including:

1. The need for and uses of computers in personnel management.
2. The design of a personnel management information system (PMIS).
3. New uses of the PMIS concept.
4. The implications of information systems for future personnel development.

COMPUTERS FOR PERSONNEL MANAGEMENT

Technological Change and the Personnel Function

Advancing computer technology and the availability of more sophisticated tools of analysis have made many traditional approaches to personnel management somewhat out-dated. Unfortunately, there is a large gap between available technology and general personnel practices. While many personnel departments are becoming increasingly concerned with developing information for decision making, few of them are using computers. Current personnel applications of computers include payroll processing, record keeping, and limited information on skills. But most personnel directors have done little to provide usable information to line managers for better management of human resources. Of course, there are exceptions such as Continental Bank (data base for career planning), Standard Oil of Indiana (manpower projections), and Illinois Bell Telephone (data base for personnel assignment), but unfortunately these are the exceptions rather than the rule.

In this chapter we will explain how to design a personnel management information system and put it into use to humanize and enrich both jobs and people. Organizations need better human resource planning and control systems and the technology necessary to put them into practice. There is no reason to feel that computer technology must necessarily debase the individual and society. Personnel departments can take the lead in reaching important human goals using available technology.

Personnel Management Information Systems: An Overview

Every personnel department needs good information to make good decisions—or at least to avoid making really bad ones. An information system enables a manager to get information quickly and easily. Exhibits 15–1 and 15–2 illustrate such a system. Basic data inputs are environmental (labor market trends, government regulations), biographical (address, age, marital status, dependents, test scores, references, etc.), skills, educational background, employment experience, significant achievements, work and geographical preferences, and personal goals. These data are available in most organizations, but they usually are spread throughout several departments and difficult to locate. For example, in a study within the IBM Corporation, it was found that over 2,000 elements of personnel data were being maintained, but that in fact there were only 145 unique elements. The rest were repetitions (Bricker, 1970). In another study of fifteen large companies, it was found that between 145 and 160 items were needed to accurately describe an employee.

As is indicated in Exhibits 15–1 and 15–2, there are limitations to the kind of data that can be introduced into the system. Antidiscrimination laws may prevent the storage of information about race, creed, and, maybe in the future, age and sex. Labor market conditions and corporate policies will also limit uses of data in the system. During a period of an expanding economy, labor is difficult

EXHIBIT 15-1 Broad Perspective on Personnel Management Information Systems

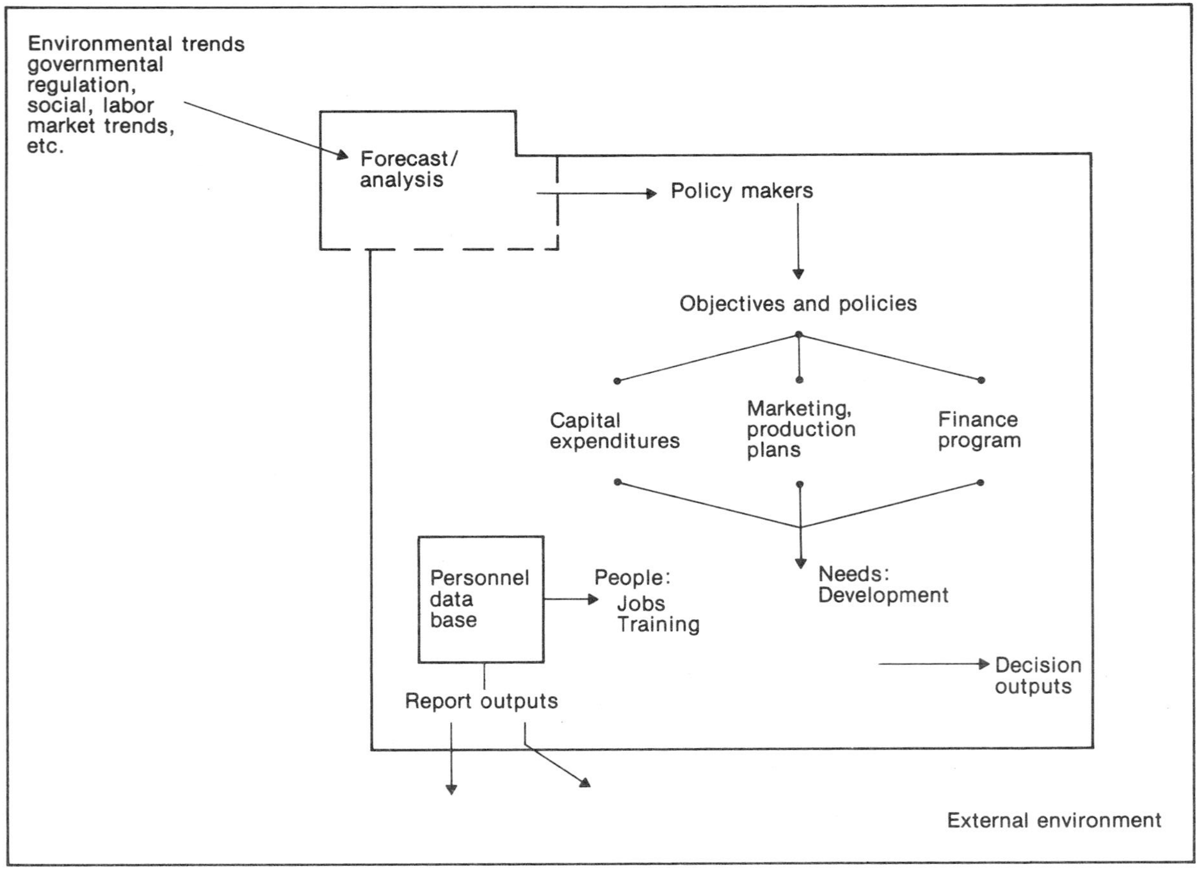

Environmental trends governmental regulation, social, labor market trends, etc.

Forecast/analysis

Policy makers

Objectives and policies

Capital expenditures

Marketing, production plans

Finance program

Needs: Development

People: Jobs Training

Personnel data base

Report outputs

Decision outputs

External environment

EXHIBIT 15-2 Personnel Data for Decision Making: Utilizing a Personnel Information System

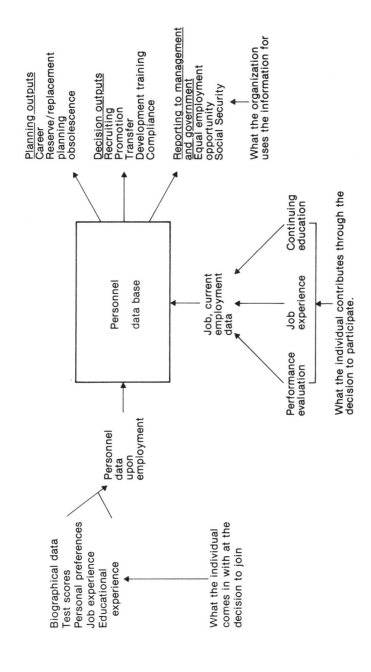

431

to locate, which means that a manager may have to change selection ratios (i.e., ratio of those hired to those interviewed). Once the data are centrally stored, however, the manager can use mathematical models to develop more efficient recruiting plans, manpower forecasts, placement policies, promotion criteria, and so forth.

Anatomy of PMIS: A Case of Failure

Several organizations had disappointing experiences with their early attempts to construct personnel information systems and computerized skills inventories. A very ambitious human resource program begun in 1963 and significantly modified in 1971 by a computer manufacturer provides useful insights into potential problem areas when developing personnel systems (Jabel, 1972). It should be pointed out that the corporation learned much from its early experiences and has since developed a more workable system.

In 1963 the system had several objectives:

1. The provision of information about interests and capabilities of employees
2. Location of personnel for specific vacancies
3. Giving all job candidates equal opportunity
4. Assisting management to plan training programs
5. Analysis of skills required for all corporate positions
6. Improvement of personnel record keeping.

The company published an extensive dictionary containing some 3,300 skills or areas of knowledge related to its operations. Once skills were categorized, other information including foreign language proficiency, extent of knowledge of company products, and management experience was obtained. Then 100,000 employees were asked to volunteer information; the great majority of people supplied what was asked. Programmers and analysts were assigned to the personnel system, which was given complete support by upper and middle level management. Yet, according to Jabel, the system failed.

The problem was "too much and not enough." The original system included 3,300 aspects of human performance; much of this was unnecessary detail and did not contribute to achievement of system objectives. (The company has since reduced the size of its dictionary to 600 skills at about one-tenth the cost.) Analysts learned that employees tend to exaggerate their experiences and skills on a skills questionnaire. Younger employees, thinking that the number of skills they put down would improve their chances for promotion in the future, tended to overstate their skills. Validation of skills data proved to be politically sensitive and expensive. In the final analysis, management decided that a skills inventory could provide only rough screening, that the question of when an employee will be available for transfer is a critical piece of data, and that there must be strong commitment to transferring the most qualified people.

Modern Personnel Systems: More Emphasis on Users' Needs

In the early 1970s many larger organizations began to experiment with *management-oriented* personnel systems, which used terminals and a data base of employee profiles. Formerly, managers resisted computerization because it was expensive to maintain current records on large numbers of employees. Also, employees resisted the invasion of privacy they associated with the computerization of their personal history and work preferences.

Systems analysts now realize that they must reorient their approaches to systems design. Their systems are used by people for people and must first meet the needs of the user rather than the programmer's need for precision or sophisticated programming. As systems become more user oriented, they also become much more defensible and attractive to both managers and employees.

The following approach adopted by a major bank illustrates such a user orientation. Employee records are placed in a direct-access computer file. Managers are provided with three hours of instruction on use of terminals and a simple language they can use to ask questions. Either managers or analysts then write eight to ten statement programs to get the information into the computer files. Naturally, users must have the proper password and identification numbers:

```
10  File personnel
20  For salary <15,000
30  And education >16
40  Print last:name
50  Print job:title
60  Print performance:index
70  Next
80  End
 *  Run
```

In a few seconds the person querying the file has the last names and performance reviews (indexes) of all employees who earn less than $15,000 but have more than 16 years of education. From this point it is easy for the manager to use statistical models to make wage and salary analyses. For example, a manager might wish to know if there is a significant difference between the salaries of males and females in a given area, an answer easily and quickly supplied through the personnel information system.

Personnel Systems and the Federal Government

Several experimental projects are being funded by the federal government in an attempt to introduce computer-supported personnel systems into government agencies. These efforts have been supported largely by grants from the U.S. Civil Service Commission under the Intergovernmental Personnel Act and from the

Urban Information Systems Interagency Committee in the Department of Housing and Urban Development. Unfortunately, most of the systems are specialized and designed to meet special problems of the moment (e.g., EEO questions) without concern for an overall design (Lee, 1975).

DESIGN OF A PERSONNEL MANAGEMENT INFORMATION SYSTEM

Setting System Objectives

The first step in designing a system is to define its objectives. Personnel managers should set objectives for the following areas: planning, recruiting, selection, evaluation, training, development, and compensation.

Many personnel managers have made common but costly errors when they first approach computers. They fail to set objectives for the system. Instead they merely accumulate as much data as possible to be used if the need ever arises. This method is inefficient; it adds unnecessarily to storage, updating, and search-and-retrieval expense. Instead, the manager should first define the objectives of the system and include data that will help meet them. For example, if a firm wishes to develop a more scientific recruiting strategy, the manager might include the following kinds of data: name of original recruiter and subsequent interviewers, source of contact, performance of employees after being recruited, number and characteristics of applicants who accept jobs versus those who reject offers, and the number and type of skills required by the organization's manpower plan.

The following set of objectives might be used by a personnel organization. This set is not meant to be comprehensive, but it should serve as a useful practical example.

1. *Human resource planning objectives.* To determine the number and types of personnel required for each department for the next year, the next three years, and the next five years.

2. *Recruiting objectives.*
   a. To generate a minimum of ten applicants for each open scientific and managerial position (salary level $14,000 and above) and five applicants for each technical, clerical, and skilled labor position (salary level below $14,000).
   b. To maintain the recruiting cost per hire between $800 and $1,000 for salary level $14,000 and above, and $200 to $300 on the average for salary level below $14,000.

3. *Selection objectives.*
   a. To bring those personnel into the organization who have the highest probability of success where success is defined as:
      1) performance appraisal score (index score) of .75 or above
      2) retention for five years within the organization. (Figures are hypothetical; in practice they will depend on size of the firm, type of industry, labor supply, etc.)

b. To place 90 percent of all employees in one of their top three specified job preferences.

4. *Development and training objectives.*

To provide a minimum of 40 hours of training per year for all personnel who demonstrate a need (e.g., performance indexes between .25 and .75) and 60 hours for those who demonstrate a potential for higher positions (e.g., performance indexes greater than .75).

5. *Performance evaluation objectives.*

To objectively and reliably evaluate each employee at least once every year, or after six months in a position if a transfer has been made to a new position.

6. *Compensation subsystem objectives.*

a. To provide merit increases to all those who show significant improvement or potential (e.g., greater than 5 percent increase in overall performance index, or two standard deviations above the mean for a particular work group).

b. To maintain wage levels within 7 percent of prescribed industry standards across all departments for all hourly workers.

Human Resource Data Base

A personnel information system requires current biographical data as well as educational, skills performance, and work preference data. We have already mentioned, in a general way, why this is important. We will be a little more specific here. A human resource file does away with the need to spend thousands of dollars on recruiting specialists. Existing personnel who have various kinds and combinations of skills can immediately be identified as specific needs arise. Computerized inventories can be especially helpful for situations like government contracts, where an employer-contractor must provide a detailed analysis of human resource capabilities. The system can also improve the development of personnel by identifying potential strengths and weaknesses and provide better direction for training and self-development programs.

A carefully prepared data base can be used as the starting point for long-range personnel planning and development by providing exact definitions of the aptitudes and abilities the organization has and needs. It can be used to evaluate the growth potential of the present work force, help to identify group strengths, and help to plan future recruiting strategies. It may uncover imbalances (e.g., understaffing) that can cause future personnel problems throughout the organization. Most importantly, management can use the system as a motivating device. It tells employees that the organization has a systematic approach to personnel management and is eager to develop each person to his or her full potential.

It is evident that there is little uniformity in the selection, development, and use of personnel data, even though certain basic data are needed by all organizations. The following are types of files in common use:

Payroll (salary, hourly, and special executive)

Benefits (e.g., deferred compensation and stock options)

Personnel descriptive data and work history

Training and education

Performance appraisal

Foreign service and foreign language competence

Skills inventory

Management development information

Labor reporting

Timekeeping

Absences

Vacation scheduling

Medical data

Attitude survey information

Accession/separation

Some personnel data files contain only biographical data, while others include work history, training and education, performance appraisal data, and language abilities. The combinations are numerous.

Once the initial expenditure and effort have been made to capture the data needed for the required reports, a matrix sheet may be used to display the data elements and the reports on which they appear (see Figure 15–3). The matrix sheet can also be used to determine the cost of present reports or to estimate the cost of future reports.

What Managers Can Expect from a PMIS

What kind of decision-making and record-keeping help should a user expect from a personnel management information system? In this section we will provide specific examples of what should be expected, although the illustrations are only a beginning. Creative managers will undoubtedly find other uses.

All data entered in the system should automatically be edited and verified. Then, if an employee changes jobs, the system should automatically provide an updated job title and salary data relevant to the new job code. Wide variations in salary among individuals working in similar jobs should automatically be brought to the attention of the salary administrator. Scheduled performance and salary review dates and budget data should be generated. Available manpower and open positions can be balanced against each unit's personnel budget. Conditions specified in labor contracts, such as bumping routines (displacement of people in one department by those in another), seniority privileges, and benefits based on wage increases or calendar dates, should be provided by the system.

Personnel systems should be designed to provide answers to the following types of questions:

EXHIBIT 15–3   Matrix for Determining Cost of Personnel Reports

Report name / Employee Information Items	Department Lists	New Hires	Terminations	EEO Reports	Skills Lists	Payroll Lists	Insurance Roster	Promotability	Performance	
1. Employee number										
2. Check sort										
3. Payroll type										
4. Employee class										
5. Status										
6. Turnover or terminating date										
7. Terminating type										
8. Location state										
9. Location city										
10. Current labor grade										
11. Nonhourly pay-period rate										
12. Shift										
13. Department number										
14. Federal income tax code										
15. Current overtime rate										
16. Current hourly rate										
17. Monthly salary										
18. Life insurance deduction amount										
19. United fund deduction amount										

1. How much will it cost over the next four years to increase vacation benefits if the vacation allowance is extended one additional week for employees with twenty years instead of twenty-five years of experience?

2. How many employees have not had a raise in the past twelve months and how does that number correlate with the last two performance evaluations?

3. What specific jobs will become available over the next five years due to retirement?

4. Where can four mechanical engineers be found in the company who would be available for temporary assignment overseas, who have no dependents, and who have worked on the F4H engine?

According to Seamans (1973), an effective computerized system must combine the traditional autobiographical skills inventory with an individualized development plan that reflects a management by objectives approach. Then the manager can use computer retrieval techniques to analyze individual goals and create departmental or divisional goals. An organization can plan its projects more realistically when it knows its existing skills. Seamans states that "implementation of a total human resource system that combines skills of employees with individual development plans will enable an organization to more effectively identify its human resource assets and invest in their expansion and maintenance."

Measuring the Effectiveness of a Personnel System

Every system has several levels of objectives, and each level should be used to measure a system's effectiveness. The simplest way to measure effectiveness is to begin at the first level with the individual employee. Managers then can relate individual performance figures with other personnel system objectives. This method provides a straightforward, integrated approach to personnel management. Perhaps a few examples will help to clarify this somewhat optimistic assertion.

If the annual performance evaluation process identifies a group of executives who are weak in the areas of planning, communication, and motivation of subordinates and if the personnel manager can involve them in a development program covering these areas, a later performance review should indicate improvement. If the executives do not improve, the development program (or evaluation method) itself may need improvement because it, *not* the executives, is not working well.

Another example is "new blood." If new employees perform significantly better than the remainder of the work force and if other factors such as training, incentive systems, and leadership styles have not changed, the recruiting people probably are functioning at a high level of effectiveness.

Individual employee performance is only one variable that can be evaluated. All of the usual personnel-related concerns can be measured and, in turn, used to measure the effectiveness of the system as a whole. Some of the standard measures are employee turnover, absentee rate, number and quality of suggestions from employees, number and type of grievances and arbitration awards, accident and health records, participation in tuition-refund plans, requests for transfers, scrap losses, and trends and comparisons of personnel costs.

Attitude surveys can also be used to evaluate a personnel program. Attitudes can be compared with demographic, performance, skills, and cost data to identify personnel problems. Causal relationships can then be established, enabling decisions that will eliminate the causes of the problems.

Feedback on employee performance is another important source of information for any personnel department. This kind of information lends itself to tracing performance from the bottom to the top of the organization. A manager can evaluate feedback from one employee, then the group, then the department, and so on, to the various systems in the organization. Exhibit 15–4 provides a set

---

EXHIBIT 15–4   Practical Guidelines and Principles for PMIS Development and Implementation

---

1. Information has value only if it improves the quality of decisions. Masses of information in skills inventories or human resource data banks will not help management make better decisions unless meaningful comparisons, ratios, and trends are provided from which analyses can be made and causality inferred.

2. Emphasis on PMIS must be upon better decisions and not the computer. An effective PMIS permits an organization to match its manpower demands with properly qualified people, to design appropriate training programs, to reward employees equitably, to bargain more effectively with unions, and, in general, to measure the effectiveness of the overall personnel human resource program.

3. Get user and top management involvement and agreement from the very earliest stage of systems analysis.

4. Establish clear-cut objectives and measures of effectiveness for the system (Exhibit 15–5).

5. Skills inventories are useful only in organizations where conditions are right (i.e., managers must be willing to use the inventories; the organization should be large; there should be a high degree of internal mobility, such as in organizations that use project teams; or the government requires the organization to maintain such a system).

6. Changes to the system should be made quickly and accurately.

7. Access should be simple for authorized users (i.e., computer specialists should not be required to get information from the system).

8. Employees should have a clear understanding of all data stored about them and have at least annual opportunity to see and update their personal files.

9. If higher levels of management do not use the system or do not release people for promotion when they are identified, the system will die.

---

of guidelines which can be applied to the design of a personnel information system.

Personnel Management Information Systems and the Right to Privacy

In recent years, concern over potential invasion of privacy has become widespread, and personnel data banks have become only one of the issues. The Federal Privacy Act, passed in 1974, applies to federal agencies and the private companies supplying services to them. By 1975 several states and foreign countries had enacted similar laws, and in 1976 nearly a hundred privacy bills were pending before various state legislatures.

In general, privacy laws cover three main categories: controls on operating procedures, access rights of subjects, and control of use by subjects (Goldstein and Nolan, 1975). Organizations using a PMIS must use several controls, such as keeping a log of the uses of each person's record, taking precautions against natural hazards and other threats to the system. They also must establish procedures for responding to inquiries from individuals about their records and for resolving disputes about the accuracy of such records. An employee may examine his own records, correct any false information, and add a statement to the record if he is not satisfied with the change. Also, employees must be told what the information will be used for when it is collected, and they must have opportunity to refuse to provide it.

Organizations should anticipate problems related to these new regulations. Proper planning will save time, conversion costs, and excessive interference from government agencies. An effective plan should include a statement identifying the potential impact upon privacy for all new personnel systems. The plan should also include a statement about privacy controls (location, access, use, and subject). Employees who handle data should be trained, and employees themselves informed of the organization's plans to protect their privacy.

Time-Sharing and PMIS

As the demands of a personnel system grow, the available devices, programs, and personnel to service the system often lag far behind. One solution has been the use of time-sharing programs. Time-sharing (i.e., using another's computer and consultant) enables an organization to get the information it needs quickly and easily by using "interactive processing" instead of traditional processing methods. Time-sharing also reduces cost and helps to avoid interference with main-line applications as in marketing or production. Cost and accessibility obviously are important considerations. Time-sharing allows personnel departments to get the information they need without conflicting with other departments.

Since the system uses a common data base rather than the more cumbersome method of maintaining separate files for each personnel application, a personnel manager can add, change, and delete records as needed and in a variety of ways (e.g., batch, random access, sequential search).

The time-sharing approach is also quite important for smaller firms that cannot afford their own in-house computers, operations staff, or systems analysts and programmers. In principle, the time-sharing idea can be used whether one has an in-house computer or rents time. By using the computer facilities of an outside service, many of the advantages of data base systems and computerized personnel applications discussed in this chapter can be made cost effective for the small organization (Michaels, 1975). Regardless of the method used, a personnel manager must be careful to analyze and design the computer models and information flows that will meet objectives at the lowest possible cost. A detailed approach to systems analysis and design may be found in Gross and Smith (1976). A sample set of effectiveness criteria is provided in Exhibit 15–5.

Relationship Between Personnel and Other Organization Systems

After the personnel information system has been designed and is in operation, the personnel department can interact with other departments' information systems more easily. Research and development planning, for example, will have better direction if R&D managers have access to the personnel department's technical skills data. R&D planners can know whether the organization has the

---

EXHIBIT 15–5   Effectiveness Criteria for PMIS

Human resource planning
  Number of *un*predicted new jobs opening up within the company
  Deviation between forecasted and actual needs
  Year-to-year improvement in skill balance within total organization

Recruiting
  Source of referrals (newspaper and journal ads, agency, other divisions, etc.)
  Advertising cost per referral
  Advertising cost per hire
  Ratio of offers to acceptances
  Number of offers, acceptances, and rejections per recruiter
  Individual performance indexes of new employees identified by recruiter and source
    of referral

Selection and placement
  Turnover and absentee rates
  Ratio of various application blank scores to performance indexes
  Ratio of psychological test scores to performance indexes
  Physical examination results related to subsequent health records

Training and development
  Training courses attended related to subsequent job performance
  Product and service quality before and after training
  Training costs per employee and employee salary level

Compensation
  Number of employees significantly above or below standard wage and salary rates
  The relationship between merit increases and personal performance
  Consistency of wage patterns among departments and divisions
  Effects of incentive systems on productivity and costs
  Number and types of employees participating in profit sharing plans
  Number and types of employees using recreational facilities, insurance plans, and food
    services provided by the company

---

skills needed for a new project or whether they will have to go outside the organization for new talent, which of course can be quite costly. For instance, research tools such as the morphological box (Smith and Klafehn, 1971) establish relationships between research objectives and available skills.

Computer Data Bases for Personnel Research

The computer has provided inestimable help to personnel research. Personnel data can be used for specific employee problems that were almost impossible to get at in the past. The turnover situation is one example. According to Cleff and Hecht (1971), "It is estimated that workers under 35 change jobs on the average of once in one-and-a-half years, while those over 35 stay on their jobs about twice as long." Furthermore, "In today's labor market, employer after employer has revealed that virtually every business has its own trigger point, that when employment passes a certain level an annual ratio of between 3.5 and 5.0 hires per job is not unusual." It is easy to see that if an organization can lower these figures, it will be able to save a substantial amount of time, effort, and money.

Texas Instruments' computer data bank included some 38,000 employees. The main objective of the bank is to lower turnover. According to Patterson (1971), "With the system, we can produce computer-generated profiles, based on actual records, of the average high-risk employee, who is most likely to leave the company at an early date, and the low-risk employee, who is more likely to justify the company's investment in hiring and training." For example, "In a moment's time . . . we can learn whether graduates of certain high schools do better or worse in our work environment than graduates of other schools or than high school dropouts. By age, by address, by any meaningful category, we can spot both high-risk and low-risk areas." Of course the danger exists that they may turn away some potentially good employees just because they went to the wrong high school.

Eaton Corporation used a data system that separates employees into groups depending on whether they are promotable, not promotable, or promotable after further training (Zimmerman, 1971). While this does not directly attack the problem of turnover, it tends to reduce it somewhat. According to Farris (1972), turnover is positively associated with the perception that turnover will help one's career. This kind of system may tend to cause the employee to feel that he can succeed at Eaton as well as anywhere else, so consequently will not seek other employment.

The Reynolds Tobacco Company has a somewhat different type of system covering some 21,000 blue-collar employees. It is a skills inventory system that selects factory workers for training as technicians as the need arises ("Skills Inventory System," *Data Management*, 1971).

Another area where a personnel data base can be most helpful is in job matching. The personnel department develops a profile for every job within the company and then matches people to those jobs. Cleff and Hecht (1971), spent two-and-a-half years developing a universal language, or common set of variables, that would describe the content of any semi- to low-skilled job in the economy as well as the preferences and past experiences of potential employees. They then found that they could identify the best candidates for a particular job by using job applicant profiles made possible by their universal language. They found that their "experimental validation study . . . developed average people-to-job correlations with four to five times the predictive power of the 'normal' psychological test battery validation with similar work groups."

This type of system has far-reaching potential. It can be useful for student guidance and placement, as well as for matching the hardcore unemployed with jobs they keep—apparently because they find them fulfilling. It might even be feasible to expand a system of this type to plan business-related education. A counselor might develop a profile and then attempt to fit the curriculum to this profile or, in the same vein, to match vocational training classes to industry profiles. In 1976 the federal government announced that it would sponsor a national computer network for person-job matching.

Wittreich and Miner (1971) point out that "the current advance in personnel performance predictive accuracy is based on four independent factors: modern computers, acknowledgement of the unique corporate personality, emergence of a projective/objective test, and development of a selection procedure that is highly responsive to change." Our feeling is that all of these factors can be aided through the use of carefully designed, computer-assisted personnel data systems.

INNOVATIVE EXTENSIONS OF THE PMIS CONCEPT

Manpower Planning and Human Resource Inventories

If organizations maintain an accurate count of human skills, it is easier to plan for future employee needs. Matching human skills with potential research and development projects has other benefits. It increases the potential for innovation because employers have a bigger stake—their interest—in what they are doing.

Another approach to the problem of matching available skills to job requirements is described by Grey and Waas (1974). They identify nineteen kinds of information that the Grumman Data Systems Corporation gathers about personnel. The system makes it easy for managers to report personnel transfers. The Grumman system identifies personnel who think they can benefit by additional training. And it specifies the kind of training they want. The system is dependent on voluntary inputs, but the authors claim that attention to the behavioral aspects of the system's operations has minimized distrust and maximized participation.

Traum (1973) illustrates a method for analyzing availabilities and needs. Exhibit 15–6 demonstrates a human resource inventory for three levels of management in four functional areas (systems, production, marketing, and finance). The top part of the box (cell in the matrix) represents persons available for the position for the coming year, while the bottom half identifies projected needs for the coming year. There is a resource gap between management levels 6 and 7 in the finance function because the managers do not expect anyone to be ready for level 7 next year. At the same time, there is a resource surplus in the production

EXHIBIT 15–6   Personnel Planning Inventory

	Systems	Production	Marketing	Finance
Level 7	6 / 4	3 / 1	3 / 3	0 / 3
Level 6	5 / 3	14 / 6	6 / 5	4 / 3
Level 5	9 / 12	29 / 22	9 / 9	6 / 3

Top = availabilities

Bottom = needs

function as a whole. This type of reporting device can be effectively used to pinpoint staffing needs before they become critical problems or shortages.

If the inventory system is integrated with the salary system, another important source of information will be generated. For example, the system can reveal how well managers in different divisions are developing their subordinates. If management in one division is increasing salaries for everyone regardless of performance while other managers are holding people down for significantly longer periods of time than the average, personnel mismatches (employees held back in less challenging jobs) and morale problems will be noticeable—if not now, then in the near future. The PMIS can easily generate data for measuring the rate of salary increases by performance, by division, or by operating unit. If "high potentials" are kept in a place for too long a period, the information can and should be brought to the attention of upper management.

Computer systems for performance reviews and control. Usually the personnel manager is responsible for management of some, if not all, of the performance evaluation program. Promotions and raises often are based on these evaluations. Top management also uses them to exercise general control of operations. Searles (1975) reports a "top three/bottom three" evaluation technique used at the Honeywell Information Systems Division of North America. Basically, the system is a control device that tracks the actions of managers. It shows whether or not managers are promoting their best people and either upgrading or dismissing those who do poorly. An evaluation program identifies the "top three" and "bottom three" persons in each subunit of the company. Periodic reports establish a percentage of the top three who 1) have not moved since the past period, and 2) were promoted from their present position. The system also shows any trends from past periods. For the bottom three, it indicates 1) rating, 2) percentage terminated, 3) if performance improved to a satisfactory level, and 4) those on active status. While the system relies on ranking managers by number and is essentially an extension of "management by exception," it does give a comparative look at the actions of management from top to bottom. In so doing, it helps to rationalize promotion and termination actions.

The American Greeting Corporation has taken a different approach to computerized performance measurement. Polster and Rosen (1974) report a system that measures each employee on a scale in seven dimensions (relations with others, planning and controlling, work approach, decision making, development of subordinates, initiative and advancement potential, and motivation). A frequency table constructed from the total scores allows each individual to establish his percentile rating. To control for bias by individual raters, each rater is compared with each other rater in terms of the average ratings given. Thus, the performance system—when used in conjunction with a computer—allows for its own internal control and rationalization. Unfortunately, it also gives numbers to events that are sometimes accorded more than their real significance.

Wage and salary surveys. Information necessary for wage and salary surveys can be easily and quickly obtained from the personnel information system. It can show a variety of factors, such as age breakdowns, which indicate the average age and seniority for particular skilled and nonskilled jobs. If the majority of firms participating in the survey have personnel information systems, the survey itself could be computerized.

System Development Corporation of California had been active in forming a group of thirty firms that agreed to contribute to a large centralized compensation data base on a semiannual basis. Standard job codes and company job description codes were developed. Data were collected on rate ranges, actual high and low salaries, and the number of job holders. Three reports were available to each company: 1) a complete breakdown of all rates within the requesting company, 2) compensation data for key jobs from all participating companies, and 3) detailed comparisons with selected companies with whom the requesting company had a mutual agreement (Flippo, 1971).

Absenteeism. One area where the personnel information system can be particularly useful is in pinpointing chronic absenteeism among employees, one of the main reasons for low productivity within organizations. Using industry absentee figures, the personnel department can search the personnel information system for an absentee exception listing. The listing would contain only those employees above the plant average (e.g., 7 percent and up). Since these employees are the worst offenders, they are the ones who should be investigated for purposes of possible disciplinary action. Some degree of absenteeism will always exist, but by investigating the chronic cases, the personnel department can save line supervisors the many nonproductive hours required to check all absenteeism.

Sickness and accident claims. In a similar manner, the personnel department can correlate data about chronic absentee employees and those employees filing sickness and accident insurance claims. If there is a positive correlation, claims may be reduced by counseling the employees. Counseling could pinpoint the causes of past absenteeism or sickness.

The importance of pinpointing and correcting both absenteeism and sickness problems by the personnel department is that it not only benefits the company, but also the personnel manager has tangible dollar proof of the merit of the personnel information system.

Community-Related Uses of Personnel Systems

Blood donor program. Organizations generally encourage their employees to support blood donation drives. It is a humanitarian act, the full significance of which is probably not recognized by either management or donors.

Personnel departments often establish employee blood donor lists. The Red Cross supplies the input information—employee name, number, and blood type. This information is then placed in the personnel data file so that with the proper retrieval process, the department can have a list of blood donors by blood type, name, number, address, and the accumulative amount in pints of previous donations. The employee blood donor listing can then be made available to the Red Cross and all hospitals within a 100-mile radius and updated regularly. The list can be updated after every visit by the Bloodmobile and as new employees are added to the employment roles.

This information is beneficial for more than strictly humanitarian purposes. In emergencies requiring a quick supply of special types of blood, donors can be identified quickly—and, possibly, a life saved.

The personnel department could recognize the donors through the company newspaper as well as provide employees time off with pay to make the blood donations. This kind of program could boost employee morale.

Internships. Increasing numbers of organizations are using internship programs with high schools and colleges. In many cases they have become a vital information link between education and industry. Personnel departments are instrumental in implementing these programs.

Advances in computers make it possible for these programs to be more sophisticated in the future. After establishing contact with a school, a committee made up of personnel and educational representatives could map out an exchange program. Once the program was outlined, it would be relatively easy to select the employees and educators who would switch positions. The personnel data bank could be used to find two people who best matched. The employees would receive their regular pay while the internship program was in effect.

A major computer company conducted an internship-in-industry program to help teachers keep pace with rapidly changing technology. According to Jack Lindon, one of Honeywell's program coordinators:

> In our highly technological society, innovations occur so rapidly that technology is often outdated just as it reaches the textbook stage, so it is essential for teachers to study constantly to keep up to date (*Automation*, 1972).

Personnel departments have learned from their experiences in hiring and training large numbers of so-called disadvantaged youths and adults. They have been able to convince management that it is in their best interest to help schools. They have found these people to be deficient not only in job-seeking and job-retention skills but also in the basic fundamentals. They have found it necessary to bridge the education gap as well as provide health and other social services for the disadvantaged new employees. Internship programs can help.

Volunteers. The personnel information system can be used to compile a list of employees who are interested in doing volunteer work, and the skills they possess. A recent advertisement in a major newspaper appealed for volunteers who had the following skills:

> CARPENTER to remodel 12 wooden boxes used for educational kits; kits need repair and painting; plexiglas front to be added.
> ACCURATE TYPIST 2–3 hours a week to develop a membership roster for a new youth program. Electric typewriter. Urgent.

EXPERIENCED PLASTICS WORKER to construct several small box-like covers for exhibit of small sculpture in children's home.

Many important jobs need to be done in any community, and a considerable number of volunteers can be recruited from industry if the various volunteer agencies and local industry cooperate in a data service. And participation in outside activities benefits both the company and the employee. It provides the satisfaction of feeling needed in the community and a pride in worthwhile accomplishment. Outside activities can relieve the boredom of daily routine and provide an outlet for other creative drives (Moseman, 1970).

Retirees as well as active employees could be recruited from the personnel information system. Many companies keep information on retired employees to keep them informed of company activities, changes in policy benefits, and to mail them pension checks. Since their skills are still recorded in the system, it would be relatively simple to inform retirees of volunteer activities that match their particular talents. If the volunteer agencies approach a firm that has a personnel information system, they may get a response beyond their most optimistic expectations.

Industrial planning and growth boards. More and more people have become actively concerned with the planned growth of their communities. A listing of employees living in an area could help local industrial planning boards. Supposedly, the industrial exodus has left the cities with unskilled workers who are without resources or transportation to get to suburban jobs. If a planning board can pinpoint where factory workers live and the distances they are willing to travel to good jobs, they can be more effective in persuading new businesses to locate in the areas they suggest. Several cities have reversed the process of losing jobs to the suburbs with the industrial park concept, a concept perfected in the very suburbs that industry has found so spacious and appealing.

Some city planners, contrary to many predictions, emphasize that since 1963 large cities have no longer been net losers of jobs. This is certainly true for manufacturing jobs. Large cities presently contain as large a share of rapidly growing activities as the suburban ring.

An employee residence list can be useful for an organization. It can help assess growth patterns for the general area in which the plant is located, as well as help transportation planners and traffic surveyors study the origin and destination of large segments of rush-hour traffic.

PERSONNEL INFORMATION SYSTEM CASE STUDIES

The U.S. Air Force System

One of the more advanced human resource management systems is found in the United States Air Force even though its designers admit that initial attempts to develop a computerized personnel information system were ineffective and discouraging. ("Personnel Data Systems," U.S. Air Force *Study Guide,* 1970).

Each major command involved in early design attempts had its own rules and many operated with different types of computers. This made it most difficult for AF Headquarters to extract valid information for planning purposes. It became obvious that without controls the system would not work effectively. This initial bad experience has paid off. System controls were established at headquarters through standardization of record content, codes, techniques, and methods of operation, and all policies and procedures were established at a central location. Requests for deviation are approved before procedures are put into operation.

At present there are two basic computerized personnel systems in the Air Force, one for enlisted grades and the other for officers. The data base for officers is extensive and the listing of its components (see Exhibit 15–7) shows the decision-making potential available to all levels of management. It is also evident that individuals within the system have a far greater probability of achieving their maximum career potential than those who are not in the system.

The computer files are divided into record areas and given a data identification number. When data are transmitted, they are edited by the computer before being stored. Data that are not edited are returned to where they originated.

EXHIBIT 15–7   Air Force Officer Personnel Data Base

Identification data (name, grade, SSN, current date)
Promotion dates (grade and category)
Duty listing (date of assignment, job code number)
Last officer efficiency index (performance rating)
Special experience (e.g., missile systems, engineering, science)
Combat experience (detailed)
Decorations and awards
Overseas duty
Education (for college level work, entries are made for each fifteen semester hours)
Professional specialty courses
Professional military courses
Security data
Testing data (e.g., AF Officer Qualification Test, Language Aptitude Test)
Remarks section (open for miscellaneous data)
Languages
OER Data (historical effectiveness information)
AFSC Data (primary, secondary, tertiary job qualifications)
Personal data (birthplace, home of record—classified and coded)
Physical data (complete coded physical profile)
Payroll data
Career and separation data
Last records review
Projected grade date
Flying rated data
Current temporary duty data
Current assignment data
Projected assignment
Assignment preference data (major command headquarters, specialty, length of tour preferred)

When data pass edit, computer records are updated in one of three ways: direct replacement, resequencing, or automatic data maintenance. Immediate retrieval can be made of a single record, but the Direct English Statement Information Retrieval System (DESIRE) provides personnel technicians to request from the computer a wide variety of output products dealing with more than one record. Real-time requests of single records are returned to remote terminals within a few seconds; DESIRE requests are returned on a deferred basis.

Statistical reports provide managers with tools for determining work load, unfavorable personnel trends, and areas where additional training is needed. A third phase in the development of Personnel Information Systems for the Air Force, MPMIS 70's, is designed to extend the present data gathering system to satisfy information requirements at all levels by providing a feedback loop that compares transactions with planned actions. It is also anticipated that operating managers will have greater accessibility to the system and the flexibility to deal with it in order to more effectively manage a decentralized operation.

General Electric Corporation Personnel System

Another example of computer systems application in personnel is turnover analysis conducted by the General Electric Corporation (Bassett, 1970). Computers were used to evaluate the patterns of turnover within the various units of a division. After developing a standardized exit interview and evaluating data obtained from it, managers realized that lack of opportunity to move into new positions within the organization seemed to cause turnover. Thus, the picture became clear—there was a relationship between the conflicting needs for productive stability, which requires experienced workers on the job, and opportunity for employee development, which demands varied exposure to a mix of different jobs. G.E. also discovered that, up to a point, turnover is necessary to provide openings and permit flexibility for management development. Additional research showed that in stable, slow-growth types of businesses, low rates of turnover were positively related to low rates of profit. While too much turnover can disrupt production, too little apparently leads to stagnation and loss of adaptability to changing conditions. At the time, the company was using its personnel information system to continuously update and evaluate two previously unrecognized measures of effectiveness: average position tenure and position turnover.

Kaiser Aluminum and Chemical Corporation

At the Kaiser Aluminum and Chemical Corporation, managers have used computers in several personnel functions. Their conclusion is that computers have helped improve efficiency, profitability, and effective management of human resources (Handy, 1970). Personnel managers at Kaiser have been heavily involved in systems development. Short courses in the fundamentals of data processing have been given to employees affected by automation.

Programmers developed a master file integrating payroll, skills, and performance. Examples of output reports included 1) the "comparatio," indicating the relationship between the average salary and the average midpoint salary, and 2) the percent of range utilization, showing the position of the average salary within the total salary range. Reports are also generated to show whether outstanding employees are receiving outstanding salary treatment and vice versa. All managers receive a report of each employee's last three salary increases together with a report showing the amount of increase and the reason for it. They also receive a report of average percent and frequency increases. Analysis of the relative pay of employees in similar positions in various parts of the total organization is also provided, along with summaries of external averages for the same job category. Further measures of external and internal consistency are provided in reports covering year of bachelor's degree versus salary and year of hire versus salary.

SUMMARY AND CONCLUSIONS

While it may appear to many that computers tend to depersonalize the management process, the responsible application of contemporary technology can actually improve the welfare of employees and assist in humanizing the work place. In this chapter we have illustrated systems that can provide accurate, objective, timely, relevant, and important information about people that personnel managers can use to help employees plan their careers. Personnel managers are also better able to develop relevant training programs, reward performance fairly, and choose the most interested and qualified applicant for a position. Naturally, technology can be abused, and we caution against the unplanned and unsecured development of data bases containing private information that is not handled confidentially.

The first phase in the development of a personnel management information system is to define the objectives of the personnel function. Objectives should normally be set in the areas of human resource planning, recruitment, selection, evaluation, development and training, promotion, and compensation. Once the objectives are set, the types and nature of decisions must be identified: personnel information systems can help make decisions about who to recruit, where and when to recruit, who to send on interviews at various campuses, and who to invite for interviews. The system can identify general weaknesses in management planning, decision making, communications, human relations, control, and technical competence. These weaknesses can be used to develop training and development programs. Personnel with special skills can also be identified for one-time projects or special problem situations.

When the required decisions have been defined, it is possible to identify the types of data needed. For example, a manpower plan is a necessary data input to make a decision involving recruiting strategy; performance evaluations provide data for preliminary promotion decisions; and work preferences provide data regarding job transfer. When the data base is complete, models can be introduced to enhance the use of data through simulation, exponential smoothing, regression analysis, and other operations research approaches (Greenlaw, 1973).

A final point in this discussion of technology and models in human resource management concerns the human factor. It is our contention that technology exists to serve people. The great danger, however, is not that machines will begin to think like people but that people will begin to think as machines. Ignorance can make us slaves to technology, so we should realize the fact that computers are here to stay. Whether they make us their slaves or not is up to us.

DISCUSSION QUESTIONS

1. Discuss how computers and information systems can improve the personnel function.

2. What are the major advantages and limitations of computers as they relate to organizations and society in general?

3. Discuss a situation in which you have had a positive experience as a result of a computer application.

4. What do you feel are the most important future uses of computers in human resource management?

5. Using an organization with which you have some familiarity (e.g., part-time job, school, athletic club), list five ways a computerized system might improve the personnel function in that organization.

6. Which are the major components of a personnel information system (e.g., hardware, software)?

7. Review recent issues of personnel and psychological journals to determine the present state of the art of computer applications in human resource administration.

8. Do you feel that a well-managed computerized skills inventory can increase the motivation of employees? Why? Why not?

9. Discuss a method whereby a small business (less than 500 employees) might make use of computer methods in its personnel function.

10. How might labor unions benefit from the computerization of personnel data?

11. What important design steps should be followed in developing a personnel information system?

12. "All personnel systems should be cost justified." Discuss.

13. A noted systems analyst suggests that top management need not understand the systems that they are expected to use. Do you agree?

14. If personnel managers have more and better information, they will make better decisions. Discuss this statement.

15. Following is a summary description of an actual personnel management information system designed and implemented by a major United States manufacturing organization. The system, implemented in early 1975 has many positive and some negative attributes. Read the description and be prepared to discuss what you feel are the values and limitations of the system.

The Glenwood Company Personnel Management Information System (PMIS)

PMIS is a comprehensive information system used by various levels of management to store, change, and report personnel information on an accurate and timely basis. PMIS provides a centralized information source in a company that is diverse in its organization, products, and geography.

Each employee record is capable of maintaining up to 8,000 characters of information based on over 300 individual "elements" of data. Each element is governed by a transaction code or block number, and may be added, changed or deleted by the employee, or appropriate management, or by both.

When additions, changes, or deletions occur within an employee's record, a new personnel document is created and a varying number of reports are created to communicate those modifications of records to those departments needing to know of them. The individual records are updated and these "select" reports are created three times each week.

Other reports are created on a weekly, quarterly, semiannual, or annual basis to summarize the personnel activity occurring in the reporting period. These reports cover such areas as merit budget controls, enrollment reports, compensation administration, and benefits administration.

Another system, used in conjunction with PMIS, gives management the ability to call for special reports for use in job candidate searches, Federal EEO reporting, forecasting manpower needs and budget generation, to name but a few areas.

PMIS utilizes Indexed Sequential Access Method (ISAM) tables to store information common to a multitude of individual records, such as division name, department name, job titles, etc. Use of the ISAM tables provides the capability of updating a number of individual records by entering a single change to an element stored on the tables.

There are four basic personnel documents used to maintain employee records. The first one, the employment requisition, describes the position and acts as the authorization to fill the position once approved by appropriate management. The employment application describes the individual selected to fill a position. These two documents, when combined, form the basis of each employee record.

Whenever changes occur to an employee's record, either an employee profile (describing company-related information) or an employee resume (containing personal information) or both of these documents (when common data changes) are created. These documents are sent to the divisional Employee Relations unit for further divisional distribution. These documents may also be used by appropriate management to process additional changes. Thus, the output document becomes an input document and comes, full circle, to the system that produced it. It is a turn-around document.

PMIS makes use of indicators to trigger the creation of some reports produced independently of data input. For example, a compensation adjustment proposed for a specific date will cause report generation thirty days prior to the proposed date; if critical data were not entered in a record, PMIS will create a report requesting the missing information until it is entered; another report is created, in the case of a termination, that warns of an outstanding advance.

PMIS recently underwent a massive technical rewriting to achieve faster processing, to facilitate more cost-effective resource utilization and to pave the way for future developments. All domestic employee records (wage and salary) were targeted for inclusion in PMIS in mid-1976—prior to that time, only salary records were maintained by PMIS. Such expanded coverage enables PMIS to better service Benefits Administration. Key-to-disk input, computer output, microfiche and remote terminal inquiry are among the possible future enhancements to PMIS.

BIBLIOGRAPHY

Akron Beacon Journal (February 15, 1972):66.

Baker, J. "Scheduling Part-Time and Full-Time Staff for Cyclical Changes." *Operations Research Quarterly* (March 1974):65–76.

Bassett, Glenn. "Personnel Systems Within Business." Paper presented at National Industrial Conference Board, January 1970.

Berry, W. E. "What a Personnel EDP System Should Do." *Personnel* (January–February 1969):18–21.

"Blood Brother." *Newsweek* 74 (September 29, 1969):80–83.

Bricker, J. J. "The Personnel System Concept." In *Personnel Management: A Management Science Approach,* P. F. Greenlaw and R. D. Smith, eds. Scranton, Pa.: International Textbook Company, 1970:37–43.

Burt, Samuel M. "Education and Industry Can Make a Great Team." *Today's Education* 59 (December 1970):34.

Carlson, Elliot. "Education and Industry: A Troubled Partnership." *Saturday Review* 53 (August 15, 1970):45–47.

Cleff, Samuel H., and Robert M. Hecht. "Job/Man Matching in the 70's." *Datamation* (February 1, 1971):22–27.

Conboy, Bernard M. "Do's and Don'ts for Wooing Industry." *Nation's Business* (October 1970):92.

Dukes, C. W. "The Role of Time-Sharing Consulting Services for Personnel." *Personnel Journal* 53.3 (March 1975).

Fahnline, R. H. "The Skills Inventory Put On." *Journal of Systems Management* (May 1974):14–21.

Farris, George F. "A Predictive Study of Turnover." *Personnel Journal* (January 1972):59–60.

Flippo, Edwin B. *Principles of Personnel Management.* 3d ed., rev. New York: McGraw-Hill, 1971.

Foster, Kenneth E. "Job Worth and the Computer." *Personnel Journal* 47 (September 1968):619.

Goldstein, R. C., and R. L. Nolan. "Personal Privacy Versus the Corporate Computer." *Harvard Business Review* (March–April 1975):62–70.

Greenlaw, Paul. "Management Science and Personnel Management." *Personnel Journal* (November 1973):946–54.

Grey, J. W., and R. E. Waas. "A Mini Human Resources Inventory System." *Personnel* (November–December 1974):59–64.

Gross, P. F., and R. D. Smith. *Systems Analysis and Design for Management.* New York: Dun-Donnelley Publishing Company, 1976.

Handy, A. A. "A Management Information System for Personnel." Address before National Industrial Conference Board, January 1970.

"Internship in Industry Helps Profs Keep Pace with Technology." *Automation* (February 1972):12.

Jabel, H. W. "Examining Skills Inventories." Presented to Training Specialists Institute, Cornell University, June 13, 1972.

Lee, R. D., and W. M. Lucianovic. "Personnel Management Information Systems for State and Local Governments." *Public Personnel Management* (March–April, 1975):38.

Lenniger, R. A. "Personnel Management and the Computer." *The Personnel Administrator* (January 1975):55–57.

MacGuffie, J. "Computer Programs for People." *Personnel Journal* (April 1969).

Michaels, R. F. "Computerizing Personnel Data in Small Companies." *Personnel Administrator* (April 1975).

Morrison, Edward J. *Developing Computer-Based Employee Information Systems.* New York: American Management Association, Inc., 1969.

Moseman, Verne R. "Brother Can You Spare The Time." *Nation's Business* 58 (February 1970):85.

Patterson, Eldon Roy. "The Computer Helps in Hiring and Keeping 'Top' Personnel." *Personnel Journal* (February 1971):141–43.

"Personnel Data Systems." *Study Guide*, 3AZR73270–1–3. Keesler Air Force Base, Mississippi: Keesler Technical Training Center, 1970.

Polster H., and H. Rosen. "Use of Statistical Analysis for Personnel Review." *Personnel Journal* (July 1974):498–517.

Seamans, L. H. "What's Lacking in Most Skills Inventories." *Personnel Journal* (February 1973):101–5.

Searles, J. R. "Top Three/Bottom Three: A Personnel Evaluation Technique." *The Personnel Administrator* (January 1975):50–53.

"Skills Inventory System." *Data Management* (May 1971):21.

Smith, R. D. "Information Systems for More Effective Use of Executive Resources." *Personnel Journal* 48.6 (June 1969):452–58.

Smith, R. D., and P. S. Greenlaw. "Simulation of a Psychological Decision Process in Personnel Selection." *Management Science* 13.8 (April 1967):409–19.

Smith, R. D., and K. Klafehn. "Computerized Manpower Inventories for Research and Development Planning." *Research/Development* 22.8 (April 1971):12–15.

Temeski, E. A., and H. Lazarus. "Information Systems in Personnel." *Journal of Systems Management* (August 1973):18–21.

Tetz, F. F. "System for Managing Human Resources." *Journal of Systems Management* (October 1974):10–14.

Traum, R. "Manpower Bank and Reward Systems for Professionals." *Personnel* (July–August 1973):19–27.

Wittreich, Warren J., and John B. Miner. "People: The Most Mismanaged Asset." *Business Horizons* (April 1971):69–77.

Zimmerman, Arthur. "Keeping Tabs on Ability." *International Management* (May 1971):47–49.

Chapter 16

CAREER
PLANNING
AND MANAGERIAL
DEVELOPMENT

LEARNING OBJECTIVES

This chapter will explore some of the newer concepts and techniques used to help individuals plan for and develop their careers. At the completion of the study of this chapter, the reader should be able to:

Distinguish individual from organizational development approaches

Distinguish the concept of jobs from careers

Develop planning systems and job design approaches for career and development

Clarify the crucial role of the personnel information, processing and feedback capabilities in supporting career or development approaches

Illustrate the use of the assessment center concept as a diagnostic and planning mechanism for career development

Apply basic skills of needs analysis

KEY TERMS AND CONCEPTS

careers (versus jobs)

career planning

management development (individual)

training (versus development)

career path

needs analysis

rating scales

in-basket

role play

assessment center

human capital

human resource accounting

PREVIEW

This chapter is divided into three main sections:

1. Career planning introduces the concept of a career path and relates it to the individual. The discussion enlarges on the motivational aspects of careers and points out the pitfalls of these approaches.

2. Important approaches and techniques of management development are described and a means of establishing requirements for development—needs analysis—is presented.

3. Two attempts to systematically evaluate the costs and returns of personnel programs—human resource capital and human resource accounting—are discussed.

Preparing individuals for new responsibilities is an important, exciting, and difficult challenge. For an individual, a career means far more than a particular job. A career can mean more money, prestige, and professional recognition. Having a job is one thing; having a career is something quite different. It is *really* something. A career gives a sense of accomplishment. It means opportunity, challenge, psychic rewards, and a better life-style.

Everyone needs a sense of direction. *Career planning* is a process of clarifying personal goals and abilities and matching them with future organizational needs and opportunities. The plan represents the career objectives and the program to achieve them.

Development has to do with a planned sequence of education, training, and work experience that moves an individual toward his or her career objectives efficiently. Development provides new abilities, knowledge and perspectives. It may be programmed through education (e.g., college degree or continuing education), internal organization programs, self-study programs, coaching on the job, specific skill training, or rotating job assignments. Currently organizations' development efforts emphasize the job assignment. Where this is the main approach for development, we will want to question the conditions needed for success.

Management development, the preparation of people for managerial positions (whether professional, technical, administrative, or line), is comparatively new. Approaches have been formalized largely since World War II (1945) as organizations have relied on management development to prepare enough people for key functions. Consequently, the development effort, through its preparation of vital human resources, has come to be viewed as the key to renewal and future growth.

Training versus development. A last matter of definition concerns the distinction between training and development. Historically, personnel managers have attempted to confine the term *training* to shorter-term technical skill improvement, usually on the job. Training has also been associated with laboratory procedures or exercises used to build supervisory skills. *Development*, on the other hand, has been related to managerial or professional positions. Modern literature and numerous articles have greatly blurred these distinctions. We will attempt to maintain these distinctions and elaborate on particular points to avoid misunderstanding.

The experiences described in the following scenario announce most of the main themes of this chapter. The relationships between individual careers and organizational requirements are the topics of all the subsequent discussions.

MARVIN KLEIN, "FAST TRACKER"

Marv Klein was a member of the Trust Department of the First City Bank of Chicago. He was recruited for bank employment almost six months before graduation from the M.B.A. program at the University of Illinois. Although Marv had a B.S. in Electrical Engineering from the California Institute of Technology, he felt that "big business was really where all the action (and also jobs!) was." Marv was in the upper quarter of his graduating class at Cal Tech. He wasn't an exceptional scholar, but he was a solid performer who participated in various school activities and was able to relate well to people.

Job Interviews

Marv had just started the second year of his two-year M.B.A. program at Illinois when he was advised to start taking job interviews. "It's ridiculous—interviews a year before graduation—they must be kidding!" In any case, Marv decided to go along with things and scheduled campus interviews with recruiters from several major businesses, mostly manufacturing ones, because of his engineering background. As a lark he scheduled himself for an interview "with a bank guy" just to get a "different slant on handling interviews." The interview with the bank recruiter went better than Marv expected, and he started to wonder if "maybe a technical person with an M.B.A. might really do some good at a bank."

In November of his second year Marv received an invitation to visit the First City Bank of Chicago. His interview at the bank was quite successful and in late November, Marv received a job offer—to join the "M.B.A. fast track" program at the bank. His first assignment would be in the Trust Department and the second most likely in Systems, in which he had expressed interest. The vice-president of personnel indicated, "We have an extensive and advanced concept of career development—which we practice—and have the personnel system, people, and information to back it up. Fast track will assure you of immediate responsibilities and permit you to move at your own pace as far and fast as your demonstrated performances warrant."

The Bank Job

Marv accepted the bank's offer in December and, after graduation in June, relocated in Chicago. Marv spent the entire morning of his first day at City Bank in the Personnel Department filling out forms, including a very extensive one called "Career Planning at First City Bank." The Career Planning form requested all kinds of information regarding past jobs, interests, skills, and career plans for the future. However, Marv was so busy from that point on that he quickly forgot the "bureaucratic red tape" and got immersed in banking matters.

Marv was reminded of his first day at City Bank when he received an "update card" at the end of his first year. The "reminder" was a computer print-out requesting update (new) information for his career file. Marv almost dropped the note in the wastebasket when he remembered a two-day seminar and workshop he had attended several months earlier. He filled in the information and returned the form to the manager of career planning.

Second Thoughts on Marv's Career

In Marv's second year of employment at the bank—he wasn't sure exactly when—he started to have some misgivings regarding his upcoming move to Systems.

Marv made an appointment with the career planning manager, and when they got together Marv had a good chance to discuss his doubts regarding himself and his future work.

"Marv, it's quite understandable—your interests are shifting as you gain experience and are better able to test out various career alternatives. Based on what we've been discussing, why don't we plan something quite different than that originally scheduled for your next move? Your thought about going into the personnel field is not far out—it's a good one and the experience will be valuable. I'll talk it over with the fast-track manager and systems manager, and we'll get it moving."

Comments on the Scenario

Many types of large organizations are at the cutting edge of change in career planning and development. Size of organization has been both a positive and negative aspect of career programs. It has been positive because substantial economic and personnel resources have been available, but size itself often has been the cause of personnel problems (e.g., getting lost in the organization).

Newer programs have been addressed to these problems. They create a positive influence on individual decisions about joining organizations (future opportunity) and maintaining affiliation (better than other alternatives), they encourage individual performance (a chance to demonstrate one's ability). Organizations have mainly used career planning and development for their managers and professionals such as Marv. However, there already are clear signs of incorporating semiprofessional, white collar, and other employees in these programs, especially as computer technology continues to reduce record keeping costs (see Chapter 15).

Alternative career routes. This scenario suggests that a person may take many different routes through the educational system toward a particular career. In Marv's case, his interests started to shift while he was in school. The management field seemed to be interesting—and jobs were available. But Marv knew very little about many of the occupations he was potentially qualified for. In recent years, some organizations have looked closely at their experiences with new or younger employees. Personnel officials have learned from these experiences and they have used their knowledge to develop new employee recruiting and placement policies.

The scenario brings out some features of an effective system which supports and administers career programs. Acquiring, processing, and "outputting" needed information is the basis for successful systems performance. Up-to-date information on future occupational and human resource requirements establishes need. Needs are met by recruiting and career pathing, which is a process of planning future jobs so that an employee can gain experience that will lead to promotion. Career pathing can help an organization develop talent from within.

PLANNING FOR CAREERS

Concepts

First we will examine an overall career-planning model and show how it helps identify individual career goals (see Exhibits 16–1 and 2). The major difference between the two exhibits is that Exhibit 16–1 reflects preliminary analysis to match desires of people and possibilities in the organization, while Exhibit 16–2 reflects the working out of a career program.

Preliminary Career Analysis

Exhibit 16–1 shows that both individual desire and organizational need must be jointly worked out. The difference between what an individual may be capable of achieving and what he says he wants to do can be very great. This point receives greater attention in a subsequent discussion.

Organization needs. This subject has already been covered rather extensively by the earlier discussions in Chapters 3 and 4, where it was related to human resource markets and forecasting human resource needs. The only point we want to stress here is that individual career plans are greatly improved or limited by the realities of an organization's future needs. If an organization anticipates

EXHIBIT 16–1   Reconciling Individual Preferences and Organization Need

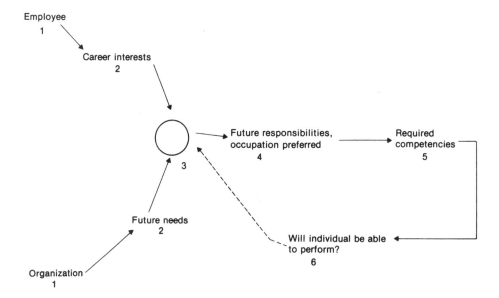

EXHIBIT 16–2   Career Planning: Career Pathing

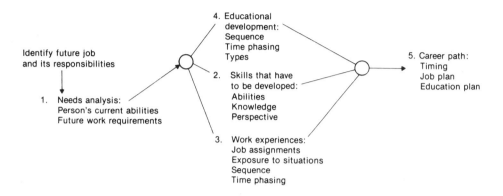

rapid expansion, it can absorb many types of specialists. But if an organization is stable and has few new openings, employees will tend to stay in the same positions. In this situation, planning would be more concerned with meeting the organization's replacement needs and improving working conditions.

Individual potential.   Recent research underscores the lack of appreciation for what an individual can accomplish. In many walks of life we keep establishing standards or measures of the best, the highest, the greatest—yet people keep surpassing them. And who hasn't heard of the "average" student who gets top grades or who accomplishes simply because of a desire to succeed? And similarly, there is the individual with high potential who has never been able to turn it on and come even close to his potential. Unless a particular occupation requires certain physical qualities a person just doesn't have (e.g., physical stamina), managers involved in career planning and development will be increasingly inclined *not* to judge in advance—or they will pay the consequences of such judgments. A more pragmatic approach is gaining acceptance: managers are trying to help diagnose and provide thoughtful advice and assistance and let the individual "prove out" or "bomb out."

·Career Pathing.   The career path analysis in Exhibit 16–2 concerns a program combining education (4) and work (2) to enlarge individual capabilities. Individual skill (5) is developed by job, education, and training. The individual gains a broad range of experience by working in a variety of planning, operating, and problem situations. If these experiences are reviewed carefully with the participant on an on-going basis, they will help improve the worker's skills. The elements of this kind of program should be closely related, and training should reflect skills needed on the job.

The Career Path—A Motivational View

The career path—a set of related jobs designed to lead to a more responsible position—is closely related to designing approaches that motivate individual achievement and performance. A motivational model such as the path-goal approach (Chapters 4, 7, 9) seeks to identify the best ways to meet valued, personal goals. Best, of course, is relative, but a manager can help an employee explore alternative paths of growth. A path-goal approach can also keep plans on a concrete and realistic footing. The model specifies goals and can describe how quickly those goals can be reached.

These motivational concepts are the basis of the career path. What is sought are those experiences (alternatives) that will best meet individual career objectives—yet meet organization requirements also. Career planning and definition of a career path should provide a highly motivating experience for the individual as the individual realizes that this is a path highly likely to achieve a valued goal. The reality is that organizations may try to do what is best but the personnel officer is forced to be pragmatic and do what's possible—this can fall far short of what the person may want.

There are, of course, the dangers. Quite naturally, an individual's expectations rise as he realizes that his career path can help him reach his personal goals. A career path takes a long time to follow. Many events, such as an economic downturn, can delay or even cancel a career program. Poor support and lack of feedback may also reduce the impact of the development program. Several department heads have a vital role in an individual's career program, and a single supervisor's incompetence or lack of interest have been stumbling blocks in many career programs.

The plan. As we have mentioned, objectives must be set for the career path. Generally, the larger the organization, the more formal the plan. The type of industry is also a factor and will affect how the plan is structured. For example, banks with 2,000 employees and manufacturing firms with 20,000 employees may both have career programs, though they will differ in many respects.

TOOLS FOR ANALYSIS

Needs analysis presents an excellent opportunity to illustrate the application of job analysis, job evaluation, and individual performance assessment. The purpose of needs analysis is to identify the educational and development experiences that will best meet the individual's career plans and the organization's future needs and set objectives for them. For instance, the Continental Bank of Chicago has developed highly refined tools for needs analysis. Although our description of needs analysis would not have been possible without the work of company specialists or groups such as Kepner-Tregoe, the following descriptions can apply to any company.

Overview of Needs Analysis

Needs analysis can get somewhat complex, so we will begin a brief summary of the essence of this technique. Needs analysis has several parts:

1. Determining which areas of individual knowledge, skill, and abilities require modification

2. reconciling future organization needs with organizational alternatives and individual desires

3. identifying the specific experiences or learning and education that will help transform the individual from the current state to the desired future state

4. individual counseling and programming.

These points are described in detail in the following material and illustrated in Exhibit 16–3.

Where the Individual Stands Today

Identifying an employee's need for training often starts with finding out what position that employee wants and then deciding what that position requires. For purposes of illustration, we will consider a management job, though the same approach can be applied to a variety of positions.

Determining needed managerial abilities. Organizations have become increasingly pragmatic; they are placing more and more emphasis on what the individual has to do on the job to be successful. A *classification scheme* that describes the need to be able to "plan," "organize," "communicate," is somewhat helpful, but more specific descriptions are necessary. Instead of listing "planning" a manager might put down "establishes specific objectives for short- and long-range activities and determines priorities to be assigned to these." This degree of detail is sufficient for the initial stage, but still more detail will be required when an individual development program is prepared.

The next step is to determine the critical requirements of the planned-for job. An employee's present position may be supervisor, and his target may be

---

EXHIBIT 16–3 Needs Analysis Procedure

Use the classification scheme of abilities to establish the relative importance of each ability

Identify the planned-for job.

Use the classification scheme of abilities to establish the relative importance of each ability in job success.

Compare the person's current span and degree of abilities to those needed in the planned-for job.

Carry out similar analyses for other employees who may seek a similar position which provides reference points for comparisons.

---

assistant manager. This is where needs analysis begins. Consider the function of planning as carried out by a manager and a supervisor. The supervisor's planning duties may include "establishes specific activities to meet short-range objectives and the appropriate priorities for these." The assistant manager may have to be able to develop both short- *and* long-range objectives. These differences should be shown in the job analysis and position descriptions. This initial analysis shows that the more highly rated job (assistant manager) calls for an additional ability: the ability to conduct long-range planning. Long-range planning has a greater effect on the affairs of most businesses, which is why it is more important for an assistant manager's position.

However, an important question still remains: How much planning ability does the employee already have and how much more will be needed? Planning ability must be defined more precisely. The following illustrates the requirements:

Sales Supervisor *Planning*	Assistant Manager *Planning*
1. Sets monthly sales quotas	1. Assists manager in setting yearly sales quotas
2. Determines six-month schedule of assignments of sales people	2. Reviews the six-month salesperson schedule with each sales supervisor
3. Plans quarterly sales program for dealers	3. Assists manager in planning yearly sales program
4. Identifies sales and promotion incentives for future sales campaigns.	4. Contracts with suppliers to secure sales and promotion incentives for future sales campaigns.

These four points show the different planning responsibilities and abilities needed for both positions.

Rating schemes and individual ability.   The supervisor now has a more specific idea of what he must be able to do to become an assistant manager. Higher-level abilities such as long-range planning may reflect more field experience, computer ability, and company knowledge. If the person has the mental abilities to meet the requirements of the higher-rated job, he can get additional knowledge through education and experience.

In this illustration the person might require some (rather than much) added experience, and exposure to the whole range of assistant managerial functions might be needed (the supervisor might substitute during vacation time). On the other hand, the supervisor may only need training in special skills, such as market research concepts, including statistics, to conduct long-range planning. In this case, training would not have to include so many different skills.

EXHIBIT 16–4 Use of Rating Scales in Assessing Individual Abilities

Assistant manager (needed planning abilities)	Underlying abilities and skills	Rating of individual's current abilities				
		Not present	Low	Some proficiency	Good	Very good
"Assists manager"	Understands general market research concepts			X		
"Reviews"	Uses elementary statistics		X			
"Assists sales personnel"	Works with people				X	
"Contracts with"	Prepares yearly sales quotas					X

Assessment itself can be conducted in several ways. An employee's skills can be rated descriptively or on rating scales such as the one in Exhibit 16–4. This exhibit illustrates a basic approach to rating abilities. One note of warning here: terms such as *fair* or *excellent* must be defined clearly.

Quantitative ratings of abilities. Some organizations want a quantitative measure of an employee's abilities or deficiencies, so they develop a composite numerical score. However, these numerical or composite scores can be difficult to interpret because some type of judgment must be used in any rating scheme, whether it is descriptive or quantitative. Also, the computations can get so complex that there is a tendency to oversimplify rating forms. For example, instead of dealing with the various abilities that are a part of an assistant manager's planning duties, an organization might simply deal with the general function of *planning*. This approach undoubtedly simplifies ratings and calculations, but critical information is lost. Though detailed analyses can be difficult to handle, they give better results than gross assessments. Numerical assessments can be useful in initial determinations, but care must be exercised in preparing individual development plans based on these approaches.

Before we proceed, we will briefly summarize needs analysis. Needs analysis defines abilities an employee must have to move into a more responsible position. The individual learns *what* is needed and *how* to get it. The career plan helps the employee acquire new abilities through various combinations of experience, formal education, and specific training. Successful needs analysis will involve the actual performance expected, the *relative* importance of skills needed for higher level performance, and accurate assessment of where the individual stands at the time of the needs analysis.

NEEDS ANALYSIS SCENARIO

Fairmont Stores, Inc., a national chain of department stores, provides the basis for the career planning procedure described in this section. Stores are classified as A (large) or B (small) on the basis of sales. Most large stores are in or near metropolitan centers.

The amount of information needed to program individual career planning activities is substantial. Aside from interviews and special testing to help establish ability and interests, an employee's career form is the basic input document to a career planning system. This input form provides previous job experiences, career interests, and the abilities an individual feels he offers the organization to further his career interests.

Several points about this form are not obvious and require clarification. First, sections 1 and 2 relate specifically to employees' experiences before they joined Fairmont. Second, the "specific experiences or abilities acquired," section is an attempt to identify:

1. significant knowledge areas
2. how-to-do-it skills
3. problem solving abilities
4. supervisory and/or decision making skills, gained from past work experience.

Section 4 requests a detailed description of education and training. This section asks for college degrees, major and minor fields, and schools attended. In addition, if one has attended special development programs or received skill training, these are to be noted (3).

Section 5 reflects the individual's attempt to spell out occupational preferences and to describe work features he values. As already indicated, an accurate and comprehensive description of personal preferences must reflect one's abilities. Also, the description of personal preferences assumes access to good information about future work opportunities in the organization and an understanding of the organization's work system.

Designing a Career Plan

Fairmont has standardized the main procedural steps in designing a career development plan. Fairmont's program involves the following steps:

1. Develop employee background data
2. Discuss career interests with employee
3. Establish the abilities or competencies required to perform the planned-for career activity
4. Conduct needs analysis to determine development needs
5. Discuss development needs with employee
6. Relate employee career desires to company needs

EXHIBIT 16-5 Fairmont Stores, Inc.: Job History and Career Objectives

Today's date _____

Current department _____

Company start date _____   Current title _____   Months in latest job _____

Individual's name _____

1. Previous job titles   Location   Division   From to   2. Specific experiences or skills acquired

_____   _____   _____   ___ ___   _____

_____   _____   _____   ___ ___   _____

_____   _____   _____   ___ ___   _____

_____   _____   _____   ___ ___   _____

_____   _____   _____   ___ ___   _____

3. Previous company experience   From to

_____   ___ ___

_____   ___ ___

4. Special training _____

5. Education _____

6. Career interests and objectives _____   7. Travel restrictions or special needs

_____   _____

_____   _____
(signature)

7. Formalize feasible career objective(s) for the employee

8. Identify needed education, training, and job experiences

9. Design the individual's career development plan.

It should be noted that the above steps may not always be followed in the specified sequence. In fact, steps 6 and 7 may be repeated or modified several times during the design of individual career development plans. Fairmont Stores, Inc., uses a general set of managerial job abilities that is then used to determine individual development requirements. The company uses its job description information to establish a profile of the "career job"—which is defined in terms of managerial job abilities. The same set of abilities is assessed against the individual —the difference determines the development need. These determinations are indicated in Exhibit 16–6 for the position of floor manager.

Information and analysis illustrated in this exhibit for Fairmont reflect that company's customized approach to career design.

Features of Fairmont's needs analysis. Fairmont uses a set of seven ability areas it considers common to all managerial jobs. Consequently, considerations that differ in job-to-job comparisons are the relative importance of the ability area to job functioning and specific work-related activities. Part C of Exhibit 16–6 illustrates the assessment of the importance of abilities for the floor manager—class A store job. Also illustrated in part C is the assessment of a particular individual and the resultant needs. What is not provided in this exhibit are the detailed job activities of the floor manager (*what* is planned, organized, etc.) and of the benchmark jobs which furnish the standards for comparison.

Comment on the specific needs analysis. Three main categories of needs are used for determining individual career development approaches: *immediate* training ("now"); to begin *within the year* ("near term"); or periodic doses over an *extended time* interval ("long term"). For example, the ability "implementation" (Exhibit 16–6) is considered to be extremely important ("critical")—the individual's current level of achievement is considered only "fairly good" by his supervisor. Periodic and regular attention will be required for an extended time period, until the desired level of ability is developed.

The career development plan. The next step in Fairmont's career planning program is the review of the needs analysis with the individual. From this point the manager and the employee can develop a step-by-step program of jobs and education or training that will best meet both Fairmont's and the employee's needs. A portion of this career development plan is illustrated in Exhibits 16–7 and 16–8.

Individual career programming. Fairmont's program provides the step-by-step progression of jobs to build managerial competency and confidence. Each new job adds to the scope or depth of responsibility and problems that will have to be handled. Variables in this program include location in the country (varying

EXHIBIT 16-6 Fairmont Stores, Inc.: Needs Analysis Work Skills

A. Position being evaluated *Floor Manager—Class A Store*

B. *Abilities required—definitions*

1. Planning—establishes clear goals, objectives, and priorities.
2. Organization—establishes schedules for short and long-term projects; brings together various resources; programs to carry out plans.
3. Decision making—able to reach thoughtful conclusions based upon available data—take risks—make judgments.
4. Problem analysis—able to gather relevant information, use appropriate tools of analysis, define central problems or issues and propose alternative solutions.
5. Implementation—able to launch programs, develop needed rules or guidelines, provide needed support, display initiative and follow through.
6. Management practices—possesses needed skills for analysis, control, budgeting, dealing with personnel, salary administration.
7. Relationships with people—able to develop and motivate individuals and communicate to groups: able to develop effective oral and written communications; facilitates two-way communications between self, colleagues, and work-group members; establishes good communication relationships with own supervisor or manager.

C. *Assessment of required abilities*

Abilities	Importance of abilities on job				Capability of individual today					Needs		
	Some	General	High	Critical	Low	Fairly good	Operating	Quite good	Expert	Now	Near term	Long term
Planning			X		X					0		
Organization			X				X				0	
Decision making			X				X					0
Problem analysis		X			X					0		
Implementation				X		X						0
Management practices				X				X		0		
Relationship with people, communications				X					X	—	—	—

469

EXHIBIT 16–7 Fairmont Stores, Inc.: Individual Career Programming

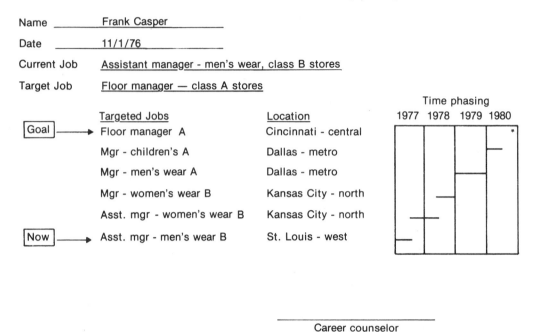

Name _____ Frank Casper _____

Date _____ 11/1/76 _____

Current Job   Assistant manager - men's wear, class B stores

Target Job   Floor manager — class A stores

	Targeted Jobs	Location	Time phasing 1977 1978 1979 1980
Goal ──►	Floor manager A	Cincinnati - central	
	Mgr - children's A	Dallas - metro	
	Mgr - men's wear A	Dallas - metro	
	Mgr - women's wear B	Kansas City - north	
	Asst. mgr - women's wear B	Kansas City - north	
Now ──►	Asst. mgr - men's wear B	St. Louis - west	

_____
Career counselor

consumer trades and regional preferences), store size (differences in sales volume), and types of clothing departments to build familiarity with lines. All of these experiences will help potential managers develop necessary skills.

Career support experiences.   The education and training shown in Exhibit 16–8 combine a wide range of tactics designed to increase managerial competency. The programmed approaches and the individual's responsibility to study independently make assumptions that are different from attending classes in school.

One education-training experience that may be of particular interest is that of the store management committee. Within the Fairmont store organization, this management committee is a valuable training ground where individuals come to understand the complexities of decision making and the practical considerations with which one must deal.

MANAGEMENT DEVELOPMENT

Assessment Centers, A Diagnostic Approach

We discussed the assessment center concept in Chapter 12 as a diagnostic tool for performance evaluation. Since the mid-1960s, more and more organizations have also used assessment centers for career planning and development. In this section the focus will be on individual diagnosis and will relate to career planning and development programs.

EXHIBIT 16–8   Fairmont Stores, Inc.: Career Support Experiences

For   Frank Casper

Date   11/1/76

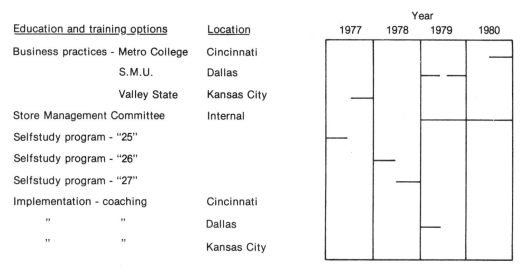

Education and training options	Location	Year 1977	1978	1979	1980
Business practices - Metro College	Cincinnati				—
S.M.U.	Dallas			——	
Valley State	Kansas City	—			
Store Management Committee	Internal				
Selfstudy program - "25"		—			
Selfstudy program - "26"			—		
Selfstudy program - "27"			——		
Implementation - coaching	Cincinnati				
" "	Dallas			—	
" "	Kansas City				

decision

The Diagnostic Approach—An Application

The passage of various manpower acts and equal employment opportunity legislation set the stage for economically disadvantaged and/or minority people to enter the world of work. Yet, success of the minority worker depends on learning new, sometimes basic, skills. Next, those people who already have necessary skills (as well as those who develop them in response to new opportunity) should have a real chance for security and job success. Yet even after gaining entrance to an organization, minorities often find that jobs turn out to be dead ends that do not provide a real opportunity for moving up. The situation described here is of this type.

Needs analysis: preliminaries. The first step in this program was to establish the overall number of managerial positions to be filled by minority personnel in conformity to EEO guidelines. As a result, management needed to make a careful analysis of future business plans, personnel turnover, and retirements. This analysis provided the basis for establishing a three-year development program, which called for developing three hundred minority supervisors and managers for store operations. Examination of store operations and managerial responsibilities indicated that there were three different types of management positions.

Although all managers had many common responsibilities, such factors as size of store and location led to specific types of problems which set some stores apart from others.

Needs analysis: critical incidents.   The responsibilities and activities of supervisory and managerial jobs were developed by the critical incidents technique. The key work-related activities that a manager had to carry out to be successful were detailed. Each position involved between seventy and one hundred different critical incidents, which were subsequently organized into eight areas of major responsibility. This process established an accurate picture of development objectives and abilities needed on the job.

Program recruitment.   Minority candidates for the program were recruited from various areas of company operations; additional candidates were recruited from outside the organization. Employees were proposed for the program by their supervisors on the basis of past performance and possibilities for the future. All of them went through a preliminary assessment center to define their qualifications and needs for future development. All candidates were to receive the benefits of diagnostic feedback if they wanted it—even if they weren't chosen for the program.

The Assessment Center.   The assessment center was physically housed in a conference facility leased by the company. A two-stage diagnostic procedure was used. The first set of procedures helped establish qualifications for the program, and the second developed a detailed career development plan for those chosen.

A six-member panel made the diagnosis. The chairperson was experienced in personnel evaluation techniques, had formal education in personnel, and had a background in psychology. The rest of the panel was comprised of senior operating managers who had been selected because of maturity, their own potential in the organization, and rapport with employees. All panel members were trained in group assessment and in the specifics of the methods employed.

The first stage.   The initial diagnosis lasted a day and a half. It was based on a management game centered on common managerial problems and several exercises. This initial procedure helped identify, for example, basic managerial qualities related to temperament (disposition under difficult conditions), time used for making decisions, and the quality of decisions made. Although some people failed to meet these requirements, each candidate was provided with a diagnosis of strengths and weaknesses and suggestions, if requested, on how to strengthen his or her abilities.

The second stage.   This activity covered three-and-a-half days. It included games, exercises, interviews, discussions with the panel, and a closed door review session among panel members. At the conclusion of the diagnostic period each candidate's performance was reviewed with the individual by the personnel specialist on the panel and the person's supervisor. A career plan and development strategy were then worked out for each participant, and the efforts of the participants were followed closely in subsequent months. Panel members were given progress reports about their candidates' problems. It was estimated that minority management assessment led to about a 50 percent improvement in successful program completion over past efforts. The diagnostic approach improved production, increased candidate confidence, provided more useful development information, and helped to gain better organization support for the program because it involved line management.

The improvement of career planning and development efforts requires that these efforts be evaluated periodically. Evaluations center around such questions as: Are the programs providing the needed number of personnel? How effective are the educational efforts? How well do people perform?

Evaluating a Development Program

An evaluation of a managerial development program should include an accurate picture of what changes have taken place in the individual, how long they took, and how much they cost. In general, this procedure involves: 1) performance assessments by one's supervisor, 2) self-assessment by the development candidate, and 3) actual success (measured by sales, costs, etc.) in subsequent job assignments.

If a management development candidate fails, there are two logical places for a personnel manager to examine: the development system itself and personal factors of the candidate.

The system. A management development system involves both the conditions and procedures under which an individual is expected to grow. But it also involves those people responsible for reinforcing individual learning or change during and after the planning stage. Lack of feedback, lack of organizational commitment to the program, and failure to identify specific training objectives are commonly encountered in program failures.

Personal factors. An individual's desire to learn, to commit needed time and energy, and to succeed are indispensable for a successful development effort. Because programs take place over an extended time period, an individual must have considerable self-discipline and perseverance.

In individually oriented development programs, these qualities are quite important. In group approaches (Chapter 17) one can often get support from other colleagues and trainees, while in an individual program, the employee is on his own.

Acceptance. Once the developed individual is back on a job or in a newly assigned position, new and challenging problems usually emerge. First, the individual's expectations for change are high, especially in the light of new or enlarged abilities. But are his associates prepared to change? Second, an individual who has completed a new program supposedly has new abilities and outlooks. Will they be accepted by work associates and subordinates? Does the person have the confidence and the skills required to perform successfully in the work situation? These questions will go through the minds of supervisors and co-workers. Clearly, evaluation is necessary to improve the program and the success of candidates.

The final major section of this chapter provides an overview of some newer concepts and procedures for judging the costs and benefits of personnel's efforts.

HUMAN RESOURCE CAPITAL AND ACCOUNTING

The concept of human capital has started to come to the attention of personnel officials. They see it as a basis for improving personnel analyses and decision making. The area of career planning and managerial development is a good context in which to introduce and clarify what human capital means.

Personnel-related costs traditionally have been viewed as current expenses rather than capital expenditures. Consequently, the costs of security, hiring, training, and management development, to name a few—to the extent that they were or could be calculated—were charged off to costs of current operations. Yet, the central focus of career planning and managerial development is the future. Thus current expenditures should be made against possible future returns to the organization as well as the individual.

The forward-looking nature of development programs and the anticipated returns are more similar to capital than to current costs. They are current investments in professional careers. Long-range returns are and should be expected to justify initial expenditures. This central idea is reflected in human resource accounting (HRA). The concept is intuitively attractive, but it has posed significant calculation problems. And managers have considered it skeptically.

The notions of human resource capital and accounting as tools of economic policy arose in conjunction with the rapidly expanding social welfare base of the 1960s. Somehow, costs and benefits had to be dealt with jointly in order to assess the effectiveness of particular social programs and to choose the best ones. Human resource capital appeared to provide one of the needed tools for this analysis. Subsequently, interest grew in the assessment (with human resource accounting) of personnel programs and returns within individual organizations.

Traditional and Human Resource Accounting Concepts

The selection of individuals for development programs has often depended on conventional personnel information such as experience, education, and other factors we have discussed. These characteristics establish a basis for determining less concrete factors.

Human resource accounting approaches seek to reduce subjectivity in personnel decisions by providing criteria that are more objective than traditional approaches. Consequently, typical calculations may involve costs of development, separation, and initial expenditures for recruiting, orientation, and training. Calculations also can include the estimated "percent worth" of future expenditures for employee salary, benefits, and cost of replacement if the employee is terminated. HRA approaches have also attempted to assess and estimate the value of individual contributions to innovation, productivity, and the like.

Developing Human Resource Accounting Data

Instruments have been developed to record human asset losses resulting from turnover, obsolescence, and health deterioration. Turnover is immediately identifiable. Obsolescence, a much more elusive variable, is judged periodically by each employee's supervisor. Health deterioration may be judged by using actuarial data. This data will indicate how serious an employee's medical problem is—that is, what the odds are that a disability will harm productivity. Computer-based systems may provide a more accurate approach to measuring human value through the use of various output indexes, thus giving a dynamic picture of human capital worth in the organization.

The Barry Corporation

In a report to the National Industrial Conference Board, Pyle (1970) indicated how managers at Barry Corporation (an oft-quoted application) were using human resource accounting information. The president said that the data were used to evaluate alternative investment opportunities. The personnel vice-president stated that costs of turnover and reorganization were recognized more clearly and quickly with the human resource accounting system. The corporate treasurer indicated that the techniques were helpful in evaluating the human resource value of potential candidates.

As might be expected, one problem with human investment analysis is convincing the employee that the investment calculation indicates only what a particular job has cost the company to fill and maintain, not the employee's value as a person. For example, Barry estimated that a foreman represented a $4,000 investment, a middle manager $16,000, and a top-level manager $34,000. These figures represented an approximation of what it would cost to replace these personnel. If organizations decide to move heavily in the direction of human asset accounting, the personnel data base is an essential ingredient for calculating necessary cost and replacement information.

Critique of Human Resource Accounting

In concept, HRA has proven highly attractive, but it has been difficult to put into practice. First, as already noted, many of the costs needed for analysis are not accumulated in conventional accounting systems. This is regrettable. But in fairness to cost analysts, it must be said that some costs are extremely difficult to isolate and, at best, arbitrary. Some skeptics add that "if you are going to make all of those guesses and compromises, you'll have no better decision bases than we now have—and maybe worse."

Second, and posing at least equal difficulty, is the fact that many decision makers can't accept the idea of equating people to dollars or dollars to people.

Many managers and officials refuse to be convinced that the dollar figures and calculations are capable of revealing human potential.

Regardless of one's viewpoint on this, almost everyone agrees that the growing complexity of organizational affairs and magnitude of personnel expenditures indicates that better information must be accumulated for improving personnel decision making.

SUMMARY

Career planning and management development have been presented as two closely linked activities in human resource management efforts. The thrust of this planning is forward looking. It combines organizational needs and opportunity with those of the individual who seeks a meaningful work experience.

Needs analysis provides the main vehicle for determining individual development requirements. Future work requirements are examined in terms of individual abilities, skills, and desires. Then there is an attempt to simultaneously reconcile individual desires and capabilities with organizational needs and possibilities. A detailed, step-by-step program is then developed—individual skill, knowledge level, and perspective are the focus of the development effort. The future sequence of jobs, and work activity through which individual learning and experience go is the career path.

The assessment center was described as a new personnel technique for diagnosing individual needs and potential. Group techniques for assessment and evaluation bear the promise of increasing considerably the accuracy and usefulness of procedures for evaluating human performance potential and developing well-planned career building efforts.

Evaluating the costs and benefits of management development efforts is important if useful guides are to emerge for future efforts. The concepts of human capital and human resource accounting represent attempts to evaluate development programs. Given the cost of career and development programs, this will be an important concern in the future.

In Chapter 17, the concluding chapter, discussion is shifted from developing the individual to developing work and organizational units.

DISCUSSION QUESTIONS

1. What should employees have to say about their own career plan?

2. From an organizational viewpoint, what considerations regarding:
   a. the individual
   b. organization features, policies, etc.
must be dealt with before developing an individual's career plan?

3. Defend or attack the premise that career planning should be confined to managerial or professional positions.

4. What major assumptions underlie the education and training features of a career plan that take into account organization personnel, resources, and jobs?

5. Needs analysis: The job analysis department of an insurance company was asked to carry out a needs analysis in conjunction with Mary Baker. Mary was currently assigned to public relations and had requested consideration for assignment to a new divisional sales organization as a sales representative for major customer accounts. The following information represents a portion of a much more comprehensive job analysis file. For the information given, provide an example of needs analysis. Be sure to name and explain your assumptions.

JOB DESCRIPTION ABSTRACT: Features of Managerial, Administrative, and Sales Positions

---

Responsibility—organization
Deal with people and resources so as to initiate needed work activities or to maintain their performance.

Work with staff and line departments to acquire assistance or counsel when needed.

Work with outside supplier, clients, etc., and so arrange contacts and meetings for best use of time.

Responsibility—planning
Identify important developments likely to affect department, area, or territory.

Develop objectives that reflect likely future developments.

Use needed tools and computer information for analysis and problem solving.

Key activities—Sales Representative, Major Accounts
Develop new insurance plans
Anticipate future needs
Deal with claims problems
Maintain good client relationships
Contact and work with all-regional departments in working out problems and programs
Mary Baker—survey of current experience
Age—23
Education—B.A. History
Experience—1½ years; assistant to vice-president for public affairs 1 year; public relations; and community affairs—presentations, news releases, government contracts, meetings with major clients.

---

6. In the Fairmont Stores example, reference is made to the specific job activities within ability categories (planning, organizing, etc.) for the education/training to be provided. Select any two of the seven ability categories described in Exhibit 16–6 and illustrate some of the possible work-related activities (be sure to develop along work-related lines as described and illustrated in the needs analysis discussion).

7. Critically evaluate the Fairmont Store career planning approach. Make and state whatever assumptions may be necessary in your response.

8. For the Fairmont Store illustration (Exhibits 16–6, 16–7), what assumptions would have to be made concerning Frank Casper's study habits and mobility?

BIBLIOGRAPHY

Anderson, S. D. "Planning for Career Growth." *Personnel Journal* 52.5 (May 1973): 357–62.

Becker, G. *Human Capital.* New York: National Bureau of Economic Research, 1964.

Bray, Douglas W., R. J. Campbell, and D. L. Grant. *Formative Years in Business: A Long Term AT&T Study of Managerial Lives.* New York: Wiley, 1974.

Brenner, B. J. *New Priorities in Training.* New York: American Management Association, 1969.

Brummet, R. Lee, Eric G. Flamholtz, and William C. Pyle. "Human Resource Accounting: A Tool to Increase Managerial Effectiveness." *Management Accounting* 51.15 (August 1969):15.

Burack, Elmer H. *Strategies for Manpower Planning and Programming.* Morristown, N.J.: General Learning Press, 1972.

Burack, Elmer H., and Gopal Pali. "Technology and Managerial O *MSU Business Topics* 18.2 (Spring 1970):49–56.

Byham, William C. "The Assessment Center as an Aid in Management Development." *Training and Development Journal* 25, 12 (December 1971).

Darew, Dean C., and A. J. Fredian. "Executive Career Guidance." *Personnel Administration* 31.2 (March–April 1971):26–30.

Ferguson, Lawrence F. "Better Management of Manager's Careers." *Harvard Business Review* 44.2 (March–April 1966):139–52.

Flamholtz, Eric. "A Model for Human Resource Valuation." *The Accounting Review* (April 1971).

Grusky, O. "Career Mobility and Organizational Commitment." *Administrative Science Quarterly* 10.4 (March 1966):488–503.

Jackson, T. A. "Turned Off by Your Job?" Parts I, II, III. *Industry Week* 176.5, 6, and 7 (January–February 1973).

Jolson, M. A., and M. J. Gannon. "Wives—A Critical Element in Career Decisions." *Business Horizons* 15.1 (February 1972):83–88.

Kellogg, Marian S. *Career Management.* New York: American Management Association, 1972.

Leider, R. J. "Emphasizing Career Planning in Human Resource Management." *Personnel Administrator* 18.2 (March–April 1973):35–38.

Lippitt, Gordon L. "Developing Life Plans." *Training and Development Journal* 24.5 (May 1970):2–7.

Moment, David, and D. Fisher. "Management Career Development and Confrontation." *California Management Review* 15.3 (Spring 1973):46–55.

Palmer, W. J. "An Integrated Program for Career Development." *Personnel Journal* 51.6 (June 1972):398–406.

Pinto, Patrick R., et al. *Career Planning and Career Management: An Annotated Research Bibliography.* Minneapolis: Industrial Relations Center, University of Minnesota, 1975.

Pyle, W. C. "Monitoring Human Resources On-Line." Presentation to the National Industrial Conference Board, New York City, January 20, 1970.

Schoomaker, A. N. "Individualism in Management." *California Management Review* 11.2 (Winter 1968):9–22.

Schultz, Theodore W. *Investment in Human Capital.* New York: The Free Press, 1971.

Vaughan, James A., and Samuel D. Deep. *Program of Exercises for Management and Organizational Behavior.* Beverly Hills, Calif.: Glencoe Press, 1975.

Vroom, Victor, and K. R. MacCrimmons. "Toward a Stochastic Model of Managerial Careers." *Administrative Science Quarterly* 13.1 (June 1968):26–46.

Walters, Rory W. *Job Enrichment for Results: Strategies for Successful Implementation.* Reading, Mass.: Addison-Wesley, 1975.

Wnuk, J. J., Jr. "Career Paths." *Training and Development Journal* 24.5 (May 1970): 38–40.

Chapter 17

ORGANIZATION DEVELOPMENT AND PERSONNEL RESEARCH

LEARNING OBJECTIVES

As a result of studying this chapter the reader should be able to:

Define organization development (OD)

Illustrate conditions required for successful implementation of OD efforts

Specify strengths and limitations of OD as a tool for changing organizations

Measure individual needs related to the job and suggest realistic strategies for fulfillment of these needs

Specify the directions of change in the field of human resource management and discuss the type of research necessary to bring about these changes.

KEY TERMS AND CONCEPTS

organization development
change
intervention

change agent
individual needs
personnel research

PREVIEW

Organization development, a systems approach to change, has become an increasingly important tool for personnel management. In this chapter we will discuss:

1. The strengths and weaknesses of organization development programs.
2. The relationship between organizations' operations and individual needs.
3. Areas requiring extensive personnel research in the 1980s.
4. The changing image of personnel management.

ORGANIZATION DEVELOPMENT

Organization development is used broadly and often loosely throughout management literature. Its meaning varies from company to company and frequently refers to activities that bear little relation to one another. For our purposes, we will adopt a definition constructed through research of the Conference Board Incorporated (1973): "Organization development is a planned, managed, systematic process (used) to change the culture, systems, and behavior of an organization in order to improve the organization's effectiveness in solving problems and achieving its objectives." Organization development (OD) is a reeducating process that uses applied behavioral science techniques focusing on the total organization. Management development, on the other hand, tends to be primarily concerned with the individual. OD philosophy suggests that an employee's value increases through the improvement of the organization.

Action is the cornerstone of OD: problem-oriented *research* and the use of a *change agent*. Before change processes are introduced, the culture, values, and problems of an organization are evaluated scientifically. Change is applied where change is needed; what is good is kept. Change for the sake of change is avoided. To facilitate this distinction, OD processes are ideally undertaken with large amounts of timely, relevant, and accurate scientific information about attitudes and areas that need to be changed.

Historical Perspective

Organization development has gained increasing acceptance since its appearance in the middle 1950s. In the early days OD was based solely on sensitivity training, or T-groups, and was synonymous with "laboratory training." In the early 1960s sensitivity training was expanded from concern for the individual's increased psychological awareness to concern for work-related problems and organization objectives.

In early OD seminars a person from outside the organization functioned as a laboratory trainer but took a more active role in gathering hard data for application within the seminar. The outsider then fed back personal observations and conclusions to the group.

In the middle 1960s the managerial grid was introduced (Blake and Mouton, 1968). The grid approach consists of six phases and is a long-range OD process directed from within the organization. It begins with a laboratory seminar that identifies, analyzes, and relates managerial behavior to concern for both people and production. This session is followed by a team-building phase, an intergroup building and conflict resolution phase, a development of long-range organization goals phase, an implementation phase, and a measurement and followup phase.

By 1976 organization development specialists were using many different approaches to change. These include attitude measurement, diagnosis of organization climate, communication improvement, management by objectives, conflict resolution, job enrichment, sensitivity training, team building, problem solving, and transactional analysis.

Ideally, OD specialists adopt a systems orientation so they can view events as they relate to the organization as a whole rather than in isolation. Thus they approach a particular problem with the view that if part of a system is changed, the whole system will be affected. They emphasize the importance of experience-based learning. In summary, the OD process requires diagnosis to identify and define problems and opportunities; intervention related to objectives; and measurement to evaluate the effects of attempted change.

Differences Between OD and Non-OD Organizations

In 1973 the Conference Board conducted a survey to compare organizations that were using and were not using recognized organization development processes. A panel of thirty consultants* identified forty-seven organizations they called "OD companies" and two hundred "non-OD companies." They sent both groups detailed questionnaires to determine if they engaged in specific OD-type activities (e.g., opinion measurement, interviewing for diagnosis, goal setting, communication improvement, conflict resolution, measurement, etc.). The survey also had other purposes: it was designed to determine why the activities were used, how they were implemented, who served as the change agent, and how the effects were measured. Ninety-six percent of the OD companies returned the questionnaires and 50 percent of the non-OD companies reported. Both small and large companies were represented, and most major industries participated. Results of the study indicate that 71 percent of the OD companies and 38 percent of the non-OD companies used attitude surveys to measure the organizational climate. While 51 percent of the OD companies used interviewing for diagnosis, only 25 percent of the non-OD companies did so.

The question "Does your company perform any special exercises to identify existing or potential conflict between individuals or groups?" elicited a positive response from 73 percent of the OD companies and only 22 percent of the non-OD companies. Participative techniques, such as problem identification and solving, were used by 98 percent of OD and 47 percent of non-OD companies.

The study also indicated the extent to which these companies used management by objectives (Chapter 12). Eighty percent of the OD and 66 percent of the non-OD companies reported that they used some form of MBO to evaluate performance. The use of group objectives for the same purpose was reported by only 49 percent of the OD and only 12 percent of the non-OD groups.

Among the OD companies, 40 percent reported that they have some objective measures of effectiveness, while 7 percent of the non-OD companies reported similar measures for their development efforts. Of all companies surveyed, 41 percent used employee attitude questionnaires at all levels in the organization. The majority of all companies using such surveys fed the results back to all participants.

* Among these consultants were: Argyris, Beer, Bennis, Blake, Burke, Kahn, Lawler, Lawrence, Lippitt, Lorsch, Mouton, Schein, Seashore, Shepard, and other noted experts in the field.

An interesting difference between the two groups emerged with regard to the use of internal versus external change agents (third parties) for OD intervention work. OD companies were using external change agents much more frequently than the non-OD groups. However, the use of outside or external consultants varied for different OD activities. The OD companies used external agents approximately 50 percent of the time for communication improvement and conflict resolution but only 25 percent of the time for diagnostic interviewing and problem-solving activities.

Evaluation of the Impact of Organization Development

Another study attempted to answer the question "What happened in this organization as a result of the OD experience?" (Armenakis, Field, and Mosley, 1975). This study used a sample of approximately 50 percent of the North American membership of the OD network coordinated by the National Training Labs Institute for Applied Behavioral Science. The survey asked those members who had served as consultants (change agents) what evaluation techniques they used and also asked for workable methods of testing results.

Results of the study indicate that evaluation practices usually include one of two major types of criteria. "Soft" criteria for evaluation are those perceptive judgments such as "leadership style." "Hard" criteria can be either internal or external. For instance, productivity is an internal hard criterion, while sales revenue is an external hard criterion.

Seventy-three percent of the change agents used both soft and hard criteria to evaluate OD efforts with a profit-oriented organization. Twenty-six percent employed soft criteria alone, and only one percent used only hard criteria. A majority of the change agents said that they preferred to tailor their own written instruments for each situation (59 percent). Thirty-six percent used existing instruments, most notably the Likert Profile of Organizational Characteristics.

Assumptions About People

According to French and Bell (1973), OD experts generally make the following assumptions about people:

1. Most individuals have drives toward personal development and growth if provided with an environment that is supportive and challenging.
2. Most people are capable of making a greater contribution to organizational goals than organizational environments will permit.
3. Work groups have strong influences on their members; members want to belong to groups.
4. Formal leaders can't make all the decisions for all of the group at all times.
5. Suppressed feelings hurt problem solving.
6. Trust and cooperation among people is lower than necessary or desirable.
7. Solutions to most problems in work groups are transactional. That is, one

must focus on how A and B can both modify behavior rather than on how A can convince B to change.

8. The way a manager acts with peers and superiors will influence how he acts toward subordinates. For example, the manner in which a meeting is conducted between Smith and his superior will influence the way Smith will act toward his subordinates.

9. Situations in which one group must win and another group must lose are not productive.

10. OD works best if there are sustained changes in the reward, performance, training, and communication systems within the organization.

The behaviorally oriented change agent believes that long-run opportunities for personal growth are critical for all people in the organization. The agent is convinced that both work and every-day living can become more meaningful, more effective, and more enjoyable for most people. He is committed to research, action, and generally a participative way of life.

Conditions Required for Successful Implementation of OD

Implementing a successful OD program depends on several key conditions. Managers of the OD effort must have a visible strategy (map, plan, milestones, measurement) and must coordinate among large organizational units after problems are recognized by key people. These same key people must genuinely believe in the behavioral sciences and have a visible commitment to action-oriented research through a change agent.

The early success of the development program should be made clearly visible to everyone involved. Results should be monitored by internally developed OD professionals. In addition to the specific individual motivation and OD requirements we have mentioned, recent studies in the field (e.g., Evans, 1974) have led to consideration of a broader and more far-reaching concept. Managers who establish personnel policies (e.g., salary, training, promotion) must understand the nature of motivation. We have discussed this previously: an employee must feel that goals are important and that higher performance will help him reach those goals. This is a basic, obvious, and often overlooked principle of motivation. An employee must be able to see a strong connection between his performance for the organization and his personal goals.

A related principle is equally important. If an employee doesn't believe that performance will help him reach his personal goals, his motivation will be low. Even though a person values money, if salary increments are automatic and based on simple seniority rather than merit, they will do little to motivate him. The employee sees that he can get what he wants. But he sees no connection between salary increases and a high level of job performance. Satisfying his needs depends on only doing adequate work for a long time rather than performing at the highest possible level.

Growing evidence suggests that a model of this type is a good predictor of job performance and satisfaction. Moreover, a motivation model incorporating this idea introduces a set of variables that is actually under the control of the organization—the performance-reward links. Whether managers like it or not, an organization's own policies determine how employees see the connection between reward and performance. Each time, for instance, the organization makes a salary or a promotion decision based on seniority or other similar considerations, the individual's belief in performance as a way to satisfy personal needs drops. Like-wise, an individual's motivation decreases if someone is promoted who is regarded as incompetent. Motivation will increase, though, if competency is rewarded.

To summarize earlier discussions, there are at least three basic conditions that enhance motivation for high performance. A task that provides a challenge and some degree of freedom to meet that challenge will motivate some employees to seek high self-esteem or self-actualization through performance. Second, management should understand the value of being both task-oriented *and* person-oriented: being person-oriented means that a manager can give rewards that meet the particular needs and desires of the individual. Since the rewards also are task-oriented, they will then depend on high performance. Third, a pay increase should very clearly be linked to high performance, for it then has added value: it is a status symbol as well as a concrete benefit. It is especially beneficial if the employee can choose the form of pay and benefits (e.g., insurance, pensions, holidays).

Personnel Practices and Effective Organization Development

One particular problem that managers in all organizations must then confront is that employee attitudes toward personnel are based on past experience. In most organizations, weak links between high performance and need satisfaction have been established, while strong links between goal attainment and such conditions as seniority already exist. An OD program must specifically concentrate on strengthening these links. This, in turn, necessitates a change in emphasis, especially for personnel managers. The following three factors merit consideration in this area:

Compensation policy.   What should be the organization's mix of remuneration among possibilities such as salary, fringe benefits, pensions, and stock options? How frequently should changes be made and what should be the basis for a change? In many instances, if the organization instituted a "cafeteria" style plan, it would be delivering more valuable and thus more motivating rewards. To avoid administrative complications, pay plans could be handled through computerized accounting or even contracted outside the organization; to banks, for example.

Promotion.   In addition to linking promotions clearly to performance, an organization might take the particular wishes of its employees into account. Could the employee, for instance, refuse a certain promotion without destroying his chances for future promotions?

Human resource planning.   Besides the familiar questions of future vacancies, skills needed, and employee training, organizations must confront the question of who is to make such choices and at what levels the choices are to be made.

Problems with OD: Some Noted Limitations

OD intervention generally involves a preoccupation with human social dynamics. At times, managers have lost sight of the task to be accomplished. When this has happened, some serious problems have resulted. Additionally, OD programs are sometimes ineffectively linked with personnel management functions, computer information systems, or the external environment. In some cases they are not linked at all. The long period of time required for implementation and high cost are other problems. If upper management does not commit itself wholeheartedly to OD, there will be additional problems (Greiner, 1972).

According to Halal (1974), some of the original enthusiasm for OD has declined for a variety of other reasons. Many of the considerable benefits promised by OD have not been attained, and programs have not been economically justified. The implicit stress on subjective techniques and values has proven to be undesirable on many occasions. We feel that most organizations should continue their OD programs, but that they should aim at smaller, more realistic goals, more performance-oriented than earlier ones and more quantitative in focus.

Bowers (1976) concludes that there is little evidence to suggest that benefits obtained from OD have always been worth the high prices paid. Superficiality, commercialism, and consultants who could not accurately diagnose problems have given the OD field poor initial momentum, according to Bowers. He notes that OD, when it is done well, is a complex venture requiring substantial resources, careful and rigorous problem definition, and a consulting style capable of responding in a variety of ways as different situations are diagnosed.

Organizations and Organization Development in the Future

The future of OD undoubtedly hinges on the future of organizations in general. Kahn and Wiener (1967) and others predict that future organizations will be even larger and more complex than they are today. In all probability, they will be more geographically dispersed as well. This growth and dispersion will make informal methods even more obsolete. Technology, including management science, computer science, and information systems, will continue to play significant roles in organizations. What, then, does all of this mean for personnel management and organization development?

First, increased size and complexity plus greater dispersion can increase human problems such as dissatisfaction, apathy, turnover, absenteeism, and monotony. Social issues, as well as complex problem-solving technologies, will become increasingly important. Because of these factors we may expect certain characteristics to be prevalent in OD systems of the future. Basic OD programs will have to be redesigned somewhat in order to be more effective. OD will use a comprehensive systems approach with less emphasis on process and more emphasis on content. How managers make their decisions will continue to be important, but there will be an increased emphasis on the right decisions. OD will perform in an even more systematic fashion, and with continued development of newer, more far-reaching models, substantially higher levels of accuracy in dealing with variables may be reached.

Secondly, OD professionals will begin to apply new technology to their methods of diagnosis and intervention. Just as computers have enhanced marketing and financial problem solving, so will they become an integral part of the personnel and OD program. Hard data on human assets will be collected, evaluated, and used for planning and measuring OD efforts. Researchers and analysts will study more variables as they relate to and cause productivity, motivation, and organizational goal achievement. Personnel management information systems will become an integral part of the OD process. These new systems will enable personnel managers to collect many kinds of data from throughout the organization, transmit it to a central location, process it, and tabulate and analyze it. Reports will be disseminated to users throughout the organization. This process in itself raises urgent questions concerning the nature of future OD programs. How will they be managed? Will they result in a decided centralization of power at the top of the organization? Will they foster an inhuman control and manipulation of people? How will they influence individual privacy?

In coming years the management of OD programs will focus on economic and social goals that make organizations more efficient and more competitive. New structures in pay systems and personnel plans will be used to produce more satisfactory structures. OD models may be tested on a limited scale in separate parts of the organization similar to the way scale models are tested today. Specialists in behavioral sciences and systems analysis will be included on OD teams.

Managing the OD program of the future will require even more sophisticated measurement and testing procedures. Measuring changed behavior and improved results leads to new types of problems. Training will emphasize actual operating groups that will study subject content and teaching techniques that can be measured accurately. Consultants alone will not analyze results. The consultant and manager working as a team with other outside experts, if necessary, will make evaluations (Mack, 1974). Evaluation periods will be lengthened to handle the greater complexity and geographic dispersion of the organizations of the future. In some cases, this may mean evaluation periods of several years.

The question of the focal point of power within an organization will inevitably concern centralization or decentralization. Will the fact that executives can have comprehensive information at their fingertips in a matter of seconds result in a centralized power structure? The sheer availability of information will provide the means for greater centralization, but since more and better information should yield superior measures of performance, will there be a need to exert centralized control if performance is goal oriented and meets standards? OD systems probably will be used to reflect management philosophy toward centralization and decentralization.

A final question, whether or not such systems will ever result in control of human beings by machines for machines, is of the gravest importance. In early

OD programs many managers refused to make adequate use of hard criteria since they had only recently discovered the value of an intuitive, subjective view of the world. But as complexity increased, a swing towards the hard measuring theories developed. A key question about the more formal OD programs is what will be their effect on the rights and privacy of the individual human being as computers store more and more personal data.

Fortunately, both approaches, the science of the formal and the art of the intuitive, have differing strengths that complement each other. Formal quantitative measuring, while using the hard economic view, provides too limited a perspective, allows a greater chance of misinterpretation, and discourages optimization. Formal procedures can best be used to support qualitative judgments. The intuitive approach adds wider flexibility of judgments but also brings in the possibility of serious error and bias. Thus either approach alone seems to have serious drawbacks, but when used together, the drawbacks can be avoided. For example, planning and implementing future OD programs will require interdisciplinary teams of specialists from such fields as systems analysis, computer science, research and statistical design, the behavioral sciences, and law. The makeup of these teams should reflect a balanced mix of the objective and the impressionistic.

The personnel manager should recognize that what we have been discussing so far—the future of OD programs—fits general patterns of change and evolution. There are alternative patterns of organizational change being proposed, and since the future is, after all, more speculation than knowledge, it is appropriate to briefly summarize some of these alternatives (Hinrichs, 1974).

It is possible to reduce the hierarchical (bureaucratic) structure of organizations. While admitting that somebody somewhere has to run the show and provide direction of movement, still there is no doubt that bureaucracy has overgrown us. The key idea is to connect main-line managers with some type of long-term continuing need. These positions then form the skeleton bureaucracy.

When members of the slimmed-down bureaucracy need staff functionaries, they could turn to middle-level managers or other professionals to fill temporary position needs. These middle-level personnel would be grouped by specialty area according to their competence and assigned to the bureaucratic staff as consultants. Each position would be eliminated as its work was finished. Employees would move to other temporary positions. These mid-level personnel would work mainly through the concept of a competence center from which they would be assigned to organization units and staff projects as needed. The personnel management information system would assist in locating, scheduling, and evaluating these employees.

These competence centers might function as "profit centers." That is, they would function as a sort of outside consultant center, and their services would be paid for by the demand for their work from the bureaucracy. A benefit of this approach is to encourage the search for areas where an individual can make a significant contribution. Many operations research (management science) personnel function in this manner.

If these new forms of career development emerge, they will then be associated with the members of the competence centers. Since assignments to each center would be temporary, the concept encourages self-development and greater growth because the center member would have to "sell" personal skills, develop proposals, and look for problems within his sphere of competence. Titles and levels in the competence centers might even be determined by peer nominations solely on the basis of ability. As in the university, an individual would be an assistant, an associate, and then a full specialist. For those low in the hierarchy, on-the-job development and training by senior members would be a built-in benefit. Those higher up might have a guarantee of security after fulfilling certain expectations.

There are certain advantages to this form of organization. The fluidity permits a flexibility that reduces job decay. Many superficial tasks can be eliminated, and bureaucracy can be streamlined. The system can highlight competence, since the inability to sell personal services is a clear indicator of lack of competence. Moreover, the skills of a competent individual can be put to maximum use, and actual organization needs for employees can be measured by the demand for services.

Admittedly, there are certain disadvantages to this form, the chief of which is unfamiliarity. But the bare framework presented here may be typical of the thinking needed in OD programs and management development of the future.

IMPROVING ORGANIZATION EFFECTIVENESS THROUGH RESEARCH OF INDIVIDUAL NEEDS

Up to this point we have focused on diagnosis, intervention, and change at the organization level. This section is designed to approach *individual* behavior through the diagnosis of employee needs (desires) and to provide guidelines for meeting unfulfilled needs. Exhibits 17–1, 17–2 and 17–3 are examples of how the process of diagnosis and managerial action might be implemented.

Most managers realize that they will have a far greater motivational impact on their subordinates if they can influence employee needs. However, in order to understand and motivate subordinates, the supervisor must first know what they want from their jobs. Exhibit 17–1 is an example of a survey form that can be used to determine a subordinate's attitude toward his job. This is not a typical attitude questionnaire. It is used to relate the ideal and the actual conditions of the job. Needs that are not being met on the job provide great potential for effective intervention on the part of the manager.

Research of Job Needs: An Exercise for the Reader

At this point we suggest that the reader complete the questionnaire provided in Exhibit 17–1. Practicing managers and full-time employees may use their present jobs as a reference point, while students may use a part-time or recent summer job to complete the questionnaire. A self-scoring key is provided in Exhibit 17–2 but should not be checked until after the questionnaire has been completed.

EXHIBIT 17–1 Dowell Need Satisfaction Questionnaire

Considering what you ideally would like from your job *and* what is currently present in your job, rate your *satisfaction* with each of the following characteristics.

1 = Extremely dissatisfied	5 = Satisfied
2 = Dissatisfied	6 = Very satisfied
3 = Somewhat dissatisfied	7 = Extremely satisfied
4 = Only slightly dissatisfied	

Circle one number for each characteristic

1. Opportunity to know what you will be doing from day to day 1 2 3 4 5 6 7
2. Opportunity to do things for your coworkers 1 2 3 4 5 6 7
3. The respect you receive from others 1 2 3 4 5 6 7
4. Opportunity for worthwhile accomplishment on the job 1 2 3 4 5 6 7
5. Opportunity to develop your abilities 1 2 3 4 5 6 7
6. The extent to which your work is orderly and predictable 1 2 3 4 5 6 7
7. Opportunity on the job to help others 1 2 3 4 5 6 7
8. Opportunity to direct the work of others 1 2 3 4 5 6 7
9. Opportunity to do your job the best you can 1 2 3 4 5 6 7
10. Opportunity to gain knowledge 1 2 3 4 5 6 7
11. Opportunity to have your work well planned and organized 1 2 3 4 5 6 7
12. Opportunity to work closely with other people 1 2 3 4 5 6 7
13. The responsibility you have for the work of others 1 2 3 4 5 6 7
14. Opportunity to do work you can be proud of 1 2 3 4 5 6 7
15. Opportunity to try out new ideas 1 2 3 4 5 6 7
16. Opportunity to know what is expected of you 1 2 3 4 5 6 7
17. Opportunity to work as part of a team with other people 1 2 3 4 5 6 7
18. The extent to which you are looked to for leadership by your coworkers 1 2 3 4 5 6 7
19. Opportunity to make use of your best abilities 1 2 3 4 5 6 7
20. Opportunity to set your own goals 1 2 3 4 5 6 7
21. The extent to which you do not have to worry about losing your job 1 2 3 4 5 6 7
22. Opportunity to have friends at work 1 2 3 4 5 6 7
23. The extent to which your coworkers recognize your abilities 1 2 3 4 5 6 7
24. Opportunity to complete the things you start 1 2 3 4 5 6 7
25. Opportunity to develop new ways of doing your job 1 2 3 4 5 6 7
26. The extent to which there are no sudden changes in your work .. 1 2 3 4 5 6 7
27. Opportunity to talk to others while working 1 2 3 4 5 6 7
28. The extent to which you are valued by your coworkers 1 2 3 4 5 6 7
29. Opportunity to do something meaningful 1 2 3 4 5 6 7
30. Opportunity to develop new skills 1 2 3 4 5 6 7

Source: Dr. Ben Dowell, Department of Administrative Sciences, Kent State University, 1976. By permission.

This exercise will help identify important needs that are being fulfilled and pinpoint those job characteristics that would be found in the employee's "ideal" work environment. Knowledge of the ideal is helpful because it establishes a standard. For example, if an employee's need for esteem or recognition from others is extremely high but he desires little responsibility or opportunity for

---

EXHIBIT 17-2 Dowell Need Satisfaction Questionnaire Scoring Key

Need area	Questionnaire numbers
Security	1, 6, 11, 16, 21, 26
Belongingness (social)	2, 7, 12, 17, 22, 27
Esteem from other (recognition)	3, 8, 13, 18, 23, 28
Self-Actualization	
Achievement	4, 9, 14, 19, 24, 29
Growth	5, 10, 15, 20, 25, 30

---

achievement, he probably would not aspire to or perform well in a managerial position. High needs for security might indicate a search for a job with a large, stable organization rather than with a small business operating in a high-risk product market.

Results can be tabulated by adding the scale scores for each major need area. Those major areas with the lowest total score indicate potential opportunities for managerial intervention. For example, if the answers to statements 3, 8, 13, 18, 23, and 28 totaled only 7, it would indicate that an employee has a need for esteem or recognition from others but is not fulfilling the need in his or her current position.

Once needs are assessed and weak areas discovered, Exhibit 17–3 will provide various intervention strategies that a manager may wish to consider in order to increase leadership effectiveness and employee motivation.

PERSONNEL MANAGEMENT IN TRANSITION: THE NEED FOR RESEARCH

Why Research Is Needed

Progress in personnel continues at a relatively slow pace in view of growing complexities of the business world. Presently, personnel is at a crucial turning point. Changes in economic patterns and technology and a vast and growing body of knowledge about managerial decision making are creating new problems and challenges for personnel executives. The personnel function is in a period of organizational stress. Managers are attempting to adapt to rapid changes occurring both inside and outside organizations. Third and fourth generation microcomputers and distributed-information systems have been playing an increasingly significant role in personnel. Expanding markets, international operations, new laws, and social pressures are constantly creating new demands. Personnel executives must recognize these changes and their effects. If personnel fails to maintain a necessary degree of creativity, actions to meet changing conditions will come from outside the personnel department.

It is unfortunate that organizations spend so much less on personnel research than on other research activities. A functional breakdown reveals that most R&D

Security needs

Provide assurance of job continuation and stability

Be predictable in your relations with subordinates

Issue clear and concise directives and regulations

Communicate performance standards and assure they are understood

Show hazard of nonproductive work by stressing that organization will not be able to compete effectively

Emphasize fringe benefit program (especially hospitalization and retirement)

Demonstrate the history of growth and stability of the organization

Provide sound training and development programs

Prepare people carefully for changes that will affect their jobs

Apply rules and regulations uniformly

If turnover rate is low, emphasize this fact to personnel

Provide information about strengths of the organization

Belongingness (affiliation) needs

Provide good communications through two-way discussion, newsletters, bulletins, etc.

Emphasize the friendly and cooperative nature of the organization

Stimulate strong interpersonal relations within groups

Establish good orientation program for new group members

Provide for unofficial get-togethers and social functions

Organize special project teams around personnel with compatible (not necessarily equal) value systems and personalities

Assign undesirable work as equitably as possible

Permit each employee to contribute his or her share to the overall effectiveness of the organization

Allow informal work groups to interact reasonably on the job

Use regular and well-planned group meetings

Have an up-to-date organization chart, possibly with pictures

Give personal attention to employee's family, hobbies, athletic interests

Esteem and recognition needs

Provide merit salary increases

Base promotion on merit

Assign tasks so as to permit individuals to display special skills

Use positive reinforcement when performance meets or exceeds standard

Stress the importance of the work that is being performed

Show how work affects the overall performance of work group or total organization

Provide goals that are achievable and recognizable by personnel

Give public recognition for outstanding performance through awards, news bulletins, or news releases to local papers

Use a suggestion system with quick feedback on acceptability of suggestions

Invite people to attend special staff meetings on particular occasions when the individual's job may be concerned

Place personnel on special task groups, committees, or boards where their talents can be recognized by those outside the immediate work group

Whenever possible, use indirect rather than direct controls

Self-actualization (growth and achievement) needs

Redesign tasks so personnel can perform a more complete set of duties; that is, permit employees to see the end result of their labor if possible

Encourage creativity and imagination through personal involvement in work design

Provide for autonomy and risk taking without the constant fear of negative feedback or reprisals if a wrong decision is made

Encourage self-development through university or postsecondary school credit or nondegree continuing education

Stress personal freedom and growth opportunities of present position

Give complete information on personal progress

funds are devoted to new products and processes. Personnel research is generally not of sufficient importance to be mentioned in most breakdowns of research spending by companies. Thus a nation that must attribute much of its economic success to research may not be allocating enough money to research into one of the basic factors of its success: people.

Types of Personnel Research

Executives need sound information on which to base decisions. Research about consumers helps an executive make manufacturing and marketing decisions. Personnel research is also necessary to enable personnel directors to make better personnel decisions.

Presently, there are two main kinds of personnel research: descriptive research and the more deeply-rooted behavioral research. Descriptive research is conducted to satisfy management's need for information about the personnel situation in its company and in competing companies. This kind of research usually involves compiling data about employees who have comparable jobs in the same community or industry. Examples of this kind of research include turnover data and wage surveys. Descriptive research is an important source of information and is conducted in varying degrees by most companies.

Behavioral research makes use of techniques from the social sciences. It provides a company with detailed data about its employees. This kind of research usually addresses the deeper questions about employee behavior, such as who to employ, how to reduce turnover, and how to increase job satisfaction. It uses the traditional techniques of test validation, opinion surveys, training evaluations, and motivational research. The purpose of behavioral research is to develop theories of interest, motivation, and adaptation to change.

Most contemporary personnel research is applied rather than basic. It usually is used to answer specific questions and solve specific problems. Basic personnel research is directed at developing a more fundamental understanding of people in a work situation. Most of it is conducted in university and government laboratories rather than in private industry.

Byham (1968) illustrated areas in which forty-four firms were conducting research. Most firms in the sample used only traditional areas of personnel management as bases for analysis. The research areas noted in the survey were:

(Percentage of the 44 companies)			
Selection and placement	98	Supervision	Less than 10
Opinion measurement and		Managerial and tech-	
communications research	75	nical obsolescence	Less than 10
Training and development	30	Accident prevention	Less than 10
Appraisal	20	Emotional stress	Less than 10
Motivation and job satisfaction	18	Counseling	Less than 10
Organizational effectiveness	16	Recruitment	Less than 10
		Basic research	Less than 10

Fortunately, the focus and methods of personnel research indicated in the Byham survey are gradually changing. Increasingly sophisticated tools and procedures are being used. More use is being made of computers to analyze statistical data and to store research findings for further reference. Today there is as much concern with development and placement as with selection.

At present, in-house researchers have a mixed status. Some researchers feel the most important part of their job is to advise management on behavioral matters. And this is how managers view them. Management's feeling as to the proper role of the researcher is mixed. Most managers insist that the researcher function in a behavioral capacity. But some large corporations also use their researchers to conduct clinical evaluations of employees and potential employees and to act as the personnel advisor and counselor of management and non-management employees.

The efforts of corporate researchers are currently finding added encouragement from the growing number of studies undertaken by universities and the armed forces. Universities mainly conduct basic personnel research, while the military is more directed toward applied research. Within the U.S. Air Force, substantial personnel research is conducted by the Human Resources Laboratory at Lackland AFB, Texas (formerly Personnel Research Laboratory). Feedback between and among industrial, university, and military researchers helps refine new ideas and approaches.

Industrial research in personnel has suffered in four respects. First, the inability of managers to place a dollar figure on the value of personnel research has made them reluctant to support it. Second, researchers have not communicated well with managers. The inability of many executives to understand what researchers *actually do and say* has made it difficult to develop long-range research programs. Third, time is an important factor. Personnel research may be slow in producing results or action, a situation that is often not acceptable to the high speed executives of modern industry. Fourth, many executives have yet to comprehend the purpose of personnel research.

Areas of Needed Research in Personnel

Selection.   Managers are making greater use of personnel research in selection and placement activities. And there's good reason for this change. Technological advances have required more scientific approaches to personnel functions because previous methods, which were based on subjective factors, are not entirely reliable. Selection mistakes are costly because technological advances have required a greater initial investment in training. New machines that multiply efforts also magnify mistakes. Further, union contracts in many instances have made it increasingly difficult to replace nonproductive workers. Therefore, better methods of selection and placement are imperative and can be developed only through research. Behavioral science research has helped interviewers interpret information on application forms and has provided a system for weighting the data. It has also provided interpretation of test scores to aid in differentiating among applicants and has provided validated test programs by which to screen applicants without violating the provisions of the Civil Rights Act of 1964. The objective of this research has been to minimize or eliminate errors in selection and placement.

Attitudes. Opinion and attitude surveys continue to be used effectively because management has learned that policies and plans are more effective if they are based on consideration of the employee's opinions and feelings. The most common topics for these surveys are communications, quality of supervision, training, company organization, safety, education and development, employee benefit plans, promotions, wage and salary administration, employee services, and transfers. The prime reasons for these surveys are to determine the desires of management and the workers, to identify units or plants needing special attention, and to identify policies or areas of operation that are causing unusual dissatisfaction. These surveys have been useful in identifying supervisors who may need more training or a new orientation toward their responsibilities.

Appraisal. Research into the realm of employee appraisal represents another important contemporary endeavor. The areas most usually studied are the accuracy of appraisal ratings and psychological tests, validating objective measures for management and nonmanagement assessment, and developing new methods of appraisal. This line of research is important because it provides efficient direction for training, compensation, and development efforts and has also provided useful insight into the motivations and social patterns of successful executives.

Training. The cost effectiveness of development programs has been an important area for research because these programs represent an expense that should yield substantial benefits to the company. The object of this research endeavor is to cut labor and training costs, increase employee satisfaction, determine who needs to be trained or developed and what areas and specific topics are essential to the training programs, evaluate the training techniques and procedures, and evaluate the program effectiveness.

Motivation. Past assumptions concerning effective motivation centered around money. However, researchers are increasingly recognizing that other factors can be very important. Contemporary research is focusing on the influence of work groups, supervisors, and the organizational climate as well as compensation and benefit programs.

Human resource planning. Planning has benefited significantly from research studies. Armed with an increasing amount of knowledge about employees, researchers have been able to estimate quantitative and qualitative factors about the future work force. Researchers are becoming able to predict the effects of planned changes and changing business conditions on the size and nature of the future work force.

Social responsibility. Corporations are taking a more serious view of their social responsibilities to the community and society. We feel applied research into job structures will promote new possibilities for providing gainful employment for physically handicapped persons, including blind persons, as well as the mentally retarded. In considering the poverty sector in our society, we believe corporations will take a greater interest in providing job training to produce employable people and restore human dignity. Personnel research will have a vital role in devising training techniques that will permit effective training of the less educated. Cost-benefit analysis will be a consideration but not the sole influential determinant.

Retirement and leisure.   Personnel research should take a more basic look at retirement programs and the increase in leisure time available to its employees. Most retirement programs are inadequate because they often terminate the services of employees who possess sorely needed experience and wisdom. Perhaps corporations should practice selective retirement of people to a management advisory group. Attainment of age sixty or sixty-five should no longer mark the boundary of productivity. Perhaps a system of granting extended vacations or sabbaticals throughout a person's productive years will change retirement programs or at least supplement them.

Research is needed to determine the effects of leisure time on employees. Contemporary labor movements are slowly producing a work force that is employed only part time. This may produce some significant changes in employees' motivation and attitudes which should be explored. As working hours are reduced, companies may find difficulty in maintaining company loyalty. A worker who spends thirty hours per week with a company may soon feel more allegiance toward his golf clubs or fishing tackle. Perhaps more company-sponsored recreation activities or a company-owned recreation area will be needed to maintain company-labor ties. One such project was conducted by Riegel Paper Corporation. During the Great Depression the company used the workers to build a company community center. This provided not only a recreation facility for the employees, which still enjoys great popularity, but at least two to three days work per week when employment was nonexistent. Employee gratitude and allegiance to the company were unrivaled in that location.

Some aspects of personnel research have applications outside the personnel area. Studies of behavior patterns, for example, are useful to the marketing department. Corporations will profitably merge some of their research resources into, perhaps, a human studies center. Of course, such a concept would probably have application only in the large corporations with substantial research budgets.

International forces.   International operations have many implications for the personnel executive in which research could be beneficial. Measurement must be developed to assist in selecting employees who can adapt to foreign cultures and will be good representatives. Research has already produced training techniques to facilitate rapid learning of a foreign language. Familiarization training should be developed for the employee and his family to prepare them to live in a foreign land.

A second aspect of international operations is in the employment of foreign people. Every traditional personnel function, from recruitment to retirement, should be studied for applicability in a different culture. Merely adapting programs developed from research on the American society may lead to severe labor difficulties.

Human obsolescence.   Another beneficial area for management to investigate is personnel obsolescence. An executive, as well as a technical employee, who allows himself to become obsolete represents a waste of training and development expenditures. Therefore, research should provide executives with some indication of factors that may be in evidence as this process occurs. The study by Frederick C. Haas (1968) into this area has upset some traditional notions that obsolescence is a function of age. Such diverse characteristics as poor health and prosperity have been found as indicators of possible obsolescence.

Perhaps the most vital task of personnel research will be to devise a method of effectively placing the enlarged work force. In addition to handling a normal accession rate that exceeds the loss rate from the labor force, government and industry are making greater efforts to add other groups to employment rolls. Such groups as the hard-core unemployed, handicapped persons, and retarded persons will eventually be added to the total labor force.

THE CHANGING IMAGE OF PERSONNEL MANAGEMENT

Some personnel departments in contemporary organizations are hampered in their efforts to innovate because of an image problem. Line managers may view the department merely as a record keeper, or perhaps as a firefighter, or maybe a counseling office. Odiorne (1974) illustrated that at least some of the image problem may be justified. A majority of corporate personnel directors could not state their organization's sales volume, profit level, or return on investment. The reader may ask why the personnel officer need be concerned about marketing and financial matters. The answer lies in our attempt to build a systems approach to human resource management. If the personnel managers don't understand the company's major financial and marketing goals and achievements, they probably will not be able to develop a well-integrated human resource planning system.

Foulkes (1975) suggests that the image problem faced by certain personnel departments can, in part, be resolved if less weight is given to traditional experience when key personnel people are hired. Line experience for personnel managers is recommended. Development and communication of a modern philosophy concerning the firm's approach to human resource management is also an important image builder. Additionally, top personnel officers should report directly to the chief executive officer of the organization. Personnel and labor relations should be at least of equal status, with preference hopefully extended to the personnel officer. General Motors, Weyerhauser, AT&T, Burlington Industries, and Babcock and Wilcox, to name a few, split their personnel and industrial relations functions by 1976.

In addition to their basic concerns for selection, compensation, training, and evaluation, chief personnel officers should be knowledgeable of the organization's objectives and problems. This knowledge should extend to the same depth as that possessed by marketing, financial, and operating executives. In this way, personnel officers should be able to contribute effectively to the short- and long-range planning efforts of top management.

Personnel managers of the 1980s will need increased skills. The changing nature of work, job design, organizational effectiveness, and career development programs will be a daily part of the overall human resource manager's concern. Knowledge of various communications programs, understanding of computers and information systems applied to personnel management, and skills in budgeting will also be required. In addition to all these background skills, the future personnel executive should have a working knowledge of organization theory, economics, and psychology. If this array of talent begins to look like the job description for a "superperson," then the reader has begun to realize the challenge and responsibilities of effective personnel management.

SUMMARY AND CONCLUSION

Accelerating change, reams of new government regulations, and increasing demands from various advocacy groups require personnel departments that can respond to pressures before they become problems or court cases. An effective information system and applied research using a data base will assist in fulfilling this responsive role. As we have pointed out in previous chapters, modern personnel officers should be able to offer new approaches that add to the organization's overall productivity and employee satisfaction. In this concluding chapter we have offered brief insights into organization development as a mechanism for bringing about needed changes in the management of human resources. We have also illustrated areas where research should be considered in personnel.

We suggest that personnel managers must be able to interpret the impact of social and political change on their organizations. Areas of prime social concern during the 1980s will be government regulations pertaining to age discrimination, occupational safety, affirmative action, hiring of the handicapped, pension reform, and quality of the work life. These, and undoubtedly more, interventions have a significant bearing on an organization's personnel policies as well as its profits. Thus, the modern personnel manager should be ready to play an increasing role in forming organization objectives and strategies through sound research, yielding evidence to support all recommendations.

DISCUSSION QUESTIONS

1. Recall the definition given for organization development at the beginning of this chapter: How do you think you would like to change that definition? Would you leave it the same? Why? Do you think that different types of organizations should look upon the OD concept from different viewpoints? Why or why not?

2. Imagine that you are a "change agent," approaching a company for the first time.

How would you prepare? Consider the lack of information, the need for establishing authority, and your own prejudices.

3. Briefly list results from some of the recent research in the field of OD. What conclusions are you most likely to accept? Least likely? What conclusions will be hardest to sell to management? Why? How could some of the research results be applied to a company's problems?

4. Briefly explain some of the differences between the use of "hard" and "soft" data methods in OD evaluation. What are the advantages of both "internal" and "external" hard data? The disadvantages? What type of methods might be best in a profit-making organization? In a nonprofit organization? In the military?

5. Often, unsuccessful programs are based on faulty assumptions. Do you think there are any basic assumptions you would quarrel with in the field of OD? More importantly, do you think there are any basic assumptions company management might quarrel with simply because they are company management?

6. The authors list various strengths and weaknesses of OD programs. Do you perceive these as equally weighted? (That is, are you more impressed with the related strengths or the related weaknesses or neither?)

7. OD theorists and even those outside the field seem confident that there can be a happy marriage of "science and art" in organizational development. Is this your viewpoint? Do you think that people and their technology can get along? Do you think there is really any choice? Why or why not?

8. The authors seem convinced that larger organizations the future will thrust upon us can best be handled through emphasis on such scientific methods as improved data gathering, the coordination of different sciences, the introduction of sound methods of information science, and a less intuitive feel for the organization. Do you agree? As our needs become more and more specialized, will the organization become more or less centralized?

9. Clearly, although OD seems destined for a more scientific and better informed niche in the overall management concept, there are also those who believe that new and different ideas must be given a trial. Since the entire OD concept will be of major interest to you in the future, how do you view such possibilities as the hiring of special "creative people"? Do you believe that these should be part of the new program? Part of your answer might be directed toward why they are not part of current programs. How can ideas such as these be integrated in the OD system of the future?

10. Some critics have pointed out that many of the OD models have never achieved stated goals. Do you think stated goals for OD in general may be too high? Too low? Just right? How must management perception of goals change in the future?

11. Assume you are a change agent–consultant coming to a particular organization with a problem: both students and faculty of an American university are discontented with the educational process. The specific problem seems to be the perceived quality of the teaching, the harsh loads imposed on faculty, and the failure of the university to keep up with faculty salary standards. How might you approach all or one of these problems? Consider a research design, motivation, testing, interaction with the change agent (you), and personal prejudices of all involved, including the change agent.

12. Using Exhibits 17–1 and 17–2, administer the needs assessment questionnaires to one of your associates or fellow students. Based on the results of the assessments decide on a strategy that could be used to increase the motivation of the individual completing the survey.

13. In what ways do you feel the tasks of modern personnel managers differ from those of the 1960s?

BIBLIOGRAPHY

Armenakis, A. A., H. S. Field, and D. C. Mosley. "Evaluation Guidelines for the OD Practitioner." *Personnel Journal* 53.4 (February 1975):99–103.

Blake, R. R., and J. S. Mouton. *Corporate Excellence Through Grid Organization Development.* Houston: Gulf Publishing Company, 1968.

Bowers, D. G. "Organization Development: Promises, Performances, Possibilities." *Organizational Dynamics* (Spring 1976):50–62.

Burke, W. W. "A Comparison of Management Development and Organization Development." *Journal of Applied Behavioral Science* 7 (1971):569–78.

Byham, William C. "The Uses of Personnel Research." *AMA Research Study* 91. American Management Association, Inc., New York, 1968.

Evans, M. G. "Failure in OD Programs—What Went Wrong?" *Business Horizons* 17.2 (April 1974):18–22.

Foulkes, F. K. "The Expanding Role of the Personnel Function." *Harvard Business Review* (March–April 1975):71–84.

French, W., and C. Bell. *Organization Development.* Englewood Cliffs, N.J.: Prentice-Hall, 1973.

Friedlander, Frank. "OD Reaches Adolescence: An Exploration of its Underlying Values." *Journal of Applied Behavioral Science* (January–March 1976).

Greiner, L. E. "Red Flags in Organization Development." *Business Horizons* 4.3 (June 1972):17–24.

Haas, Frederick C. "Executive Obsolescence." *AMA Research Study* 90. American Management Association, Inc., New York, 1968.

Halal, W. E. "Organizational Development in the Future." *California Management Review* 16.3 (Spring 1974):35–41.

Hinrichs, J. R. "Restructuring the Organization for Tomorrow's Needs." *Personnel* (March–April 1974):9–19.

Huse, Edgar. *Organizational Development and Change.* Minneapolis: West Publishing Co., 1975.

Kahn, H., and A. Wiener. *The Year 2000: A Framework for Speculation.* New York: Macmillan, 1967.

Mack, H. "Evaluating the Organization Development Effort." *Training and Development Journal* 28.3 (March 1974):42–47.

Odiorne, G. *Management by Objectives Newsletter* (July 1974).

"Organization Development: A Reconnaissance." *The Conference Board Report,* No. 605, 1973:74.

Scott, D. "Motivation from the TA Viewpoint." *Personnel* 51.1 (January–February 1974):8–19.

Schein, E. H. *Process Consultation: Its Role in Organization Development.* Reading, Mass.: Addison-Wesley, 1969.

*

GLOSSARY

Accretion-type change. Slow, paced modifications or changes over time.

Agency shop. Union security measure whereby employees are not forced to join or remain in the union but those who elect not to join must pay a service charge equal to the dues charged by the union to members.

Aggregate models. Forecasting approaches that attempt to determine overall measures of business, economic achievement, units of production, etc. These models may be used as a first step in determining the more precise figures required for human resource planning.

Alienation. Refers to a sense of strangeness, being left on the outside, and isolation felt by organization members regarding the purposes, rewards, and activities of the organizations. "I'm just a cog in the machinery" reflects this feeling of estrangement.

Alpha (beta) exams. Administered during World War I (alpha and beta) and World War II as intelligence tests in order to judge acceptability for the armed services and to judge potential for occupational specialties or officer candidacy.

Alternative career paths. Different choices people may make in selecting careers and also the different combinations or selections of work experience (with education) which help one obtain a career objective.

Apparatus of government. Refers to the governmental functions or administrative units, plus procedures for undertaking activities in conformity with various laws—of special concern are those related to labor or human resources.

Aptitude. A measure of learning ability.

Arbitration. Generally, the final step in the grievance process involving a neutral third party who listens to both sides of the case and issues a decision.

Area wage differences. The differences in pay between geographic areas for a particular type of occupation.

Assessment center. A systems approach to diagnosing individual potential or assessing individual performance based on group techniques. When used for *diagnosis*, a battery of exercises, games, or tests is administered to judge current abilities and future potential. Some portion of individual performance is judged by observation and evaluation of a panel of experts numbering perhaps four to six people. The results of individual performance and judgments of potential are then fed back to the person for further discussion. In an *assessment* approach, many of the same techniques and approaches are employed, but here the emphasis is on evaluation of potential, often in competitive situations—for example, when a position is open and several people are being considered.

Benchmark jobs. A set of jobs that provides the foundation for a wage program. The jobs are designated *benchmark* when they are well recognized and lend themselves to comparison.

Benefits (fringe benefits). Refers to all nondirect wage-associated costs including such elements as insurance, vacation, medical expense, retirement contributions, and company contributions to profit sharing.

Behavior modification. The use of positive or negative reinforcements to alter individual or group behavior.

BFOQ. Bona fide occupational qualification; pertains to civil rights and permits (legal) discrimination on the basis of sex. The difficulty lies in proving a BFOQ is justified.

Bias (test). Elements of a test or technique which favor particular people or circumstances.

Binding arbitration. Third-party dispute settlement, which is binding on both parties and reached by mutual agreement.

Boycott. Refusal of a union to permit its members to patronize an enterprise where there is a labor dispute. Going a step further, a secondary boycott may be induced through third parties (suppliers and customers) to refrain from doing business with the employer. Secondary boycotts are generally illegal under the Taft-Hartley Act.

Budgetary model. Refers to the use of budgetary procedures in establishing the relationships between human resources variables and business or economic variables. This model is essentially short run and determines the specific program for the most immediate forthcoming period (recruiting, training, and other personnel activities).

Career management. Formal organization programs for counseling and planning future work activities; development of abilities and responsibilities of individuals.

Career path. The route of jobs, experiences, training, and learning experiences taken by an individual in proceeding from a current state (job status or education situation) to a valued state in the future.

Career planning. This term is employed in an organizational context. It is a systemic program on the part of organizations to connect individual desires for themselves and their futures with organizational needs, and to then attempt to work out a joint accommodation between the objectives (individual and organization).

Career. Term employed to contrast the view that work serves the primary purpose of income or meeting immediate needs (a "job") with the view that work is a longer-term activity using a fuller range of abilities and likely to bring greater psychic and social returns.

Centralization/decentralization. Establishing formal decision authority for an activity such as personnel near the top level (centralization) or further down in the organization (decentralization).

Change strategy. Developing thoughtful means of causing new programs, policies, or directions to be introduced into the organization.

Check-off. A procedure whereby the employer deducts membership dues and assessments from the pay of employees and turns these monies over to the union.

Closed shop. Union security measure whereby employer may hire only union labor.

Collective bargaining. A process for negotiating wages and terms of employment which govern all workers in a bargaining unit. Collective bargaining prevents an employee from negotiating different terms on his or her own behalf, but the law does provide for employees to discuss their grievances with management on an individual basis. Collective bargaining is involved in both negotiating for a new contract and in the administration of an existing contract. Collective bargaining is generally a ritualistic process beginning with exaggerated demands, which are scaled down as negotiations proceed.

Communications. Two different approaches are described in this text. One deals with information flow between people. Of interest are the characteristics of information flow between individuals. The second approach relates to description and analysis of communications systems. The approach is largely impersonal and deals with the structure, flows, blockages, and media involved in developing, transmitting, storing, and interpreting data and information.

Compensable factors. Those items of individual ability (e.g., mental, physical), indirect measures of ability (e.g., amount or type of education), functional qualities (e.g., related to planning), or direct work-related measures that an organization values and which become the basis for wage payment. These factors are usually standardized for most or all of the employee group to facilitate comparisons. In larger organizations, the managerial group might use a set that is different from factors used for the employee group.

Compulsory unionism. Contract between employer and union which requires employees, as a condition of employment, to join or support the union within a specified period of time.

Conciliator. Individual whose responsibility is to keep negotiations moving when the two parties to a labor dispute refuse to continue discussion. The conciliator, unlike the mediator, does not attempt to develop a solution.

Concurrent validity. The extent to which test scores are associated with a criterion measure that is available at the same time. It is generally developed by administering tests to the current employees and using these results to predict success of future job applicants.

Content validity. The extent to which a predictor reflects actual job requirements.

Contingency approach to personnel. A flexible means of approaching the design of personnel organization; it seeks to identify the critical features of environment, organization, and work in a specific situation affecting the features of a personnel unit.

Critical incident. The description of work activity based on what a person actually does in performance of a job. There is also some degree of selectivity, in the sense that *critical* means important.

Critical mass. Refers to the combination of law, social changes, economic circumstances, etc. necessary for important or large-scale changes to take place.

Criterion. The dimension used to distinguish "good" from "bad." For selection purposes, the criterion generally accepted and used is some measure of job performance.

Data. Unorganized (unprocessed) information; e.g., personnel recruiting activities for all divisions identified by applicant name; once the names are alphabetized by division, they can be viewed as information.

Data base. Integrated file of data used by many processing applications throughout an organization, as contrasted with an individual data file, which can be used for only one particular application.

Decision outputs. When the results of data processing lead to the actual decision without the need for human intervention at the output stage.

Decision to join, produce, maintain affiliation. Three primary decisions made by individuals regarding employment: to become a member of a particular organization (to join), to perform at a good level of performance (to produce), and to continue to maintain organization membership (to maintain affiliation).

Delphi technique. Technique involving a group of experts for securing some type of estimate or forecast where no single individual possesses all of the needed information. Delphi involves a structured technique for gaining this information so that agreement can be obtained in a comparatively short time.

Direct compensation. The wages or salary received by the worker in the form of the pay check as opposed to other benefits. The amount is usually the gross payment, but variation in usage occasionally arises here.

DOT. *Dictionary of Occupational Titles*, prepared by the U.S. Department of Labor. The most recent edition contains over 20,000 different occupational titles and descriptions. The DOT is the basic job evaluation document in virtually all classification work and employment analyses involving governmental employees.

Due process. A legalistic approach to corrective or punitive discipline which requires that all employees be appraised of work rules and penalties for violating the rules in advance of any infractions.

Encounter group. A type of sensitivity training which usually includes nonverbal interaction such as feeling and touching. This type of group interaction is seldom used in business organization development programs.

Environmental stability. A descriptive term for the rate at which change is taking place and the degree of change and turbulence—here suggests slow or gradual change.

ERISA. Employee Retirement Income Security Act of 1974; a complex government act intended to increase employee security through regulation of pension plans provided by employers.

Exchange. A process of give and take between two parties and, as used in the text, between organization and individual. Each party accepts a combination of inducements ("take") and contributions ("give") which the party views as acceptable at the time of employment or during the course of employment. The latter applies to situations where, for example, maintaining employment may be the major consideration.

Exclusive jurisdiction. One union serves as the sole representative for all employees in a plant or bargaining unit. (In certain governmental agencies different unions may represent the same workers for different purposes.)

Extrinsic work features. Factors surrounding the job rather than a part of the job; often refers to benefits, treatment of workers, working conditions, etc. A convenient means of classification but lacks predictive power.

Facilitator. A person who serves as a catalyst in group processes with the objective of improving the interaction among group members.

Fact-finding session. Meeting usually held before formal negotiation to clarify objectives and lay ground rules for collective bargaining.

Factor clusters. Refers to a technique of statistical analysis in which a group of individual job elements is examined to determine if the elements are related by a single idea or description that defines the essence of the group.

Factor comparison. This technique of job evaluation combines the ranking and point systems. In the ranking approach, it rates jobs by comparing one with another. In the point system, it subdivides jobs in compensable factors, and ratings are expressed in points or, more frequently, in dollar amounts. This approach generally uses fewer compensable factors than point schemes do.

Feedback. Knowledge of results, whether desirable or undesirable, which are communicated back to a worker, supervisor or unit.

Fishbowl. A technique used to improve communication between two groups. Two groups are arranged in concentric circles; one group in the inner and the other in the outer circle. The inner group discusses the other group (i.e., the inner group discusses among its members the problems the group as a whole has with members of the outer group). Meanwhile the outer group listens and watches. Subsequently the process is repeated, with the groups exchanging positions. The inner group moves outside and observes, while the initial outer group moves into the fishbowl.

Flexitime. A technique that supposedly increases employee motivation; it permits the employee to choose when to start work between designated hours (e.g., between 7:30 and 9:30 A.M.) and when to leave work between designated hours (e.g., 4:30 and 6:30 P.M.), as long as the normal work day is completed (e.g., as long as a total of eight hours is worked).

Forced choice. A rating method that in chapter discussions uses four behavioral statements per grouping and the rater is expected to check two of the four items, one of which is the most and the other the least like the person being rated.

Forced distribution. A rating method whereby the evaluator is forced to place all ratees in specified classes (e.g., 10 percent of all subordinates are placed in the highest class, 20 percent in the next class, etc.).

Grievance. An allegation by an employee or employer that the labor agreement has been violated.

Halo effect. Tendency for raters (evaluators) to be influenced in rating a particular factor by the kind of rating given on other factors. For example, if the rater has a general feeling that a person is good, high ratings may be given on all factors.

Hawthorne Experiments. Refers to an industrial research study undertaken by Dr. Elton Mayo *et al.* in the 1920s at a division of the Western Electric Company in Chicago, Illinois.

Human capital. A way of viewing employees or human resources which recognizes these as capital in the very same sense as financial capital; it reflects an investment by the organization in human potential where expectancies exist for some type of returns for the organization's investment.

Human relations. Personnel approaches arising out of the Hawthorne Experiments and emphasizing such things as good communications, job satisfaction, and human interaction.

Human resources. Redefinition of term *personnel* to emphasize its new role in the planning and implementation of human resource systems.

Human resource accounting. An attempt to quantify the costs and benefits associated with the personnel programs involving organization employees who are considered as human capital (see human capital).

In-basket. An exercise used to develop people. It involves communications, letters, or the like which have been carefully organized in advance to bring out a certain understanding, build confidence in one's abilities to handle these situations, and create awareness of practical problems in a systematic way. Evaluation may be on the basis of predetermined "best" responses, observations of an assessment panel, etc.

Industrial relations. A title often assigned to a unit that deals with unions and sometimes used in place of the more conventional term *personnel.*

Information system. A broadly used and abused term usually referring to computerized and integrated files of data which can be accessed by users of information to improve decision-making and problem-solving activities.

Input system. Function concerned with recruiting and selecting people.

Integrated system. Components of work activity displaying logical interrelationships, conscious design, and purpose.

Intrinsic work features. Elements of work within the job itself which are thought to contribute to challenge, identification, purposefulness, etc.

Job classification. The process of determining the appropriate job group to which a job belongs. This is a nonquantitative technique of job evaluation.

Job design. Structuring the elements of a work task in such a way as to contribute to good performance and satisfaction of the job holder.

Job enlargement. Increasing the number of tasks that a person does while at work.

Job enrichment. Delegation of some of the planning and control aspects of the job to the person actually doing the job—elements thought to be psychologically satisfying.

Job evaluation. Judging the relative importance of a job preliminary to assigning dollar values for compensation.

Job structure. The relationships formed from intercomparison among most or all the jobs in an organization based on job evaluation points or some other systematic technique for estimating relative job importance.

Job specification. Indirect measures of the mental and physical skills needed for a job plus equipment or devices used in conducting work. Items included might be education level, educational area of concentration, motor skills, special features of personality, etc.

Labor markets (internal, external). Refers to the two main divisions of people considered a part of the work force: internal refers to those currently employed, while external considers those interested in work, actively seeking jobs but unemployed currently. The labor market term also has a geographic dimension; one may be dealing with local, city, state, regional, or national areas depending on the interests of the analyst or the major source of employable labor for an organization.

Laboratory training. See T-group training.

Learning function. Describes the gain in skill over time for a specific job or occupation —100 percent normally designates an individual who has fully learned a job.

Life planning. A variation of career planning which usually includes variables relating to family, religion, and other personal objectives besides strictly work-related objectives.

Life-style. A person's desired manner of dress, social pursuits, and valued activities.

Lockout. A lockout occurs when the employer closes down operations in an effort to force the union to cease certain harassing activities or to accept certain work rules demanded by the employer.

Maintenance. Identifies traditional personnel functions concerned with securing and servicing employment-related needs of employees in rather routine fashion.

Man-machine model. A description applied to the traditional approach of work study engineers, especially Fredrick W. Taylor. In this model, man was considered as an adjunct to machine—largely as a means to the end (production).

Management development. The expansion of individual knowledge, outlook, perspective, and skills in preparation for promotion and so that the person can better handle some current situation.

Manpower forecasting. A planning approach in which statistical or other mathematical methods are used to predict the how many, type, and when aspects of future human resource needs.

Manpower planning and programming. A group of interrelated activities for providing the right number of people at the right place and with support activities to assure fulfillment of human and organization needs.

Markov model. A mathematical model used in human resource planning to determine the numbers and extent of occupational needs in the future based on a set of assumptions involving past relationships. In this application to people planning, the paths of people are traced out as they experience various moves such as promotion, leaving an organization, or joining the organization. The model tracks the movement of people from one state (job or situation) to another and uses math to project both individual and total movements of people into future time periods so long as basic assumptions remain valid.

Mediator. The mediator is a stronger third party than a conciliator to deadlocked union negotiations since he or she generally recommends a solution to the situation, drawing the parties closer together and enabling discussion to continue.

Mobility. The ease with which a particular person or class of employees moves between employers or across geographic boundries.

Monetary incentives. Wages that are paid in proportion to the amount of work performed.

Motion and time study. Analyzing a job to determine its basic work elements and the time needed to carry these out, and proposing job designs to improve performance.

National Alliance of Businessmen (NAB). A national organization run by private enterprise to assist in providing jobs and job opportunities for the economically disadvantaged. NAB attempts to gain commitments from employers regarding making jobs available and/or providing needed training to facilitate employment. The government provides needed training funds under the Comprehensive Employment and Training Act to support these company training programs.

Needs analysis. A basic approach to establishing the requirements of a particular situation prior to initiating any program of activity.

Negotiation. The exchange of ideas with the intention of changing relationships, compensation arrangement, conditions of work, etc.

New life-style. Refers to the changes in living patterns and priorities assigned by younger people to all manner of activities and life goals. Among these would be attitudes regarding the importance of education and work, which have an impact on work dedication and desire to live the "good life" now.

Nonquantitative job evaluation. Refers generally to job ranking and the job classification (grade description) systems for evaluating jobs. Both schemes have in common the explicit use of comparisons and judgments to determine relative importance of jobs.

Normal (work) pace. Closely related to "average" and "standard"; thought to represent the energy expenditure or amount of work performed by a typical worker without undue physical exertion.

Open system. Vulnerability of organizational activities to developments external to the firm.

OSHA. Occupational Safety and Health Act of 1970; a part of the U.S. labor law which attempts "to assure so far as possible every working man or woman in the nation safe and healthful working conditions."

Past practice. A term typically used in grievance sessions to denote employee behavior or company approach to particular situations which was accepted (or overlooked) in the past as part of the traditional work environment. Past practice is not part of current contract language.

Path-goal model. Considered a part of a broader body of motivational theory called *expectancy theory*. This model takes an approach to motivation which examines the means by which an individual achieves valued goals, the relative attractiveness of alternative paths, and the likelihood that a particular path or means will achieve the valued goal.

Planning horizon. Length of a planning period, generally measured in years.

Point method. Easily the most popular job evaluation scheme, in which point values are assigned to compensable factors to yield a total point value for a particular job.

Position analysis questionnaire. An instrument developed by Dr. Ernest McCormick and his associates at Purdue University containing some 192 different questions concerning the critical features of a given job.

Predictive validity. Calculated on a past relationship that existed in an earlier sample (locking up the test scores of a batch of job applicants and subsequently determining who succeeds and who fails and using these data in the selection of future applicants).

Predictor. In relation to tests or selection tools, the predictor is that which forecasts success on the criterion measure. For example, the score on a typing test supposedly predicts success as a typist.

Pressure points. Situations or events existing in an organization which can be used as a "legitimate" reason for undertaking an action or program that would otherwise be difficult.

Primary work system. Part of the terminology of sociotechnical systems—has to do with work activity for producing an organization's product or delivery of its services.

Productivity. A measure of individual, department, or organizational performance relating costs or effort to accomplish work to the outcomes of the costs or effort; a measure of outputs divided by inputs.

Random access storage. A storage technique in which the time required to obtain data is independent of the location of the data most recently obtained or stored; random or direct access is contrasted with sequential access, which requires that all data be searched in sequence until the required bit of data is retrieved.

Ranking method. A nonquantitative technique for determining the relative importance of jobs based on judgment and knowledge of each individual job.

Rate of participation. A technical term used by labor economists or manpower analysts to indicate the relative numbers or percentages of a class of workers or general category of people (e.g., women, blacks, etc.) who are working or employed.

Rating scales. A formal or organized way of judging the performance or potential of an individual. Descriptive terms are arranged in order from "good" to "bad," often with intermediate points so as to permit some degree of choice by the rater. When employed properly, each degree or rating level is defined so that an assessment of "good," for example, is not completely subjective.

Reaction management. The practice of dealing only with immediate circumstances or responding to the pressures of the moment.

Reinforcement. Encouragement for performing in a desired manner.

Reliability. The characteristic of a selection tool which assures that similar results will be obtained when the tool is used on different occasions with the same individual.

Remote access. When a computer user is located some distance from the computer such as in a different building, city, or state.

Representative work conditions. Refers to the many variables that surround a job and influence its performance; representative refers to typical, or what can usually be expected. Items included under conditions might be temperature and lighting.

Rewards (extrinsic and intrinsic). This term distinguishes between those rewards which are extrinsic to the job (pay, vacations, treatment by supervisors, etc.) as opposed to those which are part of the job itself (challenge, interest, variety, etc.) and which lead to various job-related satisfactions. The concept provides a convenient basis for classifying the work-environment factors.

Role playing. A developmental technique using unrehearsed dramas. Participants become actors and actresses who are assigned specific roles to play. They are usually told about the circumstances that led to a given situation or problem they are to act out. Roles are often rotated to teach empathy and to broaden the participant's perspective on the given problems. Observers are generally used to feed back reactions and to analyze the behaviors of the participants.

Salary experience curves. A portrayal, usually in chart form, of the change in income (individual or occupation) over time as experience is gained.

Secondary support system. The wide range of activities, services, departments, and units which facilitate the activities of the primary work system. Typical activities would include engineering departments, personnel units, marketing departments, and accounting departments.

Sensitivity training. See T-group training.

Shop steward. Union representative, typically a work force member who is generally elected by members within the area.

Simulation. As used in the personnel field, simulation refers to a broad range of techniques in which trainees act out samples of real organizational behavior in order to obtain practice in making decisions or interact without interfering with ongoing operations.

Social secretary. A name given to people in organizations, mostly in the era of 1910–30, whose responsibilities were primarily concerned with employee welfare.

Social welfare legislation. Generally, laws passed with the idea of uplift or betterment of the life of people. In the book context, refers more specifically to a growing list of work-related laws and acts starting largely with Social Security and relating to retirement, health, work conditions, pension reform, safety, and support during unemployment.

Sociotechnical systems. A way of viewing an organization as a combination of both human and technical elements, both of which are needed to conduct the work of the organization. This view was developed to emphasize the crucial role of the human element in meeting the objectives of the organization. In turn, the concept led to the use of terms such as social performance or social efficiency to further emphasize the importance of the human dimension. Secondly, this concept set out in clearer fashion the distinctions between those elements concerned directly with the main products or services of the organization (the primary work system) as opposed to those elements and activities supporting the primary system (secondary support/work system). Finally, the system idea describes the great interdependence existing between the various human and technical elements and primary and secondary units, plus the logical organization of these to meet performance objectives.

Strike. Any concerted refusal to perform job-related duties as part of a labor dispute, including sick outs, slowdowns, blue flu, etc.

SUB. Supplementary unemployment benefits; contract provisions obtained primarily by steel, auto, rubber, and cement unions which, when combined with ordinary unemployment insurance, can bring the laid-off employee's income very close to prelayoff earnings.

T-group training. Deals with real, not simulated, problems existing within the actual training group. T-group training seeks to change underlying attitudes and thus job behavior rather than merely teaching skills and knowledge. T-groups are laboratories where people generate data about themselves and experiment with the data.

Time-sharing. A data processing method which enables several users to interact with a computer concurrently.

Tower Amendment. An amendment to Civil Rights Act of 1964 which gives employers the right to administer "and act upon the results of any professionally developed ability test provided that such test, its administration, or action upon the results is not designed, intended, or used to discriminate because of race, color, religion, sex, or national origin."

Training. This term attempts to make a distinction between approaches to building skills for immediate needs (training) versus approaches that build perspective for longer range *development* of the individual. Traditionally, much of training was associated with building physical skills as in factory-type jobs.

Transactional analysis. This technique was originally used in psychotherapy to assist persons with difficulties in forming personal relationships. Behaviors between people (transactions) are analyzed and categorized into three ego states: parent, adult, and child (PAC). Transactions are satisfactory if the behavior of one person is responded to with the corresponding ego state of another. For example, adult-adult is considered satisfactory. Transactions that are crossed (parent-child) may cause behavioral problems. TA is a relatively new technique for organizational development but is being used at the time of writing by several companies interested in improving the relationships between employees and customers.

Turnover. The percentage of the total workforce which has to be replaced in a given time period, such as one year. Also may be calculated for particular jobs.

Union shop. Union security measure whereby employer may hire nonunion members but once hired, employees must join union within a specified time period in order to maintain job.

Validation. As applied to tests and interviews or other selection tools, validation exists if the tool actually predicts what it purports to predict. A tool is said to be valid if it can distinguish effectively between those who will be successful from those who will fail on the job.

Wage level. Refers to the average wage for an organization or to the average wages for an occupation in a particular city, region, or labor market area.

Wage progression. A series of successively higher wage rates that can be earned by an individual, generally in a particular job or occupation. The upward movement may take place on the basis of length of employment, merit, or a combination of both.

Wage structure. The relationship between type of job and the wage rate or salary paid. Also used to describe the relationship between points assigned to a job and dollar worth, as in a point plan (see structure).

Wage survey. A process of acquiring information from other employers related to wages, benefits, and type of work.

Wildcat strike. Refusal of a group of employees to perform assigned jobs generally without taking a vote of the full membership or without following contract provisions for such strike action.

Work design. Used synonymously with job design to indicate the analysis of job or work activities for the purpose of securing two main objectives: improve performance and increase the individual's sense of personal accomplishment and identification with work.

Work ethic. Values of the general population or individual concerning the importance and meaning of work activity.

*

INDEX

†